Communication and Social Cognition

Theories and Methods

LEA's COMMUNICATION SERIES
Jennings Bryant and Dolf Zillmann, General Editors

Selected titles include:

Berger • Planning Strategic Interaction: Attaining Goals Through Communicative Action

Bryant/Zillmann • Media Effects: Advances in Theory and Research, Second Edition

Ellis • Crafting Society: Ethnicity, Class, and Communication Theory

Fortunato • Making Media Content: The Influence of Constituency Groups on Mass Media

Greene • Message Production: Advances in Communication Theory

Reichert/Lambiase • Sex in Advertising: Perspectives on the Erotic Appeal

Singhal/Rogers • Entertainment Education: A Communication Strategy for Social Change

Zillmann/Vorderer • Media Entertainment: The Psychology of Its Appeal

---

For a complete list of titles in LEA's Communication Series, please contact Lawrence Erlbaum Associates, Publishers at www.erlbaum.com

Communication and Social Cognition
Theories and Methods

Edited by

David R. Roskos-Ewoldsen
University of Alabama

Jennifer L. Monahan
University of Georgia

LAWRENCE ERLBAUM ASSOCIATES, PUBLISHERS

2007 Mahwah, New Jersey London

Lawrence Erlbaum Associates, Inc., Publishers
10 Industrial Avenue
Mahwah, New Jersey 07430
www.erlbaum.com

Cover design by Tomai Maridou

Library of Congress Cataloging-in-Publication Data

National Communication Association (U.S.) Meeting (2002 : New Orleans, LA)
Communication and social cognition : theories and methods / edited by David R. Roskos-Ewoldsen and Jennifer L. Monahan.
p. cm.
Includes bibliographical references and index.
ISBN 978-0-8058-5355-1 — 0-8058-5355-3 (cloth)
ISBN 978-1-4106-1469-8 — 1-4106-1469-7 (e book)
1. Social perception—Congresses. 2. Interpersonal communication—Congresses. I. Roskos-Ewoldsen, David R. II. Monahan, Jennifer L. III. Title.
BF323.S63N38 2006
302.2—dc22 2006012793
CIP

Books published by Lawrence Erlbaum Associates are printed on acid-free paper, and their bindings are chosen for strength and durability.

Printed in the United States of America
10 9 8 7 6 5 4 3 2 1

Contents

II INTERPERSONAL COMMUNICATION

III MASS MEDIA

IV SOCIAL INFLUENCE

Preface

This volume is an outgrowth of a panel at the 2002 meeting of the National Communication Association (NCA) in New Orleans. Jim Weaver asked David Roskos-Ewoldsen to put together a panel celebrating the renaming of the Intrapersonal Communication Division to the Social Cognition and Communication Division. That panel provided a fascinating look at current work in the field of social cognition and communication. From that panel, David Roskos-Ewoldsen and Linda Bathgate of Lawrence Erlbaum Associates conceived this volume. Jennifer Monahan, a member of the panel, was brought on to the book project soon after.

During that meeting at NCA, the book *Social Cognition and Communication*, edited by Mike Roloff and Chuck Berger (1982) received the Communication and Social Cognition Commission Publication Award. *Social Cognition and Communication* was and still is highly valued by communication and social cognition researchers. Yet, it has been close to 25 years since this seminal collection of articles on social cognition and communication was published. In part, this volume celebrates the pivotal impact Roloff and Berger's book had on the study of communication and social cognition. A second important reason for this volume is that we believe the explosion of work in communication and social cognition since 1982 merits an update.

This volume brings together several authors, each an expert in social cognition research within a specific area of communication. We gave the authors several tasks. First, we asked them to inform the reader about the state of social cognitive theorizing and research in their area of study when *Social Cognition and Communication* was published. Second, we asked authors to summarize the major trends in their area of research since 1982. We asked them to highlight both theoretical and methodological aspects of social cognition research in hopes that an emphasis on how theory is translated into methods will encourage more communication scholars to include social cognition in their research and more social cognition researchers to include communication in their research. Third, authors were asked to speculate about the future of social cognition in their area: Where did they think scholarship should be moving? What are the theories with the most promise? What are the methods that are yielding promising results?

The volume is structured into four major sections on message production, interpersonal communication, media, and social influence. In our estimation, these are four major areas in which social cognition theories have become integral in our understanding of communicative processes. In all four areas, we have seen an explosion of scholarship concerning well-established theories and phenomena, as well as new theoretical developments and exciting new methods.

This volume was conceived with a number of audiences in mind. We believe that the focus on both the major theories and methods will make the volume appealing to both researchers and to those teaching senior undergraduate classes and graduate classes on social cognition and communication. In addition, this volume may also prove useful in teaching classes that rely heavily on social cognition theories. The editors and chapter contributors teach advanced undergraduate or graduate courses in social cognition, social influence, message production, interpersonal communication, media effects, and message design. Students in these and related courses should find that the volume provides comprehensive updates on this important literature.

We also thought it important that each chapter articulate methodological challenges to collecting social cognition data and highlight some of the methodological innovations in the field. We especially wanted to highlight method because social cognitive work often requires methods that go beyond self-report, and we hope that a basic exposition on methodology will be of use to newcomers to this perspective. Although social cognition theory testing still remains primarily the domain of experimental research, it is exciting to see the changes being made to survey research to help accommodate more precise measures of social cognitive processes. A second primary audience is our colleagues in departments of communication and psychology. We hope this volume's emphasis on both cognitive and communicative processes will provide even more impetus for continual collaborative efforts between our disciplines.

ACKNOWLEDGMENTS

We owe a debt of gratitude to Jim Weaver. Without his request for a special panel on social cognition at NCA, it is highly doubtful this volume would have come into existence. We and many others owe a special debt to Chuck Berger and Mike Roloff for taking on the task of editing *Social Cognition and Communication* more than 20 years ago. They were pioneers in bringing social cognition theories and methods into communication departments and they remain two of its preeminent scholars today.

We would like to thank Linda Bathgate at Lawrence Erlbaum Associates for her helpful suggestions and support through the process. In addition, Jennifer Monahan would like to thank Jennifer Samp and Jerry Hale at the University of Georgia and Cynthia Zuckerman of North Carolina State for providing helpful criticism and guidance as well. April Lofsinger at the University of Georgia was a miracle worker on the author and subject indexes and other editorial tasks as well. Finally, Jennifer Monahan would like to thank her husband, Bill Ryland, and children Caitlin and Kerry Monahan and Erin and Rachel Ryland for their love and for all they have contributed to her life. David Roskos-Ewoldsen would like to thank his wife, Beverly Roskos-Ewoldsen, and children Andrew and Jonathan for their love and support.

—David Roskos-Ewoldsen and Jennifer Monahan

1

Celebrating Social Cognition and Communication

Jennifer L. Monahan
University of Georgia

David R. Roskos-Ewoldsen
University of Alabama

We see the goal of this volume as celebrating and affirming the study of communication from a social cognition perspective. There is much to celebrate as scholars working in such disparate subdisciplines as political communication, social influence, group communication, information systems, health communication, and mass communication have incorporated social cognition into their research programs. The reader will find that this volume provides a synthesis of some of the most exciting research in social cognition and communication research over the past 25 years.

Defining social cognition often depends on the interests of the authors involved in the writing. From a psychological perspective, social cognition research is often conceived of as the study of the specific cognitive processes that are involved when we think about or perceive the social world. From such a perspective, memory, perception, and thought are critical cognitive concepts and researchers ask questions about how social information is encoded, stored, and retrieved from memory; how social knowledge is structured and represented in memory; and what processes are involved when individuals make judgments and social decisions.

In Roloff and Berger's (1982) volume, *Communication and Social Cognition, social cognition* is defined as "the organized thoughts people have about human interaction" (p. 21). Thus, their definition focuses almost exclusively on interpersonal interactions (see Eveland & Seo, chap. 13, this volume). In this volume, we take a broader perspective than Roloff and Berger to include mass communication, yet a more interaction-oriented perspective than do most psychologists. We suggest there are four broad ways in which communication scholars study social cognition processes: (a) the processes that impact the generation of messages, (b) the processing of messages and social information, (c) the generation and storage of mental models, and (d) the generation and perception of shared cognitions. In this volume, you will find exemplars of each of these broad perspectives. Some chapters examine the cognitive processes that underlie how individuals form messages to communicate with or influence others (see, e.g., Berger, chap. 3; Greene & Graves, chap. 2; Hamilton, chap. 18; Meyer, chap. 17; Solomon & Theiss, chap. 6; Wilson & Feng, chap. 4). This perspective, as Greene and Graves (chap. 2) note, tries to account for the "activities carried out in social interaction, by social actors pursuing social ends, in contexts governed by social rules and norms" (p. 18). Other chapters focus not so much on how social cognition affects message production, but rather on how individuals form impressions, attitudes, and beliefs via the media or interpersonal messages (see, e.g., Arpan, Rhodes, & Roskos-Ewoldsen, chap. 15; Eveland & Seo, chap. 13; Lannutti & Monahan, chap. 10; Manusov, chap. 7; Nabi, chap. 16; Oliver, Ramasubramanian, & Kim, chap. 12; Shrum, chap. 11). This perspective tries to account for how people process messages generated by others or the media and the outcomes of these messages on behavior such as stereotype formation, voting, and risk decision making. Other chapters focus on *shared cognitions,* or how individuals jointly form cognitions via communication (see, e.g., Koerner, chap. 9; Roloff & Van Swol, chap. 8; Solomon & Theiss, chap. 6). Finally, other chapters examine mental model formation and change when the models we construct are about other people and of media events (see, e.g., Roloff & Van Swol, chap. 6; Roskos-Ewoldsen, Roskos-Ewoldsen, Yang, & Lee, chap. 14). Thus, like all social cognition researchers, our interests involve how humans process and use social information. However, because this volume is not only about social cognition but also about communication, the work represented in this volume examines social cognition processes as such processes inform our understanding of or engagement in communicative acts.

With this broad-based understanding of communication and social cognition, we easily could have generated three volumes but, alas, the publisher requested but one. We lament there was insufficient space for separate chapters on social cognition theories in health communication, organizational communication, advertising, or marketing. Moreover, we did not have the space to do an entire section on personality-based theories. When making decisions about what to include and what to regrettably leave out, we began by considering the areas in which social cognition appears to have made great strides since 1982. In our estimation, message production and compliance or social influence are two areas that have seen an explosion of scholarship, theories, and exciting new developments. In addition, we see a wide-ranging use of social cognition theories in both interpersonal and mass communication. Therefore, the book is divided into these four major parts: Message Production, Interpersonal Communication, Mass Media, and Social Influence. Although this organizing scheme highlights certain aspects of each scholar's contributions, it may hide the fact that many chapters apply across the sections. For example, although the attribution chapter is located in the interpersonal communication section, attribution theory is used widely in the social sciences to explain message production, media effects, and social influence processes as well. In the final analysis, chapters were grouped together in terms of the primary focus of the research.

A secondary consideration when selecting areas to cover in this volume was to include chapters on areas in which we would like to encourage more scholarship in communication and social cognition. Thus, within each part we include chapters on research areas that we feel deserve more attention from scholars in the next 20 years. Specifically, we highlight arguments, family communication, comprehension, and the importance of understanding the effects of specific emotions on persuasion processes as areas of communication research that are poised to take off in the near future.

PART I: MESSAGE PRODUCTION

The first set of chapters focuses on the role of social cognition in message production. Message production research, at the most general level, is research that attempts to explain the mental process that result in communicative behavior. Message design has become a very active area in communication research with a special issue of *Communication Theory* (Wilson, Greene, & Dillard, 2000), countless research articles, and a book (Greene, 1997) devoted to the topic. We lead this section with Greene and Graves's chapter (chap. 2), which provides a general theoretical overview of developments in cognitive models of message production processes. In reviewing the literature, they answer the following questions about theoretical work on message production: What is the theory about? What theoretical terms are invoked? What methods and data are brought to bear? Thus, this first chapter offers an overview of the contribution of social cognition theory to message production.

Planning is the mental processes by which goals are put into communication action. In chapter 3, Berger examines planning research with an emphasis on message production. His chapter draws on a wide variety of research including artificial intelligence, cognitive science, communication, linguistics, and philosophy to demonstrate the importance of plans in explaining discourse comprehension and message production.

In chapter 4, Wilson and Feng trace how interaction goals have been conceptualized in theories of message production. Four theories are comprehensively examined: Brown and Levinson's (1978) politeness theory; O'Keefe's (1988) goal complexity–behavioral complexity account; Dillard's (2004) goals-plans-action (GPA) model; and Wilson, Aleman, and Leatham's (1998) revised analysis of face threats and facework. All four theories employ a goal pursuit metaphor and view message production as a process of reconciling multiple goals, but differ in their characterization of goals and in terms of how multiple goals are managed.

The final chapter in the part on message production is written by Hample (chap. 5) on argumentation. Hample notes that argumentation is an activity in which humans engage and argumentation functions to create new meanings because the goal of an argument is to change how someone sees or understands the world. Starting with this basic observation, Hample convincingly defends his central thesis that most message production scholarship is about arguing and he integrates argument-specific research into the message production literature.

PART II: INTERPERSONAL COMMUNICATION

The second part of the book delves more deeply into social cognition in interpersonal contexts such as close relationships, family, and groups. Solomon and Thesis (chap. 6) lead off this section with an examination of current research on the forms of social cognition models of close relationships. This chapter also highlights the processes by which conclusions about relationships are extracted from conversation and the research on the cognitive antecedents and consequences of communication in close relationships.

Manusov (chap. 7) takes on the challenging job of summarizing the wide body of work on attributions in interpersonal interaction and relationships. She describes how attribution principles are a fundamental part of everyday sense making and our interactions with others. The attribution chapter focuses on findings relevant to social interaction and examines the use of attribution models to understand social meaning making as well as communication effects and outcomes of attribution processes.

In chapter 8, Roloff and Van Swol focus on social cognition in negotiation and group decision making with a specific emphasis on shared cognitions. In their review of the literature, the authors demonstrate how the success of group decision-making and negotiation processes depends on the ability of individuals to generate and accurately interpret messages that describe and forward their interests. Moreover, they suggest that a key "function of groups is to develop a shared reality among the members. Having shared cognition in the group allows for coordination of movement, facilitates communication and consensus, and promotes the maintenance of the group" (p. 172). Thus, this chapter demonstrates key ways in which shared cognitions affect outcomes of group decision making and negotiation processes.

In chapter 9 on family communication research, Koerner simultaneously illustrates how social cognition has not been an important theoretical perspective in this area and also provides a compelling argument for why more work should be done. He examines some of the key social cognition work that is emerging from the family literature and discusses the difficult methodological issues that arise when one wants to study social cognition within families.

Finally, chapter 10 focuses on interpersonal communication under the influence of alcohol. Lannutti and Monahan note that most major theories that examine the influence of alcohol on social interaction assume alcohol affects social behavior via cognitive impairment. This chapter traces both the pharmacological effects and the expectancy effects of alcohol consumption on social perception and communication and examines the effects of alcohol on such interpersonal behaviors as verbal aggression, compliance gaining, and communication anxiety.

PART III: MASS MEDIA

In many ways, media scholars were slow to understand the utility of social cognitive approaches for advancing our understanding of the media, which may explain why there was only one chapter on the media in Roloff andBerger's (1982) volume. As the label *media effects* would suggest, the research tradition that characterized early research on the media focused on the consequences of media use and tended to ignore the mechanisms underlying these consequences. As a result, cognitive mechanisms were ignored. Unfortunately, the uses and gratification perspective spent an inordinate amount of research focusing on people's motivations for media use instead of moving to the next generation of research, which would have focused on the cognitive consequences of the functions that media use served for individuals (Morley, 1992). However, the 1980s saw an explosion of research utilizing social cognitive approaches to understand the media. The first chapter in the part on media is an analysis of current cultivation research that focuses on the cognitive processes that mediate the relation between television viewing and judgment. Consequently, Shrum (chap. 11) examines what he refers to as the weighing and balancing (Shapiro & Lang, 1991) and the accessibility models (Shrum, 2002) and demonstrates how these models each account for the information processing stages of cultivation (i.e., encoding, storage, retrieval, judgment). Importantly, Shrum extends the present work with cultivation theory, which focuses on offline cognitive processing to consider the importance of online processing when one is examining how media can change existing attitudes and beliefs.

Racism is a problem that continues to confront this country as events that occurred during Hurricane Katrina highlighted in 2005. What role do the media play in reinforcing or promoting racism? In chapter 12, Oliver, Ramasubramanian, and Kim examine research that demonstrates how media and racism interact and the mechanisms that explain how media creates and perpetuates stereotypes and racism. In their chapter, such social cognition processes as cultivation, exemplification, priming, selective attention, and selective recall are explored as they relate to racism. In addition, Oliver and her colleagues note that research on media and racism needs to take into account recent advances in our understanding of racism, including the important work that is going on regarding implicit racism (Devine, 1989; Dovidio, Kawakami, Johnson, Johnson, & Howard, 1997; Fazio & Towles-Schwen, 1999).

In chapter 13, Eveland and Seo examine social cognitive processes that help explain how individuals process news and political communication. They focus on cognitive processing of and learning from media, the influence of news on perceptions of opinion climates, agenda setting, media priming, framing effects, and the role of expertise or sophistication as moderator of many of these effects. Methodologically, they highlight some of the changes that have occurred in survey methodologies that allow researchers to test social cognitive explanations of news via surveys, but they also note the need for more development in this area.

Finally, in the last chapter explicitly on media, Roskos-Ewoldsen, Roskos-Ewoldsen, Yang, and Lee (chap. 14) look at how people comprehend media stories. Despite numerous critiques of media scholarship because it seems to assume a perfect audience that interprets the media stimuli presented by experimenters in an identical manner (Hall, 1980/2001, 1994; Morley, 1992, 1980/1999), Roskos-Ewoldsen and colleagues note that little research has actually focused on how audiences understand media messages. As they note in their chapter, extensive research and theorizing has been conducted on text comprehension, but not much is known about how well theories of text comprehension will apply to visual media. Research in this area is complex and requires a number of different methodologies, which they highlight in this chapter.

PART IV: SOCIAL INFLUENCE

The final part of this book is comprised of four chapters on the role of social cognition in social influence or persuasive communication. Social influence, as with message design, is an area of the discipline that has embraced social cognition theories. Arpan, Rhodes, and Roskos-Ewoldsen (chap. 15) lead this part with an up-to-date analysis of attitude accessibility research. They define *attitude accessibility* as "the ease with which an attitude is activated from memory" (p. 351). The chapter demonstrates how accessible attitudes are more resistant to counterpersuasion attempts, are more likely to last longer, are better at predicting future behavior, and also are more likely to affect how future information is interpreted. In addition, they highlight new research in this area including research on implicit attitudes and racism and norm accessibility. This chapter concludes with a useful guide for gathering reaction time data.

In the 1980s, much of the research utilizing social cognition ignored or downplayed the role of affect and emotion. Since that time, scholars have come to realize the dynamic relation between emotion and cognition. In chapter 16, Nabi examines the current research on discrete emotions in social influence processes. Clearly, fear has been the most studied emotion as it relates to persuasion. However, in this chapter, Nabi summarizes her cognitive function model and several recent lines of research that move away from the simple bifurcation of positive and negative affect and offers intriguing ideas for where this work on discrete emotions and persuasion will be going.

Chapter 17, by Meyer, takes a social cognition perspective on one of the most studied aspects of social influence: compliance gaining. In this chapter, Meyer reviews research programs that examine (a) multiple goals in request messages; (b) the cognitive structures connecting influence goals and contextual features to behaviors; and (c) how perceptions of a situation influence the retrieving, designing, and editing of a compliance-gaining plan. Meyer's model—the implicit rules model—is one of the first models that utilizes principles from connectionist models of memory, which are becoming more common within cognitive psychology (McLeod, Plunkett, & Rolls, 1998).

Dual-process models of persuasion such as the elaboration likelihood model (Petty & Cacioppo, 1986) and the heuristic systematic model (Chaiken, Liberman, & Eagly, 1989) have had an enormous influence on persuasion research by scholars in both psychology and communication. Hamilton (chap. 18) reviews the theories that led up to the development of dual-process models. In addition, the chapter summarizes some of the weaknesses of these models as it outlines important issues that communication scholars need to consider as theorizing in this area moves beyond the basic dual-process models of the 1980s.

SYNTHESIS

It was illuminating for the editors to read the full set of chapters in this volume because in doing so certain commonalities emerge across this wide range of scholarship. First, we note that accessibility of information is becoming a critical concept for a wide array of scholars. Although it is not surprising to find accessibility highlighted in the chapter on attitude accessibility, a wide array of chapter authors talked about the importance of information accessibility, from Shrum's (chap. 11) discussion of cultivation theory to Meyer's (chap. 17) work with the implicit rules model to Berger's (chap. 3) work with the hierarchy principle. In addition, both Nabi (chap. 16) and Eveland and Seo (chap. 13) highlight the importance of accessible information in framing messages. Oliver et al. (chap. 12) inform us as to how priming affects the accessibility of stereotypes, and Solomon and Theiss (chap. 6) note that the accessibility of relational schemata affects current communication in relationships. Finally, Arpan et al. (chap. 15) highlight the importance of both attitude and norm accessibility in understanding how persuasion can influence behavior. Although each author may highlight a different aspect of accessibility, the focus on accessibility demonstrates the importance that research in this area is attaching to how information is being processed. Information that is accessible from memory is more likely to be processed. However, as many of these chapters illustrate, accessibility also influences how incoming information is likely to be processed. Along these same lines, several of the chapters focus on limited capacity models of attention that have important implications for understanding how information presented via the media is processed (Lang, 2000; Lang & Potter, 1999).

A second thread we saw across several chapters was a new interest in narrative. Several authors saw narrative as an important direction for social cognition and communication research to be heading in. Nabi (chap. 16) argues that the study of persuasive messages embedded in narrative or dramatic content should become a priority for those interested in persuasion and emotion. Shrum (chap. 11) also suggests that one of "the more interesting directions in recent social cognition research is a focus on narrative processing and its implications for social judgment" and how narrative offers a link between individual-level and cultural-level social cognition (p. 264). Greene and Graves (chap. 2) provide the link between narrative and message production by noting that message production work, to a large degree, is about how individuals produce narratives for others. Solomon and Theiss (chap. 6) demonstrate how relationship narratives that individuals hold can serve to constrain and shape current communication patterns between relational partners. Finally, Roskos-Ewoldsen and colleagues (chap. 14) point to the difficulties in processing narrative in addition to arguing for the importance of studying narrative comprehension for understanding many communication-related phenomenon such as cultivation effects, impression formation, and attributional processes.

A third trend that is evident is an increased focus on how information is represented in memory. The issue of how information is represented in memory has until recently largely been ignored by communication scholars interested in studying social cognition and communication. Clearly, there are exceptions to this (cf. Greene, 1984; Kellermann, 1995), but the major focus of research on communication and social cognition has been on the relation between how information is processed and communication. For example, in Roloff and Berger's (1982) introduction to their volume, they open with the observation that *"First, social cognition involves thought processes"* (p. 10). Although Roloff and Berger did later acknowledge the role of various factors such as attitudes, implicit theories, schemas, and scripts in organizing information, how that information is represented in memory is relatively ignored. Every chapter in Roloff and Berger's (1982) volume that did discuss how information was represented within the cognitive system focused on schemas or related concepts such as scripts. In the intervening more than 20 years, research and theorizing in this area has embraced basic distinctions between declarative and procedural memory, draws heavily on general models of cognition including associative or network models or memory and parallel distributed processing or connectionist models, and discusses many different ways in which information is theorized to be represented in memory, including schemas, scripts, memory organizational packets, procedural records, mental and situation models, prototypes, and exemplars. In addition, the research on traditional concepts such as schemas and scripts has become much more sophisticated. One may think that discussing so many different ways in which information is represented in memory may represent a fundamental fragmentation in our thinking about social cognition and communication. However, all of the chapters seem to appreciate that different types of representations almost certainly co-occur within the cognitive system. Even theories that were traditionally viewed as diametrically opposed to each other such as network models and connections models are now theorized to be complementary systems dealing with explicit and implicit processing, respectively (see, e.g., Sun, 2002).

METHODS

We were gratified to see the authors take the charge of considering methodology very seriously. Communication researchers often use self-report measures and, indeed, each author in this volume relies quite extensively on self-report in their own research. For social cognition theories and constructs such as cultivation effects, goals, planning, attributions, and perception, self-report measures are an excellent way of generating information to test theory. As the authors note, self-report is measured in a wide variety of ways including diary studies, free recall, questionnaires, critical incidents, focus groups, generating responses to hypothetical situations, generating request strategies, and video-assisted recall of goals in conversations.

Although self-report remains an important method, communication researchers interested in social cognition also have a wide array of other methods of measurement to assess processes and constructs that are not usually available to conscious awareness. It is critical that researchers go beyond self-report if they hope to make claims about process, how information is represented, or if they want to make arguments about how social cognition processes affect communication outcomes. The authors in this volume use three types of measures to capture feelings and thoughts unavailable to conscious awareness, those that might be misrepresented by asking a participant, and social cognitive processes that effect perception and behavior: measures of time, behavioral observations, and physiological measures.

First, most, if not all, authors highlight the importance of measuring time. For example, research examining message generation and responses to media messages often uses response latencies that measure how fast one responds to a given stimuli. Response latencies are effective at assessing the strength of association between a stimulus and other concepts in memory as well as providing an assessment of the accessibility of information in memory. Time has also been examined using secondary-task reaction time measures to tap residual attentional resources not being used in the primary processing tasks. Such tasks as lexical decision making, semantic priming, and the implicit attitude test use response latencies to assess implicit attitudes and perceptions. Implicit measures are helpful when overt measures (e.g., self-report measures) are subject to bias (e.g., when asking about racial stereotyping). Implicit measures using time as the dependent measure are helpful in that researchers are not interested in what specific answer participants give but in how long it takes them to make decisions. For example, Monahan, Shtrulis, and Brown Givens (2005) found that participants more quickly associate positive words with Whites than with African Americans. In addition, participants more quickly associate negative words with African Americans than they do with Whites. Overall, social cognition and communication researchers examine time as a way of assessing cognitive processing in such a way that the researcher is not dependent on either self-report or evaluative responses.

Second, authors examining message processing and interpersonal processes often rely on behavioral observations—especially when one is interested in examining dyadic interactions, family communication patterns, or negotiators—any situation in which shared cognitions are important. A nice aspect to behavioral observation is that such methods allow researchers to examine speech production measures to assess errors, verbal fluencies, patterns of repetition, and the relation between the verbal and nonverbal channels of communication. Moreover, by tracing a conversation about a particular issue, one can see how shared cognitions are formed.

Third, physiological measures are utilized when researchers examine the interplay between emotion and cognition as well as to examine the stages of social information processing (e.g., attention, arousal, encoding, and storage). In media research physiological measures assess orienting responses, attention, arousal, and other cognitive processing that occurs in response to media stimuli. A wide array of measures are used, including physiological measures of facial affect, heart rate, skin conductance, eyes-on screen measures, and so on. Researchers also use neurophysiological techniques such as functional magnetic resonance imaging (fMRI), positron emission tomography (PET), and tracking fluctuations in the alpha frequency of the electroencephalogram (EEG), which provide new opportunities to observe brain activity in response to social stimuli.

The research innovations of the past 20 years demonstrate the inventiveness of various scholars and a dedication to capturing the dynamic processes that are involved in the study of communication and social cognition. The research traditions that have developed also demonstrate the importance of triangulation. As these chapters demonstrate, no single method is enough to answer the myriad questions that remain to be addressed. The study of communication and social cognition demands a commitment to multiplicity of research methods.

CONCLUSION

The desire to understand how we generate, process, and understand communication behaviors has puzzled communication researchers since Aristotle. This desire has led a wide array of scholars across several disciplines to focus their attention on social information processing. Each chapter in this volume offers a state-of-the-art analysis of current social cognition research in communication. Given new exciting discoveries using neuroscience techniques; our ability to understand how and why people form the messages they do; what they perceive in the media and why such perceptions affect their decision making; and how our mental models of family, friends, and coworkers are updated, changed, and affect social discourse seem endless. Although these research traditions have long histories, each of the chapters demonstrates the authors' zeal for theorizing and research in these areas. Much has been accomplished, but the excitement that exists in this area is palatable and infectious. We hope you enjoy reading this volume as much as we did editing it.

REFERENCES

Brown, P., & Levinson, S. C. (1978). Universals in language usage: Politeness phenomena. In E. Goody (Ed.), *Questions and politeness: Strategies in social interaction* (pp. 56–289). Cambridge, UK: Cambridge University Press.

Chaiken, S., Liberman, A., & Eagly, A. H. (1989). Heuristic and systematic information processing within and beyond the persuasion context. In J. S. Uleman & J. A. Bargh (Eds.), *Unintended thought* (pp. 212–252). New York: Guilford.

Devine, P. G. (1989). Stereotypes and prejudice: Their automatic and controlled components. *Journal of Personality and Social Psychology, 56,* 5–18.

Dillard, J. P. (2004). The goals-plans-action model of interpersonal influence. In J. S. Seiter & R. H. Gass (Eds.), *Perspectives on persuasion, social influence, and compliance gaining* (pp. 185–206). Boston: Allyn & Bacon.

Dovidio, J. F., Kawakami, K., Johnson, C., Johnson, B., & Howard, A. (1997). On the nature of prejudice: Automatic and controlled processes. *Journal of Experimental Social Psychology, 33,* 510–540.

Fazio, R. H., & Towles-Schwen, T. (1999). The MODE model of attitude–behavior processes. In S. Chaiken & Y. Trope (Eds.), *Dual-process theories in social psychology* (pp. 97–116). New York: Guilford.

Greene, J. O. (1984). A cognitive approach to human communication: An action assembly theory. *Communication Monographs, 51,* 289–306.

Greene, J. O. (Ed.). (1997). *Message prcduction: Advances in communication theory.* Hillsdale, NJ: Lawrence Erlbaum Associates.

Hall, S. (1994). Reflections upon the encoding/decoding model: An interview with Stuart Hall. In J. Cruz & J. Lewis (Eds.), *Viewing, reading, listening: Audiences and cultural reception* (pp. 253–274). Boulder, CO: Westview.

Hall, S. (2001). Encoding/decoding. In M. G. Durham & D. M. Kellner (Eds.), *Media and cultural studies: Keyworks* (pp. 166–176). Malden, MA: Blackwell. (Original work published 1980)

Kellermann, K. (1995). The conversation MOP: A model of patterned and pliable behavior. In D. E. Hewes (Ed.), *The cognitive bases of interpersonal communication* (pp. 181–221). Mahwah, NJ: Lawrence Erlbaum Associates.

Lang, A. (2000). The limited capacity model of mediated message processing. *Journal of Communication, 50,* 46–70.

Lang, A., & Potter, R. F. (1999). Something for nothing: Is visual encoding automatic? *Media Psychology, 1,* 145–154.

McLeod, P., Plunkett, K., & Rolls, E. T. (1998). *Introduction to connectionist modeling of cognitive processes.* Oxford, UK: Oxford University Press.

Monahan, J. L., Shtrulis, S., & Brown Givens, S. (2005). Priming welfare queens and other stereotypes: The transference of media images into interpersonal contexts. *Communication Research Reports, 22,* 195–205.

Morley, D. (1992). *Television, audiences & cultural studies.* London: Routledge.

Morley, D. (1999). The nationwide audience: Structure and decoding. In D. Morley & C. Brunsdon (Eds.), *The nationwide television studies* (pp. 111–228). London: Routledge. (Original work published 1980)

O'Keefe, B. J. (1988). The logic of message design. *Communication Monographs, 55,* 80–103.

Petty, R. E., & Cacioppo, J. T. (1986). The elaboration likelihood model of persuasion. In L. Berkowitz (Ed.), *Advances in experimental social psychology* (Vol. 19, pp. 123–205). New York: Academic.

Roloff, M., & Berger, C. R. (1982). *Social cognition and communication.* Beverly Hills, CA: Sage

Shapiro, M. A., & Lang, A. (1991). Making television reality: Unconscious processes in the construction of social reality. *Communication Research, 18,* 685–705.

Shrum, L. J. (2002). Media consumption and perceptions of social reality: Effects and underlying processes. In J. Bryant & D. Zillmann (Eds.), *Media effects: Advances in theory and research* (2nd ed., pp. 69–95). Mahwah, NJ: Lawrence Erlbaum Associates.

Sun, R. (2002). *Duality of the mind: A bottom up approach toward cognition.* Mahwah, NJ: Lawrence Erlbaum Associates.

Wilson, S. R., Aleman, C. G., & Leatham, G. B. (1998). Identity implications of influence goals: A revised analysis of face-threatening acts and application to seeking compliance with same-sex friends. *Human Communication Research, 25,* 64–96.

Wilson, S. R., Greene, J. O., & Dillard, J. P. (2000). Introduction to the special issue on message production: Progress, challenges, and prospects. *Communication Theory, 10,* 135–138.

I

Message Production

2

Cognitive Models of Message Production

John O. Greene
Purdue University

Angela R. Graves
Oral Roberts University

It is of no small consequence, and a happy circumstance, that this chapter is titled as it is rather than, say, something like "Psychological Models of Speech Production." The project suggested by such an alternative title would be a daunting one indeed—we suspect that it would not be possible to do justice to that topic in less than several hundred pages. Fortunately, our task is made considerably more tractable by limiting the focus to message production rather than speech production and by restricting the domain of models under examination to those that reflect the particular stance of cognitive science as opposed to the broader constellation of approaches that address issues of behavioral production by invoking psychological constructs of one sort or another.

The roots of the study of speech production can be traced at least as far back as the 1950s, and to a pair of seminal events, the publication of Chomsky's (1957) *Syntactic Structures* and the birth of cognitivism (a date pegged as September 11, 1956 by Gardner [1987]). Work on speech production is most closely associated with the fields of psycholinguistics and neurolinguistics (and to a lesser extent, developmental psychology) and has tended to focus on the acquisition and representation of phonological, syntactic, and semantic knowledge and the corresponding production of words, clauses, sentences, and more extended narratives (see, e.g., Aitchison, 1998; Miller & Eimas, 1995; Tomasello & Bates, 2001).

The study of *message production* obviously shares much in common with that of *speech production*, but differs in the emphasis that scholars working in this tradition place on the conception of message behavior as a *social activity*.[1] Fundamental to the message production approach is the conception of activities carried out in social interaction, by social actors pursuing social ends, in contexts governed by social rules and norms. People are seen to construct their messages in light of some model or understanding of their interlocutors, a model of the unfolding interaction, their goals, situational constraints, and so on. The essential point of distinction, then, lies in the fundamental apprehension of what people are doing when they speak. From the point of view of the message production tradition, rather than producing words, sentences, and narratives, people are *communicating by producing messages*.[2]

Limiting the focus of this chapter to cognitive approaches is as significant as the editors' request to focus on message production. There are different views of exactly what cognitivism entails (see Churchland, 1992; Flanagan, 1991), but in general, cognitive approaches seek to explain behavior by describing the system of mental structures and processes that produced those behaviors. Cognitive models, then, are a subset of the larger world of psychological approaches that also includes a variety of other sorts of theoretical constructs and formulations.[3]

SOME HISTORICAL CONTEXT

During the 1970s scholars in the field of communication became increasingly interested in the implications of developments in the cognitive sciences for understanding communication processes (see, e.g., Craig, 1978, 1979; Miller, 1976). By the end of that decade the assumptions, experimental paradigms, and models of cognitive science had come to exert considerable influence on the thinking of communication scholars. Thus, by the

---

[1]This is not to say, of course, that scholars engaged in the study of speech production do not conceive of speech production as a communicative act. The distinction we are suggesting here is one of relative emphasis. What we have characterized as the speech production and message production traditions are, doubtless, best conceived as fuzzy sets without a distinct boundary, but with central and peripheral members, and where specific research programs might legitimately be held to belong to both domains.

[2]If the social thrust of message production has the effect of restricting the boundaries of that tradition relative to that of speech production, there are two other characteristics of the message production approach that actually make it broader and more encompassing than the study of speech production. First, message production has given relatively greater emphasis to the nonverbal components of communicative behavior. Second, as noted later in this chapter, message production encompasses both intra- and interindividual processes (see Greene, 1997a).

[3]Examples of other psychological traditions include "trait" approaches that ground explanations in presumed general dispositions (e.g., extroversion) and "cognitive neuroscience" which seeks to explain behavior in terms of brain structures and processes.

early 1980s titles like "A Cognitive Model of ..." and "An Information Processing Approach to ..." had become relatively commonplace in the field's convention programs. The publication of Roloff and Berger's (1982a) *Social Cognition and Communication* was a signal event in that it evidenced a critical mass of scholars working to apply insights derived from the study of the mind to problems of interest to people in the field of communication.

A survey of the contents of that volume, however, reveals two features that merit note in the context of this chapter. First, as suggested by the book's title, the particular slice of the broad spectrum of cognitive science reflected in the various chapters tends to be that of *social cognition;* that is, an amalgam of traditional social psychology and cognitivism concerned with social sense-making (Fiske & Taylor, 1984; see also Reeves, Chaffee, & Tims, 1982; Roloff & Berger, 1982b). Second, and in keeping with the general thrust of the social-cognition perspective at that time, the chapters in Roloff and Berger (1982a) are primarily concerned with input processing and social perception, and relatively little space is devoted to the production of behavior. Only two chapters, those by O'Keefe and Delia (1982) and by Street and Giles (1982), give much consideration to processes pertinent to message production. The O'Keefe and Delia chapter summarizes research by scholars, primarily at (or trained at) the University of Illinois, on the impact of variations in the nature of people's interpersonal construct systems on the production of listener-adapted messages. More specifically, the authors suggest that individuals who possess more differentiated and abstract constructs for apprehending others are more likely to arrive at complex configurations of social objectives, and, by extension, to produce messages that reflect a concern with multiple ends (for more recent reviews of work in the constructivist tradition, see Burleson, 1987; Gastil, 1995; Wilson, 2002). The Street and Giles (1982) chapter is more broadly concerned with mutual influence processes; that is, patterns of increasing similarity and dissimilarity in behavior that emerge during the course of an interaction. The authors review and critique three of the models of mutual influence that had been developed by the early 1980s, but their primary focus is on explicating speech accommodation theory. The thrust of this theory is that social actors enact patterns of convergence and divergence to gain social approval, communicate more effectively, establish positive social identities, dissociate from the other, and so on. The specific cognitive mechanisms by which behavioral changes are enacted are not the primary focus of the theory, but Street and Giles did suggest that preestablished memory structures may permit people to manifest behavioral changes with little or no conscious awareness (for more recent reviews of speech accommodation theory, see Burgoon, Stern, & Dillman, 1995; Giles, Coupland, & Coupland, 1991).

The fact that comparatively little space in *Social Cognition and Communication* is devoted to message production should not be taken as an indication that such work had not yet begun to develop. The aforementioned study of speech production that began in the 1950s had, by the early 1980s, resulted in an impressively large body of theory and data (see, e.g., Aaronson & Rieber, 1979; Butterworth, 1980; Dechert & Raupach, 1980; Fromkin, 1980; Rosenberg, 1977). More important, one can discern, here and there in that literature (e.g., Clippenger, 1977; Coulmas, 1981; Siegman & Feldstein, 1979), a rising awareness of speech as message production. There were other research programs and traditions bearing directly on message production as well. For example, in addition to the models of mutual influence reviewed by Street and Giles (1982), the decade of the 1970s witnessed the development of a number of other models of mutual influence processes (e.g., Argyle & Cook, 1976; Burgoon, 1978; Patterson, 1976). Another prominent example of the growing interest in message production is the work on verbal and nonverbal correlates of deception (see Knapp & Comadena, 1979; Zuckerman, DePaulo, & Rosenthal, 1981); yet a third example can be seen in the rising recognition that understanding the experience and overt manifestation of social anxiety and apprehension would require consideration of the thought processes of the anxious person (see Daly, 1978; Greene & Sparks, 1983). As one final example, and perhaps most pertinent, throughout the decade of the 1970s Motley and his associates (see Motley, Camden, & Baars, 1979, 1981) were engaged in the systematic investigation of phoneme transposition errors.

Thus, although it is not well reflected in Roloff and Berger's (1982a) book (again, doubtless a consequence of that volume's focus on social cognition), there was at that time a gathering momentum of cognitive approaches to the study of message production. In relatively short order, then, there appeared a number of seminal treatments of cognitive mechanisms involved in the production of various features of message behavior, including discrepancy–arousal theory (Cappella & Greene, 1982), action assembly theory (Greene, 1984), and work by several authors on message planning (e.g., Berger, 1988; Hobbs & Evans, 1980; Infante, 1980; McLaughlin et al., 1985). Since the mid-1980s, work on cognitive approaches to message production has continued to develop, and a number of surveys of advances in the area have appeared (e.g., Burleson, 1995; Cody & McLaughlin, 1990; Greene, 1997b; Greene & Cody, 1985; Hewes, 1995; Palmer, 1994; Wilson, 2002; Wilson, Greene, & Dillard, 2000).

THREE TOOLS FOR UNDERSTANDING COGNITIVE MODELS OF MESSAGE PRODUCTION

Message production takes in a lot of territory—the complexity of human message behavior is such that it can be conceptualized, partitioned, and analyzed in countless ways. For example, one might focus on how it is that people develop the specific *ideas* that they wish to communicate to others; alternatively, one could focus on how people are able to generate overt *utterances* that, to some degree, convey those ideas. The utterances themselves reflect selection of specific *words* and *syntax*. The verbal component of message behavior is embedded in a constellation of *nonverbal features* (facial expressions, eye behavior, gestures, etc.). The verbal and nonverbal elements of message behavior may be enacted in pursuit of certain social *goals*, and may have been the result of *plans* for accomplishing those goals. What a person says and does may reflect greater or lesser knowledge of *social rules*, understanding of the *perceptions of his or her interlocutor*, and *strategic sophistication*. Message features may be well-worn *routines* (e.g., "How's it going?"), or they may be *novel*—something the person has never said or done before.

Obviously, then, there are a great many aspects of message production that a scholar might legitimately choose to focus on. There is also a virtually limitless number of ways that he or she might seek to explain the specific characteristics of message production that are of interest. As an approach to building theory, cognitivism emphasizes that it is possible to arrive at multiple, distinct models, all equally adequate to explain some phenomenon. In fact, the specific details of a cognitive model are ultimately limited only by the theorist's imagination (constrained, of course, by the standard criteria for evaluating theory; i.e., predictive accuracy, heurism, falsifiability, parsimony, etc.). As a result, the potential exists for a weltering array of models of message production—models focused on any of the enormous number of properties of message production, coupled with the endless variety of cognitive formalisms that might be devised to explain those message phenomena. Fortunately, in reality, the situation is not quite that complicated. Cognitive scientists have developed a relatively limited number of generally recognized conceptions of mental structures and processes that have proven applicable and useful in understanding many different domains of human behavior. Moreover, by applying a few basic questions to cognitive models of message production it is possible to impose some order on what might otherwise appear to be a rather chaotic body of work. The answers to such questions reveal points of both similarity and difference in the various models and provide a conceptual scheme for reviewing work in the area. Perhaps the three most obvious and fundamental of these questions are: (a) What is the theory about? (b) What sorts of theoretical terms are invoked?, and (c) What methods and data are brought to bear?

What Is the Theory About?

As noted earlier, there are any number of characteristics of message production that a researcher might select for analysis. An essential first question, then, involves identifying what set of message phenomena are addressed by a given theory or research program. At a very fine-grained level of analysis, any theory will almost certainly emphasize some unique constellation of message features and processes. As a result, even two theories that appear to be focused on the same phenomenon, may, in fact, be addressing slightly different aspects of that process. When characterizing any particular theory, then, we need to attend carefully to answering the question, "What is the theory about?"

Of course, such a fine-grained level of analysis will not meet the exigencies of a chapter such as this. At a much more general level, then, it is possible to discern certain broad categories of cognitive models of message production based on the general classes of phenomena with which they are concerned. Figure 2.1 provides a schematic representation of

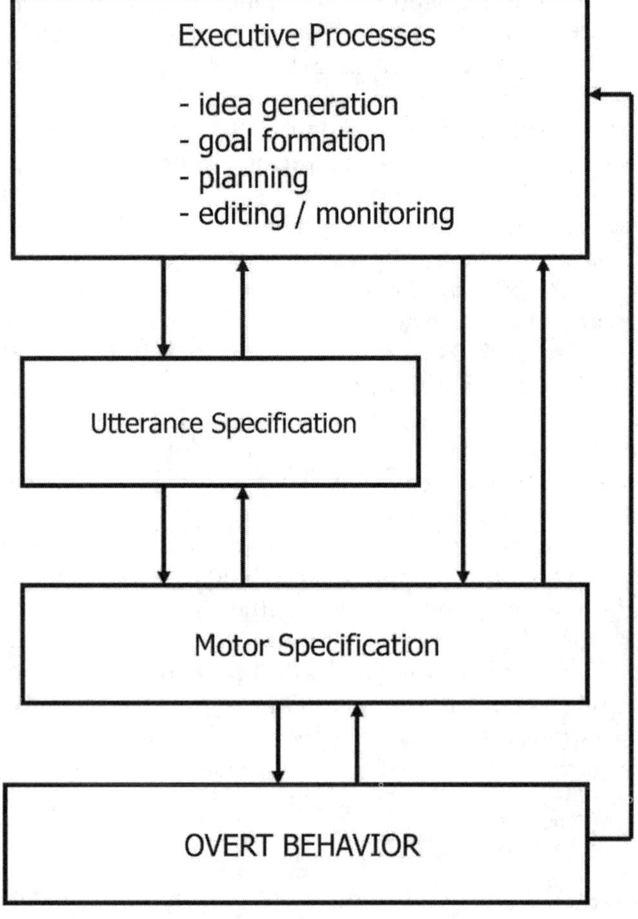

FIGURE 2.1.

some of the essential functions thought to be involved in message production. *Executive processes* refer to higher order activities such as idea generation, goal formation, planning, and editing or monitoring of potential and actual behavior. *Utterance specification* involves the processes of arriving at specific words and syntax that will be expressed in the verbal component of a message. *Motor specification* encompasses the formulation of programs for actually pronouncing verbal strings, as well as for all the nonverbal features that will accompany the verbal message. Finally, *overt production* involves the execution of those motor programs. Beyond these basic components, it is significant that the model in Figure 2.1 includes various bidirectional arrows and feedback loops to indicate that message production need not proceed unidirectionally from idea to verbal plan to overt behavior (and by the same token, there is no assumption of a temporal ordering of the various executive processes.) Even so, the model in Figure 2.1 is obviously quite rudimentary, but it does provide a framework for answering questions about the focus or domain of a given theory. Moreover, because scholars have devoted considerable attention to some of the processes highlighted in the model while subjecting others to less scrutiny, the model suggests areas where more intensive research efforts might be directed.

What Sorts of Theoretical Terms Are Invoked?

The question of the nature of the cognitive formalism(s) invoked to explain some message production phenomena concerns the very nuts and bolts of the explanation; that is, what are the mechanisms that produce the phenomenon of interest? This is obviously the central question in understanding any cognitive model, but preliminary to exploring this issue we need to consider the nature of cognitive explanations in general. As we noted earlier, there are differing views about where the precise boundaries of cognitive theories lie, but probably the most widely accepted position among cognitivists themselves is that of metaphysical functionalism (Flanagan, 1991). The essence of functionalism is to cast explanations in terms of mental structures and events rather than physical (i.e., brain) structures and events. The functionalist accepts that mental processes must have some instantiation in the brain (and seeks to be informed about neural processes), but holds that there is value to pursuing explanations that involve structures and processes of the mind (e.g., intentions, planning, scripts, etc.). Thus, cognitivism is distinct from behaviorism (in its various manifestations) on one hand because it accords explanatory prominence to mental states and processes, and on the other, from neuroscience, which pursues explanations grounded in physical entities and processes.

Working within a functionalist framework, then, it is possible to make a general distinction between two types of explanatory constructs. In a seminal essay, Dennett (1971) showed that the behavior of a complex system (like the message behavior of a human being) can be apprehended via three alternative approaches. The first of these, the *physical stance,* involves attempts to explain and predict the system's behavior in terms of its physical construction and operation, as in neuroscientific approaches to the study of speech production. The remaining two approaches involve recourse to functionalist constructs, and thus would fall within the realm of cognitive models (as that domain was delimited in the preceding paragraph). Dennett noted that, on one hand, the behavior of a system can be apprehended from an *intentional stance;* that is, by ascribing to it some goal, or goals, and information relevant to accomplishing those goals. In the realm of message behavior, then, an intentional stance account for what a person said might involve notions of what he or she wanted, knew, and expected.

Intentional stance accounts have obvious intuitive appeal—they invoke the terms of our everyday experience of, and talk about, mental processes. On the other hand, they have certain limitations as psychological explanations. Among these are that intentional stance accounts assume rationality; that is, an explanation based on goals and information will work only when the system does what it should do, given its goals and knowledge. In the realm of human message behavior, however, people often fail to say and do what they should in light of the things they know and that they want to accomplish (see Greene & Geddes, 1993). A second, related concern is that although the sort of mental states invoked as explanatory constructs in intentional stance models have a commonsense appeal because social actors may be aware of their goals and beliefs, much of what goes on in message production is not available to the person himself or herself. As one example, the ordering of words in a clause is governed by processes that almost certainly are not available to consciousness (see Bock, 1982), and, more generally, people are simply unaware of many of the features of their own verbal and nonverbal behavior (see Hample, 1987; Kellermann, 1992; Palmer & Simmons, 1995).

The third alternative identified by Dennett (1971), the *design stance,* provides a means of overcoming some of the limitations of the intentional stance. The essence of the design stance is to describe the functional units thought to be responsible for a system's behavior. Put another way, the idea is to specify the tasks the system must be executing to perform as it does. Consider Figure 2.1 once again; this could be considered a design stance model, albeit a very rudimentary one, in the sense that the model identifies functional units devoted to goal formation, planning, and so on. Of course, such "white boxology" does not take us very far toward understanding the processes involved in message production. The sorts of macro functions identified in Figure 2.1 can be seen to involve still more fundamental processes, and the real potential of design stance approaches comes from more fine-grained specification of the functional units involved in carrying out goal formation, planning, and what have you. Developing design stance models requires specifying how information is represented in a particular mental subsystem and how that information is processed (e.g., accessed, transformed, used) to carry out the system's functions (see J. R. Anderson, 1976). In other words, the theorist seeks to describe (a) what kind of information is held in the system and how that information is structured, and (b) the nature of the processes that operate over that information (see Greene, 1995).

One way of answering the question "What sort of theoretical terms are invoked?" in a cognitive model of message production, then, is simply to discern whether the explanation is cast in intentional stance terms, design stance terms, or, as is often the case, a hybrid that incorporates both types of constructs. At a deeper level of analysis answering this question requires examination of the specific design stance formalisms employed in the model.

What Methods and Data Are Brought to Bear?

The fact that cognitive theories are cast in functional terms rather than physical terms (i.e., at the level of mind rather than brain) makes the task of the cognitivist rather different from that of the neuroscientist. Rather than examine neural structures and processes, the cognitive scientist relies primarily on the method of *transcendental deduction* (see Flanagan, 1991). That is, he or she observes relations between inputs and responses and infers what must be the nature of the mental system that could have produced such regularities. This approach to theory building makes almost any sort of behavioral response potentially relevant for understanding the mind, and in fact, scholars have relied on a wide array of output variables in developing their models (see Greene, 1988); among the most important categories of clues to the nature of the output system are verbal reports, message regularities, and temporal measures.

Verbal Reports. Perhaps the most obvious means of gaining a window on people's thought processes is simply to ask them what they are thinking and doing. Such verbal reports are particularly relevant for accessing the sorts of higher level cognitive constructs that are available to conscious introspection, such as goals and plans (e.g., Daly, Weber, Vangelisti, Maxwell, & Neal, 1989; Infante, 1980). At the same time, relying on verbal reports requires caution. As we noted earlier, there are many aspects of message production that are not typically available to consciousness. Moreover, even when asked to report on activities that they might reasonably be expected to have access to, people's reports of what they were thinking can be erroneous. In an important paper, Ericsson and Simon (1980) argued that retrospective reports and reports on mental contents that must be recoded into verbal form are less likely to be valid. Although concerns about the validity of verbal reports are real, there are techniques for reducing these concerns (see Waldron & Cegala, 1992; see also Ericsson & Simon, 1984), and verbal reports remain a potentially important source of data for illuminating certain of the processes involved in message production.

Message Regularities. A second source of clues about the nature of the message production system is recurrent patterns of various message features. The basic idea is that an observed pattern in what people say and do must be the product of what is represented in the mind and how that information is processed, and for this reason, such regularities can be used to draw inferences about the nature of those representations and processes. A good example of such recurrent patterns is found in Kuiper's (1996) analysis of the speech behavior of auctioneers and horse-race announcers. Kuiper argued that people in these professions are able to maintain very high rates of speech while responding to changing situational conditions because they rely on preestablished formulae (e.g., "they're off and running," "round the turn they come") that are stored in long-term memory. There are numerous other examples of recurrent patterns in message behavior (see Coulmas, 1981), ranging from the structure of initial conversations with a stranger (Kellermann, 1995) to paying someone a compliment (Manes & Wolfson, 1981), and again, the idea is that the very fact that such patterns do occur must reveal something about the mental system that produced them.[4]

A slightly different type of message regularity used to draw inferences about the nature of the output system is speech errors (see Fromkin, 1980). One might suppose that speech errors are just random "glitches," but, in fact, such errors are not random, and the very fact that they reflect underlying regularities tells something about how the message production system functions even when speech is error-free. There

---

[4]It is important to note that caution is in order when attempting to draw conclusions about the nature of the message production system based on observed message regularities. Having ascertained some recurrent message feature, it may be tempting to infer that this feature corresponds in some relatively direct way to the contents of long-term memory. However, Greene (1990) showed that such an inferential leap may not be warranted.

are at least a couple of important senses in which speech errors are not random. First, they tend to occur under certain conditions and not under others. For example, we are more likely to experience the "tip-of-the-tongue" phenomenon when the word we are searching for is one we do not use too often (Brown & McNeill, 1966; MacKay, 1980), a fact that suggests that models of message production need to incorporate some formalism that captures the effects of familiarity and practice. A second sense in which speech errors reflect an underlying regularity is that certain types of errors are relatively common, whereas others almost never occur. As an example, Boomer and Laver (1968) found that when syllables are transposed between adjacent words, the first syllable of one word may be transposed with the first syllable of the second (e.g., when intending to say "well made" someone might actually say "mell wade") but never will the second syllable of the first intended word be transposed with the first syllable of the next word (e.g., "wem lade"). Other regularities are simply tendencies to make one sort of error more frequently than another. For example, when people are induced to make slips of the tongue in which they transpose syllables, they are more likely to utter actual words than nonwords (see Motley, Baars, & Camden, 1983).

A third sort of message regularity involves patterns that occur across distinct behavioral channels. There are many such interchannel regularities, including familiar examples such as the relation between direction of gaze and speech (e.g., Beattie, 1979, 1981), which suggest that speakers avert their gaze when faced with difficulties in encoding a verbal message. Other examples would include relations between gestural activity and verbal production, as in the case of the link between filled pauses and gestures (e.g., Christenfeld, Schachter, & Bilous, 1991), or between the form of hand and arm gestures and the semantic content of speech (McNeill, 1992). In these and numerous other examples, the covariation of cues in different message channels yields clues to the nature of the output system that could not be garnered from examination of a single message channel (see Cappella & Palmer, 1990).

Temporal Measures. A third class of cues examined to draw inferences about message production processes are various temporal measures of speech (see Greene, 1988; Siegman, 1979). Examples of temporal measures include speech-onset latency and speaker-turn latency (i.e., the time required to begin speaking), and various measures of silent pausing after the onset of speech such as pause–phonation ratio and speech rate. The significance of temporal measures like these stems from two considerations. On one hand, because the cognitive processes involved in message production unfold over time, examining how long it takes to formulate or produce a response provides a window on those underlying processes. If a theorist believes that he or she has specified the mechanisms involved in some aspect of message production, then it should be possible to impact the speed of message production in predictable ways by systematically varying some factor that is implicated by his or her construal of those mechanisms. So, for example, if a particular model suggests that sentence encoding is sensitive to syntactic complexity, the time to begin producing complex sentences should be longer than the time required to initiate less complex constructions (see Ferreira, 1991). As an extension of this basic idea, many models assume that certain processes involved in message production make demands on a limited pool of processing resources (e.g., Greene, 1984; Levelt, 1989), and when demands on this finite reserve are high, message production will be slowed. Thus, experimental manipulations that are posited to increase cognitive load should affect the speed with which people are able to speak.

Distinguishing Data and Domain

One final comment is in order regarding the analytic tools for understanding cognitive models of message production that we have presented here. People sometimes fail to appreciate that the first question posed earlier (i.e., "What is the theory about?") is, in fact, different from the third (i.e., "What methods and data are brought to bear?"). To illustrate the distinction, suppose a model is developed that describes the memory structures and processes involved in producing narratives. The specific nature of the formalisms invoked in the model may yield the prediction that certain types of stories will result in greater cognitive load than others, and the theorist may embark on a series of studies examining silent pauses to test the theory. The fact that pauses are the dependent variable examined in these studies (i.e., the data) should not obscure the fact that the domain of the model is narrative production. Just as physicists may examine the production and decay of a particular subatomic particle (the data) to test theories about the nature of all matter (the domain), cognitivists may study a particular message feature to test theories with a focus that extends well beyond that individual message feature.

MODELS OF MESSAGE PRODUCTION

Any of the three questions posed in the preceding section could be used to organize a discussion of cognitive models of message production. That is, one could structure the discussion according to the message phenomena of interest in various models, or the nature of the theoretical terms invoked in those models, or by the types of methods and data that have been used to shed light on message production processes. It is probably the case that any of these approaches would serve our purposes,[5] but in what follows we have taken the first option. In keeping with the editors' vision for the book, our aim in this section is to highlight representative and seminal models, rather than attempt a comprehensive review of work in the area.

The essence of science is to describe regularities or patterns, and to explain, predict, and perhaps control, those regularities. In the realm of message production research one can discern two broad traditions of inquiry distinguished by the nature of the regularities that are of primary interest (see Greene, 1997a). On one hand are studies of intraindividual processes and patterns. Work in this tradition focuses on questions such as how people generate ideas about what to say, how they formulate plans for conveying those ideas to others, and how it is possible to produce overt verbal and nonverbal behaviors that in some sense correspond to their ideas and plans. The second tradition gives greater emphasis to interindividual regularities and processes; that is, on interdependencies between people engaged in interaction. This work includes investigations of turn taking, interaction synchrony, development of shared frames of reference, and so on.

Of the large body of work on interindividual regularities, much of it quite sophisticated (e.g., Sanders, 1997), a relatively small portion involves efforts to ground explanations in cognitive (i.e., functional) terms. One area where there have been attempts to develop models that explicitly incorporate cognitive constructs is that of mutual influence processes (i.e., patterns of increasing similarity and dissimilarity) mentioned earlier in this chapter. Even though the primary focus of these models is interindividual dynamics, theorists working in the area have recognized that understanding those regularities requires consideration of processes transpiring within each individual. Thus it is common to find appeals to memory stores of social knowledge, processes of drawing on that social knowledge to form expectations for the behavior of others, processes of assessing or evaluating deviations from those expectations, processes of integrating or combining multiple relevant factors, and processes of controlling or effecting changes in one's own behavior (e.g., P. A. Anderson, 1998; Burgoon et al., 1995; Patterson, 1982). As might be expected given the interaction phenomena of interest in these models, however, their characterizations of cognitive structures and processes tend to be cast in very general terms, or to be altogether unspecified.

[5]Of course the most comprehensive approach would be to construct a three-dimensional matrix defined by domain, theoretical terms, and data, within which specific models could be positioned.

Turning to the realm of models focused to a greater degree on intraindividual processes, one finds more emphasis devoted to explicating cognitive mechanisms (albeit typically with a corresponding deemphasis on interpersonal regularities). Among these, even if only for expository purposes, it is useful to draw a distinction between models devoted to explaining some particular subprocess involved in message production (e.g., goal formation, planning) and what might be termed more "comprehensive" models that attempt to incorporate and explicate a broader range of the cognitive phenomena that underlie and give rise to verbal and nonverbal messages.[6] In the remainder of this section we consider examples of each of these.

Message Production Subprocesses

Idea Generation. We typically think of message production as a process in which ideational content (i.e., one's thoughts or understandings) is, in some way, manifested as overt verbal and nonverbal cues. The process of idea generation, then, is an essential component of message production. Idea generation in many models sets in motion the operation of the other components of the output system. Despite its centrality to the overall message production process, idea generation has received relatively little attention in models of message production—it tends to be assumed rather than treated as a process in need of explication. Moreover, where idea generation is addressed, the treatments are sometimes rather rudimentary. It is possible to conceive of idea generation in three increasingly sophisticated ways. One approach is to view idea generation essentially as a process of selection; that is, the person is assumed to possess a repository of ideas, or propositions, and idea generation simply involves the selection of some particular elements from that repository. A somewhat more sophisticated approach is to view idea generation as sequencing; that is, selection from a repository of ideational content reflects a chaining or temporal ordering, thereby introducing the potential for novelty stemming from a unique sequencing of existing propositions. Finally, at a more sophisticated level still, one can think of idea generation as creation; rather than relying solely on the contents of a preexisting repository of ideas, people are able to assemble more elemental cognitive units to formulate ideas and understandings that they have never thought or encountered before. In the main, models of message production have tended to rely on one of the first two senses of idea generation, rather than the last. Where

---

[6]In reality, of course, the distinction is more one of degree than of kind, and even what we have termed comprehensive models can readily be seen to focus on certain of the subprocesses involved in message production while shedding little light on others.

models do acknowledge the sense of idea generation as creation, the mechanisms that give rise to the creation of new ideas typically are not explicated.

A typical example of the somewhat more refined approaches to idea generation is found in the model of message production developed by Herrmann (1983).[7] Like other comprehensive models (see later) of message production, in the hierarchical system Hermann proposes, a speaker's intended meaning passes through a series of successively more concrete stages, culminating with overt expression. In the terminology of the model, the *propositional base* that gives rise to a message consists of an activated body of declarative information that comprises a speaker's intended meaning. From the very large number of cognitions in the propositional base, some small portion is selected to form the *semantic input* to the remainder of the message production system where lexical, syntactic, and prosodic features of the eventual utterance are formulated. What is particularly germane in the context of a discussion of idea generation is the nature of the processes by which the propositional base is formed, and Hermann suggests two possibilities: On one hand, existing declarative information is selectively activated on the basis of the speaker's goals and construal of the situation. Here, then, is the notion of idea generation as selection—the speaker possesses a body of declarative information, and from this store, some subset is activated. There is, however, a second sense of idea generation embodied in Hermann's (1983) formulation. He notes that the elements of declarative knowledge that comprise the propositional base are not always preformulated, but rather are sometimes created to "enrich and elaborate" (p. 36) the body of activated knowledge. Here we find allusion to the sense of idea generation as creation—the generation of novel thoughts and understandings—but the model is mute with respect to the nature of the mechanisms that give rise to such novel cognitions.

Goal Formation Processes. One of the most influential conceptions to emerge in the study of message production is that people formulate social goals, that these goals precipitate planning, which in turn results in actions intended to accomplish one's goals (see Dillard, 1990). From the perspective of this goals-plans-action (GPA) framework, then, the processes underlying goal formation are an essential piece of the message production puzzle, and scholars have devoted considerable effort to ascertaining the nature of social goals (see Dillard, 1990, 1997; Wilson & Feng, chap. 4, this volume) and goal-formation processes (see Austin & Vancouver, 1996).

---

[7] A more recent extension of Hermann's model is found in O'Keefe and Lambert (1995).

Among the various approaches to goal formation, one of the earliest and most highly developed is Powers's (1973) perceptual control theory. Powers was not specifically concerned with message production per se, but rather with the nature of the system responsible for all behavioral regulation. Although the model was not developed with an eye toward communication processes, it has served as a foundation for work in social psychology (e.g., Carver & Scheier, 1981) and communication (e.g., Greene & Frandsen, 1979; Parks, 1994). The architecture of the model rests on the conception of a system comprised of numerous simple "comparators" that serve to match input signals to reference signals. In the event of a mismatch between the two, an output signal is generated. The operation of the output system, then, serves to restore congruence between the input and reference signals. The reference signals themselves reflect a hierarchy of increasing abstraction; at lower levels they control simple stimulus intensity, but at higher orders they may represent aspects of self-concept and principles of personal conduct. As an approach to goal formation, perceptual control theory has a number of important attributes, among them the fact that the theory makes explicit that the goals people pursue in interactions do reflect varying levels of abstraction, only some of which may be available to consciousness at any particular instant. Thus, the output system may be engaged in moment-by-moment regulation of lower level perceptions (as in the case of many of the behavioral features examined in models of mutual influence processes) quite out of phenomenal awareness. A second noteworthy attribute of the theory is that people need not ever have experienced a particular situation or perceptual input to generate goals relevant to that context; instead, the very fact of a mismatch between an input signal and a reference signal will result in an impetus to eliminate that incongruity.

An alternative approach to goal formation is found in Wilson's (1990, 1995) cognitive rules model and in Meyer's (e.g., 1997) work on message editing discussed later. Both of these models posit associative network memory structures (i.e., nodes and links) that represent knowledge that people have acquired about goals appropriate to particular social situations. The nodes in these memory structures correspond to situational features and to goals that are relevant to that context. So for example, one hypothetical and doubtless oversimplified structure might link a situational feature like "meeting a distressed friend" with the goal of "offer encouragement." The assumption of such network models is that when a person encounters a particular configuration of situational features, the nodes corresponding to those features will be activated, and this activation will spread to the associated goals. In the cognitive rules model many memory structures may be activated at any given time, but only those whose level of activation exceeds some minimum threshold will actually be triggered. The model further specifies a set of factors that determine just how highly activated a particular situation–goal rule will become when relevant contexts are encountered. In simplest terms, rules will be more highly activated when their situational nodes closely match the features of the current situation, when they have been used often in the past and hence have greater "strength," and when they have been activated very recently and carry over some level of residual activation from that previous instantiation.

Planning Processes. As noted earlier, the standard GPA framework suggests that goal formation leads to planning a course of action for accomplishing those goals.[8] Of course, planning is not restricted to making message plans, and theorizing about planning processes over the last 50 years has produced some of the most influential work in the entire realm of the study of human behavior (e.g., Bratman, 1987; Hayes-Roth & Hayes-Roth, 1979; Miller, Galanter, & Pribram, 1960; Newell & Simon, 1972; Sacerdoti, 1977; Schank & Abelson, 1977; Wilensky, 1983). Progress in understanding the nature of planning was quickly incorporated into models of message behavior (e.g., Cohen & Perrault, 1979; de Beaugrande, 1980; Hobbs & Evans, 1980; Weiner & Goodenough, 1977), and more recent work on message planning has produced several important refinements and extensions of these initial models. A particularly noteworthy example is found in Berger's (e.g., 1997a) treatment of planning, which is reviewed elsewhere in this volume.[9]

By their nature, plans specify a series of steps for accomplishing a goal. They are transitory cognitive representations, formulated to meet the demands of a current or anticipated situation. Moreover, the process of planning is typically held to be cognitively demanding in the sense that a focus on planning limits one's ability to carry out other cognitive activities. These considerations have led theorists to propose the existence of more enduring memory structures that preserve sequences of actions, and that can be invoked without the heavy processing demands associated with planning. The idea is that in addition to planning, people may be able to rely on preestablished routines for solving certain types of action-sequencing problems.

---

[8]An expanded discussion of developments in models of planning processes is available by contacting John O. Greene.

[9]One final thread that merits mention in the context of a discussion of message planning involves attempts to examine the interplay of social (i.e., interindividual) and intraindividual processes in planning (see Waldron, 1997; Wilson, 2002). An example, again from Berger (1997b), links properties of plans and planning to the uncertainty that one experiences concerning his or her interlocutor.

Conceptions of such long-term memory structures have been developed in numerous academic disciplines over the last century, they have been given a variety of names, and the specific features ascribed to them vary (see Hastie, 1981; Rumelhart & Ortony, 1977). The most familiar term used to refer to such structures is *scripts,* a label most closely associated with Schank's (e.g., 1975; Schank & Abelson, 1977) conceptual dependency theory. The focus of conceptual dependency theory was on input processing (i.e., comprehension) rather than behavioral production, but the use of the term script to refer to memory structures representing familiar sequences of action that can be used in guiding behavior arose early on (e.g., Abelson, 1981). Schank (1982) subsequently refined and extended his earlier work by developing a model that incorporated a set of memory structures more general and flexible than scripts. In his dynamic memory model *scenes* are memory structures that preserve information relevant to pursuit of instrumental goals in particular settings (e.g., ordering in a restaurant). Scenes, in turn, are ordered by still more general structures, *memory organization packets* (MOPs). The MOP concept has been invoked to explain observed regularities in the sequencing of a variety of communication behaviors including initial interactions (see Kellermann, 1995), development of intimate relationships (e.g., Honeycutt, Cantrill, & Greene, 1989), and group discussions (Pavitt, 1993).

Editing and Monitoring Processes. In addition to forming goals and planning courses of action to achieve those goals, people engage in both editing of message features prior to execution and monitoring of their behavior as it unfolds. Models of editing and monitoring processes can be divided into those primarily concerned with lower level utterance specification and production on one hand and those focused on more abstract social ramifications of message activity on the other. Among the former is the aforementioned model of prearticulatory editing developed by Motley et al. (1983). In that model, a lexically based editing mechanism serves to compare fully formulated (but unarticulated) verbal messages to the most highly activated nodes in an associative network lexicon. The activation levels of particular nodes in the lexicon are themselves a product of several factors including situational and social features, communicative intent, and syntactic constraints. In the event that the lexical elements of the message formulation do not correspond to highly activated nodes of the lexicon, the editor rejects that formulation and a new, presumably more adequate, message is formulated.

As might be expected, models of utterance-level editing are typically cast in design stance terms. Thus, the editing mechanism in the model developed by Motley et al. (1983) operates in the absence of volition and phenomenal awareness of the comparisons it executes (see also Laver, 1980). Other models of prearticulatory editing (e.g., Dell & Reich, 1980) dispense with the conception of a dedicated editing mechanism altogether and instead view the editing function as a natural result of more general design stance encoding processes.

In contrast to models of prearticulatory editing are those models of higher level editing processes centering on relational, communicative, and self-relevant ramifications of message choices. Not surprisingly, these models tend to be cast in intentional stance terms, or as intentional-design hybrids, rather than at the design level. A prominent example of models of this sort is found in the work of Hample and Dallinger (1987, 1990). These authors propose that people decide either to express or suppress potential arguments based on three clusters of concern: *effectiveness* (i.e., perceptions of whether the argument is likely to work and whether it is too negative to use), *person-centered factors* (implications of the use of a strategy for self, other, and the relationship), and *discourse competence* (i.e., the truthfulness and relevance of an argument). Thus a person may formulate a potential argument and yet decide not to use it because he or she perceives that it would not work, would not be consistent with his or her self-image, would damage the relationship, and so forth.[10]

As we noted previously, Meyer's (e.g., 1997) model of message encoding explicitly addresses editing phenomena. This model, couched in associative network terms, posits that among other long-term memory structures, people possess knowledge of outcomes that are likely to arise from the display of various message behaviors. When a person formulates an initial message plan, relevant action–consequence associations are activated, potentially causing the speaker to become aware of previously unrecognized relational consequences of the intended message. In the event that the newly realized relational consequences of the anticipated message are negative, the person may abandon or modify the original message plan.

One other model, relevant to monitoring processes, merits mention here. Vallacher and Wegner's (1985, 1987) action identification theory (AIT) is a general model of output processes and was not developed as a theory of message production per se, but the tenets of the theory can be seen to apply to message production, and AIT has been employed as the conceptual foundation for experimental investigations of message production phenomena (e.g., Vallacher, Wegner, & Somoza, 1989).

[10]A similar line of thought is found in Berger's aforementioned work on planning processes (see Berger, 1995, 1997a) and in Kellermann's related work on compliance gaining (e.g., Kellermann & Park, 2001; Kellermann & Shea, 1996). In both these cases the authors argued that strategic choices are based on overarching criteria of efficiency (i.e., expediency and economy of effort) and social appropriateness.

Vallacher and Wegner noted that a person can conceive of his or her own ongoing activity at any of a variety of levels of abstraction. At abstract levels, people characterize what they are doing in terms of the behavior's larger meanings and implications; at lower levels they focus on the details of the activity itself. Thus, an assembly line worker may apprehend the same action in low-level terms (e.g., "tightening this screw"), at some intermediate level (e.g., "installing the component board"), or in a highly abstract way (e.g., "providing for my family"). The particular characterization that an individual adopts at any given moment is termed the *prepotent act identity,* and this act identity serves as the standard for monitoring and evaluating one's behavior. Central to AIT is the notion that there are competing forces that push people toward more and less abstract act identities. On one hand, there is a natural tendency to move toward more abstract act identities as people entertain broader understandings and implications of their actions. On the other, when activities require attending to the details of what one is doing, abstract act identities may not be particularly useful and people will tend to adopt lower level characterizations. The upshot is the optimality hypothesis, which suggests that performance suffers when people adopt a prepotent act identity that is either too abstract (so that the requisite details for carrying out the action are lost) or too concrete (resulting in a loss of coordination or integration that comes from having a "big-picture" conception of what one is doing).

Comprehensive Models of Message Production

As we noted previously, models of message production can be distinguished on the basis of the extent to which they address and explicate the entire range of subprocesses that underlie speech and action. In contrast to models such as those reviewed to this point that are more narrowly focused, other models reflect attempts to encompass multiple subprocesses within a single conceptual framework. One hallmark of models of this sort is a hierarchical conception of the output system akin to that depicted in Figure 2.1. In essence, these models attempt to incorporate higher order conceptual activities as well as lower level utterance formulation and articulatory processes. A second feature of these models is that the explanatory mechanisms they posit typically reflect a hybrid intentional–design stance. Thus, they meld intentional stance conceptions of goals, expectations, and so on, with design stance specifications of underlying structures and processes.

One example of more comprehensive, hierarchical models is found in MacKay's (e.g., 1982, 1987) node structure theory (NST). NST posits a system of nodes and relations organized into three major levels: the sentential system, the phonological system, and the muscle movement system. Each of these levels is itself a hierarchy of constituent subsystems. Thus, at the highest level of the sentential system there are nodes corresponding to entire propositions (e.g., "fast pedaling builds lung power"). At an intermediate level of the sentential system there are conceptual compound nodes (e.g., "fast pedaling," "builds lung power"), and at the lowest level there are lexical nodes (e.g., "fast," "pedaling"). In similar fashion, the phonological and muscle movement systems reflect a hierarchical arrangement of increasingly fine-grained action specifications. The model invokes a standard conception of links among nodes that permit an activated node to prime associated nodes, and, as is commonly posited in such models, linkage strength is held to be a function of the frequency with which a given link has been activated in the past. There are, however, some ways in which NST differs from standard associative network models. For example, the model makes a distinction between priming and activation: In NST, nodes may be primed by the activation spreading from other nodes, but priming itself cannot cause a node to become activated. Instead, a triggering mechanism is required to activate a primed node. The primary focus of NST (at least insofar as it is concerned with behavioral production) is on the processes responsible for the overt expression of propositions as utterances rather than the production of social actions, and thus, the theory is probably more accurately characterized as a model of speech production rather than message production as we drew that distinction at the outset of this chapter. Nonetheless, the theory does shed light on phenomena such as the impact of practice on speech fluency that are of interest to communication scholars.

An example of a comprehensive model that is decidedly more communicative in focus is that developed by Levelt (1989). The model assumes that message production begins with the formulation of a communicative intention to impact the understanding of one's interlocutor in some way. In designing a message to accomplish this intention the speaker draws on his or her store of declarative and procedural information (see J. R. Anderson, 1976). The model assumes a standard production system architecture (see Newell & Simon, 1972), and the primary representational formalism, then, is the production; that is, units of procedural memory that code information in a condition–action format and are brought into play when the conditions represented in the production arise.

The model specifies four major subcomponents involved in message production: (a) a *conceptualizer* that generates a preverbal message by selecting information for expression, (b) a *formulator* that both translates the preverbal message into an ordered string of lexical items and establishes an articulatory plan for producing that utterance, (c) an *articulator* that executes the articulatory plan as overt behavior, and (d) a *speech-comprehension system* that allows a person to monitor his or her own internal and overt speech. Levelt argued that these four systems function incrementally in the sense that the output of a given level need not be fully specified before the next successive level can begin to operate. However, he also stipulated that lower levels of the hierarchy cannot influence the content of those above it. He further suggested that the operation of the conceptualizer and the monitoring system are subject to processing-capacity restrictions associated with the limitations of working memory, whereas the operation of the formulator and articulator are essentially automatic and not typically subject to executive control. Of particular note in this regard is Levelt's contention that working memory contains all of the information that can be employed in the conceptual and monitoring components of the output system at any given moment.

A third example of a comprehensive model offers a very different view of the message production process. Like the other models reviewed here, second-generation action assembly theory (AAT2; Greene, 1997c) posits a hierarchical output system that permits high-level, abstract action specifications to be manifested as overt behavior. In AAT2, the basic units of long-term memory, *procedural records,* code relations among elemental action specifications, situational features, and outcomes. Action specifications are activated, then, when a person's goals correspond to the outcomes represented in procedural records and when current conditions match the situational features in various records. According to AAT2, a very large number of action specifications will be activated at any moment, but these memory elements will quickly decay back toward their resting levels unless they coalesce with other action features. So, for example, an abstract action specification corresponding to the concept "automobile" might coalesce with the lexical action specification "car" and with the syntactic frame specification "noun–verb–direct object." The effect of binding action specifications in coalitions is to keep those features activated longer and to make it more likely that those features will be able to marshal still more features, perhaps leading a particular coalition to be manifested in overt behavior.

Several attributes of AAT2 distinguish it from other hierarchical models. Unlike the models developed by Herrmann (1983) and Levelt (1989), for example, AAT2 does not suggest that all of the understandings that contribute to an individual's message production activities are held in working memory. Indeed, the image of the nature of thought and action in AAT2 suggests that people are not even aware of the majority of the content of the output system that colors their messages. As a second example, AAT2 posits upward hierarchical influences such that lower level action specifications can actually drive higher level thought. Moreover, in AAT2, the third sense of idea generation discussed earlier in this chapter (i.e., idea generation as creation) is seen as the natural consequence of assembling elemental action specifications. Finally, rather than treat executive processes such as planning, monitoring, and editing, and the conscious experience of engaging in such activities, as different in kind from the other mechanisms of the output system, these processes are seen simply to be manifestations of coalition formation.

A LOOK TO THE FUTURE: CREATIVITY, EVANESCENCE, INTERACTION, AND THE NOT-SAID

It should be clear that the years since the publication of Roloff and Berger's (1982a) *Social Cognition and Communication* have witnessed remarkable growth in our understanding of message production processes, both with respect to describing message-relevant regularities and in the development of theoretical accounts of the cognitive mechanisms that underlie and give rise to those regularities. Moreover, there is every reason to believe that the empirical and theoretical sophistication that characterizes this domain of study will continue grow in the coming years. Doubtless, future developments in our understanding of message production processes will involve exploration of many issues that are currently unforeseen. However, even now it seems likely that certain questions will attract the attention of scholars in the future. For example, the question of the nature of the processes that give rise to novel verbal and nonverbal messages strikes us as one that almost certainly will be the focus of increased scrutiny and conceptual sophistication. Similarly, we expect that future work will more fully engage the rapid, shifting nature of message-relevant cognitions (see Greene, 2000). As a third example, future models will doubtless address both intra-individual and inter-individual message phenomena in increasingly sophisticated and rigorous ways (see Greene, 1997a). Finally, most of the progress of the last few decades has centered on understanding of what is said; we have come considerably less far in explicating the not-said—the universe of thoughts not voiced, those incapable of being voiced, and those of which we are unaware. As fascinating as are the things we have learned to date, the future of work on message production holds even greater challenge and promise.

REFERENCES

Aaronson, D., & Rieber, R. W. (1979). *Psycholinguistic research: Implications and applications*. Hillsdale, NJ: Lawrence Erlbaum Associates.

Abelson, R. P. (1981). Psychological status of the script concept. *American Psychologist, 36*, 715–729.

Aitchison, J. (1998). *The articulate mammal: An introduction to psycholinguistics* (4th ed.). London: Routledge.

Anderson, J. R. (1976). *Language, memory, and thought.* Hillsdale, NJ: Lawrence Erlbaum Associates.

Anderson, P. A. (1998). The cognitive valence theory of intimate communication. In M. T. Palmer & G. A. Barnett (Eds.), *Progress in communication sciences: Vol. 14. Mutual influence in interpersonal communication: Theory and research in cognition, affect, and behavior* (pp. 39–72). Stamford, CT: Ablex.

Argyle, M., & Cook, M. (1976). *Gaze and mutual gaze.* Cambridge, UK: Cambridge University Press.

Austin, J. T., & Vancouver, J. B. (1996). Goal constructs in psychology: Structure, process, and content. *Psychological Bulletin, 120,* 338–375.

Beattie, G. W. (1979). Planning units in spontaneous speech: Some evidence from hesitation in speech and speaker gaze direction in conversation. *Linguistics, 17,* 61–78.

Beattie, G. W. (1981). A further investigation of the cognitive interference hypothesis of gaze patterns during conversation. *British Journal of Social Psychology, 20,* 243–248.

Berger, C. R. (1988). Planning, affect, and social action generation. In R. L. Donohew, H. Sypher, & E. T. Higgins (Eds.), *Communication, social cognition, and affect* (pp. 93–116). Hillsdale, NJ: Lawrence Erlbaum Associates.

Berger, C. R. (1995). A plan-based approach to strategic communication. In D. E. Hewes (Ed.), *The cognitive bases of interpersonal communication* (pp. 141–179). Hillsdale, NJ: Lawrence Erlbaum Associates.

Berger, C. R. (1997a). *Planning strategic interaction: Attaining goals through communicative action.* Mahwah, NJ: Lawrence Erlbaum Associates.

Berger, C. R. (1997b). Producing messages under uncertainty. In J. O. Greene (Ed.), *Message production: Advances in communication theory* (pp. 221–244). Mahwah, NJ: Lawrence Erlbaum Associates.

Bock, J. K. (1982). Toward a cognitive psychology of syntax: Information processing contributions to sentence formulation. *Psychological Review, 89,* 1–47.

Boomer, D. S., & Laver, J. D. M. (1968). Slips of the tongue. *British Journal of Disorders of Communication, 3,* 1–12.

Bratman, M. E. (1987). *Intentions, plans, and practical reason.* Cambridge, MA: Harvard University Press.

Brown, R., & McNeill, D. (1966). The "tip of the tongue" phenomenon. *Journal of Verbal Learning and Verbal Behavior, 5,* 325–337.

Burgoon, J. K. (1978). A communication model of personal space violations: Explication and an initial test. *Human Communication Research, 4,* 129–142.

Burgoon, J. K., Stern, L. A., & Dillman, L. (1995). *Interpersonal adaptation: Dyadic interaction patterns.* Cambridge, UK: Cambridge University Press.

Burleson, B. R. (1987). Cognitive complexity. In J. C. McCroskey & J. A. Daly (Eds.), *Personality and interpersonal communication* (pp. 305–349). Newbury Park, CA: Sage.

Burleson, B. R. (Ed.). (1995). *Communication yearbook 18.* Thousand Oaks, CA: Sage.

Butterworth, B. (Ed.). (1980). *Language production: Vol. 1. Speech and talk.* London: Academic.

Cappella, J. N., & Greene, J. O. (1982). A discrepancy-arousal explanation of mutual influence in expressive behavior for adult and infant–adult interaction. *Communication Monographs, 49,* 89–114.

Cappella, J. N., & Palmer, M. T. (1990). The structure and organization of verbal and non-verbal behavior: Data for models of production. In H. Giles & W. P. Robinson (Eds.), *Handbook of language and social psychology* (pp. 141–161). New York: Wiley.

Carver, C. S., & Scheier, M. F. (1981). *Attention and self-regulation: A control-theory approach to human behavior.* New York: Springer-Verlag.

Chomsky, N. (1957). *Syntactic structures.* The Hague, Netherlands: Mouton.

Christenfeld, N., Schachter, S., & Bilous, F. (1991). Filled pauses and gestures: It's not a coincidence. *Journal of Psycholinguistic Research, 20,* 1–10.

Churchland, P. M. (1992). *Matter and consciousness: A contemporary introduction to the philosophy of mind* (Rev. ed.). Cambridge, MA: Bradford.

Clippenger, J. H., Jr. (1977). *Meaning and discourse: A computer model of psychoanalytic speech and cognition.* Baltimore: Johns Hopkins University Press.

Cody, M. J., & McLaughlin, M. L. (Eds.). (1990). *The psychology of tactical communication.* Clevedon, UK: Multilingual Matters.

Cohen, P. R., & Perrault, C. R. (1979). Elements of a plan-based theory of speech acts. *Cognitive Science, 3,* 177–212.

Coulmas, F. (Ed.). (1981). *Conversational routine: Explorations in standardized communication situations and prepatterned speech.* The Hague, Netherlands: Mouton.

Craig, R. T. (1978). Cognitive science: A new approach to cognition, language, and communication. *Quarterly Journal of Speech, 64,* 439–450.

Craig, R. T. (1979). Information systems theory and research: An overview of individual information processing. In D. Nimmo (Ed.), *Communication yearbook 3* (pp. 99–121). New Brunswick, NJ: Transaction–ICA.

Daly, J. A. (1978). The assessment of social-communicative anxiety via self-reports: A comparison of measures. *Communication Monographs, 45,* 204–218.

Daly, J. A., Weber, D. J., Vangelisti, A. J., Maxwell, M., & Neal, H. (1989). Concurrent cognitions during conversations: Protocol analysis as a means of exploring conversations. *Discourse Processes, 12,* 227–244.

de Beaugrande, R. (1980). The pragmatics of discourse planning. *Journal of Pragmatics, 4,* 15–42.

Dechert, H. W., & Raupach, M. (Eds.). (1980). *Temporal variables in speech: Studies in honour of Frieda Goldman-Eisler.* The Hague, Netherlands: Mouton.

Dell, G. S., & Reich, P. A. (1980). Toward a unified model of slips of the tongue. In V. A. Fromkin (Ed.), *Errors in linguistic performance: Slips of the tongue, ear, pen, and hand* (pp. 273–286). New York: Academic.

Dennett, D. C. (1971). Intentional systems. *Journal of Philosophy, 68,* 87–106.

Dillard, J. P. (1990). The nature and substance of goals in tactical communication. In M. J. Cody & M. L. McLaughlin (Eds.), *The psychology of tactical communication* (pp. 70–90). Clevedon, UK: Multilingual Matters.

Dillard, J. P. (1997). Explicating the goal construct: Tools for theorists. In J. Greene (Ed.), *Message production: Advances in communication theory* (pp. 47–69). Mahwah, NJ: Lawrence Erlbaum Associates.

Ericsson, K. A., & Simon, H. A. (1980). Verbal reports as data. *Psychological Review, 87,* 215–251.

Ericsson, K. A., & Simon, H. A. (1984). *Protocol analysis: Verbal reports as data.* Cambridge, MA: MIT Press.

Ferreira, F. (1991). Effects of length and syntactic complexity on initiation times for prepared utterances. *Journal of Memory and Language, 30,* 210–233.

Fiske, S. T., & Taylor, S. E. (1984). *Social cognition.* Reading, MA: Addison-Wesley.

Flanagan, O. J., Jr. (1991). *The science of the mind* (2nd ed.). Cambridge, MA: Bradford.

Fromkin, V. A. (Ed.). (1980). *Errors in linguistic performance: Slips of the tongue, ear, pen, and hand.* New York: Academic.

Gardner, H. (1987). *The mind's new science: A history of the cognitive revolution.* New York: Basic Books.

Gastil, J. (1995). An appraisal and revision of the constructivist research program. In B. R. Burleson (Ed.), *Communication yearbook 18* (pp. 83–104). Thousand Oaks, CA: Sage.

Giles, H., Coupland, N., & Coupland, J. (1991). Accommodation theory: Communication, context, and consequence. In H. Giles., J. Coupland, & N. Coupland (Eds.), *Contexts of accommodation: Developments in applied sociolinguistics* (pp. 1–68). Cambridge, UK: Cambridge University Press.

Greene, J. O. (1984). A cognitive approach to human communication: An action assembly theory. *Communication Monographs, 51,* 289–306.

Greene, J. O. (1988). Cognitive processes: Methods for probing the black box. In C. H. Tardy (Ed.), *A handbook for the study of human communication: Methods and instruments for observing, measuring, and assessing communication processes* (pp. 37–66). Norwood, NJ: Ablex.

Greene, J. O. (1990). Tactical social action: Towards some strategies for theory. In M. J. Cody & M. L. McLaughlin (Eds.), *The psychology of tactical communication* (pp. 31–47). Clevedon, UK: Multilingual Matters.

Greene, J. O. (1995). An action-assembly perspective on verbal and nonverbal message production: A dancer's message unveiled. In D. E. Hewes (Ed.), *The cognitive bases of interpersonal communication* (pp. 51–85). Hillsdale, NJ: Lawrence Erlbaum Associates.

Greene, J. O. (1997a). Introduction: Advances in theories of message production. In J. O. Greene (Ed.), *Message production: Advances in communication theory* (pp. 3–13). Hillsdale, NJ: Lawrence Erlbaum Associates.

Greene, J. O. (Ed.). (1997b). *Message production: Advances in communication theory.* Hillsdale, NJ: Lawrence Erlbaum Associates.

Greene, J. O. (1997c). A second generation action assembly theory. In J. O. Greene (Ed.), *Message production: Advances in communication theory* (pp. 151–170). Hillsdale, NJ: Lawrence Erlbaum Associates.

Greene, J. O. (2000). Evanescent mentation: An ameliorative conceptual foundation for research and theory on message production. *Communication Theory, 10,* 139–155.

Greene, J. O., & Cody, M. J. (Eds.). (1985). Cognition in social interaction: Production principles [Special issue]. *Journal of Language and Social Psychology,* 4(3 & 4).

Greene, J. O., & Frandsen, K. D. (1979). Need-fulfillment and consistency theory: Relationships between self-esteem and eye contact. *Western Journal of Speech Communication, 43,* 123–133.

Greene, J. O., & Geddes, D. (1993). An action assembly perspective on social skill. *Communication Theory, 3,* 26–49.

Greene, J. O., & Sparks, G. G. (1983). Explication and test of a cognitive model of communication apprehension: A new look at an old construct. *Human Communication Research, 9,* 349–366.

Hample, D. (1987). Communication and the unconscious. In B. Dervin & M. J. Voigt (Eds.), *Progress in communication sciences* (Vol. 8, pp. 83–121). Norwood, NJ: Ablex.

Hample, D., & Dallinger, J. M. (1987). Individual differences in cognitive editing standards. *Human Communication Research, 14,* 123–144.

Hample, D., & Dallinger, J. M. (1990). Arguers as editors. *Argumentation, 4,* 153–169.

Hastie, R. (1981). Schematic principles in human memory. In E. T. Higgins, C. P. Herman, & M. P. Zanna (Eds.), *Social cognition: The Ontario symposium* (Vol. 1, pp. 39–88) Hillsdale, NJ: Lawrence Erlbaum Associates.

Hayes-Roth, B., & Hayes-Roth, F. (1979). A cognitive model of planning. *Cognitive Science, 3,* 275–310.

Herrmann, T. (1983). *Speech and situation: A psychological conception of situated speaking.* Berlin: Springer-Verlag.

Hewes, D. E. (Ed.). (1995). *The cognitive bases of interpersonal communication.* Hillsdale, NJ: Lawrence Erlbaum Associates.

Hobbs, J. R., & Evans, D. A. (1980). Conversation as planned behavior. *Cognitive Science, 4,* 349– 377.

Honeycutt, J. M., Cantrill, J. G., & Greene, R. W. (1989). Memory structures for relational escalation: A cognitive test of the sequencing of relational actions and stages. *Human Communication Research, 16,* 62–90.

Infante, D. A. (1980). Verbal plans: A conceptualization and investigation. *Communication Quarterly, 28,* 3–10.

Kellermann, K. (1992). Communication: Inherently strategic and primarily automatic. *Communication Monographs, 59,* 288–300.

Kellermann, K. (1995). The conversation MOP: A model of patterned and pliable behavior. In D. E. Hewes (Ed.), *The cognitive bases of interpersonal communication* (pp. 181–221). Hillsdale, NJ: Lawrence Erlbaum Associates.

Kellermann, K., & Park, H. S. (2001). Situational urgency and conversational retreat: When politeness and efficiency matter. *Communication Research, 28,* 3–47.

Kellermann, K., & Shea, B. C. (1996). Threats, suggestions, hints, and promises: Gaining compliance efficiently and politely. *Communication Quarterly, 44,* 145–165.

Knapp, M. L., & Comadena, M. E. (1979). Telling it like it isn't: A review of theory and research on deceptive communications. *Human Communication Research, 5,* 270–285.

Kuiper, K. (1996). *Smooth talkers: The linguistic performance of auctioneers and sportscasters.* Mahwah, NJ: Lawrence Erlbaum Associates.

Laver, J. (1980). Monitoring systems in the neurolinguisitc control of speech production. In V. A. Fromkin (Ed.), *Errors in linguistic performance: Slips of the tongue, ear, pen, and hand* (pp. 287–305). New York: Academic.

Levelt, W. J. M. (1989). *Speaking: From intention to articulation.* Cambridge, MA: Bradford.

MacKay, D. G. (1980). Speech errors: Retrospect and prospect. In V. A. Fromkin (Ed.), *Errors in linguistic performance: slips of the tongue, ear, pen, and hand* (pp. 319–332). New York: Academic.

MacKay, D. G. (1982). The problems of flexibility, fluency, and speed–accuracy trade-off in skilled behavior. *Psychological Review, 89,* 483–506.

MacKay, D. G. (1987). *The organization of perception and action: A theory for language and other cognitive skills.* New York: Springer-Verlag.

Manes, J., & Wolfson, N. (1981). The compliment formula. In F. Coulmas (Ed.), *Conversational routine: Explorations in standardized communication situations and prepatterned speech* (pp. 115–132). The Hague, Netherlands: Mouton.

McLaughlin, M. L., Louden, A. D., Cashion, J. L., Altendorf, D. M., Baaske, K. T., & Smith, S. W. (1985). Conversational planning and self-serving utterances: The manipulation of topical and functional structures in dyadic interaction. *Journal of Language and Social Psychology, 4,* 233–251.

McNeill, D. (1992). *Hand and mind: What gestures reveal about thought.* Chicago: University of Chicago Press.

Meyer, J. R. (1997). Cognitive influences on the ability to address interaction goals. In J. O. Greene (Ed.), *Message production: Advances in communication theory* (pp. 71–90). Mahwah, NJ: Lawrence Erlbaum Associates.

Miller, G. A., Galanter, E., & Pribram, K. H. (1960). *Plans and the structure of behavior.* New York: Holt, Rinehart, & Winston.

Miller, G. R. (1976). The person as actor—Cognitive psychology on the attack. *Quarterly Journal of Speech, 62,* 82–87.

Miller, J. L., & Eimas, P. D. (Eds.). (1995). *Speech, language, and communication.* San Diego, CA: Academic.

Motley, M. T., Baars, B. J., & Camden, C. T. (1983). Experimental verbal slip studies: A review and an editing model of language encoding. *Communication Monographs, 50,* 79–101.

Motley, M. T., Camden, C. T., & Baars, B. J. (1979). Personality and situational influences upon verbal slips: A laboratory test of Freudian and prearticulatory editing hypotheses. *Human Communication Research, 5,* 195–202.

Motley, M. T., Camden, C. T., & Baars, B. J. (1981). Toward verifying the assumptions of laboratory-induced slips of the tongue: The output-error and editing issues. *Human Communication Research, 8,* 3–15.

Newell, A., & Simon, H. (1972). *Human problem solving.* Englewood Cliffs, NJ: Prentice-Hall.

O'Keefe, B. J., & Delia, J. G. (1982). Impression formation and message production. In M. E. Roloff & C. R. Berger (Eds.), *Social cognition and communication* (pp. 33–72). Beverly Hills, CA: Sage.

O'Keefe, B. J., & Lambert, B. L. (1995). Managing the flow of ideas: A local management approach to message design. In B. R. Burleson (Ed.), *Communication yearbook 18* (pp. 54–82). Thousand Oaks, CA: Sage.

Palmer, M. (Ed.). (1994). Cognition and interpersonal communication [Special issue]. *Communication Studies, 45*(2).

Palmer, M. T., & Simmons, K. B. (1995). Communicating intentions through nonverbal behaviors: Conscious and nonconscious encoding of liking. *Human Communication Research,* 22, 128–160.

Parks, M. R. (1994). Communicative competence and interpersonal control. In M. L. Knapp & G. R. Miller (Eds.), *Handbook of interpersonal communication* (2nd ed., pp 589–618). Thousand Oaks, CA: Sage.

Patterson, M. L. (1976). An arousal model of interpersonal intimacy. *Psychological Review, 83,* 235–245.

Patterson, M. L. (1982). A sequential functional model of nonverbal behavior. *Psychological Review, 89,* 231–249.

Pavitt, C. (1993). Describing know-how about group discussion procedure: Must the representation be recursive? *Communication Studies, 43,* 150–170.

Powers, W. T. (1973). *Behavior: The control of perception.* Chicago: Aldine.

Reeves, B., Chaffee, S. H., & Tims, A. (1982). Social cognition and mass communication research. In M. E. Roloff & C. R. Berger (Eds.), *Social cognition and communication* (pp. 287– 326). Beverly Hills. CA: Sage.

Roloff, M. E., & Berger, C. R. (Eds.). (1982a). *Social cognition and communication.* Beverly Hills, CA: Sage.

Roloff, M. E., & Berger, C. R. (1982b). Social cognition and communication: An introduction. In M. E. Roloff & C. R. Berger (Eds.), *Social cognition and communication* (pp. 9–32). Beverly Hills, CA: Sage.

Rosenberg, S. (1977). *Sentence production: Developments in research and theory.* Hillsdale, NJ: Lawrence Erlbaum Associates.

Rumelhart, D. E., & Ortony, A. (1977). The representation of knowledge in memory. In R. C. Anderson, R. J. Spiro, & W. E. Montague (Eds.), *Schooling and the acquisition of knowledge* (pp. 99–135). Hillsdale, NJ: Lawrence Erlbaum Associates.

Sacerdoti, E. D. (1977). *A structure for plans and behavior.* Amsterdam: Elsevier.

Sanders, R. E. (1997). The production of symbolic objects as components of larger wholes. In J. O. Greene (Ed.), *Message production: Advances in communication theory* (pp. 245–277). Mahwah, NJ: Lawrence Erlbaum Associates.

Schank, R. C. (1975). The structure of episodes in memory. In D. G. Bobrow & A. Collins (Eds.), *Representation and understanding in cognitive science* (pp. 237–272). New York: Academic.

Schank, R. C. (1982). *Dynamic memory: A theory of reminding and learning in computers and people.* Cambridge, UK: Cambridge University Press.

Schank, R. C., & Abelson, R. P. (1977). *Scripts, plans, goals, and understanding.* Hillsdale, NJ: Lawrence Erlbaum Associates.

Siegman, A. W. (1979). Cognition and hesitation in speech. In A. W. Siegman & S. Feldstein (Eds.), *Of speech and time: Temporal speech patterns in interpersonal contexts* (pp. 151–178). Hillsdale, NJ: Lawrence Erlbaum Associates.

Siegman, A. W., & Feldstein, S. (Eds.). (1979). *Of speech and time: Temporal speech patterns in interpersonal contexts.* Hillsdale, NJ: Lawrence Erlbaum Associates.

Street, R. L., Jr., & Giles, H. (1982). Speech accommodation theory: A social cognitive approach to language and speech behavior. In M. E. Roloff & C. R. Berger (Eds.), *Social cognition and communication* (pp. 193–226). Beverly Hills, CA: Sage.

Tomasello, M., & Bates, E. (Eds.). (2001). *Language development: The essential readings.* Malden, MA: Blackwell.

Vallacher, R. R., & Wegner, D. M. (1985). *A theory of action identification.* Hillsdale, NJ: Lawrence Erlbaum Associates.

Vallacher, R. R., & Wegner, D. M. (1987). What do people think they're doing? Action identification and human behavior. *Psychological Review, 94,* 3–15.

Vallacher, R. R., Wegner, D. M., & Somoza, M. P. (1989). That's easy for you to say: Action identification and speech fluency. *Journal of Personality and Social Psychology, 56,* 199–208.

Waldron, V. R. (1997). Toward a theory of interactive conversational planning. In J. O. Greene (Ed.), *Message production: Advances in communication theory* (pp. 195–220). Mahwah, NJ: Lawrence Erlbaum Associates.

Waldron, V. R., & Cegala, D. J. (1992). Assessing conversational cognition: Levels of cognitive theory and associated methodological requirements. *Human Communication Research, 18,* 599–622.

Weiner, S. L., & Goodenough, D. R. (1977). A move toward a psychology of conversation. In R. O. Freedle (Ed.), *Discourse production and comprehension* (pp. 213–225). Norwood, NJ: Ablex.

Wilensky, R. (1983). *Planning and understanding: A computational approach to human reasoning.* Reading, MA: Addison-Wesley.

Wilson, S. R. (1990). Development and test of a cognitive rules model of interaction. *Communication Monographs, 57,* 81–103.

Wilson, S. R. (1995). Elaborating the cognitive rules model of interaction goals: The problem of accounting for individual differences in goal formation. In B. R. Burleson (Ed.), *Communication yearbook 18* (pp. 3–25). Thousand Oaks, CA: Sage.

Wilson, S. R. (2002). *Seeking and resisting compliance: Why people say what they do when trying to influence others.* Thousand Oaks, CA: Sage.

Wilson, S. R., Greene, J. O., & Dillard, J. P. (Eds.). (2000). Message production: Progress, challenges, and prospects [Special issue]. *Communication Theory, 10*(2).

Zuckerman, M., DePaulo, B. M., & Rosenthal, R. (1981). Verbal and nonverbal correlates of deception. In L. Berkowitz (Ed.), *Advances in experimental social psychology* (pp. 1–59). New York: Academic.

3

Communication: A Goal-Directed, Plan-Guided Process

Charles R. Berger
University of California, Davis

The era during which the volume *Social Cognition and Communication and Communication* (Roloff & Berger, 1982a) was published was an exciting one in the communication discipline's history. The cognitive approach to the study of communication was in its nascent stages and its effects were beginning to be reflected in the work of several communication researchers, especially those with interests in social interaction (Berger & Bradac, 1982; Delia, O'Keefe, & O'Keefe, 1982; Greene, 1984; Hewes & Planalp, 1982, 1987; Planalp & Hewes, 1982). One source of excitement surrounding this surging interest in cognitive approaches stemmed from the promise that they would spawn theoretical frameworks that would illuminate basic communication processes. The hope was that these theories would transcend and integrate such ostensibly unique domains of communication inquiry as health, intercultural, interpersonal, mass, organizational, and political communication, as well as others (Berger & Chaffee, 1987, 1988; Roloff & Berger, 1982b). Cognitively based approaches have continued to exerted considerable influence within these subdomains of the communication discipline, as the contributions to this volume attest; however, it remains to be seen whether the promised theoretical integration of these areas will occur.

One perspective that emerged within this cognitive turn concerns the roles that knowledge structures in general and plans in particular play in the production and comprehension of discourse, actions, and text (Berger, 1988b, 1989). This approach was strongly influenced by the work on knowledge structures and discourse comprehension (Abelson, 1976, 1981; Galambos, Abelson, & Black, 1986; Schank, 1982; Schank &

Abelson, 1977; Schank & Berman, 2002). This chapter provides an overview of the development of this planning framework, with an emphasis on message production. As this presentation demonstrates, researchers from a wide variety of fields, including artificial intelligence, cognitive science, cognitive psychology, communication, developmental psychology, linguistics, and philosophy have found the constructs of plans and planning to be useful in their attempts to explain and model discourse comprehension and the production of intentional action. This chapter seeks to show that plans and planning processes have the potential to provide significant insights into the reasons individuals display considerable variability in their abilities to employ verbal and nonverbal communication to achieve their interaction goals. Although this chapter focuses on the social interaction domain, plans and planning processes are not only in play when individuals engage in face-to-face interaction. Individuals who seek to achieve various goals by communicating with audiences through mass media must also rely on mental representations of plans to guide the design and implementation of their messages.

The ability to make reasonably accurate inferences regarding cointerlocutors' goals and plans is a critical prerequisite for realizing individual and socially shared goals during social intercourse. Indeed, Bogdan (1994, 1997, 2000) suggested that the ability to "read" others or the ability to interpret others' intentions and actions evolved from the necessity for understanding others' goals to attain one's own. If others' goals potentially interfere with the satisfaction of one's own, it is vital to know others' intentions. The ability to make inferences concerning their goals and plans is at the heart of this interpretative process. Moreover, the human capacity for forethought and planning undergirds the ability of humans to engage in metamentation (Bogdan, 2000). Within the domain of language use, Green (1996) observed, "Understanding a speaker's intention in saying what she said the way she said it amounts to inferring the speaker's plan, in all of its hierarchical glory, although there is room for considerable latitude regarding the details" (p. 13). The dual role that plans play in guiding both message production and message comprehension makes the plan construct a strong candidate to play a significant role in explaining communicative competence and communicative performance (Berger, 1997, 2002; Wilson & Sabee, 2003). Although this chapter focuses on face-to-face interaction, goal- and plan-based knowledge is vital for functioning effectively in communication contexts that are interactive but not necessarily face-to-face. Technologically mediated social interaction is one such case (Walther & Parks, 2002), and interactions that involve the thwarting of potentially harmful actions of nonpresent adversaries, as might occur in international relations, is another (Carbonell, 1981).

The plan construct has also been accorded a central role in accounts of intentional action by action philosophers (Brand, 1984; Bratman, 1987, 1990); those interested in the folk concept of intentional action have taken linguistic expressions of having a plan to reach a goal to be a potential indicator of intention rather than desire (Malle & Knobe, 1997, 2001). Thus, the verbal assertion of desire, for example, "I want/hope to go to Tokyo" can be differentiated from the verbal assertion of intending to achieve the goal, "I intend/plan to go to Tokyo," or "I have decided to go to Tokyo." Others have suggested that plans are bundles of intentions or intentions "writ large" (Bratman, 1987). Although the place of the plan and planning concepts within the broader philosophical project of characterizing the nature of intentional action is not pursued in this chapter, the fact that they are viewed by some as integral to intentions attests to their importance in explaining both message production and message comprehension processes.

GOALS, PLANS, AND PLANNING

Students of language have frequently observed that language is a tool or an instrument for attaining goals (Austin, 1962; Semin, 1998; Wittgenstein, 1953). As Clark (1994) put it,

> People engage in discourse not merely to use language, but to accomplish things. They want to buy shoes or get a lost address or arrange a dinner party or trade gossip or teach a child improper fractions. Language is simply a tool for achieving these aims. (p. 1018)

However, the very simplicity of this notion may be somewhat misleading, especially when language use occurs in the dynamic crucible of social interaction where the multiple goals pursued by cointerlocutors may be at once both opaque to interaction parties and, at the same time, highly unstable over time (Berger, 1997; Dillard, 1997). Of course, many everyday encounters are so transparent that social actors need not use any verbal communication to understand each others' goals and plans. For instance, the question "Why are you standing there looking at me?" when uttered by either a shopper holding a basket full of grocery items while standing in a supermarket checkout line or a grocery checker facing the waiting shopper would seem more than somewhat odd. This same query posed within the context of many everyday commercial transactions seems pointless. In these instances, the mere presence of social actors in the physical situation acts to define their likely goals, plans, and intentions. Of course, in rare instances these highly transparent social encounters turn out to be far from routine, as in the case of a bank teller being asked by a bank robber to hand over all of his or her money. Other social encounters such as negotiations or adversarial interactions are routinely fraught with indirectness and the intentional deployment of covering moves designed to mask goals and plans and uncovering moves calculated to unmask these covering moves (Goffman, 1969; Miller, 2003). These latter social situations pose major challenges to cointerlocutors' abilities to detect each other's intentions, goals, and plans and are akin to exercises in intelligence gathering (Berger & Kellermann, 1989; Goffman, 1969). Nonetheless, whether social encounters are highly transparent or profoundly opaque, cognitive representations of goals and plans are in play, guiding message comprehension and interpretation as well as message production.

Typically, goals are viewed as desired end states for which individuals strive. Cognitive representations of these desired end states are assumed to be hierarchically organized in long-term memory with abstract goals located at the tops of the hierarchies and concrete goals nested at lower hierarchical levels. Under this hierarchical view, the achievement of lower level goals enables the attainment of more abstract goals; however, because of inherent limitations in attention, goals may be activated and pursued outside of conscious awareness (Berger, 1995, 1997; Dillard, 1997; Dillard, Anderson, & Knobloch, 2002). When individuals directly observe goal-directed action sequences or read written descriptions of the same sequences, they show better memory for higher level goals than for the subgoals that enable them (Lichtenstein & Brewer, 1980). It is also commonly assumed that individuals often pursue multiple goals simultaneously during their social interactions with others; a number of alternative typologies have been proposed to characterize these goals (Dillard, 1997). Individuals may seek to attain a variety of instrumental goals such as obtaining information, goods, services, and the like during their interactions, at the same time attempting to satisfy such interpersonal goals as maintaining a friendship, not threatening the face of their cointerlocutors, or avoiding threats to their own face (Brown & Levinson, 1978, 1987; Goffman, 1959).

Regardless of the number and types of goals being pursued, relevant knowledge must be activated and accessed to guide actions and discourse in ways calculated to reach desired end states. This knowledge is organized in memory in plan-like fashion. Plans are cognitive representations of goal-directed action sequences. Plans are not the action sequences themselves but representations of these sequences in long-term memory (Berger, 1995, 1997; Wilensky, 1983). Like goals, it is assumed that plans are organized hierarchically in long-term memory with more abstract action units represented at the tops of these hierarchies and more concrete action units at lower hierarchical levels. Thus, a plan to gain compliance from another might include the abstract unit "offer a reward" with lower level units specifying the nature of the reward, for example, "verbal praise" or "material reward," or both. Successively lower level units would further specify the nature of the verbal praise or the material reward. If it were to continue, the process could cascade down to the level of specific utterances ("If you take the garbage, I'll give you $1.00") and actions (a smile and a pat on the back). Consistent with this account, some have proposed that phonetic plans are activated to encode conceptual representations of message plans into speech sounds (Levelt, 1989). Similar to the notion of plans as hierarchically organized knowledge structures, proponents of action identification theory have argued that actions can be identified at various levels of abstraction (Vallacher & Wegner, 1985; Vallacher, Wegner, & Somoza, 1989). Hierarchical models imply that there are numerous alternative combinations of utterances and actions that can fulfill the requirements of representing abstract message plan units for reaching goals.

The plan construct can be distinguished from the concept of planning. As Wilensky (1983) suggested, "Planning concerns the process by which people select a course of action—deciding what they want, formulating and revising plans, dealing with problems and adversity, making choices, and eventually performing some action" (p. 5). Under this notion, planning is a process that produces a plan as its product. Although planning may largely be a conscious activity, plan retrieval, plan following, and even plan alteration may occur outside of conscious awareness (Berger, 1997). Some have suggested that plans for attaining recurring goals may become attached to these goals and be activated automatically when the goals arise, thus eliminating the necessity for any conscious planning activity (Hammond, 1989). Moreover, when exigencies arise that require low-level adjustments to these "canned plans," they too may be carried out outside of conscious awareness (Alterman, 1988; Hammond, 1989).

The notion of planning, as presented here, may encourage the mistaken belief that plans are devised consciously and only in advance of particular encounters. Although individuals may imagine interactions with others before or after they actually engage in them (Honeycutt, 2003), evidence strongly suggests that when individuals are engaged in goal-directed interactions, they frequently report formulating and altering goals and plans online, as the interaction unfolds, and much of this online planning activity is in response to both perceived and anticipated changes in the goals and plans of cointerlocutors (Waldron, 1990, 1997; Waldron & Applegate, 1994). Thus, planning occurs as individuals converse, and this planning activity may or may not be carried out consciously.

Typically, plan-based approaches to message production, as represented in the goals-plan-action (GPA) model of persuasion (Dillard,

1990, 1997) and more general plan-based approaches to strategic interaction (Berger, 1995, 1997, 2002, 2003), have bracketed the question of how the goals arise in the first place. That is, these approaches presume that individuals have formulated a set of goals, some of which may exist outside of conscious awareness, that they anticipate pursuing. As noted previously, these approaches recognize that these goals are dynamic, but they make no attempt to explain how they arise and transmute over time. Although questions concerning the genesis of goals fall outside the scope of this discussion, models have been devised to illuminate the processes by which goals arise (Wilson, 1990, 1995, 1997, 2002).

GOAL FAILURE AND THE HIERARCHY PRINCIPLE

Utilizing this general conception of goals, plans, and planning we initiated a research program designed to explore the relations between plan attributes, especially their complexity, and the rapidity with which individuals are able to marshal alternative actions when they fail to reach their goals. Two ostensibly competing hypotheses were examined in the studies. First, individuals whose plans anticipate potential failures at different points in their execution by stipulating contingent actions should be faster in retrieving alternative actions to circumvent goal failures than those whose plans do not include contingent actions. Second, because plans that include contingent actions are, by default, more complex than plans that do not include contingencies, retrieving alternative actions from complex plans could increase the time necessary to retrieve alternative actions when goal failure occurs.

In an early study, individuals wrote plans to persuade another person to accept their opinions on two issues (Berger, 1988a). Immediately after writing their plans, the actions contained in them were questioned with respect to what the participant would do if the enacted action failed to bring about the desired outcome. The time it took participants to respond to these questions was averaged over each plan. One week later, participants were asked to try to persuade a resistant experimental confederate to accept their position on one of the two issues. Judges rated the participants' verbal fluency during the persuasion task. Average response latencies for answering the questions were significantly and negatively correlated with the fluency judgments for the issue argued ($r = -.36$, $p < .001$). By contrast, the correlation between the response latencies and verbal fluency for the issue that was questioned but not argued was nonsignificant ($r = .04$, *ns*), and the two correlations were significantly different ($p < .05$).

Although these results support the hypothesis that increased accessibility of contingent actions reduces the time necessary to respond to goal failures, other evidence suggests support for the second hypothesis (Berger, Karol, & Jordan, 1989). One of the conditions in this study's first experiment employed a procedure similar to the study just described; that is, planned actions were again questioned. In a second condition, individuals wrote plans that were not questioned, and in a third condition participants wrote no plan. Immediately after writing plans, individuals tried to persuade a resistant confederate. Those whose plans were questioned were marginally less fluent than those whose plans were not questioned. However, within the plan-question condition, those who generated more specific arguments were judged to be significantly less verbally fluent ($r = -.62$) and were significantly more likely to show increased vocalized pausing ($r = .33$), nonvocalized pausing ($r = .52$), and frequency of false starts ($r = .43$). By contrast, the same correlations with the plan-only condition were nonsignificant with the exception of the nonvocalized pauses parameter ($r = .43$). In a third experiment, individuals were given the opportunity to devise a second plan after generating their first plan. This experiment revealed that individuals whose plans were questioned produced significantly more new arguments in their second plan than did those whose first plans were not questioned, demonstrating that questioning plans tends to increase their complexity. Thus, under some conditions enhanced plan complexity may undermine verbal fluency when individuals are forced to retrieve actions to circumvent goal failures.

Although the results of these two early studies appear to conflict, in all likelihood they demonstrate quite different processes. In the first study (Berger, 1988a), all participants' plans were questioned, and thus potentially made more complex. The issue was whether response latencies to queries would predict verbal fluency 1 week later when participants participated in the persuasion task. Presumably, the response latencies indexed the accessibility of contingent actions, not necessarily the complexity of the plans themselves. The second study dealt more directly with the complexity of plans, as indexed by the number of specific arguments generated by participants (Berger et al., 1989). In this case, the increased plan complexity, induced by questioning plans, tended to undermine verbal fluency.

Subsequent research has revealed nonlinear relations between plan complexity or the number of alternative plans one has available to achieve a particular goal and duration of latencies in response to goal failure. In one of these studies, individuals drew one, three, or six alternative maps depicting walking routes from the laboratory in which the study was conducted to a well-known campus location. They then provided their directions from memory to an experimental confederate (Knowlton & Berger, 1997, Experiment 1). Those in a control condition gave their directions without preparing any maps. After participants provided the first rendition of their directions, confederates indicated that they had difficulty following the route used in the directions and requested that participants provide an alternative route. The latency between the end of the confederates' requests and the beginning of the second rendition of the participants' directions was recorded. The speech onset latencies of those in the three maps condition were significantly less than those observed in the one and six maps conditions. Apparently, those who drew only one map were hard pressed when an alternative route was requested, whereas those who prepared six maps experienced elevated decision uncertainty arising from the proliferation of alternative routes.

Virtually identical results were found in a second experiment in which participants generated one, three, or six alternative arguments supporting their position on an issue and then attempted to persuade a resistant experimental confederate (Knowlton & Berger, 1997, Experiment 2). Individuals who generated three arguments showed significantly shorter latencies in response to goal failure than did those who prepared one or six arguments. Although it would be premature to claim that these two experiments provide support for a magical number 3 ± 0 with respect to the optimal number of alternatives, they show that onset latencies behave similarly when the number of alternative plans (Experiment 1) and the number of alternative actions within a plan (Experiment 2) are varied. That is, a specific route depicted in the map plans devised in Experiment 1 could have been made more or less complex by including more or less detail in the description of the route, for example, more or fewer landmarks. Instead, entirely different routes were requested to induce complexity. By contrast, the complexity of the persuasion plans devised in Experiment 2 was varied by requesting different numbers of arguments within them. In any case, these findings suggest that message plans may have optimal complexity levels, at least in terms of their ability to generate alternative actions in the event of goal failure.

A second line of research that developed within this plan-based theoretical perspective explored the relations between plan alterations at various hierarchical levels and cognitive load. One study revealed that when elementary school children were given the opportunity to replan the order in which they would perform a series of classroom chores after school, the alterations they made to their plans involved changes at concrete plan levels rather than changes in abstract plan units (Pea & Hawkins, 1987). Similarly, another study showed that when individuals provided geographic directions to others who indicated failure in understanding the directions, direction givers rarely altered the walk routes in the second rendition of their directions, but, the direction givers were more likely to increase their vocal intensity and lower their speech rate in response to the understanding failure (Berger &

diBattista, 1993). When plans fail and individuals wish to continue to pursue them, they tend to make lower level rather than higher level alterations to their plans. The hierarchy principle grew out of these studies and was subsequently evaluated in a series of experiments.

The hierarchy principle suggests that one reason individuals show a proclivity for altering concrete rather than abstract plan elements is that abstract alterations to plans potentiate more cognitive demands than do concrete alterations (Berger, 1997). Changes to abstract message plan units cascade down the plan hierarchy, thus implicating changes at less abstract levels. By contrast, alterations to concrete levels of message plans, for example, varying vocal intensity or speech rate, require the alteration of only one paralinguistic parameter. The remainder of the plan can be reenacted as it was the first time. Under the assumption that individuals tend to be "cognitive misers" (Fiske & Taylor, 1991), one would expect a preference for alterations to less abstract plan levels. A series of laboratory and field experiments was undertaken to determine whether required changes at different plan hierarchy levels would eventuate in the predicted levels of cognitive load. These studies again employed the direction-giving understanding-failure paradigm and speech onset latencies as a measure of cognitive load.

In two laboratory experiments (Berger, Knowlton, & Abrahams, 1996, Experiments 1 & 2), participants were asked to provide geographic directions to experimental confederates who expressed difficulty in understanding them. In Experiment 1, confederates attributed their understanding failures either to the direction givers' excessively rapid speech rate or to their inability to follow the directions' walking route. In a third condition, the locus of the understanding failure was unspecified. In all conditions, participants were asked to give a second rendition of their directions; direction givers were either asked to speak more slowly or to provide an alternative walk route. Analyses revealed that speech onset latencies in the route change condition were significantly longer than those in the speech rate and unspecified conditions. Experiment 2 employed the speech rate and route change conditions used in Experiment 1 and a landmarks condition in which direction givers were asked to provide more landmarks in the second rendition. Again, speech onset latencies were longest in the route change condition and shortest in the speech rate condition with the landmarks condition between these extremes.

The two field experiments involved two confederates approaching lone pedestrians at an intersection. One of the confederates asked a target pedestrian for directions to another well-known location in the city (Berger et al., 1996, Experiments 3 & 4). After receiving the directions, the direction asker expressed difficulty in understanding the directions for different reasons. The second confederate recorded speech onset latencies using a concealed stopwatch. Three different plan failure loci were represented in the speech rate, landmarks, and route change conditions. The speech rate and route change conditions were employed in the second experiment. The pattern of onset latency means observed in these two field experiments replicated the one found in the two laboratory studies. Movement up the plan hierarchy from speech rate alterations through the addition of landmarks to route changes resulted in significant increases in speech onset latencies, lending support to the hierarchy principle (Berger, 1997).

OFFLINE PLANNING AND TASK EFFECTIVENESS

The notion that the opportunity to plan before engaging in certain tasks improves performance has received considerable support. In one study, individuals who were given the chance to plan before trying to solve a traveling salesman problem, one requiring them to schedule a series of client calls in the most efficient order, produced more efficient routes for making their client calls than did those who did not plan before making their schedules (Battman, 1989). Children given the task of scheduling a series of classroom chores such as cleaning blackboards and putting away books devised progressively more efficient plans when given the opportunity to revise their schedules (Pea & Hawkins, 1987). Apparently, good planners engage in cycles of plan revision and simulation to develop and test increasingly efficient plans. Plans may become more efficient when individuals are given the opportunity to revise them because replanning may enable planners to recognize previously unseen opportunities for improving their plans' efficiency and perhaps their effectiveness. Indeed, some researchers have suggested that this kind of opportunistic planning is more the rule than the exception in everyday planning situations (Hayes-Roth & Hayes-Roth, 1979).

For a variety of reasons, it may not be possible or desirable to initiate action in pursuit of a goal at a particular point in time. Holding a goal or goals in abeyance for some period of time may be an optimal course of action. However, once the opportunity to pursue a goal arises, having a plan available to pursue it should facilitate goal achievement. Evidence suggests that when people plan for goals to be pursued later, they are more sensitive than those who have not devised plans to future opportunities to achieve these goals when the opportunity arises (Patalano & Seifert, 1997). Thus, just as planning may be opportunistic, having plans available for attaining future goals may sensitize individuals to opportunities to achieve them when such opportunities arise. Other research has demonstrated that the effectiveness of offline plans designed to reach such social goals as obtaining a date or ingratiating one's self to a new roommate is related to social loneliness (Berger & Bell, 1988; Berger &

diBattista, 1992). In these studies individuals wrote plans to achieve the goals of obtaining a date and ingratiating one's self to a new roommate. Untrained judges read the plans and rated their potential effectiveness. Judges' effectiveness ratings were correlated with responses given to the revised version of the UCLA Loneliness Scale (Russell, Peplau, & Cutrona, 1980). In both studies date-request plan effectiveness was inversely related to social loneliness for men only. Given that these studies both indicated that the burden of date requesting still falls disproportionately on men's shoulders, ineffective date-request plans should be associated with more negative outcomes for men than for women. By contrast, in both studies, roommate ingratiation plan effectiveness was inversely related to loneliness among women. Plans that were judged to be more effective contained more actions than were plans judged to be potentially less effective, thus suggesting a relation between plan complexity and effectiveness (Berger & Bell, 1988).

ONLINE PLANNING AND TASK EFFECTIVENESS

Several of the experiments considered thus far involved the generation of message plans offline, prior to using them during social interactions. Such planning may occur before some everyday social encounters in the form of imagined interactions (Honeycutt, 2003) and in communication contexts in which individuals typically have the time to plan the messages they will ultimately disseminate to audiences, as they do in the mass media and advertising industries. However, if planning occurred only offline in this preparatory mode, its usefulness as a theoretical construct for explaining social interaction would be limited. When individuals are engaged in conversations, plans may have to be instantiated rapidly and any conscious planning must be done on the fly, most likely when individuals find themselves in the listener role. Methods other than those used in the offline planning studies must be used to study online planning during interactions. A series of studies employing a cued-recall method undertook this task (Cegala & Waldron, 1992; Waldron, 1990, 1997; Waldron & Applegate, 1994; Waldron, Caughlin, & Jackson, 1995; Waldron & Cegala, 1992). Several of these studies have linked attributes of plans and planning, as revealed by the cued-recall procedure, and the degree to which individuals are effective in achieving their interaction goals.

In these studies, individuals were given goals to pursue prior to their interactions; for example, obtain specific information from their partner or engage in a conversation about a topic on which they disagree. Immediately after concluding their conversation, participants were taken to a room where they individually reviewed a videotape of the just-completed conversation. They were instructed to stop the tape whenever they could recall what they were thinking during the conversation and record what it was they were thinking at that time. In one of the studies, approximately 44% of the some 2,273 thoughts participants listed were concerned with the goals they were pursuing during the conversation and the plans they were using to attain these goals (Waldron, 1990). Similar results were obtained in a later study (Waldron et al., 1995). Because individuals may pursue goals and instantiate plans for doing so outside of conscious awareness, these results probably underestimate the extent to which online planning occurs during conversations, although the fact that research participants were instructed to pursue specific goals during the conversations may have made them more conscious of both their goals and plans as they conversed.

After a conversation during which they engaged in verbal disagreements, participants completed the cued-recall procedure described earlier (Waldron & Applegate, 1994). Participants also individually completed a measure of cognitive complexity with respect to other people (Applegate, 1990). The videotapes were analyzed to determine how competent each person was in using various disagreement tactics. The plans that people developed during the conversation were scored in terms of their complexity, specificity, and sophistication. Plan complexity was determined by the number of distinct actions contained in the plan, more actions indicated greater complexity. Plan specificity was determined by the degree to which planned actions were abstract or concrete. Plan sophistication concerned the degree to which planners relied solely on canned plans versus their propensity to accommodate their plans to the current situation. Results showed that highly sophisticated planners took into account the actions of their conversational partners, and they anticipated future conversational moves that might help them achieve their goals. Also, people who developed more complex, specific, and sophisticated online plans used more effective disagreement tactics than did those whose plans were simple, general, and less sophisticated. The plans of those who were more effective looked further ahead into the conversational future than did those who performed less well at the task, and those who were more effective tended to incorporate their partner's arguments into their own message plans. Although the complexity with which individuals construe others was significantly and positively correlated with plan complexity, only plan complexity proved to be a significant predictor of arguing effectiveness. Thus, plan complexity may mediate or enable relations between the complexity of person construal and interaction effectiveness.

In another study, in which individuals tried to elicit from their partners as much information about AIDS as they could, individuals whose online plans were more complex elicited significantly more information than did those whose plans were relatively simple. In addition, those whose online plans focused on concrete actions were more successful at eliciting the desired information than were those whose plans were dominated by highly abstract, undifferentiated actions (Waldron et al., 1995). Similar findings were reported in a study in which clients involved in a welfare-to-work program devised job interview plans offline. Those who generated more complex and specific job interview plans were more likely to obtain employment and remain on their jobs longer than those whose plans were simple and abstract (Waldron & Lavitt, 2000). During mock interviews, individuals with more complex and specific plans were better able to address interviewers' questions about their job qualifications. Those whose plans were simple and abstract tended to repeat what they had said before in response to interviewers' questions and to provide such vague responses as "I like to work with other people" when answering interviewers' questions about their job qualifications.

Although the previously reviewed studies suggested that highly complex plans tend to undermine verbal fluency (Berger et al., 1989; Knowlton & Berger, 1997), the studies just reviewed seem to support the proposition that those who enter interactions with more complex plans developed offline and those who generate more complex plans online are more effective at achieving their interaction goals than are those whose plans are relatively simple and abstract. However, the potential conflict between these two sets of studies may be more apparent than real. There is considerable literature demonstrating that reduced verbal fluency tends to undermine judgments of speaker credibility (Burgoon, Birk, & Pfau, 1990; Miller & Hewgill, 1964), thus suggesting that reduced verbal fluency arising from high plan complexity levels may diminish effectiveness. However, although individuals employing highly complex plans may be somewhat less fluent than their less complex counterparts, because they have more alternative actions available to them, they are better able to overcome obstacles that arise during the interaction. Their ability to deploy effective actions calculated to surmount these problems rapidly may outweigh any negative judgments that might accrue from complexity-driven reductions in their verbal fluency. Of course, there remains the possibility that the communication context modulates the potential negative effects of reduced verbal fluency. In the formal context of a speech or presentation, fluency reductions may be particularly problematic; whereas in informal social contexts, lack of verbal fluency may not have as negative an impact on effectiveness judgments.

ON THE SOCIALIZATION OF PLANS AND PLANNING

Some critics have raised questions about the usefulness of cognitive approaches to the study of social interaction in general and the kinds of psychologically oriented, plan-based models described in this chapter. On the general level it has been claimed that planning, intentions, and other cognitive structures and processes are too far removed from interaction behavior, and when people engage each other in conversation, "the communication patterns of an interaction partner may gain prepotency over one's own cognitions and affect as determinants of communication behavior" (Burgoon & White, 1997, p. 280). Although patterns of reciprocity and compensation discerned in the study of social interaction may sometimes be the product of automatic processes, certainly cognitive structures and processes enable such patterns to emerge, even though social actors may be unaware of them (Lewicki, 1986; Nisbett & Wilson, 1977). Thus, for example, reciprocal increases in the speech rates of cointerlocutors involve the processing, albeit nonconscious, of changes in each other's speech rates. Unless one embraces the tenets of radical behaviorism, it is difficult to see how, even in this case, cognitively oriented explanations can be bracketed.

As discussed previously, the understandings individuals derive from observing each other's discourse and actions are critically dependent on inferences they make about each other's goals and plans. Moreover, individuals' communicative conduct flows from their understandings of each other's goals and plans. Indeed, individuals may choose not to initiate interaction or withdraw from it if they infer that interaction partners harbor highly malevolent intentions toward them. Moreover, individuals must have some understanding of others' goals and plans to conduct coherent conversations. Such basic questions as, "What is this interaction about?" or "Why are we talking?" are answered by recourse to goal–plan inferences, which enable individuals to respond in sensible ways to the utterances and actions of fellow interlocutors. These goal–plan inferences enable understanding at progressively less abstract levels as well.

A critique more directly related to the work on goals, plans, and planning concerns the idea that these concepts, when viewed strictly from the individual perspective, are inadequate to account for the complexities of ongoing social interaction (Waldron, 1997).

This problem was recognized more than two decades ago, and was addressed by the notion of interactive planning (Bruce & Newman, 1978). These researchers argued that stories, like conversations, must be understood in terms of the interactions that take place between story characters' goals and plans rather than by recourse to each individual story characters' goals and plans in isolation. They devised a complex system to represent story characters' interacting goals and plans and used it to analyze characters' actions in Grimm's (1944) fairy tale "Hansel and Gretel." In the story, Hansel becomes aware of his stepmother's plan to abandon him and his sister in the forest and his father's complicity in the nefarious plot. As a result, Hansel devises a counterplan to foil the plan. His plan involves dropping pebbles while he and his sister are being led into the forest so that they can retrace their steps to their house. Being appraised of the interactions between the stepmother's plans and Hansel's plans enables the story reader to understand the story characters' actions, such as Hansel and Gretel being led deep into the forest by their father where they are left alone and Hansel dropping white pebbles while walking. The complexities created by the interacting plans of the story characters would very likely have been amplified if Hansel had not first overheard the conversation in which his stepmother revealed her plan. What if Hansel had been left to infer the stepmother's wicked plot solely on the basis of its perpetrators' actions? Presumably, this less obvious scenario would have required considerably more time and inferential work for Hansel to achieve an understanding of the stepmother's goals and plans.

The difference between the way that the "Hansel and Gretel" story was written and the alternative version of the story offered here suggests a continuum on which social situations can be ordered with respect to goals, plans, and planning, as suggested earlier. One end of this continuum is anchored by situations that are highly transparent with respect to social actors' goals and plans, as represented by numerous face-to-face commercial transactions in everyday life. At the other end of this continuum are social situations in which the goals and plans of the involved parties are highly opaque to each other. This opaqueness might arise from intentional efforts to conceal goals and plans either through misdirection or restriction of information through covering moves and counteruncovering moves (Goffman, 1969). Strategic interactions involving negotiations and interactions between adversarial parties such as governments and competitors provide such examples. Located toward the middle of this continuum are situations in which interaction partners do not intentionally attempt to obfuscate their goals and plans but that, for a variety of reasons, are less transparent than the routines that define the transparent end of the continuum. In these situations, individuals may have a general understanding of others' goals and plans but not possess detailed knowledge that would enable them to fashion messages and actions that might address these goals and plans.

Although social interactions that fall toward the opaque pole of the continuum may attract more research attention because of their apparent complexity, work in the areas of linguistic formulaicity and conversational routines suggests that people's everyday lives are dominated by highly transparent social interactions. Students of language use have asserted that up to 70% of adult language use may be formulaic (Altenberg, 1990), "despite a rich superficial variation" (Sinclair, 1991,

p. 121). These formulaic utterances may be used during social interactions to achieve such goals as manipulating others (satisfying physical, emotional, and cognitive needs), asserting a separate identity (being taken seriously), or asserting a group identity (establishing a place in a hierarchy; Wray & Perkins, 2000). This view holds that everyday language production and comprehension relies on the statistical likelihood of the expected rather than the potential for the unexpected (Wray, 1992), and linguistic formulaicity enables individuals to cope with the memory demands individuals incur during social interactions (Wray & Perkins, 2000). Others have observed that conversational routines are commonplace in everyday social behavior because the same interaction goals tend to recur frequently during social encounters (Aarts & Dijksterhuis, 2000; Coulmas, 1981).

Interaction routines associated with transparent social contexts may become so well established that few, if any, verbal exchanges are necessary to reveal goals and plans. In such instances, prefabricated or canned plans (Hammond, 1989) are instantiated with minimal cuing and little conscious calculation. The plans themselves are social in the sense that they specify the actions of all parties to the routine (Schank, 1982; Schank & Abelson, 1977; Schank & Berman, 2002). In enacting such transparent routines, individuals need not go to the trouble of consciously calculating their cointerlocutors' next moves or looking ahead in the conversation. Their individual representations of the social situation are sufficient for attaining their goals.

In transparent interactions, it is only when anomalies arise that conscious calculation about the goals and plans of one's partners becomes necessary; however, when "all goes as planned," social actors individually execute their roles in a mutually shared plan. Because only minimal cuing is necessary to carry out these routines, participants' actions may be appropriately interleaved but not necessarily mutually influence each other, except in the sense that they are performed in a particular, well-defined sequence (Cappella, 1987). Even though they involve only minimal cuing, most of the time in daily social commerce these transparent interactions are executed without difficulty. The high reliability of interaction routines with respect to producing desired outcomes is nicely illustrated by a colleague's revelation about her non-English-speaking mother who looks forward with great anticipation to grocery shopping by herself in American supermarkets because she can do it successfully without having to speak English, except perhaps to say "Thank you."

In spite of the fact that they are highly taken for granted, there are a number of important research questions that can be asked about transparent social interactions. First, how do children acquire the information necessary to build cognitive representations of the goals pursued and the plans enacted during transparent interactions? Second, although it is probably rare, why do some individuals sometimes experience difficulty in enacting transparent interactions within the linguistic community in which they have been socialized? Third, situations may arise that are transparent for some interlocutors but not others. Cross-cultural interactions might be the occasion for such disjunctions, but they could involve individuals from the same culture with differing funds of knowledge. How are the operative goals and plans made manifest to the uninitiated? Finally, to what degree does the goal–plan knowledge associated with specific transparent social interactions generalize across other transparent situations? Such generalized representations in the form of scenes have been suggested by the work on memory organization packets (Kellermann, 1995; Schank, 1982).

Movement from the transparent end of the continuum toward the highly opaque pole creates a number of exigencies. On the input side, cointerlocutors must deploy increasing amounts of attention to each other's discourse and actions to ascertain their goals and plans (Berger, 2000; Bogdan, 1994, 1997). Goal–plan detection must occur before one can retrieve and modify canned plans or generate a set of goals and plans from scratch. However, what if it takes time to detect others' goals and plans? Short of terminating the interaction to try to solve this problem, there may be routines that can be invoked to continue the interaction while "buying time" so that a larger sample of discourse and actions can be sampled in an effort to build inferences about cointerlocutors' goals and plans. Such a routine might involve a conversational gambit such as, "You just said something about X, could you tell me more (explain more) about that?" This gambit has the effect of shifting the conversational burden to the cointerlocutor and allowing the individual time to engage in inference making regarding the cointerlocutor's goals and plans. More pointed questions might be deployed to elicit specific information that could provide more direct clues about the other person's likely goals and plans. In extreme cases, individuals might ask cointerlocutors to reveal their goals and plans—for example, "What is it that you want from me?"—although this level of directness is rarely reached in social encounters.

On the message production side, increasingly opaque interactions necessitate an increase in the amount of online planning and a shift in the planning style. As social actors become aware that cointerlocutors may be intentionally employing concealment and deception to obfuscate their goals and plans, an activity that perhaps serves to define the opaque pole of the transparent–opaque continuum, they must build more contingencies into their own plans in case their inferences turn out to be erroneous. The complexity of their message plans must of necessity increase because second-, third-, and *n*-guessing of cointerlocutors' goals and plans is required. Individuals may be forced to make inferences about their cointerlocutor's inferences. When these metainferential levels are activated, it may be useful to distinguish between observable social interaction on the one hand and the conversation of intentions and inferences on the other. As people search for clues to their cointerlocutors' goals, plans, and intentions, verbalizations may not be treated literally, simply because they cannot be trusted. Rather, individuals may use cointerlocutors' verbal discourse and nonverbal actions to try to diagnose the nature of their true goals and plans, rather than interpret them literally. Because these levels of inferencing and planning are highly demanding of cognitive resources, individuals engaged in everyday pursuits are not likely to reach them very often. However, as they ply their trade, intelligence professionals, as well as corporate and political strategists, must engage in these exercises in strategic interaction on a routine basis.

Social encounters falling somewhere between the transparent and opaque poles of this continuum are not routine, but they also do not involve intentional deception. For example, individuals involved in an escalating romantic relationship may be unsure of the degree to which their partner is attracted to them and the degree to which they are committed to their relationship. Although not intentionally created, these uncertainties may require increased vigilance to resolve, as well as increased contingent planning, although the complexity of these plans would probably be less than those encountered in the case of deceptive communication. However, even at these reduced opacity levels, some second guessing and metainferencing of necessity may occur, thus activating the conversation of intentions and inferences.

An important implication of this analysis is that, for the most part, transparent interactions do not demand that plans be socialized as they are carried out during an encounter. By their nature and design, routinized interactions do not require elaborate adjustments and accommodations; they are geared toward the efficient attainment of instrumental goals. Thus, concerns that plan and planning constructs are insufficiently "social" for explaining such interactions seems misplaced. By contrast, when interactions become more opaque, plans and planning must, of necessity, take on a more "social" character. Making inferences about others' intentions and inferences about others' inferences regarding one's own intentions in the conversation of intentions and inferences is itself a social process. Although the opaque nature of adversarial interactions has been emphasized in this regard, individuals may sometimes cooperatively lead each other to accurate inferences about their intentions, as when individuals escalate the intimacy level of a romantic relationship. In such cases, acts more than words may be taken to be diagnostic of intentions, and, in extreme cases talk may itself become cheap. How individuals intentionally guide each other's inferences regarding their goals and plans is a potentially fruitful area for future research.

In a symposium dedicated to the question of the degree to which social interaction is conducted consciously or automatically, one participant observed that communication is at once both strategic and automatic (Kellermann, 1992). Although this assertion is tenable, the view articulated here suggests that the relative mix of conscious calculation and automaticity varies considerably depending on the degree of situational transparency. Furthermore, highly opaque interactions, whether they involve individuals, institutions, or governments, may be much more about the conversation of intentions and inferences than they are about observable interaction behavior, at least at the level of the meaning of particular verbal exchanges. When it is crucial to ascertain the intentions of a potentially dangerous adversary, individuals are compelled to participate in the conversation of intentions and inferences, and message cues that might not ordinarily be heeded may take on considerable significance. For example, a potential precursor to a large-scale military attack by one country on another may be very high levels of radio traffic on military and government communication links of the attacking country followed by complete radio silence, rather than battle plans conveyed in the content of particular communiqués. Message content may be intentionally misleading, but variations in the pattern of message volume on communication networks are diagnostic of invasion intentions. In such interactions the automatic component is minimal and the content of messages suspect. The conversation of intentions and inferences is all important.

Although language and social interaction can be usefully viewed as instruments for achieving goals, when social interactions locate themselves toward the opaque end of the transparency continuum, these language tools must be augmented by another level of communication, the conversation of intentions and inferences. Language may be deployed and monitored as ways of providing information about goals, plans, and intentions; however, in parallel with these efforts, cognitive effort must be expended to determine cointerlocutors' range of possible goals and plans and then winnow these alternatives to the most probable candidates, ones on which individuals, institutions, and governments are willing to predicate their own goals, plans, messages, and actions. Some have suggested that these cognitive processes be left to psychologists to study and that communication researchers should focus mainly on discourse and actions (Burgoon & White, 1997). However, because conversational discourse and the conversation of intentions and inferences may run in parallel and mutually influence each other, especially when interactions become opaque, it is difficult to see how communication researchers seeking to understand social interaction processes can possibly ignore one of these conversations at the expense of the other.

REFERENCES

Aarts, H., & Dijksterhuis, A. (2000). Habits as knowledge structures: Automaticity in goal-directed behavior. *Journal of Personality and Social Psychology, 78,* 53–63.

Abelson, R. P. (1976). Script processing in attitude formation and decision-making. In J. S. Caroll & J. W. Payne (Eds.), *Cognition and social behavior* (pp. 33–45). Hillsdale, NJ: Lawrence Erlbaum Associates.

Abelson, R. P. (1981). Psychological status of the script concept. *American Psychologist, 36,* 715–729.

Altenberg, B. (1990). Speech as linear composition. In G. Caie, K. Haastrup, A. L. Jakobsen, J. E. Nielsen, J. Sevaldsen, H. Specht, et al. (Eds.), *Proceedings from the Fourth Nordic Conference for English Studies* (Vol. 1, pp. 133–143). Copenhagen, Denmark: University of Copenhagen, Department of English.

Alterman, R. (1988). Adaptive planning. *Cognitive Science, 12,* 393–421.

Applegate, J. L. (1990). Constructs and communication: A pragmatic integration. In G. Neimeyer & R. Neimeyer (Eds.), *Advances in personal construct psychology* (Vol. 1, pp. 203–230). Greenwich, CT: JAI.

Austin, J. L. (1962). *How to do things with words.* Oxford, UK: Oxford University Press.

Battman, W. (1989). Planning as a method of stress prevention: Will it pay off? In C. D. Spielberger, I. G. Sarason, & J. Strelau (Eds.), *Stress and anxiety* (Vol. 12, pp. 259–275). New York: Hemisphere.

Berger, C. R. (1988a, May). *Communication plans and communicative performance.* Paper presented at the annual meeting of the International Communication Association, New Orleans, LA.

Berger, C. R. (1988b). Planning, affect, and social action generation. In L. Donohew, H. Sypher, & E. T. Higgins (Eds.), *Communication, social cognition, and affect* (pp. 93–116). Hillsdale, NJ: Lawrence Erlbaum Associates.

Berger, C. R. (1989). Goals, plans, and discourse understanding. In J. J. Bradac (Ed.), *Message effects in communication science* (pp. 75–101). Newbury Park, CA: Sage.

Berger, C. R. (1995). A plan-based approach to strategic communication. In D. E. Hewes (Ed.), *The cognitive bases of interpersonal communication* (pp. 141—179). Hillsdale, NJ: Lawrence Erlbaum Associates.

Berger, C. R. (1997). *Planning strategic interaction: Attaining goals through communicative action.* Mahwah, NJ: Lawrence Erlbaum Associates.

Berger, C. R. (2000). Goal detection and efficiency: Neglected aspects of message production. *Communication Theory, 10,* 156–166.

Berger, C. R. (2002). Goals and knowledge structures in social interaction. In M. L. Knapp & J. A. Daly (Eds.), *Handbook of interpersonal communication* (3rd ed., pp. 181–212). Thousand Oaks, CA: Sage.

Berger, C. R. (2003). Message production skill in social interaction. In J. O. Greene & B. R. Burleson (Eds.), *Handbook of communication and social interaction skills* (pp. 257–289). Mahwah, NJ: Lawrence Erlbaum Associates.

Berger, C. R., & Bell, R. A. (1988). Plans and the initiation of social relationships. *Human Communication Research, 15,* 217–235.

Berger, C. R., & Bradac, J. J. (1982). *Language and social knowledge: Uncertainty in interpersonal relations.* London: Edward Arnold.

Berger, C. R., & Chaffee, S. H. (1987). The study of communication as a science. In C. R. Berger & S. H. Chaffee (Eds.), *Handbook of communication science* (pp. 15–19). Newbury Park, CA: Sage.

Berger, C. R., & Chaffee, S. H. (1988). On bridging the communication gap. *Human Communication Research, 15,* 311–318.

Berger, C. R., & diBattista, P. (1992). Information seeking and plan elaboration: What do you need to know to know what to do? *Communication Monographs, 59,* 368–387.

Berger, C. R., & diBattista, P. (1993). Communication failure and plan adaptation: If at first you don't succeed, say it louder and slower. *Communication Monographs, 60,* 220–238.

Berger, C. R., Karol, S. H., & Jordan, J. M. (1989). When a lot of knowledge is a dangerous thing: The debilitating effects of plan complexity on verbal fluency. *Human Communication Research, 16,* 91–119.

Berger, C. R., & Kellermann, K. A. (1989). Personal opacity and social information gathering. *Communication Research, 16,* 314–351.

Berger, C. R., Knowlton, S. W., & Abrahams, M. F. (1996). The hierarchy principle in strategic communication. *Communication Theory, 6,* 111–142.

Bogdan, R. J. (1994). *Grounds for cognition: How goal-guided behavior shapes the mind.* Hillsdale, NJ: Lawrence Erlbaum Associates.

Bogdan, R. J. (1997). *Interpreting minds: The evolution of a practice.* Cambridge, MA: MIT Press.

Bogdan, R. J. (2000). *Minding minds.* Cambridge, MA: MIT Press.

Brand, M. (1984). *Intending and acting: Toward a naturalized theory of action.* Cambridge, MA: MIT Press.

Bratman, M. E. (1987). *Intentions, plans, and practical reason.* Cambridge, MA: Harvard University Press.

Bratman, M. E. (1990). What is intention? In P. R. Cohen, J. Morgan, & M. E. Pollack (Eds.), *Intentions in communication* (pp. 15–31). Cambridge, MA: MIT Press.

Brown, P., & Levinson, S. (1978). Universals in language use: Politeness phenomena. In E. Goody (Ed.), *Questions and politeness* (pp. 56–289). Cambridge, UK: Cambridge University Press.

Brown, P., & Levinson, S. (1987). *Politeness: Some universals in language use.* Cambridge, UK: Cambridge University Press.

Bruce, B., & Newman, D. (1978). Interacting plans. *Cognitive Science, 2,* 195–233.

Burgoon, J. K., Birk, T., & Pfau, M. (1990). Nonverbal behaviors, persuasion, and credibility. *Human Communication Research, 17,* 140–169.

Burgoon, J. K., & White, C. H. (1997). Researching nonverbal message production: A view from interaction adaptation theory. In J. O. Greene (Ed.), *Message production: Advances in communication theory* (pp. 279–312). Mahwah, NJ: Lawrence Erlbaum Associates.

Cappella, J. N. (1987). Interpersonal communication: Definitions and fundamental questions. In C. R. Berger & S. H. Chaffee (Eds.), *Handbook of communication science* (pp. 184–238). Newbury Park, CA: Sage.

Carbonell, J. G. (1981). Counterplanning: A strategy-based model of adversary planning in real-world situations. *Artificial Intelligence, 16,* 295–329.

Cegala, D. J., & Waldron, V. R. (1992). A study of the relationship between communication performance and conversation participants' thoughts. *Communication Studies, 43,* 105–125.

Clark, H. H. (1994). Discourse in production. In M. A. Gernsbacher (Ed.), *Handbook of psycholinguistics* (pp. 985–1021). San Diego, CA: Academic.

Coulmas, F. (1981). Introduction: Conversational routine. In F. Coulmas (Ed.), *Conversational routine: Explorations in standardized communication situations and prepatterned speech* (pp. 1–17). The Hague, Netherlands: Mouton.

Delia, J. G., O'Keefe, B. J., & O' Keefe, D. J. (1982). The constructivist approach to communication. In F. E. X. Dance (Ed.), *Human communication theory: Comparative essays* (pp. 147–191). New York: Harper & Row.

Dillard, J. P. (1990). The nature and substance of goals in tactical communication. In M. J. Cody & M. L. McLaughlin (Eds.), The psychology of tactical communication (pp. 70–90). Clevedon, UK: Multilingual Matters.

Dillard, J. P. (1997). Explicating the goal construct: Tools for theorists. In J. O. Greene (Ed.), *Message production: Advances in communication theory* (pp. 47–69). Mahwah, NJ: Lawrence Erlbaum Associates.

Dillard, J. P., Anderson, J. W., & Knobloch, L. K. (2002). Interpersonal influence. In M. L. Knapp & J. A. Daly (Eds.), *Handbook of interpersonal communication* (3rd ed., pp. 425–474). Thousand Oaks, CA: Sage.

Fiske, S. T., & Taylor, S. E. (1991). *Social cognition* (2nd ed.). New York: McGraw-Hill.

Galambos, J. A., Abelson, R. P., & Black, J. B. (1986). Goals and plans. In J. A. Galambos, R. P. Abelson, & J. B. Black (Eds.), *Knowledge structures* (pp. 101–102). Hillsdale, NJ: Lawrence Erlbaum Associates.

Goffman, E. (1959). *The presentation of self in everyday life.* Garden City, NY: Doubleday.

Goffman, E. (1969). *Strategic interaction.* Philadelphia: University of Pennsylvania Press.

Green, G. M. (1996). *Pragmatics and natural language understanding* (2nd ed.). Hillsdale, NJ: Lawrence Erlbaum Associates.

Greene, J. O. (1984). A cognitive approach to human communication: An action assembly theory. *Communication Monographs, 51,* 289–306.

Grimm, B. (1944). *Grimm's fairy tales.* New York: Pantheon.

Hammond, K. J. (1989). *Case-based planning: Viewing planning as a memory task.* New York: Academic.

Hayes-Roth, B., & Hayes-Roth, F. (1979). A cognitive model of planning. *Cognitive Science, 3,* 275–310.

Hewes, D. E., & Planalp, S. (1982). There is nothing so useful as a good theory...The influence of social knowledge on interpersonal communication. In M. E. Roloff & C. R. Berger (Eds.), *Social cognition and communication* (pp. 107–150). Beverly Hills, CA: Sage.

Hewes, D. E., & Planalp, S. (1987). The individual's place in communication science. In C. R. Berger & S. H. Chaffee (Eds.), *Handbook of communication science* (pp. 147–183). Newbury Park, CA: Sage.

Honeycutt, J. A. (2003). *Imagined interactions: Daydreaming about communication.* Cresskill, NJ: Hampton Press.

Kellermann, K. (1992). Communication: Inherently strategic and primarily automatic. *Communication Monographs, 59,* 288–300.

Kellermann, K. (1995). The conversation MOP: A model of patterned and pliable behavior. In D. E. Hewes (Ed.), *The cognitive bases of interpersonal communication* (pp. 181–221). Hillsdale, NJ: Lawrence Erlbaum Associates.

Knowlton, S. W., & Berger, C. R. (1997). Message planning, communication failure, and cognitive load: Further explorations of the hierarchy principle. *Human Communication Research, 24,* 4–30.

Levelt, W. J. M. (1989). *Speaking: From intention to articulation.* Cambridge, MA: MIT Press.

Lewicki, P. (1986). *Nonconscious social information processing*. Orlando, FL: Academic.

Lichtenstein, E. H., & Brewer, W. F. (1980). Memory for goal directed events. *Cognitive Psychology, 12,* 412–445.

Malle, B. F., & Knobe, J. (1997). The folk concept of intentionality. *Journal of Experimental Social Psychology, 33,* 101–120.

Malle, B. F., & Knobe, J. (2001). The distinction between desire and intention: A folk–conceptual analysis. In B. F. Malle, L. J. Moses, & D. A. Baldwin (Eds.), *Intentions and intentionality: Foundations of social cognition* (pp. 45–67). Cambridge, MA: MIT Press.

Miller, G. R., & Hewgill, M. A. (1964). The effect of variations in nonfluency on audience ratings of source credibility. *Quarterly Journal of Speech, 50,* 36–44.

Miller, W. I. (2003). *Faking it*. Cambridge, UK: Cambridge University Press.

Nisbett, R., & Wilson, T. (1977). Telling more than we can know: Verbal reports on mental processes. *Psychological Review, 84,* 231–259.

Patalano, A. I., & Seifert, C. M. (1997). Opportunistic planning: Being reminded of pending goals. *Cognitive Psychology, 34,* 1–36.

Pea, R. D., & Hawkins, J. (1987). Planning in a chore-scheduling task. In S. L. Friedman, E. K. Skolnick, & R. R. Cocking (Eds.), *Blueprints for thinking: The role of planning in cognitive development* (pp. 273–302). New York: Cambridge University Press.

Planalp, S., & Hewes, D. E. (1982). A cognitive approach to communication theory: Cogito ergo dico. In M. Burgoon (Ed.), *Communication yearbook 5* (pp. 49–77). New Brunswick, NJ: Transaction.

Roloff, M. E., & Berger, C. R. (Eds.). (1982a). *Social cognition and communication.* Beverly Hills, CA: Sage.

Roloff, M. E., & Berger, C. R. (1982b). Social cognition and communication: An introduction. In M. E. Roloff & C. R. Berger (Eds.), *Social cognition and communication* (pp. 9–32). Beverly Hills, CA: Sage.

Russell, D. W., Peplau, L. A., & Cutrona, C. E. (1980). The revised UCLA Loneliness Scale: Concurrent and discriminant validity evidence. *Journal of Personality and Social Psychology, 39,* 472–480.

Schank, R. C. (1982). *Dynamic memory: A theory of reminding in computers and people.* New York: Cambridge University Press.

Schank, R. C., & Abelson, R. P. (1977). *Scripts, plans, goals, and understanding: An enquiry into human knowledge structures.* Hillsdale, NJ: Lawrence Erlbaum Associates.

Schank, R. C., & Berman, T. R. (2002). The pervasive role of stories in knowledge and action. In M. C. Green, J. J. Strange, & T. C. Brock (Eds.), *Narrative impact: Social and cognitive foundations* (pp. 287–313). Mahwah, NJ: Lawrence Erlbaum Associates.

Semin, G. R. (1998). Cognition, language, and communication. In S. R. Fussell & R. J. Kreuz (Eds.), *Social and cognitive approaches to interpersonal communication* (pp. 229–257). Mahwah, NJ: Lawrence Erlbaum Associates.

Sinclair, J. (1991). *Corpus, concordance, collocation.* Oxford, UK: Oxford University Press.

Vallacher, R. R., & Wegner, D. M. (1985). *A theory of action identification.* Hillsdale, NJ: Lawrence Erlbaum Associates.

Vallacher, R. R., Wegner, D. M., & Somoza, M. (1989). That's easy for you to say: Action identification and speech fluency. *Journal of Personality and Social Psychology, 56,* 199–208.

Waldron, V. R. (1990). Constrained rationality: Situational influences on information acquisition plans and tactics. *Communication Monographs, 57,* 184–201.

Waldron, V. R. (1997). Toward a theory of interactive conversational planning. In J. O. Greene (Ed.), *Message production: Advances in communication theory* (pp. 195–220). Mahwah, NJ: Lawrence Erlbaum Associates.

Waldron, V. R., & Applegate, J. L. (1994). Interpersonal construct differentiation and conversational planning: An examination of two cognitive accounts for the production of competent verbal disagreement tactics. *Human Communication Research, 21,* 3–35.

Waldron, V. R., Caughlin, J. P., & Jackson, D. W. (1995). Talking specifics: Facilitating effects of planning on AIDS talk in peer dyads. *Health Communication, 7,* 247–264.

Waldron, V. R., & Cegala, D. J. (1992). Assessing conversational cognition: Levels of cognitive theory and associated methodological requirements. *Human Communication Research, 18,* 599–622.

Waldron, V. R., & Lavitt, M. (2000). Welfare-to-work: Assessing communication competencies and client outcomes in a job training program. *Southern Communication Journal, 66,* 1–15.

Walther, J. B., & Parks, M. R. (2002). Cues filtered out, cues filtered in: Computer-mediated communication and relationships. In M. L. Knapp & J. A. Daly (Eds.), *Handbook of interpersonal communication* (3rd ed., pp. 529–563). Thousand Oaks, CA: Sage.

Wilensky, R. (1983). *Planning and understanding: A computational approach to human reasoning.* Reading, MA: Addison-Wesley.

Wilson, S. R. (1990). Development and test of a cognitive rule model of interaction goals. *Communication Monographs, 57,* 81–103.

Wilson, S. R. (1995). Elaborating the cognitive rules model of interaction goals: The problem of accounting for individual differences in goal formation. In B. R. Burleson (Ed.), *Communication yearbook 18* (pp. 3–26). Thousand Oaks, CA: Sage.

Wilson, S. R. (1997). Developing theories of persuasive message production: The next generation. In J. O. Greene (Ed.), *Message production: Advances in communication theory* (pp. 15–43). Mahwah, NJ: Lawrence Erlbaum Associates.

Wilson, S. R. (2002). *Seeking and resisting compliance: Why people say what they do when trying to influence others.* Thousand Oaks, CA: Sage.

Wilson, S. R., & Sabee, C. M. (2003). Explicating communicative competence as a theoretical term. In J. O. Greene & B. R. Burleson (Eds.), *Handbook of communication and social interaction skills* (pp. 3–50). Mahwah, NJ: Lawrence Erlbaum Associates.

Wittgenstein, L. (1953). *Philosophical investigations.* Oxford, UK: Basil Blackwell.

Wray, A. (1992). *The focusing hypothesis: The theory of left hemisphere lateralized language re-examined.* Amsterdam: John Benjamins.

Wray, A., & Perkins, M. R. (2000). The functions of formulaic language: An integrated model. *Language and Communication, 20,* 1–28.

4

Interaction Goals and Message Production: Conceptual and Methodological Developments

Steven R. Wilson and Hairong Feng
Purdue University

Theories of message production attempt to explain why individuals say what they do during everyday interaction. Such theories have shed light on how adolescents refuse drug offers from peers (Miller, Alberts, Hecht, Trost, & Krizek, 2000), adult children confront elderly parents about problem behaviors (e.g., unsafe driving; Morgan & Hummert, 2000), organizational members exert influence with supervisors at work (Olufowote, Miller, & Wilson, 2005), and pharmacists confront physicians with concerns about medications prescribed to patients (Lambert, 1996). The same theories offer a lens on the "dark side" of relationships such as child physical abuse (Wilson, 2000) and obsessive relationship intrusion and stalking (Cupach & Spitzberg, 2004). Aside from practical insights, theories of message production address a number of intrinsically interesting questions about communication such as why individuals often say such different things in the same situation (O'Keefe, 1988), why individuals from different cultures might view the "same" message as more or less appropriate or effective (Kim & Wilson, 1994), and how we are judged to be communicatively (in)competent by others (Wilson & Sabee, 2003).

The concept of *interaction goal* figures prominently in theorizing about message production. Goals, broadly speaking, are future states of affairs that individuals desire to attain or maintain (Austin & Vancouver, 1996). Desired end states become interaction goals when they involve or necessitate communication and coordination with others (Wilson, 2002). Goals have not always been at the forefront of theorizing about message production; rather, a shift occurred during the 1980s and 1990s from theories based on a metaphor of strategy selection to ones grounded in goal pursuit (Seibold, Cantrill, & Meyers, 1994; Wilson, 2002). One important development in this evolution of metaphors was a chapter in which O'Keefe and Delia (1982) forwarded what then was a new conception of message production: "It is simply not plausible that messages begin as packages of potential arguments or contents; obviously messages begin as purposes .... Messages can be seen as the product of multiple communicative intentions and message design as the product of reconciling multiple objectives in performance" (pp. 51–52). This chapter traces how interaction goals have been conceptualized in message production theories since their work. Rather than trying to cover all possible theories, we describe and compare four in detail (for a summary of our comparisons, see Table 4.1). Initially we review Brown and Levinson's (1978, 1987) politeness theory as it has served as an important backdrop for O'Keefe and Delia as well as other communication scholars. We then present O'Keefe's (1988; O'Keefe & Delia, 1982) situation complexity/behavioral complexity account; Dillard's (1990, 2004) goals-plans-action (GPA) model; and Wilson, Aleman, and Leatham's (1998) identity implications theory (IIT). All four view message production as a process of balancing multiple goals but differ in their precise characterization of goals as well as how multiple goals are managed. For each theory, we clarify what it was proposed to explain, describe key concepts and assumptions, and analyze how goals have been conceptualized and measured within it. At the end, we offer some brief closing remarks regarding goals and message production.

POLITENESS THEORY

Purpose of Theory

Brown and Levinson (1978, 1987) developed politeness theory based on extensive fieldwork of speakers in three cultures: English as spoken in Great Britain; Tamil, a dialect spoken in southern India; and Tzetlal, the language of the Mayan Indians in Mexico. They sought to account for the "extraordinary parallelism in the linguistic minutia of the utterances with which persons choose to express themselves in quite unrelated languages and cultures" (Brown & Levinson, 1987, p. 55), such as why speakers in all three cultures often used conventionally indirect requests (e.g., "Could you tell me the time?") rather than imperatives (e.g., "Tell me the time").

Central Constructs and Assumptions

Brown and Levinson (1987) accounted for observed linguistic regularities by constructing a "model person," which they described as follows:

Table 4.1

A Comparison of Four Theories of Goals and Message Production

	Message Production Theory			
Point of Comparison	*Politeness Theory*	*Situational/Behavior Complexity*	*GPA Model*	*Identity Implications Theory*
Purpose of theory	Account for observed linguistic regularities in diverse cultures	Reconceptualize individual/developmental differences in communication	Provide theoretical grounding for compliance-gaining literature	Address limits of politeness theory
Central constructs	Rationality Politeness vs. efficiency Positive/negative face Intrinsic FTAs (rules) Power/distance/rank Five superstrategies	Possible vs. actual goals Situation complexity Individual differences Selection/separation/integration Behavioral complexity	Primary vs. secondary goals Goal structure complexity Decision to engage Plan generation Tactic implementation/ monitoring Behavioral intensity vs. quality	Rules/primary goals Intrinsic vs. potential FT Secondary goals - face Facework Personality/cultural differences
Conception of interaction goals	Arise from universal human wants and interdependence; tacit	Arise from generalized problems posed by social situations; individuals differ in likelihood of recognizing them	Arise from implications of the momentarily understood purpose of talk for cross-situational concerns; in principle accessible to conscious awareness	Arise from implications of the momentary purpose of talk for situated face wants; in principle accessible to awareness
Goal measurement	Inferred from discourse	Inferred from discourse	Self-reports or inferred from discourse	Self-reports

Note. GPA = goals–plans–actions; FTAs = face = threatening acts; FT = face-threatening.

> All our Model Person (MP) consists in is a willful fluent speaker of a natural language, further endowed with two special properties—rationality and face. By "rationality" we mean something very specific—the availability to our MP of a precisely definable mode of reasoning from ends to the means that will achieve those ends. By "face" we mean something quite specific again: our MP is endowed with two particular wants—roughly the want to be unimpeded and the want to be approved of in certain respects. (p. 58)

Although the authors did not use the term *goal* explicitly, their MP is willful, has "wants," and possesses the ability to reason from desired end states to linguistic means for pursuing goals.

Brown and Levinson (1987) assumed that speakers in any culture possess both positive face (i.e., the desire to have their ideas and actions approved of by others important to them) and negative face (i.e., the desire not to be impeded or constrained without reason) and are aware that other conversational participants do so as well. Because face wants can be satisfied only in conjunction with others (i.e., they are interaction goals), people typically have some interest in maintaining each other's face. Despite this, many speech acts, given their defining conditions (see Searle, 1969, 1976), threaten the hearer or speaker's own face; such acts are labeled *intrinsic FTAs.* Of course, not all intrinsic FTAs threaten face equally. According to Brown and Levinson, the weightiness of any FTA depends on three factors: the speaker's power relative to the hearer (P), the relational distance between speaker and hearer (D), and the ranking of impositions in a culture (R).

Brown and Levinson (1987) viewed politeness as a linguistic means of addressing the hearer's face. When contemplating performing an FTA, a speaker might enact any of five superstrategies that are presumed to be ordered from least to most polite: (a) do the FTA baldly, without redress; (b) do the FTA on record, with positive politeness; (c) do the FTA on record with negative politeness; (d) do the FTA off record; and (e) do not do the FTA. Brown and Levinson documented a host of concrete linguistic means (what they termed *output strategies*) by which speakers can enact each superstrategy; for example, they recorded 10 specific forms of negative politeness (e.g., hedge, be pessimistic, apologize) used by speakers in all three cultures.

Brown and Levinson predicted that as the weightiness of an FTA increases speakers will choose an increasingly polite (i.e., higher numbered) strategy. Speakers also have motivations, however, not to use excessive politeness. Speakers have an interest in not expending more time, effort, or resources than is necessary; indeed, in some situations (e.g., emergencies) concerns about face may be set aside entirely in the interest of efficiency (Brown & Levinson, 1987; Kellermann & Park, 2001). By using more politeness than is expected, a speaker also might mistakenly convey that the FTA is more face-threatening than it is in reality or that the relationship is more distant than the hearer otherwise would have presumed.

Politeness theory has been extremely heuristic and widely criticized (for reviews, see Brown & Levinson, 1987, pp. 1–54; Watts, 2003; Wilson, 2002). Rather than sorting through these issues here, we analyze the theory's conception of goals and message production.

Conception and Measurement of Interaction Goals

People's interaction goals, according to Brown and Levinson (1987), reflect universal human wants that we both possess ourselves and recognize as being desired by others (see Table 4.1):

> Central to our model is a highly abstract notion of "face" which consists of two specific kinds of desires ("face wants") attributed by interactants to one another .... This is the bare bones of a notion of face which (we argue) is universal, but which in any particular society we would expect to be the subject of much cultural elaboration. (p. 13)

Who has the right to impose on whom, from whom we want approval, what counts as a serious criticism or a large request, and other matters are taken to be culturally specific, but the basic human desires for approval and autonomy are underpinnings for interaction goals in any culture. Because face wants inherently are interdependent, how participants impact each other's face is salient in virtually any interaction.[1] Message production is thus the process of balancing face wants with other motivations (e.g., efficiency, clarity).

Speakers typically are not conscious of how the precise wording of their speech acts reflects this balancing act (Brown & Levinson, 1987). Interaction goals are thus inferred from discourse, and along with other key concepts (interdependence; P, D, and R; the five superstrategies)

[1]This claim should not be interpreted as saying that interactants never attack each other's face. As already noted, a speaker may set aside supporting a hearer's face when efficiency is paramount, and a speaker also may attack a hearer's face if he or she perceives that the hearer already has threatened his or her own face. In addition, Brown and Levinson (1987) argued that face and the relational parameters of power and distance are related reciprocally. For example, a speaker who has more power relative to the hearer is likely to use less politeness than if the situation were reversed because the speaker's power diminishes the weightiness of the FTA. However, speakers who wish to highlight or expand their power may do so by using less politeness than normally would be expected as a way of demonstrating that they do not have to attend to the hearer's face needs (Brown & Levinson, 1987, pp. 228–230). Wilson and Morgan (2004) developed this point in more detail in their analysis of politeness, persuasion, and power in families.

provide a post-hoc explanation for "the degree of detail in convergence" in the authors' field recordings from three the cultures that lie "far beyond the realm of chance" (Brown & Levinson, 1987, p. 59).

THE SITUATION COMPLEXITY/BEHAVIORAL COMPLEXITY ACCOUNT

Purpose of Theory

O'Keefe and Delia (1982) offered their situation complexity/behavioral theory as a reinterpretation of findings from the long-standing constructivist program of research on developmental and individual differences in communication (see Table 4.1). To contextualize their own account, we briefly describe the listener-adaptation model of communication it was designed to reinterpret (for reviews, see Burleson, 1987; Wilson, 2002).

As a theoretical perspective, constructivism emphasizes that people's messages arise from and reflect the interpretive structures they bring to the social world (Gastil, 1995). People rely on "constructs" or bipolar dimensions of judgment (e.g., good–bad, big–small) to anticipate, interpret, and evaluate objects and events. As children mature, their construct systems become more differentiated, psychologically abstract, and integrated. Construct systems develop in a domain-specific fashion; for example, some individuals are more differentiated about art, automobiles, or other people. Because of this, adults or children of the same age will include persons who possess more and less developed systems of constructs about any particular domain.

Constructivist scholars asserted that individuals who possessed more developed (i.e., differentiated, psychologically abstract) systems of constructs about other people would have an advantage over those with less developed interpersonal construct systems in terms of recognizing differences in how particular others might interpret their messages and hence in adapting messages to the unique perspective of their interaction partner. Several studies showed that listener adaptation in messages was associated with developmental and individual differences in interpersonal construct system development (see Burleson, 1987). In their chapter, O'Keefe and Delia (1982) proposed a significant reinterpretation of what these research findings actually meant. To understand their argument, it is necessary to clarify the key constructs in their situation complexity/behavioral complexity theory (see Table 4.1).

Central Constructs and Assumptions

O'Keefe (1988) began by distinguishing two senses of the goal construct: "goals as generalized constraints defined and activated by social structures and goals as they are recognized and pursued by individuals" (p. 82). O'Keefe's first sense of goal refers to general problems posed by a social situation given its constituent features (e.g., the tacitly understood task, culturally defined roles and relationships occupied by the participants). In this sense, goals are demands implicit within the nature of social situations themselves; they are identified through an analysis of "the predefined activities of human cultures and the general norms of consideration, self-respect, cooperation, and so on, that govern group life" (p. 82). Because goals in this first sense are generalized problems arising from social situations, they exist independent of the desires of any specific individual. O'Keefe provided the following example:

> For any situation, some *possible goals* are intrinsically relevant and some are not. For instance, in a committee meeting any goal related to the accomplishment of the committee business is naturally relevant and a committee member can be held accountable for meeting such a goal whether or not that particular member identifies with the committee and its objectives. (p. 82, italics added)

O'Keefe's second sense of goal refers to future states of affairs that an individual wants to attain or maintain. Goals in this second sense are mental states, and, as such, one identifies them by asking an individual what he or she is to trying to accomplish or by inferring what he or she is trying to accomplish from the individual's behavior in context. To avoid confusion, we refer to O'Keefe's first sense of goals as *possible goals* and the second sense as *actual goals.* Complex situations make multiple possible goals relevant to pursue, but individual actors may or may not actually recognize and form multiple goals in complex situations.

O'Keefe and Delia (1982) also distinguished complex and simple situations. A situation is complex when (a) its constituent features create multiple relevant possible goals, (b) significant obstacles to achieving those possible goals are present, or (c) actions that help accomplish one possible goal conflict with those that help accomplish other relevant possible goals. As an example, a conversational argument—in which participants hold different positions on an issue and attempt to justify their position—inherently is a complex situation (O'Keefe & Shepherd, 1987). Multiple possible goals are made relevant by the situation (e.g., explaining why one disagrees with the other's position in a clear, truthful fashion; maintaining both parties' face), significant obstacles to achieving those possible goals are present (e.g., the other party may be firmly committed to his or her position or feel defensive about disagreement), and actions that help accomplish one potential goal (e.g., presenting evidence inconsistent with the other's position) may run contrary to another potential goal (e.g., supporting the other's face).

Although many communicative situations are complex, individuals do not always form and pursue multiple goals. According to O'Keefe and Delia (1982), individuals with more developed interpersonal construct systems should be more likely than those with less developed systems to define communicative situations in a manner that makes multiple potential goals salient. The former group, who spontaneously rely on a larger number of abstract, psychological constructs to interpret others' actions, is more skilled than the latter at taking the perspective and inferring the affective states of others (see Burleson, 1987). Given these differences in person perception, O'Keefe and Delia argued that persons with highly developed interpersonal construct systems are also more likely than those with less developed systems to actually form multiple goals as well as to use behaviorally complex communication strategies that address multiple goals.

O'Keefe and Delia (1982) identified three strategies for managing multiple goals. *Selection* involves giving priority to one possible goal while ignoring others. *Separation* involves addressing multiple possible goals in temporally or behaviorally distinct aspects of a message. *Integration* involves attempting to address multiple goals simultaneously by redefining the situation in a way that reduces conflict between multiple possible goals.[2] O'Keefe and Delia argued that separation and integration reflect greater concern about accomplishing multiple goals and hence are more behaviorally complex than selection.

According to O'Keefe and Delia (1982), this situation complexity-behavioral complexity account offered an alternative interpretation for prior studies of construct system development and listener-adapted communication. Specifically, they argued the coding systems that had been used to assess listener adaptation plausibly could be reinterpreted as assessing behavioral complexity. For example, persuasive strategies that paid attention to only one's own concerns were similar to selection, whereas those that attended to the hearer's perspective and concerns were similar to separation and integration. O'Keefe and Shepherd (1987) demonstrated that people's interpersonal construct system development did predict how frequently they included separation and integration strategies in their talk during face-to-face conversational arguments.

---

[2]O'Keefe (1988) eventually argued that these three goal management strategies (selection, separation, integration) were not just different behavioral strategies, but rather behavioral manifestations of different message design logics or systems of reasoning from possible goals to means for accomplishing those goals. Because O'Keefe's theory of message design logic moves away from an emphasis on interaction goals to highlight different fundamental conceptions of communication itself, we do not review it here.

Conception and Measurement of Interaction Goals

O'Keefe's (1988; O'Keefe & Delia, 1982) conception of interaction goals and message production is similar to but extends Brown and Levinson's (1978) conception (see Table 4.1). Possible goals are general problems arising from shared construals of communicative situations. To identify possible goals, one begins not by asking a particular individual what he or she hoped to accomplish (actual goals) but rather with an analysis of communicative tasks. Given the defining features of a type of situation that are recognizable within a culture as well as general norms for interaction (e.g., efficiency, face support), what possible goals are relevant to pursue and how are those goals in conflict? Possible goals should be distinguished from actual goals because the latter arise from the former, not all individuals actually will recognize multiple relevant potential goals, and different individuals who actually pursue the "same" possible goal may label it differently (e.g., one person might say she was supporting the other party's face, whereas another might say he was maintaining a relationship with the other).

As with Brown and Levinson, message production is viewed here as a rational process. Messages are seen "as efforts to meet the demands of social situations, and not as efforts to meet individually selected and consciously recognized sets of goals" (O'Keefe, 1988, p. 82). Individuals do form (actual) goals, but goal formation and message production are not highly conscious processes and most messages "are produced without extensive monitoring and editing" (O'Keefe & Delia, 1982, p. 52). Given these assumptions, O'Keefe assesses individual differences in recognition and pursuit of possible goals from the type of goal-management strategies employed in response to written scenarios (O'Keefe, 1988) or during face-to-face interaction (O'Keefe & Shepherd, 1987) rather than from asking individuals about their goals.

THE GPA MODEL

Purpose of Theory

Dillard (1990) proposed a GPA model of interpersonal influence in response to limitations of the traditional compliance-gaining literature. In the late 1970s, Miller and colleagues developed a source-oriented perspective on persuasion in interpersonal contexts (Miller, Boster, Roloff, & Seibold, 1977; Miller & Burgoon, 1978). Their program of research set out to answer three questions: (a) What types of strategies do individuals use when seeking to change a target person's behavior? (b) How does people's choice of strategies vary across situational and relational factors? and (c) What individual difference variables predict strategy choice? Although this program of research focused attention on important questions about message production, theoretical and methodological problems limited the number of conclusions that could be drawn from these studies (see Kellermann & Cole, 1994; Wilson, 2002). To fill this theoretical void, Dillard (1990) argued that the production of interpersonal influence messages can be modeled as a sequence of involving goals, plans, and actions.

Central Constructs and Assumptions

According to Dillard (2004) goals are "future states of affairs that an individual is committed to achieving or attaining," whereas plans are "cognitive representations of the behaviors intended to enable goal attainment" (p. 185). Goals and plans are mental states, whereas actions are overt behaviors enacted in pursuit of goals.

Among the range of interaction goals individuals might pursue, Dillard (1990, 2004) distinguished primary and secondary goals. At any point in a conversation, the *primary goal* is the objective that for the moment defines the situation or answers the question "What is going on here?" The primary goal "brackets the situation" and "helps segment the flow of behavior into a meaningful unit; it says what the interaction is about" (Dillard, Segrin, & Harden, 1989, p. 21). Primary goals play a social meaning function in the sense that they offer "culturally viable explanations of the discourse produced by two or more interlocutors" (Dillard, 2004, p. 188). Primary goals also play a motivational function in that they energize the actor, stimulate planning and consideration of other goals, and push the actor toward engaging the target person.

A series of studies investigated specific primary goals related to influence, or reasons why individuals attempt to change other people's behavior (Cody, Canary, & Smith, 1994; Dillard, 1989; Kipnis, Schmidt, & Wilkinson, 1980; Rule, Bisanz, & Kohn, 1985; Yukl, Guinan, & Sottolano, 1995). Although these studies investigated multiple relationships (e.g., family members, romantic partners, work colleagues) using varied data collection methods (critical incidents, diaries, and hypothetical scenarios), they produced remarkably similar findings. Common reasons for attempting to influence a target person identified in two or more of these studies include seeking the target person's assistance (favors), giving the target advice, obtaining permission from the target, getting the target to fulfill an obligation, eliciting support from the target for a third party, proposing that the target join one in a shared activity, and (de)escalating the intimacy of one's relationship with the target. Rather than viewing themselves as seeking compliance, people conceive of their actions in terms of much more specific goals.

Although the GPA model initially was proposed as a theoretical account for the production of influence messages, recent research explores types of primary goals that do not inherently involve influence. For example, Sabee and Wilson (2005) explored how students conceived of interactions in which they discussed a disappointing grade with their instructor. Four possible answers to "What is going on here?" emerged in students' responses; specifically, different students said they were attempting to (a) understand and master important course concepts (learning), (b) convince the instructor to raise the disappointing grade (persuading), (c) convince the instructor that the low grade did not accurately reflect their real abilities (impressing), and (d) attack the instructor for what was perceived to be an unjustified grade (attacking). Students with different primary goals tended to make different attributions for the disappointing grade and to enact different face-threatening acts and politeness strategies. As this example makes clear, the GPA model can be applied to situations beyond seeking compliance such as when individuals meet a new acquaintance (Waldron, 1997), attempt to increase the level of intimacy with a romantic partner (Honeycutt, Cantrill, Kelly, & Lambkin, 1998), or refuse unwanted intimacy from a cross-sex friend or dating partner (Lannutti & Monahan, 2004).

Secondary goals are concerns that arise in a wide range of situations and shape how individuals pursue primary goals (Dillard, 1990). Rather than defining and driving interaction, secondary goals set boundaries on behavioral options available to the message source. In influence situations, secondary goals act as a "pull" force that shapes and constrains how the message source seeks compliance. Dillard et al. (1989) proposed five categories of secondary goals: (a) identity goals, or desires to act consistently with one's beliefs, morals, and values; (b) conversation management goals,[3] or desires to maintain a positive self-image, maintain other people's face, and say things that are relevant and coherent in light of the larger conversation; (c) relational resource goals, or desires to maintain valued relationships; (d) personal resource goals, or desires to avoid unnecessarily risking or wasting one's time, money, or safety; and (e) arousal management goals, or desires to avoid or reduce anxiety or nervousness. A replication of Dillard et al.'s research in the context of computer-mediated communication identified these same five secondary goals categories (Wilson & Zigurs, 2001).

Any category of secondary goals can become primary if it moves from being a constraint on how other goals are pursued to the objective that for the moment frames the situation and motivates one to engage

[3]Although Dillard (1990) originally labeled this category of secondary goals as interaction goals, he recently relabeled it conversation management goals (Dillard, 2004) to avoid confusion with the definition of interaction goal presented at the start of this chapter; that is, any goal (primary or secondary) that can only be accomplished via coordination with others.

others. In Sabee and Wilson's (2005) study, the desire to maintain a positive self-image (conversation management) functioned as a secondary goal for students with learning, persuading, or attacking primary goals, but for students classified as having impressing goals, this desire was the primary goal that framed the interaction and motivated them to speak. The labels primary and secondary thus refer to goal function (what goals do) rather than goal importance. For example, young adults who perceive that their romantic partner or adult sibling could benefit from advice (primary goal) still may refrain from giving it because they place even greater importance on not sounding "parental" and not making their partner or sibling defensive (secondary goals; Goldsmith & Fitch, 1997).

The GPA model also explicates a number of cognitive processes that underlie message production (Dillard, 1990). Goal assessment refers to an individual evaluating the importance of primary and secondary goals when facing a concrete situation. When concern about the primary goal outweighs secondary goals, the actor decides to engage the other person, which results in plan generation and editing. Plan generation involves retrieving mental representations of verbal and nonverbal actions that might modify the behavior of the other party. Retrieved actions may be edited in light of primary and secondary goals, the importance of which in turn is a joint function of situational and individual difference variables such as benefits to self or other and verbal aggressiveness (Hample & Dallinger, 1987; Meyer, 2004). When primary and secondary goals are weighted about equally, the decision about whether to engage the other may depend on whether a means can be found for pursuing the primary goal without interfering with secondary goals and hence plan generation and editing may precede the decision to engage. If suitable means are found, the speaker attempts to put the plan into action, which is tactic implementation. The final step in the GPA model is monitoring of the target person's response, which provides continuous feedback for ongoing goals assessment. Very little research has investigated these specific claims about planning processes (Hullett, 2004) but developments since Dillard initially proposed the GPA model suggest that such processes occur much faster, at more levels of abstraction, and with less coordination than the model seems to imply (Greene, 2000). In sum, the lasting contribution from the GPA model is its conception of primary and secondary goals.

The distinction between primary and secondary goals suggests that two broad dimensions of behavior are important to examine: the intensity with which the actor pursues the primary goal and the manner in which secondary goals shape such attempts. Dillard et al. (1989) found that participants' ratings of the importance of their primary goal predicted how intensely they pursued the primary goal (i.e., their self-reports of planning and effort), whereas their importance for secondary goals predicted how they went about pursuing the primary goal (i.e., coders' ratings of how explicit they were about what they wanted as well as whether they emphasized positive consequences if the target complied or negative consequences if the target refused to comply).

Conception and Measurement of Interaction Goals

Interaction goals in the GPA model arise from how the momentarily understood purpose of talk implicates an actor's cross-situational concerns (see Table 4.1). Primary goals are culturally viable explanations regarding what, for the moment, is going on in an interaction. If an actor says to a target person "Can I ask you a favor?" then both participants have some idea of what type of interaction will follow. Asking a favor may implicate concerns in both parties about acting consistently with core values, maintaining face, keeping arousal within comfortable levels, and so forth. Whether and how the actor asks and the target refuses depends on the relative importance of obtaining or providing assistance versus these other concerns.

Message production is conceived as a process of balancing primary and secondary goals; the decision to engage the other, the intensity with which the primary goal is sought, and the manner in which a request is made (or refused) all reflect this balancing act. Actors continuously monitor how targets respond to their efforts (and vice versa), and hence the importance of secondary goals may change rapidly over time (Dillard, 2004; Waldron, 1997). In addition, the mutually understood purpose of talk also may change quickly or participants may not even agree about what primary goal defines their talk, which may lead to shifts in both types of goals (Feng & Wilson, 2004; Wilson & Morgan, 2006). Although the GPA model may seem to imply a high degree of consciousness, Dillard (2004) argued that many of these processes just described occur with little or no conscious awareness:

> People often find themselves embroiled in conversation without ever having made a reflective decision to enter that interaction. They expel air from their lungs to power their vocal apparatus, moving their tongue and lips in (usually) well-coordinated ways to produce sounds—all without awareness. (p. 200)

Having said this, the GPA model does assume that in principle primary and secondary goals are accessible to conscious awareness (Dillard, 2004, p. 200). People are likely to have momentary, albeit fleeting, awareness of their goals when primary and secondary goals conflict or when their initial attempts to accomplish goals are thwarted (Greene, 2000; Motley, 1986). Due to these assumptions, primary and secondary goals most often have been assessed via a host of self-report procedures. Participants have been asked to complete Likert scales assessing the importance of a list of primary and secondary goals after recalling a past conversation (Dillard et al., 1989), after completing a simulation (Wilson & Zigurs, 2001), or while watching a videotape of a recently completed conversation (Waldron, 1997). Other studies have coded participants' open-ended goal reports (e.g., Honeycutt et al., 1998; Lannutti & Monahan, 2004; Sabee & Wilson, 2005). At least one study also has employed raters to infer the degree to which actors were pursuing primary and secondary goals based on hearing what they would say (Lannutti & Monahan, 2004). Conversational partners also presumably make such inferences under at least some conditions, although GPA research has not addressed this directly.

IDENTITY IMPLICATIONS THEORY

We present a theory of the identity implications of primary goals to explain how face threats arise and get managed during interpersonal influence episodes. The central assumptions of IIT were presented by Wilson et al. (1998), but we clarify and elaborate some points here. IIT is designed to address limits of Brown and Levinson's (1987) politeness theory; hence, IIT embraces several assumptions from politeness theory but modifies others. IIT also draws on Dillard's (1990) distinction between primary and secondary goals.

IIT was proposed to address two difficulties with politeness theory. First, politeness theory cannot predict when seeking another person's compliance will create multiple face threats. Politeness theory assumes that any individual speech act primarily threatens one type of face. Brown and Levinson (1987) included directives, or speech acts designed to get a target person to do something she or he otherwise might not have done (Searle, 1976), in their list of acts that intrinsically threaten the target's negative face. In reality, directives often create multiple threats to both the speaker's and hearer's face (Kellermann, 2004; Wilson, Kim, & Meischke, 1991/1992; Wilson & Kunkel, 2000). A mother who tells her son "You need to start trying in math class" not only attempts to constrain her son's future options (negative face), but also communicates disapproval of her son's current effort (positive face). Politeness theory has little to say regarding when or why these additional potential face threats are likely to occur.

Second, politeness theory pays limited attention to how participants make sense of what is going on during influence episodes and what implications such sense making could have for their own and the other party's face. Failing to explore how participants are defining the situation is an important omission if one hopes to understand how messages can be heard as communicating disapproval or constraint. IIT explains which face threats potentially might arise when speakers have different reasons (primary goals) for seeking to change a target's behavior.

Key Constructs and Assumptions

IIT adopts several constructs and assumptions from politeness theory. Specifically, IIT assumes that individuals in all cultures (a) desire approval from significant others (positive face) and autonomy (negative face) and realize that others do as well, (b) have motives to support other people's face given the interdependent nature of face wants, (c) perform actions that have the potential to threaten both their own and other people's face during interaction, and (d) possess the ability to reason from goals to linguistic means for pursuing those goals.

Despite these points of convergence, IIT also departs from politeness theory in several respects. Rather than analyzing face threats at the level of individual speech acts, IIT argues for a more "episodic" analysis of how face threats arise and get managed. For example, an influence episode begins when one or both parties recognize that a speaker is attempting to alter a target person's behavior and ends when either the target person complies or the speaker at least temporarily halts seeking the target's compliance (Oldershaw, Walters, & Hall, 1986). How would participants in a conversation anticipate what threats to face might arise during an influence episode? According to IIT, people rely on two sources of implicit knowledge to do so: the preconditions for performing directives and the primary goal being sought (see Table 4.1).

Directives (e.g., requests, recommendations) are the class of speech acts at the heart of any influence episode because such episodes by definition involve attempts by a speaker to get a target person to do something that the target otherwise might not have done (Searle, 1976). Directives are defined by a number of preconditions or constitutive rules. When making a request a speaker presumes that some desired action needs to be performed, the target was not already planning to perform that action (otherwise there is no need to ask), the target plausibly might be willing and able to perform that action (otherwise there is no sense in asking), and he or she has the rights to make the request and sincerely wants the requested action performed (Labov & Fanshel, 1977; Searle, 1969). By seeking to change a target person's behavior, a speaker explicitly or implicitly asserts that these preconditions exist at the present time. When seeking a target person's compliance, speakers usually perform other actions in addition to the core directive (e.g., assertions, promises), but these additional acts often are designed to show that the preconditions for performing the directive do exist (e.g., they establish a need for action or attempt to create willingness by the target; Tracy, Craig, Smith, & Spisak, 1984).

Rather than presenting a static analysis of constitutive rules, IIT explores how the implications of these preconditions change depending on what participants believe is going on during an influence episode. Following Dillard (1990), IIT argues that participants in an influence episode conceive of the speaker's actions in terms of the specific reasons why the target person's compliance is being sought. By overlaying the primary goal defining an influence episode onto the constitutive rules for directives, the full range of potential face threats that might arise during the episode can be understood. Wilson et al. (1998) used this procedure to analyze the identity implications of pursuing three primary goals: giving advice, asking a favor, and enforcing an unfulfilled obligation (see Table 4.2). Kunkel, Wilson, Olufowote, and Robson (2003) recently offered a similar analysis for episodes in which participants understand that a speaker is attempting to initiate, intensify, or end a romantic relationship with the target person.

IIT distinguishes potential versus intrinsic face threats. Seeking to alter a target person's behavior intrinsically places some constraint on the target's autonomy, although the degree of constraint varies considerably depending on the primary goal. Seeking to alter a target person's behavior also creates many other potential face threats depending on the reason compliance is being sought. Potential face threats are those that plausibly could, although not necessarily will, arise given the primary goal that defines an influence episode.

IIT predicts that different primary goals are associated with different sets of potential face threats. As one example, giving advice has the potential to make a speaker appear to be "nosy" (e.g., if given when advice is not needed or when the speaker has no right to give it; see Table 4.2). Speakers do not always appear to be nosy when giving advice, yet appearing nosy is a potential face threat when giving advice in a way that it is not when pursuing many other primary goals (e.g., asking a favor). We may disapprove of a speaker who asks for assistance when help really is not needed (see Table 4.2), but we do so not because the speaker is being "nosy."

A key claim of IIT is that the potential face threats associated with primary goals are culturally invariant. Both of the sources of tacit knowledge that people rely on to anticipate potential face threats appear to be widely shared across cultures: Constitutive rules describe logical preconditions for performing speech acts such as directives (for debate on this point, see Ellis, 1999) and primary goals such as advice and favors appear in analyses of influence across cultures (e.g., Fitch, 1994; Kim & Wilson, 1994). Consistent with this claim, female and male students from a variety of ethnic backgrounds in the United States make similar judgments about which face threats are most likely to occur depending on whether speakers are giving advice, asking favors, or enforcing un-

Table 4.2

Constitutive Rules for Directives and Potential Face Threats Associated With Three Primary Goals

	Primary Goal		
Rules for Directives	*Advice*	*Favor*	*Obligation*
Need for action	Does the target understand what needs to be done?	Does the source understand what needs to get done?	Does the target understand what needs to be done?
Need for directive	Does the target need to be given advice? Why?	Does the source really need help in this situation? Why?	Why hasn't the target complied already?
Ability	Is the target capable of carrying out the advice?		Is the target capable of fulfilling the obligation?
Willingness	Is the target willing to listen to the advice?	Is the target willing to help?	Is the target willing to fulfill his or her obligations?
Rights	Does the source have the right to give this advice?	Does the source have the right to ask this favor?	
Sincerity		Is the source going to be willing to help in return?	

Note. From "Identity Implications of Influence Goals: A Revised Analysis of Face-Threatening Acts and Application to Seeking Compliance With Same-Sex Friends," by S. R. Wilson, C. Aleman, & G. Leatham, 1998, Human Communication Research, p. 72. Copyright 1998 by the International Communication Association. Adapted with permission.

fulfilled obligations (Wilson, Anastasiou, Aleman, Kim, & Oetzel, 2000; Wilson & Kunkel, 2000). In contrast, IIT assumes the likelihood that any potential face threat actually will be perceived by participants during a specific conversation is dependent on a host of culturally specific factors. When giving advice, people are more likely to worry about appearing nosy rather than lazy; however, the likelihood of actually appearing nosy when giving advice depends on who has rights to give advice to whom at what times and about what matters within a particular culture as well as whether participants themselves have unique advice-giving norms. IIT thus sets parameters on which potential face threats might occur and which are unlikely during influence interactions based on the underlying primary goal.

IIT presumes that in most cases speakers want to mitigate potential face threats; for example, speakers typically want to avoid making themselves appear nosy or the target person appear incompetent when giving advice.[4] For this reason, particular primary goals should be associated with particular secondary goals pertaining to face. Cai and Wilson (2000) found that students from both Japan and the United States varied the importance they placed on maintaining their own positive and negative face as well as supporting the target's positive and negative face in a similar fashion depending on whether they asked a favor or enforced an obligation.

IIT assumes that speakers employ a variety of message features as facework or attempts to make whatever is being done consistent with face (Goffman, 1967). Because different primary goals are associated with different potential face threats and secondary goals, speakers should vary their attempts to seek a target person's compliance depending on their primary goal. Studies testing IIT show that speakers vary how likely they are to actually confront the target person, make direct requests, exert pressure on the target to comply, use a variety of positive and negative politeness strategies, provide reasons focused on themselves or the target, and persist in the face of target resistance depending on the particular primary goal (Cai & Wilson, 2000; Kunkel et al., 2003; Kunkel, Wilson, Robson, Olufowote, & Soliz, 2004; Wilson et al., 1998; Wilson et al., 2000; Wilson & Kunkel, 2000). Speakers' perceptions of potential face threats also are associated with several of these message features (Kunkel et al., 2004; Wilson & Kunkel, 2000).

---

[4]Speakers at times may choose not to mitigate potential face threats. Enforcing an unfulfilled obligation, for example, has the potential to make the target person appear irresponsible because the target already should have complied without having to be asked. Speakers who enforce obligations often report that they want to both threaten the target's positive face (to make the target feel guilty) but also support the target's positive face (to avoid losing them as a friend; Wilson, 1990; Wilson et al., 1998).

Finally, individual differences play several roles in IIT. Although attachment anxiety does not moderate which specific face threats students associate with initiating, intensifying, and ending romantic relationships, students high in attachment anxiety are more likely than those lower in anxiety to perceive that both participants will lose face during any attempt to redefine a relationship (Kunkel et al., 2004). Similarly, self-construals do not qualify which face threats are seen as most probable with giving advice, asking favors, and enforcing obligations, but people with interdependent self-construals rate all face threats as more likely to occur in situations defined by any of these goals (Kim, Wilson, Anastasiou, Aleman, & Oetzel, 2003). Aside from being more or less sensitized to face threats, individuals also differ in the degree to which they are concerned with maintaining and supporting face (Hample & Dallinger, 1987; Meyer, 2004) as well as in their ability to produce messages that skillfully redress potential face threats.

Conception and Measurement of Interaction Goals

Interaction goals in IIT arise from how the momentarily understood purpose of talk implicates participants' situated desires for approval and autonomy (see Table 4.1). Different primary goals provide different explanations regarding what, for the moment, is going on during an interpersonal influence episode; indeed, different primary goals animate the speaker's implicit assertion that the preconditions for performing a directive exist in the current situation with different meanings (see Table 4.2). IIT thus offers a more situated view of face threats and secondary goals than does politeness theory or the GPA model. Just as participants conceive of influence episodes in terms of specific primary goals (e.g., advice, favors) rather than a global goal of seeking compliance, they also conceive of face in more situated terms than positive and negative. Speakers do not worry about being disapproved of for random reasons (at least most do not); rather, speakers worry about specific types of disapproval that could arise given their primary goal. When giving advice, speakers plausibly may worry about not making the target appear incompetent or themselves appear nosy; when enforcing obligations, speakers plausibly may worry about not making the target appear irresponsible (Wilson et al., 1998). Speakers also do not worry about random threats to their autonomy; speakers worry about specific constraints that could be created given the primary goal. When seeking to intensify a romantic relationship, speakers plausibly may worry that they will lose the current relationship if their partner does not desire greater connection or that they will preclude future relationships with others if their partner does desire greater connection (Kunkel et al., 2003). Message production is thus the process of balancing concern about the primary goal with these more situated face concerns. Participants may use many types of facework during episodes of interpersonal influence to preempt or redress potential face threats.

Like the GPA model, IIT assumes that people have momentary, albeit fleeting, awareness of their interaction goals. Participants in all of the studies testing IIT to date have rated the likelihood of potential face threats and the importance of face-related secondary goals after reading hypothetical scenarios defined by different primary goals (e.g., Cai & Wilson, 2000; Kunkel et al., 2003; Kunkel et al., 2004; Wilson et al., 1998; Wilson & Kunkel, 2000). Because these studies were designed to test IIT's claim that people associate the same potential face threats with particular primary goals regardless of personality, gender, or culture, having large samples respond to multiple scenarios that clearly instantiate each primary goal has made sense.

Hypothetical scenarios and ratings scales alone are not adequate to address other questions arising from IIT. As one example, parents in some cases attempt to regulate their children's computer use (e.g., instant messaging, Web sites, or video games). Parents may view such interactions to be about protecting their children from possible exploitation and unhealthy activities, whereas children and adolescents may view such interactions to be about parents attempting to limit their autonomy and interaction with peers (Jennings & Wartella, 2004). Obtaining permission is a common influence goal (Wilson, 2002), and IIT can be used to predict potential face threats for both parties when children ask permission. But what occurs when children believe they should not have to ask? Do children negotiate with their parents about whether they need permission to use the computer? If so, are there developmental patterns to such interactions? Does a family's conversation or conformity orientation influence such interactions (Koerner & Fitzpatrick, 2004)? Observational and interview data would help clarify what occurs when the legitimacy of the primary goal itself becomes a topic of discussion.

CLOSING REMARKS

Interaction goals have occupied a central place in theorizing about message production during the past 25 years. We offer two remarks about our hopes for future research on goals. First, we would like to see a détente between scholars advocating psychological and social approaches to communication. Goal-based approaches to communication have been criticized as being too individualist, psychological, and mechanistic (e.g., Lannamann, 1991; Shepherd, 1998). Inspection of Table 4.1, however, reveals no lack of awareness regarding the social origins of interaction goals. Goals are states of affairs that individuals desire to attain or maintain, but goals arise from universal human wants, culturally defined roles, relational interdependence, and general norms of consideration, respect, and cooperation. One can identify possible goals only by analyzing general problems posed by social situations given the mutually understood communicative task and context, just as one can identify potential face threats only by analyzing identity implications arising from mutually understood purposes for talk. Goals energize individual actors, motivate planning, and shape and constrain action, but goals also are at the heart of the social negotiation of meaning, a point that is especially evident when actors disagree about what goal defines (or should define) their current reality. Psychologists are showing renewed interest in understanding the cognitive processes by which individuals form and pursue goals (e.g., Bargh, Gollwitzer, Lee-Chai, Barndollar, & Troetschel, 2001; Shah, 2003). Communication scholars are positioned to contribute to these efforts (e.g., Greene, 1995, 2000; MacGeorge, 2001; Meyer, 2003; Wilson, 1990, 1995) but also to compliment this work with social analyses of the origins of interaction goals as well as the role goals play in mutually constructed definitions of situations (Wilson & Morgan, 2006). The goal construct offers theoretical grist for social as well as psychological approaches to communication.

Aside from theoretical détente, we hope to see greater methodological pluralism and triangulation in future research on interaction goals. Studies to date have typically either inferred goals from discourse or asked individuals to report or rate goals—most often in response to hypothetical scenarios (see Table 4.1). Many of the factors that influence people's interaction goals operate largely out of awareness (Kellermann, 1992); hence, scholars might supplement goal self-reports with data on response times (Greene, 1995) or from priming techniques (Shah, 2003; Wilson, 1990). Asking people to provide rationales for things they would not say or do during conversation also can raise their awareness of concerns that otherwise might remain tacit, such as managing arousal or making relevant contributions (Dillard et al., 1989; Hample & Dallinger, 1987). Analyses of goals in discourse also would benefit from supplemental techniques such as stimulated recall to understand how conversational participants alter the importance placed on their own goals over time (Waldron, 1997), make inferences about each other's goals (Sillars, Roberts, Leonard, & Dun, 2000; Simpson, Orina, & Ickes, 2003), and adjust their understandings of the momentary, mutually accepted purpose for talking. Although various methods have been or could be used to assess interaction goals, we know surprisingly little about how findings from these methods converge, diverge, or compliment one another.

As we noted at the outset, the theories reviewed in this chapter address intrinsically interesting and pragmatically important questions about communication. We are optimistic that our understanding of interaction goals and message production will be refined and elaborated in years to come.

REFERENCES

Austin, J. T., & Vancouver, J. B. (1996). Goal constructs in psychology: Structure, process, and content. *Psychological Bulletin, 120,* 338–375.

Bargh, J. A., Gollwitzer, P. M., Lee-Chai, A., Barndollar, K., & Troetschel, R. (2001). The automated will: Nonconscious activation and pursuit of behavioral goals. *Journal of Personality and Social Psychology, 81,* 1014–1027.

Brown, P., & Levinson, S. C. (1978). Universals in language usage: Politeness phenomena. In E. Goody (Ed.), *Questions and politeness: Strategies in social interaction* (pp. 56–289). Cambridge, UK: Cambridge University Press.

Brown, P., & Levinson, S. C. (1987). *Politeness: Some universals in language usage.* Cambridge, UK: Cambridge University Press.

Burleson, B. R. (1987). Cognitive complexity. In J. C. McCroskey & J. A. Daly (Eds.), *Personality and interpersonal communication* (pp. 305–349). Newbury Park, CA: Sage.

Cai, D., & Wilson, S. R. (2000). Identity implications of influence goals: A cross-cultural comparison of interaction goals and facework. *Communication Studies, 51,* 307–328.

Cody, M. J., Canary, D. J., & Smith, S. W. (1994). Compliance-gaining goals: An inductive analysis of actors' goal types, strategies, and successes. In J. A. Daly & J. M. Wiemann (Eds.), *Strategic interpersonal communication* (pp. 33–90). Hillsdale, NJ: Lawrence Erlbaum Associates.

Cupach, W. R., & Spitzberg, B. H. (2004). *The dark side of relationship pursuit: From attraction to obsession and stalking.* Mahwah, NJ: Lawrence Erlbaum Associates.

Dillard, J. P. (1989). Types of influence goals in personal relationships. *Journal of Social and Personal Relationships, 6,* 293–308.

Dillard, J. P. (1990). A goal-driven model of interpersonal influence. In J. P. Dillard (Ed.), *Seeking compliance: The production of interpersonal influence messages* (pp. 41–56). Scottsdale, AZ: Gorsuch Scarisbrick.

Dillard, J. P. (2004). The goals-plans-action model of interpersonal influence. In J. S. Seiter & R. H. Gass (Eds.), *Perspectives on persuasion, social influence, and compliance gaining* (pp. 185–206). Boston: Allyn & Bacon.

Dillard, J. P., Segrin, C., & Harden, J. M. (1989). Primary and secondary goals in the production of interpersonal influence messages. *Communication Monographs, 56,* 19–38.

Ellis, D. G. (1999). *From language to communication.* Mahwah, NJ: Lawrence Erlbaum Associates.

Feng, H., & Wilson, S. R. (2004, May). *A critical review of the primary/secondary goal framework.* Paper presented to the annual meeting of the International Communication Association, San Diego, CA.

Fitch, K. L. (1994). A cross-cultural study of directive sequences and some implications for compliance-gaining research. *Communication Monographs, 61,* 185–209.

Gastil, J. (1995). An appraisal and revision of the constructivist research program. In B. R. Burleson (Ed.), *Communication yearbook 18* (pp. 83–104). Thousand Oaks, CA: Sage.

Goffman, E. (1967). *Interaction ritual: Essays on face-to-face behavior.* Chicago: Aldine.

Goldsmith, D. J., & Fitch, K. (1997). The normative context of advice as social support. *Human Communication Research, 23*, 454–476.

Greene, J. O. (1995). Production of messages in pursuit of multiple goals: Action assembly theory contributions to the study of cognitive encoding processes. In B. R. Burleson (Ed.), *Communication yearbook 18* (pp. 26–53). Thousand Oaks, CA: Sage.

Greene, J. O. (2000). Evanescent mentation: An ameliorative conceptual foundation for research and theory on message production. *Communication Theory, 10*, 139–155.

Hample, D., & Dallinger, J. M. (1987). Individual differences in cognitive editing standards. *Human Communication Research, 14*, 123–144.

Honeycutt, J. M., Cantrill, J. G., Kelly, P., & Lambkin, D. (1998). How do I love thee? Let me consider my options: Cognition, verbal strategies, and the escalation of intimacy. *Human Communication Research, 25*, 39–63.

Hullett, C. R. (2004). A test of the initial processes of the goal-plans-action model of interpersonal influence. *Communication Studies, 55*, 286–299.

Jennings, N., & Wartella, E. (2004). Technology and the family. In A. L. Vangelisti (Ed.), *Handbook of family communication* (pp. 593–608). Mahwah, NJ: Lawrence Erlbaum Associates.

Kellermann, K. (1992). Communication: Inherently strategic and primarily automatic. *Communication Monographs, 59*, 288–300.

Kellermann, K. (2004). A goal-directed approach to compliance-gaining: Relating differences among goals to differences in behaviors. *Communication Research, 31*, 397–445.

Kellermann, K., & Cole, T. (1994). Classifying compliance-gaining messages: Taxonomic disorder and strategic confusion. *Communication Theory, 4*, 3–60.

Kellermann, K., & Park, H. S. (2001). Situational urgency and conversational retreat: When politeness and efficiency matter. *Communication Research, 28*, 3–47.

Kim, M. S., & Wilson, S. R. (1994). A cross-cultural comparison of implicit theories of requesting. *Communication Monographs, 61*, 210–235.

Kim, M. S., Wilson, S. R., Anastasiou, L., Aleman, C. G., & Oetzel, J. (2003, June). *The relationship between self construals, perceived face threats, and facework during the pursuit of influence goals.* Paper presented to the annual meeting of the International Communication Association, Seoul, South Korea.

Kipnis, D., Schmidt, D., & Wilkinson, I. (1980). Intraorganizational influence tactics: Explorations in getting one's way. *Journal of Applied Psychology, 65*, 440–452.

Koerner, A. F., & Fitzpatrick, M. A. (2004). Communication in intact families. In A. Vangelisti (Ed.), *Handbook of family communication* (pp. 177–196). Mahwah, NJ: Lawrence Erlbaum Associates.

Kunkel, A. D., Wilson, S. R., Olufowote, J., & Robson, S. (2003). Identity implications of influence goals: Initiating, intensifying, and ending romantic relationships. *Western Journal of Communication, 67*, 382–412.

Kunkel, A. D., Wilson, S. R., Robson, S., Olufowote, J., & Soliz, J. (2004). *Changes of heart from start to part: Identity implications of (re)negotiating romantic relationships.* Manuscript under review.

Labov, W., & Fanshel, D. (1977). *Therapeutic discourse: Psychotherapy as conversation.* New York: Academic.

Lambert, B. L. (1996). Face and politeness in pharmacist–physician interaction. *Social Science & Medicine, 43*, 1189–1198.

Lannamann, J. W. (1991). Interpersonal communication as ideological practice. *Communication Theory, 1*, 179–203.

Lannutti, P. J., & Monahan, J. L. (2004). Resistance, persistence, and drinking: Examining goals of women's refusals of unwanted sexual advances. *Western Journal of Communication, 68,* 151–169.

MacGeorge, E. L. (2001). Support providers' interaction goals: The influence of attributions and emotions. *Communication Monographs, 68,* 72–97.

Meyer, J. R. (2003). Cognitive representations of request situations: The relative importance of specificity and situation features. *Western Journal of Communication, 67,* 292–317.

Meyer, J. R. (2004). Effect of verbal aggressiveness on the perceived importance of secondary goals in messages. *Communication Studies, 55,* 168–184.

Miller, G. R., Boster, F. J., Roloff, M. E., & Seibold, D. (1977). Compliance-gaining message strategies: A typology and some findings concerning effects of situational differences. *Communication Monographs, 44,* 37–51.

Miller, G. R., & Burgoon, M. (1978). Persuasion research: Review and commentary. In B. D. Ruben (Ed.), *Communication yearbook 2* (pp. 29–47). New Brunswick, NJ: Transaction.

Miller, M. A., Alberts, J. K., Hecht, M. L., Trost, M. R., & Krizek, R. L. (2000). *Adolescent relationships and drug use.* Mahwah, NJ: Lawrence Erlbaum Associates.

Morgan, M., & Hummert, M. L. (2000). Perceptions of communicative control strategies in mother–child dyads across the lifespan. *Journal of Communication, 50,* 48–64.

Motley, M. T. (1986). Consciousness and intentionality in communication: A preliminary model and methodological approaches. *Western Journal of Speech Communication, 50,* 3–23.

O'Keefe, B. J. (1988). The logic of message design. *Communication Monographs, 55,* 80–103.

O'Keefe, B. J., & Delia, J. G. (1982). Impression formation and message production. In M. E. Roloff & C. R. Berger (Eds.), *Social cognition and communication* (pp. 33–72). Beverly Hills, CA: Sage.

O'Keefe, B. J., & Shepherd, G. J. (1987). The pursuit of multiple objectives in face-to-face persuasive interaction: Effects of construct differentiation on message organization. *Communication Monographs, 54,* 396–419.

Oldershaw, L., Walters, G. C., & Hall, D. K. (1986). Control strategies and noncompliance in abusive mother–child dyads: An observational study. *Child Development, 57,* 722–732.

Olufowote, J. O., Miller, V. D., & Wilson, S. R. (2005). The interactive effects of role change goals and relational changes on employee upward influence tactics. *Management Communication Quarterly, 18,* 385–403.

Rule, B. G., & Bisanz, G. L., Kohn, M. (1985). Anatomy of a persuasion schema: Targets, goals, and strategies. *Journal of Personality and Social Psychology, 48,* 1127–1140.

Sabee, C. M., & Wilson, S. R. (2005). Students' primary goals, attributions, and facework during conversations about disappointing grades. *Communication Education, 54,* 185–204.

Searle, J. R. (1969). *Speech acts: An essay in the philosophy of language.* Cambridge, UK: Cambridge University Press.

Searle, J. R. (1976). A classification of illocutionary acts. *Language in Society, 5,* 1–25.

Seibold, D. R., Cantrill, J. G., & Meyers, R. A. (1994). Communication and interpersonal influence. In M. L. Knapp & G. R. Miller (Eds.), *Handbook of interpersonal communication* (2nd ed., pp. 542–588). Thousand Oaks, CA: Sage.

Shah, J. (2003). Automatic for the people: How representations of significant others implicitly affect goal pursuit. *Journal of Personality and Social Psychology, 84,* 661–681.

Shepherd, G. J. (1998). The trouble with goals. *Communication Studies, 49,* 294–299.

Sillars, A., Roberts, L. J., Leonard, K. E., & Dun, T. (2000). Cognition during marital conflict: The relationship of thought and talk. *Journal of Social and Personal Relationships, 17,* 479–502.

Simpson, J. A., Orina, M. M., & Ickes, W. (2003). When accuracy hurts, and when it helps: A test of the empathic accuracy model in marital interactions. *Journal of Personality and Social Psychology, 85,* 881–893.

Tracy, K., Craig, R. T., Smith, M., & Spisak, F. (1984). The discourse of requests: Assessment of a compliance-gaining approach. *Human Communication Research, 10,* 513–538.

Waldron, V. R. (1997). Toward a theory of interactive conversational planning. In J. O. Greene (Eds.), *Message production: Advances in communication theory* (pp. 195–220). Mahwah, NJ: Lawrence Erlbaum Associates.

Watts, R. J. (2003). *Politeness.* Cambridge, UK: Cambridge University Press.

Wilson, E. V., & Zigurs, I. (2001). Interpersonal influence goals and computer-mediated communication. *Journal of Organizational Computing and Electronic Commerce, 11,* 59–76.

Wilson, S. R. (1990). Development and test of a cognitive rules model of interaction goals. *Communication Monographs, 57,* 81–103.

Wilson, S. R. (1995). Elaborating the cognitive rules model of interaction goals: The problem of accounting for individual differences in goal formation. In B. R. Burleson (Ed.), *Communication yearbook 18* (pp. 3–25). Thousand Oaks, CA: Sage.

Wilson, S. R. (2000). Developing planning perspectives to explain parent–child interactions in physically abusive families. *Communication Theory, 10,* 210–220.

Wilson, S. R. (2002). *Seeking and resisting compliance: Why people say what they do when trying to influence others.* Thousand Oaks, CA: Sage.

Wilson, S. R., Aleman, C. G., & Leatham, G. B. (1998). Identity implications of influence goals: A revised analysis of face-threatening acts and application to seeking compliance with same-sex friends. *Human Communication Research, 25,* 64–96.

Wilson, S. R., Anastasiou, L., Aleman, C. G., Kim, M. S., & Oetzel, J. O. (2000, June). *Identity implications of influence goals: Ethnicity and face work.* Presentation at the annual meeting of the International Communication Association, San Francisco.

Wilson, S. R., Kim, M. S., & Meischke, H. (1991/1992). Evaluating Brown and Levinson's politeness theory: A revised analysis of directives and face. *Research on Language and Social Interaction, 25,* 215–252.

Wilson, S. R., & Kunkel, A. W. (2000). Identity implications of influence goals: Similarities in face threats and facework across sex and close relationships. *Journal of Language and Social Psychology, 19,* 195–221.

Wilson, S. R., & Morgan, W. M. (2004). Persuasion and families. In A. Vangelisti (Ed.), *Handbook of family communication* (pp. 447–471). Hillsdale, NJ Lawrence Erlbaum Associates.

Wilson, S. R., & Morgan, W. M. (2006). Goals-plans-action theories: Theories of goals, plans, and planning processes in families. In D. O. Braithwaite & L. A. Baxter (Eds.), *Engaging theories in family communication: Multiple Perspectives* (pp. 66–81). Thousand Oaks, CA: Sage.

Wilson, S. R., & Sabee, C. M. (2003). Explicating communicative competence as a theoretical term. In J. O. Greene & B. R. Burleson (Eds.), *Handbook of communication and social interaction skills* (pp. 3–50). Mahwah, NJ: Lawrence Erlbaum Associates..

Yukl, G., Guinan, P. J., & Sottolano, D. (1995). Influence tactics used for different objectives with subordinates, peers, and superiors. *Group & Organizational Management, 20,* 272–296.

5

Arguments

Dale Hample
Western Illinois University

Although a few remarkable scholars undertake their work with a decades-long perspective that illuminates a grand insight into communication, most of us have a different working orientation. We find an interesting question, pursue it, and follow the evidence wherever it leads, letting one study frame the next. We do what Kuhn (1970) called normal science. Once in a while, one of us will write a paper that catches a topic on the sweet part of the bat, but usually, like slow base runners, we just move from station to station. This scholarly reality makes it important to undertake periodic stock taking, to look back and to try to glimpse the immediate future. This joint venture is of that sort.

Our pretense is that we are approaching the 25th anniversary of the publication of Roloff and Berger's (1982) *Social Cognition and Communication,* a project that, in its own day, synthesized a relatively new approach to the study of communication. Although quantitative research had emerged from the rhetoric wars of the 1960s as a legitimate approach to communication, most of the work in the 1960s and 1970s had been concerned with personality measures or with attitude theories drawn from social psychology. Cognition, studied for its own sake, had been suspiciously regarded as obscure and pointlessly technical by the field's mainstream scholars. The Roloff and Berger book helped others to see what the emerging cognitive paradigm could add to the discipline, and the impressive credentials of the volume's contributors cemented positive perceptions of the general approach.

The Roloff and Berger (1982) volume does not, however, include either a chapter or any focused attention on arguing, the topic of this chapter. The sociology and history of the discipline make this omission predictable, and these problems continue to some extent today. Historically, argumentation has been the domain of debate coaches, who have generally been regarded as taking a merely pedagogical orientation to the field. In decades past, many communication faculty debated as undergraduates, and quite a few coached forensics early in their careers. Those who were research oriented generally left the activity behind, either spontaneously or with mentors' encouragement. Recent decades have seen the decay of intercollegiate debating, and so even this connection with argumentation has been dwindling. Very early work on argumentation tended to concern itself with the practicalities of debating, and such papers rarely had any implications for more naturally occurring argumentation or communication. Those coaches or former debaters who continued to concern themselves with argumentation typically had a rhetorical bent, and pursued the topic of reason giving through the lens of political communication and public address. Those of us who received our doctoral training in the 1960s or later, decades in which interpersonal, organizational, and mass communication research began to mature, normally migrated to those areas, leaving argumentation aside.

Argumentation, in spite of what I hope will soon be its apparent importance to communication phenomena, continues to be poorly represented on doctoral faculties. Those few schools that have, or have had, concentrations of argumentation scholars rarely approach the subject cognitively, or even experimentally. The faculties of Northwestern University, the University of Iowa, the University of Utah, and the University of Southern California have a nearly exclusive rhetorical orientation. Other schools, such as the University of Amsterdam and the University of Arizona, are committed to a particular theory of the standards for rational critical discussions. The latter approach has produced at least a few empirical studies that bear on cognitive issues (e.g., several of the chapters in van Eemeren & Grootendorst, 1994), but this can hardly be said to be the main impetus of the research program. Straightforwardly cognitive work has been done, as we will see, but the researchers tend to be solitary and unaffiliated with the field's major schools. Much of the central work is not even explicitly identified as being about arguing.

As it has not won a featured place in doctoral programs, the argumentation community has therefore had to establish its own opportunities for publication. Setting aside the forensics journals and newsletters, argumentation studies has several journals focused on sophisticated research: *Argumentation and Advocacy, Argumentation,* and *Informal Logic.* Only a few articles on argumentation break into mainstream journals. The research community is a nearly underground movement, and probably more of its published scholarship appears in fugitive proceedings than in accessible journals. The biennial conference in Alta, Utah, has now published a dozen sets of proceedings, collectively containing more than 1,000 papers. Every 4 years since 1986, scholars have met in Amsterdam as the International Society for the Study of Argumentation, and those five multivolume proceedings are even more massive than the Alta products. The biennial meetings of the Ontario Society for the Study of Argumentation also generate quite substantial sets of papers. The smaller biennial Wake Forest meetings (the 10th was in 2004) do not normally publish proceedings, but important work is quietly presented at that conference as well. People who do not attend these meetings have little idea of what work is being done in argumentation, even when that scholarship would be pertinent to more well-known research programs in communication.

Therefore, I intend this chapter to be at once informative and evangelical. My thesis is that most message production scholarship is actually about arguing, because it is oriented to content and reasons. In developing my claim, I integrate argument-specific research into the message production literature. Not incidentally, this should result in a description of the process of argument production. Besides the informative value of this chapter, I am hopeful that it will also stimulate more attention to argument-specific research, and encourage readers to undertake their own investigations.

To those ends, I wish to cover three main topics. The first is a definition of argument. I offer a somewhat nonstandard stipulation (Rowland, 1987) of argument's structure and function. This, I hope, will abstract argument's nature from the narrower definitions that are common in the literature. The second topic is how argument, as defined, connects with the message production literature. Third, I make some general remarks about methodology, and finally comment on the future of argumentation studies.

DEFINING ARGUMENT

My understanding of argument is based on an important principle, one that strikes me as obvious, but seems too rarely appreciated by some other writers: Arguing is done by people. It is an essentially human activity, and can only be done by humans. Propositions cannot argue, syllogisms cannot argue, paragraphs cannot argue, cartoons cannot argue, and speeches cannot argue. This chapter cannot argue. Only a person can argue. As Brockriede (1975) observed, "arguments are not in statements but in people" (p. 179).

The texts that we casually describe as arguments are literally only their artifacts. Sometimes, when we study a speech from another era or culture, it might be more accurate to say that we are looking at the fossil of an argument. The first scholarly task in such work is to understand the fossil well enough to reconstruct the person who created it, and the people who engaged it. When we write that some text is (or has made) an argument, we are expressing ourselves figuratively, and it is a mistake to forget that.

Definitions of argument ordinarily specify either the structure or function of arguing, or both. In a recent book, I offered a two-part definition of argument (Hample, 2005a). The form of argument is reason in support of a conclusion. The function of argument is to create meaning. Notice that the structural specification is not in terms of textual propositions. I intend it to apply to mental representations of ideas even more directly than it describes discursive artifacts. Reasoning and concluding are human actions, not grammatical relations. A portion of a paragraph that serves as a justification only does so when that passage is taken as a reason by a human reader, and the same applies to conclusions. The connection between reason and claim must also be recognized by a person. Otherwise the paragraph will appear incoherent. Many textual or artistic expressions of reasons and conclusions are relatively transparent, and we rarely make substantial mistakes in our critical understandings of them. However, at bottom, arguing and its form are sited only within human minds. This is obviously a cognitive orientation to arguing, one that has a modest history in argumentation studies (e.g., Cummings, 2004; Hample, 1980, 1985).

In saying that the function of arguing is to create meaning, I am making an effort to express the most basic thing that arguments do. Arguments are designed to make conclusions seem more likely, and therefore arguments naturally arise when claims are thought not to be obvious to the hearer. The conclusion to an argument is supposed to be a new thought, a new attitude, a new shading of a previous impulse, or a reinforcement of an indifferently held cognition. I count all of these, loosely, as referring to the creation of meaning.

Function is an important word, and must be closely distinguished from some similar ideas that I also discuss in this article (earlier treatments are Dace & Hirokawa, 1987; Hample, 1983). In particular, functions and goals are different. A goal is something intended, and it may or may not eventuate. A function simply happens, consistently. Often, goals and functions work out to be the same things, and this is why many people elide the two terms. Here is a useful example that displays the potential contrast. A main goal of public education in the United States is to produce a more knowledgeable citizenry. A consistent function of public education in the United States is to shrink the available labor force by preventing people in their middle and late teens from competing for full-time jobs. I think it is better in a definitional effort to focus on the functions of arguing rather than its goals, because different people will have wonderfully variable intentions for engaging in argumentation. Sometimes the statement of argumentation's goals reveals more about the scholar than about any naive arguers.

Although this two-part definition differs in detail from more standard ones, I think it has the capacity to subsume them, or at least to exist comfortably alongside them. Many structural definitions refer to a reason-claim relation (e.g., Govier, 2001; Toulmin, 1958), even if these scholars have propositions in view, rather than beliefs. I depart here only in that I think the structure is psychological rather than textual, but the idea of proving is consistent. Several scholars see arguing as a sort of interpersonal interaction (e.g., Jackson & Jacobs, 1980; O'Keefe, 1977; Willard, 1989), and Gilbert (1997) identified this as the basic view of naive actors. Here, the form is abstracted from the nature of conversation. I recognize that interaction imposes constraints on arguing and provides structural resources, but the reason–claim relation will still need to be apparent to participants.

Many scholars consider that arguing has a particular purpose. Some say that we argue to regulate disagreement (e.g., Jackson & Jacobs, 1980). Others orient more to argument's capacity to achieve rational outcomes (e.g., van Eemeren & Grootendorst, 2004). Another common point of view is that arguments serve to persuade (e.g., Perelman & Olbrechts-Tyteca, 1969). The conjunction of disagreement resolution, rational outcomes, and persuasion undergirds the standard pedagogical claim that argument is at the heart of democratic processes.

Notice that these views are best understood as being about goals. I am unwilling to say that arguing has one goal, because people have many reasons for arguing. Some argue for fun, some to resolve a disagreement rationally, and others to hurt the other person (cf. Hample, 2003a). It is surely productive to study all these goals, and to try to make sense of their connections. However, in each case, the creation of meaning is necessary to achieve the arguer's aim. That is why argument is so often selected as a means to those goals: because it serves the function of creating or shaping meaning.

So as we move into the second substantial section of this article, we have in mind a two-part definition of argument: Its structure is reason–conclusion, and its function is meaning creation.

THE CENTRALITY OF ARGUMENT TO MESSAGE PRODUCTION RESEARCH

Message production theory and research are aimed at describing why people say what they do. Although some nonverbal work has been done (e.g., Burgoon & White, 1997), the bulk of scholarship is concerned with verbal messages. The usual focus is on a single actor, and this is understood as a current limitation (Waldron, 1997). With some important exceptions, the basic model in all this work is the goals-plan-action (GPA) model (Dillard, 2004). Confronting a social situation, people form goals that stimulate plans, and the resulting actions are messages. Although this is the core theory, recent research has expanded on the model, primarily studying things that precede the goal and other elements that intervene between the goal and the message. My contention is that much of this work is, or can be assimilated to, part of the study of argumentation.

Let me try to work through this literature in a sort of theoretical chronology. I start with the earliest moments in argument production, and move forward until actual expression occurs. Because clear and detailed explanations of the message production work are available elsewhere (Greene, 1997; Hample, 2005a; Wilson, 2002), I treat those topics briefly to permit us to concentrate on the connections between this scholarship and argumentation. Figure 5.1 contains a schematic summary of the main processes involved. The first and final elements in Figure 5.1 are public matters, and everything within the large central rectangle is a cognitive process that we need to examine.

A message begins with a situation. Normally, the stimulating circumstances can be nicely analyzed with traditional ideas (Bitzer, 1968), but some matters may be so complex as to require something like Goodnight's (2003) notion of predicament. In any case, the situation generates some sense of immediacy, some exigency that must be addressed communicatively.

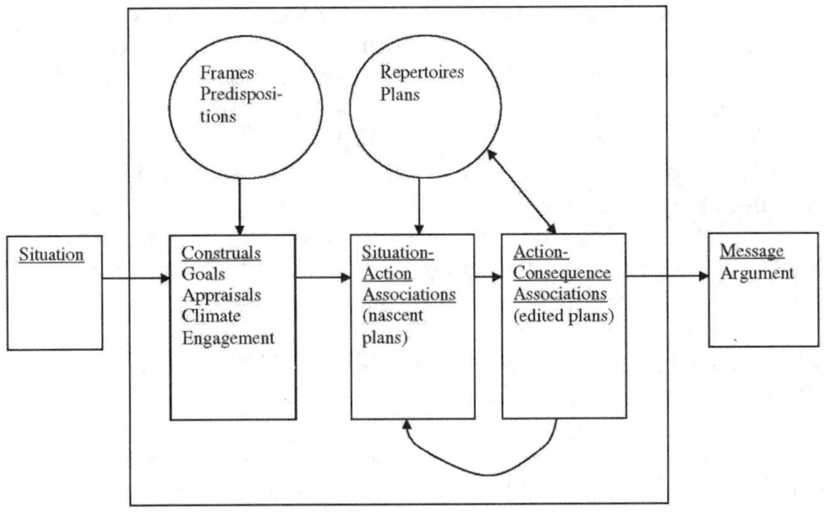

FIGURE 5.1. Diagram of the argument production process.

These circumstances are not registered: They must be construed. The interpretations are what guide the production of messages (Hample, 1997). In a series of studies, Wilson (1995) showed that ambiguous situations are understood differently by people varying in interpersonal construct differentiation. A consequence of these distinct interpretations is that people make different attributions about the exigence, and so understand various sets of goals to be in play. The principle that situations must be construed—that they are not given—is an important one. This interpretation creates the context to which an argument's meanings must be directed.

Two key sorts of construals have been studied at some length. The first has to do with the constellation of goals that are active. Dillard (1990, 2004; Dillard & Solomon, 2000; also see Feng & Wilson, 2004; see Wilson & Feng, chap. 4, this volume) distinguishes between primary and secondary goals. These terms do not indicate relative motivational force. Instead, the primary goal is the one that frames the situation—phenomenally defines it as advice giving, or compliance seeking, or comforting, and so forth. If the primary goal is the verb in the motivational syntax, the secondary goals are rather like the adverbs. They index matters such as politeness, identity, and anxiety, and constrain how the framing goal should be pursued, if it is pursued at all. All these objectives must eventually be addressed by the generation of meaning, and the secondary goals in particular may direct the editorial processes that shape the core meanings into satisfactory forms (Hample & Dallinger, 1990; Meyer, 1997). Much of the work on secondary goals is directed to politeness issues (e.g., Meyer, 2002), which should remind us that Jackson and Jacobs (1980) explained that conversational arguments are essentially repair devices.

A second important kind of situational construal has to do with the feelings that it rouses. Appraisal theory (Dillard, Kinney, & Cruz, 1996; Scherer, Schorr, & Johnstone, 2001) insists that situaions do not directly stimulate emotions. Instead, the process is mediated by appraisals. These are perceptual and interpretive cognitions that connect external events to personal matters. It is the appraisal pattern, not the situation, that immediately stimulates feelings, whether these feelings are theorized dimensionally (positive–negative valence, self–other directed, etc.) or discretely (love, anger, sadness, etc.).

We are only in the first stages of understanding the place of emotion in interpersonal arguing (e.g., Friemann, 2000; Gilbert, 1997; Hample, 2004b; Hample, Thompson-Hayes, Wallenfelsz, Wallenfelsz, & Knapp, in press; Willard, 1979). Perhaps our most immediate points of contact are climate and willingness to engage. The climate of an argument may be described in many ways: competitive or cooperative, positive or negative, energized or lifeless (Hample, 1997). However, climates have in common that they facilitate some sorts of action (e.g., threats) and impede others (e.g., cute analogies). Some, for instance, may seem to require objectified cost–benefit analysis (Willard, 1989), and others may want freewheeling emotionality (Gilbert, 1997). Not only may climates thereby constrain what reasons are appropriate, but they may also affect what claims are open to discussion (e.g., "Don't talk to your mother that way!").

An even more fundamental relevance of emotion to argumentation has to do with whether the argument happens at all—that is, whether the person engages. The decision to engage is rarely discussed in message production work (an exception is Dillard, 2004), but argumentation research on this point has a considerable history. We know, for instance, that many people have such negative impressions of the act of arguing that they avoid it if at all possible (Benoit, 1982; Dallinger & Hample, 2002; Martin & Scheerhorn, 1985). Infante's work on argumentativeness is perhaps the best known on this topic (e.g., Infante & Rancer, 1996). Argumentative people are highly motivated to argue about issues, but the opposite is true of people low on this trait. Berger (2004) began some interesting work on speechlessness, and trying to describe the circumstances, feelings, and cognitions that result in a person not being able to say anything at all. Work on climate and willingness to engage are most central to this chapter, but other research on the emotional experience and aftermath of arguing also needs to be undertaken.

If situations must be construed to stimulate argumentation, we should also give some heed to the interpretive predispositions people bring to potentially arguable matters. People clearly differ in the frames they apply to arguing (e.g., Hample, 2005a, 2005b; Hample, Conklin, Hodge, & Jacky, 2004). Participants vary in the degree to which they see arguing as productive, cooperative, enjoyable, domineering, intemperate, and so forth. These prejudices will frame the situational construal, affect the decision to engage, shape the constellation of relevant goals, and presumably therefore end by altering what arguments, if any, are actually produced.

Situational construal involves recognition of the situation type (resulting in activation of a framing goal), application of one's predispositions about that sort of situation, emotional appraisal, making salient attributions about the other person, and stimulation of secondary goals. Frankly, the timing of these processes has not yet been worked out very well, nor have all the connections among these cognitive and affective systems. It does seem clear, however, that situational construal is a dynamic process, with different psychological elements rising to the foreground at different moments, and with many of them susceptible to modification as the argument production process moves along.

As we have seen, the interpretation of the situation is theorized to involve the formation of one's message goals. This starts the GPA model in earnest. Although goals have been conceptually discussed in several venues (e.g., Craig, 1986; Dillard, 1997), only a few approaches are very clear about how the goals are stored and activated in long-term cognitive systems. Perhaps the most interesting approach on this point is Meyer's (1997; see also Meyer, chap. 17, this volume).

Meyer says that, in the context of the goals stimulated by the situation, message producers activate what she calls situation–action associations. These are patterns, stored in long-term memory, that connect (construed) situational features to message types (or, perhaps, exact messages). Spontaneously, a recognized situation immediately nominates one or more possible messages for utterance. This is a nascent plan, a first draft if you will, and if no more processing takes place, the message with the highest activation level will be produced. Notice that these associations can be modeled as conditional syllogisms: The situation has feature X; if the situation has feature X, then message Y should be produced; so produce message Y. Each association (or syllogism) appears in the context of competing ones, and the most pressing connection is the one that survives.

She also posits a second cognitive system that normally comes into play immediately after this step. This consists of action–consequence associations. These are also patterns, but in this case they connect message types to their results (e.g., aggressive messages cause negative reactions). They can also be modeled as conditional syllogisms. This is the point at which secondary goals assert their importance, and therefore the point at which editing takes place. Depending on the motivational and other resources available, an arguer might cycle through these latter systems several times (see Figure 5.1), until a satisfactory message is invented and shaped. Only then is the action generated.

Few message production scholars give much specification about how this cycling takes place. Commonly, readers are left with the impression that testing messages against goals is a simple matter of applying activated goals and messages to one another in a test-operate-test-exit unit (Miller, Galanter, & Pribram, 1960), and this is a good preliminary model. However, the observation that both situation–action and action–consequence associations can be understood as the major premises of conditional syllogisms invites us to consider that these processes, vaguely described as associating or cycling, are actually instances of reasoning, or private arguing, that need not be conscious (Hample, 1986a, 1986b). We can add detail to our understanding of argument production by applying a Bayesian model of inference, originally developed as a description of how arguments are processed by their recipients (e.g., Allen & Burrell,

1992; Allen & Kellermann, 1988; Hample, 1977; see Stiff & Mongeau, 2003, for a summary). The core equation is this:

$$p(C) = \beta 1\ p(C \mid D)\ p(D) + \beta_2\ p(C \mid {\sim}D)\ p({\sim}D),$$

where p(C) is the subjective probability that the argument's claim is true, p(C | D) is the subjective probability that the claim is true assuming that the data are true, p(D) is the subjective probability that the data are true, p(C | ~D) is the subjective probability that the claim is true assuming that the data are false, p(~D) is the subjective probability that the data are false, and the βs are beta weights from multiple regression. Supposing that the claim is modeled as being equivalent to "I should say X" and that the data are equivalent to "Y is a feature of the situation," the equation should generate good predictions of whether or not X will be produced. In the terms p(C | D) and p(C | ~D), the equation implies the idea that people may have a standard for acceptability, a quality level they require of anything they might say in those circumstances. Should that threshold be unachieved, the person may well decline engagement. For the most part, however, we expect that the X–Y connections that produce the highest (or most immediately satisfactory) p(C) will be most important in producing public arguments.

Most theorists have little to say about where the precise content of the messages comes from (an interesting exception is O'Keefe & Lambert, 1995). At its present stage of development, message production theory is working on the relatively simple problem of connecting one's felt needs to one's messages by means of plans. Only a few projects have shown much capacity to predict either exact utterances or even general lines of argument (an exception is work on the obstacle hypothesis; Francik & Clark, 1985). The main potential on this point is probably to be found in studies of planning (e.g., Berger, 1997; Kellermann, 1995; see Berger, chap. 3, this volume). These research methods often involve elicitation of potential lines of action, either from one individual or from a sample. For instance, Berger (1988) listed steps involved in plans for asking for a date: introducing oneself, searching for common ground, comparing schedules, and so on. These possible lines of action are the message repertoires from which content can be drawn, either for immediate production or for editing prior to utterance.

I have recently been doing some more focused work on message repertoires (Hample, 2003b, 2004a). The basic method is to provide people with a situation description, and ask them to list the things they could say. When given situations framed by a persuasive goal, about 85% of the items respondents list are argumentatively relevant: They are either reasons or conclusions. Most of the remainder is facework of some sort. Some people have significantly larger repertoires than others; that is, they are able to list more things. Those who have the most material at hand are the respondents who have more academic ability and higher levels of creativity. Predispositions, such as argumentativeness and verbal aggressiveness, make little difference in either the size of the repertoires or their argumentative content. This line of research has not matured to the point where elements from the repertoire can be traced through from situation construal to goal activation, to message stimulation, to message revision, to message production. However, the methodology may provide a means for doing just that. Repertoires and plans are key cognitive resources for an arguer, and by studying them we will come closer to being able to predict exact message content.

So scholars say that the basic message production sequence is this: situation construal, goal formation, plan generation and revision, and utterance. Each of these steps is detailed in the literature, including other chapters in this volume (especially Meyer, chap. 17, and Wilson & Feng, chap. 4), and involve more nuance than I have tried to convey here. But perhaps this broad outline will help to show the connections between this body of scholarship and argumentation. What is normally produced, especially in the persuasion settings that are most often studied in the message production tradition, is not merely a message, but a message with a meaning that is fairly well understandable as reasons and claims.

METHODOLOGY

Part of the contributors' brief for these chapters was to address methodological issues on each topic. Little is methodologically unique about scholarship on argument production (see Billig, 1998). When the research focus is conversational, ordinary conversation analysis methods will be appropriate; when interactional, the usual armament of interpersonal investigation strategies will be available; when cognitive, the typical instruments for elicitation, rating, or coding goals, plans, feelings, and beliefs will suggest themselves. To demonstrate that one's study is explicitly about arguing, the researcher will need to pay some attention to message content, of course, and data bearing on reasons and conclusions will be most on point. However, those acts, processes, interpretations, or abilities (depending on the scholar's immediate conceptualization) can be measured in a substantial variety of ways: through free-form coding of texts or transcriptions (e.g., Hample, 2004a), qualitative analysis (e.g., Jackson & Jacobs, 1980), response time measures (e.g., Graves et al., 2004), respondent ratings (e.g., Roskos-Ewoldsen, 1997), standardized questionnaires (but see Follman, Lavely, & Berger, 1997a, 1997b), behavioral observation (e.g., Hample, 2004b), perhaps eventually physiological instrumentation (e.g., Heisel & Beatty, 2004), and as many other methods as there are for observing people, their actions, and their thoughts.

Having made this practical point, perhaps readers will tolerate a more abstract one. Methodologies are normally subordinate to the topic of study, in the sense that they are used in service of theoretical advance. Argumentation and methodology have this relation, too, but they also have another one, one that may be unique in the field of communication. Arguing generates methodology. This is because all research methods are argument schemata (Hample, 1990; Jackson, 1989). Decades of scientific dialectic eventually resolve themselves into particular argument forms, forms that are endorsed as more or less automatically generating unexceptional conclusions. These forms presuppose certain kinds of data, and supply particular warrants. Here are examples of such warrants: things that might occur by chance less than 5% of the time are regarded as really being so; only measurements with known reliability can generate legitimate information; only replicable work has any scientific merit; experiments are needed for clear evidence of causality; and the more variables accounted for, the more informative is the analysis. Readers can certainly supply more warrants of this type and may, in a particular application, be able to counterargue. Still, the point should be clear: Our design decisions and interpretive judgments are the results of argumentation. Elements of these arguments become taken for granted, so that a person can simply be "trained" in statistical methods, but these taken-for-granteds are actually the residue of prior arguing by the pertinent scholarly community. So argumentation both advances and is advanced by methodology.

CONCLUSION

This chapter has been simultaneously aimed at two audiences that I believe would profit from more contact. For the message production community, I encourage consideration of argumentation. This move will sharpen our understanding of message content, and will encourage us to see goals as the first wellsprings of reasons. It will be interesting to see when goals are actually expressed as rationales and claims, and when the editorial process causes some other phrasing or reasoning to be supplied in support of the conclusion dictated by one's impulses. It may well be productive to regard goals as the first drafts of arguers' reasons. From such a beginning, we can begin to trace the emergence and shaping of content throughout the production process. By entertaining a loose initial connection between an arguer's primary goal and his or her eventual projection of meaning, we may be able to make more precise predictions about message details.

For the argumentation community, I encourage attention to the process of argument production. As we become increasingly interested in interpersonal arguing, we should develop more useful understandings of invention. Work on face-to-face argument has shown us how the constraints of conversational structure affect what sorts of things can be said, and in what slots. However, the specific remarks are also responsive to the arguer's own construals and other cognitive processes. Our understanding of argumentation can only be improved if we strive to develop theory that conjoins cognitive, microsocial, and public matters.

I see no inherent difficulty in studying argumentation simultaneously from footing in several disciplines. From philosophy and informal logic we learn the structural and rational details of arguments, whether they are parts of imagined interactions or national constitutions. From rhetoric, we see how arguments must adapt to publics, and what features of popular groups must be abstracted and used enthymematically. From discourse studies, we derive the social facts of conversation that mold the form and rhythm of our critical discussions. From social psychology, we observe the predispositions and interpretive impulses that incline us to behave in generally predictable ways. From cognitive psychology, we learn about the private processing that constitutes our personal production of reasons, conclusions, and meaning. All this, in fact, has been done for years, but mostly by disconnected scholarly communities.

Argumentation is so basic a human process that the vast majority of methodologies used in the humanities and social sciences find application to the topic. Particular questions will naturally call out particular research designs, but the field as a whole is remarkable in its hospitality to different methods. This openness is even evident in the professional histories of individual argument scholars, who have made use of radically different investigative techniques in their work. We have pragma-dialecticians who do rhetorical criticism, conversation analysts who do syllogism studies, argument theorists who do meta-analyses of evidence and conclusions, debate coaches who generate personality instruments, and rhetorical critics who do quantitative studies of persuasion dynamics. I believe that this is because we all understand that arguments are at the core of most elements of the human experience, and that we need to follow the evidence wherever it leads.

ACNOWLEDGMENTS

An earlier version of this chapter was presented to the biennial Wake Forest University Argumentation Conference, June 2004, Venice, Italy. I am grateful to the participants who discussed that paper with me after the presentation.

REFERENCES

Allen, M., & Burrell, N. (1992). Evaluating the believability of sequential arguments. *Argumentation and Advocacy, 28,* 135–144.

Allen, M., & Kellermann, K. (1988). Using the subjective probability model to evaluate academic debate arguments. *Argumentation and Advocacy, 25,* 93–107.

Benoit, P. J. (1982, November). *The naïve social actor's concept of argument.* Paper presented at the annual conference of the Speech Communication Association, Louisville, KY.

Berger, C. R. (1988). Planning, affect, and social action generation. In L. Donohew, H. E. Sypher, & E. T. Higgins (Eds.), *Communication, social cognition, and affect* (pp. 93–116). Hillsdale, NJ: Lawrence Erlbaum Associates.

Berger, C. R. (1997). *Planning strategic interaction: Attaining goals through communicative action.* Mahwah, NJ: Lawrence Erlbaum Associates.

Berger, C. R. (2004). Speechlessness: Causal attributions, emotional features and social consequences. *Journal of Language and Social Psychology, 23,* 147–179.

Billig, M. (1998). Rhetoric and the unconscious. In H. V. Hansen, C. W. Tindale, & A. V. Colman (Eds.), *Argumentation & rhetoric* [CD-ROM]. St. Catharines, ON: Ontario Society for the Study of Argumentation.

Bitzer, L. F. (1968). The rhetorical situation. *Philosophy and Rhetoric, 1,* 1–14.

Brockriede, W. (1975). Where is argument? *Journal of the American Forensic Association, 11,* 179–182.

Burgoon, J. K., & White, C. H. (1997). Researching nonverbal message production: A view from interaction adaptation theory. In J. O. Greene (Ed.), *Message production: Advances in communication theory* (pp. 279–312). Mahwah, NJ: Lawrence Erlbaum Associates.

Craig, R. T. (1986). Goals in discourse. In D. G. Ellis & W. A. Donohue (Eds.), *Contemporary issues in language and discourse processes* (pp. 257–274). Hillsdale, NJ: Lawrence Erlbaum Associates.

Cummings, L. (2004). Argument as cognition: A Putnamian criticism of Dale Hample's cognitive conception of argument. *Argumentation, 18,* 331–348.

Dace, K., & Hirokawa, R. Y. (1987). The role of argumentation in group decision-making efficacy: A functional perspective. In J. W. Wenzel (Ed.), *Argument and critical practices* (pp. 405–410). Annandale, VA: Speech Communication Association.

Dallinger, J. M., & Hample, D. (2002). The image of the ideal arguer. In G. T. Goodnight (Ed.), *Arguing, communication & culture* (Vol. 1, pp. 285–291). Washington, DC: National Communication Association.

Dillard, J. P. (1990). The nature and substance of goals in tactical communication. In M. J. Cody & M. J. McLaughlin (Eds.), *The psychology of tactical communication* (pp. 70–91). Philadelphia: Multilingual Matters.

Dillard, J. P. (1997). Explicating the goal construct: Tools for theorists. In J. O. Greene (Ed.), *Message production: Advances in communication theory* (pp. 47–70). Mahwah, NJ: Lawrence Erlbaum Associates.

Dillard, J. P. (2004). The goals-plan-action model of interpersonal influence. In J. S. Seiter & R. H. Gass (Eds.), *Perspectives on persuasion, social influence, and compliance gaining* (pp. 185–206). Boston: Allyn & Bacon.

Dillard, J. P., Kinney, T. A., & Cruz, M. G. (1996). Influence, appraisals, and emotions in close relationships. *Communication Monographs, 63,* 105–130.

Dillard, J. P., & Solomon, D. H. (2000). Conceptualizing context in message-production research. *Communication Theory, 10,* 167–175.

Feng, H., & Wilson, S. R. (2004, May). *A critical review of the primary/secondary goal framework.* Paper presented to the annual meeting of the International Communication Association, New Orleans, LA.

Follman, J., Lavely, C., & Berger, N. (1997a). Critical thinking: Concurrent validity. *Informal Logic, 18,* 268–272.

Follman, J., Lavely, C., & Berger, N. (1997b). Inventory of instruments of critical thinking. *Informal Logic, 18,* 261–267.

Francik, E. P., & Clark, H. H. (1985). How to make requests that overcome obstacles to compliance. *Journal of Memory and Language, 24,* 560–568.

Friemann, R. (2000). A consideration of empathy in argumentation. In C. W. Tindale, H. V. Hansen, & E. Sveda (Eds.), *Argumentation at the century's turn* [CD-ROM]. St. Catharines, ON: Ontario Society for the Study of Argumentation.

Gilbert, M. A. (1997). *Coalescent argumentation.* Mahwah, NJ: Lawrence Erlbaum Associates.

Goodnight, G. T. (2003). Predicaments of communication, argument, and power: Towards a critical theory of controversy. *Informal Logic,* 23, 119–138.

Govier, T. (2001). *A practical study of argument* (5th ed.). Belmont, CA: Wadsworth.

Graves, A., Morgan, M., Greene, J., Vibber, K., Kordas, J., & Stanforth, L. (2004, November). *A phrase well turned: Creative facility in narrative production.* Paper presented to the annual meeting of the National Communication Association, Chicago.

Greene, J. O. (Ed.). (1997). *Message production: Advances in communication theory.* Mahwah, NJ: Lawrence Erlbaum Associates.

Hample, D. (1977). Testing a model of value argument and evidence. *Communication Monographs, 14,* 106–120.

Hample, D. (1980). A cognitive view of argument. *Journal of the American Forensic Association, 17,* 151–158.

Hample, D. (1983). The functions of argument. In D. Zarefsky, M. O. Sillars, & J. Rhodes (Eds.), *Argument in transition* (pp. 560–575). Annandale, VA: Speech Communication Association.

Hample, D. (1985). A third perspective on argument. *Philosophy and Rhetoric, 18,* 1–22.

Hample, D. (1986a). Argumentation and the unconscious. *Journal of the American Forensic Association, 23,* 82–95.

Hample, D. (1986b). Logic, conscious and unconscious. *Western Journal of Speech Communication, 50,* 24–40.

Hample, D. (1990). Future directions in argumentation research. In R. Trapp & J. Schuetz (Eds.), *Perspectives on argumentation: Essays in honor of Wayne Brockriede* (pp. 298–314). Prospect Heights, IL: Waveland.

Hample, D. (1997). Framing message production research with field theory. In J. O. Greene (Ed.), *Message production: Advances in communication theory* (pp. 171–192). Mahwah, NJ: Lawrence Erlbaum Associates.

Hample, D. (2003a). Arguing skill. In J. O. Greene & B. R. Burleson (Eds.), *Handbook of communication and social interaction skills* (pp. 439–478). Mahwah, NJ: Lawrence Erlbaum Associates.

Hample, D. (2003b). Inventional capacity. In F. H. van Eemeren, J. A. Blair, C. A. Willard, & A. F. Snoeck-Henkemans (Eds.), *Proceedings of the fifth conference of the International Society for the Study of Argumentation* (pp. 437–440). Amsterdam: SicSat.

Hample, D. (2004a, May). *Inventional capacity: Conceptualization, operationalization, and findings.* Paper presented to the annual meeting of the International Communication Association, New Orleans, LA.

Hample, D. (2004b, May). *A methodology for observing emotions during interpersonal arguments.* Paper presented to the annual meeting of the International Communication Association, New Orleans, LA.

Hample, D. (2005a). *Arguing: Exchanging reasons face to face.* Mahwah, NJ: Lawrence Erlbaum Associates.

Hample, D. (2005b). *Argument frames: An initial investigation into operationalizations.* In C. A. Willard (Ed.), Critical problems in argumentation (pp. 568–576). Washington, DC: National Communication Association.

Hample, D., Conklin, M., Hodge, M., & Jacky, J. (2004, November). *Frames for the general orientation to argumentative situations.* Paper presented to the annual meeting of the National Communication Association, Chicago.

Hample, D., & Dallinger, J. M. (1990). Arguers as editors. *Argumentation, 4,* 153–169.

Hample, D., Thompson-Hayes, M., Wallenfelsz, K., Wallenfelsz, P., & Knapp, C. (in press). Face-to-face arguing is an emotional experience: Triangulating methodologies and early findings. *Argumentation and Advocacy.*

Heisel, A. D., & Beatty, M. J. (2004, November). *Do people rely on knowledge structures during routine interactions or do they improvise? An investigation of prefrontal cortex activity and message coding.* Paper presented to the annual meeting of the National Communication Association, Chicago.

Infante, D. A., & Rancer, A. S. (1996). Argumentativeness and verbal aggression: A review of recent theory and research. *Communication Yearbook, 19,* 319–351.

Jackson, S. (1989). Argument as method. In B. E. Gronbeck (Ed.), *Spheres of argument: Proceedings of the sixth SCA/AFA conference on argumentation* (pp. 1–8). Annandale, VA: Speech Communication Association.

Jackson, S., & Jacobs, S. (1980). Structure of conversational argument: Pragmatic bases for the enthymeme. *Quarterly Journal of Speech, 66,* 251–265.

Kellermann, K. (1995). The conversation MOP: A model of patterned and pliable behavior. In D. E. Hewes (Ed.), *The cognitive basis of interpersonal communication* (pp. 181–221). Hillsdale, NJ: Lawrence Erlbaum Associates.

Kuhn, T. S. (1970). *The structure of scientific revolutions* (2nd ed). Chicago: University of Chicago Press.

Martin, R. W., & Scheerhorn, D. R. (1985). What are conversational arguments? Toward a natural language user's perspective. In J. R. Cox, M. O. Sillars, & G. B. Walker (Eds.), *Argument and social practice* (pp. 705–722). Annandale, VA: Speech Communication Association.

Meyer, J. R. (1997). Cognitive influences on the ability to address interaction goals. In J. O. Greene (Ed.), *Message production: Advances in communication theory* (pp. 71–90). Mahwah, NJ: Lawrence Erlbaum Associates.

Meyer, J. R. (2002). Contextual influences on the pursuit of secondary goals in request messages. *Communication Monographs, 69,* 189–203.

Miller, G. A., Galanter, E., & Pribram, K. H. (1960). *Plans and the structure of behavior.* New York: Holt, Rinehart, & Winston.

O'Keefe, B. J., & Lambert, B. L. (1995). Managing the flow of ideas: A local management approach to message design. In B. Burleson (Ed.), *Communication yearbook 18* (pp. 54–82). Thousand Oaks, CA: Sage.

O'Keefe, D. J. (1977). Two concepts of argument. *Journal of the American Forensic Association, 13,* 121–128.

Perelman, C., & Olbrechts-Tyteca, L. (1969). *The new rhetoric: A treatise on argumentation* (J. Wilkinson & P. Weaver, Trans.). Notre Dame, IN: University of Notre Dame Press.

Roloff, M. E., & Berger, C. R. (Eds.). (1982). *Social cognition and communication.* Beverly Hills, CA: Sage.

Roskos-Ewoldsen, D. R. (1997). Implicit theories of persuasion. *Human Communication Research, 24,* 31–63.

Rowland, R. C. (1987). On defining argument. *Philosophy and Rhetoric, 20,* 140–159.

Scherer, K. R., Schorr, A., & Johnstone, T. (Eds.). (2001). *Appraisal processes in emotion: Theory, methods, research.* Oxford, UK: Oxford University Press.

Stiff, J. B., & Mongeau, P. A. (2003). *Persuasive communication* (2nd ed.). New York: Guilford.

Toulmin, S. (1958). *The uses of argument.* Cambridge, UK: Cambridge University Press.

van Eemeren, F. H., & Grootendorst, R. (Eds.). (1994). *Studies in pragma-dialectics.* Amsterdam: SicSat.

van Eemeren, F. H., & Grootendorst, R. (2004). *A systematic theory of argumentation: The pragma-dialectical approach.* Cambridge, UK: Cambridge University Press.

Waldron, V. R. (1997). Toward a theory of interactive conversational planning. In J. O. Greene (Ed.), *Message production: Advances in communication theory* (pp. 195–220). Mahwah, NJ: Lawrence Erlbaum Associates.

Willard, C. A. (1979). Propositional argument is to argument what talking about passion is to passion. *Journal of the American Forensic Association, 16,* 21–28.

Willard, C. A. (1989). *A theory of argumentation.* Tuscaloosa: University of Alabama Press.

Wilson, S. R. (1995). Elaborating the cognitive rules model of interaction goals: The problem of accounting for individual differences in goal formation. *Communication Yearbook, 18,* 3–25.

Wilson, S. R. (2002). *Seeking and resisting compliance: Why people say what they do when trying to influence others.* Thousand Oaks, CA: Sage.

II

Interpersonal Communication

6

Cognitive Foundations of Communication in Close Relationships

Denise Haunani Solomon
Pennsylvania State University

Jennifer A. Theiss
Rutgers University

Some 25 years after Skinner eschewed mental processes as hidden within an impenetrable black box (Skinner, 1953), social psychology underwent a "cognitive revolution" (Fiske & Linville, 1980, p. 543) marked by renewed appreciation for memory, cognitive processes, and schemas as fundamental to social experiences. In the seminal text, *Social Cognition and Communication,* Roloff and Berger (1982) took this revolution to the communication discipline, and provided a foundation for incorporating cognition into perspectives on interpersonal communication and facets of relationship development, escalation, and maintenance. Although Roloff and Berger were largely limited to drawing links between separate bodies of work on social cognition and communication in relationships, their contribution signaled the beginning of sustained efforts to integrate these literatures. In the ensuing two decades, the conceptions of social cognition that were the focus of scholarly attention in the 1980s have been applied to increasingly sophisticated portrayals of relationships.

Although contemporary thinking about interpersonal communication accepts the link between people's communication behavior and the ways they conceptualize their relationships as inherent and axiomatic, the complex nature of this relationship continues to inspire theory and research. People define and come to understand their relationships based on the meanings that are derived from interaction (Duck, 1995;

Wish, Deutsch, & Kaplan, 1976). In turn, cognitive perceptions of the relationship are used to enact relationally appropriate behaviors (Honeycutt & Cantrill, 2001) and interpret a partner's actions (Dillard, Solomon, & Samp, 1996). Yet questions remain about how close relationships are simultaneously defined in the minds of individuals and sustained by the communication that occurs between partners. Thus, interpersonal communication scholars are challenged to understand how both thoughts and words create, define, modify, maintain, and dissolve close relationships.

To provide a platform for continued efforts in this quest, this chapter highlights developments in research on cognition and communication in the context of close relationships that have emerged in the past 20 years. Whereas research leading up to the 1980s focused on discerning the structure of memory, a substantial amount of work in subsequent years has addressed the form and function of cognitive models of interpersonal relationships. Likewise, efforts to clarify the process of knowledge acquisition laid a foundation for theories examining how people draw inferences about their relationships from communication episodes. In addition, links drawn in the 1970s and 1980s between cognitive activity and message effects on attitudes are now being examined in the context of interactions between intimates. Because these lines of inquiry represent prominent themes in contemporary research on cognition, communication, and close relationships, we examine them each at length. To conclude this chapter, we suggest directions for future research that both advance and integrate these themes.

COGNITIVE MODELS AND RELATIONSHIPS

Cognitive models of relationships refer generally to knowledge structures or schemas that organize expectations, beliefs, information, and experiences associated with types of social relations and specific interpersonal relationships. Schemas can be further distinguished in terms of the function and content of information contained therein. *Declarative knowledge* encompasses semantic knowledge of the world, such as general facts, definitions, and prototypes. *Procedural knowledge* consists of information about typical or normative sequences of activity. Although the dichotomy between declarative and procedural knowledge is not absolute, it does provide a framework for organizing the substantial literature applying these concepts to close relationships. Thus, the following sections discuss cognitive models of relationship states and cognitive models of relationship processes, in turn. After reviewing these lines of inquiry, we discuss methodological trends in the study of cognitive models of close relationships.

Declarative Relationship Knowledge Structures

One prominent theme in work on cognitive models of relationships focuses on the structures that organize knowledge about relationship qualities. These abstract information stores are independent of the concrete experiences on which they are based, and they provide frames of reference for perceiving, comprehending, and making inferences about new experiences (e.g., Rumelhart, 1984). These structures can be further parsed by level of abstraction to distinguish the representation of relationship prototypes, expectations for specific behaviors within interpersonal situations, and experiences within a relationship with a specific partner (Fehr, 1988; Planalp, 1985; Shaver, Schwartz, Kirson, & O'Connor, 1987). In this section, we showcase characterizations of cognitive models at each of these levels.

A prototype is a special category of schema that contains information about the typical features that define the focal construct. Just as people have attributes that they associate with, for example, a prototypical bird (i.e., feathers, a beak, and an ability to fly), individuals develop prototypes for categories of social relations. Instantiations of the category might be more or less consistent with the prototype (e.g., a sparrow vs. an emu); nonetheless, the prototype exerts a substantial influence on people's expectations for experiences with members of the category. Whereas early work on social prototypes focused on the characteristics associated with personality traits (Cantor & Mischel, 1977, 1979) or social situations (Cantor, Mischel, & Schwartz, 1982), more recent work has explored prototypes for personal relationships. For example, Davis and Todd (1985) proposed a set of nine characteristics associated with friendships, and they argued that variations in the presence of these features differentiate types of friendship. Accordingly, Davis and Todd found that best friends, close friends of the same sex, close friends of different sexes, social acquaintances, and former friends were distinguished by the perceived viability, support, intimacy, enjoyment, spontaneity, success, and stability within those associations. In a line of research focused on a particular relationship quality, Fehr and Russell (1991; see also Fehr, 1988, 1993) mapped the prototype for love by identifying a variety of love subtypes (e.g., romantic love, motherly love, brotherly love). Although Davis and Todd's work focused on a type of social relationship and Fehr and Russell examined a relational quality, both lines of inquiry assume that people organize social knowledge using prototypical feature sets.

Whereas prototypes are embodied by a list of typical features, the term *relational schema* usually refers to a more integrated system of knowledge about an interpersonal association. In her foundational work on this topic, Planalp (1985) defined relational schemas as "coherent frameworks of relational knowledge that are used to derive relational implications of messages and are modified in accord with ongoing experience with relationships" (p. 9). Although Planalp recognized that relational schemas could address general to specific relationship knowledge, her research examined schemas for types of relationships. In particular, Planalp examined patterns of recall for a generic student–professor interaction, and she concluded that relational schemas specify the behavioral rights and obligations that characterize types of relationships (cf. Smith, 1995).

An alternative explication of the relational schema construct offered by Baldwin (1992) articulated three elements of relational schemas. The *self schema* is a sense of identity as experienced in relation to another person. The *partner schema* represents the impression individuals have of their partner, influenced by what that person is typically like, as well as what he or she is like within the context of the relationship. The *interpersonal script* combines procedural and declarative information to represent a typical sequence of actions and events for interaction; conceptualized as a set of if–then contingencies, interpersonal scripts link specific behaviors to responses or outcomes. Consistent with this view, the activation of relational schemas has been found to exert an impact on evaluations of the self (e.g., Baldwin, 1997), such that priming of a critical versus accepting significant other corresponds with reports of more negative versus positive self-evaluations (Baldwin, 1994; Baldwin, Carrell, & Lopez, 1990; Baldwin & Holmes, 1987). Similarly, the activation of positive interpersonal expectations has been found to correspond with increased emotional support-seeking behaviors (Pierce & Lydon, 1998). Notably, Baldwin presented an interdependent model of relational schema as the perception of self in relation to another (Holmes, 2000).

Of course, individuals also have a wealth of specific information about particular others; accordingly, several scholars have proposed that relationship-specific schemas exist to represent knowledge that is relevant to a particular other person and one's relationship with that person (Markus & Zajonc, 1985; Park, 1986). Relationship-specific schemas are likely to contain references to the qualities of the relationship, information about the self in relation to the partner, evaluations of the particular relationship in comparison to other relationships, and expectations based on typical interactions or action sequences involving the partner (Planalp, 1985; Wyer & Srull, 1986). Importantly, relationship-specific knowledge structures are more than the sum total of episodic memories involving the partner; they are abstractions of that wealth of information that, in turn, guide expectations, information processing, and behavior.

Procedural Relationship Knowledge Structures

Procedural knowledge is distinguished from declarative knowledge by its focus on sequences of activity. Procedural knowledge is activated by cues in the situation, including the setting, participants, activities, and goals, that have become associated over time with behavioral routines (e.g., Schank & Abelson, 1977). Whereas declarative knowledge captures the "what is" that characterizes social relations, procedural knowledge addresses the "how to" associated with enacting relationships. Baxter (1987) highlighted two types of relationship process cognitions: (a) those related to trajectories of relationship development and dissolution, and (b) those focused on strategies for achieving particular outcomes within relationships. The following paragraphs discuss research examining these facets of relationship knowledge structures.

Research on cognitive models of relationship trajectories is best exemplified by Honeycutt's work on memory structures for the rise and fall of close relationships (Honeycutt, 1995; Honeycutt, Cantrill, & Allen, 1992; Honeycutt, Cantrill, & Greene, 1989). Honeycutt and Cantrill (2001) defined a relational memory structure as "a type of schema that reflects time-ordered behaviors in the development of a relationship" (p. 104). Honeycutt et al. (1989) concluded that scripts for relational escalation could be parsed into the following six phases: (a) meeting and making small talk; (b) dating, displaying physical affection, and sharing informal activities; (c) self-disclosing; (d) having sexual intercourse; (e) meeting parents, exchanging gifts, talking about the other, and stating a commitment; and (f) marrying. Likewise, Honeycutt et al. (1992) sequenced relational deescalation into six phases: (a) stopping self-disclosures; (b) disagreeing, arguing, and making aversive statements; (c) decreasing contact; (d) reevaluating the relationship; (e) increasing attention to others; and (f) terminating the relationship. Taken together, these studies document the nature of scripts for relationship trajectories, and the features of those scripts that are typical among college-aged individuals.

People also have scripts for performing more specific routines that occur within interpersonal relationships. In their most general form, social scripts reflect culturally shared expectations for behavioral sequences that are relevant to a type of interaction and goal. For example, Rose and Frieze (1989; see also Pryor & Merluzzi, 1985) documented typical scripts for behaving on a first date that encompassed (a) preparing for the date, (b) meeting the date, (c) engaging in shared activities, and (d) ending the date. Similarly, Miller (1991) documented scripts for conflict in friendship, which typically included (a) the offended party questioning the friend, (b) the friend apologizing or making excuses, (c) the first party accepting or rejecting the friend's position, and (d) the friends resolving the conflict to some degree. In this body of work, scripts are comprised of the actions that are reported by a sizable subset of study participants; therefore, they are best conceived of as cultural scripts for addressing interaction situations.

At a more idiosyncratic level, individuals develop their own scripts for interaction situations or for interactions with particular partners. For example, Douglas (1984) documented differences between high and low self-monitors in their scripts for initial interactions, such that the scripts of high self-monitors included more goal-related conversation topics and specified more conditional conversation behaviors. Partners within a relationship also jointly develop scripts for recurrent interaction scenarios. For instance, within the cultural norms for sexual behavior that exist (see Baumeister, 2000; Simon & Gagnon, 1986), couples also negotiate their own sexual scripts that identify the appropriate content, sequence, and boundaries of sexual contact (Metts & Spitzberg, 1996). Because relationship-specific scripts reflect the routines that individuals develop for particular situations or the patterns that evolve and are shared between partners, they may exert a particularly strong influence on behavior in close relationships.

The research reviewed in this section reveals the significant advances in the study of social cognition and relationship processes since the early 1980s. The notion of behavioral scripts predates Berger and Roloff's (1982) publication (e.g., Abelson, 1981; Bower, Black, & Turner, 1979; Schank & Abelson, 1977), and was just gaining a foothold in close relationship research at the time of Berger and Roloff's review of the literature. In the time since, however, scripts detailing sequences of behaviors associated with both relationship trajectories, in general, and specific situations within close relationships have been documented. To the extent that these knowledge structures become guideposts for behavior, they exert a profound influence on communication in close relationships.

Approaches to Studying Cognitive Models and Relationships

The study of cognitive models and relationships has its foundation in research on schemas and scripts, in general. Accordingly, the methods employed in this body of work often mirror the procedures used to evaluate the content and structure of human memory. Three main approaches to assessing cognition are apparent in the literature previously reviewed: self-reports of the content of knowledge structures, ratings of features proposed to characterize knowledge structures, and recall of or recognition for information implicated by knowledge structures.

The use of self-report methods is most frequently employed to document the content of cognitive models relevant to close relationships. For example, prototype analysis typically begins with an open-ended solicitation of features or subtypes associated with the focal construct (e.g., Fehr & Russell, 1991). Likewise, identifying the sequences defining relationship trajectories or interaction scripts involves asking study participants to report, in order, the actions that occur to transform a relationship or to accomplish an interaction goal (e.g., Douglas, 1984; Honeycutt et al., 1992; Honeycutt et al., 1989; Miller, 1991; Rose & Frieze, 1989). In all of these cases, the methodology presumes that those features or actions that come easily to mind for participants reflect core content within their relational knowledge structures.

Beyond open-ended self-report, some scholars have asked participants to rate a predetermined list of relationship features or behaviors in a script on dimensions designed to reveal each item's centrality in the knowledge structure. For example, Davis and Todd (1985) asked participants to rate the extent to which relationship features characterized their friendships. Likewise, Miller (1991) asked respondents to report which of three responses they would enact at four stages of conflict in five different conflict scenarios. Similarly, Honeycutt and his colleagues (Honeycutt, 1995; Honeycutt et al., 1992; Honeycutt et al., 1989) verified the structure of procedural knowledge for relationships by soliciting ratings of how typical and how necessary each event was to relationship change. Again, these procedures assume that people's self-reports of beliefs about relationships reflect underlying cognitive structures.

Because the form and content of relational knowledge is expected to influence information processing and recall, a third category of methods has examined recall or recognition memory for schema-relevant or irrelevant details. Planalp (1985) and Smith (1995) evaluated patterns of recalled items, forgotten items, and incorrectly remembered items to reach conclusions about the content of relational schemas. Baldwin (e.g., Baldwin, Fehr, Keedian, Seidel, & Thompson, 1993; Baldwin & Meunier, 1999; Baldwin & Sinclair, 1996) used a lexical decision task to assess the cognitive structure of relationship knowledge; these procedures involve activating a relational schema and then examining response times for recognizing related or unrelated stimuli. In their explication of love as a prototype, Fehr and Russell (1991) examined response times for judging whether an experience (e.g., patriotic love) was a type of love to determine the centrality of subtypes within the love prototype. In contrast to the methods previously discussed, recall and response time measures focus on information retrieval and accessibility to draw inferences about the contents and structure of relational knowledge.

Just as querying the nature of human memory was a dominant theme in the reemergence of social cognition in the 1970s, the application of cognitive principles to close relationships has prioritized clarifying the form of relational knowledge. These points of emphasis no doubt reflect the pervasive impact that information storage systems exert on information processing and behavior. At the same time, research on knowledge structures tells us little about how people gather the information that allows them to access or build those cognitive models. In the following section, we examine the role of cognition as people extract social knowledge from their interpersonal interactions.

COGNITION AND RELATIONAL INFORMATION PROCESSING

Relational information processing encompasses the methods by which people draw inferences about their relationships from messages exchanged during interaction. A long history of research spanning a variety of disciplines has examined the dimensions on which people define their associations with others (Bateson, 1935, 1958; Burgoon & Hale, 1984; Kemper, 1973; Leary, 1957; Rogers & Farace, 1975; White, 1980; Wiggins, 1982). Likewise, a variety of theoretical perspectives have been offered to describe how people generate and use judgments about relationships (e.g., expectancy violations theory, Burgoon & Hale, 1988; discrepancy arousal theory, Cappella & Greene, 1982; a functional perspective on nonverbal messages, Patterson, 1983). Relative to research on relational knowledge structures, the study of relational communication places greater emphasis on the messages communicated between interaction partners, and cognitive processes are often only implied. One exception is relational framing theory (Dillard, Solomon, & Palmer, 1999; Dillard et al., 1996), which positions cognitive processes as essential to drawing relational inferences from ambiguous social cues. To illustrate how social cognition is at the core of relational communication processes, we review the claims advanced by relational framing theory. Then, we discuss the methods employed in this body of work.

Relational Framing Theory

As noted previously, a wealth of research has attended to the substance of relational communication. With remarkable consistency, these efforts have identified elements of dominance or power, liking or affiliation, and intensity or engagement as central to conceptions of the social domain. Although more nuanced distinctions have been validated (Burgoon & Hale, 1987; Hale, Lundy, & Mongeau, 1989), these gradations align with the broader characterizations of relationship dimensions (Dillard et al., 1999). Of course, social cues themselves are often ambiguous. Even a message as explicit as a profession of love has different connotations depending on the relational context (family members or romantic partners), the relational history (a new romance or an established partnership), and aspects of the situation (over a romantic dinner or as a prelude to separation). Relational framing theory draws on thinking about the fundamental dimensions of social relationships to explain how people use social cues to support conclusions about their relationships.

A central assumption of relational framing theory is that interactions tend to be framed in terms of either dominance–submission or affiliation–disaffiliation (Dillard et al., 1999; Dillard et al., 1996). *Relational frames,* defined as mental structures consisting of organized knowledge about social relationships, simplify the problem of interpreting social reality by directing attention to particular behaviors, resolving ambiguities, and guiding inferences. Because many behaviors and messages may convey either dominance or affiliation information, effective processing requires that cues activate one relational frame and inhibit the competing interpretive frame. In other words, the theory suggests that dominance–submission and affiliation–disaffiliation frames displace each other as a necessary part of comprehending otherwise ambiguous relational cues.

Relational framing theory characterizes frame activation as dependent on a variety of situational parameters (Mundinger, 2001; Solomon, Dillard, & Anderson, 2002; Tusing, Dillard, & Morrill, 2001). Certainly, specific utterances ("I'm in charge here" or "I hate you") can signal the relevance of either the dominance–submission or affiliation–disaffiliation frame. In addition, the type of interaction episode (Dillard et al., 1999; Dillard et al., 1996), the prior relationship between participants (Mundinger, 2001), individual differences (Solomon et al., 2002; Tusing, 2000), and social norms (Tusing et al., 2001) are assumed to inform relational frame activation. The integration of these sources of information results in a cognitive set that privileges interpretations of messages in terms of the most relevant relational frame. In the meantime, the alternative frame is relegated to the background, from which it can be easily retrieved as warranted by changing circumstances. In this sense, relational framing theory characterizes dominance–submission and affiliation–disaffiliation as mutually inhibitory, but not mutually exclusive frameworks for processing social interaction (Lannutti & Monahan, 2002; Tusing, 2000).

We previously noted a third dimension of relational communication emerging from prior research: *involvement* or the intensity of engagement in an interaction. Although relational framing theory suggests that all social cues are understood in terms of dominance–submission and affiliation–disaffiliation, the role of relational frames is most apparent when social cues are polysemic. Because involvement has no experiential content, it can inform judgments of either dominance or affiliation. More specifically, relational framing theory specifies that the active relational frame gives meaning to content-free involvement cues. In this manner, involvement contributes to the perceived intensity of either affiliation or dominance, depending on the salient relational frame.

To clarify how cognitive structures and interaction cues work in tandem to support relational inferences, consider the process by which people comprehend letters, words, and sentences in written form (e.g., van Dijk & Kintsch, 1983). Of course, the marks on a page are essential inputs into discourse processing. At the same time, the top-down application of syntactic and semantic rules facilitates people's ability to recognize letters and words. As readers progress through a text, they formulate a mental model of the discourse, which not only directs their attention to relevant interpretations of a passage, but also suppresses alternative meanings. Thus, people rely on both existing knowledge and developing expectations to decode written discourse. In an analogous fashion, relational information processing occurs when individuals observe cues within interaction, and they interpret those cues through the lens of their existing knowledge.

As this review makes clear, social cognition and communication are interwoven in relational information processing. The activation or suppression of cognitive structures provides the context in which interaction behaviors become meaningful. In turn, communicated messages are among the cues that activate the relational frames through which subsequent messages are viewed. Over the course of an interaction, the top-down structure provided by cognitive structures brings order to the somewhat unpredictable, ambiguous, and fast-paced course of interaction. In this sense, social cognition provides the steadying beat that grounds the rapid melodies of interpersonal interaction.

Approaches to Studying Social Cognition and Relational Information Processing

As noted at the opening of this section, cognition has taken a back seat to an analysis of relational messages in research on relational communication. As a result, the methods for assessing relational judgments have become increasingly sophisticated, whereas the measurement of cognitive structures and processes remains rather simple. Self-report scales on which participants and observers report relational judgments have been developed, validated, and subjected to meticulous measurement analysis (Burgoon & Hale, 1987; Dillard et al., 1999). In addition, experimental paradigms and interaction studies designed to manipulate and parse relational messages have been crafted (e.g., Burgoon, 1991; Burgoon & Buller, 1994; Walther & Burgoon, 1992). Conversely, the cognitive structures or processes assumed to participate in relational information processing have been operationalized in largely unsophisticated ways.

The general procedures employed in tests of relational framing theory require participants to consider a variety of interaction scenarios and to rate the relevance of concepts associated with dominance–submission and affiliation–disaffiliation to making sense of those episodes (see Dillard & Solomon, 2005, for details). The procedures commence with an example designed to clarify the difference between relevance judgments and evaluations of the amount of dominance, submission, affiliation, or disaffiliation that is communicated. Then, participants are instructed to rate the relevance of each of a series of word pairs to interaction scenarios. In the first use of this measure (Dillard et al., 1996), the items assessing activation of the dominance–submission frame were dominance–submission, persuade–concede, influence–comply, and controlling–yielding; the affiliation–disaffiliation scales were affection–disaffection, liking–disliking, attraction–aversion, and positive regard–negative regard. In every case, judgments are made on a 5-point scale ranging from 1 (*completely irrelevant*) to 5 (*completely relevant*). Although these scales have demonstrated reliability and are distinct from judgments of relational qualities themselves (Tusing, 2000), self-report scales remain at best an indirect measure of cognitive activation.

The cognitive processes posited by relational framing theory largely complement the roles ascribed to prototypes, schemas, and scripts that we reviewed previously in this chapter. In both cases, existing cognitive structures are assumed to guide people's communication within specific interaction episodes. Shifting the focus to relational information processing, however, highlights more fluid aspects of social cognition. In particular, relational framing theory characterizes cognitive structures as shifting with the dynamics of interaction, while imparting meaning to relational messages. In the following section, we examine programs of research that focus directly on the interplay of cognitive states and interaction in close relationships.

COGNITION AND INTERACTION IN RELATIONSHIPS

Thus far in this chapter, we have examined the cognitive structures or mechanisms that organize the relational implications of interpersonal communication. We now shift attention to research on the intersection of specific cognitive states and interaction in close relationships. In doing so, we demonstrate (a) how characteristics of close relationships produce cognitive states that shape communication, and (b) how communication influences cognition in ways that have implications for close relationships. We conclude this section of the chapter with a discussion of the methods employed in these pursuits.

Relationship Qualities, Cognition, and Communication

Fletcher and Kininmonth (1991) suggested that partners "attitudes, expectations, or other cognitions existing prior to an interaction episode are related in a fundamental way to broader relationship processes" (p. 238). Put differently, a variety of relationship qualities have implications for cognitive states that are immediately relevant to interactions with a relationship partner. Of course, a myriad of individual characteristics or states are germane to communication (e.g., self-esteem, anxiety). Moreover, other chapters in this volume reveal a variety of cognitive phenomena that influence communication behavior (e.g., goals, plans, attitude accessibility). Within the context of close relationships, we see increasingly sophisticated models linking relationship characteristics to cognitive states and, in turn, to communication experiences (Bradbury & Fincham, 1991; Solomon & Knobloch, 2004). As two examples, research on relational instability and satisfaction illustrate how relationship qualities affect cognition in ways that shape communication in close associations.

The path of relationship development and maintenance is marked by fluctuating levels of intimacy and involvement, and these periods correspond with efforts to make sense of relationships. Solomon and Knobloch (2001, 2004) reasoned that the transition from casual to serious dating corresponds with heightened levels of uncertainty about involvement in the relationship. Consistent with that model, Knobloch and Solomon (2002) observed that hypothetical uncertainty-provoking events prompted more doubts about the relationship among individuals at moderate levels of intimacy in dating relationships. Moreover, Fletcher, Fincham, Cramer, and Heron (1987) found that conscious cognitive activity is greater when (a) involvement in the relationship is increasing or decreasing, (b) relationships are of shorter duration, (c) relationships are perceived as unstable, (d) partners are separating, or (e) commitment to the relationship is increasing. In addition, Surra and Bohman (1991) reported that cognitive processing during periods of instability is characterized by three goals: (a) to obtain information about the partner, (b) to identify characteristics of the relationship and evaluate interpersonal qualities and abilities, and (c) to explain partners' behaviors and the occurrence of relationship-relevant events. Taken together, these efforts suggest that periods of instability or transition spark unique cognitive states for relationship participants.

Empirical evidence indicates that the cognitive outcomes of relational instability influence communication in close relationships. Knobloch and Solomon (2003b) found that uncertainty-increasing events are more likely than certainty-increasing events to elicit communication behaviors marked by distance, distributiveness, and avoidance. Likewise, doubts about relationship involvement correspond with more topic avoidance (Afifi & Burgoon, 1998; Knobloch & Carpenter-Theune, 2004; Knobloch & Solomon, 2002) and less direct communication about relational irritations (Theiss & Solomon, in press). Knobloch and Solomon (2005) also found that relational uncertainty compromises people's ability to draw strong inferences about their relationship from interactions with partners. Thus, the cognitive outcomes of relational instability or change, in this case relational uncertainty, are manifest in communication within close relationships.

The role of cognition in linking relationship qualities to communication outcomes is also demonstrated in the substantial body of research on attribution in close relationships. The association between relationship satisfaction and attributions is well documented (e.g., Bradbury & Fincham, 1990). In a satisfying relationship, a partner's positive behaviors are attributed to internal and stable causes, and his or her negative behaviors are explained in terms of external and unstable causes. Conversely, people who are dissatisfied with their relationship locate a partner's positive behaviors in external and unstable causes, whereas negative behaviors are attributed to internal and stable causes. Not surprisingly, longitudinal studies have shown that these patterns of adaptive and maladaptive attributions lead to the perpetuation of relationship satisfaction or dissatisfaction over time (Fincham & Bradbury, 1987, 1993; Karney & Bradbury, 2000).

As was the case in our example of relational instability, research clearly indicates that the cognitive outcomes of relationship satisfaction are manifest in communication between partners. An extensive body of research demonstrates the impact of attributions on communication behavior in relationships (for reviews, see Fincham & Bradbury, 1991; Manusov & Harvey, 2001). For example, Bradbury and Fincham (1992) found that maladaptive attributions in marriage are associated with less effective problem-solving behaviors, more negative behaviors, and a greater tendency to reciprocate negative behaviors during interaction. Similarly, Miller and Bradbury (1995) reported that wives who make maladaptive attributions are less integrative, more negative, and more likely to reciprocate their husband's negative behaviors; husbands who make maladaptive attributions are more likely to behave negatively in response to wife's neutral behaviors. Coupled with evidence linking relationship satisfaction and attributions, findings such as these clarify how relational qualities influence cognitions in ways that shape communication in close relationships.

Research on social cognition in the last two decades has documented a wide range of cognitive phenomena that are relevant to communication behavior. Within the domain of close relationships, these efforts have emphasized cognitive states that arise from relationship circumstances and affect interactions with partners in important ways. Our review of research on the cognitive and communicative consequences of relational instability and satisfaction illustrate the advances made on this front. In the following section, we examine the complementary process by which communication influences cognitive outcomes in relationships.

The Cognitive Consequences of Communication in Close Relationships

Interaction imposes demands on cognition as communicators interpret ambiguous verbal and nonverbal signals, integrate multiple or conflicting pieces of information, plan and adapt to complex behavioral sequences, reconcile conflicting goals, and respond in real time (Kellerman, 1992; Waldron & Cegala, 1992). In turn, the cognitive outcomes of interaction are influenced by the inherent properties and requirements of the communication process (Sillars, Roberts, Dun, & Leonard, 2001). Others in this volume address the effect of communication on cognition during interpersonal interactions (e.g., Berger, chap. 3, this volume); these consequences take on heightened importance in the context of close relationships. Recent work by Sillars and his colleagues (Sillars, 1998; Sillars et al., 2001; Sillars, Roberts, Leonard, & Dun, 2000) exemplifies contemporary developments in research on the cognitive consequences of communication in close relationships.

Sillars (1998) advanced the somewhat counterintuitive claim that properties of communication in close relationships might render intimate associations more vulnerable to misunderstanding than less intimate alliances. Sillars argued that although familiarity in close relationships might promote greater understanding, familiarity also breeds greater subjectivity, emotionality, and opportunity for selective recall (see also Sillars & Scott, 1983). Sillars also noted that communication's intrinsic ambiguity is not ameliorated by intimacy; in fact, close relationship partners may be more likely to tackle abstract and ambiguous relational topics with misplaced confidence in the accuracy of their perceptions. In addition, Sillars highlighted how people can draw selectively from a close relationship's rich history to construct narratives that cast themselves in a positive or persuasive light. When these circumstances of intimacy coincide with the demands of interaction, the cognitive consequences are nontrivial.

Although any interaction with a close relationship partner is subject to the biasing forces outlined by Sillars (1998), he emphasized how the demands of conflict interactions tax information processing in critical ways. In his view, "relationship conflicts are often one-sided affairs, in which the parties neither participate in the same issues nor observe the same sequence of events" (p. 89). Empirical evidence supports this pessimistic view of cognition during conflict in close relationships. For example, Sillars et al. (2000) found that thoughts during conflict interactions were limited in complexity, concerned predominantly with relationship issues or the communication process, and rarely reflected perspective taking. Likewise, Sillars et al. (2001) found that 58% of thoughts following conflict interactions were either evaluations of partner, self, or relationship, or inferences about interaction goals and strategies. Moreover, the majority of person appraisals that occur during conflict interactions are negatively valenced thoughts about the partner (Sillars et al., 2001; Sillars et al., 2000).

Sillars and his colleagues are not alone in their conclusion that conversation poses cognitive demands that can undermine comprehension. Nonetheless, their work brings to light the importance of the relationship as the context for communication and cognition. This line of inquiry emphasizes the additional constraints and demands introduced by a history of shared experiences, presumed insight, and an investment in shaping the relationship narrative. Coupled with evidence that cognitions during problem-solving interactions correspond with relational distress (Halford & Sanders, 1988; Sillars et al., 2000), these findings highlight how communication in close relationships produces cognitive outcomes of consequence for partners.

Approaches to Studying Cognition and Interaction in Relationships

The research reviewed in this section highlights the methodological techniques that have been used to assess the interplay of cognition and interaction. Research on the impact of cognition on communication must begin by measuring or stimulating various cognitive states that are believed to influence interaction. Conversely, studying the effect of communication on cognitive processes employs interaction as the starting point, and measures cognitions evoked by the episode. We discuss these approaches in turn.

Studies focused on the impact of cognition on communication typically begin with self-report measures to assess the relationship characteristics considered relevant to cognitive states (e.g., Miller & Bradbury, 1995; Surra & Bohman, 1991). Likewise, self-report measures are used to index the cognitive phenomena that link relationship qualities to communication behaviors. In fact, the conceptualization and measurement of both relational uncertainty (Knobloch & Solomon, 1999) and relational attributions (Fincham & Bradbury, 1992) have been subjected to careful scrutiny. Finally, these studies include procedures to instantiate communication. In some cases, participants are asked to engage in a videotaped interaction with their relationship partner (e.g., Miller & Bradbury, 1995). Alternatively, participants are asked to recall or imagine a communication situation and to characterize their actual or probable interaction behaviors on self-report scales (e.g., Knobloch & Solomon, 2002, 2003b). Although some exceptions are noted, our review highlighted the prominence of self-report measures to index relationship qualities, cognitions, and communication within this body of work.

Research examining the impact of communication on cognition also relies heavily on self-report to operationalize cognition; however, procedures are designed to ground these accounts within the dynamics of interaction. One method that has become increasingly popular is the use of video-assisted recall (Ickes & Tooke, 1988; Waldron & Cegala, 1992). As a first step, participants engage in a conversation with their partner that is typically focused on a point of disagreement within their relationship. Then, individuals review a videotape of the interaction and report on the thoughts they recall having at various points throughout the exchange. In this way, self-reports of cognitions are tied to very recent communication experiences and aided by the cues provided in the video. As a final step, the self-reported thoughts are coded into categories based on their content (e.g., Sillars, Dun, & Roberts, 1999).

The body of research on the associations between cognition and communication is somewhat more diffuse than work defining the domains previously discussed. To demonstrate how social cognition has informed the study of close relationships, we focused our discussion in this section on cognitive states that arise from relationship characteristics and communication episodes that are unique to intimate partners. Although our review is by no means exhaustive, it reveals the integration of social cognition into models of intimate relating that is characteristic of current research.

FUTURE DIRECTIONS FOR RESEARCH ON SOCIAL COGNITION IN RELATIONSHIPS

Throughout this chapter, we have seen the substantial and focused attention afforded questions about the form of cognitive models of close relationships. In considering the processes by which conclusions about relationships are extracted from conversation, we showcased one recent perspective on relational information processing. Finally, we examined research on the cognitive antecedents and consequences of communication in close relationships. Although these lines of inquiry represent important advances over the last 20 years, their limitations reveal several avenues for the future. Thus, we conclude this chapter by identifying directions for research on social cognition and communication in relationships.

First and foremost, we see a need for research methods that do justice to the cognitive structures or processes implicated in communication between relationship partners. Our discussions of the procedures typically employed to study cognitive models of relationships, relational information processing, and cognition as it relates to interaction within close relationships consistently highlighted the predominance of self-report instruments in this literature. Certainly, cognitive phenomena such as relational uncertainty and attributions may be accessible only by asking participants to report their states, perceptions, or thoughts. Of greater concern is the use of self-reported information to draw inferences about cognitive processes that are inaccessible to respondents (Nisbett & Wilson, 1977).

What alternatives do we see on the horizon? Within the body of work on relationship prototypes and schemas, we noted examples of indirect methods for diagnosing cognitive phenomena that circumvent the problems of self-report data. For example, reaction time studies that index patterns of concept activation can reveal both the structure of cognitive stores and the activation of particular states. Accordingly, these procedures could provide an important test of the accessibility of the information processing frames that figure so prominently within relational framing theory. Similarly, methods that involve the subliminal priming of concepts (e.g., Ratcliff & McKoon, 1981) might be fruitfully applied in efforts to link cognitive states to communication behavior. To the extent that future efforts position social cognition as integral to communication in close relationships, we anticipate the adoption of increasingly sophisticated measures of cognitive processes.

Within the body of work on cognitive models of relationships, the dominant focus on relationship types or cultural scripts, in general, constitutes an important limitation. Although Planalp (1985) conceptualized relational schemas as applicable to the wealth of knowledge people have about particular interpersonal associations, the call to document the nature and operation of relationship-specific knowledge stores has largely been ignored (but see Ostrom, Pryor, & Simpson, 1981). Mapping an individual's schema for a particular relationship and then observing how that schema interacts with communication experiences would seem to defy a social scientific focus on patterns that transcend individuals. Nonetheless, progress toward understanding how people store, access, and revise information about their own particular relationships is the next step in clarifying how cognitive models of relationships influence people's interpersonal communication and relationship experiences.

Within the domain of relational information processing, we saw theorizing about the operation of cognitive systems that far outstripped the methods used to assess cognition. Thus, the need to develop alternative measures of cognition noted previously is a high priority for research on this topic. More generally, research on relational communication has emphasized the content of relational messages largely to the exclusion of questions about the processes by which relational judgments are made. The assumption that interpersonal interaction functions to define the relationship between participants is a long-standing claim within the communication discipline (Watzlawick, Beavin, & Jackson, 1967); more than 35 years later we still know very little about how people extract relational information from their conversations with others. Relational framing theory and research on the conditions under which relational judgments may be compromised (Knobloch & Solomon, 2005) are promising signs of developments in this arena, and we look forward to future efforts to disentangle the link between interpersonal communication and conceptions of relationships (e.g., Knobloch & Solomon, 2003a).

The variety of cognitive antecedents and consequences discussed in our review of communication in close relationships highlights a need to integrate different conceptions of cognition in future work on this topic. We drew from diverse research programs to illustrate the interplay of cognition and communication in close relationships. As a result, we noted conceptions of cognition ranging from specific thoughts during interaction (e.g., Sillars et al., 2001; Sillars et al., 2000) to confidence in one's knowledge about relationship involvement (Knobloch & Solomon, 1999). Moreover, the cognitive phenomena emphasized as antecedent to communication behavior were often of a different order than the cognitive responses examined as communication outcomes. Cognition can be characterized in terms of the amount of cognitive activity, the contents of short- and long-term information stores, the processes that act on inputs, the organization of information, and an individual's style or way of thinking (Cloven, 1992). As models of interaction that position cognition as the context for interaction continue to gain ground (e.g., Bradbury & Fincham, 1991; Sillars, 1998), we call for research that brings together different facets of cognitive inputs and outputs within interpersonal episodes.

Our mission in this chapter was to illuminate prominent themes in contemporary research on cognition and communication within interpersonal relationships. In doing so, we drew on distinct areas of research representing a focus on cognitive models of relationships, relational information processing, and the interplay of cognition and interaction within intimate associations. As our final call for future research, we note the need to assimilate these levels of analysis. Certainly, cognitive models such as prototypes and schemas inform relational information processing (e.g., Planalp, 1985); nonetheless, further research is needed to reveal the processes by which knowledge about relationships is used to make sense of the relational implications of interaction episodes. Correspondingly, we see a need for perspectives on relational information processing to clarify how cognitive models of relationships participate in the activation of relational frames and the development of relational judgments. Finally, both conceptions of relational knowledge and relational information processing need to be informed by what we know about the dynamics of interaction. Social cognition encompasses the relatively static information stores that organize knowledge about communication and relationships, the mechanisms by which people process messages and their relational implications, and the states and thoughts that are proximal to interaction. The foundation laid by Roloff and Berger (1982) has come to fruition in the advances made in each of these areas. As we look forward to the next 20 years, we encourage researchers to begin weaving these threads together in the study of cognition, communication, and close relationships.

REFERENCES

Abelson, R. P. (1981). Psychological status of the script concept. *American Psychologist, 36,* 715–729.

Afifi, W. A., & Burgoon, J. K. (1998). "We never talk about that": A comparison of cross-sex friendships and dating relationships on uncertainty and topic avoidance. *Personal Relationships, 5,* 255–272.

Baldwin, M. W. (1992). Relational schemas and the processing of social information. *Psychological Bulletin, 112,* 461–484.

Baldwin, M. W. (1994). Primed relational schemas as a source of self-evaluative reactions. *Journal of Social and Clinical Psychology, 13,* 380–403.

Baldwin, M. W. (1997). Relational schemas as a source of if–then self-inference procedures. *Review of General Psychology, 1,* 326–335.

Baldwin, M. W., Carrell, S. E., & Lopez, D. F. (1990). Priming relationship schemas: My advisor and the pope are watching me from the back of my mind. *Journal of Experimental Social Psychology, 26,* 435–454.

Baldwin, M. W., Fehr, B., Keedian, E., Seidel, M., & Thompson, D. W. (1993). An exploration of the relational schemata underlying attachment styles: Self-report and lexical decision approaches. *Personality and Social Psychology Bulletin, 19,* 746–754.

Baldwin, M. W., & Holmes, J. G. (1987). Salient private audiences and awareness of the self. *Journal of Personality and Social Psychology, 52,* 1087–1098.

Baldwin, M. W., & Meunier, J. (1999). The cued activation of attachment relational schemas. *Social Cognition, 17,* 209–227.

Baldwin, M. W., & Sinclair, L. (1996). Self-esteem and "if ... then" contingencies of interpersonal acceptance. *Journal of Personality and Social Psychology, 71,* 1130–1141.

Bateson, G. (1935). Culture and contact with schismogenesis. *Man, 35,* 178–183.

Bateson, G. (1958). *Naven* (2nd ed.). Stanford, CA: Stanford University Press.

Baumeister, R. F. (2000). Gender differences in erotic plasticity: The female sex drive as socially flexible and responsive. *Psychological Bulletin, 126,* 347–374.

Baxter, L. A. (1987). Cognition and communication in the relationship process. In R. Barnett, P. McGhee, & D. Clarke (Eds.), *Accounting for relationships* (pp. 192–212). London: Methuen.

Berger, C. R., & Roloff, M. E. (1982). Thinking about friends and lovers: Social cognition and relational trajectories. In M. E. Roloff & C. R. Berger (Eds.), *Social cognition and communication* (pp. 151–192). Beverly Hills, CA: Sage.

Bower, G. H., Black, J. B., & Turner, T. J. (1979). Scripts in memory for text. *Cognitive Psychology, 11,* 177–220.

Bradbury, T. N., & Fincham, F. D. (1990). Attributions in marriage: A review and critique. *Psychological Bulletin, 107,* 3–33.

Bradbury, T. N., & Fincham, F. D. (1991). A contextual model for advancing the study of marital interaction. In G. J. O. Fletcher & F. D. Fincham (Eds.), *Cognition in close relationships* (pp. 127–147). Hillsdale, NJ: Lawrence Erlbaum Associates.

Bradbury, T. N., & Fincham, F. D. (1992). Attributions and behavior in marital interaction. *Journal of Personality and Social Psychology, 63,* 613–628.

Burgoon, J. K. (1991). Relational message interpretations of touch, conversational distance, and posture. *Journal of Nonverbal Behavior, 15,* 233–259.

Burgoon, J. K., & Buller, D. B. (1994). Interpersonal deception: III. Effects of deceit on perceived communication and nonverbal behavior dynamics. *Journal of Nonverbal Behavior, 18,* 155–184.

Burgoon, J. K., & Hale, J. L. (1984). The fundamental topoi of relational communication. *Communication Monographs, 51,* 193–214.

Burgoon, J. K., & Hale, J. L. (1987). Validation and measurement of the fundamental themes of relational communication. *Communication Monographs, 54,* 19–41.

Burgoon, J. K., & Hale, J. (1988). Nonverbal expectancy violations: Model elaboration and application to immediacy behaviors. *Communication Monographs, 55,* 58–79.

Cantor, N., & Mischel, W. (1977). Traits as prototypes: Effects on recognition memory. *Journal of Personality and Social Psychology, 35,* 28–48.

Cantor, N., & Mischel, W. (1979). Prototypicality and personality: Effects on free recall and personality impressions. *Journal of Research in Personality, 13,* 187–205.

Cantor, N., Mischel, W., & Schwartz, J. (1982). Social knowledge: Structure, content, use, and abuse. In A. H. Hastorf & A. M. Isen (Eds.), *Cognitive social psychology* (pp. 35–68). New York: Elsevier/North Holland.

Cappella, J. N., & Greene, J. O. (1982). A discrepancy-arousal explanation of mutual influence in expressive behavior for adult and infant–adult interaction. *Communication Monographs, 45,* 89–114.

Cloven, D. H. (1992, April). *Verbalization measures of cognitive phenomena.* Paper presented at the annual meeting of the Central States Speech Communication Association, Cleveland, OH.

Davis, K. E., & Todd, M. J. (1985). Assessing friendship: Prototypes, paradigm cases and relationship description. In S. Duck & D. Perlman (Eds.), *Understanding personal relationships* (pp. 17–37). Beverly Hills, CA: Sage.

Dillard, J. P., & Solomon, D. H. (2005). Measuring the relevance of relational frames: A relational framing theory perspective. In V. Manusov (Ed.), *The sourcebook of nonverbal measures: Going beyond words* (pp. 325–334). Mahwah, NJ: Lawrence Erlbaum Associates.

Dillard, J. P., Solomon, D. H., & Palmer, M. T. (1999). Structuring the concept of relational communication. *Communication Monographs, 66,* 49–65.

Dillard, J. P., Solomon, D. H., & Samp, J. A. (1996). Framing social reality: The relevance of relational judgments. *Communication Research, 23,* 703–723.

Douglas, W. (1984). Initial interaction scripts: When knowing is behaving. *Human Communication Research, 11,* 203–219.

Duck, S. W. (1995). Talking relationships into being. *Journal of Social and Personal Relationships, 12,* 535–540.

Fehr, B. (1988). Prototype analysis of the concepts of love and commitment. *Journal of Personality and Social Psychology, 55,* 557–579.

Fehr, B. (1993). How do I love thee? Let me consult my prototype. In S. Duck (Ed.), *Individuals in relationships* (pp. 87–120). Newbury Park, CA: Sage.

Fehr, B., & Russell, J. A. (1991). The concept of love viewed from a prototype perspective. *Journal of Personality and Social Psychology, 3,* 425–438.

Fincham, F. D., & Bradbury, T. N. (1987). The impact of attributions in marriage: A longitudinal analysis. *Journal of Personality and Social Psychology, 53,* 510–517.

Fincham, F. D., & Bradbury, T. N. (1991). Cognition in marriage: A program of research on attributions. In W. H. Jones & D. Perlman (Eds.), *Advances in personal relationships* (Vol. 2, pp. 159–203). Oxford, UK: Jessica Kingsley.

Fincham, F. D., & Bradbury, T. N. (1992). Assessing attributions in marriage: The relationship attribution measure. *Journal of Personality and Social Psychology, 62,* 457–468.

Fincham, F. D., & Bradbury, T. N. (1993). Marital satisfaction, depression, and attributions: A longitudinal analysis. *Journal of Personality and Social Psychology, 64,* 442–452.

Fiske, S. T., & Linville, P. W. (1980). What does the schema concept buy us? *Personality and Social Psychology Bulletin, 6,* 543–557.

Fletcher, G. J. O., Fincham, F., Cramer, L., & Heron, N. (1987). The role of attributions in close relationships. *Journal of Personality and Social Psychology, 53,* 481–489.

Fletcher, G. J. O, & Kininmonth, L. (1991). Interaction in close relationships and social cognition. In G. J. O. Fletcher & F. D. Fincham (Eds.), *Cognition in close relationships* (pp. 235–255). Hillsdale, NJ: Lawrence Erlbaum Associates.

Hale, J. L., Lundy, J. C., & Mongeau, P. A. (1989). Perceived relational intimacy and relational message content. *Communication Research Reports, 6,* 94–99.

Halford, W. K., & Sanders, M. R. (1988). Assessment of cognitive self-statements during marital problem solving: A comparison of two methods. *Cognitive Therapy and Research, 12,* 515–530.

Holmes, J. G. (2000). Social relationships: The nature and function of relational schemas. *European Journal of Social Psychology, 30,* 447–495.

Honeycutt, J. M. (1995). Predicting beliefs about relational trajectories as a consequence of typicality and necessity ratings of relationship behaviors. *Communication Research Reports, 12,* 3–14.

Honeycutt, J. M., & Cantrill, J. G. (2001). *Cognition, communication, and romantic relationships.* Mahwah, NJ: Lawrence Erlbaum Associates.

Honeycutt, J. M., Cantrill, J. G., & Allen, T. (1992). Memory structures for relational decay: A cognitive test of sequencing of de-escalating actions and stages. *Human Communication Research, 18,* 528–562.

Honeycutt, J. M., Cantrill, J. G., & Greene, R. W. (1989). Memory structures for relational escalation: A cognitive test of the sequencing of relational actions and stages. *Human Communication Research, 16,* 62–90.

Ickes, W., & Tooke, W. (1988). The observational method: Studying the interaction of minds and bodies. In S. Duck, D. Hay, S. Hobfoll, W. Ickes, & B. Montgomery (Eds.), *The handbook of personal relationships: Theory, research, and interventions* (pp. 79–97). Chichester, UK: Wiley.

Karney, B. R., & Bradbury, T. N. (2000). Attributions in marriage: State or trait? A growth curve analysis. *Journal of Personality and Social Psychology, 78,* 295–309.

Kellerman, K. (1992). Communication: Inherently strategic and primarily automatic. *Communication Monographs, 59,* 288–301.

Kemper, T. D. (1973). The fundamental dimensions of social relationship: A theoretical statement. *Acta Sociologica, 16,* 41–58.

Knobloch, L. K., & Carpenter-Theune, K. E. (2004). Topic avoidance within developing romantic relationships: Associations with intimacy and relational uncertainty. *Communication Research, 31,* 173–205.

Knobloch, L. K., & Solomon, D. H (1999). Measuring the sources and content of relational uncertainty. *Communication Studies, 50,* 261–278.

Knobloch, L. K., & Solomon, D. H. (2002). Intimacy and the magnitude and experience of episodic relational uncertainty within romantic relationships. *Personal Relationships, 9,* 457–478.

Knobloch, L. K., & Solomon, D. H. (2003a). Manifestations of relationship conceptualizations in conversation. *Human Communication Research, 29,* 482–515.

Knobloch, L. K., & Solomon, D. H. (2003b). Responses to changes in relational uncertainty within dating relationships: Emotions and communication strategies. *Communication Studies, 54,* 282–306.

Knobloch, L. K., & Solomon, D. H. (2005). Relational uncertainty and relational information processing: Questions without answers? *Communication Research, 32,* 349–388.

Lannutti, P. J., & Monahan, J. L. (2002). When the frame paints the picture: Alcohol consumption, relational framing, and sexual communication. *Communication Research, 29,* 390–421.

Leary, T. (1957). *Interpersonal diagnosis of personality.* New York: Ronald Press.

Manusov, V., & Harvey, J. H. (2001). *Attribution, communication behavior, and close relationships.* New York: Cambridge University Press.

Markus, H., & Zajonc, R. B. (1985). The cognitive perspective in social psychology. In G. Lindzey & E. Aronson (Eds.), *The handbook of social psychology* (Vol. 1, pp. 137–230). New York: Random House.

Metts, S., & Spitzberg, B. H. (1996). Sexual communication in interpersonal contexts: A script-based approach. In B. R. Burleson (Ed.), *Communication yearbook 19* (pp. 49–91). Thousand Oaks, CA: Sage.

Miller, G. E., & Bradbury, T. N. (1995). Refining the association between attributions and behavior in marital interaction. *Journal of Family Psychology, 9,* 196–208.

Miller, J. B. (1991). Women's and men's scripts for interpersonal conflict. *Psychology of Women Quarterly, 15,* 15–29.

Mundinger, E. L. (2001). *Applying relational framing theory to perceptions of psychological abuse in dating relationships.* Unpublished master's thesis, University of Wisconsin, Madison, WI.

Nisbett, R. E., & Wilson, T. D. (1977). Telling more than we can know: Verbal reports on mental processes. *Psychological Review, 84,* 231–259.

Ostrom, T. M., Pryor, J. B., & Simpson, D. D. (1981). The organization of social information. In E. T. Higgins, C. P. Herman, & M. P. Zanna (Eds.), *Social cognition: The Ontario symposium* (Vol. 1, pp. 3–38). Hillsdale, NJ: Lawrence Erlbaum Associates.

Park, B. (1986). A method for studying the development of impressions of real people. *Journal of Personality and Social Psychology, 51,* 907–917.

Patterson, M. L. (1983). *Nonverbal behavior: A functional perspective.* New York: Springer-Verlag.

Pierce, T., & Lydon, J. (1998). Priming relational schemas: Effects of contextually activated and chronically accessible interpersonal expectations on responses to a stressful event. *Journal of Personality and Social Psychology, 75,* 1441–1448.

Planalp, S. (1985). Relational schemata: A test of knowledge as guides to communication. *Human Communication Research, 12,* 3–29.

Pryor, J. B., & Merluzzi, T. V. (1985). The role of expertise in processing social interaction scripts. *Journal of Experimental Social Psychology, 21,* 362–379.

Ratcliff, R., & McKoon, G. (1981). Automatic and strategic priming in recognition. *Journal of Verbal Learning and Verbal Behavior, 20,* 201–215.

Rogers, L. E., & Farace, R. V. (1975). Analysis of relational communication in dyads: New measurement procedures. *Human Communication Research, 1,* 222–239.

Roloff, M. E., & Berger, C. R. (1982). *Social cognition and communication.* Beverly Hills, CA: Sage.

Rose, S., & Frieze, I. H. (1989). Young singles' scripts for a first date. *Gender and Society, 3,* 258–268.

Rumelhart, D. E. (1984). Schemata and the cognitive system. In R. S. Wyer & T. K. Srull (Eds.), *Handbook of social cognition* (pp. 161–186). Hillsdale, NJ: Lawrence Erlbaum Associates.

Schank, R., & Abelson, R. (1977). *Scripts, plans, goals, and understanding: An inquiry into human knowledge structures.* Hillsdale, NJ: Lawrence Erlbaum Associates.

Shaver, K. R., Schwartz, J., Kirson, D., & O'Connor, C. (1987). Emotion knowledge: Further exploration of a prototype approach. *Journal of Personality and Social Psychology, 52,* 1061–1086.

Sillars, A. (1998). (Mis)Understanding. In B. H. Spitzberg & W. R. Cupach (Eds.), *The dark side of close relationships* (pp. 73–102). Mahwah, NJ: Lawrence Erlbaum Associates.

Sillars, A., Dun, T., & Roberts, L. J. (1999). *Interaction cognition coding scheme.* Unpublished manuscript, University of Montana, Missoula.

Sillars, A., Roberts, L. J., Dun, T., Leonard, K. (2001). Stepping into the stream of thought: Cognition during marital conflict. In V. Manusov & J. Harvey (Eds.), *Attribution, communication behavior, and close relationships* (pp. 193–210). New York: Cambridge University Press.

Sillars, A., Roberts, L. J., Leonard, K. E., & Dun, T. (2000). Cognition during marital conflict: The relationship of thought and talk. *Journal of Social and Personal Relationships, 17,* 479–502.

Sillars, A., & Scott, M. D. (1983). Interpersonal perception between intimates: An integrative review. *Human Communication Research, 10,* 153–176.

Simon, W., & Gagnon, J. H. (1986). Sexual scripts: Permanence and change. *Archives of Sexual Behavior, 15,* 97–120.

Skinner, B. F. (1953). *Science and human behavior.* New York: Macmillan.

Smith, S. W. (1995). Perceptual processing of nonverbal-relational messages. In D. E. Hewes (Ed.), *The cognitive bases of interpersonal communication* (pp. 87–112). Hillsdale, NJ: Lawrence Erlbaum Associates.

Solomon, D. H., Dillard, J. P., & Anderson, J. W. (2002). Episode type, attachment orientation, and frame salience: Evidence for a theory of relational framing. *Human Communication Research, 28,* 136–152.

Solomon, D. H., & Knobloch, L. K. (2001). Relationship uncertainty, partner interference, and intimacy within dating relationships. *Journal of Social and Personal Relationships, 18,* 804–820.

Solomon, D. H., & Knobloch, L. K. (2004). A model of relational turbulence: The role of intimacy, relational uncertainty, and interference from partners in appraisals of irritations. *Journal of Social and Personal Relationships, 21,* 795–816.

Surra, C. A., & Bohman, T. (1991). The development of close relationships: A cognitive perspective. In G. J. O. Fletcher & F. D. Fincham (Eds.), *Cognition in close relationships* (pp. 281–305). Hillsdale, NJ: Lawrence Erlbaum Associates.

Theiss, J., & Solomon, D. H. (in press). A relational turbulence model of communication about irritations in romantic relationships. *Communication Research.*

Tusing, K. J. (2000). *Relational framing theory: Factors governing the absolute and relative activation of relational communication frames.* Unpublished doctoral dissertation, University of Wisconsin, Madison, WI.

Tusing, K. J., Dillard, J. P., & Morrill, J. (2001, May). *Environmental factors governing the absolute and relative activation of relational communication frames.* Paper presented at the annual meeting of the International Communication Association, Washington, DC.

van Dijk, T. A., & Kintsch, W. (1983). *Strategies of discourse comprehension.* New York: Academic.

Waldron, V. R., & Cegala, D. J. (1992). Assessing conversational cognition: Levels of cognitive theory and associated methodological requirements. *Human Communication Research, 18,* 599–622.

Walther, J. B., & Burgoon, J. K. (1992). Relational communication in computer-mediated interaction. *Human Communication Research, 19,* 50–88.

Watzlawick, P., Beavin, J. H., & Jackson, D. D. (1967). *Pragmatics of human communication.* New York: Norton.

White, G. M. (1980). Conceptual universals in language. *American Anthropologist, 82,* 759–781.

Wiggins, J. S. (1982). Circumplex models of interpersonal behavior in clinical psychology. In P. C. Kendall & J. N. Butcher (Eds.), *Handbook of research methods in clinical psychology* (pp. 183–221). New York: Wiley.

Wish, M., Deutsch, M., & Kaplan, S. J. (1976). Perceived dimensions of interpersonal relations. *Journal of Personality and Social Psychology, 33,* 409–420.

Wyer, R. S., & Srull, T. K. (1986). Human cognition in its social context. *Psychological Review, 93,* 322–359.

7

Attribution and Interpersonal Communication: Out of Our Heads and Into Behavior

Valerie Manusov
University of Washington

The term *attribution* is common in our everyday social vocabularies. We think and we talk about things that happened in our personal or social worlds, identifying our best guesses (our attributions) for why those events or behaviors happened as they did and who or what is responsible for them. We also try to understand others and their actions—as well as our behaviors and ourselves—by figuring out what could have motivated or contributed to a particular behavior. These attempts to understand behavior, as reflected in our thoughts and talk, we often call attributions. Attributions in this everyday sense involve the inferences, assumptions, beliefs, and other explanatory forms that frequent our thoughts and our talk (Burleson, 1996; Hilton, 1990); they are our commonplace efforts to understand what underlies our own and others' actions.

These efforts have been given ample attention by research scholars with an interest in social cognition, especially as it relates to attributions of achievement (for a review, see Bell-Dolan & Anderson, 1999). The past 20 years have also seen particular attention to attributions by communication scholars. Bolstered by two key chapters written in 1982 (Seibold & Spitzberg, 1982; Sillars, 1982), attribution now shows up as a key word in an array of organizational (e.g., Dugan, 1989), intercultural (e.g., Armstrong & Kaplowitz, 2001; Ehrenhaus, 1983; Gao & Gudykunst, 1995), instructional (e.g., Beatty & Friedland, 1990; Bippus & Daly, 1999), and media studies (e.g., Power, Murphy, & Coover, 1996; Quist & Wiegand, 2002), typically as (a) the reasons given or inferred for responding to another in a certain way, or (b) the character traits that we apply to ourselves or others. This chapter, however, focuses on scholarship concerned with interpersonal interaction and relating. What will be seen is a vigorous array of work on particular communication activities (e.g., interpersonal conflict, influence, support) derived directly from and informing attribution principles and practices.

To show some of the ways that the study of attribution processes and outcomes has allied with scholarship on interpersonal communication, this chapter moves in a somewhat different direction than have other similar projects and some of the other chapters in this volume. Rather than providing a chronological account of initial attribution theorizing and the scholarship that emerged from it over time, in this chapter I instead identify some of the primary attribution theories created by social psychologists. It then embeds within each of the theory discussions some of the communication scholarship that blends, reflects on, and often extends those original perspectives. My hope in using this format is to show the important influence that attribution theorizing has had on our work as well as to identify some of the many ways that a communication perspective provides new or extended applications of attribution principles.

SOME DEFINING, HISTORY, AND CONTEXTUALIZING

Finding the best way to describe attributions from a research perspective is not easy. Certainly, definitions abound, but the scope of each tends to be limited. The most common definition, however, refers to attributions as "the processes [as well as the products] by which an individual interprets events as being caused by a particular part of relatively stable environment" (Kelley, 1967, p. 193). This definition, like most, stems from Heider's (1958) foundational argument about human nature: We are sense-making beings, who try, with various levels of success, to understand the world, in part so that we may control it. In some research, the processes of attribution are called attributional, whereas the products (i.e., a particular formed attribution) are labeled attributions. In this chapter, however, I use the latter term to describe both the process and the product of attribution sense making.

As noted, two important chapters appeared in the early part of the 1980s offering communication researchers clarity about and suggestions for use of attribution theories in our part of the communication discipline (Seibold & Spitzberg, 1982; Sillars, 1982). Although not the first to suggest the applicability of attribution processes to interpersonal communication (see, e.g., McMahan, 1976), each of these chapters presented an overview of the primary perspectives from psychology that the authors believed were applicable to communication processes.

The authors also provided an array of suggestions for places in interpersonal communication where attribution applications could be useful.

Sillars (1982), for instance, asked the question, "Are people 'naïve scientists' [as Heider, 1958, suggested] or just naïve?" (p. 73). His answer was that "[p]eople are both reflective and spontaneous, rational and rationalizing, logical and illogical" (p. 96). That is, we sometimes act on inferences, and other times we act more automatically. According to Sillars, people are most likely to make attributions as part of communication in at least three instances: (a) when people attempt to reduce their uncertainty with others (see also Berger & Roloff, 1982), (b) during metacommunication, and (c) when punctuating or communication sequences. For Sillars, these communicative activities are ripe for attributional exploration.

Seibold and Spitzberg (1982) also argued for some ways in which interpersonal communication scholars get value from taking an attributional perspective. Most notably, they suggested that attribution theories provide a conceptual framework for understanding the interpretation of identities, situations, and relationships we encounter in our interactions with others. Like Sillars (1982), Seibold and Spitzberg (1982) provided possible applications in which attribution principles may inform or explain communicative action.

Sillars (1982) and Seibold and Spitzberg's (1982) chapters stood on the precipice of a relatively strong welcoming of attribution principles by many interpersonal communication scholars. To help trace the legacy of these chapters in our field, the remainder of this chapter is divided into sections, each beginning with a prominent attribution theory or perspective and then showing some exemplary work that has used the specific principles of that particular theory. I hope to show both the breadth and depth of interpersonal communication scholarship informed by and informing attribution principles. In so doing, I also hope to help identify specifically the myriad ways in which attributions and communication are linked. Finally, I show ways that the study of attributions has developed because it has been done by communication scholars. I start this journey by returning to its launching.

AN EXPLORATION OF ATTRIBUTIONS IN COMMUNICATION

Heider's (1958) Conception of Causal Locus

This history of studying attributions within a scientific framework is typically traced back to the 1920s and dissertation work by Heider, first articulated widely in 1958 (for reviews, see Harvey, 1989; Harvey & Omarzu, 2001). Heider (1958) is credited with providing a metaphor to capture the human proclivity to act as sense makers, particularly in our attempts to try to discern why something happened. He argued that much of people's everyday thinking (i.e., their attributions) mirrors to some degree the more systematic processes done by scientists as they attempt to understand why events occur. Heider argued that this mirroring shows people acting as naive scientists, pursuing everyday explanations in a similar but less formulaic way than what scientists pursue in their scholarship.

The primary type of attribution that Heider (1958) discussed was what he called a *causal locus*. Specifically, "[i]n common sense psychology (as in scientific psychology) the result of an action is felt to depend on two sets of conditions, namely, factors within the person and factors within the environment" (p. 82), a distinction that he also called *internal–external*. In addition, Heider discussed attributions of *responsibility* (i.e., determining who or what was culpable for an action) and asserted that people whose actions are thought to be done intentionally are also attributed more personal responsibility for the outcome of those actions. Following Heider, interpersonal communication and relationship researchers have worked a great deal with these two different types of attributions. The following section highlights some work that has done so for each of the attribution types as well as looking across them in the same studies. The section also helps identify some of the primary communicative activities in which attributions occur.

Considerations of Causal Locus. One of the events in which interpersonal communication researchers have seen the implication of causal attributions is relational break-ups. Krahl and Wheeless (1997), for example, asked their participants to report about who initiated a break-up and what caused the break-up to be initiated. In assessing the latter, they extended Heider's (1958) conception of causal locus by including self, other, and situation as potential sources. The authors then looked at the interplay between whom participants stated initiated the relationship and who or what was attributed as the cause for the break-up. Their results showed a range of interesting findings, including that attributions of cause were seldom to self when the other was the one who initiated the break-up.

More common in interpersonal communication research, however, is an investigation of causal locus in compliance situations. Wilson and Kang (1991), for instance, looked at causal locus to determine what caused noncompliance (see also Wilson, Cruz, & Kang, 1992). In this study, attributions were made for the target and source of a compliance attempt. The authors found that people did make attributions about causal locus as expected, but only when they had high levels of cognitive complexity. Wilson, Cruz, Marshall, and Rao (1993) likewise looked at attributions in compliance interactions, finding an important link between attributions for obstacles to compliance and people's willingness to continue to pursue compliance attempts (e.g., message sources were more persistent when they attributed the other's noncompliance as more internal, especially when the attributions were also more unstable). Ifert and Roloff (1994) found similar projected results in a study with hypothetical scenarios.

Additional work on causal locus references attributions made about discourse. For instance, Bippus (2003) investigated attributions given to a speaker's use of humor during interpersonal conflict (the site of several attribution studies in communication; see, e.g., Canary & Spitzberg, 1990; Sillars, 1980). In particular, Bippus (2003) was concerned with the outcomes of such attributions. Based on questionnaire data of actual conflict interactions, the author found that more internal attributions for humor use were associated with more negative outcomes (e.g., conflict escalation, progress, and face loss). The perceived quality of the humorous statements was also linked with attribution outcomes, such that attributors "must perceive the humorous message to actually be funny and appropriate for it to mitigate escalation and facilitate progress in the interaction" (Bippus, 2003, p. 422).

Responding to Responsibility. Other work focuses more specifically on responsibility attributions. Often, responsibility is attributed in these studies as part of the process of blame (for a theoretical and methodological discussion of the connection between responsibility and blame attributions, see Bradbury & Fincham, 1992). As Cameron and Stritzke (2003) noted, "an attribution of blame presupposes an attribution of responsibility" (p. 983), although sometimes blame is seen as its own attributional dimension (see Wilson & Whipple, 2001).

Much of the research focusing on responsibility attributions concerns decisions about who is to blame for such things as rape, physical or verbal abuse or violence, and incest (e.g., Bugental, Shennum, Frank, & Ekman, 2001; Feiring, Taska, & Lewis, 2002; Staley & Blumberg Lapidus, 1997). Sometimes the work looks at how other factors may moderate a person's responsibility and, subsequently, blame for an untoward event. For instance, in Cameron and Stritzke's (2003) work, the authors found that alcohol use affected judgments of responsibility for rape perpetrators and victims, but it did so in different ways: "[I]ntoxicated victims [in their study were] assigned more responsibility than sober victims, but intoxicated perpetrators [were] assigned less responsibility than sober perpetrators" (p. 983; for more on the rape attribution process, see Littleton & Axsom, 2003).

Combining Locus and Responsibility. Whereas the preceding studies investigated a specific attribution—causal or responsibility—for an event, typically because that type of attribution seems most salient to the context, other work has looked at both types of attribution that Heider (1958) suggested. In their assessment of attributions given by couples to changes in relationships, for instance, Noller, Feeney, and Blakeley-Smith (2001) identified an array of attributions that occurred as couples talked about their own relationships and the dialectical tensions (i.e., the positional tensions) they may face. In assessing the cause of a change, the couples pointed toward particular movements in their relational dialectic. That is, spouses talked about changes in their relationship over time and attributed the change, sometimes a problematic one, to a shift of levels in dialectic poles, such as the one delimiting autonomy from connection. Importantly, in some cases, couple members provided a dialectic shift as the cause of another behavior. One husband queried his wife, for example, "whether you took [a language course in] Indonesian because it was something totally separate to anything I would have done" (Noller et al., 2001, p. 161).

Although many more studies fall within these descriptions, those addressed help show some of the ways that interpersonal communication researchers apply Heider's (1958) concepts. The studies also point to some of the communicative activities and contexts studied most commonly by interpersonal communication and relationship researchers: relational communication and outcomes, compliance, and the darker sides of communication (Cupach & Spitzberg, 1994).

E. E. Jones and Correspondence Inference Theory

As can be seen, Heider's (1958) influence is quite clear on interpersonal communication and relationship scholarship in the past two decades. Part of this influence can be credited to Jones and his colleagues' work (for a retrospective on Jones, see Darley & Cooper, 1998). Jones and colleagues' correspondence inference model was created to formalize Heider's (1958) more general framework. In particular, Jones and Davis (1965) continued Heider's (1958) conception of causality and responsibility attributions, primarily by focusing on how dispositional (i.e., more internal and personally responsible) attributions are or should be made. Specifically, they argued that there are cognitive paths through which an attributor will or should go to draw a dispositional rather than an external cause (also known as personal or environmental causes; Kelley, 1991).[1]

[1]Kelley's (1991) work on the analysis of variance model of attributions has been very important in the development of subsequent work on attributions by social psychologists. It has not, however, generated a significant amount of scholarship by interpersonal communication scholars. Thus, it is mentioned only briefly in this chapter.

One of the primary gains from a focus on dispositions was an understanding of the importance of intentionality. That is, for Jones and Davis (1965; Jones, 1979), as for Heider (1958), dispositional attributions could be made only when an action was judged as intended. Interpersonal communication researchers, of course, are interested in judgments of intentionality, often as a basis for what counts and does not count as communication (e.g., Andersen, 1991; Motley, 1990; Stamp & Knapp, 1990). In some of my earlier work, for example, I looked specifically at both whether and how people decide that another's nonverbal behavior was sent intentionally. This research was part of a larger definitional argument surrounding the degree to which people think about (i.e., make attributions for) nonverbal cues as potentially purposeful or intentional (see Manusov, 1990). Across several studies, I found evidence that people do appear to think about whether or not a nonverbal behavior, such as an attentive face, was done intentionally or spontaneously and that such attributions both affect other meanings given to the nonverbal behaviors or are affected by those other meanings. Specifically, whether a behavior was judged as positive or negative is often linked with intentionality attributions, with positive cues more commonly seen as intentional, especially if directed toward the attributor (Manusov, 1996; Manusov & Rodriguez, 1989).

However, attributions of intentionality have other implications, most obviously for the resultant effects on judgments of the other, on emotional response, on relational quality, and on behavior. I have argued, for instance, that attributions of intent for nonverbal behavior, particularly whether or not someone else's synchrony with another interactant was seen as intentional, will affect how positively those other interactants will judge their partners (Manusov, 1991, 1993). Likewise, Vangelisti and her colleagues (e.g., Vangelisti, 1994, 2001; Vangelisti & Young, 2000) have focused part of their work on hurtful messages on determining when people make attributions of intent to hurtful messages and investigating the consequences of those attributions.

Vangelisti (2001) argued that people sometimes interpret what others say to them as an emotional injury. She asserted that "[w]hen people feel hurt, they perceive that they have been emotionally injured or wounded .... They have [attributed] something that someone else said or did as a transgression" (p. 41). Although people may be hurt by another's message whether or not it was intended to be hurtful, Vangelisti and her colleagues found that the impact is greater when a hearer makes an intentionality attribution; that is, the listener infers that the behavior was sent intentionally to be hurtful (Vangelisti, 1994; Vangelisti & Young, 2000).

Vangelisti found that intentionality attributions are related to decreases in relational satisfaction and increases in the emotional distance the attributor feels from the other. In a recent extension of Vangelisti's work, Mills, Nazar, and Farrell (2003) found that hurtful messages directed at mothers by their children that were seen as intentional increased the mothers' sense of rejection; those directed by mothers at children and attributed as intentional decreased the children's self-image, increased their feelings of rejection, and altered their feelings toward their mothers. Additional work shows, however, that certain communicative forms, such as humor, "may make hurt-evoking statements more palatable" (Young & Bippus, 2001, p. 35).

Attribution Errors and Biases. In addition to a focus on intent, another legacy of Jones's work is an awareness that, despite our ability to do so, people do not always choose attributions in a purely logical way (i.e., the way that they "should" according to correspondent inferences). Jones and Nisbett (1972) made this argument most notably when their work showed that people assessing the cause of someone else's behaviors appear to use different information and arrive at different attributions than do people when they make attributions for their own action. What has been called since then the *actor–observer bias,* Jones and Nisbett (1972) revealed the importance of perspective in making attribution decisions.

The actor–observer bias has helped to explain or provoke several interpersonal communication studies. For example, Canary and Spitzberg (1990) studied dyads who were in close relationships and who had a recent conflict. The researchers asked the participants to report on the conflict strategies that they and their partners had used in their conflict as well as attributions of competence, again for themselves and for their partners. They found an interesting association with the valence of the conflict strategy and the actor–observer bias such that the actor–observer difference in attributions was strongest with the most negative conflict choices (i.e., distributive strategies).

Other biases have been found in interpersonal communication studies. Most notable, perhaps, are three others, however: the *fundamental attribution error* or correspondence bias (Ross, 1977), *self-serving biases* (Crittenden & Wiley, 1985; Heider, 1958) such as the *egocentric bias* (i.e., the extent to which people make attributions for behaviors that place them, the attributors, in a positive light; Baucom, 1987), and the *salience bias* (Kellermann, 1984, 1989). I explain each of these and provide additional exemplary work from interpersonal communication researchers that shows their application.

One of the first biases noticed and explored by attribution scholars is known as the fundamental attribution error or correspondence bias (Ross, 1977). This error involves the overattribution of internal causes to others' behaviors and is perhaps due to the perspective of an onlooker's focus on the person himself or herself rather than on external circumstances.[2] Floyd and Voloudakis (1999), however, hypothesized that the fundamental attribution error may take a different form when attributions are looked at within close relationships and during interaction. In their study of friendship dyads, the researchers proposed that instead of overattributing internal causes to another's behavior, these dyads would overattribute external causes. As the authors argued, "[c]ertain attributions (e.g., internal attributions for increased affection) may force receivers to attend to relational implications of the behavior, whereas other attributions (e.g., external attributions for increased affection) would not" (Floyd & Voloudakis, 1999, para. 56). Their data supported their countertheoretical hypothesis.

The preceding finding suggests that people may make attributions in such a way as to preserve their own image or in some other way confirm a positive self-view. In that way, the bias that Floyd and Voloudakis (1999) found works as a form of self-serving bias. Self-serving or egocentric biases exist in a number of forms but tend to be attributions (particularly those that are communicated) that make the attributor "look good" to themselves or others (Bradley, 1978; Crittenden & Wiley, 1985).

In one extension of the egocentric bias in interpersonal communication, for example, my colleagues and I (Manusov, Floyd, & Kerssen-Griep, 1997) had couples interact in our laboratory while talking about an upcoming vacation or other plans. Following the interaction, both couple members made attributions about the same set of behaviors (their own and their spouse's) that had occurred during the interactions, allowing us to look at two sets of attributions for each set of behaviors. As expected, people tended to make more favorable attributions for their own behaviors than they did for their partners (evidence of the egocentric bias and the actor–observer bias). More notably, however, we also found that couple members who reported higher marital satisfaction tended to attribute their partners' behaviors in the same egocentric manner as they used for their own (i.e., a sort of relationship-centric bias for those who are happily married).

In determining when attributions will most likely be made, and what type of information people draw on to construct their attributions, researchers have also found certain types of behaviors to be most salient. In particular, those behaviors that are most likely to instigate attributions—and to be used in deciding what an attribution should be—are most often those that are novel, unexpected, negative, or occur in the

[2]Scholars (e.g., Krull et al., 1999) have found evidence that the fundamental attribution error as described here occurs in cultures that are described as valuing independence. In those cultures where interdependence is emphasized (e.g., Korea, China, India), the pattern on this error tends to be reversed.

initial stages of a relationship (Berger & Roloff, 1982; Pszyszynski & Greenberg, 1981; Wong & Weiner, 1981).

Kellermann (1984) was one of the first to look particularly at the salience of a message's valence and found what she called a *negativity bias* in the ways we process information. That is, people tend to notice and give more weight to negative behaviors than they do to positive ones when they are interpreting someone else's actions. Kellermann (1986) also found a *positivity bias,* however, when attributions could be made to the attributor's behavior. That is, when attributions were made within interactions, and one possible cause of the other's actions was the attributor, the interpreters tended to make more benign attributions. Manusov (1993), Burgoon and Newton (1991), and Floyd and Voloudakis (1999) found similar valence-based (and actor–observer-based) biases in their work.

Weiner's (1986, 1995) Attribution Theories

The lines of investigation just discussed allude to an important link between attributions and valence or the emotive tone of a message. Substantial links were also identified between attributions and emotions in an attribution theory proposed by Weiner (1985), a theory that has, perhaps more than any other, affected the development of attribution principles in interpersonal research. In a seminal work, Weiner (1986) made two particularly important contributions. First, he made a case for connecting the ways in which people infer others' motivations with their subsequent emotional responses to the precipitating event. Weiner suggested that common outcomes of attributions are feelings of anger or guilt (see also Weiner, 1985; Weiner, Amirkhan, Folkes, & Verette, 1987).

The second fundamental contribution from Weiner's (1986) work involves the extension of attribution dimensions. Weiner (1985, 1986) argued that within the general attribution types, there are different forms of attribution, and these forms are based on some identifiable dimensions. According to Weiner (1985), "among the internal causes [for example], some fluctuate, whereas others remain relatively stable" (p. 551). He thus added *stability* (i.e., the degree to which a cause is likely to remain constant over time), *controllability* (i.e., the degree to which a person has the ability to control the cause), and *globality* (i.e., the degree to which the cause underlies a range of effects or can be generalized across settings) as "other possible causal structures" (Weiner, 1985, p. 548), dimensions, or properties that may differentiate one attribution from another. Bradbury and Fincham (1990) and Fincham and Bradbury (1992) argued later that locus, globality, and stability are dimensions of causal attributions; intentionality, controllability, and personal responsibility are aspects of responsibility attributions.

MacGeorge (2001, 2003; MacGeorge, Gillihan, Samter, & Clark, 2003) found evidence to support Weiner's (1985, 1986) claims. Specifically, MacGeorge (2001, 2003) looked at the association between emotions and responsibility in social support contexts. Using a series of hypothetical scenarios that altered the perceived degree of responsibility, stability, and effort (the latter is, according to Heider [1958], a common characterization of causes in achievement contexts), MacGeorge (2001) followed Weiner's (1995) claim that attributions of greater responsibility, stability, and effort would induce greater anger and reduce sympathy for another's plight. Such emotional reactions, based on attributions directly, should predict a decrease in supportive or helping behavior.

The results of MacGeorge's (2001) work both supported and extended Weiner's (1995) model. Because she looked at a range of support goals and behaviors, MacGeorge (2001) was able to provide a more complex set of relations among thought, emotion, and action. In subsequent work on the data, MacGeorge (2003; MacGeorge et al., 2003) added sex differences into the complicated mix, finding such things as a greater proclivity to anger by males toward other males to whom responsibility was given. Other research by interpersonal communication scholars has also found important links between emotions and communication (e.g., Honeycutt & Eidenmuller's [2001] investigation of the influence of moods on attributions; Segrin & Dillard [1991], who found some but not full support for Weiner's [1986] model).

There are a number of ways that the discussion of the multidimensionality of attributions has played out in the interpersonal communication and relationship literature, although much of it has focused on marriage and, to a lesser degree, on other family-based relationships (for a recent review, see Manusov, 2006). One of the preeminent findings, at least within the work on married couples, has been the recognition of attribution biases that differentiate satisfied from dissatisfied couples. Holtzworth-Munroe and Jacobson (1988) argued that certain combinations of attribution dimensions work together to characterize what they called *distress-maintaining* (i.e., multidimensional attributions for negative events that accentuate their impact and that are minimizing for positive behavior) and *relationship-enhancing* attributions (i.e., attributions that minimize the impact of negative events and maximize it for positive behavior). For instance, attributions for a negative behavior that place blame internally, are seen as stable, and that are global would be considered distress maintaining when applied to a spouse's actions because they perpetuate the negative tone in a relationship and imply little chance for positive change. Conversely, more external, unstable, and specific attributions for a negative behavior would be judged as a relationship-enhancing attribution, as it works to lessen the negative valence of the attribution and places less blame on the spouse for the action and its consequences. Evidence for these biases has been found across several cultures (e.g., Stander, Hsiung, & MacDermid, 2001).

Bradbury and Fincham (1990) summarized much of the research on attributions in marriage done until that time. In addition to documenting (and qualifying) evidence for distress-maintaining and relationship attributions, they also argued that the preceding biases "underlie the patterns of behavior exchange that differentiate distressed and nondistressed couples" (p. 4). Subsequent work has reflected some of the potential cognition–behavior links (e.g., Davey, Beach, Fincham, & Brody, 2001; Johnson, Karney, Rogge, & Bradbury, 2001; Manusov, 2002; Miller & Bradbury, 1995), although much remains to be explored.

The focus on attributions in relationships brings forward an additional way in which attribution research has expanded within communication scholarship. Some researchers, while staying true to the general premise of attributions, have moved away from the traditional attribution dimensions and looked instead at attributions as particular categories of meaning given to an action within a particular context. For instance, other dimensions may constitute distress-maintaining attributions has also been investigated. Sillars, Leonard, Roberts, and Dunn (2002) looked at what couple members said that they were thinking (and what they believed their partner was thinking) during a conflict discussion. Among other things, Sillars et al. found that aggressive spouses tended to attribute less constructive engagement and more avoidance to their partner than they attributed to themselves, reflecting an actor–observer bias and additional dimensions or meanings for attributions. The authors also speculated on the effect of these attributions on future behavior as well as the future of the relationship: Given the tendency for husbands in aggressive relationships to pay heightened attention to communication, and the likelihood that their attributions for their wives' communication will be distress maintaining, the link between attributions and communication "presents a combustible situation" (Sillars et al., 2002, p. 101) in these situations.

Interpersonal and relational researchers have taken Weiner's (1986) idea that there are other important dimensions embedded in our sense making and run wild with it. A large number of scholars, especially those working from the content of attributions to derive dimensions, have offered an array of other underlying structures for interpersonally based attributions. For example, researchers have identified relational attributions, where an aspect of the relationship is identified as the cause of a behavior (Berscheid, Lopes, Ammazzalorso, & Langenfeld, 2001; Vangelisti, Corbin, Lucchetti, & Sprague, 1999); interpersonal attributions (Fletcher, Fincham, Cramer, & Heron, 1987; Newman, 1981;

Vangelisti et al., 1999) where "interaction between partners is the focus" (Manusov & Koenig, 2001, p. 142) of the attribution; and communication attributions, where explanations for behavior are tied directly to what was being communicated (Manusov & Koenig, 2001). These dimensions would likely not have emerged if attributions were not studied within the interaction and relational environment.

Another notable example of a study using different forms of attribution is by Lim and Roloff (1999). In this study, the researchers were looking specifically at verbal and nonverbal messages preceding sexual behavior; the nature of the attributions sought were interpretations of consent that could be derived from the communicative cues. Lim and Roloff found, among other things, that direct verbal statements of consent to engage in sex were judged as indicating more actual consent than were nonverbal consent cues. They also found some limited evidence for *discounting,* an idea proposed by Kelley (1991) in which certain information (in this case, the verbal consent) was not given as much weight because of other situational information (in this case, impaired judgment based on alcohol or drug use).

Summary

This section reviewed some of the primary attribution principles derived from social psychology and applied within interpersonal communication scholarship. From this selective review, it is clear that there is a robust set of research programs using attribution principles effectively for understanding interpersonal communication processes. As well, this work has expanded how attributions should be seen and the communicative activities to which it should be applied. Specifically, the research has shown the importance of mediating factors, such as cognitive complexity, goals, and relationship type in the use of attributions. It also reflects that in addition to more traditional contexts of achievement and conflict, behaviors such as support, aggression, and compliance gaining all involve attribution making and are therefore important activities to investigate with attribution principles.

AN EXPLORATION OF COMMUNICATED ATTRIBUTIONS

Perhaps the greatest contribution of communication researchers to the revelation of attributions in interpersonal interaction, however, revolves around what has been variously called expressed, spoken, or communicated attributions (Harvey & Weary, 1985; Roghaar & Vangelisti, 1996; Weber & Vangelisti, 1991). These spoken forms of attributions have much in common with accounts (Antaki, 1988) but may also be seen as different enough in both form and intent that they are usefully distinguished (for elaborations on this distinction, see Manusov & Koenig, 2001; Weber & Vangelisti, 1991). Certainly communication scholars are not the only ones to look at attributions as they occur in conversation, but they make up the bulk of scholars whose work focuses in this area.

Burleson (1986) was one of the first to delineate the importance of expressed attribution. In his chapter, Burleson stated that "[a]lthough it is certainly the case that attributional processes occur overtly within the minds of individuals, it is also the case that people frequently *talk* to one another about why someone acted in some way; indeed exploring why someone behaved as he or she did is probably one of the most ubiquitous conversational topics" (p. 64). According to Burleson's analysis, "the *outcome* of a collaborative, publicly conducted attribution process ... is a product that was socially constructed, tested, and verified" (p. 79). "The resulting personal attribution (that the student is 'stupid' or lacks ability) thus is an *intersubjective* attribution, one carrying the force of social consensus" (p. 78).

An example of discourse about attributions (i.e., expressed attributions) can be found in work by Pittam and Gallois (1997), who studied talk about AIDS and HIV in small groups. Four-person groups of heterosexual Australian university students were asked to have a general discussion about HIV and AIDS. In transcripts made from the audio-recorded conversations, Pittam and Gallois found 151 statements that were coded as attributions of blame, and the blame-based statements came from 31 of the 33 groups the authors studied. The high frequency of attribution-type statements in the groups' talk provided evidence for Burleson's (1986) claim about the occurrence of attributions in talk.

It also, however, provided additional confirmation that people reveal in their talk that they think about why certain events occur and who is responsible for their occurrence. In potentially negative contexts, such as the contracting of HIV, people seem to talk particularly about who is (and who is not) to blame. For instance, two of Pittam and Gallois's (1997) participants engaged in the following collaborative discussion:

M1: And the babies and stuff that come our um (0.3) from their mother's having it.
M2: Yeah they had nothing to do with it.
M1: Their lives are wrecked for (0.3) you know no no fault of their own (0.8) doesn't seem right. (p. 211)

Other communication-oriented investigations mirror Pittam and Gallois's transcripts in many ways by finding evidence of talk infused with responsibility and blame attributions for violent or aggressive behavior (e.g., Benson et al., 2003, who called such talk "discourses of blame"), rape, incest (e.g., McKenzie & Calder, 1993; Monahan, 1997;

Staley & Blumberg Lapidus, 1997), and abuse (e.g., Silvester, Bentovim, Stratton, & Hanks, 1995).

These investigations reveal that not only do people express their attributions to others; they appear to do so in very strategic (and potentially moralistic) ways. In a very clear test for this belief, Weber and Vangelisti (1991) reinforced that whereas "attributional processes are traditionally regarded as intrapersonal phenomena, attributional statements are a common feature of interpersonal communication" (p. 606). In their study, the authors solicited recollections of both nontactical and tactical attributions, with the latter described as causal statements designed "to get something: a sympathetic response, forgiveness, a pat on the back, or a favor" (Weber & Vangelisti, 1991, p. 611). Not only did they observe an array of reported expressed attributions, primarily positively valenced, Weber and Vangelisti also found that people made attributions for those expressed attributions (i.e., meta-attributions), judging spoken attributions that were external, for example, to be more sincere than tactically generated.

Other evidence about the strategic use of spoken attributions exists. Returning to the context of much of the early attribution research, for instance, Roghaar and Vangelisti (1996) studied the projected attribution expressions that adolescents and young adults reported that they would use when confronted with failure or success on an exam. In addition to hypothesized developmental differences between the two groups, which ties into arguments about the cognitive requirements of forming attributions, the authors also found evidence that speakers are motivated by their attributions of others' reactions to provide a spoken attribution that justifies the failure rather than just revealing the failure without a causal explanation. In this way, attribution processes occur in at least two places: as a motivation for talk and within the talk itself.

The assumption that internal attributions may drive people toward (or away) from conversation about an event is seen in scholarship by Derlega and Winstead (2001). Specifically, in their work on the social consequences of disclosure about HIV and AIDS, Derlega and Winstead found several attributions people provided for telling (or not telling) others (i.e., the event for which they were providing a causal attribution was their decision to tell or not tell another about their HIV status). Basing their conclusions on interviews with people who were HIV-seropositive, Derlega and Winstead labeled attributions for disclosure by both their goal and relationship characteristics: catharsis/self-expression, seeking help, duty to inform, desire to educate, desire to test the other's reaction, the fact that they had an emotionally close relationship, and similarity of backgrounds and experiences. The authors also found attributions people gave to their own decisions not to disclose. These were labeled privacy, self-blame or self-concept difficulties, communication difficulties, fear of rejection or being misunderstood, and superficial relationships. The authors found that the degree to which any of the attributions was salient or endorsed depended for them in part on the relationship they had with the person to whom they disclosed or did not disclose.

The preceding studies suggest that people form attributions that may influence whether or not they provide information to others and provide additional evidence that there may be a strategic basis for expressing (or withholding) attributions. One way to help determine the strategic nature of communicated attributions is to explore possible differences between attributions that are expressed and those that are withheld. Overall, the work in this area shows consistently that attributions people choose to withhold tend to be of a different nature than those they choose to communicate (Folkes, 1982; Weiner et al., 1987). Dickson, Manusov, Cody, and McLaughlin (1996), in a study of private (withheld) and public (communicated) attributions for hypothetical compliance failures, for instance, found that those attributions people said that they would communicate tended to be more unintentional, uncontrollable, unstable, and external than those they said they would not express. We argued that such strategic attribution making reflected a clear self-presentational bias in expressed attributions. Interestingly, such a bias tends to be more important when communicating with friends than with strangers (Manusov, Trees, Reddick, Carrillo Rowe, & Easley, 1998).

There is also evidence suggesting that communicated attributions appear to have very important effects, supporting communicators' decisions to express or withhold attributions. In his study of perceptions of people convicted of a crime, for example, Weisman (2004) argued that people make attributions as to whether or not another feels remorse over a crime. Basing his work on Goffman's (1961) concept of a moral career, Weisman (2004) claimed that "these [remorse] attributions may be the most important factor in how jurors ... decide who among the convicted should be executed" (para. 4). In part because remorse is seen as involuntary and caused by (attributed to) emotional collapse, signs of remorse are equated with sincere apologies and movement away from a moral transgression. They are thus likely to be seen by jurors as a reason for benevolence in sentencing. Given that people who have not committed a crime, although they have been convicted, may not be seen as remorseful, the full impact of this attribution on subsequent actions becomes even more apparent.

DISCUSSION

My goal in this chapter has been to show many of the ways in which interpersonal communication scholars (and their allies in related fields) have used attribution principles to understand interactive and relational processes. Embedded within this discussion have been several different ways in which attributions can be thought about in relation to interpersonal communication. As well, the studies mentioned provide exemplars for looking at different types of methodologies that allow researchers to alter and assess attributions. These connections and methods are reviewed here.

Connections Between Communication and Attributions

As I have argued elsewhere (e.g., Manusov, 2001), the research on interpersonal communication and attributions helps show myriad paths through which communication and attributions are intertwined. One of these connections involves identifying attributions for people's communicative behaviors. That is, many of the research projects talked about in this chapter are concerned with how the attributions people make reflect the meaning that they have given to those communication behaviors. Behaviors that may be ambiguous, such as sexual consent (Lim & Roloff, 1999), affection (Floyd & Voloudakis, 1999), or nonverbal affect (Manusov, 1996), are particularly likely to have diverse interpretations given to them, and assessing attributions is one useful way to capture this diversity (Manusov, 1990).

Second, attributions made for events and behavior may also be reflected in subsequent interpersonal communication. Work in conflict contexts suggests that the nature of attributions made for a conflict event will influence the type of conflict strategy the attributor will choose to use (Sillars, 1980) and the possibility that conflict will escalate (Bippus, 2003). I have also found attributions for one spouse's nonverbal cues influences the nonverbal cues the other spouse uses in return (Manusov, 2002). These lines of research suggest that attributions link to communication behaviors when our thoughts affect the ways we act and communicate subsequently.

A third connection between attributions and communication occurs when communication is about the attributions themselves. That is, rather than conceptualizing attributions as in-the-head processes that may be pertinent to interpersonal communication, attributions have also been studied as communicative acts. Expressed or communicated attributions, whether found in recalled reports or naturally occurring discourse, provide a potential glimpse at the ways in which attributions work as communication. Weber and Vangelisti (1991), Roghaar and Vangelisti (1996), and Dickson et al. (1996) all helped exemplify this connection and reflected the inherently interactive nature of this type of attribution.

Methodological Issues

An additional advantage that comes from looking across interpersonal communication studies using an attribution framework is an opportunity to see the many ways in which attributions can be operationalized. Some of the empirical studies discussed in this chapter involved manipulated attributions—embedded in an array of experimental designs—designed to alter the attributions made for behavior. Commonly, hypothetical examples that present specific attribution-based scenarios have proved effective in looking at reactions to certain attribution types (e.g., Roghaar & Vangelisti, 1996). Other times, reported attributions from people's previous experiences have been chosen from a large pool of responses as best exemplifying certain types of attributions, and these derived-from-real-life scenarios are then judged by others (e.g., Ifert & Roloff, 1994; Wilson et al., 1993).

Several of the experiments attempting to manipulate attribution dimensions have used confederates as part of the control over attributions. In one study (Manusov, 1991), for instance, I had confederates change their degree of actual intentionality behind their facial expressions, vocal tones, and so on, to look for differences in the ways the nonverbal behaviors—and the confederates—were judged. In another project on interaction synchrony and intentionality attributions (Manusov, 1992), confederates mirrored participants' behaviors in similar ways across all of the conditions. Attributions were manipulated, however, by my telling the participants afterward that the other interactant (the confederate) had told me that they had mirrored the other intentionally or had done so unintentionally (both of these groups differed significantly in their assessments from the control group, which was not told anything about the confederate's degree of intentionality).

Confederates (often people who were partners with someone else in the study) have also been used to help garner attributions from the participants. Floyd and Voloudakis (1999), for instance, had one friend in each of their dyads increase or reduce his or her amount of affection in the second of two interactions. The other friend then made attributions for the "confederate's" behavior following the interaction. Some of my work with married couples used similar manipulations (e.g., Manusov, 1990; Manusov et al., 1997). As with research confederates, this type of study design requires behavioral training and manipulation checks.

These latter studies also typically require additional assessment of attributions. Such assessments have been done typically in one of two ways. First, many researchers ask their participants to complete an attribution measure following the interaction. In these cases, the researcher provides scales for the attributions of interest (e.g., "Your partner's affectionate behavior was caused by something internal (1) to external (7) to him or her"). Other researchers use a similar methodology following recalled interactions (e.g., Wilson & Kang, 1993). A recent summary of some forms that these scales may take can be found in Manusov (2004) and is also reflected in Table 7.1.

Table 7.1

Types of Rating Measures for Assessing Attributions From Open-Ended Responses

Dichotomous categories

This behavior was (these behaviors were):

internal [1] or external [2]

stable [1] or unstable [2], etc. or

intentional; yes [1] no [0], unintentional; yes [1] no [0]

Bipolar scales

"This behavior was caused by something":

Global 1 2 3 4 5 6 7 Specific

Used as a Likert-type measure

To what extent do you agree with the following statement:

"The event was controllable"

Strongly disagree 1 2 3 4 5 6 7 Strongly agree

Notes. These scales can be used by coders/raters and by participants. As well, the rating scales do not have to be 7-point scales; when using raters, a 5-point scale may lead to higher reliability. The measures can also be more detailed, as in this 6-point scale that purposefully has no midpoint (e.g., 1 = *strongly disagree*, 2 = *disagree*, 3 = *somewhat disagree*, 4 = *agree somewhat*, 5 = *agree*, 6 = *strongly agree*).

Second, researchers have asked participants to write or speak about their explanations, and these open-ended answers are coded or rated later by trained researchers to assess the degree of particular attribution dimensions apparent in the participants' responses (e.g., Floyd & Voloudakis, 1999; Manusov, 1990; Manusov et al., 1997). Some researchers argue that having participants write open-ended responses better ensures that attributions are not "forced on" participants in the ways that they may be when respondents are asked to complete a previously constructed scale (see Bradbury & Fincham, 1992).

Third, scholars, especially those who desire to get attributions about behaviors that are hard to observe in a laboratory setting, may give various questionnaires to their participants to complete about events that have happened in their interactions with others. Russell (1982), for example, had a general causal dimension scale, used in Segrin and Dillard's (1991) study comparing depressed and nondepressed people's attributions in an interpersonal influence context. Wilson and Whipple (2001) developed their own scale reflecting commonly used attributions (locus and blame) and attributions new to their study (generality and knowledge). Fincham and Bradbury (1992) likewise had a psychometrically strong measure of couples' attributions designed to tap into the kinds of causal and responsibility sense making that occurs in dyadic interactions. Fincham, Beach, Arias, and Brody (1998) also developed a measure suited to assessing children's attributions, which reflect a different level of reasoning than do adults' attributions (see Roghaar & Vangelisti, 1996, for a similar argument about adolescents). Scales to assess attribution styles are also available (e.g., Fletcher, Danilovics, Fernandez, Peterson, & Reeder, 1986; Seligman, Abramson, Semmel, & von Baeyer, 1979).

Fourth, scholars use the open-ended responses on questionnaires or actual discourse as a starting place to develop a set of attributions relevant to a particular context. Peterson, Troth, Gallois, and Feeney (2001) used assessment of talk in interactions about safe sex to determine attribution dimensions (i.e., open–closed, friendly–hostile) that occurred in their data. Derlega and Winstead (2001) content analyzed open-ended interview data to gauge several attribution forms reflected in their respondents' reasons for or against disclosing HIV status. Likewise, Booth-Butterfield and Trotta (1994) found a variety of attributions for love in their respondents' descriptions. Importantly, in all of these cases, the authors developed category or rating schemes that differed from previous studies but were tied directly to the uniqueness of their context and attribution content.

Any attempt to code or rate attributions requires development and elaboration of definitions for the attributional dimensions. Given that the terms are often used in everyday language, having research participants or assistants judge the nature of attributions runs the risk of the attributors meaning different things from one another. Providing definitions that are consistent with previous research allows for researchers to be more certain that whomever is making the attributional judgments is doing so in a way that allows for comparisons to other research. Thus, an important pointer for research on attributions is to think through how the particular terms (e.g., stability, responsibility) should be conceptualized and to inform those applying the terms about these conceptualizations.

Limitations

Overall, the theoretical and methodological rigor of attributions-in-and-as communication appears to be strong within interpersonal communication research. However, not all scholars are sanguine about the use of attribution principles within our research. Shotter (1985), for instance, at a very general level, criticized attribution and other cognition research for its presumption that people think alike and should be described in social scientific terms. That is, Shotter asserted that we find evidence of causal sense making only because we ask for it.

In doing so, we create a reality where we think and act as social scientists, a reality that would not exist without our interference.

Ironically for cognitive scholars, communication scholarship on attributions may be criticized from another direction. According to Hilton (1990), communicated attributions may be better conceptualized as a language move than as a social cognition, and thus, for Hilton, a communication approach makes the study of attributions less about social cognition than about patterns of social behavior. Although in most ways the assumption that attributions as part of an interactive process and not just a psychological one is beneficial to our study, it may also take us too far away from studying the underlying cognitive processes that produced expressed attributions.

For those who do promote an integration of interpersonal communication and attributions, the scope of our work has been described both as too broad and all encompassing (Fincham, 1985, 2001; Metts, 2001) and as too narrow (i.e., that it can be subsumed under social cognition more generally; Abelson, Leddo, & Gross, 1987; Read, 1987). It has also been suggested that our ways of approaching attributions has hurt rather than helped our ability to theorize about attributions (Spitzberg, 2001). One of our remaining challenges as a discipline, then, may be to determine what may be most fruitfully thought of as attributions and what is best labeled and studied as a different set of processes.

Future Contributions

For many of us, however, attribution principles appear to lie at the base of much of our everyday sense making, both what we do internally and how we present that to—or negotiate it with—others. Thus, attribution principles likely have a long and productive life ahead in the study of interpersonal communication processes and outcomes. One of the most important contributions interpersonal communication scholars can make, however, is to look further at much of our research (e.g., Floyd & Voloudakis, 1999; MacGeorge, 2001; Segrin & Dillard, 1991; Wilson & Kang, 1993) that has found some, but inconsistent, support for claims made by attribution theorists. These interpersonal communication scholars have argued that there may be some vital mediating factors, such as communicators' goals, that affect the path that attribution making may take. Thus, one of the many additions that interpersonal communication scholars can make to understanding the role of attributions in communication is to build theoretical models that tap into this more mediated understanding.

An additional line of research germane to interpersonal communication scholars is to look further at the communicative effects of attributions. As noted, some scholars (e.g., Bradbury & Fincham, 1992;

Manusov, 2002; Sillars, 1980) have evidenced both the real and reported implications of attributions. Certain nonverbal reactions, conflict strategies, and problem-solving techniques may vary based on the attributions given to other behaviors. However, the causal ties between attributions and many communication behaviors are still relatively unknown, and our work as scholars interested in both cognition and communication should develop further along these lines. In particular, research that extends attributions for behaviors such as aggression and abuse (Benson et al., 2003; McKenzie & Calder, 1993; Pittam & Gallois, 1997) to the ways in which attributions lead to destructive communication would be particularly important lines of inquiry.

Both of these roads will help show the complexity and the consequences of attributions in interpersonal communication, particularly if we make the methodological maps we use as creative and diverse as we can. In these ways, interpersonal scholars' tendency to move from what goes on inside our heads and into our actions will have the most theoretical, methodological, and applied impact that we can.

ACKNOWLEDGMENT

I wish to thank Dru Williams for his help in searching for contemporary communication scholarship on attributions.

REFERENCES

Abelson, R. P., Leddo, J., & Gross, P. (1987). The strength of conjunctive explanations. *Personality and Social Psychology Bulletin, 13,* 141–155.

Andersen, P. A. (1991). When one cannot communicate: A challenge to Motley's traditional communication postulates. *Communication Studies, 42,* 309–325.

Antaki, C. (1988). Explanations. In C. Antaki (Ed.), *Analyzing everyday explanation* (pp. 1–14). Beverly Hills, CA: Sage.

Armstrong, G. B., & Kaplowitz, S. A. (2001). Sociolinguistic inference and intercultural coorientation: A Bayesian model of communicative competence in intercultural interaction. *Human Communication Research, 27,* 350–381.

Baucom, D. H. (1987). Attributions in distressed relations: How can we explain them? In D. Perlman & S. Duck (Eds.), *Intimate relationships: Development, dynamics, and deterioration* (pp. 177–206). Beverly Hills, CA: Sage.

Beatty, M. J., & Friedland, M. H. (1990). Public speaking state anxiety as a function of selected situational and predispositional variables. *Communication Education, 39,* 142–147.

Bell-Dolan, D., & Anderson, C. A. (1999). Attributional processes: An integration of social and clinical psychology. In R. M. Kowalski & M. R. Leary (Eds.), *The social psychology of emotional and behavioral problems* (pp. 37–67). Washington, DC: American Psychological Association.

Benson, A., Secker, J., Balfe, E., Lipsedge, M., Robinson, S., & Walker, J. (2003). Discourses of blame: Accounting for aggression and violence on an acute mental health inpatient unit. *Social Science & Medicine, 57,* 917–927.

Berger, C. R., & Roloff, M. E. (1982). Thinking about friends and lovers: Social cognition and relational trajectories. In M. E. Roloff & C. R. Berger (Eds.), *Social cognition and communication* (pp. 151–192). Beverly Hills, CA: Sage.

Berscheid, E., Lopes, J., Ammazzalorso, H., & Langenfeld, N. (2001). Causal attributions of relationship quality. In V. Manusov & J. H. Harvey (Eds.), *Attribution, communication behavior, and close relationships* (pp. 115–133). Cambridge, UK: Cambridge University Press.

Bippus, A. M. (2003). Humor motives, qualities, and reactions in recalled conflict episodes. *Western Journal of Communication, 67,* 413–426.

Bippus, A. M., & Daly, J. A. (1999). What do people think causes stage fright? Naïve attributions about the reasons for public speaking anxiety. *Communication Education, 48,* 63–72.

Booth-Butterfield, M., & Trotta, M. R. (1994). Attributional patterns for the expression of love. *Communication Reports, 7,* 119–129.

Bradbury, T. N., & Fincham, F. D. (1990). Attributions in marriage: Review and critique. *Psychological Bulletin, 107,* 3–33.

Bradbury, T. N., & Fincham, F. D. (1992). Attributions and behavior in marital interaction. *Journal of Personality and Social Psychology, 63,* 613–628.

Bradley, G. W. (1978). Self-serving biases in the attribution process: A reexamination of the fact or fiction question. *Journal of Personality and Social Psychology, 36,* 56–71.

Bugental, D. B., Shennum, W., Frank, M., & Ekman, P. (2001). "True lies": Children's abuse history and power attributions as influences on deception detection. In V. Manusov & J. H. Harvey (Eds.), *Attribution, communication behavior, and close relationships* (pp. 248–265). Cambridge, UK: Cambridge University Press.

Burgoon, J. K., & Newton, D. A. (1991). Applying a social meaning model to relational message interpretations of conversational involvement: Comparing observer and participant perspectives. *The Southern Journal of Communication, 56,* 96–113.

Burleson, B. R. (1986). Attribution schemes and causal inference in natural conversations. In D. G. Ellis & W. A. Donohue (Eds.), *Contemporary issues in language and discourse processes* (pp. 63–85). Hillsdale, NJ: Lawrence Erlbaum Associates.

Cameron, C. A., & Stritzke, W. G. K. (2003). Alcohol and acquaintance rape in Australia: Testing the presupposition model of attributions about responsibility and blame. *Journal of Applied Social Psychology, 33,* 983–1009.

Canary, D. J., & Spitzberg, B. H. (1990). Attribution biases and associations with outcomes between conflict strategies and competence outcomes. *Communication Monographs, 57,* 139–151.

Crittenden, K. S., & Wiley, M. G. (1985). When egotism is normative: Self-presentational norms guiding attributions. *Social Psychology Quarterly, 48,* 360–365.

Cupach, W. R., & Spitzberg, B. H. (Eds.). (1994). *The dark side of interpersonal communication.* Hillsdale, NJ: Lawrence Erlbaum Associates.

Darley, J. M., & Cooper, J. (Eds.). (1998). *Attribution and social interaction: The legacy of Edward E. Jones.* Washington, DC: American Psychological Association.

Davey, A., Beach, S. R. H., Fincham, F. D., & Brody, G. H. (2001). Attributions in marriage: Examining the entailment model in dyadic context. *Journal of Family Psychology, 15,* 721–734.

Derlega, V. J., & Winstead, B. A. (2001). HIV-infected persons' attributions for the disclosure and nondisclosure of the seropositive diagnosis to significant others. In V. Manusov & J. H. Harvey (Eds.), *Attribution, communication behavior, and close relationships* (pp. 266–284). Cambridge, UK: Cambridge University Press.

Dickson, R. E., Manusov, V., Cody, M. J., & McLaughlin, M. L. (1996). When hearing's not believing: Perceived differences between public and private explanations for two compliance failures. *Journal of Language and Social Psychology, 15,* 27–39.

Dugan, K. W. (1989). Ability and effort attributions: Do they affect how managers communicate performance feedback information? *Academy of Management Journal, 32,* 87–114.

Ehrenhaus, P. (1983). Culture and the attribution process: Barriers to effective communication. In W. B. Gudykunst (Ed.), *Intercultural communication theory* (pp. 259–270). Beverly Hills, CA: Sage.

Feiring, C., Taska, L., & Lewis, M. (2002). Adjustment following sexual abuse discovery: The role of shame and attributional style. *Developmental Psychology, 38,* 79–93.

Fincham, F. D. (1985). Attributions in close relationships. In J. H. Harvey & G. Weary (Eds.), *Attribution: Basic issues and applications* (pp. 203–234). New York: Academic.

Fincham, F. D. (2001). Thanks for the curry: Advancing boldly into a new millennium of relationship attribution research. In V. Manusov & J. H. Harvey (Eds.), *Attribution, communication behavior, and close relationships* (pp. 211–223). Cambridge, UK: Cambridge University Press.

Fincham, F. D., Beach, R. H., Arias, I., & Brody, G. H. (1998). Children's attributions in the family: The children's relationship attribution measure. *Journal of Family Psychology, 12,* 481–482.

Fincham, F. D., & Bradbury, T. N. (1992). Assessing attributions in marriage: The relationship attribution measure. *Journal of Personality and Social Psychology, 62,* 457–468.

Fletcher, G. J. O., Danilovics, P., Fernandez, G., Peterson, D., & Reeder, G. D. (1986). Attributional complexity: An individual differences measure. *Journal of Personality and Social Psychology, 51,* 875–884.

Fletcher, G. J. O., Fincham, F. D., Cramer, L., & Heron, N. (1987). The role of attributions in the development of dating relationships. *Journal of Personality and Social Psychology, 53,* 481–489.

Floyd, K., & Voloudakis, M. (1999). Attributions for expectancy violating changes in affectionate behavior in platonic friendships. *Journal of Psychology, 133,* 32–48.

Folkes, V. S. (1982). Communicating the causes of social rejection. *Journal of Experimental Social Psychology, 18,* 235–252.

Gao, G., & Gudykunst, W. E. (1995). Attributional confidence, perceived similarity, and network involvement in Chinese and American romantic relationships. *Communication Quarterly, 43,* 431–445.

Goffman, E. (1961). *Asylums: Essays on the social situation of mental patients and other inmates.* New York: Doubleday Anchor.

Harvey, J. H. (1989). Fritz Heider (1896–1988). *American Psychologist, 44,* 570–571.

Harvey, J. H., & Omarzu, J. (2001). Are there superior options? Commentary on Spitzberg's "The status of attribution theory qua theory in personal relationships." In V. Manusov & J. H. Harvey (Eds.), *Attribution, communication behavior, and close relationships* (pp. 372–380). Cambridge, UK: Cambridge University Press.

Harvey, J. H., & Weary, G. (Eds.). (1985). *Attribution: Basic issues and applications.* New York: Academic.

Heider, F. (1958). *The psychology of interpersonal relations.* New York: Wiley.

Hilton, D. J. (1990). Conversational process and causal explanation. *Psychological Bulletin, 107,* 65–81.

Holtzworth-Munroe, A., & Jacobson, N. S. (1988). Toward a methodology for coding spontaneous causal attributions: Preliminary results with married couples. *Journal of Social and Clinical Psychology, 7,* 101–112.

Honeycutt, J. M., & Eidenmuller, M. E. (2001). Communication and attribution: An exploration of the effects of music and mood on intimate couples' verbal and nonverbal conflict resolution behaviors. In V. Manusov & J. H. Harvey (Eds.), *Attribution, communication behavior, and close relationships* (pp. 21–37). Cambridge, UK: Cambridge University Press.

Ifert, D. E., & Roloff, M. E. (1994). Anticipated obstacles to compliance: Predicting their presence and expression. *Communication Studies, 45,* 120–130.

Johnson, M. D., Karney, B. R., Rogge, R., & Bradbury, T. N. (2001). The role of marital behavior in the longitudinal associations between attributions and marital quality. In V. Manusov & J. H. Harvey (Eds.), *Attribution, communication behavior, and close relationships* (pp. 173–193). Cambridge, UK: Cambridge University Press.

Jones, E. E. (1979). The rocky road from acts to dispositions. *American Psychologist, 34,* 107–117.

Jones, E. E., & Davis, K. E. (1965). From acts to dispositions: The attribution process in person perception. In L. Berkowitz (Ed.), *Advances in experimental social psychology* (Vol. 2, pp. 219–266). New York: Academic.

Jones, E. E., & Nisbett, R. E. (1972). The actor and the observer: Divergent perceptions of the causes of behavior. In E. E. Jones, D. E. Kanouse, H. H. Kelley, R. E. Nisbett, S. Valins, & B. Weiner (Eds.), *Attributions: Perceiving the causes of behavior* (pp. 79–94). Morristown, NJ: General Learning Press.

Kellermann, K. (1984). The negativity effect and its implication for initial interaction. *Communication Monographs, 51,* 37–55.

Kellerman, K. (1986). Anticipation of future interaction and information exchange in initial interaction. *Human Communication Research, 13,* 41–75.

Kellermann, K. (1989). The negativity effect in interaction: It's all in your point of view. *Human Communication Research, 16,* 147–183.

Kelley, H. H. (1967). Attribution theory in social psychology. *Nebraska Symposium on Motivation, 14,* 192–241.

Kelley, H. H. (1991). *Attribution in social interaction.* Morristown, NJ: General Learning Press.

Krahl, J. R., & Wheeless, L. R. (1997). Retrospective analysis of previous relationship disengagement and current attachment style. *Communication Quarterly, 45,* 167–187.

Krull, D. S., Loy, M. H-M., Lin, J., Wang, C-F., Chen, S., & Zhao, X. (1999). The fundamental attribution error: Correspondence bias in individualistic and collectivistic cultures. *Personality & Social Psychology Bulletin, 25,* 1208–1209.

Lim, G. Y., & Roloff, M. E. (1999). Attributing sexual consent. *Journal of Applied Communication Research, 27,* 1–23.

Littleton, H. L., & Axsom, D. (2003). Rape and seduction scripts of university students: Implications for rape attributions and unacknowledged rape. *Sex Roles: A Journal of Research, 49,* 465–476.

MacGeorge, E. L. (2001). Support providers' interaction goals: The influence of attributions and emotions. *Communication Monographs, 68,* 28–48.

MacGeorge, E. L. (2003). Gender differences in attributions and emotions in helping contexts. *Sex Roles, 48,* 175–183.

MacGeorge, E. L., Gillihan, S. J., Samter, W., & Clark, R. A. (2003). Skill deficit or differential motivation? Testing alternative explanations for gender differences in the provision of emotional support. *Communication Research, 30,* 272–303.

Manusov, V. (1990). An application of attribution principles to nonverbal messages in romantic dyads. *Communication Monographs, 57,* 104–118.
Manusov, V. (1991). Perceiving nonverbal messages: Effects of immediacy and encoded intent on receiver judgments. *Western Journal of Speech Communication, 55,* 235–253.
Manusov, V. (1992). Mimicry or synchrony: The effects of intentionality attributions for nonverbal mirroring behavior. *Communication Quarterly, 40,* 69–83.
Manusov, V. (1993). "It depends on your perspective": Effects of stance and beliefs about intent on person perception. *Western Journal of Communication, 57,* 27–41.
Manusov, V. (1996). Intentionality attributions for naturally-occurring nonverbal behaviors in intimate relationships. In J. E. Aitken & L. J. Shedletsky (Eds.), *Intrapersonal communication processes* (pp. 343–353). Plymouth, MI: Midnight Oil Multimedia.
Manusov, V. (2001). Preface. In V. Manusov & J. H. Harvey (Eds.), *Attribution, communication behavior, and close relationships* (pp. xvii–xxi). Cambridge, UK: Cambridge University Press.
Manusov, V. (2002). Thought and action: Connecting attributions to behaviors in married couples' interactions. In P. Noller & J. A. Feeney (Eds.), *Understanding marriage: Developments in the study of couple interaction* (pp. 14–31). Cambridge, UK: Cambridge University Press.
Manusov, V. (2004). Measuring attributions given to nonverbal cues. In V. Manusov (Ed.), *The sourcebook of nonverbal measures: Going beyond words* (pp. 335–346). Mahwah, NJ: Lawrence Erlbaum Associates.
Manusov, V. (2006). Attribution theories: Assessing interpretation processes in families. In D. O. Braithwaite & L. A. Baxter (Eds.), *Family communication theories* (pp. 181–196). Mahwah, NJ: Lawrence Erlbaum Associates.
Manusov, V., Floyd, K., & Kerssen-Griep, J. (1997). Yours, mine, and ours: Mutual attributions for nonverbal behaviors in couples' interactions. *Communication Research, 24,* 234–260.
Manusov, V., & Koenig, J. (2001). The content of attributions in couples' communication. In V. Manusov & J. H. Harvey (Eds.), *Attribution, communication behavior, and close relationships* (pp. 134–152). Cambridge, UK: Cambridge University Press.
Manusov, V., & Rodriguez, J. S. (1989). Intentionality behind nonverbal cues: A perceiver's perspective. *Journal of Nonverbal Behavior, 13,* 15–24.
Manusov, V., Trees, A. R., Reddick, L. A., Carrillo Rowe, A. M., & Easley, J. M. (1998). Explanations and impressions: Investigating attributions and their effects on judgments of friends and strangers. *Communication Studies, 49,* 209–223.
McKenzie, B. J., & Calder, P. (1993). Factors related to attributions of blame in father–daughter incest. *Psychological Reports, 73,* 1111–1122.
McMahan, E. M. (1976). Nonverbal communication as a function of attribution in impression formation. *Communication Monographs, 43,* 287–294.
Metts, S. (2001). Extending attribution theory: Contributions and cautions. In V. Manusov & J. H. Harvey (Eds.), *Attribution, communication behavior, and close relationships* (pp. 338–350). Cambridge, UK: Cambridge University Press.
Miller, G. E., & Bradbury, T. N. (1995). Refining the association between attributions and behavior in marital interaction. *Journal of Family Psychology, 9,* 196–208.
Mills, R. S. L., Nazar, J., & Farrell, H. M. (2003). Child and parent perceptions of hurtful messages. *Journal of Social and Personal Relationships, 19,* 731–754.
Monahan, K. (1997). Crocodile talk: Attributions of incestuously abused and nonabused sisters. *Child Abuse and Neglect, 21,* 19–35.

Motley, M. T. (1990). One whether one can not(not) communicate: An examination of traditional communication postulates. *Western Journal of Speech Communication, 54,* 1–20.

Newman, H. (1981). Communication within ongoing intimate relationships: An attributional perspective. *Personality and Social Psychology Bulletin, 7,* 59–70.

Noller, P., Feeney, J. A., & Blakeley-Smith, A. (2001). Handling pressures for change in marriage: Making attributions for relational dialectics. In V. Manusov & J. H. Harvey (Eds.), *Attribution, communication behavior, and close relationships* (pp. 153–172). Cambridge, UK: Cambridge University Press.

Peterson, C. C., Troth, A., Gallois, C., & Feeney, J. (2001). Attributions about communication styles and strategies: Predicting couples' safe-sex discussions and relationship satisfaction. In V. Manusov & J. H. Harvey (Eds.), *Attribution, communication behavior, and close relationships* (pp. 285–304). Cambridge, UK: Cambridge University Press.

Pittam, J., & Gallois, C. (1997). Language strategies in the attribution of blame for HIV and AIDS. *Communication Monographs, 64,* 201–218.

Power, J. G., Murphy, S. T., & Coover, G. (1996). Priming prejudice: How stereotype and counter-stereotypes influence attribution of responsibility and credibility among ingroups and outgroups. *Human Communication Research, 23,* 36–58.

Pszyszynski, T. A., & Greenberg, J. (1981). Role of disconfirmed expectancies in the instigation of attributional processing. *Journal of Personality and Social Psychology, 40,* 31–38.

Quist, R. M., & Wiegand, D. M. (2002). Attributions of hate: The media's causal attributions of a homophobic murder. *American Behavioral Scientist, 46,* 93–108.

Read, S. J. (1987). Constructing causal scenarios: A knowledge structure approach to causal reasoning. *Journal of Personality and Social Psychology, 52,* 288–302.

Roghaar, L. A., & Vangelisti, A. L. (1996). Expressed attributions for academic success and failure by adolescents and young adults. *Western Journal of Communication, 60,* 124–145.

Ross, L. (1977). The intuitive psychologist and his shortcomings: Distortions in the attribution process. In L. Berkowitz (Ed.), *Advances in experimental social psychology* (Vol. 10, pp. 174–177). New York: Academic.

Russell, D. (1982). The Causal Dimension Scale: A measure of how individuals perceive causes. *Personality and Social Psychology, 42,* 1137–1145.

Segrin, C., & Dillard, J. P. (1991). (Non)depressed persons' cognitive and affective reactions to (un)successful interpersonal influence. *Communication Monographs, 58,* 115–134.

Seibold, D. R., & Spitzberg, B. H. (1982). Attribution theory and research: Review and implications for communication. In B. Dervin & M. J. Voight (Eds.), *Progress in communication sciences* (pp. 85–125). Norwood, NJ: Ablex.

Seligman, M. E., Abramson, L. Y., Semmel, A., & von Baeyer, C. (1979). Depressive attributional style. *Journal of Abnormal Psychology, 88,* 242–247.

Shotter, J. (1985). Social accountability and self specification. In K. J. Gergen & K. E. Davis (Eds.), *The social construction of the person* (pp. 167–189). New York: Springer-Verlag.

Sillars, A. L. (1980). Attributions and communication in roommate conflicts. *Communication Monographs, 47,* 180–200.

Sillars, A. L. (1982). Attribution and communication: Are people "naïve scientists" or just naïve? In M. E. Roloff & C. R. Berger (Eds.), *Social cognition and communication* (pp. 73–106). Beverly Hills, CA: Sage.

Sillars, A. L., Leonard, K. E., Roberts, L. J., & Dunn, T. (2002). Cognition and communication during marital conflict: How alcohol affects subjective coding of interaction in aggressive and nonaggressive couples. In P. Noller & J. A. Feeney (Eds.), *Understanding marriage: Developments in the study of couple interaction* (pp. 85–112). Cambridge, UK: Cambridge University Press.

Silvester, J., Bentovim, A., Stratton, P., & Hanks, H. G. I. (1995). Using spoken attributions to classify abusive families. *Child Abuse and Neglect, 19,* 1221–1233.

Spitzberg, B. (2001). The status of attribution theory qua theory in personal relationships. In V. Manusov & J. H. Harvey (Eds.), *Attribution, communication behavior, and close relationships* (pp. 353–371). Cambridge, UK: Cambridge University Press.

Staley, J. M., & Blumberg Lapidus, L. (1997). Attributions of responsibility in father–daughter incest in relation to gender, socio-economic status, ethnicity, and experiential differences in participants. *Journal of Clinical Psychology, 53,* 331–348.

Stamp, G. H., & Knapp, M. L. (1990). The construct of intent in interpersonal relationships. *Quarterly Journal of Speech, 76,* 282–299.

Stander, V. A., Hsiung, P., & MacDermid, S. (2001). The relationship of attributions to marital distress: A comparison of mainland Chinese and U.S. couples. *Journal of Family Psychology, 15,* 124–134.

Vangelisti, A. L. (1994). Messages that hurt. In W. R. Cupach & B. H. Spitzberg (Eds.), *The dark side of interpersonal communication* (pp. 53–82). Hillsdale, NJ: Lawrence Erlbaum Associates.

Vangelisti, A. L. (2001). Making sense of hurtful interactions in close relationships. In V. Manusov & J. H. Harvey (Eds.), *Attribution, communication behavior, and close relationships* (pp. 38–58). Cambridge, UK: Cambridge University Press.

Vangelisti, A. L., Corbin, S. D., Lucchetti, A. E., & Sprague, R. J. (1999). Couples' concurrent cognition: The influence of relational satisfaction in the thoughts couples have as they converse. *Human Communication Research, 25,* 370–398.

Vangelisti, A. L., & Young, S. L. (2000). When words hurt: The effects of perceived intentionality on interpersonal relationships. *Journal of Social and Personal Relationships, 17,* 393–424.

Weber, D. J., & Vangelisti, A. L. (1991). "Because I love you ... ": The tactical use of attributional expressions in conversation. *Human Communication Research, 17,* 606–624.

Weiner, B. (1985). An attributional theory of achievement motivation and emotion. *Psychological Bulletin, 92,* 548–573.

Weiner, B. (1986). *An attributional theory of motivation and emotion.* New York: Springer-Verlag.

Weiner, B. (1995). *Judgments of responsibility: A foundation for a theory of social conduct.* New York: Guilford.

Weiner, B., Amirkhan, J., Folkes, V. S., & Verette, J. A. (1987). An attributional analysis of excuse giving: Studies of a naïve theory of emotion. *Journal of Personality and Social Psychology, 52,* 316–324.

Weisman, R. (2004). Showing remorse: Reflections on the gap between expression and attribution in cases of wrongful conviction. *Canadian Journal of Criminology and Criminal Justice, 46,* 121–138.

Wilson, S. R., Cruz, M. G., & Kang, K. H. (1992). Is it always a matter of perspective? Construct differentiation and variability in attributions about compliance gaining. *Communication Monographs, 59,* 350–367.

Wilson, S. R., Cruz, M. G., Marshall, L., & Rao, N. (1993). An attributional analysis of compliance-gaining interactions. *Communication Monographs, 60,* 352–373.

Wilson, S. R., & Kang, K. H. (1991). Communication and unfulfilled obligations: Individual differences in causal judgments. *Communication Research, 18,* 799–824.

Wilson, S. R., & Whipple, E. E. (2001). Attributions and regulative communication by parents participating in a community-based child physical abuse prevention program. In V. Manusov & J. H. Harvey (Eds.), *Attribution, communication behavior, and close relationships* (pp. 227–247). Cambridge, UK: Cambridge University Press.

Wong, P. T. P., & Weiner, B. (1981). When people ask "why" questions, and the heuristics of attributional search. *Journal of Personality and Social Psychology, 40,* 650–663.

Young, S. L., & Bippus, A. M. (2001). Does it make a difference if they hurt you in a funny way? Humorously and non-humorously phrased hurtful messages in personal relationships. *Communication Quarterly, 49,* 35–52.

8

Shared Cognition and Communication Within Group Decision Making and Negotiation

Michael E. Roloff
Lyn M. Van Swol
Northwestern University

Human beings are social animals. As such, they are drawn into contact with each other and this ongoing interaction gives rise to a variety of collective arrangements ranging from dyadic relationships to societies. These associations involve a degree of interdependency such that the decisions and actions of one person can influence those of others. Because individuals may have limited knowledge of how their behavior might aversely impact other people or in some cases, they may be indifferent or even antagonistic toward others, conflicting actions may arise that can escalate and threaten individual and collective well-being. In addition, isolated actors often miss opportunities to capitalize on their insights and resources.

To prevent such outcomes, individuals often communicate in a manner intended to coordinate their behavior. In doing so they might avoid conflict and mobilize resources into joint actions that are mutually beneficial. Two symbolic tools are group decision making and negotiation. Scholars note that these interaction forms typically differ with regard to both context and process (Roloff, Putnam, & Anastasiou, 2003). Negotiation often takes place in a mixed motive environment in which individuals enter with preset interests and proposals that are subsequently modified through concession making. In contrast, group decision making often occurs in an environment in which interests are less clear and proposals are generated during deliberation. Although the aforementioned distinctions do not always hold true, separate literatures have developed around each of the two types of processes (e.g., Gouran,

2003; Roloff et al., 2003). Moreover, researchers within these traditions have developed distinct theories, constructs, and methods.

In spite of distinct research traditions, both group decision making and negotiation are intended to create agreements that will guide future behavior. As such, they are minimally successful if sufficient consensus is formed so that the parties understand and accept how each will coordinate their actions. When held to a higher standard, these agreements should serve the interests of all parties affected by them, including those of individuals who did not participate. In our view, the success of these processes depends on the ability of individuals to generate and accurately interpret messages that describe their interests and advance solutions that might serve them. By doing so, the parties may achieve a shared view of what needs to done. If so, then understanding the conditions that lead to successful group decision making and negotiation requires us to explore the link between shared cognition and communication.

One can identify a variety of cognitive approaches within the separate literatures and several excellent reviews examine the totality of this literature at various points in its development (Bazerman, Curhan, Moore, & Valley, 2000; Bazerman & Neale, 1983; Neale & Bazerman, 1991). Because we believe that shared cognition is most centrally related to communication, this chapter is narrowly focused on that phenomenon within the group decision making and negotiation literatures. We examine the relevant literature and point out future areas of research. To that end, we first review perspectives focused on shared cognition and group decision making and then move to an analysis of shared cognition and negotiation. We end with a section that highlights future directions.

SHARED COGNITION IN GROUPS

When individuals are brought together in groups and aggregates, they operate in an environment that is more than just the sum of the individuals' contributions; rather the group often creates a shared reality in which to work and complete its task. One of the functions of groups is to develop a shared reality among the members. Having shared cognition in the group allows for coordination of movement, facilitates communication and consensus, and promotes the maintenance of the group. Communication plays an integral role in the development of shared cognition, and communication processes benefit from the development of shared cognition. In this way, communication is both a process and product of shared cognition. This section examines the meaning of shared cognition in groups, the benefits of shared cognition, the role that communication plays, and methodological limitations associated with the aforementioned research.

Shared cognition can refer to many different group processes. Much research on shared cognition has examined how groups reach agreement and convergence in opinions during a group discussion (Davis, 1973; Laughlin, 1980; Lorge & Solomon, 1955; Steiner, 1972). In this case, shared cognition often refers to sharing the same opinions or information. Prior to the mid-1980s the majority of research on shared cognition in groups focused on how individual members' opinions converged to a group opinion. However, starting with Stasser and Titus's (1985) article examining information sampling in groups, more research has considered how information sharing among group members affects group decision making. Also, starting in the 1990s research on shared mental models began to examine how group members share a common understanding of the group's task and coordination mechanisms (Cannon-Bowers, Salas, & Converse, 1993; Stout, Cannon-Bowers, Salas, & Milanovich, 1999). When group members share mental models, they do not necessarily have to have a convergence of opinion. For example, all Supreme Court justices, even those who have the most severe disagreements on the most important constitutional questions, share a commitment to the Court's existence, purposes, and freedom from any influence by the political branches of government.

Research on Shared Cognition and Group Decision Making

Tindale, Meisenhelder, Dykema-Engblade, and Hogg (2001) stated that "things that are shared among group members have a stronger impact on both group process and performance than do things that are not shared" (p. 8). Shared cognition plays a crucial role in group decision making, especially in influencing a group toward consensus. For example, groups often follow a majority-wins rule when making decisions such that the sharedness of opinion becomes the group's opinion (Kameda, Tindale, & Davis, 2003). Also, groups tend to discuss and focus on information shared in common by all group members more than information unique to one member (Savadori, Van Swol, & Sniezek, 2001; Stasser & Titus, 1985; Wittenbaum & Stasser, 1996), and members who discuss more information shared in common are more influential in the group (Kameda, Ohtsubo, & Takezawa, 1997). For example, Wittenbaum, Hubbell, and Zuckerman (1999) found that partners who provided more information shared in common with the participant were rated as more task competent and knowledgeable.

In other words, a basis for persuasion in the group is the degree of sharedness of cognition between members, either in discussion of information or opinions. The more a member's opinion or information is shared with others, the more likely the person's view is going to predominate. Sharedness lays the groundwork from which a group can converge to a common vision. In fact, even when members are in the minority opinion in a group, they can heavily influence the group's decision if they have other forms of shared cognition in the group like shared information or a shared belief system. For example, with the truth-supported (Laughlin & Ellis, 1986) model of group decision making, in which one correct group member can predominate over an incorrect majority, the correct member is able to persuade the group to his or her opinion through demonstration of the correctness of his or her opinion through a shared belief system. Also, Van Swol and Seinfeld (2004) gave participants common and unique information about the decriminalization of marijuana and then had participants come to consensus on the issue in groups. They found that minority members whose opinion prevailed as the group's opinion mentioned more information shared in common with the other group members and less information unique to only the minority member than minority members whose opinion did not prevail as the group opinion. In other words, minority members who mentioned more information shared in common were more persuasive in shaping the group's decision. Finally, Smith, Tindale, and Steiner (1998) had groups come to consensus on a sunk costs problem and found that sunk-costs minorities were more persuasive than rational minorities. Smith et al. (1998) reasoned that because individuals are more prone to sunk-cost thinking than rational thinking, a minority supporting his or her position with sunk cost thinking was more persuasive because the minority appealed to a shared representation of the task. Tindale et al. (2001) stated "Whenever a 'shared task representation' exists, alternatives consistent with the representation will be easier to defend and ... end up as the group's collective choice" (p. 13). Thus, shared information, shared preferences, and shared belief systems play a crucial role in group decision making. Shared cognitions are a powerful glue drawing a group toward consensus. Other research on shared cognition has examined how shared mental models can improve a group's performance.

Research on Shared Mental Models and Group Decision Making

Shared mental models refer to the often implicit understandings that group members have of the situation, task, and one another's responsibilities (Macmillan, Entin, & Serfaty, 2004). Group members do not have to agree to have a shared mental model, and in fact, opposing factions in a group can develop a very strong shared mental model by discussing their differences (Brauner, 1996). Generally, shared mental models in groups are studied by assessing "the degree of common understanding, overlap, agreement, congruence, or sharedness of cognitions" (Rentsch

& Woehr, 2004, p. 13). Group members hold thoughts about specific processes in the group, and the extent to which these thoughts are held in common with other group members determines the extent of the shared mental model in the group (Rentsch & Woehr, 2004). Groups are said to have shared mental models about many different aspects of the group. For example, group members can have shared mental models about the task, the team process, or members' expertise (Levine & Choi, 2004).

Shared mental models are created through communication and, in turn, improve and facilitate communication once they are formed. Macmillan et al. (2004) stated, "Team cognition requires communication ... in order for the team to build and maintain a shared mental model of the situation" (p. 61). Orasanu (1990, 1993) found that flight crews purposely would communicate to build shared mental models to prepare for stressful, high-taskload situations. This helped coordinate action and implicit understandings so that stressful situations could be handled more easily. Tindale et al. (2001) asserted that communication helps build a convergence of mental models among group members. For example, Hastie and Pennington (1991) mentioned how communication among jurors helps lead to a shared vision of the evidence.

Once shared mental models are firmly established, they can streamline communication. For example, they can reduce the amount that groups need to communicate because members have implicit understandings of responsibilities. In this way, shared mental models can reduce the communication overhead in the group, which can benefit team performance (Macmillan et al., 2004). However, established shared mental models can also help facilitate and increase the communication of important information. For example, Tindale et al. (2001) discussed a training system for airplane crews to improve crew members' mental models of fellow crew members' areas of expertise and roles in the airplane. By having a strong shared mental model of each crew member's area of expertise, members are better able to communicate information in their area of expertise because other members are more likely to listen and pay attention to each other's expertise. Similarly, research on transactive memory has found that groups can communicate more efficiently about the distribution of knowledge when members share a mental model about each other's areas of expertise (Wegner, 1995). Hence, shared mental models improve communication in the group, which should positively affect the group's performance.

"Coordinated action lies at the heart of effective team performance" (Macmillan et al., 2004, p. 63), and Cannon-Bowers et al. (1993) suggested that the extent to which group members share mental models about aspects of the group can improve group performance. For example, Minionis, Zaccaro, and Perez (1995) found that teams working on tasks that required interdependence between members had improved performance with shared mental models, and Peterson, Mitchell, Thompson, and Burr (2000) found that classroom groups with more shared mental models received higher grades in the class project than groups with fewer shared mental models. Liang, Moreland, and Argote (1995) trained participants to assemble a radio either individually or in three-person groups. Then, all participants assembled the radio as part of a three-person group. Groups whose participants were trained together, rather than individually, performed better because they had developed a shared mental model about each other's expertise on the assembly task during training. In conclusion, communication plays an integral role in building shared mental models in groups, and shared mental models, in turn, help facilitate communication and improve group performance. We next take a closer look at the role of communication in shared cognition in groups.

Role of Communication in Shared Cognition in Groups

Communication is at the core of shared cognition because shared cognition in groups requires communication among people, whereas individual cognition has no such requirement. Hence, socially shared cognition is a product of communication shared and created among a group of people. Also, shared cognition can in turn facilitate communication in the group because collective meaning is essential to meaningful communication.

Moscovici (1984) examined how social cognition underlies communication in collectives with his research on social representations. Social representations are shared meanings and beliefs about what is common sense that provide a background from which people communicate. The sharedness of social representations develops from common human experience, mores, education, geographic norms, and customs. An example of a social representation in the United States is the concept of individualism (Lorenzi-Cioldi & Clemence, 2001). Groups rely on a shared reality as a background for their interaction, and in this sense, social representations provide a background and context from which group members can more easily communicate and organize their discussion. These social representations are in constant flux as people interact and communicate to change them. For example, social representations about gender roles have changed significantly in the last 100 years in Western cultures due to a continuing discussion about women's rights (Lorenzi-Cioldi & Clemence, 2001). This perspective is also shared by the symbolic interactionist approach (Thompson & Fine, 1999), which argues that collective meaning underscores social life and social order. Interaction and communication are central to the social interactionist approach, as shared cognition is necessary for communication to occur and, yet, is also shaped by interaction among individuals. Thompson and Fine (1999) stated that "social interaction is the engine that drives the creation of collective meaning" (p. 292). Therefore, shared cognition and communication have a dynamic relation in which shared cognition improves communication and communication improves the extent and quality of shared cognition.

An example of the role of communication in shared cognition is Weick's (1993; Weick & Roberts, 1993) work on sense making in organizational groups. Weick argued that much of the decision making and work done within an organization is done through the medium of groups of individuals communicating to make sense of a chaotic situation and create a shared meaning. Weick (1993) stated, "organizations become important because they can provide meaning and order in the face of environments that impose ill-defined, contradictory demands" (p. 632). For example, in his discussion of a group of smokejumpers sent to fight the Mann Gulch wildfire in Montana, he stressed how the inability of the group to create a shared socially constructed reality of the situation contributed to the tragic death of 13 of them. He argued that the disintegration of communication among the group of smokejumpers due to poor leadership, increasing physical isolation, and noise and smoke from the fire created "individuals (that) were isolated and left without explanations or emotional support for their reactions" (p. 234). Without the ability to create a shared understanding of the situation with the other smokejumpers, many of them panicked and responded poorly to the fire. However, Weick (1993) discussed how the only three smokejumpers who survived maintained a sense of group and shared understanding of the situation that allowed them to make sense of the situation, forestall panic, and find an escape route. Weick stated, "It is intriguing that the three people who survived the disaster did so in ways that seem to forestall group disintegration" (p. 234). In this way, groups communicating and negotiating a shared sense of a situation gives the group resilience and support and helps prevent disorganization and chaos in the group.

Another example of the role of communication in creating shared cognition is research on transactive memory. A transactive memory system is "a set of individual memory systems in combination with the communication that takes place between individuals" (Thompson & Fine, 1999, p. 287). It consists of individuals' memory, external memory, and the process of creating a transactive memory through communication. External memory refers to information stored in sources external (i.e., other people) to the individual. Through a process of communication and interaction, individuals in a group learn about each other's areas of expertise and learn what information is stored externally in the memories of fellow group members. This information about what others in the group have in their memories allows members access to this external memory, and in this way, the transactive memory system offers a group memory that is more than "its individual components" (Wegner, 1987, p. 190). Hollingshead (1998) highlighted the importance of communication in building a transactive memory system between individuals. In her study, when dyads could not communicate, dating couples had better collective recall on a memory task than a pair of strangers because the partners in a dating couple had a transactive memory system in place and could infer what their partner would be more likely to remember. However, when Hollingshead allowed the dyads to communicate, the pair of strangers performed better because they were able to explicitly establish a transactive memory system of who would remember what. Thus, the transactive memory system exists only at the level of the group and is created and maintained by the act of group members communicating about members' roles in the process of group memory.

In conclusion, Fiore and Salas (2004) remarked how "team cognition can be like a field-dependence task, where it may be the figure or it may be the ground" (p. 244). The same can be said of the role of communication in socially shared cognition. As the preceding research attests, communication plays the role of both developing shared cognition and benefiting from established shared cognition, as in the case of shared mental models. However, in both cases communication plays a central role in socially shared cognition in groups.

Method and Issues

Little research has examined how groups create shared cognition. It is often assumed that shared cognition is the result of communication and possibly some sense of shared social categorization, but theory often does not get much more sophisticated than this (Tindale et al., 2001). Research needs to address what types of processes and communication are more significant toward creating and maintaining socially shared cognition. For example, Hollingshead (1998) found that intact groups are better able to use their transactive memory systems when interacting face to face than through the computer. Therefore, the type and length of communication along with the context in which the communication is occurring can all affect how a shared cognition is created, used, and maintained in groups.

Research on shared mental models has also often failed to examine exactly how groups create shared mental models. Shared mental models refer to cognitive representations of how a certain system works that is shared among members of a group such that all members understand the system in a similar way. One problem with studying shared mental models is that because they are created over time, they are difficult to study in a controlled laboratory situation. Therefore, it is difficult to study the actual process of groups creating a shared mental model. Most often research assumes that groups that have interacted with each longer have more shared mental models (Hastie & Pennington, 1991) or research assesses areas of agreement in the group after interaction without determining how these shared mental models were created. For example, Peterson et al. (2000) measured group members' mental models of structure, process, and task after working together on a semester-long class project. They found that some groups developed more agreement on their mental models than others, but did not actually study interaction within the groups to determine how these mental models were created and why some groups were better at creating them. However, given the complexity and difficulty of studying group interaction, examining how groups create shared cognition offers a challenge to any researcher.

In conclusion, more research needs to examine the process by which shared cognition and shared mental models are created. Often research examining shared cognition has a black box for how the shared cognition or shared mental model actually comes into existence. It is often assumed that this black box implicitly contains communication among group members, but research needs to get more sophisticated about what types of communication facilitate shared cognition. Thompson and Fine (1999) stated, "In traditional models of socially shared behavior, an exogenous force (a 'black box') determines perceptions of reality. In contemporary models, interaction itself creates perceptions of reality ... there can be no substitute for actual interaction" (p. 296). This has implications for research and methodology for studying shared cognition in groups and negotiation (Thompson & Fine, 1999), as the new paradigm demands studying interaction among individuals, rather than assuming it as a background variable or a black box.

SHARED COGNITION AND NEGOTIATION

Prior to the 1980s, negotiation research took a somewhat limited approach. Much of it was guided by a game theoretic model or method in which negotiators were given the choice to cooperate or compete with minimal opportunity to communicate (see Putnam & Jones, 1982). However, since that time, three trends emerged. First, researchers became increasingly interested in the processes that lead to the discovery of integrative agreements. According to Pruitt (1981), an integrative agreement is one that "reconciles (i.e., integrates) the parties' interests and thus provides high benefits to both of them" (p. 137). Second, researchers recognized that cognitive processes limit the ability of individuals to identify the integrative potential within a situation and hence, doom many to substandard agreements. Neale and Bazerman (1991) articulated this view in the introduction to their book: "The central argument of this book is that to negotiate most effectively negotiators need to make more rational decisions. Making such decisions requires the negotiators understand and reduce the cognitive errors that permeate their decision processes" (p. 2). Although a wide variety of biases have been uncovered, a particularly consequential one arises from a lack of perspective taking in which negotiators make simplifying assumptions about their opponent's cognitions and hence make inaccurate predictions about their negotiation behavior (Carroll, Bazerman, & Maury, 1988). Such misperceptions are an impediment to developing a shared outlook. Finally, researchers have recognized that communication can play a central role in either reinforcing or attenuating the influence of cognitive errors. In particular, by sharing information, negotiators may be able to overcome some of the incorrect assumptions about each other that inhibit the discovery of integrative agreements. To more fully elaborate on these trends, we first examine research focused on shared cognition and move to a discussion on shared mental models. We end the section by examining the role of communication in the development of shared perspectives and critiquing the methods employed by researchers.

Research on Shared Cognition and Negotiation

Pruitt (1981) argued that some degree of integrative potential exists within all negotiation situations. Integrative potential means that some alternative settlements afford higher joint benefits than do others. The potential is lowest in single-issue negotiations that are often characterized as zero sum (i.e., one party gains at the other's expense) and at best, only afford a compromise solution in which both parties sacrifice something of value (Raiffa, 1982). By adding issues, integrative potential increases because parties may be able to identify issues in which they have identical interests or trade-off between issues of differing priority. However, the addition of issues does not ensure that integrative potential will be realized; negotiators must develop a shared understanding of their interests. Unfortunately, issues may be quite complex or negotiators may be unfamiliar with one another; hence, they experience a great deal of uncertainty about each other's perspective. Carroll et al. (1988) argued that to manage their uncertainty, negotiators often make simplifying assumptions about their opponents that prove to be problematic. One particularly pernicious simplifying assumption is called the fixed pie bias. Negotiators often believe that an opponent's interests are opposed to their own (Bazerman & Neale, 1983). This bias diminishes the ability of negotiators to detect compatible issues and to identify issues of differing priorities.

When analyzing issues, negotiators often begin by focusing on the degree to which their preferences are compatible with those of their opponents (Keeny & Raiffa, 1994). For some issues, negotiators have shared interests such that agreements yield common value to both (Lax & Sabenius, 1986). For example, in a real estate transaction, a buyer and a seller may both want an early closing date. The lack of conflicting preferences should increase the likelihood and efficiency of reaching an integrative agreement. Unfortunately, there is evidence from bargaining experiments that individuals often enter negotiation assuming that they have incompatible preferences (Thompson & Hastie, 1990; Thompson & Hrebec, 1996) and after completing a negotiation over issues of common value, they continue to believe that their interests were incompatible (Thompson & Hastie, 1990). Indeed, even when provided with postnegotiation information demonstrating the compatibility of each other's interests, some negotiators persist in believing that they had incompatible preferences (Thompson & DeHarpport, 1994). Furthermore, the ability to accurately identify issues of common value does not increase with experience (Thompson, 1990a) or generalize across bargaining contexts (Thompson, 1990b). Sadly, this misperception yields lose–lose agreements in which negotiators agree to suboptimal alternatives (Thompson & Hrebec, 1996).

The fixed pie bias also leads to misperceptions of priorities. When multiple issues are negotiated, integrative potential is increased when they are of differing priorities to the negotiators and hence, they may log roll by trading concessions on low-priority issues for gains on high-priority ones (Pruitt, 1981; Roloff & Jordan, 1991). So, a seller of a house may want to close early on the deal, but is indifferent to the amount of down payment that is provided. The buyer may be indifferent about the closing date, but can only afford a modest down payment. Hence, they can trade off among the issues and both of their issues are served.

To identify log-rolling potential, it is helpful if negotiators have insight into each other's priorities. Indeed, there is evidence that insight is positively related to discovering integrative agreements (Pruitt, 1981; Thompson & Hastie, 1990). Unfortunately, the fixed pie bias reduces the likelihood that negotiators will develop insight. Thompson and Hastie (1990) found in a bargaining experiment that almost 70% of participants assumed at the outset of the negotiation that their high-priority issue was also their opponent's high-priority issue. However, unlike the incompatibility error, misperceptions of priorities can be self-correcting. There is evidence that negotiators correct these errors soon after negotiation begins, which facilitates log rolling and the discovery of integrative agreements (Thompson & Hastie, 1990). Furthermore, priority misperceptions are amenable to correction when feedback about the opponent's priorities is provided after a negotiation (Thompson & DeHarpport, 1994). Finally, the ability to identify issues of differing importance improves with experience (Thompson, 1990a) and generalizes across bargaining contexts (Thompson, 1990b).

Because the fixed pie bias is pervasive and aversely influences bargaining effectiveness, researchers have tried to discover its origin. For example, Bottom and Paese (1997) argued that it stems from a lack of definitive information about the opponent. When entering a negotiation, opposing parties may have insufficient information about each other from which to make confident judgments about their stance on issues. Because they know their own positions, they tend to generalize them to their counterpart. The researchers conducted an experiment in which they activated stereotypes of the opponents for some negotiators and not for others. Negotiators for whom stereotypes were activated suffered less from the fixed pie bias and negotiated more efficiently than did those for whom stereotypes were not activated. For the latter group, they relied on their own preferences to infer those of the opponents. In some conditions, stereotypes that did not accurately fit the negotiator were activated and although they initially prompted inaccurate perceptions of the opponent, they eventually were corrected and led to more efficient negotiation relative to when no stereotypes were activated.

Although the absence of reliable information about the opponent may play an important role in the fixed pie bias, some evidence suggests the fixed pie bias may reflect the culture of the negotiator. Gelfand and Christakopoulou (1999) argued that the fixed pie bias results from cultural expectations. Specifically, individualistic cultures stress the importance of distancing from others and focusing on one's own internal characteristics (Markus & Kitayama, 1991). Hence, negotiators from such cultures should focus their attention on their own interests, which inhibits them from developing an accurate assessment of their partners. Collectivistic cultures encourage a greater connection among individuals and outward focus. This should increase understanding. They had students from an individualistic culture (United States) negotiate with someone from a collectivistic culture (Greece) and assessed the fixed pie bias. Consistent with their expectations, U.S. negotiators were more likely than those from Greece to show evidence of the fixed pie bias both in their private perceptions of each other and in the statements they made during the negotiation.

Although cultural expectations may promote the fixed pie bias, that does not mean that the effect is uniform among cultural members. A number of studies conducted in the United States indicate not all individuals suffer from it and that certain conditions can undercut its influence. For example, instructional sets can influence the occurrence of the fixed pie bias. In a bargaining experiment, Pinkley, Griffith, and Northcraft (1995) created either fixed pie (instructional material indicated that most negotiations involve incompatible issues) or mixed motive negotiation expectations (instructional material indicated that most negotiations involve a mixture of compatible and incompatible interests). Prior to inducing the expectation and entering into a bargaining simulation, the participants were provided with either full information about their partner's preferences (including areas of compatibility and incompatibility) or provided with no information. The researchers found that negotiators analyzed the information in a manner consistent with the activated expectations. Fixed pie negotiators looked for areas of incompatibility, and hence overlooked areas of compatibility, whereas mixed motive negotiators looked for both incompatibility and compatibility. Not surprisingly, mixed motive negotiators were more likely to discover integrative agreements than were fixed pie negotiators.

Kemp and Smith (1994) looked at whether altering negotiators from the fixed pie bias might stimulate the discovery of integrative agreements. Prior to engaging in a negotiation simulation, participants were asked to identify within a profit schedule which issues were most and least important to them. Afterward, they were admonished that their opponents might not have the same priorities, although they were not given access to the opponent's profit schedule. Relative to negotiators who were not asked about priorities, the primed negotiators reached more integrative agreements and had more accurate insights into their opponent's priorities.

Finally, De Dreu, Koole, and Steinel (2000) hypothesized that the fixed pie bias might result from insufficient motivation to systematically process information. To stimulate motivation, some negotiators in a bargaining simulation were told that they would be held accountable for their actions (i.e., they were told that they would be interviewed by an experienced negotiator and psychologist about their negotiation behaviors), whereas others were given no such expectation. Consistent with their predictions, accountability appears to undercut the fixed pie bias and increased the likelihood of discovering integrative agreements.

In a follow-up study, De Dreu (2003) looked at the degree to which time pressure to reach an agreement might also aversely impact motivation to systematically process information and therefore allow the fixed pie bias to go unabated. He found that negotiators under time pressure were less motivated to process information about the opponent; hence, they were less likely to correct their fixed pie errors and subsequently were less able to find integrative agreements.

Research conducted on the fixed pie bias clearly indicates that the inability of negotiators to understand each other's stance on positions is a detriment to finding integrative agreements. Although there is evidence that the origin of this bias may stem from cultural expectations, to some degree, the bias may result from insufficient information. However, simply providing negotiators with complete information about their issue preferences seems insufficient to overcome the error. Negotiators must be motivated to closely examine the information for compatible issues and for those of differing priority.

Research on Shared Mental Models

Relative to the literature on shared cognition, research on shared mental models is relatively new and consequently it is not as well developed. To our knowledge, only one study has focused on the mental models of negotiators. Van Boven and Thompson (2003) referred to mental models as "cognitive representations of the causal relationships within a system that allow people to understand, predict and solve problems within that system" (p. 388). With regard to negotiation, they conceive of mental models varying on a continuum ranging from those that are purely integrative to those that are purely distributive. Purely integrative models reflect "a belief that negotiation situations offer opportunities for joint gain through 'creation,'" whereas purely distributive models signal "a belief that negotiations do not offer opportunities for joint gains, and that gains for one party necessitate losses for the other party" (p. 389).

To empirically validate the existence of negotiation mental models, Van Boven and Thompson (2003) had undergraduates engage in a bargaining simulation that contained both compatible and incompatible issues and issues of differing priorities. Afterward, they judged how related 15 negotiation terms were to each other. The terms focused on specific aspects of the negotiation simulation (e.g., issues, roles) as well as features related to collaboration (e.g., information exchange, both gain, same interests, trade-off) and competition (e.g., compromise, even split, give away). The linkages among the terms constituted the mental model. They first compared participants who found integrative agreements with those who did not. Their analysis indicated that the mental models of successful negotiators had a greater number of links to information exchange, the structure of the task, and trade-off issues than did those of unsuccessful negotiators. In addition, the mental maps of successful negotiators reflected fewer fixed pie biases in that they included compatible issues and issues of differing importance to each negotiator than did unsuccessful negotiators. The researchers also were able to compare negotiators who had been trained in integrative bargaining with those who had not. Relative to untrained, unsuccessful negotiators, experienced ones had mental models that stressed making trade-offs, identifying preferences, and sharing information. Relative to untrained successful negotiators, the mental models of experienced negotiators had fewer linked terms, which implies that the maps were organized around general principles that guide negotiation, whereas untrained negotiators focused more on the surface characteristics of the situation. Finally, the researchers discovered that the mental models of opposing negotiators who were successful were more substantially correlated than were those who were unsuccessful.

Although the dearth of research warrants caution, this study implies an alternative and useful way of approaching cognition in negotiation. Prior research has been heavily focused on individual cognitive processes in isolation from one another. Consequently, the literature is fragmented and often appears to be a laundry list of biases and errors. Mental models afford the possibility of identifying the interrelations among the various processes. Hopefully, this preliminary research on mental models will stimulate more interest.

Role of Communication in Shared Cognition in Negotiation

Because communication is a process by which individuals seek and disclose information, researchers have investigated its role in developing shared cognition. One body of research has focused on how information exchange might diminish the fixed pie bias. Pruitt's (1981) experimental research identified three types of information exchange that afford negotiators insight into their respective priorities and facilitate the discovery of log-rolling agreements (i.e., those in which they trade concessions on low-priority issues for concession on high-priority ones). First, and not surprisingly, directly disclosing numerical information about profits and priorities are positively related to developing insight and to the discovery of log-rolling agreements. Second, when trust is low, negotiators may indirectly transmit information by noting areas in which their opponent's offers might be improved and such directed information exchange increases insight and the discovery of log-rolling agreements. Finally, negotiators may effectively signal their priorities by stating their preference for one of their opponent's offers relative to another offer.

Pruitt (1981) also argued that negotiators are more likely to reach integrative agreements when they simultaneously considered all of the issues as a package rather than in a sequence (i.e., one at time). Weingart, Bennett, and Brett (1993) found that the advantage of simultaneous consideration of issues stems from the impact it has on information exchange and insight into priorities. Negotiating teams who considered issues as a package exchanged more priority information than did those teams who sequentially negotiated issues and that simultaneous consideration of issues led to a greater degree of insight into priorities and greater likelihood of discovering integrative agreements.

Thompson (1991) looked at the degree to which the development of insight into priorities was affected by whether one negotiator sought or disclosed priority information. Through experimental instructions, she prompted one member of a dyad to ask questions or to disclose priority information. She then compared their insights and bargaining success with negotiators to whom she provided complete information about priorities prior to the start of the negotiation or were not prompted to seek or disclose information. The results indicated that having one member of a negotiation dyad seek or disclose information was sufficient to prompt greater mutual insight and to enhance the discovery of integrative agreements.

Thompson, Peterson, and Brodt (1996) examined information exchange and the fixed pie bias in negotiations involving negotiation parties of different size. In an experiment, they compared negotiations involving (a) two opposing teams, (b) a team and an individual, and (c) two individuals. The researchers hypothesized that because of the greater number of parties at the table, team negotiations should stimulate greater uncertainty than those involving single individuals. To reduce their ambiguity, team members are more likely to exchange information with each other and the opposing team relative to individuals. Consistent with this view, they found that individuals in interteam negotiations exchanged more information, were better able to identify each other's priorities and compatible interests, and were better able to reach integrative agreements than those involving two individuals. Importantly, when negotiations were between a team and an individual, negotiators were better at garnering information and reaching integrative agreements than when negotiations were between two individuals.

Although useful, the aforementioned research did not fully test the degree to which insight into a bargainer's priorities mediates the relation between information exchange and the discovery of integrative agreements. Two studies have provided such evidence. Tutzauer and Roloff (1988) found a three-part path leading to log-rolling agreements: (a) information seeking stimulates mutual insight into priorities; (b) mutual insight leads to the discovery of log-rolling agreements; and (c) discovering log-rolling agreements increases negotiation satisfaction. Interestingly, they found no evidence that disclosing information played a role in this path. In part, this may have resulted from the tendency of some negotiators to unilaterally disclose false information that undercuts the development of insight. O'Connor (1997) looked at the degree to which social motivations might play a role in information seeking and insight. She conducted a bargaining simulation and found a two-part sequence among cooperatively motivated negotiators: (a) information exchange stimulated mutual insight; and (b) mutual insight facilitated reaching log-rolling agreements. Interestingly, these sequences were not statistically significant for individualistically motivated negotiators.

Not all research indicates that information disclosure facilitates integrative bargaining. In particular, disclosing information about compatible issues does not always seem to facilitate understanding or reaching integrative agreements. In the O'Connor study (1997), there was no statistically significant relation among sharing information about common value issues, accuracy of assessing common value issues and reaching agreements for either cooperatively or individualistically motivated negotiators. Furthermore, Murnighan, Babcock, Thompson, and Pillutla (1999) looked at whether information disclosure might actually be to one's disadvantage. They argued that although sharing information about issue preferences may be useful in settings in which there are compatible issues, it could lead to exploitation when the context is distributive (i.e., few issues are compatible and there is limited possibility of trade-offs) and especially when bargainers are experienced and bargaining incentives are high. Indeed, they found that experienced bargainers seeking incentives used information about their opponent's preferences to maximize their own outcomes rather than to reach integrative agreements. Indeed, when discussing compatible issues, experienced negotiators who knew their partner's preferences lied about their own preference. This could reflect a negotiation strategy. O'Connor and Carnevale (1997) found that some negotiators misrepresent their position on a compatible issue to their opponent to extract concessions on other issues (i.e., they pretend to disagree on the issue to gain concessions on one about which they have different preferences). In most cases, negotiators enacted this strategy by not expressing their actual position rather than overtly lying about it. It was most common among individualistically motivated negotiators and it proved to be a highly effective means of maximizing individual outcomes. Although shared information about compatible issues generally discouraged its use and effectiveness, some fully informed negotiators fell prey to it.

The previous research has focused on the fixed pie bias and communication. Other research has focused on communication and the framing bias. The framing bias examines how negotiators view their outcomes (Bazerman & Neale, 1983). Negotiators with gain frames focus on how much they gain from reaching an agreement, whereas those using a loss frame focus on how much they lose by reaching an agreement. Because individuals are more averse to losses than they are attracted by gains (Kahneman & Tversky, 1979), bargainers in loss frames are less willing to make concessions even at the risk of deadlocking and foregoing the benefits of a proposed settlement. Indeed, research generally indicates that gain framed negotiators are less demanding, make more concessions, and are more likely to reach agreements than are those that are loss framed (e.g., Bazerman, Magliozzi, & Neale, 1985; Neale, Huber, & Northcraft, 1987). However, none of these studies addressed the degree to which bargainers communicated their frames to each other and with what effect.

To provide insight into the effect of expressed frames, De Dreu, Emans, and Van de Vliert (1992) conducted a study in which negotiators received information about their opponent's frames and found support for what they labeled the frame adoption hypothesis. Because of the interdependent nature of negotiation, each party must to some degree accommodate each other's frames to reach agreement. When two negotiators have the same frame, communication about the frames simply reinforces the existing one. However, because individuals find losses to be more averse than gains are beneficial, expressed loss frames will cause opponents to shift their gain frame to a loss frame to a greater extent than expressed gain frames will prompt opponents to shift from a loss frame to a gain frame. Consistent with this reasoning, negotiators who expressed a gain frame (e.g., "I make little gains with this offer") stimulated lower goals and greater concessions in their opponents than did those who expressed a loss frame (e.g., "I make big losses with this offer."), but primarily among opponents who had a gain frame from the outset. However, when a negotiator expressed a loss frame, the opponent adopted a loss frame regardless of the opponent's initial frame and resisted lowering goals and making concessions. De Dreu, Carnevale, Emans, and Van de Vliert (1994) replicated this pattern but discovered that it only occurs when the expressed frame is consistent with prenegotiation impressions of the opponent's frame.

Research on communication and shared cognition is reasonably well developed. It shows that communication can reinforce or alter cognitive biases that in turn influence the ability to reach beneficial agreements.

Method and Issues

As is characteristic of social cognition research, much of the literature we reviewed relied on self-reports. Typically, research participants are asked about their negotiation goals, priorities, and frames as well as those of their opponents. Because many of the perspectives assume that negotiators are self-aware, these assessments are reasonable. Furthermore, researchers often code the content of negotiations and directly tested the relation among cognition, communication, and negotiation outcomes. In such cases, there has been a movement away from reporting a series of bivariate correlations toward more rigorous statistical techniques that test causal sequences. Moreover, recent research has drawn samples from several cultures that can provide useful insights into the impact of culture on cognitive processes. These are important strengths of research in this area.

However, there are four limitations. First, the bulk of the research continues to rely on student samples of undergraduates or MBAs. It is an open question as to how well results from these samples generalize to actual negotiators. Students are well educated and trained and their expertise seems to fall between actual negotiators who are novices and those that are experienced professionals. Second, much of the research employs experimental methods and role-play simulations. Although researchers have used scenarios that are created from actual negotiations, they are contrived, issues are defined from the outset, outcomes are initially presented to negotiators in a clear and quantitative fashion, and the personal consequences of the negotiation are relatively minor. These features may not always characterize actual negotiations and might influence shared cognition. Third, most research is conducted over a limited time frame. Most frequently, negotiations are single episodes completed within an hour with no expectation of future negotiation. This approach does not provide information about how shared cognition converges or diverges throughout prolonged negotiations. Finally, the focus of much research is on dyadic rather than group negotiation. Adding more than two individuals to the negotiation mix increases the complexity of the negotiations with regard to the ability to understand the perspectives of multiple opponents as well as those of one's colleagues on the team.

FUTURE DIRECTIONS

As noted in this chapter, important insights have emerged from research focused on shared cognition. There are also a variety of challenges facing researchers in this area that if addressed, could yield important directions for future research.

First, as with many research areas, there is a need to diversify our samples. Although research in group decision making has been conducted with a variety of samples, a great deal of research continues to be conducted with educated individuals from the United States. Expanding the diversity of the samples not only indicates whether the findings generalize, but allows researchers to test hypotheses about the impact of culture (e.g., Gelfand, & Christakopoulou, 1999), education, or socioeconomic status on shared cognition.

Second, there is a pressing need for more diversified study designs. If we assume that shared cognition develops over time, then longitudinal studies are required. Although some researchers have employed such designs, they are infrequent and are typically restricted to two points in time, preinteraction and postinteraction. Hence, we have little idea of how they are modified during the course of deliberation or negotiation. Certainly, assessing online cognition is a substantial methodological challenge, but unless we do so, the manner in which the substance of interaction influences cognition will remain a mystery. Moreover, much research is episodic (i.e., it only investigates one deliberation or negotiation rather than viewing them as part of a serial process that takes place over an extended period of time). There is evidence that some negotiations occur over multiple episodes and include group deliberations between representatives and constituencies to interpret what has transpired and to formulate strategy (Putnam, Wilson, & Turner, 1990). Current research does not inform whether shared cognition changes as episodes unfold. Researchers should consider using a method employed by Kuhn and Corman (2003) for studying organizational change as a model for doing so.

Third, researchers need to refine their conceptualization of shared cognition. For example, it is unclear what should constitute sharedness. It seems reasonable that decision makers and negotiators differ to some degree in their perspectives of what occurred during the interaction. Is there a threshold of agreement that must be reached for participants to believe that an accord exists? Can there be subgroups whose viewpoints do not match those of the majority? If so, how do we identify them?

Fourth, researchers need to assess whether reaching an agreement necessarily yields an effective solution. As we have noted, aspects of shared cognition allow groups to reach decisions and negotiators to reach integrative ones, the research does not address whether those decisions are actually implemented and if they are, whether they prove to be effective. In other words, reaching an accord that seems optimal at the time may not mean that it proves to be workable later or that it will serve the interests of others not present but who are impacted by it.

Fifth, researchers should also focus on the degree to which shared cognition developed during one interaction is used and modified in future ones. To some extent, negotiation researchers have recognized this need and a number of studies are being reported that look at knowledge transfer (e.g., Bereby-Meyer, Moran, & Unger-Aviram, 2003; Nadler, Thompson, & Van Boven, 2003) and hopefully more research will be conducted on this topic.

Sixth, it is our hope that this review will stimulate greater collaboration and mutual awareness among researchers focused on group decision making and those studying negotiation. As we noted at the outset, the two literatures form separate streams, each with its own theories and research questions. Although one can identify some researchers who work in both areas and apply principles from one context in the other (e.g., Weingart, Bennett, & Brett, 1993), many are specialists. Given the common set of concerns facing each set, it would seem useful that the streams be merged. For example, group researchers note that individuals are prone to communicate ideas that they perceive are shared with others while ignoring important unique insights. That perspective could afford important insights into negotiation. Not all integrative agreements flow from log rolling or identifying common interests. Some involve bridging agreements wherein negotiators approach a problem by stepping beyond conventional, prominent solutions (e.g., split the difference or compromise) and hence, find a creative solution (Pruitt, 1981). In such cases, unique information is likely to help them break from the conventional and find a solution that is mutually beneficial. Perhaps the same processes that lead group decision makers to only share information that is already known operate in negotiation dyads, and hence reduce the likelihood of bridging.

Finally, as with many areas of research, there is a need for theoretical frameworks that more specifically address how interaction processes influence shared cognition. Although Pruitt's (1981) perspective provides insights into the forms of information exchange that are related to developing insight into the opponent's perspective, there is still no theory that stimulated those discoveries, nor has one been developed. By and large, many of the discoveries seem serendipitous and in many cases, they are not investigated beyond one or two studies. As the reader may have noticed, the vast majority of studies we reviewed were not conducted by individuals in communication departments. It is possible that communication researchers could make a lasting contribution to this area by incorporating our knowledge of interaction processes into it. We hope that will be the case.

REFERENCES

Bazerman, M. H., Curhan, J. R., Moore, D. A., & Valley, K. L. (2000). Negotiation. *Annual Review of Psychology, 51,* 279–314.

Bazerman, M. H., Magliozzi, T., & Neale, M. (1985). Integrative bargaining in a competitive market. *Organizational Behavior and Human Decision Processes, 35,* 294–313.

Bazerman, M. H., & Neale, M. A. (1983). Heuristics in negotiation: Limitation to effective dispute resolution. In M. H. Bazerman & R. J. Lewicki (Eds.), *Negotiating in organizations* (pp. 51–67). Thousand Oaks, CA: Sage.

Bereby-Meyer, Y., Moran, S., & Unger-Aviram, E. (2003). When performance goals deter performance: Transfer of skills in integrative negotiations. *Organizational Behavior and Human Decision Processes, 93,* 142–154.

Bottom, W. P., & Paese, P. W. (1997). False consensus, stereotypic cues, and the perception of integrative potential in negotiation. *Journal of Applied Social Psychology, 27,* 1919–1940.

Brauner, E. (1996, June). *Stability and change of attitudes and mental models in group interaction processes.* Paper presented at the Nags Head International Conference on Groups, Networks, and Organizations, Highland Beach, Florida.

Cannon-Bowers, J. A., Salas, E., & Converse, S. (1993). Shared mental models in expert team decision making. In N. J. Castellan (Ed.), *Individual and group decision making* (pp. 221–246). Hillsdale, NJ: Lawrence Erlbaum Associates.

Carroll, J. S., Bazerman, M. H., & Maury, R. (1988). Negotiator cognitions: A descriptive approach to negotiators' understanding of their opponents. *Organizational Behavior and Human Decision Processes, 41,* 352–370.

Davis, J. H. (1973). A theory of social decision schemes. *Psychological Review, 80,* 97–125.

De Dreu, C. K. W. (2003). Time pressure and closing of the mind in negotiation. *Organizational Behavior and Human Decision Processes, 91,* 280–295.

De Dreu, C. K. W., Carnevale, P. J. D., Emans, B. J. M., & Van de Vliert, E. (1994). Effects of gain–loss frames in negotiation: Loss aversion, mismatching, and frame adoption. *Organizational Behavior and Human Decision Processes, 60,* 90–107.

De Dreu, C. K. W., Emans, B. J. M., & Van de Vliert, E. (1992). The influence of own cognitive and other's communicated gain or loss frame on negotiation behavior. *International Journal of Conflict Management, 3,* 115–132.

De Dreu, C. K. W., Koole, S. L., & Steinel, W. (2000). Unfixing the fixed pie: A motivated information-processing approach to integrative negotiation. *Journal of Personality and Social Psychology, 79,* 975–987.

Fiore, S. M., & Salas, E. (2004). Why we need team cognition. In E. Salas & S. M. Fiore (Eds.), *Team cognition: Understanding the factors that drive process and performance* (pp. 235–248). Washington, DC: American Psychological Association.

Gelfand, M. J., & Christakopoulou, S. (1999). Culture and negotiation cognition: Judgment accuracy and negotiation processes in individualistic and collectivist cultures. *Organization Behavior and Human Decision Processes, 79,* 248–269.

Gouran, D. S. (2003). Communication skills for group decision making. In J. O. Greene & B. R. Burleson (Eds.), *Handbook of communication and social interaction skills* (pp. 835–871). Mahwah, NJ: Lawrecne Erlbaum Associates.

Hastie, R., & Pennington, N. (1991). Cognitive and social processes in decision-making. In L. B. Resnick, J. M. Levine, & S. D. Teasley (Eds.), *Perspectives on socially shared cognition* (pp. 308–327). Washington, DC: American Psychological Association.

Hollingshead, A. (1998). Communication, learning, and retrieval in transactive memory systems. *Journal of Experimental Social Psychology, 34,* 423–442.

Kahneman, D., & Tversky, A. (1979). Prospect theory: An analysis of decision making under risk. *Econometrica, 47,* 263–291.

Kameda, T., Ohtsubo, Y., & Takezawa, M. (1997). Centrality in socio-cognitive networks and social influence: An illustration in a group decision-making context. *Journal of Personality and Social Psychology, 73,* 296–309.

Kameda, T., Tindale, R. S., & Davis, J. H. (2003). Cognitions, preferences, and social sharedness: Past, present, and future directions in group decision making. In S. L. Schneider & J. Shanteau (Eds.), *Emerging perspectives on judgment and decision research* (pp. 458–485). Cambridge, UK: Cambridge University Press.

Keeny, R. L., & Raiffa, H. (1994). Structuring and analyzing values for multiple-issue negotiations. In H. P. Young (Ed.), *Negotiation analysis* (pp. 131–150). Ann Arbor: University of Michigan Press.

Kemp, K. E., & Smith, W. P. (1994). Information exchange, toughness, and integrative bargaining: The roles of explicit cues and perspective-taking. *The International Journal of Conflict Management, 5,* 5–21.

Kuhn, T., & Corman, S. R. (2003). The emergence of homogeneity and heterogeneity in knowledge structures during a planned organizational change. *Communication Monographs, 70,* 198–229.

Laughlin, P. R. (1980). Social combination processes of cooperative, problem-solving groups on verbal intellective tasks. In M. Fishbein (Ed.), *Progress in social psychology* (Vol. 1, pp. 127–155). Hillsdale, NJ: Lawrence Erlbaum Associates.

Laughlin, P. R., & Ellis, A. L. (1986). Demonstrability and social combination processes on mathematical intellective tasks. *Journal of Experimental Social Psychology, 22,* 177–189.

Lax, D., & Sabenius, J. (1986). *The manager as negotiator.* New York: The Free Press.

Levine, J. M., & Choi, H. S. (2004). Impact of personnel turnover on team performance and cognition. In E. Salas & S. M. Fiore (Eds.), *Team cognition: Understanding the factors that drive process and performance* (pp. 153–176). Washington, DC: American Psychological Association.

Liang, D. W., Moreland, R. L., & Argote, L. (1995). Group versus individual training and group performance: The mediating role of transactive memory. *Personality and Social Psychology Bulletin, 21,* 384–393.

Lorenzi-Cioldi, F., & Clemence, A. (2001). Group processes and the construction of social representations. In M. A. Hogg & S. Tindale (Eds.), *Blackwell handbook of social psychology: Group processes* (pp. 311–333). Malden, MA: Blackwell.

Lorge, I., & Solomon, H. (1955). Two models of group behavior in the solution of eureka-type problems. *Psychometrica, 20,* 139–148.

Macmillan, J., Entin, E. E., & Serfaty, D. (2004). Communication overhead: The hidden costs of team cognition. In E. Salas & S. M. Fiore (Eds.), *Team cognition: Understanding the factors that drive process and performance* (pp. 61–82). Washington, DC: American Psychological Association.

Markus, H. R., & Kitayama, S. (1991). Culture ad the self: Implications for cognition, emotion and motivation. *Psychological Review, 98,* 224–252.

Minionis, D. P., Zaccaro, S. J., & Perez, R. (1995, May). *Shared mental models, team coordination, and team performance.* Paper presented at the 10th Annual Conference of the Society for Industrial/Organizational Psychology, Orlando, FL.

Moscovici, S. (1984). The phenomenon of social representations. In R. M. Farr & S. Moscovici (Eds.), *Social representations* (pp. 3–69). Cambridge, UK: Cambridge University Press.

Murnighan, J. K., Babcock, L., Thompson, L., & Pillutla, M. (1999). The information dilemma in negotiations: Effects of experience, incentives, and integrative potential. *The International Journal of Conflict Management, 10,* 313–339.

Nadler, J., Thompson, L., & Van Boven, L. (2003). Learning negotiation skills: Four models of knowledge creation and transfer. *Management Sciences, 49,* 529–540.

Neale, M., & Bazerman, M. H. (1991). *Rationality and cognition in negotiation.* New York: The Free Press.

Neale, M., Huber, V., & Northcraft, G. (1987). The framing of negotiations: Contextual versus task frames. *Organizational Behavior and Human Decision Processes, 39,* 228–241.

O'Connor, K. M. (1997). Motives and cognitions in negotiation: A theoretical integration and an empirical test. *The International Journal of Conflict Management, 8,* 114–131.

O'Connor, K. M., & Carnevale, P. J. (1997). A nasty but effective negotiation strategy: Misrepresentation of a common-value issue. *Personality and Social Psychology Bulletin, 23,* 504–515.

Orasanu, J. M. (1990). *Shared mental models and crew decision making* (CSL Rep. No. 46). Princeton, NJ: Princeton University, Cognitive Science Laboratory.

Orasanu, J. M. (1993). Decision making in the cockpit. In E. Wiener, B. Kanki, & R. Helmreich (Eds.), *Cockpit resource management* (pp. 137–172). San Diego, CA: Academic.

Peterson, E., Mitchell, T., Thompson, L., & Burr, R. (2000). Collective efficacy and aspects of shared mental models as predictors of performance over time in work groups. *Group Processes and Intergroup Relations, 3,* 296–316.

Pinkley, R. L., Griffith, T. L., & Northcraft, G. B. (1995). "Fixed pie" a la mode: Information availability, information processing, and the negotiation of suboptimal agreements. *Organizational Behavior and Human Decision Processes, 62,* 101–112.

Pruitt, D. G. (1981). *Negotiation behavior.* New York: Academic.

Putnam, L. L., & Jones, T. S. (1982). The role of communication in bargaining. *Human Communication Research, 8,* 262–280.

Putnam, L. L., Wilson, S. R., & Turner, D. B. (1990). The evolution of policy arguments in teachers' negotiations. *Argumentation, 4,* 129–152.

Raiffa, H. (1982). *The art and science of negotiation.* Cambridge, MA: Harvard University Press.

Rentsch, J. R., & Woehr, D. J. (2004). Quantifying congruence in cognition: Social relations modeling and team member schema similarity. In E. Salas & S. M. Fiore (Eds.), *Team cognition: Understanding the factors that drive process and performance* (pp. 11–31). Washington, DC: American Psychological Association.

Roloff, M. E., & Jordan, J. M. (1991). The influence of effort, experience, and persistence on the elements of bargaining plans. *Communication Research, 18,* 306–332.

Roloff, M. E., Putnam, L. L., & Anastasiou, L. (2003). Negotiation skills. In J. O. Greene & B. R. Burleson (Eds.), *Handbook of communication and social interaction skills* (pp. 801–834). Mahwah, NJ: Lawrence Erlbaum Associates.

Savadori, L., Van Swol, L. M., & Sniezek, J. A. (2001). Information sampling and confidence within groups and judge advisor systems. *Communication Research, 28,* 737–771.

Smith, C. M., Tindale, R. S., & Steiner, L. (1998). Investment decisions by individuals and groups in "sunk cost" situations: The potential impact of shared representations. *Group Processes and Intergroup Relations, 1,* 175–189.

Stasser, G., & Titus, W. (1985). Pooling of unshared information in group decision making: Biased information sampling during discussion. *Journal of Personality and Social Psychology, 48,* 1467–1478.

Steiner, I. (1972). *Group process and productivity.* New York: Academic.

Stout, R. J., Cannon-Bowers, J. A., Salas, E., & Milanovich, D. M. (1999). Planning, shared mental models, and coordinated performance: An empirical link is established. *Human Factors, 41,* 61–71.

Thompson, L. (1990a). An examination of native and experienced negotiators. *Journal of Personality and Social Psychology, 59,* 82–90.

Thompson, L. (1990b). The influence of experience on negotiation performance. *Journal of Experimental Social Psychology, 26,* 528–544.

Thompson, L. (1991). Information exchange in negotiation. *Journal of Experimental Social Psychology, 27,* 161–179.

Thompson, L., & DeHarpport, T. (1994). Social judgment, feedback, and interpersonal learning in negotiation. *Organizational Behavior and Human Decision Processes, 58,* 327–345.

Thompson, L., & Fine, G. A. (1999). Socially shared cognition, affect, and behavior: A review and integration. *Personality and Social Psychology Review, 3,* 278–302.

Thompson L., & Hastie, R. (1990). Social perception in negotiation. *Organizational Behavior and Human Decision Processes, 47,* 98–123.

Thompson, L., & Hrebec, D. (1996). Lose–lose agreements in interdependent decision making. *Psychological Bulletin, 120,* 396–409.

Thompson, L., Peterson, E., & Brodt, S. E. (1996). Team negotiation: An examination of integrative and distributive bargaining. *Journal of Personality and Social Psychology, 70,* 66–78.

Tindale, R. S., Meisenhelder, H. M., Dykema-Engblade, A. A., & Hogg, M. A. (2001). Shared cognition in small groups. In M. A. Hogg & S. Tindale (Eds.), *Blackwell handbook of social psychology: Group processes* (pp. 1–30). Malden, MA: Blackwell.

Tutzauer, F., & Roloff, M. E. (1988). Communication processes leading to integrative agreements: Three paths to joint benefits. *Communication Research, 15,* 360–380.

Van Boven, L., & Thompson, L. (2003). A look into the mind of the negotiator: Mental models in negotiation. *Group Processes and Intergroup Relations, 6,* 387–404.

Van Swol, L. M., & Seinfeld, E. (2004, November). *Confirmation bias and common information bias in consensus and non-consensus groups.* Poster presented at the Society for Judgment and Decision-Making annual meeting, Minneapolis, MN.

Wegner, D. M. (1987). Transactive memory: A contemporary analysis of the group mind. In B. Mullen & G. R. Goethals (Eds.), *Theories of group behavior* (pp. 185–208). New York: Springer.

Wegner, D. M. (1995). A computer network model of human transactive memory. *Social Cognition, 13,* 319–339.

Weick, K. E. (1993). The collapse of sense-making in organizations: The Mann Gulch disaster. *Administrative Science Quarterly, 38,* 628–652.

Weick, K. E., & Roberts, K. H. (1993). Collective mind in organizations: Heedful interrelating on flight decks. *Administrative Science Quarterly, 38,* 357–381.

Weingart, L. R., Bennett, R. J., & Brett, J. M. (1993). The impact of consideration of issues and motivational orientation on group negotiation process and outcome. *Journal of Applied Psychology, 78,* 504–517.

Wittenbaum, G. M., Hubbell, A. P., & Zuckerman, C. (1999). Mutual enhancement: Toward an understanding of the collective preference for shared information. *Journal of Personality and Social Psychology, 77,* 967–978.

Wittenbaum, G. M., & Stasser, G. (1996). Management of information in small groups. In J. L. Nye & A. M. Brower (Eds.), *What's social about social cognition? Research on socially shared cognition in small groups* (pp. 3–28). Thousand Oaks, CA: Sage.

9

Social Cognition in Family Communication

Ascan Koerner
University of Minnesota

As evident in this volume, the application of social cognition to communication research in most areas has met or exceeded the expectations expressed by the authors in Roloff and Berger's (1982) *Social Cognition and Communication*. Social cognition has been successfully employed to explain communication behaviors in a number of social contexts, ranging from mass media to interpersonal relationships. Yet, there are a few areas in the field of communication research where social cognition thus far has had little impact, and family communication might very well be first among them.

One of the main reasons for this is that most family communication researchers approach family research from a sociological rather than a psychological perspective. As a consequence, they are generally more interested in how family communication is affected by the social environment that surrounds them, how families interact with the social environment, and in the interpersonal dynamics within families than with the cognitive processes associated with these phenomena. Nonetheless, there have been consistent efforts by some family communication researchers to employ social cognition in their investigation of families. The purpose of this chapter is to briefly review this research and to show how social cognition has been used in the family context. I then discuss family communication patterns theory as an example of a family communication theory that is based on social cognition and explicate how family communication patterns fit into the more comprehensive theoretical model of family relationship schemas. Finally, I suggest future developments in theory and research methods of family communication that will ultimately, I believe, result in a comprehensive theory of family communication that is based on social cognition.

LINKING RESEARCH IN SOCIAL COGNITION AND FAMILY COMMUNICATION

Social Cognition and Family Communication

Historically, there has been little connection between the field of social cognition and family communication research. For example, family communication or family relationships are not explicitly mentioned in any of the 17 chapters of Wyer and Srull's (1984) *Handbook of Social Cognition* or in any of the 9 chapters of Roloff and Berger's (1982) *Social Cognition and Communication*. In these volumes, the only connection made between social cognition and family communication is an implied one that only exists because both volumes link social cognition to interpersonal communication. Of course, what applies to interpersonal communication in general often also applies to interpersonal communication in particular relationship contexts, such as families. Chapters in Roloff and Berger (1982) with content somewhat relevant to family communication included O'Keefe and Delia's (1982) discussion of message design, Sillars's (1982) review of attribution theory, Hewes and Planalp's (1982) chapter on information processing, and Street and Giles's (1982) consideration of speech accommodation theory. Because interpersonal communication in these chapters was considered in contexts that are different from family relationships, the chapters' applicability to family communication is suggestive at best.

The relatively small role of social cognition in family communication, however, is not necessarily limited to the past, nor is it the case that researchers concerned primarily with social cognition ignore family communication whereas family communication scholars pay a lot of attention to social cognition. Rather, both areas still operate in relative isolation from one another.

A search of the major publications in social cognition shows that the area of family communication is still largely ignored by the field of social cognition. For example, in the second edition of the *Handbook of Social Cognition* (Wyer & Srull, 1994) only two out of eight chapters on application (i.e., stereotypes and relationship functioning) even addressed interpersonal relationships, and neither of them made any direct reference to family relationships. Likewise, in the most recent fourth edition of the *Handbook of Social Psychology* (Gilbert, Fiske, & Lindzey, 1998), none of the 37 chapters addresses family communication directly. If families are mentioned at all, they are mentioned only as socialization agents (e.g., Kinder, 1998) or as examples of close interpersonal relationships (e.g., Berscheid & Reis, 1998; Buss & Kenrick, 1998).

There exist in social psychology, however, a few research programs that explicitly address family relationships and communication. In a review of this fairly limited literature, Bugental and Johnston (2000) noted that historically parental cognition and its influence on child cognition and behavior has been the focus of most research and that the influence of child cognition on parents largely has been ignored. In addition, much of the research reviewed dealt with identifying different types of cognition relevant in families (e.g., descriptive, analytical, evaluative, and prescriptive cognition) and with the intergenerational transmission of cognition. Relatively little research has been conducted on the interdependence or joint construction of family members' cognition, not the least because of the relative recent arrival of more sophisticated statistical methods that take the interdependence of family data into consideration (Kenny, Kashy, & Bolger, 1998).

Despite this paucity of research, there are some interesting theoretical models developed in social psychology that have obvious implications for family communication researchers. For example, Gottman's (Gottman, Katz, & Hooven, 1996) study of meta-emotion suggests that parents' beliefs about their own emotions and the emotions of their children are associated with their own parenting and with their children's emotion regulation ability and ultimately lead to important child outcomes, such as physical health, academic achievement, and peer relationships. This model is important for communication research because it proposes that the main link between parent cognition and child cognition and outcomes lies in parenting behavior; that is, the way that parents relate to and communicate with their children. Parents' awareness of their own and their children's emotion and their teaching of how to deal with emotions in particular stood out as important communication behaviors linking parents' and children's emotions.

Even more exclusively concerned with parents' cognition than Gottman et al. (1996), but still of great practical importance to communication scholars, is the research of Bugental (Bugental et al., 2002) linking parental cognition to child abuse. In an evaluative study of a parent education program, Bugental et al. showed that abusive parenting is often based on negative attributions made about children's behaviors and that teaching parents to make more positive attributions reduced harsh parenting by as much as 80%. Not only did this study provide further support for the association between parent cognition and parenting, but it also suggests that a particularly effective way to change parents' cognition involves teaching them problem solving and similar communication skills.

Family Communication and Social Cognition

In the area of family communication, references to social cognition are not entirely absent from current research, but they, too, are very infrequent. To wit, in a recent, comprehensive review of research on family communication that examined 1,254 journal articles published between 1990 and 2001, Stamp (2004) identified major perspectives of inquiry, guiding theories, and common concepts used in research of family communication. Of the 16 most frequently used guiding theories identified by Stamp, only 3 can be considered to belong to the field of social cognition (i.e., exchange theory, attribution theory, and equity theory), accounting for less than 15% of the research that had clearly identifiable theoretical bases. In addition, based on a grounded theoretical model of family communication developed from the reviewed research that involved concepts at four levels of abstraction, Stamp identified cognition as 1 of the 28 most basic-level concepts relevant to family communication, further demonstrating the relatively low significance of social cognition afforded by family communication researchers. Stamp grouped cognition together with gender, emotion, and personality to constitute the second-order category *personal,* which together with relationship, interaction, and communication, constituted the third-order category *substance.* The other third-order categories identified by Stamp that together constituted the fourth-order concept *family life* were form, space, and time. The paucity of social cognition in family communication research also is evident in Vangelisti's (2004) *Handbook of Family Communication.* Of 30 chapters, not one mentions cognition in its title and only two (Koerner & Fitzpatrick, 2004; Sillars, Canary, & Tafoya, 2004) make references to social cognition in their explications of family communication.

The lack of research explicitly using social cognition in the context of family communication should not be taken as evidence, however, that social cognition is irrelevant to a better understanding of family communication. Rather, the lack of interest of family communication scholars in social cognition and of social cognition scholars in family communication is a historical accident that needs to be corrected. Indeed, there are several scholars of family communication who have successfully employed ideas and models from social cognition in their attempts to explain family communication. Most frequently, such research is concerned with how relationships and relationship partners are represented in memory and how that affects family communication. For example, in his research on family understanding, Sillars (Sillars, 1998; Sillars, Koerner, & Fitzpatrick, 2005) used concepts from social cognition such as attributions and representations of others to describe and explicate the role of meta-communication in families. This research showed that different types of understanding are associated with different family processes. For example, parents' understanding of their children's self-concepts is associated with more positive self-concepts of children and more open communication and greater relationship satisfaction of parents and children. An understanding of how children perceive family conflict, in contrast, is associated with greater family conformity and less relationship satisfaction.

Investigating how family communication is associated with children's mental representations of others, Burleson, Delia, and Applegate (1995) studied the impact of different regulating and comforting messages parents use with their children. Specifically, these researchers compared the effects of person-centered messages, which they defined as "an elaborated code [that] focuses on the motivations, feelings, and intentions of individuals" (p. 39), with the effects of position-centered messages, which they defined as "a restricted code [that] fosters and expresses a focus on the identity of others and the meanings of their actions as given in conventionally defined social roles" (p.39). Results showed that person-centered messages of parents are associated with children's more complex and sophisticated mental representations of other persons' psychology, children's own use of person-centered communication in their social relationships, and children's greater success in peer relationships and school performance. Parents' position-centered communication, on the other hand, was associated with children's less complex and less sophisticated mental representations of others, children's own use of position-centered communication, and their lesser success in peer relationships and school performance.

Another example of family communication research that uses concepts from social cognition to predict behaviors and psychological outcomes for family members is Vangelisti's (Vangelisti, Crumley, & Baker, 1999) and Caughlin's (2003) work on family communication standards. These scholars conceptualize family communication standards as shared knowledge structures representing ideals for family communication that are distinct from mental representations of how one perceives one's own family to actually communicate. Family communication standards are associated with relationship satisfaction in two distinct ways. First, divergence of actual family communication from family communication standards is associated with less relationship satisfaction (Caughlin, 2003; Vangilisti et al., 1999). Thus, these findings are generally consistent with one of the fundamental assumptions of social cognition formalized by Thibaut and Kelley (1959) in their social exchange model of relationships, namely that relationship satisfaction is a function of expected relationship outcomes compared to actually obtained relationship outcomes.

The second way in which family communication standards affect relationship satisfaction is through their influence on family members' actual behaviors. Based on earlier theorizing by Epstein and Eidelson (1981; Eidelson & Epstein, 1982), Caughlin (2003) labeled this process the *distressful ideals hypothesis* and found that just having certain standards is in fact associated with relationship satisfaction, regardless of whether or not these standards are actually met in the relationship. Specifically, to the extent that family communication standards encourage behaviors that are associated with satisfying relationships, such as being open or supportive, holding such standards is associated with greater relationship satisfaction. Conversely, having standards that encourage behaviors associated with less satisfying relationships, such as avoiding self-disclosure or being very punitive in relationships, is associated with less satisfying relationships (hence the name of the hypothesis).

The most explicit use of social cognition in theorizing about family communication, however, is Koerner and Fitzpatrick's (2005) family communication patterns theory (FCPT). The previously mentioned theories employ concepts or theories from social cognition to explain fairly narrow and isolated phenomena of family communication, such as meta-communication or relationship satisfaction. In contrast, FCPT is much broader in scope and applies to a wide range of family communication phenomena and family relationship outcomes. In addition, although family communication patterns are observable behaviors, according to FCPT they are the result of underlying social cognitive processes that affect most, if not all, family processes.

FAMILY COMMUNICATION PATTERNS THEORY

The Cognitive Basis of Family Communication Patterns

The original model of family communication patterns was developed by McLeod and Chaffee (1972, 1973) to explain how families process external information, in particular mass media messages. Consequently, McLeod and Chaffee described family communication patterns as families' tendencies to develop fairly stable and predictable ways of communicating with one another about information they received through media messages. According to McLeod and Chaffee, these stable and predictable ways of communicating ultimately are based on how families create and share social reality and represent an observable indicator of these cognitive processes. At the time, mass communication and allied fields experienced a renewed interest in cognitive processes as they turned away from focusing almost exclusively on channels and messages (Reeves, Chaffee, & Tims, 1982); thus, it is no surprise that McLeod and Chaffee employed the cognitive theory of coorientation to explain family communication patterns.

The Process of Coorientation. Initially described by Newcomb (1953) coorientation is a basic concept in social cognition that refers to the situation when two or more individuals focus their attention on, and form an attitude about, the same object in their social or physical environment. In dyads and larger groups, such as families, coorientation leads to a set of cognitions that have important psychological and behavioral consequences. Coorientation is similar for dyads and groups but because it is easier to explain for dyads, I use dyads in my short review of the coorientation process.

In dyads, coorientation leads to two different cognitions for each person. The first cognition is a person's own perception and evaluation of the observed object. The second cognition is a person's perception of the other person's perception and evaluation of the object. These two cognitions determine three attributes of the cooriented dyad: agreement, accuracy, and congruence. *Agreement* refers to the similarity between the two persons' evaluations of the object. For example, assume the object the dyad is focusing on is ice cream. If Chris and Pat both perceive and evaluate ice cream positively (e.g., they both like ice cream), the dyad has agreement. *Accuracy* refers to the similarity between a person's perception of the other person's evaluation and the other person's actual evaluation. Thus, if Chris likes ice cream and Pat thinks that Chris likes ice cream, Pat has accuracy. Finally, *congruence* refers to the similarity between a person's own evaluation of the object and the person's perception of the other person's evaluation of the object. Thus, if Pat likes ice cream and thinks that Chris likes ice cream, Pat has congruence.

Because of the need to have balanced cognition and congruent beliefs (Heider, 1946, 1958) these three attributes of the dyad are linearly dependent on one another. That is, the state of any two determines the state of the third according to the same rules governing multiplication of positive and negative numbers. For example, accuracy and congruence require that there is agreement (+ * + = +), congruence and disagreement require that there is inaccuracy (+ * – = –), and inaccuracy and incongruence require that there is agreement (– * – = +).

For families to be in coorientation does not necessarily mean that they also share a social reality; that is, that they are in agreement as previously defined. Still, to coordinate behaviors and to function as a family, there is a pragmatic need for accuracy in family relationships. Without being able to accurately perceive other family members' perceptions and attitudes, misunderstandings are inevitable and coordination and functioning is inhibited. In addition, there is a psychological desire for balanced cognitions (Heider, 1946, 1958) about family members and attitude objects. Because attitudes about family members are usually positive, incongruent evaluations of attitude objects lead to imbalanced cognition. Thus, in addition to a pragmatic need for accuracy, there is psychological need for congruence in family relationships.

Given the linear dependence of accuracy, congruence, and agreement, the pragmatic need for accuracy and the psychological desire for congruence lead to agreement in family relationships, and thus to a shared social reality.

Two Ways to Come to Agreement in Families. According to McLeod and Chaffee (1972, 1973), family members can achieve agreement in two distinct ways. First, family members can agree about an evaluation of an attitude object in the environment based on its attributes. Family members discover these attributes jointly by discussing the object and its properties, characteristics, and outcomes. Because this process emphasizes a focus on the object and how family members conceptualize it, McLeod and Chaffee called this process *concept orientation.* Second, family members can come to an agreement about an attitude object by focusing on another family member's evaluation of the object and adopting that evaluation. Because this process emphasizes the relationships between family members rather than the attributes of the object itself, McLeod and Chaffee called this process *socio orientation.*

McLeod and Chaffee (1972) proposed that families vary in their use of these two strategies to achieve agreement and, consequently, that children were socialized differently in regard to the processing of information contained in media messages. Some families prefer concept orientation over socio orientation, whereas other families prefer the opposite. In addition, some families make frequent use of both strategies, whereas other families are less interested in sharing social reality and use both strategies infrequently.

Because McLeod and Chaffee's main interest was in mass media and families' information processing, the Family Communication Patterns instrument they developed to measure family communication has been widely used in media-effects research. Its utility for describing and explaining family communication more generally and not only family information processing, however, went largely unnoticed until Fitzpatrick and her colleagues started using the instrument in the early 1990s in their research on family communication.

Family Communication Patterns as Important Aspects of Family Relationships

Although social reality ultimately takes shape and resides in the cognition of individual family members, the two strategies of socio orientation and concept orientation have direct effects on the communication behaviors of family members and on family relationships. In addition, which strategies families prefer to use is not just pragmatically driven, but ties to important values and beliefs families have about themselves and their relationships (Koerner & Fitzpatrick, 2002a). Recognizing this, Fitzpatrick and Ritchie (1994; Ritchie, 1991, 1997; Ritchie & Fitzpatrick, 1990) refined and reconceptualized McLeod and Chaffee's (1972) concept orientation and socio orientation by placing a greater emphasis on family communication behaviors associated with the two strategies of achieving agreement.

Thus, in the Revised Family Communication Patterns instrument (RFCP), concept orientation was reconceptualized as conversation orientation because the communication behaviors associated with concept orientation are those of lengthy, involving, and open family discussions. In regard to socialization, children in conversation-oriented families learn to look at the concepts themselves when assigning meaning to them and to explore potential meanings by discussing them with others. In these interactions, children are learning to pay attention to the strengths of arguments rather than the social position of their advocates. Similarly, socio orientation was reconceptualized as conformity orientation because the communication behaviors associated with socio orientation are those that emphasize conformity within families, particularly that of children with parents. Children in conformity-oriented families learn to look to others to assign meaning and parents discourage open discussions and divergent opinions and expect children to conform to their views.

Although conversation orientation and conformity orientation are alternative strategies for families to agree on the meaning of concepts and to share social reality, they are not mutually exclusive. In fact, most families make use of both strategies. Consequently, the frequencies in which families use these strategies can be used to define a two-dimensional conceptual space in which to place families. Furthermore, the four quadrants of the conceptual space created by the two dimensions can be used to define four different family types (see Figure 9.1).

Dimensions of Family Communication and Family Types

Conversation Orientation. The first dimension of family communication, conversation orientation, is defined as the degree to which families create a climate where all family members are encouraged to participate in unrestrained interaction about a wide array of topics. In families on the high end of this dimension, family members freely, frequently, and spontaneously interact with each other without many limitations in regard to time spent in interaction and topics discussed. These families spend a lot of time interacting with each other and family members share their individual activities, thoughts, and feelings with each other. In these families, actions or activities that the family plans to engage in as a unit are discussed within the family, as are family decisions.

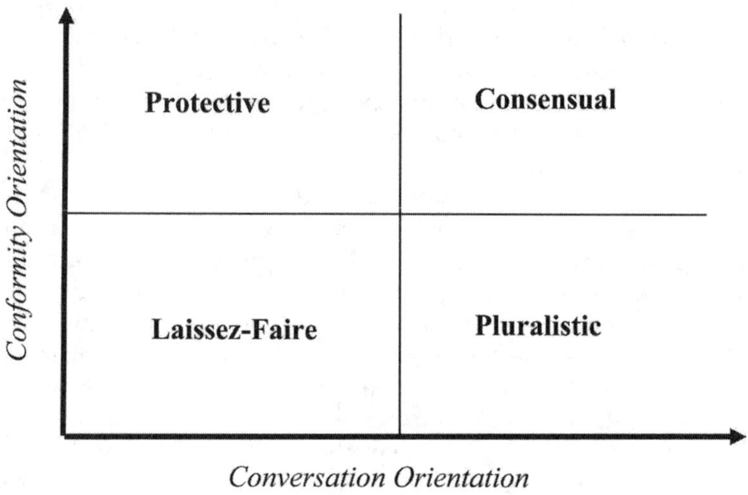

FIGURE 9.1. Family communication orientations and family types.

Conversely, in families at the low end of the conversation orientation dimension, members interact less frequently with each other and there are only a few topics that are openly discussed with all family members. There is less exchange of private thoughts, feelings, and activities. In these families, activities in which family members engage as a unit are not usually discussed in great detail, nor is everybody's input sought for family decisions.

Associated with high conversation orientation is the belief that open and frequent communication is essential to an enjoyable and rewarding family life. Families holding this view value the exchange of ideas, and parents holding this belief see frequent communication with their children as the main means to educate and to socialize them. Conversely, families low in conversation orientation believe that open and frequent exchanges of ideas, opinions, and values are unnecessary for the functioning of the family in general, and for the children's education and socialization in particular.

Conformity Orientation. The other dimension of family communication is conformity orientation. Conformity orientation refers to the degree to which family communication stresses a climate of homogeneity of attitudes, values, and beliefs. Families on the high end of this dimension are characterized by interactions that emphasize a uniformity of beliefs and attitudes. Their interactions typically focus on harmony, conflict avoidance, and the interdependence of family members. In intergenerational exchanges, communication in these families reflects obedience to parents and other adults. Families on the low end of the conformity orientation dimension are characterized by interactions that focus on heterogeneous attitudes and beliefs, as well as on the individuality of family members and their independence from their families. In intergenerational exchanges, communication reflects the equality of all family members (e.g., children are usually involved in decision making).

Associated with high conformity orientation is the belief in what might be called a traditional family structure. In this view, families are cohesive and hierarchical. That is, family members favor their family relationships over relationships external to the family and they expect that resources, such as space and money, are shared among family members. Families high in conformity orientation believe that individual schedules should be coordinated among family members to maximize family time and expect family members to subordinate personal interests to those of the family. Parents are expected to make the decisions for the family and the children are expected to act according to their parents' wishes. Conversely, families low in conformity orientation do not believe in a traditional family structure. Instead, they believe in less cohesive and hierarchically organized families. Families on the low end of the conformity orientation dimension believe that relationships outside the family are equally as important as family relationships, and that families should encourage the personal growth of individual family members, even if that leads to a weakening of the family structure. They believe in the independence of family members, they value personal space, and they subordinate family interests to personal interests.

The effects that these two core dimensions of communication in families have on actual family communication are often dependent on one another. That is, rather than having simple main effects on family communication, these two dimensions often interact with one another such that the impact of conversation orientation on family outcomes is moderated by the degree of conformity orientation of the family, and vice versa. Therefore, to predict the influence of family communication patterns on family outcomes, it is rarely sufficient to investigate only one dimension without assessing the other dimension (Koerner & Fitzpatrick, 2002b, 2004). Thus, the family types that result from crossing the two dimensions are not just convenient ways to describe the main effects of conversation orientation and conformity orientation, but they also encapsulate important qualitative differences between family types.

Consensual Families. Families high in both conversation and conformity orientation are labeled *consensual.* Their communication is characterized by a tension between pressure to agree and to preserve the existing hierarchy within the family, on the one hand, and an interest in open communication and in exploring new ideas on the other hand. That is, parents in these families are very interested in their children and what the children have to say, but at the same time also believe that they, as the parents, should make decisions for the family and for the children. They resolve this tension by listening to their children and by spending time and energy in explaining their decisions, as well as their values and beliefs, to their children in the hope that their children will understand the reasoning behind the parents' decisions and adopt the parents' belief system. Children in these families usually learn to value family conversations and tend to adopt their parents' values and beliefs. In these families, volatile conflict is generally regarded as negative and harmful to the family, but because unresolved conflict is perceived as potentially threatening to the relationships within the family, these families also value and engage in problem solving and conflict resolution (Koerner & Fitzpatrick, 1997).

Pluralistic Families. Families high in conversation orientation and low in conformity orientation are labeled pluralistic. Communication in pluralistic families is characterized by open, unconstrained discussions involving all family members and a wide range of topics. Parents in these families do not feel the need to be in control of their children by making decisions for them, nor do they feel the need to agree with their children's decisions. This parental attitude leads to family discussions in which opinions are evaluated based on the merit of arguments in their support rather than on which family members espouse them. That is, parents are willing to accept their children's opinions and to let them participate in family decision making. Because of their emphasis on the free exchange of ideas and the absence of overt pressure to conform or to obey, these families are low in conflict avoidance and openly address their conflicts with one another, engage in positive conflict resolution strategies, and usually are able to resolve their conflicts. Children of these families learn to value family conversations and, at the same time, learn to be independent and autonomous, which fosters their communication competence and their confidence in their ability to make their own decisions.

Protective Families. Families low on conversation orientation and high on conformity orientation are labeled *protective.* Communication in protective families is characterized by an emphasis on obedience to parental authority and by little concern for conceptual matters or for open communication within the family. Parents in these families believe that they should be making the decisions for their families and their children, and they see little value in explaining their reasoning to their children. Conflict in protective families is perceived negatively because of the great emphasis placed on conformity (Koerner & Fitzpatrick, 1997). Family members are expected not to have any conflicts with one another and to behave according to the interests and norms of the family. Because communication skills are not valued and not practiced much, these families often lack the necessary skills to engage productively in conflict resolution should it come to open disagreements. Children in protective families learn that there is little value in family conversations and to distrust their own decision-making ability.

Laissez-Faire Families. Families low in both conversation orientation and conformity orientation are labeled *laissez-faire*. Their communication is characterized by few and usually uninvolving interactions among family members that are limited to a small number of topics. Parents in laissez-faire families do believe that all family members should be able to make their own decisions, but unlike parents in pluralistic families, they have little interest in their children's decisions, nor do they value communicating with them. Most members of laissez-faire families are emotionally divorced from their families. Laissez-faire families value neither conformity nor communication very much. As a result, they do not experience their families as constraining their individual interests and incidents of colliding interests and thus conflicts are rare. These families do not engage much in conversation with one another and therefore tend to avoid conflict. Children of these families learn that there is little value in family conversation and that they have to make their own decisions. Because they do not receive much support from their parents, however, they come to question their decision-making ability.

FAMILY COMMUNICATION PATTERNS AND FAMILY RELATIONSHIP SCHEMAS

Although FCPT links family communication behaviors to the fundamental cognitive processes involved in coorientation, coorientation is only one of many cognitive processes relevant to family communication. A more comprehensive theoretical model is necessary to fully account for the role that cognition plays in family communication. One such more comprehensive model is Koerner and Fitzpatrick's (2002a) outline of a theoretical model of family communication that is based on family relationship schemas.

Like schemas of other relationships, family relationship schemas consist of interrelated pieces of declarative and procedural knowledge about the family that reside in long-term memory (Baldwin, 1992). In this context, declarative knowledge is defined as descriptive knowledge of the attributes and features of things, whereas procedural knowledge refers to a person's knowledge of if–then contingencies. Declarative and procedural knowledge contained in relational schemas consists of three subsets of knowledge (Baldwin, 1992). The first subset of knowledge is related to the self and corresponds to what might be called the self-concept. The second subset of knowledge concerns the others with whom one is in the relationship, in this case, family members. Knowledge of others mirrors knowledge of self in that it includes perceptions of others and of their beliefs, attitudes, and expectations they have for one's own behavior. The third subset consists of beliefs that define prototypical interactions with others. It includes knowledge of typical behavioral sequences that is used to interpret and to plan behavior. Family communication orientation belongs to this subset of knowledge, because it largely determines how families achieve agreement about their social world. Although these three subsets can be conceptualized in isolation from one another, Baldwin (1992, 1994) observed that they are so highly interdependent on one another (i.e., any change in one will effect changes in the others) that they actually all belong to the same cognitive structure.

Like schemas of other relationships, family relationship schemas are part of a hierarchically organized social cognition that stores relational knowledge at three levels of generality (Koerner & Fitzpatrick, 2002a). At the most general level is knowledge that applies to all social relationships, the general social schema. Such general social knowledge includes beliefs and pragmatic rules that apply to all interactions, like the norm of reciprocity or the need to be truthful and relevant when communicating (e.g., Grice, 1975). On the second level are relationship-type schemas that include knowledge specific to the different types of relationships one has, including family relationships. The knowledge stored in schemas on this level is different from the knowledge in the general social schema and applies to all relationships of that type (Fletcher, 1993). On the most specific level are relationship-specific schemas that contain knowledge that applies to only one particular relationship a person has with one specific other person. These schemas contain memories, attributions, and experiences made within the context of that particular relationship and allow individuals to adapt their cognition, behaviors, and interpretations to that particular relationship. In other words, these particular relationship beliefs are what make each relationship unique and distinguishable from other relationships (Fletcher, 1993).

The knowledge contained at the level of a more specific schema is different from the knowledge that exists at the more general levels and a person's mental representation of a relationship combines knowledge from all three schemas. Thus, similarities of mental representations of different relationships are the result of shared knowledge drawn from either the general social schema or the relationship type schema. By contrast, differences in mental representations of different types of relationships are due to differences between relationship type schemas, and differences in mental representations of relationships of the same type are due to differences in relationship-specific schemas. Consequently, there must be a process that determines which information is retrieved and used in relational information processing. Originally, Koerner and Fitzpatrick (2002a) proposed a sequential process in which relationship-specific knowledge is accessed first and general social knowledge last, which would explain why more specific knowledge has supremacy over more general knowledge in information processing. An equally plausible alternative that is more consistent with parallel processing is a recursive or iterative process that accesses knowledge at all levels of specificity simultaneously and that assigns more specific knowledge primacy over more general knowledge if there is a conflict between knowledge at the different levels of abstraction.

SOCIAL COGNITION, FAMILY COMMUNICATION, AND FUTURE RESEARCH

Family relationship schemas are cognitive structures that, in concert with general social schemas and relationship-specific schemas, determine social cognition in family relationships. Thus, a full understanding of family relationships and family communication without knowledge of family relationship schemas is impossible. Family relationship schemas contain declarative and procedural knowledge that applies to all relationships with family members. Clearly, beliefs about coorientation that underlie family communication patterns are an important part of that knowledge, but they alone cannot fully account for all aspects of family communication. Thus, future research must focus on identifying the additional knowledge contained in family relationship schemas.

A good starting point for this investigation might be the beliefs that other researchers already have found to have important consequences for family communication. Among those are the already discussed relationship ideals identified by Vangelisti (Vangelisti et al., 1999) and Caughlin (2003) and beliefs about the complexity of others associated with person-centered and position-centered communication (Burleson et al., 1995). In addition, Fletcher (1993; Fletcher & Thomas, 1996) identified beliefs that constitute relationship schemas of close romantic relationships that are also relevant to family relationships (Koerner & Fitzpatrick, 2002a). These beliefs include *intimacy,* which includes trust, respect, love, and affection; *individuality,* which includes independence and equity; and *external factors,* which include personal security and children. Finally, attachment beliefs are also important in family relationships and almost certainly are part of family relationship schemas.

In addition to investigating the content of family relationship schemas and how they affect cognitive processes related to family communication, future research will also focus on more sophisticated methods to investigate the cognitions and behaviors of family members. All too often, family variables are assessed only once based on reports by only one family member, usually adolescents or young adult children now in college. Clearly, research that takes the multiple perspectives of family members and the dynamic nature of family systems into consideration has to employ study designs that collect data from all family members at multiple times. Unfortunately, such designs provide such logistical and financial challenges to researchers that many find them impractical. Still, with some creativity and innovative use of technology, more complicated designs might well be within reach of even only minimally funded researchers.

Collecting data from all family members, however, creates its own set of difficulties because it requires family researchers to employ statistical techniques that account for the interdependence of family data. This is important because techniques most commonly employed to analyze psychological data (e.g., analysis of variance, multivariate analysis of variance, hierarchical regression) assume that individual observations are independent, an assumption that data based on observations of members of the same family (or marriage) clearly violate. Examples of techniques that take the interdependence of data into consideration and that have already found acceptance in research on dyadic relationships are Kashy and Kenny's (2000) actor–partner interdependence model and Gonzalez and Griffin's (1999) model of distinguishable dyads. Both methods enable researchers not only to statistically control for the interdependence of data, but also to assess to what extent partners affect each other.

Family communication researchers are well advised to use these or similar techniques in their research. Other techniques that account for the influence of families and similar groups on individual-level data that need to be more rigorously employed in family communication research include Snijders and Kenny's (1999) multilevel modeling of the social relations model to estimate individual, dyadic, and family effects, and Widmer's (1999) families as cognitive networks approach. Extending the logic of the actor–partner model to the family context with its multiple social relationships, Snijders and Kenny's (1999) multilevel modeling allows for the precise assessment of the effects that individual family members have as actors and partners in dyads; the effects of dyadic relationships on both actors and partners; and the effects the family has on actors, partners, and dyads.

Another promising approach to study the effects that individual family members have on each other is the family-as-cognitive-network approach (Widmer, 1999). In this approach, mental representations of families are assumed to be subject to Heider's (1958) balance theory and therefore tend to be transitive or balanced in regard to intrafamiliar influence. That is, if mother influences father and father influences daughter, than mother exerts a similar influence on daughter, for example. The advantage of this approach is that family networks of various sizes and compositions can be analyzed in a way that is both intuitively appealing and theoretically rigorous.

The use of social cognition in family communication research already has led to an impressive array of research and research findings explicating important processes and outcomes of family communication. With family communication researchers focusing their efforts on better understanding family relationship schemas and developing more sophisticated research methods, there are few limits on the contributions that social cognition will make to our understanding of family relationships and family communication.

REFERENCES

Baldwin, M. W. (1992). Relational schemas and the processing of social information. *Psychological Bulletin, 112,* 461–484.

Baldwin, M. W. (1994). Primed relational schemas as a source of self-evaluative reactions. *Journal of Social and Clinical Psychology, 13,* 380–403.

Berscheid, E., & Reis, H. T. (1998). Attraction and close relationships. In D. T. Gilbert, S. T. Fiske, & G. Lindzey (Eds.), *The handbook of social psychology* (Vol. 2, 4th ed., pp. 193–281). Boston: McGraw-Hill.

Bugental, D. B., Ellerson, P. C., Lin, E. K., Rainey, B., Kokotovic, A., & O'Hara, N. (2002). A cognitive approach to child abuse prevention. *Journal of Family Psychology, 16,* 243–258.

Bugental, D. B., & Johnston, C. (2000). Parental and child cognitions in the context of the family. *Annual Review of Psychology, 51,* 315–344.

Burleson, B. R., Delia, J. G., & Applegate, J. L. (1995). The socialization of person-centered communication: Parents' contributions to their children's social-cognitive and communication skills. In M. A. Fitzpatrick & A. Vangelisti (Eds.), *Explaining family interactions* (pp. 34–76). Thousand Oaks, CA: Sage.

Buss, D. M., & Kenrick, D. T. (1998). Evolutionary social psychology. In D. T. Gilbert, S. T. Fiske, & G. Lindzey (Eds.), *The handbook of social psychology* (Vol. 2, 4th ed., pp. 982–1026). Boston: McGraw-Hill.

Caughlin, J. P. (2003). Family communication standards: What counts as excellent family communication and how are such standards associated with family satisfaction? *Human Communication Research, 29,* 5–40.

Eidelson, R. J., & Epstein, N. (1982). Cognition and relationship maladjustment: Development of a measure of dysfunctional relationship beliefs. *Journal of Consulting and Clinical Psychology, 50,* 715–720.

Epstein, N., & Eidelson, R. J. (1981). Unrealistic beliefs of clinical couples: Their relationships to expectation, goals, and satisfaction. *American Journal of Family Therapy, 9,* 13–22.

Fitzpatrick, M. A., & Ritchie, L. D. (1994). Communication schemata within the family: Multiple perspectives on family interaction. *Human Communication Research, 20,* 275–301.

Fletcher, G. J. O. (1993). Cognition in close relationships. *New Zealand Journal of Psychology, 22,* 69–81.

Fletcher, G. J. O., & Thomas, G. (1996). Close relationship lay theories: Their structure and function. In G. J. O. Fletcher & J. Fitness (Eds.), *Knowledge structure in close relationships* (pp. 3–24). Mahwah, NJ: Lawrence Erlbaum Associates.

Gilbert, D. T., Fiske, S. T., & Lindzey, G. (Eds.). (1998). *Handbook of social psychology.* Boston: McGraw-Hill.

Gonzalez, R., & Griffin, D. (1999). The correlational analysis of dyad-level data in the distinguishable case. *Personal Relationships, 6,* 449–469.

Gottman, J. M., Katz, L. F., & Hooven, C. (1996). Parental meta-emotion philosophy and the emotional life of families: Theoretical models and preliminary data. *Journal of Family Psychology, 10,* 243–268.

Grice, P. (1975). Logic and conversation. In P. Cole & J. L. Morgan (Eds.), *Syntax and semantics* (Vol. 3, pp. 41–58). New York: Academic.

Heider, F. (1946). Attitudes and cognitive organization. *Journal of Psychology, 21,* 107–112.

Heider, F. (1958). *The psychology of interpersonal relations.* New York: Wiley.

Hewes, D. E., & Planalp, S. (1982). There is nothing as useful as good theory…: The influence of social knowledge on interpersonal communication. In M. E. Roloff & C. R. Berger (Eds.), *Social cognition and communication* (pp. 107–150). Beverly Hills, CA: Sage.

Kashy, D. A., & Kenny, D. A. (2000). The analysis of data from dyads and groups. In H. T. Reis & C. M. Judd (Eds.), *Handbook of research methods in social psychology* (pp. 451–477). New York: Cambridge University Press.

Kenny, D. A., Kashy, D. A., & Bolger, N. (1998). Data analysis in social psychology. In D. Gilbert, S. Fiske, & G. Lindzey (Eds.), *Handbook of social Psychology* (4th Ed., Vol. 1, pp. 233–265). Boston, MA: McGraw-Hill.,

Kinder, D. R. (1998). Opinion and action in the realm of politics. In D. T. Gilbert, S. T. Fiske, & G. Lindzey (Eds.), *The handbook of social psychology* (Vol. 2, 4th ed., pp. 778–867). Boston: McGraw-Hill.

Koerner, A. F., & Fitzpatrick, M. A. (1997). Family type and conflict: The impact of conversation orientation and conformity orientation on conflict in the family. *Communication Studies, 48,* 59–75.

Koerner, A. F., & Fitzpatrick, M. A. (2002a). Toward a theory of family communication. *Communication Theory, 12,* 70–91.

Koerner, A. F., & Fitzpatrick, M. A. (2002b). Understanding family communication patterns and family functioning: The roles of conversation orientation and conformity orientation. In W. B. Gudykunst (Ed.), *Communication yearbook 26* (pp. 37–69). Mahwah, NJ: Lawrence Erlbaum Associates.

Koerner, A. F., & Fitzpatrick, M. A. (2004). Communication in intact families. In A. Vangelisti (Ed.), *Handbook of family communication* (pp. 177–195). Mahwah, NJ: Lawrence Erlbaum Associates.

Koerner, A. F., & Fitzpatrick, M. A. (2005). Family communication patterns theory. A social cognitive approach. In D. O. Braithwaite & L. A. Baxter (Eds.), *Engaging theories in family communication: Multiple perspectives* (pp. 50–65). Thousand Oaks, CA: Sage.

McLeod, J. M., & Chaffee, S. H. (1972). The construction of social reality. In J. Tedeschi (Ed.), *The social influence process* (pp. 50–59). Chicago: Adeline-Atherton.

McLeod, J. M., & Chaffee, S. H. (1973). Interpersonal approaches to communication research. *American Behavioral Scientist, 16,* 469–499.

Newcomb, T. M. (1953). An approach to the study of communicative acts. *Psychological Review, 60,* 393–404.

O'Keefe, B. J., & Delia, J. G. (1982). Impression formation and message production. In M. E. Roloff & C. R. Berger (Eds.), *Social cognition and communication* (pp. 33–72). Beverly Hills, CA: Sage.

Reeves, B., Chaffee, S. H., & Tims, A. (1982). Social cognition and mass communication research. In M. E. Roloff & C. R. Berger (Eds.), *Social cognition and communication* (pp. 33–72). Beverly Hills, CA: Sage.

Ritchie, L. D. (1991). Family communication patterns: An epistemic analysis and conceptual reinterpretation. *Communication Research, 18,* 548–565.

Ritchie, L. D. (1997). Parents' workplace experiences and family communication patterns. *Communication Research, 24,* 175–187.

Ritchie, L. D., & Fitzpatrick, M. A. (1990). Family communication patterns: Measuring intrapersonal perceptions of interpersonal relationships. *Communication Research, 17,* 523–544.

Roloff, M. E., & Berger, C. R. (Eds.). (1982). *Social cognition and communication.* Beverly Hills, CA: Sage.

Sillars, A. L. (1982). Attribution and communication: Are people "naïve scientists" or just naïve? In M. E. Roloff & C. R. Berger (Eds.), *Social cognition and communication* (pp. 73–106). Beverly Hills, CA: Sage.

Sillars, A. L. (1998). (Mis)understanding. In B. H. Spitzberg & W. R. Cupach (Eds.), *The dark side of relationships* (pp. 73–102). Mahwah, NJ: Lawrence Erlbaum Associates.

Sillars, A. L., Canary, D. J., & Tafoya, M. (2004). Communication, conflict, and the quality of family relationships. In A. Vangelisti (Ed.), *Handbook of family communication* (pp. 413–446). Mahwah, NJ: Lawrence Erlbaum Associates.

Sillars, A., Koerner, A. F., & Fitzpatrick, M. A. (2005). Communication and understanding in parent–adolescent relationships. *Human Communication Research, 31,* 103–128.

Snijders, T. A. B., & Kenny, D. A. (1999). The social relations model for family data: A multilevel approach. *Personal Relationships, 6,* 471–486.

Stamp, G. H. (2004). Communication in intact families. In A. Vangelisti (Ed.), *Handbook of family communication* (pp. 1–30). Mahwah, NJ: Lawrence Erlbaum Associates.

Street, R. L., & Giles, H. (1982). Speech accommodation theory: A social cognitive approach to language and speech behavior. In M. E. Roloff & C. R. Berger (Eds.), *Social cognition and communication* (pp. 193–226). Beverly Hills, CA: Sage.

Thibaut, J. W., & Kelley, H. H. (1959). *The social psychology of groups.* New York: Wiley.

Vangelisti, A. L. (Ed.). (2004). *Handbook of family communication.* Mahwah, NJ: Lawrence Erlbaum Associates.

Vangelisti, A. L., Crumley, L. P., & Baker, J. L. (1999). Family portraits: Stories as standards for family relationships. *Journal of Social and Personal Relationships, 16,* 335–368.

Widmer, E. D. (1999). Family contexts as cognitive networks: A structural approach of family relationships. *Personal Relationships, 6,* 487–503.

Wyer, R. S., & Srull, T. K. (Eds.). (1984). *Handbook of social cognition* (Vol. 1). Hillsdale, NJ: Lawrence Erlbaum Associates.

Wyer, R. S., & Srull, T. K. (Eds.). (1994). *Handbook of social cognition* (2nd ed., Vol. 1 & 2). Hillsdale, NJ: Lawrence Erlbaum Associates.

10

Social Cognition Under the Influence: Drinking While Communicating

Pamela J. Lannutti
Boston College

Jennifer L. Monahan
University of Georgia

Social drinking is a ubiquitous part of American culture. Alcohol consumption in the United States has been consistently rising, with the most recent information from the National Institutes of Alcohol Abuse and Alcoholism indicating that, per capita, Americans consumed 2.20 gallons of ethanol from alcoholic beverages in 2002 (Lakins, Williams, Yi, & Smothers, 2004). For most drinkers, the majority of this alcohol was consumed in the company of others.

Although the effect of alcohol on communicative behavior was not examined in *Communication and Social Cognition,* it is included in this volume because of the literature documenting alcohol's effects on social cognitive and communication behaviors. For example, research demonstrates consuming alcohol affects relational conflict (Sillars, Leonard, Roberts, & Dun, 2002), self-disclosure (Monahan & Lannutti, 2000), social anxiety (Sayette, 1993), mood regulation (Cooper, Frone, Russell, & Mudar, 1995), communication behavior in small groups (Lindfors & Lindman, 1987), perception of sexual risk (Murphy, Monahan, & Miller, 1998), self-evaluation (Banaji & Steele, 1989), social information processing (Giancola, 2004), verbal aggression (Parrott, Zeichner & Pihl, 2003), and sexual disinhibition (Crowe & George, 1989).

Alcohol produces change in social cognition and communicative behaviors via two mechanisms: a drug mechanism that produces pharmacological effects and an expectancy mechanism that produces psychological effects. In this chapter, we first provide a brief overview of important theories that explain alcohol's pharmacological effects on social cognition and communicative behaviors. Second, expectancies—or how people think alcohol affects behavior—are reviewed. Third, three communication variables—sociability, aggression, and compliance—are examined to demonstrate the potent, yet sometimes conflicting, effects of alcohol consumption and expectancy. Finally, we offer a brief analysis of methodological issues and suggest future research for communication scholars.

Because the alcohol literature is large, with several books and academic journals devoted to research on human behavior, the scope of this chapter was narrowed to pharmacological and expectancy effects of alcohol on social cognition and interpersonal behavior. Second, although there is a large and important literature on alcoholics, that work typically does not examine the effect of consuming alcohol on the communicative behaviors of alcoholics because giving alcohol to alcoholics is unethical. Our focus, thus, is narrowed to alcohol's influence on social cognitive and communicative behaviors of social drinkers.

PHARMACOLOGICAL EFFECTS OF ALCOHOL ON SOCIAL BEHAVIOR

The major theories of alcohol's pharmacological effect on social behavior share the common theme of restricted mental processing and impaired cognitive capacity. Current neuroscience research indicates alcohol consumption affects social behavior because it impairs the executive control functioning of the brain (Hoaken, Giancola, & Pihl, 1998; Pihl, Assaad, & Hoaken, 2003). Executive control functions guide the planning, initiation, and self-regulation of goal-directed behavior and involve the ability to initiate purposeful activity and inhibit inappropriate activity (Giancola & Tarter, 1999). Cognitive abilities subsumed by executive functioning include attention, information appraisal, self- and social monitoring, cognitive flexibility, and responses to external feedback (Baddeley & Della Sala, 1998; Kimberg & Farah, 1993; Stuss & Alexander, 2000).

An assumption of social cognitive theories of alcohol's affect on social behavior is that alcohol interferes with the appraisal of something, but theories differ on what is being appraised. We review three pharmacological theories—self-awareness theory, the appraisal–disruption model, and alcohol myopia theory—to demonstrate the types of appraisals that are affected by alcohol consumption. Although there are other relevant theories that share similar characteristics, these theories are reviewed because they make specific predictions relevant to communicative behaviors.

Self-Awareness Theory

Hull and colleagues (Hull, 1981; Hull & Young, 1983) argued that self-awareness increases the correspondence between actual behavior and one's internal and external standards of how to behave. Self-awareness theory (SAT) assumes that alcohol pharmacologically impedes higher order encoding and the processing of self-relevant information, which, in turn influences the self-regulation of social behaviors (Bailey, Leonard, Cranston, & Taylor, 1983). For example, alcohol purportedly lessens self-awareness by blocking cognitive processing that encodes self-relevant information, resulting in fewer uses of self-references after alcohol consumption (Hull & Young, 1983). The relevant predictions from SAT are that (a) drinking impedes higher order encoding and processing of self-relevant information; (b) reduced self-awareness leads to decreased appropriate behaviors (i.e., behavioral disinhibition) and self-evaluation based on past performance; and (c) alcohol decreases negative self-evaluation for failure, thus inducing or sustaining drinking.

Hull (1987) argued that people who are highly self-conscious are most likely to drink alcohol to reduce self-awareness. Self-conscious people constantly evaluate their own performance and may experience stress if the result of that self-evaluation is negative. Drinking impairs the ability to encode information with respect to its relevance to the self. Consequently, both the drinker's self-awareness and his or her associated stress decline. In support of this argument, research has demonstrated that highly self-conscious people are more sensitive to alcohol's stress-reducing effects (see Hull, 1987; Sayette, 1993). Other studies, however, have produced conflicting results and other researchers have failed to reproduce Hull's finding that drinking influences self-references (Frankenstein & Wilson, 1984), or that drinking alcohol reduces the correspondence between actual behavior and one's internal standards of how to behave (Lannutti, 2001).

Appraisal–Disruption Model

Models that consider affective components such as social anxiety or tension reduction propose that alcohol can reduce negative feelings associated with stressful interactions. One such theory is the appraisal–disruption model (Sayette, 1994). The appraisal–disruption model states alcohol diminishes the power of a stressor by interrupting the cognitive processing that links a stressor to stressful events a person has experienced in the past. This theory predicts that behavior does not change as a function of alcohol consumption unless the person is experiencing a stressor.

Sayette (1994, 1999) noted alcohol reduces anxiety when it is consumed prior to the initial appraisal of a stressful situation. Therefore, anxiety should be measured during the initial appraisal of stressful information rather than after the stressful situation is over (the typical time such stress is measured in most studies). There has been substantial literature supporting the relation between drinking and anxiety proposed by this model (see Ito, Miller, & Pollock, 1996; Sayette, 1999, for reviews). However, other studies have shown that individual difference factors may mediate alcohol's anxiety-reducing effects (Lewis & Vogeltanz-Holm, 2002; Monahan & Lannutti, 2000), suggesting that the appraisal–disruption model may predict social behavior only when a person would normally feel highly anxious or threatened by a situation. For example, a study found cardiovascular stress response mediated the alcohol–aggression relation for men and women (Hoaken, Campbell, Stewart, & Pihl, 2003). Those who showed the greatest amount of cardiovascular stress response dampening in response to alcohol consumption were the ones who acted most aggressively while intoxicated. In summary, although considerable support exists for the appraisal–disruption model, research suggests the model best predicts behavior when individual differences are measured or if the amount of stress in the situation is manipulated.

Alcohol Myopia Theory

A third group of theories rely on inhibition mechanisms to account for alcohol's pharmacological effects on social behavior. One such theory that has been widely tested is alcohol myopia theory (AMT: Steele & Josephs, 1990). According to AMT, alcohol affects social perceptions such that an intoxicated person will attend to a restricted range of cues, take longer to understand them, and piece these cues together in a less coherent way than will a sober person (Tartar, Jones, Simpson, & Vega, 1971).

AMT posits that drinking affects social behavior when the individual experiences an inhibition response conflict (IRC). During an IRC, social behaviors are affected by cues that instigate a behavior (provoking cues) and cues that constrain a behavior (inhibitory cues). When sober, the inhibitory cue operates in opposition to the provoking cue to act. During intoxication, alcohol suppresses inhibitory cues, so intoxicated individuals are more likely to act on their provoking cues than are sober individuals. Alcohol consumption suppresses inhibitory cues (rather than provoking cues) because inhibiting an impulse requires more cognitive effort than simply acting on that impulse. When people act in accordance with a provoking cue rather than possible inhibitory cues, their behavior is seen as more extreme because it is not what they would "normally" do.

AMT has been applied to explain alcohol's effects on communication behaviors such as sexual negotiation (Lannutti & Monahan, 2002), flirting (Monahan & Lannutti, 2000), and request refusals (Lannutti & Monahan, 2004a, 2004b). For example, we observed alcohol consumption's effects on women interacting with an attractive flirtatious man they had just met (Monahan & Lannutti, 2000). Based on AMT, it was predicted that women with low social self-esteem (SSE) would experience an IRC between the provoking cue to play along with the man and their own internal inhibition cue to shy away from such interactions. The effects of alcohol consumption were such that intoxicated low-SSE women experienced less anxiety and engaged in more self-disclosure when interacting with the flirtatious man than did sober low-SSE women.

AMT, like SAT and the appraisal–disruption model, has most often been examined using experimental methods in which researchers manipulate or isolate a set of competing instigating and inhibitory cues. Therefore, the theory has gained support in explaining the effects of alcohol on the processing of one cue versus another, but less is known about how alcohol affects the processing of multiple instigating and inhibitory cues. Future research is needed to more fully understand the way that alcohol affects the hierarchical processing of simultaneous and numerous IRCs.

Summary

These three theoretical perspectives offer insights into alcohol's pharmacological effects on communicative behaviors. Each theory offers a unique lens on alcohol and social behavior. The models just reviewed posit no magic bullet or main effect of drinking alcohol. Instead, alcohol affects social behavior to the extent to which a person is reacting to something: a stressor, anxiety, or IRC. In the absence of a stressor, self-awareness, or inhibition cues, individuals should act similarly when drinking or sober. Thus, the theories stress the importance of considering context in studying alcohol and communicative behavior. Next, we turn from theories of alcohol's pharmacological effects to a second theoretical framework from which alcohol consumption's effect on social cognitive and communicative behavior is examined: alcohol expectancies.

ALCOHOL BELIEFS AND ALCOHOL EXPECTANCY EFFECTS

Alcohol expectancies are people's beliefs about what happens when they or others drink. Goldman modeled alcohol expectancies as information in long-term memory that represents both direct and vicarious experiences a person has had with the environment (Goldman, 1999; Goldman, Brown, Christiansen, & Smith, 1991). In this model, unique alcohol expectancies (e.g., drinking makes me feel sexy or drinking makes me argumentative) are nodes in an information network. Activation of particular nodes occurs in a predictable fashion when the individual encounters stimuli that match previously encoded material relevant to drinking. Second, these activation patterns influence drinking patterns by activating neuromotor and affective systems in the brain. Goldman (1999) stated that "this information memory system acts as a repository of the potential to consume alcohol and other drugs, and this potential is then manifested in certain stimulus circumstances" (p. 196). Research has documented that these expectancies can be activated automatically. For example, Roehrich and Goldman (1995) implicitly primed positive expectancies about drinking and found that alcohol consumption increased as a function of the priming. Thus, alcohol expectancies appear to be stored in long-term memory in a network-like structure and can be activated automatically in relevant drinking situations.

A network of alcohol expectancies has important implications. For example, studies using clustering techniques suggest that the information networks of heavy and light drinkers differ such that drinkers associate positive effects with drinking, whereas light drinkers associate the sedative effects of drinking (Rather & Goldman, 1994). Heavier drinkers also have more densely connected networks of positive beliefs. Hence, the activation of any specific expectancy is more likely to activate other expectancies.

The next section reviews some of the important expectancy findings that are relevant to communication and social cognition scholars. Before doing so, however, the reader should be aware that in the alcohol literature the term *expectancy* is used in two different ways. First, alcohol expectancies are individuals' beliefs about how alcohol affects them or how alcohol affects the behaviors of others. For the sake of clarity in our discussion, we refer to this type of alcohol expectancy as alcohol beliefs. Alcohol beliefs can range from believing that when intoxicated one is more talkative, sexual, and aggressive to beliefs that one will be more passive, compliant, and taciturn (George et al., 1995; George, Stoner, Norris, Lopez, & Lehman, 2000). The second definition of alcohol expectancy emerges from experimental studies and refers to the belief that one has consumed an alcoholic beverage when one has not. Research from this second aspect of expectancies examines to what extent changes in communicative behaviors occur because of drug effects or because of people's beliefs.

Alcohol Beliefs and Communicative Behavior

The power of alcohol beliefs was first demonstrated in an anthropological study (MacAndrew & Edgerton, 1969) that found alcohol effects were highly heterogeneous across different cultures and longitudinally within a culture. For example, the way people behave when "drunk" varied among Native American cultures such that some groups became outrageously boisterous when drinking, whereas others became very quiet and reserved. Within the same culture, such as the Irish, behaviors induced by the same amount of alcohol consumption at a pub and at a wake were markedly different.

Since MacAndrew and Edgerton's (1969) seminal work, several self-report studies found people hold relatively stable beliefs about alcohol's effects on behavior (Brown, Goldman, Inn, & Anderson, 1980; Southwick, Steele, Marlatt, & Lindell, 1981). Although Americans hold several fairly stable alcohol beliefs, a number of studies have documented that the same person may hold contradictory beliefs about the effects of alcohol (e.g., Brown, Christiansen, & Goldman, 1987; Leigh, 1987; Young & Knight, 1989). For example, alcohol beliefs can be positive (e.g., I'll be more talkative when drinking) and negative (e.g., I'll feel out of control when I drink). Similarly, beliefs assume drinking leads to greater self-efficacy (e.g., It is easier to flirt when I drink) as well as decreased self-efficacy (I can't follow complicated arguments when I'm drinking). Finally, beliefs hold that alcohol reinforces good feelings (keep drinking to keep up the good times) and it blocks painful feelings (drink so you don't think about your breakup).

Along with beliefs for the self, people also have beliefs about how alcohol affects the behavior of others (Abbey, McAuslan, Ross, & Zawacki, 1999; Corcoran, 1997; Corcoran & Thomas, 1991). People consistently report that alcohol affects others more than it affects the self. In addition, people report more positive beliefs for the self (e.g., alcohol makes me more social) and more negative beliefs for others (e.g., alcohol makes others more verbally aggressive or angry; Leigh, 1987). These beliefs are often affected by gender when the beliefs are about sexual situations. For example, Corcoran (1997) showed that men who had an initial interaction with a female partner who had been drinking believed the woman found them more likeable than when the woman was sober. Other research shows that men and women believe that sexual activity is more likely to occur on a date if the members of the couple consume alcohol (Abbey & Harnish, 1995; Corcoran & Thomas, 1991). This research also finds that women believe men will perceive them more negatively if the women drink, whereas men believe women perceive men more positively if the men consume alcohol (Corcoran, 1996; Corcoran & Michels, 1998). In summary, alcohol beliefs serve to set the guidelines for what is considered normal and acceptable social behavior when drinking, and as such, these beliefs can serve as a type of self-fulfilling prophecy about one's social behavior when consuming alcohol.

Alcohol beliefs are at the root of two related branches of alcohol research. First, alcohol beliefs serve as a goal for consuming alcohol (i.e., people who believe that drinking relaxes them will drink to relax) and thus serve as a basis for understanding people's motivation to drink alcohol. Second, alcohol expectancy effects demonstrated in studies in which people think they have consumed an alcoholic beverage but have not serve as examples of how people will enact the behaviors they believe alcohol produces despite the nonalcoholic content of their beverage.

Motivational Model of Alcohol Use

Individuals often have strong beliefs about how alcohol consumption will affect their social behavior and alcohol researchers have identified social motives for drinking such as to reduce social anxiety, to celebrate, and to make a gathering more enjoyable (Burke & Stephens, 1999; Cooper, Russell, Skinner, & Windle, 1992; Smith, Abbey, & Scott, 1993). Cooper et al. (1995) developed and tested a motivational model of alcohol use that shows how antecedents and consequences of drinking alcohol differ depending on whether one is drinking to enhance positive emotions or to cope with negative emotions.

When people drink to enhance positive feelings, the antecedents of their drinking include sensation seeking, feeling good, and strong socioemotional alcohol enhancement expectancies. Those who drink to cope have strong tension reduction expectancies, feel bad, and use alcohol as an avoidance or coping mechanism. Cooper et al. (1995) found that those who drink to cope are less able to exercise volitional control over their drinking than are those who drink to enhance positive feelings. Interestingly, expectancies were the strongest predictors among the examined antecedent variables of whether one drank to enhance or to cope. Thus, alcohol's expectancy effects help explain how people's communication behavior may change when they think they have consumed alcohol, and suggests that people's drinking behavior may be influenced by their motives to enact certain social behaviors in a given situation.

Expectancy Versus Pharmacology Effects

Alcohol beliefs are also examined in balanced placebo studies to evaluate which behaviors are most affected by pharmacology and which ones are most affected by beliefs. Balanced placebo studies are usually in the form of a 2 (alcohol: consume alcohol or not) × 2 (alcohol expectancy: believe you consumed alcohol or not) completely crossed design. These studies generally find that alcohol expectancies are powerful predictors of deviant social behaviors such as aggression and sexual inhibition, even when participants actually drank a placebo (nonalcoholic) beverage (George & Marlatt, 1986; Hull & Bond, 1986; Nagoshi, Noll, & Wood, 1992). Changes in physiological responses, psychomotor responses, cognitive processing, and mood are primarily pharmacological with little evidence suggesting any significant expectancy effects (Hull & Bond, 1986; Nagoshi et al., 1992).

ALCOHOL AND SPECIFIC COMMUNICATIVE BEHAVIORS

Having provided a basic overview of theories of alcohol's effects on social behavior, we turn to a more in-depth focus on three areas of interest to communication scholars: sociability, aggression, and compliance. For each communication behavior, alcohol's relevant pharmacological, belief, and expectancy effects are reviewed.

Sociability

Alcohol is often referred to as a social lubricant because people believe drinking reduces communication anxiety, takes away their inhibitions, and increases talkativeness. However, the literature on alcohol and sociability is remarkably mixed. This section reviews pharmacological and expectancy effects on two aspects of sociability: social anxiety and self-disclosure.

Social Anxiety. Social anxiety in the alcohol literature is analogous to communication apprehension in that the construct includes feelings of unease and nervousness in a social situation. The relation between alcohol consumption and anxiety reduction has produced countless studies and two alcohol-anxiety-specific theories: the appraisal–disruption model (Sayette, 1994) noted earlier and the attention-allocation model (Steele & Josephs, 1988), which posits that alcohol consumption reduces anxiety by allocating a person's attention to a pleasant distraction rather than a stressor. Despite the widespread interest in alcohol and social anxiety, studies in this area that specifically examine communication behaviors or interpersonal contexts are in the minority. Next, we review important studies in this area.

The first approach to examining the relation between social anxiety and alcohol consumption is to consider how alcohol beliefs about anxiety motivate drinking. In experimental studies in which participants prepare for a potentially anxiety-increasing task (e.g., giving a speech), participants preferred to increase their alcohol consumption prior to the stress-inducing event (Kidorf & Lang, 1999; Knight & Godfrey, 1993). Yet, survey studies have shown that those who experience high amounts of social anxiety drink less, both in frequency and quantity, than those who have low levels of social anxiety (Eggleston, Woolaway-Bickel, & Schmidt, 2004; Ham & Hope, 2005).

An explanation put forth to clarify these mixed results is that specific alcohol beliefs about alcohol's effect on anxiety mediate or moderate the relation between drinking and social anxiety. In other words, those who think alcohol reduces social anxiety consume more alcohol when they wish to achieve such a reduction. Again, however, there has been mixed support for this proposition. Some survey studies have found that alcohol beliefs regarding social anxiety moderate the relation between social anxiety and drinking (Burke & Stephens, 1999; Tran, Haaga, & Chambless, 1997), whereas others found no support for a moderating or mediating role of alcohol beliefs in the social anxiety–alcohol consumption relation (Eggleston et al., 2004; Ham & Hope, 2005). Thus, the results of studies examining social anxiety reduction as a motive to consume alcohol are inconsistent.

Studies using the balanced placebo design to test the effect of alcohol expectancy on anxiety have also found mixed results. Woolfolk, Abrams, Abrams, and Wilson (1979) showed that men who believed that they had consumed alcohol before talking with a female confederate used less anxious nonverbal cues than those who believed there was no alcohol in their drink. In this study, there were no significant differences in self-reported anxiety. In another study, Abrams and Wilson (1979) reported that females who expected alcohol in their drinks were coded as demonstrating more anxious behavior while interacting with a male confederate than those who expected a nonalcoholic drink. In a partial replication, de Boer, Schippers, and van der Staak (1993) found that alcohol expectancies reduced self-reported anxiety in women, but not in men. Again, the explanation usually given for these inconsistencies is that specific beliefs about alcohol's effects moderate the relation. de Boer, Schippers, and van der Staak (1994), for example, reported that alcohol expectancies resulted in reduced self-reported anxiety for women who believed consuming alcohol had a positive effect on social interaction, but expectancies had no significant effect on the anxiety for those who believed that alcohol negatively affects social interaction.

In the pharmacological literature, studies of social interactions either manipulate anxiety or measure participants' individual differences in terms of social anxiety. In general, these experimental studies find consuming alcohol reduces self-reported social anxiety (Monahan & Lannutti, 2000). De Boer et al. (1993) found that consuming alcohol reduced the self-reported anxiety of men and women who engaged in a brief social interaction with a stranger. Observational studies have also shown the anxiety-reducing effect of alcohol consumption during social interactions. For example, Lindfors and Lindman (1987) found men and women who had consumed alcohol were less anxious (operationalized as talking more) during conversations with strangers and acquaintances than were those who did not consume alcohol.

In sum, the extant data suggest that alcohol's pharmacological effect on social anxiety is more robust and stable across studies than are belief or expectancy effects. It is likely that the pharmacological effect is stronger because such effects are tested in situations with a stressor, whereas in expectancy research, individuals are often asked to reflect back on their drinking patterns. Thus, although the belief that alcohol reduces social anxiety may be widespread, the belief per se does not appear to be a reliable predictor of people's motivation to drink nor of their behavior when drinking. In addition, thinking that one has consumed alcohol has not consistently produced a reduction in self-reported social anxiety. Instead, the literature suggests that alcohol consumption leads to a reduction in social anxiety for those who suffer from social anxiety in specific situations. Second, although positive beliefs about alcohol's social effects contribute to stronger expectancy effects, the precise expectancy relationship is still unclear.

Self-Disclosure. A second aspect of sociability explored in the alcohol literature is self-disclosure. Self-disclosure is usually defined as the verbal expression of self-relevant information. Although the lay assumption may be that alcohol loosens lips, the pharmacological findings are mixed. Sayette (1994) showed that alcohol consumption increased negative self-disclosure but had no effect on positive self-disclosure for men who gave a brief speech about themselves. In Rohrberg and Sousa-Poza's (1976) study, alcohol consumption increased depth, but not amount, of self-disclosure in interactions between male strangers. Miller, Ingham, Plant, and Miller (1977) found that alcohol consumption increased amount of self-disclosure for moderate drinkers, but consumption had no significant effect on the self-disclosure of heavy drinkers. Still other studies have shown no effect of alcohol consumption on self-disclosure in stranger interactions (de Boer et al., 1994; Schippers, de Boer, van der Staak, & Cox, 1997).

These inconsistencies may best be explained using AMT. Recall that AMT posits that alcohol affects social cognitions and behavior only when a person is experiencing an IRC between provoking cues and inhibiting cues. Thus, AMT would predict that alcohol would affect self-disclosure only in situations where a person would normally experience a conflict between cues to self-disclose and cues discouraging disclosure. An example from a study by Monahan and Lannutti (2000) supports an AMT explanation of alcohol consumption's effect on self-disclosure. We predicted that women with low SSE would experience a conflict between their self-protective interpersonal style and the provoking cue of an attractive man flirting with them. Similarly, we expected that women who are high in SSE would not experience a conflict between their interpersonal style and a man flirting with them. In other words, a low-SSE woman should feel more anxious in response to flirting, whereas a high-SSE woman should not. Supporting AMT, findings showed that intoxicated low-SSE women self-disclosed significantly more than did sober low-SSE women, but that the self-disclosure of high-SSE women did not differ as a function of alcohol consumption. Studies on alcohol's pharmacological effects on self-disclosure reiterate the idea that individual differences and context remain key to predicting and explaining alcohol effects.

The influence of alcohol expectancy when experimentally manipulated so that the person believes he or she consumed alcohol has also produced mixed findings. Schippers et al. (1997) found those who were led to believe they drank alcohol did not self-disclose differently than those who were sober during interactions with strangers. Caudill, Wilson, and Abrams (1987) found that alcohol expectancy led to increased self-disclosure for men who believed that they and their female conversational partner had consumed alcohol, but women who believed they had consumed alcohol had lower self-disclosure than women who thought they had a nonalcoholic beverage. As with social anxiety, researchers have suggested that the inconsistencies when examining expectancy effects on self-disclosure may be explained by examining the moderating role of alcohol beliefs in the link between expectancy and self-disclosure (de Boer et al., 1994), but as yet no firm support for this hypothesis has been offered.

These inconsistencies in both the alcohol consumption and expectancy literatures regarding alcohol's effect on self-disclosure represent an opportunity for communication scholars. Further work is needed in these areas, especially regarding alcohol expectancy, with refinements in both operationalization of self-disclosure and context for self-disclosure (e.g., including interactions between those with an established relationship).

Verbal Aggression

Aggression, both verbal and physical, has been extensively studied in the alcohol literature and meta-analyses and reviews are available elsewhere (see Bushman & Cooper, 1990; Ito et al., 1996). Therefore, we focus on alcohol's pharmacological and expectancy effects on aggression in existing interpersonal relationships. Unlike the alcohol and sociability studies that mainly examined interactions between strangers, studies on alcohol and aggression include examinations of romantic partners in beginning and established relationships. First, we discuss the research examining alcohol's effect on sexual aggression and perceptions of sexual aggression in dating couples and then focus on studies of alcohol's effects on couple conflict.

Abbey, Ross, McDuffie, and McAuslan (1996) found that 46% of acquaintance rapes occurred when the man, the woman, or both had been consuming alcohol. Emmers-Sommer and Allen (1999) performed a meta-analysis of variables related to sexual coercion and found a positive association between alcohol consumption and coercion. Thus, it appears alcohol consumption is linked to aggression among dating couples, yet not all dates in which alcohol consumption occurs lead to aggressive and coercive behavior. How does alcohol consumption lead to relational aggression?

Research suggests that alcohol consumption contributes to an increase in verbal aggression among dating couples by distorting social cognitive processes during such interactions. Studies that present participants with depictions of interactions containing aggressive cues show that men and women who have consumed alcohol perceive aggression in these interactions to be more positive, acceptable, and less problematic than do those who are sober (Abbey, Buck, Zawacki, & Saenz, 2003; Lannutti & Monahan, 2002; Livingston & Testa, 2000; Marx, Gross, & Juergens, 1997; Norris & Kerr, 1993). This change in the understanding of aggression cues and subsequent distortion in decision making in which these cues must be weighed against other salient cues, such as sexual arousal, fit with both alcohol myopia (Lannutti & Monahan, 2002) and response inhibition models of alcohol's pharmacological effect. Interestingly, some of this work finds alcohol expectancies also lead participants to similar misperceptions of aggressive cues (Livingston & Testa, 2000; Marx et al., 1997). Thus, pharmacological effects and expectancy effects may result in both men and women distorting their perceptions of aggression cues on dates and seeing these cues as less problematic than they would when sober. This, then, opens the door to sexually coercive acts because intoxicated men may misperceive coercion as acceptable or wanted, and intoxicated women may misperceive coercion as less dangerous (Abbey et al., 1996).

Studies of alcohol's effect on aggression extend beyond dating or early couple interactions to studies of alcohol and conflict in established romantic relationships. Research has explored the negative effects of alcohol consumption and expectancy on cognitive processes, especially attributions, during couple conflict. Senchak and Leonard (1994) used interview and survey techniques to examine attributions made about husband-to-wife aggression and found that husbands who drank prior to aggressive episodes were more likely to attribute responsibility for the aggression to themselves, whereas sober husbands were more likely to attribute responsibility for the episode to their wives. In contrast, alcohol consumption did not significantly affect the perceptions of responsibility made by wives (Senchak & Leonard, 1994). Other research looks deeper into couple conflict and examines the effect of alcohol on cognitive and communication processes during the actual conflicts. Sillars et al. (2002) studied the effects of husbands' alcohol consumption and alcohol expectancy on conflicts between couples with and without a history of aggression in their relationship. Sillars et al. found that when husbands with a history of aggression were expected to have consumed alcohol, wives were more vigilant of the communication during the conflict, meaning that they spend greater cognitive energy analyzing what was said while fighting, than when husbands were not expected to have had alcohol. This effect was not found in couples in which husbands were not historically aggressive. Thus, wives of aggressive men had distinct expectancies for how alcohol consumption affected their husbands' behavior during conflicts.

Sillars et al. (2002) also found that alcohol consumed prior to the conflict increased wife-disparaging attributions made by historically aggressive husbands and increased wife-enhancing attributions by historically nonaggressive husbands. Together, the studies by Senchak and Leonard (1994) and Sillars et al. (2002) suggest that when a husband tends to be aggressive toward his wife, alcohol consumption results in more negative attributions about conflict, and conceivably his relationship and partner. However, similar relationships are not found when a husband is historically nonaggressive.

It is not only in couples with a history of aggression that alcohol increases negative cognitions during conflict. For example, MacDonald, Zanna, and Holmes (2000) found even when couples do not have a history of aggression toward each other, consuming alcohol leads to increases in negative emotion surrounding conflict and more negative perceptions of a partner's feelings. These more negative emotions and evaluations lead to more aggressive conflict. Thus, although the effects of alcohol consumption and expectancy may be more negative in the conflict of couples that already have a history of problems with aggression, the research suggests that alcohol consumption may escalate negative aspects of conflict for all couples.

Seeking Compliance and Acting Compliant

Compliance is defined as a disposition to yield to others and compliance gaining refers to interpersonal interactions during which one person attempts to influence another to perform a desired behavior (Wilson, 2002). Whereas communication researchers consider compliance or social influence to be a (if not the) primary motive for communication, alcohol researchers generally do not consider their work to be about compliance. Yet, when examined through a communication lens, much of the applied alcohol research is about compliance. Research examines pharmacological effects of drinking on compliance, alcohol beliefs about other's behaviors and strategies used to get an intoxicated friend to comply with requests, and alcohol beliefs about one's own compliance behaviors.

Pharmacological Effects. A demonstrated positive effect of drinking is that intoxicated persons can be more responsive to requests for help. For example, Steele, Critchlow, and Liu (1985) used AMT to explain how alcohol consumption created "helpful drunkards." After completing a study, participants were asked if they would do the researcher a favor by volunteering for a second tedious task. Thus, participants were presented with an IRC between the provoking cue of being asked for a favor and the inhibiting cue of the tediousness of the additional task. AMT predicts that behavior of intoxicated participants should be more affected by the provoking cue (favor being asked), whereas sober participants should be more affected by the inhibitory cues (I already finished the study I agreed to do and the task I am being asked to help with is tedious). In support of AMT, drinkers were significantly more likely to agree to help than were sober participants.

Although the literature suggests that drinking results in a higher likelihood of helping behavior, research examining other aspects of drinking and conformity has mixed outcomes. Gustafson (1988) randomly assigned women to one of three conditions (consume alcohol, placebo, or control) to examine the influence of alcohol consumption on conformity with group pressure. Participants were assigned to guess the length of lines while interacting with a group of confederates that applied pressure to influence the participants' guesses. Intoxicated participants and those in the placebo condition were significantly more likely to conform with group pressure than were sober participants. Gustafson suggested that the expectancy probably drove the compliant behavior.

There are also a few studies demonstrating the opposite outcome. Smith (1974) found no evidence that alcohol affected measures of yielding. Bostrom and White (1979) argued that alcohol creates a psychological state in which people are more resistant to persuasion. In the Bostrom and White study, individuals assessed how much they agreed with a series of cultural sayings or truisms. They then drank alcohol or were in a control condition. Next, participants read an essay attacking the validity of cultural truisms and then completed a questionnaire asking them to identify any counterarguments that occurred to them while reading the essay. Although there was no significant difference in the number of counterarguments provided by drinking and control participants, participants who drank alcohol were significantly less likely to change their attitude toward the cultural truisms than were control participants.

Alcohol Beliefs About Others. Seibold and Thomas (1994) used survey methods to examine the circumstances people would try to persuade a drunk friend to not engage in risky behavior. Participants indicated willingness to intervene in drunk-driving situations and were most likely to intervene when they perceived that harm could come to the intoxicated person, others, or themselves. Thomas and Seibold (1995) also examined strategies that college students employed to persuade a friend who had been drinking to either control his or her drinking better or to not drive while intoxicated. Although both outcomes were prosocial and in the drinking person's best interest, results indicate that although negative influence strategies, such as verbal threats, were not preferred or initially used by persuaders, they were the most successful in persuading the drinking person.

Other studies on alcohol-related personal interventions indicate persuaders employ a variety of influence strategies that differ in their degree of aggressiveness and potential for success (Jung, 1986; Rabow, Hernandez, & Watts, 1986). Results from these studies indicate that strategies most likely to be employed were those least intrusive (e.g., asking the drunken friend not to go), whereas those least likely to be employed were those most intrusive and negatively valenced (e.g., threatening the drunken friend). Although individuals prefer using unobtrusive strategies to highly intrusive ones, they also report that intrusive strategies (e.g., forcing a friend to leave) were most successful at getting the person out of the risky situation.

Beliefs About the Self. Other research has examined alcohol's influence on the persuasive strategies a person believes he or she will employ when drinking. Monahan (2005) examined people's beliefs about how drinking will affect their persuasion tactics and how amenable they will be to persuasion in two survey studies. When in the role of the influencer, people believe that when they are drunk they will be more persistent, more direct, and more likely to use negative compliance strategies in a variety of situations including trying to convince friends to do what the influencer wants on a Friday night, starting an argument with another, and trying to get someone to do them a favor. When in the role of the influencee, participants report that when drinking they would be more likely to give up their own and other peoples' secrets (in response to a request by another) and more likely to comply with a request to engage in risky behaviors.

In summary, people expect to be more compliant and expect others to be more compliant as well when drinking. This belief is supported by pharmacological studies as well as studies that measure behavioral acts as helping another. Yet, the literature is mixed when looking at changing opinions or attitudes. Second, people expect they will be more persistent, direct, and more likely to use negative persuasion strategies when they themselves are drinking, although there are scant experimental data to indicate whether or not individuals actually are more persistent and use more negative strategies as a function of alcohol consumption. Clearly one area of future research for communication scholars is to see how drinking affects both the type of strategy a persuader may use as well as the intensity (e.g., directness, persistence, etc.) the persuader uses when enacting the strategy.

METHODOLOGICAL CHALLENGES

We offer an overview of some of the challenges faced by communication researchers who want to identify the pharmacological or expectancy effects of alcohol on social cognition and communicative behaviors.

Challenges of Pharmacological Studies

Although field studies of alcohol's pharmacological effects exist (e.g., Lannutti & Cameron, 2003; Taylor & Booth-Butterfield, 1993), the most common way to examine these effects is through controlled experiments. Ethical standards require participants who drink in the lab must be sober (operationally defined as a blood alcohol content [BAC] of less that .02 g/dl, whereas "drunk" is operationally defined in most of the United States as .08 g/dl) before leaving the lab facility. Thus, these studies can take up to 4 to 6 hours per participant for those who receive alcohol. Otherwise, the researcher must provide transportation for the intoxicated participant to get home. Additionally, such research requires a breathalyzer to measure BAC as well as a set of scales, lab space, alcohol, tonic water, soft drinks, and snacks. Thus, most laboratory-based studies require some fiscal investment.

Other essential tools for studies that involve alcohol consumption are persistence and creativity. For example, when presenting a study for approval by an institutional review board (IRB), one can safely assume a full board review every time a new study is proposed. Although we have had success at three different universities in gaining IRB approval, the paperwork for approval is much more detailed and elaborate than one would expect for a typical communication study. Consider the following IRB questions and our responses to get a feel for the type of issues that a researcher must consider: What will you do if an intoxicated participant insists on leaving? Answer: Hold his or her driver's license at the beginning of the study and call the campus police. What will you do if someone gets sick? Answer: Take them to the Student Health Center or local hospital. How will you know that it is safe to give someone alcohol? Answer: Get a list of medications from the pharmacy school that contraindicate alcohol consumption and compare them to the participant's medications, and to back that list up, have a consulting pharmacist who will answer questions on a case-by-case basis.

Thus, conducting research in which participants consume alcohol presents a researcher with unique challenges, but with thought and creativity, answers to these challenges are within reach. Our recommendation for the first time one designs an alcohol consumption study is to get copies of other researchers' IRB applications to help one become familiarized with the necessary components. Second, work with someone who has done alcohol research before so you can observe their methodology before branching out on your own.

Challenges of Balanced Placebo Designs

As noted previously, experimental studies use a balanced placebo design to examine both pharmacological and expectancy effects. Although the balanced placebo design allows the researcher to parse out beliefs from pharmacological effects, it is not a simple research plan to execute. Participant screening and safety concerns of pharmacological studies discussed earlier still apply to these studies and join with additional concerns. For example, the BAC level for the alcohol consumption condition must be sufficiently low so that participants who believe they are not getting alcohol (but actually do get alcohol) will believe the manipulation. This usually means setting BAC at a dose no higher than .06 g/dl, which is less than legally drunk in most states and may not be sufficient to cause cognitive impairment. Thus, for those interested in impairment of social cognitive processes, the balanced placebo design is often unsatisfactory. Further, creating a beverage that tastes and smells like it contains alcohol but does not is a tricky endeavor, often requiring a delicate deception of rubbing the rim of a glass with alcohol and spraying a small amount of alcohol on top of the otherwise nonalcoholic beverage and having participants gargle with a very strong mouthwash so that they have a difficult time tasting the alcohol (or lack thereof) in their drinks. Finally, the multiple deceptions involved (e.g., convincing those who consumed to believe they are sober and convincing those who are sober that they received alcohol) are often unsuccessful (Sayette, Breslin, Wilson, & Rosenblum, 1994).

Challenges of Alcohol Belief Studies

Alcohol belief studies involve methods with which most communication scholars are probably familiar. Normally, such beliefs are measured with surveys, use of vignettes or scenarios, or diary methods. As in any study using survey methods to examine how social cognitive processes affect communication outcomes, demonstrating a cause-and-effect relation is unlikely. Instead, such studies are helpful in demonstrating what aspects of social cognition (e.g., cognitive impairment, attribution processes, etc.) people believe are affected by alcohol, which in turn, affects their behaviors.

A second concern with alcohol belief studies is that when one examines pharmacological effects without manipulating expectancies, one is open to the contention that perhaps it is all in the mind, not in the drug. However, expectancy studies are equally open to criticisms made of self-report measures: What people say they do when they drink may not be a reflection of what they actually do. If one is interested in alcohol belief studies, it is important to pay heed to the meta-analyses demonstrating that beliefs tend to be significant predictors of actual behavior primarily when the behavior is deviant in some aspect (e.g., date rape, verbally aggressive behavior, flirting for a normally shy person).

A third concern is that in our own experience, people will report alcohol affects almost any communicative behavior possible if one is simply asked if one engages in a behavior more or less often when one drinks. Thus, it is important to contextualize the behaviors as much as possible by use of scenarios or vignettes. In other words, have participants compare in which situations they are more likely to drink alcohol or which strategies are affected, rather than simply asking if their behavior in general changes as a function of drinking.

STUDYING ALCOHOL EFFECTS: FUTURE DIRECTIONS

Although this chapter has provided an overview of theory and findings relevant for alcohol consumption on social cognitive and communicative outcomes, it should also be clear there are ample opportunities for communication researchers to further explore this area. We see three areas of interest for social cognition and communication scholars.

First, most of the literature discussed previously, although addressing communication outcomes, comes from researchers outside of the communication field. Thus, whereas the literature can tell us about alcohol's effects on social cognitions and behaviors, it is limited in that specific speech acts, communication strategies, nonverbal behavior, and mutual influence effects are rarely examined. For example, we know surprisingly little of people's beliefs about how drinking can or does affect their own communication behaviors because past belief measures have focused on psychological outcomes. The most frequently used expectancy scale (Alcohol Expectancy Questionnaire [AEQ]; Brown et al., 1980) has been employed in various forms across hundreds of studies. However, the AEQ covers a wide array of psychological states and behavioral outcomes (sample AEQ items: Alcohol helps me to fall asleep more easily; I feel powerful when I drink, as if I can really make other people do as I want; I'm more clumsy after a few drinks) and many of these outcomes are not geared specifically toward the type of outcome of interest to communication scholars. In pharmacological studies, many of the operationalizations of dependent variables are not those that are standard within the communication field. For example, alcohol researchers have been known to measure self-disclosure by counting words rather than examining the content of the utterances, social anxiety by number of words spoken, and sociability by self-report about feelings.

The literature would also benefit from more examinations of alcohol's influence on communication outcomes in naturally occurring interactions in established relationships rather than lab interactions between strangers. Although verbally aggressive acts occur between relative strangers, the frequency of those acts between known others is much higher. Thus, we need more understanding of how drinking shapes social cognitions about aggression that, in turn, shape the form and content of arguments.

Finally, we hope to see more research on the influence of alcohol consumption and expectancy within various areas of the communication field. For example, research using theories of alcohol and alcohol expectancy to make predictions about which compliance-gaining strategies are more likely to be used by persuaders who are drunk or which strategies will be most effective in gaining compliance in a drinking partner are needed. Scholars interested in relational communication topics such as relationship initiation may also explore how drinking fundamentally affects relationship initiation discourse, as initiating new relationships often occurs at bars, parties, and other venues where drinking is present. From a health communication perspective, we need more work targeting how alcohol affects the ability to process messages discouraging risky behavior. These and other ways in which alcohol affects social cognitions and behavior are worthy of future attention from communication researchers.

REFERENCES

Abbey, A., Buck, P. O., Zawacki, T., & Saenz, C. (2003). Alcohol's effects on perceptions of a potential date rape. *Journal of Studies on Alcohol, 64,* 669–677.

Abbey, A., & Harnish, R. J. (1995). Perception of sexual intent: The role of gender, alcohol consumption, and rape supportive attitudes. *Sex Roles, 32,* 297–313.

Abbey, A., McAuslan, P., Ross, L. T., & Zawacki, T. (1999). Alcohol expectancies regarding sex, aggression, and sexual vulnerability: Reliability and validity assessment. *Psychology of Addictive Behaviors, 13,* 174–182.

Abbey, A., Ross, L. T., McDuffie, D., & McAuslan, P. (1996). Alcohol and dating risk factors for sexual assault among college women. *Psychology of Women Quarterly, 20,* 147–169.

Abrams, D. B., & Wilson, G. T. (1979). Effects of alcohol on social anxiety in women: Cognitive versus physiological processes. *Journal of Abnormal Psychology, 88,* 161–173.

Baddeley, A., & Della Sala, S. (1998). Working memory and executive control. In A. C. Roberts & T. W. Weiskrantz (Eds.), *The prefrontal cortex: Executive and cognitive functions* (pp. 9–21). New York: Oxford University Press.

Bailey, D. S., Leonard, K. E., Cranston, J. W., & Taylor, S. P. (1983). Effects of alcohol and self-awareness on human physical aggression. *Personality and Social Psychology Bulletin, 9,* 289–295.

Banaji, M. R., & Steele, C. M. (1989). Alcohol and self evaluation. Is a social cognition approach beneficial? *Social Cognition, 7,* 137–151.

Bostrom, R. N., & White, N. D. (1979). Does drinking weaken resistance? *Journal of Communication, 29,* 73–80.

Brown, S. A., Christiansen, B. A., & Goldman, M. S. (1987). The alcohol expectancy questionnaire: An instrument for the assessment of adolescent and adult alcohol expectancies. *Journal of Studies on Alcohol, 48,* 483–491.

Brown, S. A., Goldman, M. S., Inn, A., & Anderson, L. R. (1980). Expectancies of reinforcement from alcohol: Their domain and relation to drinking patterns. *Journal of Consulting and Clinical Psychology, 48,* 419–426.

Burke, R. S., & Stephens, R. S. (1999). Social anxiety and drinking in college students: A social cognitive theory analysis. *Clinical Psychology Review, 19,* 513–530.

Bushman, B. J., & Cooper, H. M. (1990). Effects of alcohol on human aggression: An integrative research review. *Psychological Bulletin, 107,* 341–354.

Caudill, B. D., Wilson, G. T., & Abrams, D. B. (1987). Alcohol and self-disclosure: Analyses of interpersonal behavior in female social drinkers. *Journal of Studies on Alcohol, 48,* 401–409.

Cooper, M. L., Frone, M. R., Russell, M., & Mudar, P. (1995). Drinking to regulate positive and negative emotions: A motivational model of alcohol use. *Journal of Personality and Social Psychology, 69,* 990–1005.

Cooper, M. L., Russell, M., Skinner, J. B., & Windle, M. (1992). Development and validation of a three-dimensional measure of drinking motives. *Psychological Assessment, 4,* 123–132.

Corcoran, K. J. (1996). The influence of gender, expectancy, and partner beverage selection on (meta) perceptions in a "blind" dating situation. *Addictive Behaviors, 21,* 273–282.

Corcoran, K. J. (1997). The influence of personality, cognition, and behavior on perceptions and metaperceptions following alcoholic beverage selection in a dating situation. *Addictive Behaviors, 22,* 577–585.

Corcoran, K. J., & Michels, J. L. (1998). Interpersonal perception and alcohol expectancies predict beverage selection in opposite sex dyadic interactions. *Journal of Child & Adolescent Substance Abuse, 9,* 29–38.

Corcoran, K. J., & Thomas, L. R. (1991). The influence of observed alcohol consumption on perceptions of initiation of sexual activity in a college dating situation. *Journal of Applied Social Psychology, 21,* 500–507.

Crowe, L. C., & George, W. H. (1989). Alcohol and human sexuality: Review and integration. *Psychological Bulletin, 105,* 374–386.

de Boer, M. C., Schippers, G. M., & van der Staak, C. P. F. (1993). Alcohol and social anxiety in women and men: Pharmacological and expectancy effects. *Addictive Behavior, 18,* 117–126.

de Boer, M. C., Schippers, G. M., & van der Staak, C. P. F. (1994). The effects of alcohol, expectancy, and alcohol beliefs on anxiety and self-disclosure in women: Do beliefs moderate alcohol effects? *Addictive Behavior, 19,* 509–520.

Eggleston, A. M., Woolaway-Bickel, K., & Schmidt, N. B. (2004). Social anxiety and alcohol use: Evaluation of the moderating and mediating effects of alcohol expectancies. *Journal of Anxiety Disorders, 18,* 33–49.

Emmers-Sommer, T. M., & Allen, M. (1999). Variables related to sexual coercion: A path model. *Journal of Social and Personal Relationships, 16,* 659–678.

Frankenstein, W., & Wilson, G. T. (1984). Alcohol's effects on self-awareness. *Addictive Behaviors, 9,* 323–328.

George, W. H., Frone, M. R., Cooper, M. L., Russell, M., Skinner, J. B., & Windle, M. (1995). A revised Alcohol Expectancy Questionnaire: Factor structure confirmation and invariance in a general population sample. *Journal of Studies on Alcohol, 56,* 177–185.

George, W. H., & Marlatt, G. A. (1986). The effects of alcohol and anger on interest in violence, erotica, and deviance. *Journal of Abnormal Psychology, 95,* 150–158.

George, W. H., Stoner, S. A., Norris, J., Lopez, P., & Lehman, G. L. (2000). Alcohol expectancies and sexuality: A self-fulfilling prophecy analysis of dyadic perceptions and behavior. *Journal of Studies on Alcohol, 61,* 168–176.

Giancola, P. R. (2004). Executive functioning and alcohol-related aggression. *Journal of Abnormal Psychology, 113,* 541–555.

Giancola, P. R., & Tarter, R. E. (1999). Executive cognitive functioning and risk for substance abuse. *Psychological Science, 10,* 203–205.

Goldman, M. K. (1999). Risk for substance abuse: Memory as a common etiological pathway. *Psychological Science, 10,* 196–199.

Goldman, M. S., Brown, S. A., Christiansen, B. A., & Smith, G. T. (1991). Alcoholism and memory: Broadening the scope of alcohol-expectancy research. *Psychological Bulletin, 110,* 137–146.

Gustafson, R. (1988). Alcohol and social influence: Female yielding to male and female group pressure. *Alcohol and alcoholism, 23,* 501–505.

Ham, L. S., & Hope, D. A. (2005). Incorporating social anxiety into a model of college student problematic drinking. *Addictive Behaviors, 30,* 127–150.

Hoaken, P. N., Campbell, T., Stewart, S. H., & Pihl, R. O. (2003). Effects of Alcohol on cardiovascular reactivity and mediation of aggressive behavior in adult men and women. *Alcohol and Alcoholism, 38,* 84–92.

Hoaken, P. N. S., Giancola, P., & Pihl, R. O. (1998). Executive cognitive functions as mediators of alcohol-related aggression. *Alcohol and Alcoholism, 33,* 47–54.

Hull, J. G. (1981). A self-awareness model of the causes and effects of alcohol consumption. *Journal of Abnormal Psychology, 90,* 586–600.

Hull, J. G. (1987). Self-awareness model. In H. T. Blane & K. E. Leonard (Eds.), *Psychological theories of drinking and alcoholism* (pp. 272–304). New York: Guilford.

Hull, J. G., & Bond, C. F. (1986). Social and behavioral consequences of alcohol consumption and expectancy: A meta-analysis. *Psychological Bulletin, 99,* 347–360.

Hull, J. G., & Young, R. D. (1983). Self-consciousness, self-esteem, and success-failure as determinants of alcohol consumption in a male social drinkers. *Journal of Personality & Social Psychology, 44,* 1097–1109.

Ito, T. A., Miller, N., & Pollock, V. E. (1996). Alcohol and aggression: A meta-analysis on the moderating effects of inhibitory cues, triggering events, and self-focused attention. *Psychological Bulletin, 120,* 60–82.

Jung, J. (1986). How significant others cope with problem drinkers. *International Journal of the Addictions, 21*, 5–22.

Kimberg, D. Y., & Farah, M. J. (1993). A unified account of cognitive impairment following frontal lobe damage: The role of working memory in complex, organized behavior. *Journal of Experimental Psychology: General, 122*, 411–428.

Kidorf, M., & Lang, A. R. (1999). Effects of social anxiety and alcohol expectancies on stress-induced drinking. *Psychology of Addictive Behaviors, 13*, 134–142.

Knight, R. G., & Godfrey, H. P. (1993). The role of alcohol-related expectancies in the prediction of drinking behaviour in a simulated social interaction. *Addiction, 88*, 1111–1118.

Lakins, N. E., Williams, G. D., Yi, H., & Smothers, B. A. (2004). Surveillance report No. 66: Apparent per capita alcohol consumption. National, state, and regional trends, 1977–2002. Retrieved April 5, 2005, from http://www.niaaa.nih.gov/publications/surveillance66/CONS02.htm

Lannutti, P. J. (2001). *Women's refusals of unwanted sexual advances: The influence of repeated requests, alcohol consumption, and self discrepancy.* Unpublished doctoral dissertation, The University of Georgia, Athens, GA.

Lannutti, P. J., & Cameron, M. O. (2003, November). *Does expectancy violations theory apply when there's an open bar? The influence of alcohol consumption on nonverbal immediacy threshold and violator assessment.* Paper presented at the annual meeting of the National Communication Association, Miami, FL

Lannutti, P. J., & Monahan, J. L. (2002). When the frame paints the picture: Alcohol consumption, relational framing, and sexual communication. *Communication Research, 29*, 390–421.

Lannutti, P. J., & Monahan, J. L. (2004b). Resistance, persistence, and drinking: Examining goals in women's refusals of unwanted sexual advances. *Western Journal of Communication, 68*, 151–169.

Lannutti, P. J., & Monahan, J. L. (2004a). "Not now, maybe later": The influence of request persistence, alcohol consumption, and relationship type on women's refusal strategies. *Communication Studies, 55*, 362–377.

Leigh, B. C. (1987). Beliefs about the effects of alcohol on self and others. *Journal of Alcohol Studies, 48*, 467–475.

Lewis, B. A., & Vogeltanz-Holm, N. D. (2002). The effects of alcohol and anxiousness on physiological and subjective responses to a social stressor in women. *Addictive Behaviors, 27*, 529–545.

Lindfors, B., & Lindman, R. (1987). Alcohol and previous acquaintance: Mood and social interactions in small groups. *Scandinavian Journal of Psychology, 28*, 211–219.

Livingston, J. A., & Testa, M. (2000). Qualitative analysis of women's perceived vulnerability to sexual aggression in a hypothetical dating context. *Journal of Social and Personal Relationships, 17*, 729–741.

MacAndrew, C., & Edgerton, R. B. (1969). *Drunken comportment: A social explanation.* Oxford, UK: Aldine.

MacDonald, G., Zanna, M. P., & Holmes, J. G. (2000). An experimental test of the role of alcohol in relationship conflict. *Journal of Experimental and Social Psychology, 36*, 182–193.

Marx, B. P., Gross, A. M., & Juergens, J. P. (1997). Of effects of alcohol consumption and expectancies in an experimental date rape analogue. *Journal of Psychopathology and Behavioral Assessment, 19*, 281–302.

Miller, P. M., Ingrham, J. G., Plant, M. A., & Miller, T. (1977). Alcohol consumption and self-disclosure. *British Journal of the Addictions, 72*, 293–300.

Monahan, J. L. (2005). *Alcohol expectancies and social influence: How people believe drinking affects their persuasive attempts as well as their responses to persuasive attempts.* Athens: University of Georgia.

Monahan, J. L., & Lannutti, P. J. (2000). Alcohol as social lubricant: Alcohol myopia theory, social self-esteem, and social interaction. *Human Communication Research, 26,* 175–202.

Murphy, S. T., Monahan, J. L., & Miller, L. C. (1998). Inference under the influence: The impact of alcohol and inhibition conflict on women's sexual decision-making. *Personality and Social Psychology Bulletin, 24,* 517–529.

Nagoshi, C. T., Noll, R. T., & Wood, M. D. (1992). Alcohol expectancies and behavioral and emotional responses to placebo versus alcohol administration. *Alcoholism: Clinical and Experimental Research, 16,* 255–260.

Norris, J., & Kerr, K. L. (1993). Alcohol and violent pornography: Responses to permissive and nonpermissive cues. *Journal of Studies on Alcohol, 11*(Suppl.), 118–127.

Parrott, D. J., Zeichner, A., Pihl, R. O. (2003). Effects of alcohol, personality, and provocation on the expression of anger in men: A facial coding analysis. *Alcoholism: Clinical and Experimental Research, 27,* 937–945.

Pihl, R. O., Assaad, J. M., & Hoaken, P. N. S. (2003). What differential responsivity to alcohol challenge adds to understanding the alcohol-aggression relationship. *Aggressive Behavior, 29,* 302–315.

Rabow, J., Hernandez, A. C. R., & Watts, R. K. (1986). College students do intervene in drunk driving situations. *Sociology and Social Research, 70,* 224–225.

Rather, B. C., & Goldman, M. S. (1994). Drinking-related differences in the memory organization of alcohol expectancies. *Experimental and Clinical Psychopharmacology, 2,* 167–183.

Roehrich, L., & Goldman, M. S. (1995). Implicit priming of alcohol expectancy memory processes and subsequent drinking behavior. *Experimental and Clinical Psychopharmacology, 3,* 402–410.

Rohrberg, R. G., & Sousa-Poza, J. F. (1976). Alcohol, field dependence, and dyadic interaction. *Psychological Reports, 39,* 1151–1161.

Sayette, M. A. (1993). An appraisal–disruption model of alcohol's effects on stress responses in social drinkers. *Psychological Bulletin, 114,* 459–476.

Sayette, M. A. (1994). Effects of alcohol on self-appraisal. *International Journal of the Addictions, 29,* 127–133.

Sayette, M. A. (1999). Does drinking reduce stress? *Alcohol Research & Health, 23,* 250–255.

Sayette, M. A., Breslin, F. C., Wilson, G. T., & Rosenblum, G. D. (1994). An evaluation of the balanced placebo design in alcohol administration research. *Addictive Behaviors, 19,* 333–342.

Schippers, G. M., de Boer, M. C., van der Staak, C. P. F., & Cox, W. M. (1997). Effects of alcohol and expectancy on self-disclosure and anxiety in male and female social drinkers. *Addictive Behaviors, 22,* 305–314.

Seibold, D. R., & Thomas, R. W. (1994). Rethinking the role of interpersonal influence processes in alcohol intervention situations. *Journal of Applied Communication Research, 22,* 177–197.

Senchak, M., & Leonard, K. (1994). Attributions for episodes of marital aggression: The effects of aggression severity and alcohol use. *Journal of Family Violence, 9,* 371–381.

Sillars, A., Leonard, K. E., Roberts, L. J., & Dun, T. (2002). Cognition and communication during marital conflict: How alcohol affects subjective coding of interaction in aggressive and nonaggressive couples. In P. Noller & J. A. Feeney (Eds.), *Understanding marriage: Developments in the study of couple interaction* (pp. 85–112). Cambridge, UK: Cambridge University Press.

Smith, M. J., Abbey, A., & Scott, R. O. (1993). Reasons for drinking alcohol: Their relationship to psychosocial variables and alcohol consumption. *International Journal of the Addictions, 28,* 881–908.

Smith, R. C. (1974). Alcohol and the acceptance of social influence: An experimental study. *Psychopharmacologia, 36,* 357–366.

Southwick, L. L., Steele, C. M., Marlatt, G. A., & Lindell, M. K. (1981). Alcohol-related expectancies: Defined by phase of intoxication and drinking experience. *Journal of Consulting & Clinical Psychology, 49,* 713–721.

Steele, C. M., Critchlow, B., & Liu, T. J. (1985). Alcohol and social behavior II: The helpful drunkard. *Journal of Personality and Social Psychology, 48,* 35–46.

Steele, C. M., & Josephs, R. A., (1988). Drinking your troubles away: II. An attention-allocation model of alcohol's effect on psychological stress . *Journal of Abnormal Psychology, 97,* 196–205.

Steele, C. M., & Josephs, R. A. (1990). Alcohol myopia: Its prized and dangerous effects. *American Psychologist, 45,* 921–933.

Stuss, D. T., & Alexander, M. P. (2000). Executive functions and the frontal lobes: A conceptual view. *Psychological Research, 63,* 289–298.

Tartar, R., Jones, B., Simpson, C. D., & Vega, A. (1971). Effects of task complexity and practice during acute alcohol intoxication. *Perceptual and Motor Skills, 33,* 307–318.

Taylor, T., & Booth-Butterfield, S. (1993). Getting a foot in the door with drinking and driving: A field study of influence. *Communication Research Reports, 10,* 95–101.

Thomas, R. W., & Seibold, D. R. (1995). Interpersonal influence and alcohol-related interventions in the college environment. *Health Communication, 7,* 93–123.

Tran, G. Q., Haaga, D. A. F., & Chambless, D. L. (1997). Expecting that alcohol use will reduce social anxiety moderates the relation between social anxiety and alcohol consumption. *Cognitive Therapy & Research, 21,* 535–553.

Wilson, S. R. (2002). *Seeking and resisting compliance: Why people say what they do when trying to influence others.* Thousand Oaks, CA: Sage.

Woolfolk, A. E., Abrams, L. M., Abrams, D. B., & Wilson, G. T. (1979). Effects of alcohol on the nonverbal communication of anxiety: The impact of beliefs on nonverbal behavior. *Environmental Psychology and Nonverbal Behavior, 3,* 205–218.

Young, R. M., & Knight, R. G. (1989). The drinking expectancy questionnaire: A revised measure of alcohol-related beliefs. *Journal of Psychopathology and Behavioral Assessment, 11,* 99–112.

III

Mass Media

11

Social Cognition and Cultivation

L. J. Shrum
University of Texas at San Antonio

Cultivation theory is now approaching its third decade of empirical research. There are few areas of research in communication that have sparked more controversy, save perhaps research on media and aggression.[1] Although cultivation research has produced a voluminous amount of data (cf. Shanahan & Morgan, 1999), the effects are typically small and sometimes elusive. These two factors have contributed to a healthy skepticism regarding the validity of the cultivation effect. Moreover, I would like to argue that this skepticism is fueled by a lack of understanding about how the process actually works from a psychological perspective. How does television information, in all of its types and forms, influence judgments?

That is the question that a social cognition perspective approach to cultivation seeks to address. It attempts to flesh out and enrich a more macro cultural phenomenon by demonstrating that more micro psychological theories can also explain cultivation. In doing so, the approach provides at least two important services: (a) It provides convergent validity for the theory, and (b) it provides an understanding of conditions that facilitate and inhibit the effect.

---

[1]Cultivation and research on media and aggression share a number of similarities, to the point of being almost indistinguishable except for the choice of dependent variable (beliefs vs. behaviors). A focus on the similarities would be instructive, but unfortunately is beyond the scope of this chapter. However, it is worth noting that many aspects of the social cognition models reviewed here, particularly the accessibility model, are similar to the mechanisms in Berkowitz's cognitive neoassociationistic model for the effects of media on aggression (cf. Berkowitz & Rogers, 1986; Jo & Berkowitz, 1994).

The goal of this chapter is to review and discuss cultivation research that has taken a social cognition perspective and to proffer some opinions about the future of social cognition-oriented cultivation research. With respect to cultivation research, I am referring to any research that looks at the relation between television program content and judgment. With respect to social cognition research, I am referring to research that focuses on the "cognitive mechanisms that mediate judgments and behavior" (Wyer & Srull, 1989, p. 2). As Wyer and Srull noted, although much of the social psychological research has indeed been concerned with cognitive issues, and often makes explicit assumptions about the cognitive processes that underlie particular effects, traditional social psychological research typically has not evaluated these assumptions directly. In contrast, social cognition research is precisely concerned with these mediating processes. This point is an important one for considering research that is relevant for this chapter. Social cognition research is not merely a psychological perspective, but is more specifically an information processing perspective. Thus, with respect to cultivation, I only address (for the most part) research that deals with—and ideally tests—the cognitive processes that underlie cultivation effects.

The structure of the chapter adheres for the most part to the mandate provided by the editors: review of the state of social cognition-oriented research in the early 1980s, discussion of the major developments since then (both theoretical and methodological), and predictions about where this area of research might be headed in the near future. The only exception is a slight bending of the time line such that the initial review starts with research through the 1980s, rather than the beginning of the 1980s. I do this for two reasons. One is that little research relevant to social cognition and cultivation had been conducted prior to the early 1980s. Second, most of the research conducted in the late 1980s was a direct outgrowth of this seminal research, and thus it seems more coherent to discuss this research together.

SOCIAL COGNITION AND CULTIVATION THROUGH THE 1980S

Given that cultivation research itself did not hit the radar screen of communication research with any impact until the seminal publication of Gerbner and Gross (1976), it is not surprising that little research on the processes underlying cultivation effects occurred prior to 1980. In fact, it was around this time that the issue of cognitive processes was first raised. The first foray into this area was research by Hawkins and Pingree (1980), appropriately titled "Some Processes in the Cultivation Effect." In a series of conceptual and empirical articles, these researchers broached the notion that couching cultivation effects in terms of learning is more descriptive than explanatory. They therefore developed hypotheses regarding the processes by which television information might influence various types of judgments. These processes included cognitive processing abilities (Hawkins & Pingree, 1980), perceptions of television reality (Hawkins & Pingree, 1980), and inference-making abilities (Pingree, 1983; for reviews, see Hawkins & Pingree, 1981, 1982).

Unfortunately, as is often the case with groundbreaking research, the initial attempts to investigate process were largely unsuccessful (cf. Hawkins & Pingree, 1980). In most cases, the research produced null findings with respect to the process-oriented hypotheses. For example, the notion that perceived reality of television might play a role in cultivation by increasing the propensity of high-realism viewers to use television information for real-world judgments received little support. Although viewers were found to differ on the extent to which they perceived television portrayals to reflect reality, these differences did not relate to the cultivation effect in any consistent manner. Other individual difference variables that might serve as surrogate measures for some type of processing (e.g., sex, current event knowledge, other media usage) likewise showed little relation with cultivation effects. One variable, children's age, did appear to exhibit some relation to cultivation. Age was used as a surrogate measure of processing ability, and results indicated that television did not appear to cultivate a mean worldview for students in Grades 5 and 8, but did for students in Grade 11. However, students in Grade 8 did evidence a cultivation effect for perceptions of the prevalence of societal violence, whereas those in Grade 11 did not. Thus, it is unclear how generalizable that effect is. Finally, the relation between inference making and cultivation yielded significant but counterintuitive results. Pingree (1983) hypothesized that those better at drawing inferences from information would thus be better at using television information to construct their judgments. However, the results showed stronger cultivation effects for those with low rather than high inference-making abilities.

Following these initial attempts to investigate process issues for cultivation effects, additional studies were conducted by Hawkins and Pingree, as well as others, that attempted to more precisely specify the component processes. As with the earlier studies, the hypotheses concerning these processes were derived from what was broadly described as learning theory (Hawkins, Pingree, & Adler, 1987; Potter, 1991). Essentially, three sequential processes were proposed: that viewers learn television facts from television (learning), that viewers construct real-world beliefs from these facts (construction), and that viewers generalize from these real-world beliefs related to TV facts (termed first-order beliefs; e.g., estimates of the prevalence of societal crime) to construct more generalized beliefs about the world (termed second-order beliefs; e.g., fear of crime; the process is termed *generalization*).

In a series of independent studies (cf. Hawkins et al., 1987; Potter, 1988, 1991), no aspect of the learning model received consistent support. In some studies a learning process was observed (Potter, 1988), but in others no effects (Potter, 1991) or even negative effects (Hawkins et al., 1987) were found. Similarly, in some studies, evidence of a construction process was observed, but only for first-order measures (Potter, 1991), whereas in other studies just the opposite pattern was noted (Potter, 1986). Finally, no consistent evidence for generalization was noted across these sets of studies, with most results showing no relation between first- and second-order judgments. Although it is possible that problems of measurement might explain many of the null findings, the lack of any consistent pattern over multiple studies suggests that a learning model cannot account for the process through which cultivation works.

So what to make of the lack of support for the learning model? One conclusion, voiced by Potter (1991), is that a lack of evidence for certain of these processes, particularly the construction process in which beliefs about the TV world are used to form judgments about the real world, would suggest that cultivation effects are artifactual, and not the result of a causal influence of viewing on beliefs. However, the logic is predicated on the notion that the learning model is the only one through which cultivation can work. In fact, there are a number of processes that could account for how television influences judgments without recourse to any consideration of beliefs about the television world. As the next section details, it is precisely the groundbreaking research in social cognition that forms the bases of these process models.

In conclusion, early research on cultivation processes was not completely successful in illuminating how the effects work. Nevertheless, as a first step toward advancing research on the cognitive processes underlying cultivation, the contribution of Hawkins and Pingree and others cannot be overemphasized. As they noted explicitly in their later writings, understanding the processes that underlie cultivation effects is a crucial step in establishing the validity of the effect (Hawkins & Pingree, 1990). A large majority of cultivation research is correlational in nature, bringing with it the threats to validity that reside in all correlational research. Thus, providing and empirically verifying a cognitive processing model that can specify clear links between television and judgments should make threats to internal validity such as spuriousness and reverse causality less plausible (Shapiro & Lang, 1991; Shrum, 2001, 2002). In the next section, research aimed at developing these types of models is discussed.

CURRENT SOCIAL COGNITION MODELS OF CULTIVATION

Although a number of studies have dealt with information processing issues in cultivation, there are only two models that have been offered that trace cultivation effects through different processing stages (i.e., encoding, storage, retrieval, judgment) and specifically focus on the cognitive processes that mediate the relation between television viewing and judgment. Although these models have been described by a number of different names, I call them the weighing and balancing model (Shapiro & Lang, 1991) and the accessibility model (Shrum, 2002).

The two models have a number of aspects in common, most of which are central to current conceptualizations in social cognition research. The first is that they look at the process in terms of memory and judgment. That is, both models look at how information from television is encoded into memory, the effects of encoding on retrieval, and the implications of both for the judgment construction process. A second common aspect is that they view the process of judgment construction, and the critical operations within it, as a relatively automatic one. Automatic processes are ones that occur without conscious knowledge of their operations (Bargh, 1997). This is an important point, because it implies that if people are not aware of these processes, they will likely not be able to accurately describe them when asked (although they will certainly try). Consequently, indirect measures are required to investigate these processes, necessitating the need for methodological innovation.

The primary point of departure of the two models pertains to perspective. The weighing and balancing model starts out with the notion that people try to scrutinize (weigh and balance) information retrieved from memory to ascertain its veracity and then use the information resulting from this process to form a judgment. Various conditions, both individual and situational, may impact how well people perform the weighing and balancing process. The accessibility model starts out from the other end. It assumes that people typically do not put out the effort to scrutinize the information they retrieve from memory, particularly for the types of judgments used to measure cultivation, but instead rely on cognitive shortcuts such as information accessibility to form their judgments.

Thus, the two models differ in terms of perspective on the default state, but agree for the most part on the processes underlying judgments. Consequently, the models are not mutually exclusive, but highly compatible. The following sections elaborate on each model, detailing their assumptions and hypotheses, and review research that has tested these possibilities.

WEIGHING AND BALANCING MODEL OF CULTIVATION

Model Description

The weighing and balancing model was the first to apply traditional social cognition principles of memory and judgment to explain the cultivation effect. The fullest treatment of the model is provided by Shapiro and Lang (1991). The model begins with the television viewing process and the encoding of information, in the form of "event memories," into episodic memory (Shapiro & Lang, 1991, p. 686). These event memories contain information about the event itself (e.g., a shooting), as well as a variety of contextual information about the event. Such contextual information would include information about the source of the event memory (television, but also whether cartoon, soap opera, news, etc.) as well as emotional reactions to the stimuli. The next step occurs when a judgment is to be made. At that point, potentially relevant information bearing on the judgment is retrieved from memory and each individual piece of information is assessed (weighed and balanced) for its degree of relevance. Contextual information, such as the source of the memory, may be considered, and information deemed to be from an unreliable source may be discarded and the judgment constructed based on the remaining information.

The preceding process certainly appears to be one that should produce good judgments, and if properly performed, television should have a minimal effect on judgments.[2] The problem is, the process is not perfect. In fact, under certain conditions, and for certain people, the process is remarkably imperfect. When attempting to ascertain source (source monitoring; Johnson, Hashtroudi, & Lindsay, 1993), people may make mistakes in ascertaining the source of their memories. This source confusion may have numerous causes. One is that the event memory may have a number of surface or contextual features that make it appear real. For example, it may have been shot on video to resemble news footage, or it may have produced an emotional response similar to a real event. A second cause of errors in source monitoring might be sheer frequency. If many memories are available and each must be checked for veracity, more mistakes would be made, and thus television information would be more likely to be used than if fewer memories were available. A third possibility is the lack of motivation to scrutinize the event memories to accurately ascertain source. Finally, a fourth possibility is that individual differences in ability to ascertain source may

[2]In fact, Shapiro and Lang (1991) suggested that minimal effects of television information predicted by the model may explain the relatively small effect sizes noted in cultivation research (see Hawkins & Pingree, 1982; Shanahan & Morgan, 1999).

contribute to errors in source monitoring. Some people may be deficient in certain cognitive abilities that allow them to accurately determine memory sources (e.g., children, the elderly; Ceci, Ross, & Toglia, 1987; Johnson et al., 1993). Others may be simply more prone to misattribute fiction as fact (Mares, 1996).

In all of the scenarios of possible causes of errors in source monitoring, there is one unifying aspect that makes the model a plausible one to explain cultivation effects: In each instance, heavy viewers are more likely to commit these errors than light viewers simply because they have more relevant event memories to be evaluated. Because the dependent variables used to assess cultivation effects pertain to constructs portrayed more often on television than occur in real life, heavy viewers by definition should encounter these constructs more often and thus have more relevant memories available for retrieval and evaluation.

There is one additional concept noted by Shapiro and Lang (1991) that has some relation to source monitoring: the perceived reality of television. Some people may be more prone to believe that television portrayals reflect reality. If so, then even when the source monitoring and weighing and balancing process is working perfectly, some people may opt not to discount televison information and thus would deliberately use it as a basis for their judgment. This would not necessarily produce a main effect for television viewing (cultivation effect) unless heavy viewing was correlated with perceived reality. However, it would imply an interaction between television viewing and perceived reality, such that those higher in perceived reality would exhibit a stronger cultivation effect than those lower in perceived reality.

Model Testing

A number of studies have provided support for various components of the model. Shapiro (1991) found that when participants were asked to recall exemplars within domains relevant to cultivation (crime, occupations), level of television viewing was positively correlated with the number of exemplars recalled. Moreover, participants were able to categorize the exemplars in terms of their source (books, movies, direct experience, etc.). However, contrary to intuition, the number of exemplars recalled was negatively correlated with estimates of societal crime and occupations. Thus, from this one study, although some of the assumptions of the model received support, it is unclear whether source discounting influenced judgments.

Other studies have looked more directly at the issue of errors in source discounting. Quite a few studies have established this general effect (for a review, see Johnson et al., 1993). In a study more directly relevant to media effects, Strange (1993) had participants read both a factual and a fictional story about the Panama Canal, after which they rated the truthfulness and source of particular statements. Strange found that participants did indeed make mistakes in attributing source and they also rated the truthfulness of statements they (mis)believed to be from the factual account higher than statements they believed to be from the fictional account.

Other studies give indirect support to the notion that increased motivation to attend to source characteristics may increase source discounting, thereby reducing the cultivation effect. Studies by Shrum and colleagues found that when participants were motivated to provide accurate judgments (Shrum, 2001), made aware of source issues (Shrum, Wyer, & O'Guinn, 1998), or had more time to construct their judgments (Shrum, 2004b), the cultivation effect was significantly reduced from when participants were not under those conditions. Presumably, under certain conditions, participants were more able or more willing to ascertain source and thus source discount.

Some studies have investigated the role that perceived reality plays in cultivation. The weighing and balancing model predicts that those higher in perceived reality should discount less simply because they think the information is veridical. Potter (1986) provided some evidence to support this reasoning. For a few dependent variables, cultivation effects were stronger for those scoring higher on a particular dimension ("magic window") of perceived reality. However, given that the cell sizes from which the correlations were derived were often quite small (e.g., < 25), these results should be interpreted with caution.

Probably the most comprehensive study to test the key components of the weighing and balancing model, particularly the component linking errors in source discounting with social reality judgments, was conducted by Mares (1996). That study looked at individual differences in propensity to make errors in judging whether information comes from a factual or fictional source. Mares established this propensity by having participants watch both news and fictional television programming, after which they were asked to recall whether specific events had been part of the news or the fictional program. The participants also provided social reality estimates pertaining to perceptions of violence and mean world beliefs (cf. Hawkins et al., 1987). Participants were then classified as to whether they tended to mistake fact for fiction (high vs. low) and whether they tended to mistake fiction for fact (high vs. low). Mares predicted two related pattern of results. First, those who tend to make more errors of mistaking fiction for fact were expected to be more likely to use fictional information to make judgments in their everyday lives (because they think it is factual), and thus should score higher on the violence perception and mean world scales than those who make fewer of those mistakes. Second, this general pattern should also be more pronounced for those who watch more television. Thus, those making more fiction-as-fact errors were expected to show a stronger cultivation effect than those making fewer of these errors. Conversely, a comparison of those who tend to make the opposite type of error (tending to mistake fact as fiction) with those who tend not to make such errors should show just the opposite pattern of results.

The results were generally supportive of these hypotheses. Fiction-as-fact errors were positively correlated with both the perceptions of violence and mean world measures, and these relations were stronger for those who watched more television. Further, as expected, those making the opposite type of errors showed negative correlations with social reality beliefs, but the expected differences between heavy and light viewers were not significant. However, given the correlational nature of the study, there could be explanations other than source confusions to explain the data. To address this limitation, Mares used some innovative methods (some measured, some experimentally manipulated) to further pinpoint process issues. She manipulated the extent to which the news and fictional segments were visually distinct versus visually similar and whether participants provided their source judgments immediately after viewing or 1 week later. She also measured level of certainty with which participants identified source. Mares expected that the time delay should increase source confusions and that making the segments visually distinct should decrease source confusions. In addition, level of certainty was expected to interact with the propensity to make source confusions: Those more certain should show greater effects than those less certain. All of these hypotheses were supported.

Summary

The weighing and balancing model provides an explanation for one of the conundrums of cultivation theory: Why would television information—particularly fictional information—be used to construct real-world judgments? To be more precise, why would individuals assess the landscape of the television world to determine the incidence of, say, doctors, and then use this assessment to form an estimate of the real-world incidence of doctors? The early research on cultivation processes assumed that people knowingly used television information to construct their judgments and that they were aware that television was the source (cf. Hawkins et al., 1987; Potter, 1991), but this process does not comport well with the way most of us at least think we construct judgments and make decisions. Shapiro and colleagues' work took a different tack: People would not generally use television information to form such judgments. However, when they attempt to recall examples of doctors (which are useful in inferring incidence), they do not always realize when the examples come from television. Thus, they use the information to construct their judgments. Moreover, this process occurs for the most part outside conscious awareness. This latter proposition provides an explanation for the lack of relations between viewing and perceptions of the television world as well as lack of relations between television-world perceptions and real-world perceptions.

ACCESSIBILITY MODEL OF CULTIVATION

Initial formulations of the accessibility model for cultivation effects were provided by Shrum (1995), but more comprehensive treatments of the model did not appear until later (Shrum, 1999b, 2002). Although initial studies on the accessibility model began much earlier than 1995, and independently of Shapiro's work, later studies and fuller model development were greatly informed by the weighing and balancing model. As noted earlier, the models are similar in many respects, and differ primarily on whether weighing and balancing, or the lack of it, is the default process for most social reality judgments.

One of the primary similarities of the weighing and balancing and the accessibility models is their exclusive focus on memory-based judgments. Memory-based judgments are ones that are constructed through the recall of information from long-term memory, as opposed to on-line judgments, which are formed as information is encountered (Hastie & Park, 1986). More specifically, the accessibility model is primarily concerned with belief judgments, as opposed to attitudes and values. Belief judgments pertain to such things as the prevalence of a construct (e.g., societal violence) or trait characteristics of individuals or society (e.g., people cannot be trusted, women are meek). Thus, the accessibility model does not address evaluative judgments such as good–bad (attitudes) or ought (values).

The following sections provide a description of the general model and supporting evidence. Because the model has been discussed extensively elsewhere (Shrum, 1999b, 2002), the descriptions are brief, with a focus on recent studies that bear on implications of the model.

Model Description and Initial Tests

The accessibility model of cultivation effects is based on two general propositions. The first is that television viewing increases the accessibility (ease of recall) of constructs and exemplars that are often portrayed on television. The second is that social reality judgments, because they are typically perceived to be difficult to answer accurately and are seldom of any importance to study participants, are made through heuristic processing. That is, rather than searching memory for all available information relevant to the judgment (systematic processing), people retrieve only a subset of relevant information, and the likelihood of retrieval of that subset is determined by its accessibility. A corollary of this second proposition is that for memory-based judgments such as prevalence, probability, or proportion (e.g., the percentage estimates often used in cultivation research), the judgments are constructed through the application of judgmental heuristics such as availability, simulation, and representativeness (see Kahneman, Slovic, & Tversky, 1982).

From these two general principles, more specific and testable propositions can be derived. The first is that television viewing enhances accessibility. The most direct support of this proposition was provided by Busselle and Shrum (2003). Participants indicated how easy it was for them to recall examples of certain constructs, some of which were frequently portrayed on television (murder, trial, highway accident). The results indicated that media examples were more frequently recalled for events portrayed often in the media but infrequently experienced personally (trial, murder). Personal experiences were more easily retrieved for events encountered frequently in real life, even when these events are frequently portrayed on television (highway accidents, dates). The results also showed that ease of retrieving media examples was related to hours of TV viewing, but only for viewing of television programs in which the events were frequently portrayed and when the direct experience with the events was likely to be low.

Indirect evidence suggesting that television viewing increases accessibility was obtained in studies that measured the speed with which participants constructed their social reality judgments. Greater accessibility was expected to result in faster judgments, and thus heavy viewers were expected to respond faster than light viewers. The expectations were confirmed in a series of studies that varied the type of dependent variables, measurement of viewing, and control variables employed (cf. O'Guinn & Shrum, 1997; Shrum, 1996; Shrum & O'Guinn, 1993).

Demonstrating that viewing enhances accessibility is only the first step in testing the model. The second proposition states that the accessibility bias resulting from viewing should mediate the cultivation effect. Indirect evidence supporting this proposition was obtained by Shrum and O'Guinn (1993), who showed that controlling for the accessibility bias (reaction time) reduces the cultivation effect to nonsignificance. In a more direct test, Shrum (1996) demonstrated via path analyses the mediating effect of accessibility across a number of social reality judgments.

Busselle (2001) used a novel procedure to provide further evidence of the mediating role of accessibility that varied the conditions under which participants provided their estimates. In one condition, participants provided estimates of the prevalence of Black doctors, shootings, and extramarital affairs, and then recalled an example of each. In the other condition, the order of the task was reversed, and participants first recalled an example before reporting their estimates. In the first condition, a cultivation effect was observed. Presumably, television examples were more accessible for those who watched relatively more television, which influenced the estimates. In the second condition, the accessibility bias for heavier viewers was eliminated by having all participants recall an example, effectively making an example equally (and easily) accessible for everyone. Under these conditions, the cultivation effect was also eliminated.

The third proposition is related to concepts articulated in the weighing and balancing model. However, unlike the weighing and balancing model, which postulates that people typically discount media exemplars, the third proposition posits that television exemplars are not discounted. This proposition is necessary to explain the somewhat counterintuitive notion that people would use information from nonveridical sources (e.g., fictional programs) to form judgments about the real world. The proposition goes back to the second general proposition regarding lack of motivation to be accurate in constructing judgments. Due to this lack of motivation, people will likely not attend to source features in constructing their judgments. Support for this proposition was provided by Shrum et al. (1998). Two experiments manipulated whether source characteristics (television) were primed (i.e., made salient) before participants provided their social reality judgments. When source was not primed, the expected cultivation effect was obtained. However, when source was primed, the cultivation effect was significantly reduced and in some cases even eliminated. Just as important was the pattern of effects: Source discounting conditions did not affect light viewers, only heavy viewers. Thus, source discounting conditions served to bring the judgments of heavy viewers to the same level as light viewers. This general pattern of results in which source priming reduces the cultivation effect has also been replicated in other contexts such as beliefs about sex (Zhang & Krcmar, 2004).

The fourth proposition relates to conditions that facilitate or inhibit heuristic processing. The second general proposition states that the default condition for constructing memory-based social reality judgments is one of heuristic processing, which results from lack of motivation to process information. However, suppose people are motivated to provide accurate judgments. Then they should be motivated to not only consider more information (rather than relying on that which is most accessible), but also be more likely to scrutinize the information retrieved from memory, notice source characteristics, and source discount when the information is deemed to come from unreliable sources. Thus, the fourth proposition states that motivation to process information will moderate the cultivation effect such that high motivation reduces the effect. Evidence supporting this proposition was obtained by Shrum (2001; see also Mares, 1996; Shrum, 1997). Some participants were motivated to engage in systematic processing via an accuracy motivation and task importance manipulation, whereas other participants were motivated to process heuristically (instructed to answer "off the top of their head"). A third, control group was given no processing instructions, thus simulating the typical method of data collection for cultivation studies. For each of four dependent variables (estimates of crime, marital discord, affluence, and occupations), the results showed that both the control and heuristic groups exhibited cultivation effects that did not differ in magnitude. However, the systematic group showed no cultivation effects. In addition, the pattern of effects that was observed in Shrum et al. (1998) was again found: Motivation to process did not affect the judgments of light viewers, but made the judgments of heavy viewers equal to those of light viewers. These same general patterns of results have also been obtained in studies using neural network simulations to model the psychological processes underlying cultivation effects (Bradley, 2004; Bradley & Payne, 2004).

Like the fourth proposition, the fifth and final proposition of the model pertains to conditions that may affect heuristic processing. However, the fifth proposition pertains to factors that may facilitate the cultivation effect. Specifically, ability to process information is proposed to moderate the cultivation effect. Those with less ability to process should show a cultivation effect of greater magnitude than those with more ability to process. Shrum (2004b) manipulated ability to process via time pressure, and time pressure was operationalized via survey method. Some participants were surveyed by phone (high time pressure) and others by mail (low time pressure). As expected, the magnitude of the cultivation was greater in the high time pressure condition than in the low time pressure condition.

Applying the Accessibility Model to Other Studies

One of the useful aspects of any model is its ability to not only account for a set of results based on specific propositions of the model, but to also account for results of other studies, particularly when those results seem counterintuitive or damaging to current theory.

Memory and Source Discounting Studies. As noted earlier in the discussion of the weighing and balancing model, Shapiro (1991) provided some counterintuitive findings regarding the relation between recall and judgments. Remember that in that study, participants were asked to recall exemplars within domains relevant to cultivation (crime, occupations), and level of television viewing was positively correlated with number of exemplars recalled. However, unexpectedly, the recall of more exemplars was related to lower rather than higher social reality estimates of crime and occupation. This result seems at odds with the accessibility model in that individuals might be expected to infer frequency from the number of examples recalled (if more examples can be recalled, it must occur frequently). It is also reasonable to think that availability (i.e., whether the information exists in memory) and accessibility (i.e, ease of retrieving information from memory) might be correlated.

Recent research, however, has demonstrated the lack of validity of these propositions. Note that a strict application of the availability heuristic posits that frequency and probability judgments will be based on "the ease with which instances and associations come to mind" (Tversky & Kahneman, 1973, p. 208). Thus, it is what Schwarz (2004) referred to as the "megacognitive" experience of ease of recall that is posited to drive judgments, not the content of the recall. Schwarz et al. (1991) provided empirical evidence for this process. They showed that participants rated themselves as more assertive when they were asked to recall 6 examples of assertive behaviors (an easy recall task) than participants who were asked to recall 12 examples of assertive behavior (a difficult recall task). The experimental procedure thus unconfounded the content (number of examples) and ease of recall. This general effect has been confirmed in a number of other studies as well (cf. Schwarz, 2004; Wänke, Bohner, & Jurkowitsch, 1997).

The implications of Schwarz et al. (1991) for the findings of Shapiro (1991) are straightforward. Participants who listed more exemplars may have found the task more difficult than participants who listed fewer exemplars. Participants may have in turn inferred frequency or likelihood of occurrence from the experienced ease of recall, resulting in lower estimates for participants who recalled more exemplars than for those who recalled fewer exemplars.

General Cultivation Studies. The accessibility model can also account for some results that would seem to be damaging to cultivation theory (see Shrum, 1995, for a fuller discussion). For example, some researchers have suggested that typical cultivation methodology may contain a response bias because virtually all items are worded in the negative direction (e.g., perceptions of crime vs. safety; mistrust vs. faith in others; cf. Hawkins & Pingree, 1980; Rubin, Perse, & Taylor, 1988). They present evidence that when items are worded more positively, no cultivation effect is noted (e.g., a negative correlation between viewing and trust would be expected). However, the accessibility model would expect just such a null finding. Because it is examples of the constructs to be estimated that are recalled during judgment construction, then making judgments of trustworthiness, safety, or trust would result in instances of these constructs being recalled (and not their opposites). Thus, if people form their judgments based on the ease with which relevant examples come to mind, and trustworthiness is not prevalent in television portrayals, there should be no accessibility bias as a result of viewing, and thus, no cultivation effect. Conversely, there should be a cultivation effect if the question is worded in terms of mistrust. This was in fact what was found. Note that part of the reasoning for why Rubin et al. (1988) might have expected a negative cultivation effect was that perceptions of how safe the world is (first-order judgment) might be expected to be used to form attitudes and beliefs regarding fear of crime (second-order judgment). However, as noted earlier, these two types of judgments have been shown to be relatively independent and likely are constructed via different processes.

Summary

The accessibility model provides additional explanatory mechanisms for processes underlying cultivation effects. The model specifies a number of mediating and moderating influences that help explicate the conditions under which cultivation effects would and would not be expected. As with the weighing and balancing model, the accessibility model provides a compelling explanation for why television information (examples) would be used to construct real-world judgments. Unlike the weighing and balancing model, however, the accessibility model does not assume that people (necessarily) make source discounting errors, but rather that they usually do not make the effort to source discount at all.

Of course, it should be obvious that both models are sometimes right and both are sometimes wrong. In this regard, the models are overstatements, and are not meant to reflect what all people do all of the time. Rather, the model's assumptions are intended to provide starting points from which deviations (i.e., moderating effects) are expected to occur. However, as with all models, there are always shortcomings. In the next section, these limitations are outlined and new models are proposed to account for these limitations.

BEYOND MEMORY-BASED JUDGMENTS: NEW JUDGMENTS REQUIRE NEW MODELS

Both the weighing and balancing model and the accessibility model focus exclusively on memory-based judgments such as estimates of prevalence and probability, and thus have little to say about cultivation processes for second-order judgments such as attitudes and values. This is unfortunate for two reasons. One is that the question of how television messages get processed and transformed into stable, evaluative beliefs perhaps better captures the true meaning of cultivation and represents inherently more interesting and important phenomena than the simple accumulation of incidental data such as frequency of occurrence. The second reason is that memory-based judgments are actually relatively rare. Not only do they not occur all that often, but they are actually difficult to produce, even in the lab (Hastie & Park, 1986). More often, people make judgments spontaneously as information is encountered (i.e., on-line), including forming impressions of others, stereotyping, making causal attributions, and forming attitudes, and preventing people from doing so is remarkably difficult.

Process Models for the Cultivation of Attitudes and Values

Unfortunately, developing process models for the cultivation of on-line judgments such as attitudes and values is not simply a matter of extending current models for memory-based judgments such as prevalence and probability to the new judgments. Because the processes underlying the construction of on-line and memory-based judgments differ in such fundamental ways, it seems likely that the ways in which television information figures into the construction of these judgments may be fundamentally different as well (Shrum, 2004a; Shrum, Burroughs, & Rindfleisch, 2004). In fact, not only are the processes different for the two types of judgments, but in some cases they appear to be exact opposites.

Cultivation as On-line Persuasion. Assume for the moment that most attitudes and values are formed via an on-line process. This means that as information is encountered in everyday life, it is used to form new attitudes or update old ones. The latter case would involve activating an existing attitude from memory and either changing or reinforcing it. Note that these processes need not occur consciously, but instead may occur automatically outside of awareness of the process (Bargh, 1997).

What are the implications of such processes for cultivation? The most obvious one is that, if attitudes and values are formed via on-line processes, and if television messages influence attitudes and values, then this process should occur during viewing. The television message represents a persuasive communication and persuasion is evidenced by attitude or values change. The second implication follows from this proposition: If the television message is viewed as a persuasive communication, then factors that facilitate or inhibit persuasion should correspondingly facilitate or inhibit the cultivation effect. What factors might those be? As Hamilton (chap. 18, this volume) details, two factors that have been shown to moderate the effects of a persuasive message are motivation and ability to process information during information acquisition. Specifically, persuasion is enhanced when motivation to process and the ability to process information are high (Chaiken, Liberman, & Eagly, 1989; Petty & Cacioppo, 1986).[3]

As noted earlier, this reasoning is based on the assumption that viewers spontaneously construct judgments related to their personal values during viewing. Is this a reasonable assumption? Research suggests that people do not form judgments unless they have an explicit goal to do so (Hastie & Park, 1986; Lichtenstein & Srull, 1987; Wyer & Srull, 1989). However, research also suggests that judgments are automatically activated when objects are encountered (Fazio, Sanbonmatsu, Powell, & Kardes, 1986) and impressions tend to be formed spontaneously (see Uleman, Newman, & Moskowitz, 1996). In addition, recent research on television viewing indicates that as a process of enjoying television, viewers readily form impressions and make causal attributions about characters, even to the point of forming close, parasocial relationships with them (Russell, Norman, & Heckler, 2004). Thus, it seems reasonable to posit that beliefs such as attitudes and values would be easily activated during the viewing situation.

Some Initial Tests of the Model. A few studies have begun to test some aspects of this very rough model of cultivation for attitudes and values. In a set of studies, Shrum, Burroughs, and Rindfleisch (2005) investigated whether motivation to process information during viewing affected the extent to which television information influenced personal values. If television influences values through an on-line process, then those who are more motivated, active, and involved during viewing should show stronger cultivation effects than those less motivated, less active, or less involved. Motivation during viewing was operationalized as the extent to which viewers pay attention during viewing (self-reported using the Rubin et al. [1988] scale) and the extent to which viewers elaborate during viewing. The latter was operationalized as need for cognition, which is an individual difference variable related to the extent to which people like to think, elaborate, and solve problems (Cacioppo & Petty, 1982). The results of a random,

[3]This is true only when arguments are strong rather than weak. The arguments are assumed to be compelling (e.g., in movies or dramas) for heavy viewers given that they have made the decision to view frequently and may often suspend disbelief (and counterarguing) in an effort to become immersed in the narrative (Shrum et al., 2005).

general population survey of the United States showed that, as expected, motivation moderated the cultivation effect for the personal value of materialism (Richins, 2004). Cultivation effects were significantly and substantially stronger for those who paid more attention and for those who elaborated more during viewing. A second study provided evidence that the moderating effect of need for cognition can be traced to greater positive elaboration and transportation (Green & Brock, 2000) for individuals with a higher need for cognition who are also heavy viewers.

The on-line nature of attitude activation also has some interesting implications for the accessibility of attitudes (for reviews of attitude accessibility and persuasion, see Arpan, Rhodes, & Roskos-Ewoldsen, chap. 15, this volume; Roskos-Ewoldsen, 1997). If attitudes are in fact activated frequently during viewing, the attitudes may be changed in ways other than simply the extremity of the attitude. A change in attitude extremity (how positive or negative) is how attitude change has been traditionally measured. However, an attitude can be made stronger (e.g., more certain, confident) without changing the extremity of the attitude (Petty & Krosnick, 1995). Thus, for example, if viewers watch a television program that contains a general message (e.g., tough on criminals) with which they agree, they may not necessarily become more positive in their attitude (they may still be a 5 on a 5-point scale) but may reinforce that evaluative belief so that it is stronger and actually more impervious to change.

Shrum (1999a) investigated this possibility by measuring attitude accessibility (i.e., how easily they are activated) for heavy and light soap opera viewers. Viewing was expected to not only affect attitude extremity (heavy viewers would indicate greater expectations of marital discord when they get married, more distrust of people, and a greater desire to own luxury products than would light viewers), but that these attitudes would also be more accessible for those who viewed relatively more television. The results partially confirmed the hypotheses: Heavy viewers were more distrustful and expected more marital problems than light viewers, but there were no differences in attitude extremity toward owning luxury products. However, over and above the affects of attitude extremity, effects of attitude accessibility were observed. For all dependent variables, attitudes for heavy viewers were more accessible than those of light viewers.

These findings have important implications for cultivation research. First, they show that, just as noted by Gerbner, Gross, Morgan, Signorielli, and Shanahan (2002), television may serve to not only change beliefs, but also to reinforce them. Second, the reinforcing nature of television on existing attitudes has implications for the extent to which people act on their attitudes. As Fazio and colleagues have conclusively shown, attitudes that are more accessible tend to be ones that are stronger, more persistent, more resistant to change, and perhaps most important, ones that are more likely to guide behavior (Fazio, 1990a; Fazio & Roskos-Ewoldsen, 1994). Thus, the findings of Shrum (1999a) suggest that heavy viewers are not just more distrustful of spouses and people in general, but they may also be more likely to act on these attitudes (e.g., perhaps through divorce, behavior toward neighbors). In addition, even though no differences were noted between heavy and light viewers on the desire to own luxury products, the accessibility differences suggest that heavy viewers may be more likely to act on their attitudes (perhaps by purchasing).

Summary

Expanding cultivation processes to include on-line judgments is an important step toward integrating all cultivation findings under a social cognition umbrella. It also helps dispel some misconceptions of what models for memory-based judgments imply. Although the accessibility model has always been explicitly and exclusively concerned with memory-based judgments (cf. Shrum, 1995), that distinction has often been lost. Thus, findings that the cultivation effect for memory-based judgments tended to occur through low involvement processes at the time of judgment elicitation (recall) were often interpreted as evidence that all judgments were so affected, and moreover, often interpreted as a low involvement process during viewing.

The results from the studies just reviewed make it clear that not only is that not the case, but the opposite actually tends to occur: Cultivation for on-line judgments such as attitudes and values seems to be enhanced by high involvement processes during viewing. It is interesting (and perhaps ironic)[4] to note that variables that have traditionally been the purview of the uses and gratifications area of research (e.g., viewer motives, individual differences) are also central to the cultivation of online judgments. In fact, motives (in social cognition terms, processing goals) play a big part in determining the types of cognitive processes in which people engage. Thus, cultivation effects may vary as a function of viewer motives because different viewer motives result in different types of processing of television information. Note that this proposition implies an interaction between amount of viewing and motives for viewing, a relation that has been considered in uses and gratifications research but not investigated with any consistency.

---

[4]Ironic because uses and gratifications is often viewed as the antithesis of social cognition research.

NEW DIRECTIONS, NEW METHODOLOGIES

So where do we go from here? The preceding discussion should make it clear that there are a whole host of possibilities. Some of these possibilities are a function of applying well-established principles of social cognition to new ways of looking at cultivation effects and other possibilities arise from new directions in social cognition research.

Experimental Manipulations of Viewing

Even contemplating the notion of experimental manipulations of viewing is probably a taboo from the perspective of Gerbner and colleagues. Their argument is that short-term manipulations that occur in experiments are problematic because (a) they are unlikely to influence most beliefs with such brief exposures, and (b) they do not capture the long-term nature of the cultivation process (Gerbner et al., 2002). I have to confess to having made this same argument on a number of occasions. In fact, the logic for deriving complex social cognition models for cultivation processes was in part a function of not being able to manipulate television viewing and still capture the concept of cultivation (Shrum, 2002).

However, the fact of the matter is, it is almost impossible to study online processes without experiments. When the judgments are memory-based, one can experimentally manipulate processing at the time of judgment elicitation to make inferences about how television influences judgments (cf. Shrum, 2001; Shrum et al., 1998). However, for online judgments, the only alternative to experiments is measuring both television and the proposed moderators (e.g., attention, involvement). Although this strategy has been useful (Shrum et al., 2005), it is extremely limited and remarkably imprecise. Consequently, to truly understand the role on-line processes play in cultivation, some manipulation of processing during viewing is vital.

Narrative Processing

One of the more interesting directions in recent social cognition research is a focus on narrative processing and its implications for social judgment (cf. Green & Brock, 2000; Green, Strange, & Brock, 2002; Wyer, 2004; Wyer & Radvansky, 1999). This research has begun to explore how traditional social and cognitive mechanisms (e.g., memory, persuasion) relate to these "metamessages" that narratives produce. Thus, as Johnson (2002) noted, "the study of narratives provides a clear bridge between examining cognition on an individual level and at the social-cultural level" (p. xi).

The relation between cultivation and narrative processing could not be more clear. As Busselle, Ryabovolova, and Wilson (2004) pointed out, cultivation has always been concerned with stories, rather than simply the various messages, characters, facts, or behaviors that comprise those stories (see Gerbner, 1999). Research in this area is already underway. For example, research has investigated the utility of mental models (how situations or events are represented in memory) for cultivation research (Roskos-Ewoldsen, Davies, & Roskos-Ewoldsen, 2004). Other research has looked at the effects of verbal and visual media, and their narrative messages, on memory and judgment (Adaval & Wyer, 1998; Wyer & Adaval, 2004). Still other research has looked at the persuasive power of narratives, including those conveyed in television programs, with a particular focus on the process of transportation during narrative processing (Busselle & Wilson, 2004; Green & Brock, 2000; Green, Garst, & Brock, 2004; Shrum et al., 2005).

Implicit Measures of Processes and Beliefs

Another promising area of research, one that is primarily methodological in nature, is on the use of implicit measures to infer both processes and beliefs. They are termed implicit because they are not direct or overt measures, but instead are measures that are assumed to imply particular processes or beliefs.

Response Latencies. Probably the most common technique is the use of response latencies. Response latencies refer to how fast someone responds to a particular stimuli. This technique has been used for many decades to show how closely linked particular concepts are in memory, allowing for assessments of associative strength. Response latencies have also been used to measure the accessibility of constructs from memory, and this technique has proved useful for linking accessibility of both exemplars (e.g., Busselle, 2001; Shrum & O'Guinn, 1993) and attitudes (Shrum, 1999a) with frequency of television viewing.

Despite their productive use in past research, however, response latencies can be messy, and particularly so for cultivation research. In most reaction time procedures, the task for respondents is to provide simple yes–no or like–dislike responses. However, these types of responses do not translate well into the typical measures used in cultivation research, particularly ones that ask for percentage estimates such as prevalence or probability. Fazio (1990b) recommended only two response categories ideally, but no more than five response categories. The reasoning is that with numerous, finely scaled options, respondents may spend an inordinate amount of time trying to make those fine distinctions (e.g., whether to press 7, 8, or 9, even though they arrived at the general number, between 7 and 9, very quickly).

Five response categories work well for most attitude measures (cf. Shrum, 1999a). However, reducing a 101-point scale to 5 points is problematic because people do not think in terms of categories such as 0% to 20%, 30% to 50%, and so forth. Thus, in the studies in which I measured response times for constructing social reality estimates (e.g., O'Guinn & Shrum, 1997; Shrum, 1996; Shrum & O'Guinn, 1993), I reduced the 0 to 100 scale to a 0 to 9 scale (0%–9%, 10%–19%, etc.). This proved workable, but nevertheless resulted in a significant amount of error variance, necessitating quite a bit of training for participants to learn the use of the scale prior to the study.

One additional, and quite unexpected, problem with using response latencies in cultivation research also became apparent at times: reluctance to provide a response. This occurred in the instances in which I used the 0 to 9 scale to measure the time it took participants to construct a social reality estimate. More specifically, it occurred when I attempted to expand external validity by using nonstudent, general population adults. For the most part, with student participants, they accept the anonymity and confidentiality statements, as well as the notion that there are no wrong answers (students seem to love those types of questions). Consequently, they are more than happy to give a quick response. Not so the adults that participated. Perhaps it was the lack of familiarity with computers (this was in the late 1980s), the intimidation of the university setting or the professor, or simply a higher level of involvement with the task. Whatever the reasons, the latencies—which averaged about 4 to 6 seconds for students, including reading time—were often well over 10 seconds. In some cases, some people took over 1 minute to respond, despite significant training for the task. The reasons for this type of behavior are still unclear, as I quickly abandoned this particular quest for external validity. However, those interested in pursuing this type of research should be cognizant of these potential problems.

Implicit Association Test. More recently, response latency techniques have been used to construct what are termed *implicit attitude measures*. The most well known is the Implicit Association Test (IAT; Greenwald, McGhee, & Schwartz, 1998). The purpose and underlying logic are straightforward. It is well known that explicit, overt measures of attitudes (e.g., Likert scales) are subject to response bias, particularly when the attitude object pertains to sensitive or threatening topics (e.g., race, sex). In addition, one of the principles of Freudian psychology is that we hold attitudes and beliefs of which we may not be consciously aware (Erdelyi & Zizak, 2004). Thus, explicit attitude scales may not be able to get at these attitudes either.

The IAT is designed to solve both problems (but see Olsen & Fazio, 2004, for a discussion of problems with the IAT). It measures attitudes implicitly via a reaction time task in which participants classify four categories of items, two of which are concepts such as race (e.g., Black, White) and two of which are evaluative attributes (like, dislike). The logic is that categorization should be easier (faster) when the pairing of a concept and attribute reflect a strong association in memory than when they reflect a weak association. Thus, a person who is racially biased against African Americans should more quickly categorize Black or White faces and positive or negative words when Black and dislike are paired together than when Black and like are paired together. The important aspect of this method is that the assessment of bias is wholly dependent on the latencies, and has nothing to do with overt evaluative responses.

Procedures such as the IAT may be useful in investigating certain types of cultivation effects. In particular, any type of dependent variable that might be subject to socially desirable responding would be a good candidate. Obvious examples would include racism, sexism, and materialism, all of which have been a focus of prior cultivation research. Thus, it might be useful to determine whether heavy and light viewers differ in terms of racism, and to compare their explicitly measured beliefs (e.g., a racism scale) with their implicitly measured beliefs.

CONCLUSION

A social cognition perspective on cultivation effects is a relatively recent phenomenon. This research adds the always needed convergent findings that are so important to theory development and validation. Although this is true for any theory, I have argued that it is particularly the case for cultivation theory. Previous cultivation research has been subject to substantial criticism, some of it clearly warranted, some of it less so. At least part of the problem was that, even though the theory was presented as sociocultural, it tended to be described in psychological terms (perceptions, beliefs, attitudes, reinforcement, learning, extrapolation), and thus made itself vulnerable to general psychological criticisms (e.g., direction of causality).

However, cultivation is a psychological theory, just as it may also be sociological and cultural. In my mind, these are not mutually exclusive, but inextricably entwined. The only difference is the level or unit of measure. A social cognition perspective simply adds an additional level of measurement, as well as more precision, to the cultivation research paradigm. New methods and theories are allowing us to gain a better understanding of how the process works. Thus, the best is ahead of us in terms of understanding how television information influences judgment.

ACKNOWLEDGMENTS

I thank Tina Lowrey, Bob Wyer, David Roskos-Ewoldsen, Mary Beth Oliver, Jan Van den Bulck, Rick Busselle, and Sri Kalyanaraman for all of the numerous thoughtful conversations that provided many of the ideas detailed in this chapter.

REFERENCES

Adaval, R., & Wyer, R. S. (1998). The role of narratives in consumer information processing. *Journal of Consumer Psychology, 7,* 207–245.

Bargh, J. A. (1997). The automaticity of everyday life. In R. S. Wyer (Ed.), *The automaticity of everyday life: Advances in social cognition* (Vol. 10, pp. 1–61). Mahwah, NJ: Lawrence Erlbaum Associates.

Berkowitz, L., & Rogers, K. H. (1986). A priming effect analysis of media influence. In J. Bryant & D. Zillmann (Eds.), *Perspectives on media effects* (pp. 57–81). Hillsdale, NJ: Lawrence Erlbaum Associates.

Bradley, S. D. (2004). *Neural network simulations support heuristic processing model of cultivation effects.* Unpublished manuscript, Indiana University, Bloomington, IN.

Bradley, S. D., & Payne, B. D. (2004). *Seeing the world through TV's lens: Brain structures and memory systems involved in the construction of social reality.* Manuscript submitted for publication.

Busselle, R. W. (2001). The role of exemplar accessibility in social reality judgments. *Media Psychology, 3,* 43–67.

Busselle, R. W., Ryabovolova, A., & Wilson, B. (2004). Ruining a good story: Cultivation, perceived realism, and narrative. *Communications, 29,* 365–378.

Busselle, R. W., & Shrum, L. J. (2003). Media exposure and the accessibility of social information. *Media Psychology, 5,* 255–282.

Busselle, R. W., & Wilson, B. (2004, May). *Transportation into the narrative and perceptions of media realism.* Paper presented at the annual meeting of the International Communication Association, New Orleans, LA.

Cacioppo, J. T., & Petty, R. E. (1982). The need for cognition. *Journal of Personality and Social Psychology, 42,* 116–131.

Ceci, S. J., Ross, D. F., & Toglia, M. P. (1987). Suggestibility of children's memory: Psychological implications. *Journal of Experimental Psychology: General, 116,* 38–49.

Chaiken, S., Liberman, A., & Eagly, A. H. (1989). Heuristic and systematic processing within and beyond the persuasion context. In J. S. Uleman & J. A. Bargh (Eds.), *Unintended thought* (pp. 212–252). New York: Guilford.

Erdelyi, M. H., & Zizak, D. M. (2004). Beyond gizmo subliminality. In L. J. Shrum (Ed.), *The psychology of entertainment media: Blurring the lines between entertainment and persuasion* (pp. 13–44). Mahwah, NJ: Lawrence Erlbaum Associates.

Fazio, R. H. (1990a). Multiple processes by which attitudes guide behavior: The MODE model as an integrative framework. In M. Zanna (Ed.), *Advances in experimental social psychology* (Vol. 23, pp. 75–109). Orlando, FL: Academic.

Fazio, R. H. (1990b). A practical guide to the use of response latency in social psychological research. In C. Hendrik & M. S. Clark (Eds.), *Review of personality and social psychology: Vol. 11. Research methods in personality and social psychology* (pp. 74–97). Newbury Park, CA: Sage.

Fazio, R. H., & Roskos–Ewoldsen, D. R. (1994). Acting as we feel: When and how attitudes guide behavior. In T. C. Brock & S. Shavitt (Eds.), *Psychology of persuasion* (pp. 71–94). Boston: Allyn & Bacon.

Fazio, R. H., Sanbonmatsu, D. M., Powell, M. C., & Kardes, F. R. (1986). On the automatic activation of attitudes. *Journal of Personality and Social Psychology, 65,* 221–233.

Gerbner, G. (1999). Foreward by George Gerbner: What do we know? In J. Shanahan & M. Morgan (Eds.), *Television and its viewers: Cultivation theory and research* (pp. ix–xiii). Cambridge, UK: Cambridge University Press.

Gerbner, G., & Gross, L. (1976). Living with television: The violence profile. *Journal of Communication, 26,* 182–190.

Gerbner, G., Gross, L., Morgan, M., Signorielli, N., & Shanahan, J. (2002). Growing up with television: Cultivation processes. In J. Bryant & D. Zillmann (Eds.), *Media effects: Advances in theory and research* (2nd ed., pp. 43–67). Mahwah, NJ: Lawrence Erlbaum Associates.

Green, M. C., & Brock, T. C. (2000). The role of transportation in the persuasiveness of public narratives. *Journal of Personality and Social Psychology, 79,* 701–721.

Green, M. C., Garst, J., & Brock, T. C. (2004). The power of fiction: Determinants and boundaries. In L. J. Shrum (Ed.), *The psychology of entertainment media: Blurring the lines between entertainment and persuasion* (pp. 161–176). Mahwah, NJ: Lawrence Erlbaum Associates.

Green, M. C., Strange, J. J., & Brock, T. C. (Eds.). (2002). *Narrative impact: Social and cognitive foundations.* Mahwah, NJ: Lawrence Erlbaum Associates.

Greenwald, A. G., McGhee, D. E., & Schwartz, J. L. K. (1998). Measuring individual differences in implicit cognition: The Implicit Association Test. *Journal of Personality and Social Psychology, 74,* 1464–1480.

Hastie, R., & Park, B. (1986). The relationship between memory and judgment depends on whether the judgment task is memory-based or on-line. *Psychological Review, 93,* 258–268.

Hawkins, R. P., & Pingree, S. (1980). Some processes in the cultivation effect. *Communication Research, 7,* 193–226.

Hawkins, R. P., & Pingree, S. (1981). Uniform messages and habitual viewing: Unnecessary assumptions in social reality effects. *Human Communication Research, 7,* 291–301.

Hawkins, R. P., & Pingree, S. (1982). Television's influence on constructions of social reality. In D. Pearl, L. Bouthilet, & J. Lazar (Eds.), *Television and behavior: Ten years of scientific progress and implications for the eighties* (Vol. 2, pp. 224–247). Washington, DC: U.S. Government Printing Office.

Hawkins, R. P., & Pingree, S. (1990). Divergent psychological processes in constructing social reality from mass media content. In N. Signorielli & M. Morgan (Eds.), *Cultivation analysis: New directions in media effects research* (pp. 33–50). Newbury Park, CA: Sage.

Hawkins, R. P., Pingree, S., & Adler, I. (1987). Searching for cognitive processes in the cultivation effect. *Human Communication Research, 13,* 553–577.

Jo, E., & Berkowitz, L. (1994). A priming effect analysis of media influences: An update. In J. Bryant & D. Zillmann (Eds.), *Media effects: Advances in theory and research* (pp. 43–60). Hillsdale, NJ: Lawrence Erlbaum Associates.

Johnson, M. K. (2002). Foreword. In M. C. Green, J. J. Strange, & T. C. Brock (Eds.), *Narrative impact: Social and cognitive foundations* (pp. ix–xii). Mahwah, NJ: Lawrence Erlbaum Associates.

Johnson, M. K., Hashtroudi, S., & Lindsay, D. S. (1993). Source monitoring. *Psychological Bulletin, 114,* 3–28.

Kahneman, D., Slovic, P., & Tversky, A. (Eds.). (1982). *Judgment under uncertainty: Heuristics and biases.* New York: Cambridge University Press.

Lichtenstein, M., & Srull, T. K. (1987). Processing objectives as a determinant of the relationship between recall and judgment. *Journal of Experimental Social Psychology, 23,* 93–118.

Mares, M. L. (1996). The role of source confusions in television's cultivation of social reality judgments. *Human Communication Research, 23,* 278–297.

O'Guinn, T. C., & Shrum, L. J. (1997). The role of television in the construction of consumer reality. *Journal of Consumer Research, 23,* 278–294.

Olsen, M. A., & Fazio, R. H. (2004). Reducing the influence of the extrapersonal associations on the Implicit Association Test: Personalizing the IAT. *Journal of Personality and Social Psychology, 86,* 653–667.

Petty, R. E., & Cacioppo, J. T. (1986). *Communication and persuasion: Central and peripheral routes to attitude change.* New York: Springer-Verlag.

Petty, R. E., & Krosnick, J. A. (Eds.). (1995). *Attitude strength: Antecedents and consequences.* Mahwah, NJ: Lawrence Erlbaum Associates.

Pingree, S. (1983). Children's cognitive processes in constructing social reality. *Journalism Quarterly, 60,* 415–422.

Potter, W. J. (1986). Perceived reality and the cultivation hypothesis. *Journal of Broadcasting & Electronic Media, 30,* 159–174.

Potter, W. J. (1988). Three strategies for elaborating the cultivation hypothesis. *Journalism Quarterly, 65,* 930–939.

Potter, W. J. (1991). Examining cultivation from a psychological perspective. *Communications Research, 18,* 92–113.

Richins, M. L. (2004). The material values scale: Measurement properties and development of a short form. *Journal of Consumer Research, 31,* 209–219.

Roskos-Ewoldsen, B., Davies, J., & Roskos-Ewoldsen, D. R. (2004, May). *Implications of the mental models approach for cultivation theory.* Paper presented at the annual meeting of the International Communication Association, New Orleans, LA.

Roskos-Ewoldsen, D. R. (1997). Attitude accessibility and persuasion: Review and transactive model. In B. Burleson (Ed.), *Communication yearbook 20* (pp. 185–225). Beverly Hills, CA: Sage.

Rubin, A., Perse, E. M., & Taylor, D. S. (1988). A methodological examination of cultivation. *Communication Research, 15,* 107–134.

Russell, C. A., Norman, A. T., & Heckler, S. E. (2004). The consumption of television programming: Development and validation of the connectedness scale. *Journal of Consumer Research, 31,* 150–161.

Schwarz, N. (2004). Meta-cognitive experiences in consumer judgment and decision making. *Journal of Consumer Psychology, 14,* 332–345.

Schwarz, N., Bless, H., Strack, F., Klumpp, G., Rittenauer-Schatka, H., & Simons, A. (1991). Ease of retrieval as information: Another look at the availability heuristic. *Journal of Personality and Social Psychology, 61,* 195–202.

Shanahan, J., & Morgan, M. (1999). *Television and its viewers: Cultivation theory and research.* Cambridge, UK: Cambridge University Press.

Shapiro, M. A. (1991). Memory and decision processes in the construction of social reality. *Communication Research, 18,* 3–24.

Shapiro, M. A., & Lang, A. (1991). Making television reality: Unconscious processes in the construction of social reality. *Communication Research, 18,* 685–705.

Shrum, L. J. (1995). Assessing the social influence of television: A social cognition perspective on cultivation effects. *Communication Research, 22,* 402–429.

Shrum, L. J. (1996). Psychological processes underlying cultivation effects: Further tests of construct accessibility. *Human Communication Research, 22,* 482–509.

Shrum, L. J. (1997). The role of source confusion in cultivation effects may depend on processing strategy: A comment on Mares (1996). *Human Communication Research, 24,* 349–358.

Shrum, L. J. (1999a). The relationship of television viewing with attitude strength and extremity: Implications for the cultivation effect. *Media Psychology, 1,* 3–25.

Shrum, L. J. (1999b). Television and persuasion: Effects of the programs between the ads. *Psychology & Marketing, 16,* 119–140.

Shrum, L. J. (2001). Processing strategy moderates the cultivation effect. *Human Communication Research, 27,* 94–120.

Shrum, L. J. (2002). Media consumption and perceptions of social reality: Effects and underlying processes. In J. Bryant & D. Zillmann (Eds.), *Media effects: Advances in theory and research* (2nd ed., pp. 69–95). Mahwah, NJ: Lawrence Erlbaum Associates.

Shrum, L. J. (2004a). The cognitive processes underlying cultivation effects are a function of whether the judgments are on-line or memory-based. *Communications, 29,* 327–344.

Shrum, L. J. (2004b). *The implication of survey method for measuring cultivation effects.* Manuscript under review.

Shrum, L. J., Burroughs, J. E., & Rindfleisch, A. (2004). A process model of consumer cultivation: The role of television is a function of the type of judgment. In L. J. Shrum (Ed.), *The psychology of entertainment media: Blurring the lines between entertainment and persuasion* (pp. 177–191). Mahwah, NJ: Lawrence Erlbaum Associates.

Shrum, L. J., Burroughs, J. E., & Rindfleisch, A. (2005). Television's cultivation of material values. *Journal of Consumer Research, 32,* 473–479.

Shrum, L. J., & O'Guinn, T. C. (1993). Processes and effects in the construction of social reality: Construct accessibility as an explanatory variable. *Communication Research, 20,* 436–471.

Shrum, L. J., Wyer, R. S., & O'Guinn, T. C. (1998). The effects of television consumption on social perceptions: The use of priming procedures to investigate psychological processes. *Journal of Consumer Research, 24,* 447–458.

Strange, J. J. (1993). The facts of fiction: The accommodation of real-world beliefs to fabricated accounts. (Doctoral dissertation, Columbia University, 1993). *Dissertation Abstracts International, 54*(2–A), 358.

Tversky, A., & Kahneman, D. (1973). Availability: A heuristic for judging frequency and probability. *Cognitive Psychology, 5,* 207–232.

Uleman, J. S., Newman, L. S., & Moskowitz, G. B. (1996). People as flexible interpreters: Evidence and issues from spontaneous trait inference. In M. P. Zanna (Ed.), *Advances in experimental social psychology* (Vol. 28, pp. 211–279). San Diego, CA: Academic.

Wänke, M., Bohner, G., & Jurkowitsch, A. (1997). There are many reasons to drive a BMW: Does imagined ease of argument generation influence attitudes? *Journal of Consumer Research, 24,* 170–177.

Wyer, R. S. (2004). *Social comprehension and judgment: The role of situation models, narratives, and implicit theories.* Mahwah, NJ: Lawrence Erlbaum Associates.

Wyer, R. S., & Adaval, R. (2004). Pictures, words, and media influence: The interactive effects of verbal and nonverbal information on memory for judgments. In L. J. Shrum (Ed.), *The psychology of entertainment media: Blurring the lines between entertainment and persuasion* (pp. 137–160). Mahwah, NJ: Lawrence Erlbaum Associates.

Wyer, R. S., & Radvansky, G. A. (1999). The comprehension and validation of social information. *Psychological Review, 106,* 89–118.

Wyer, R. S., & Srull, T. K. (1989). *Memory and cognition in its social context.* Hillsdale, NJ: Lawrence Erlbaum Associates.

Zhang, Y., & Krcmar, M. (2004, May). *Effects of television viewing of sexual content on behavioral intentions in priming and no-priming conditions: A cultivation analysis from a theory of reasoned action perspective.* Paper presented at the annual meeting of the International Communication Association, New Orleans, LA.

12

Media and Racism

Mary Beth Oliver
Pennsylvania State University
Srividya Ramasubramanian
Texas A&M University
Jinhee Kim
Pennsylvania State University

The ways that individuals learn about other people and social groups aside from their own is widely varied, including through schools, books, peers, family, and direct contact. Whereas direct contact may provide the most salient (and therefore influential) means of learning about other people, geographical and social boundaries often prevent interpersonal interaction. Consequently, alternate sources of information can be very important in shaping our attitudes and beliefs, although unfortunately, not always in accurate ways or in a manner that encourages social harmony.

The notion that media may play a role in creating or sustaining prejudice has attracted research attention since early in the 20th century when studies of viewers' reactions to cinematic portrayals were examined (Peterson, Thurstone, Shuttlesworth, & May, 1933). Since that time, numerous scholars have recognized that media portrayals likely play important roles in affecting how viewers think about and respond to different racial and ethnic groups. Much of the research on media and racism in previous decades has tended to focus on the nature of the portrayals themselves, providing evidence for the existence of stereotypical media content. In addition, studies that have explored effects of such content on viewers have often tended to employ self-report techniques, with such strategies likely reflecting both assumptions concerning the processes by which viewers' were thought to be affected, and the methodological tools that were readily available.

The last several decades have seen a large increase in interest in the importance of media's role in stereotyping, as researchers have moved beyond looking only at the content of such portrayals and viewers' self-reported responses, to examining more subtle manifestations of the role of media in affecting and sustaining stereotypes. In addition, rather than exploring questions of if media stereotypes can affect stereotyping and racism, more recent research has explored how media and racism interact, and the mechanisms that might help to explain this association. Consequently, the purpose of this chapter is to overview current theorizing concerning media and racism, to explore the mechanisms that appear to fruitfully explain how these variables are related, and to suggest directions for future research. Although the directions that we suggest hold considerable challenges, we believe that they also highlight the idea that media influence may be more pervasive than we may commonly assume, thereby making research in this area particularly urgent.

MEDIA AND THE FORMATION OF STEREOTYPES

The idea that stereotyped media portrayals could play an important role in the formation of prejudiced attitudes and beliefs has arguably garnered the majority of research attention among scholars studying media and racism. A running assumption in this research is that media portrayals represent an important source of information about social groups, and that insofar as individuals employ media in forming impressions and making judgments, beliefs and attitudes should reflect the types of content frequently encountered. With this assumption in mind, however, research exploring perceptions of social reality has emphasized different mechanisms by which media may play a role in stereotyping, with some approaches stressing effects due to long-term, cumulative viewing, and other approaches identifying how even short-term exposure to biased images or information may affect individuals' beliefs about social reality.

Cultivation and Social Reality Judgments

Research from a cultivation perspective generally suggests that long-term, cumulative viewing of television content can lead to distorted perceptions of social reality that mirror the patterns or portrayals featured in television content (Gerbner, 1998; Gerbner, Gross, Morgan, Signorielli, & Shanahan, 2002). Support for cultivation's general hypotheses as applied to media and racism has been obtained for a variety of stereotypes such as perceptions of African Americans as relatively more impoverished than Whites (Armstrong, Neuendorf, & Brentar, 1992; Busselle & Crandall, 2002) and perceptions of greater African American involvement in crime (Oliver & Armstrong, 1998).

Despite some broad support for the general notion that long-term media exposure can be associated with increased stereotypical perceptions, it is important to point out that cultivation as a theoretical approach has generated substantial debate and criticism (Doob & Macdonald, 1979; Hirsch, 1980, 1981; Potter, 1993). Arguably, one of the most serious criticisms of cultivation is that it does not clarify the specific mechanisms that explain why media portrayals should affect perceptions of social reality, and particularly when many portrayals are understood by viewers to be fictional. However, Shrum's (chap. 11, this volume; 1995, 1996, 2002; Shrum & O'Guinn, 1993) work on the role of heuristic processing in cultivation effects sheds light on the manner by which media consumption (including consumption of fictional entertainment) may affect social reality judgments. Briefly, Shrum's model suggests that when making judgments or prevalence estimates, examples that come to mind quickly or easily serve to inflate perceptions of the prevalence of the phenomenon under consideration via the availability heuristic (Tversky & Kahneman, 1973). Insofar as heavy television viewers have a larger arsenal of media examples (many of which presumably differ considerably from reality), these examples should serve to distort social reality judgments. Furthermore, such distortion is predicted to occur even when the media examples come from less-than-veridical sources provided that the decision making reflects heuristic processing whereby the reliability of sources does not come under close scrutiny.

The application of Shrum's model to the issue of media and race has several important implications. First, this model would suggest that the nature of the portrayals that viewers consume is crucial in predicting the types of judgments that may be expected. Whereas original conceptualizations of cultivation emphasized the homogenous patterns of portrayals across media genres, thereby focusing on total amount of television viewing as the primary independent variable, other researchers have suggested that it may be more fruitful to examine how consumption of certain types of content (e.g., news, sitcoms, etc.) predicts viewers' responses, as many content analyses demonstrate that portrayals substantially vary between genres (Hawkins & Pingree, 1981; Potter, 1993). Shrum's model is consistent with this argument, as television content that contains numerous examples of stereotypical portrayals should be expected to provide viewers with readily available biased examples that, in turn, affect social reality perceptions. For example, viewers who are heavy consumers of news or crime dramas may be expected to have a larger number of accessible examples of "Black criminals" than do heavy viewers of soap operas or educational programming (Dixon & Linz, 2000a, 2000b; Entman & Rojecki, 2000; Oliver, 1994), thereby implying that crime-drama consumers will report higher estimates of African American crime involvement than would others.

An additional implication of Shrum's cultivation model is that it is important to acknowledge direct experience when considering the role of media in affecting judgments (see Busselle & Shrum, 2003; Shrum & Bischak, 2001). That is, if asked to make social reality estimates on issues that are highly familiar, it may be expected that direct or firsthand experiences would provide numerous, salient, and relevant examples. Consequently, as some researchers have suggested, the influence of media on individuals' perceptions should be expected to be most pronounced when firsthand or direct experiences are lacking or limited, as media portrayals represent the only source of information available (e.g., Fujioka, 1999; Tan, Fujioka, & Lucht, 1997). On the other hand, if direct experiences are consistent with media portrayals, one might expect to see stronger relations between media consumption and judgments, as media exemplars and real-life exemplars become reinforcing (Shrum & Bischak, 2001). Applied to issues of media and racism, the importance of direct contact cannot be overlooked, as information about many other countries and cultures is arguably acquired (at least among U.S. viewers) almost entirely via news reports (e.g., the war in Iraq). At the same time, media portrayals of racial and cultural groups that viewers frequently encounter are also common and vivid, meaning that predictions concerning the role that media may play in affecting social reality judgments may be largely dependent on the nature of firsthand or direct experiences. As such, future research should consider the utility of assessing not only media consumption in predicting beliefs and perceptions concerning race, but also by examining how perceptions acquired via personal experience moderate the effect of media on stereotypes.

A final, possible implication of Shrum's cultivation model is that the influence of media on racial stereotyping may be attenuated when viewers employ more deliberative processing strategies in arriving at their judgments. Although this implication may seem to provide reason for optimism, its applicability to actual judgments occurring outside of research labs may be questionable. Namely, research on social reality judgments seems to suggest that heuristic processing is the default strategy typically employed, with individuals rarely scrutinizing the veracity of informational sources when making judgments (Shrum, Wyer, & O'Guinn, 1998). Consequently, future research may benefit from exploring how strategies such as media literacy training or the development of critical viewing skills can serve to attenuate media's cultivation of racial stereotypes (see Ramasubramanian, 2004).

Exemplification

Whereas the focus of cultivation has typically been conceptualized as an outcome of long-term or cumulative viewing, Shrum's model does not imply that long-term exposure is necessarily a requisite. Rather, media examples may be thought to exert an influence on social reality judgments, regardless of whether or not the examples arise from long-term or limited exposure. However, in keeping with the assumptions of traditional cultivation research, Shrum and colleagues have typically assessed media exposure in terms of frequency of viewing (e.g., Shrum, 1995; Shrum & O'Guinn, 1993), making it somewhat difficult to determine if accessible exemplars (and their resultant effects) reflect cumulative exposure or exposure to a limited number of media instances.

In contrast, research on exemplification has typically employed experimental designs, assessing how even a single exposure to salient examples can affect individuals' judgments (Zillmann, 2002; Zillmann & Brosius, 2000). In general, exemplification research has demonstrated that when forming judgments based on media information, individuals tend to give greater weight to examples than to any base-rate information that may also be featured. Consequently, insofar as exemplars accurately reflect population parameters, viewers' resulting beliefs or judgments about the topic at hand should accurately reflect reality. As Zillmann and Brosius (2000) pointed out, however, the finite number of exemplars that can be feasibly included in news stories, as well as reporters' tendencies to include sensational examples to enliven what might otherwise be bland information, lead to numerous situations in which exemplars can lead to distorted perceptions.

The notion of the importance of exemplars in affecting individuals' perceptions of race-related information is highlighted by content-analytic research pointing to how individuals from different racial or ethnic groups are featured as illustration of various news issues such as crime (Entman, 1992; Entman & Rojecki, 2000) or poverty (Gilens, 1996, 1999). However, whereas content-analytic research on the race of exemplars in news stories offers evidence that biases exist, such findings do not, of course, demonstrate the specific effects that such exemplars may have on viewers' social reality judgments.

However, Gibson and Zillmann's (2000) research on the effects of pictorial exemplars suggests that exemplification may be a particularly fruitful theoretical framework for exploring how media portrayals and racial beliefs may intersect. In their study, a news story concerning a fictitious tick-borne disease was manipulated to include photographs of White victims, Black victims, or both Black and White victims. Although the text of the news story itself made no reference to race, participants reported greater estimated risk for the racial groups who had been featured in the photographs. Whereas this study suggests that exemplars concerning race may play an important role in individuals' subsequent judgments, it is important to point out that the exemplars featured in this study were visual (photographic). Although other studies have revealed similar findings based on variations in textual exemplars, the importance that visual (and therefore, perhaps, salient) exemplification may play in affecting perceptions of race is deserving of greater research attention.

In addition to examining the presentational form of exemplars (text vs. visual), future research would also benefit from exploring whether or not Gibson and Zillmann's (2000) research could be replicated for judgments concerning such issues as poverty and crime. Specifically, many exemplification studies (including Gibson & Zillmann's) have employed as stimuli news stories on topics for which participants likely had very little existing information or direct experience (Aust & Zillmann, 1996; Gibson & Zillmann, 1994; Zillmann, Gibson, Sundar, & Perkins, 1996). Similarly, many news topics employed in exemplification studies have examined issues that are unlikely to be associated with strong preexisting attitudes or judgments. Given the differences between exemplars that have been examined in extant research with those typically featured in race-related news stories, it is unclear how exemplars of race or ethnicity may function in affecting viewers' attitudes or stereotypes. In some respects, exemplars may be expected to have a particularly pronounced influence, as racial information is arguably salient and, for some viewers, emotionally charged. In contrast, racial exemplars may be expected to have weaker effects on judgments, as individuals' existing beliefs, attitudes, and stereotypes may serve to attenuate the influence of media information. Given the ambiguous ways that exemplars may function, future work on race-related examples in media portrayals would benefit from identifying the variables that may be important moderators and from examining possible boundary conditions in the exemplification process.

PRIMING

In addition to exploring the ways in which media may play a role in the formation and cultivation of stereotypes, researchers have also explored the idea that media content can serve as a powerful agent in the priming of existing stereotypes. In general, media priming refers to the idea that exposure to one set of stimuli can activate or bring to mind related cognitions, with these activated cognitions affecting the way that new information is processed (see Roskos-Ewoldsen, Roskos-Ewoldsen, & Carpentier, 2002, for a recent review). Much of the work on priming and racial stereotypes in particular is based on a neo-associationistic model that employs the concepts of associative networks and spreading activation to understand priming processes (Jo & Berkowitz, 1994). Briefly, this model conceptualizes thoughts, emotions, and action tendencies as nodes in a cognitive framework, with semantically related nodes interconnected via associative pathways. When one node is activated or brought to mind, activation spreads along pathways to related nodes, resulting in a host of related cognitions being primed. In turn, these activated cognitions may affect interpretations of or responses to subsequent stimuli that are relevant to the primed cognitions, at least for a short time.

Although media researchers have most frequently examined this model in the context of media violence, its application to media and stereotyping is readily evident. For example, priming would suggest that once a stereotype is in place, the priming of any element of the stereotype can serve to prime associated characteristics. For example, Ford (1997) found evidence that the priming of racial stereotypes of African Americans as comical or buffoonish served to prime stereotypes associating African Americans with criminal behavior. Similarly, Johnson, Trawalter, and Dovidio (2000) demonstrated that exposure to music videos of violent rap music was related to subsequent judgments of African Americans as less intelligent (a stereotypical characteristic) but was unrelated to judgments that were not stereotyped (e.g., spatial skills; for additional examples, see Power, Murphy, & Coover, 1996; Ramasubramanian, 2004; Valentino, 1999).

In the aforementioned examples, the priming of racial stereotypes was facilitated via exposure to media portrayals of racial stereotypes. However, additional research suggests that stereotypes can also be primed even in the absence of explicit stereotypical portrayals. Namely, Domke and his colleagues suggested that exposure to news stories framed in such a way as to include "racial cues" but with no explicit mention or presentation of race should result in the activation of stereotypes. These activated stereotypes can, in turn, affect subsequent judgments and political attitudes (Domke, 2001; Domke, McCoy, & Torres, 1999). For example, in one study, reading a newspaper story concerning crime resulted in greater stereotyping of African Americans and Hispanics on such characteristics as lazy, unintelligent, and violent, but only if the newspaper story mentioned racial cues such as drive-by shootings or inner cities. Further, when racial cues were present, primed stereotypes of African Americans and Hispanics had a more influential role on self-reported political attitudes per se, as well as on perceptions of crime policies specifically. The important implication of this line of research is that blatant portrayals of racial stereotypes are not necessary to prime racist thoughts. Rather, more subtle framing of news stories that contain racial cues can activate stereotypes that are connected via associated pathways, with these stereotypes affecting not only judgments of the stereotyped group, but judgments of related political and social issues.

Whereas research has demonstrated that priming can influence perceptions and judgments of subsequent stimuli in consequential ways, one noteworthy aspect of this model is that the effects of media exposure on the priming of related cognitions is thought to be relatively short term (see Roskos-Ewoldsen et al., 2002). Strictly speaking, then, one would not expect media priming of stereotypes to influence judgments or behaviors beyond a very brief duration (e.g., 15–20 minutes after exposure). However, there are ways in which priming models may be applicable when considering longer term effects of media exposure. As Berkowitz (1984; Berkowitz & Rogers, 1986) noted, any given media portrayal (e.g., violence) can be associated with given cues that, when encountered later in the environment, can prime or activate cognitions associated with the portrayal (see also Olson & Fazio, 2001, 2002, for a discussion of implicit attitude formation). For example, should media portrayals of violent crime be repeatedly associated with a given racial or ethnic group, these two concepts may become linked in an associative network. As a consequence, later exposure to one of these elements (e.g., African Americans) should prime thoughts of the other (e.g., violence). Although, to our knowledge, this specific hypothesis has not been tested in the context of media and race, other studies of the influence of context cues on aggressive behavior offer some empirical support for idea that media portrayals may have this type of effect (e.g., Josephson, 1986). Given media portrayals' repeated associations of given minorities with specific behaviors (e.g., Arabs and terrorism), this direction of research may be particularly relevant.

An additional implication of neo-associationistic models of priming is that people who already have stereotypes in place should presumably be most susceptible to the priming effects of stereotypical media portrayals (see Bushman, 1995, for an illustration of this point in the context of media violence). This assumption rests on the idea that for spreading activation to occur there must be an associative network that connects cognitions associated with minority groups to stereotyped characteristics. At first glance, then, this implication would seem to suggest that people who admit to racism or who endorse stereotypes should be most influenced.

However, research on implicit stereotyping points out that regardless of the extent to which individuals endorse a particular stereotype, the pervasiveness of stereotypes through a host of socially and culturally shared experiences (including the media) implies that most people are familiar with them (Devine, 1989), and, as a consequence, have cognitive structures of stereotypes in place. This observation implies that all individuals, regardless of their levels of racial prejudice, may be susceptible to the influence of priming of racial stereotypes (Bargh, 1999; Dovidio, Kawakami, Johnson, Johnson, & Howard, 1997).

Nevertheless, it is important to recognize that the activation of stereotypes is distinct from the application of stereotypes. That is, simply because a stereotype is activated does not mean, necessarily, that it will be applied to subsequent judgments or behaviors. For example, Fazio's (1990) motivation and opportunity as determinants (MODE) model suggests that the activation of stereotypes will be most likely to affect individuals' judgments and behaviors toward minorities when the motivation and opportunity to process deliberately is absent (see also Fazio & Towles-Schwen, 1999). Consequently, although low-prejudice individuals should be less likely than high-prejudice individuals to evidence behavioral manifestations of activated stereotypes, stereotype application may be likely to occur for any individual in situations in which deliberative processing is disrupted, when there is low awareness that stereotypes have been activated, or when the task at hand seems irrelevant to activated stereotypes (Devine & Monteith, 1999; Fazio & Towles-Schwen, 1999). Applied to media priming, then, one might expect to see the strongest influence of media stereotyping when the salience of the stereotyping is minimized, as such situations should be least likely to result in controlled responding and hence any attempt to engage in stereotype suppression. Valentino, Traugott, and Hutchings (2002) argued this point in their research on racial cues in political advertisements, suggesting that as racial cues become more salient, the influence they have on priming likewise increases. However, when racial cues become too salient (e.g., when individuals become cognizant that race has been primed), attempts will be made to suppress the influence that accessible stereotypes may play on judgments.

To summarize, research from a priming perspective suggests that stereotypical media portrayals may serve to activate stereotypical cognitions, with these cognitions, in turn, affecting subsequent judgments. Furthermore, research on implicit stereotyping implies that all viewers, regardless of their levels of racial prejudice, may be susceptible to these types of effects in some circumstances. Consequently, future research would benefit from further exploration of characteristics of media content, aspects of viewing situations, and viewers' motivations for media consumption that may prove to be useful moderators of the extent to which media-induced priming of racial stereotypes affects viewers' judgments.

SELECTIVITY

In addition to examining how media may serve to create or prime racial stereotypes, additional media scholarship has also suggested that media consumption can function to sustain (or even strengthen) stereotypes and prejudicial attitudes. In large part, these types of outcomes are thought to reflect the idea that viewers' existing stereotypes act as a filter of incoming information, with media portrayals interpreted and remembered in ways that are consistent with existing cognitions and attitudes.

Selective Perception and Enjoyment

The importance of racial attitudes in moderating interpretations of race-related media content is perhaps best illustrated in Vidmar and Rokeach's (1974) now-classic study of viewers' interpretations of *All in the Family*. Consistent with the notion of selective perception, these authors reported that although most respondents, regardless of their racial attitudes, reported enjoying the show, viewers scoring higher on measures of racial prejudice generally interpreted the primary bigoted character on the program as likable and funny, and misunderstood the sitcom to be making fun of progressive politics rather than racism and prejudice. Since this early study was conducted, a number of additional studies have reported similar results for a variety of different types of content, including comedy, portrayals of welfare, and depictions of crime (Cooks & Orbe, 1993; Peffley, Hurwitz, & Sniderman, 1997; Peffley, Shields, & Williams, 1996).

Research on enjoyment of media entertainment has revealed analogous results, suggesting that individuals tend to report greater liking for media content that reflects their existing racial attitudes. For example, Oliver and Armstrong (1995) examined viewers' enjoyment of reality-based police programs, suggesting that disposition theory may explain the relation between existing racial attitudes and evaluations of these programs. In general, disposition theory suggests that individuals report high levels of enjoyment when characters that are "liked" are portrayed as winning or succeeding, and when characters who are "disliked" are portrayed as losing or suffering (Raney, 2003; Zillmann, 1985; Zillmann & Bryant, 1986). Oliver and Armstrong reasoned, therefore, that programs containing frequent depictions of racial minorities as punished or as "losing" (e.g., Black criminal suspects being arrested) should hold particular appeal among viewers who harbor racist attitudes. Consistent with these expectations, measures of racial prejudice were positively associated with greater viewing and reported enjoyment of these programs, but were unrelated to enjoyment of fictional police programs where criminal behaviors are not as strongly associated with racial minorities.

Although research on viewers' enjoyment and interpretation of race-related media content generally support the idea that people understand and are attracted to media portrayals that are consistent with their existing attitudes, such a description may paint a picture that is too simplistic to capture the full range of possible responses. For example, in terms of selective exposure, some researchers have suggested that what may appear to be selectivity on the part of viewers may actually reflect the availability of information or the usefulness of information in attaining goals (Freedman & Sears, 1965). In addition, other researchers have suggested that under some circumstances, individuals might selectively expose themselves to information that is inconsistent with existing attitudes, and particularly so if the information is easily refutable (Frey, 1986).

Similarly, in terms of selective perception, although research on viewers' interpretations of media content would seem to imply that viewers with more extreme racial attitudes would be most likely to interpret content as consistent with their existing beliefs, this prediction appears inconsistent with existing research on hostile media perceptions (Gunther & Chia, 2001; Vallone, Ross, & Lepper, 1985). In essence, the hostile media phenomenon refers to the tendency for people who are partisans on a given issue to perceive that media are hostile to their position.

What might explain the divergent predictions between hostile media and selective perception hypotheses? Recent research by Gunther and Schmitt (2004) provides one possible explanation for these divergent hypotheses that places emphasis on the respondents' focus of attention on the self versus on others when evaluating messages. These authors suggested that research demonstrating an assimilation bias has tended to employ stimuli and questions that encourage research participants to focus on their own opinions. For example, Vidmar and Rokeach (1974) asked respondents what they thought of *All in the Family* and the characters portrayed, and Oliver and Armstrong (1995) assessed viewers' own reactions to reality-based police programs. In neither of these studies were respondents asked to speculate about how other viewers might respond or how the program might influence others' attitudes—indeed, perceptions of other viewers were largely irrelevant. In contrast, research demonstrating a hostile-media effect has tended to employ stimuli (e.g., news reports) and questions that encourage participants to focus on how other people or the public at large are influenced by media messages. Why might this result in perceptions of media as hostile? Gunther and Schmidt (2004) first pointed to literature on third-person perceptions demonstrating that individuals tend to believe that others are vulnerable to harmful media messages (Davison, 1983; Perloff, 2002). These authors then suggested that this perceived vulnerability may translate into perceptions of a hostile media—or at least a fear that other viewers may interpret or be affected by media in ways that are "unfavorable or disagreeable." Applied to the issue at hand, this reasoning would suggest that future research on selective perception may find weaker, nonexistent, or even negative relations between racial attitudes and perceptions of media content insofar as it encourages participants to focus on how others may be affected. Although this reasoning is clearly in need of empirical exploration at this point, it appears to be a useful framework in exploring the limits of the audience's ability and tendency to perceive media content as consistent with their existing stereotypes.

Selective Recall

In addition to exploring selective interpretation and enjoyment, more recent research suggests that viewers' memories of race-related portrayals may also reflect cultural stereotypes associated with race (Oliver, 1999; Oliver & Fonash, 2002). In general, this research indicates that individuals are likely to misremember racial portrayals—ones that have never been explicitly featured—insofar as these portrayals are consistent with racial stereotypes (e.g., associating African Americans with violent crime). More recently, this type of research has been expanded to include an examination of the visual representations that people may construct when recalling crime-related photographs (Oliver, Jackson, Moses, & Dangerfield, 2004). Similar to prior research on mismemory of racial groups per se, this research suggests that individuals' memories of stereotypical content (crime news) are associated with distorted visual memories of race-related facial features, resulting in prototypical and stereotypical mental images accentuating Afrocentric characteristics (see Blair, Judd, Sadler, & Jenkins, 2002, for a discussion of stereotypes of physical features).

Surprisingly, research on viewers' memories of race-related information has generally not obtained evidence for the importance of individuals' racial attitudes in moderating effects. That is, unlike prior research on viewers' interpretation and enjoyment, race-related biases reflected in individuals' self-reported memory of media content appears to happen regardless of self-reported racial attitudes. Although it is unclear at this point why these seemingly similar strands of research differ in this regard, one possible explanation is that research on individuals' memories of race-related information has typically taken great pains to disguise any indications in the research procedures that the study pertained to race. In contrast, research on viewers' interpretations of media content has often measured racial attitudes immediately prior to measuring media-related variables. Consequently, in studies of perception and enjoyment, the idea that the research pertained to race may have been apparent to participants, resulting in attempts to control or suppress responses that may have been considered socially undesirable. In other words, existing research on selective perception may reflect stereotype application, whereas research on selective recall may reflect stereotype activation. Because this interpretation is only speculative at this point, future research on selective interpretation and recall would benefit from more directly assessing these distinctions.

Future research would also benefit from exploring what selective recall implies for subsequent attitudes and social reality judgments concerning race. At this point, the notion that selective interpretation and recall can serve to sustain or intensify racial stereotyping is largely speculative, albeit intuitively appealing. However, existing research on heuristic processing models of cultivation (Shrum, 2002) or on exemplification (Zillmann, 2002) may provide useful starting points for more systematic explorations of the ways in which mismemory of racial information could lead to distorted reality judgments. Both of these perspectives suggest that exemplars that readily come to mind exert strong influences on judgments, yet neither of these perspectives suggest that the exemplars be true or actual. Consequently, readily accessible media exemplars reflecting mistaken recall may affect perceptions to the same degree as accurate exemplars, and particularly given that errors in recall are likely consistent with prevailing cultural stereotypes. Of course, this interpretation calls for empirical validation—namely a closer examination of the distinction between what was actually seen versus what was misremembered, and the role that each plays in affecting individuals' judgments.

CONCLUDING COMMENTS AND FUTURE DIRECTIONS

This overview of research pertaining to media and racism provides a broad base of evidence that media portrayals of stereotyping can result in several harmful outcomes: the formation or cultivation of stereotypes, the priming of stereotypes, and the maintenance of stereotypes. Throughout this chapter we have attempted to not only describe the mechanisms that extant research suggests are important in explaining the relation between media and racism, but to also suggest avenues that future researchers may find particularly fruitful or enlightening. In this final section, we provide additional advice to scholars interested in entering this arena, with this advice focused on what existing theorizing suggests are important methodological considerations. These suggestions grow out of the recognition that whereas current scholarship has revealed important ways that media consumption may lead to stereotyping, the magnitude of the effect sizes reported in the studies that we have overviewed are often quite modest.

Ultimately, we believe that one explanation for the modest associations observed in the literature may reflect the ways that racial attitudes have been conceptualized (and hence operationalized) by media scholars over the last several decades. Namely, research from a variety of perspectives has typically employed self-report measures to assess racial attitudes, with many of these measures reflecting what are often considered to be traditional forms of racism. As such, it is important to recognize that many studies, therefore, have narrowed their focus to only those attitudes that individuals are both cognizant of and are openly willing to express to researchers. Not only are such situations vulnerable to problems associated with social desirability, they are also ill-equipped to examine effects that are likely more subtle and sometimes imperceptible to participants. As an analogy, if researchers were to employ only self-reported feelings of well-being to detect cancer among smokers, the association between cigarettes and cancer would probably be very small. However, by employing more sensitive and subtle measures, researchers are able to detect damage at the molecular level that is virtually invisible to the individual whose health is in danger.

The advice that this observation implies for future researchers is to be cognizant of the dangers involved in employing only broad or even obtuse measures of racial attitudes or stereotypes, or in employing stimulus materials that are too obvious or blatant. Racism is insidious, and recognizing its subtleties in manifestation is of crucial importance in capturing its prevalence and influence. As researchers in related disciplines continue to examine the distinctions between stereotype application and stereotype activation, we believe that future research in media and stereotyping would benefit substantially from greater attention to this issue as well. Although we do not mean to suggest that self-report measures should be abandoned, we would also like to encourage researchers to take advantage of methodological tools now readily available that enable the assessment of implicit stereotyping (e.g., response time techniques, lexical decision tasks, etc.). In addition, we would like to encourage researchers to employ creativity in the design of their studies in such a way that makes the focus of study on race and the racism in their stimuli less evident and therefore less likely to result in deliberative processing or attempts at stereotype suppression.

We realize that to a naive reader, our suggestions may sound somewhat like we are implying that researchers trick respondents into providing evidence of biased attitudes or prejudicial responses. In contrast, though, we believe that a greater acknowledgment of the pervasiveness of racial stereotypes and the extent to which such stereotypes are a commonplace element in most people's cognitive structures is an important step to take, both methodologically and socially. Consequently, if there is any trick to be noticed here, we believe that it may be an unfortunate underestimation of the strength and prevalence of the media's role in the formation and maintenance of racial stereotypes, even among those of us who like to believe that our attitudes are progressive and egalitarian. Because we all are vulnerable, although perhaps not cognizant of our vulnerability, research on the effects of media on stereotyping and the strategies we may employ to diminish such harmful outcomes is particularly urgent.

REFERENCES

Armstrong, G. B., Neuendorf, K. A., & Brentar, J. E. (1992). TV entertainment, news, and racial perceptions of college students. *Journal of Communication, 42*, 153–176.

Aust, C. F., & Zillmann, D. (1996). Effects of victim exemplification in television news on viewer perception of social issues. *Journalism & Mass Communication Quarterly, 73*, 787–803.

Bargh, J. A. (1999). The cognitive monster: A case against the controllability of automatic stereotype effects. In S. Chaiken & Y. Trope (Eds.), *Dual-process theories in social psychology* (pp. 361–382). New York: Guilford.

Berkowitz, L. (1984). Some effects of thoughts on anti- and prosocial influences of media events: A cognitive-neoassociation analysis. *Psychological Bulletin, 95*, 410–427.

Berkowitz, L., & Rogers, K. H. (1986). A priming effect analysis of media influences. In J. Bryant & D. Zillmann (Eds.), *Perspectives on media effects* (pp. 57–82). Hillsdale, NJ: Lawrence Erlbaum Associates.

Blair, I. V., Judd, C. M., Sadler, M. S., & Jenkins, C. (2002). The role of Afrocentric features in person perception: Judging by features and categories. *Journal of Personality and Social Psychology, 83*, 5–25.

Bushman, B. J. (1995). Moderating role of trait aggressiveness in the effects of violent media on aggression. *Journal of Personality and Social Psychology, 69*, 950–960.

Busselle, R. W., & Crandall, H. (2002). Television viewing and perceptions about race differences in socioeconomic success. *Journal of Broadcasting & Electronic Media, 46*, 265–282.

Busselle, R. W., & Shrum, L. J. (2003). Media exposure and exemplar accessibility. *Media Psychology, 5*, 255–282.

Cooks, L. M., & Orbe, M. P. (1993). Beyond the satire: Selective exposure and selective perception in "In Living Color". *Howard Journal of Communications, 4*, 217–233.

Davison, W. P. (1983). The third-person effect in communication. *Public Opinion Quarterly, 47*, 1–15.

Devine, P. G. (1989). Stereotypes and prejudice: Their automatic and controlled components. *Journal of Personality and Social Psychology, 56*, 5–18.

Devine, P. G., & Monteith, M. J. (1999). Automaticity and control in stereotyping. In S. Chaiken & Y. Trope (Eds.), *Dual-process theories in social psychology* (pp. 339–360). New York: Guilford.

Dixon, T. L., & Linz, D. (2000a). Overrepresentation and underrepresentation of African Americans and Latinos as lawbreakers on television news. *Journal of Communication, 50*, 131–154.

Dixon, T. L., & Linz, D. (2000b). Race and the misrepresentation of victimization on local television news. *Communication Research, 27*, 547–573.

Domke, D. (2001). Racial cues and political ideology: An examination of associative priming. *Communication Research, 28*, 772–801.

Domke, D., McCoy, K., & Torres, M. (1999). News media, racial perceptions, and political cognition. *Communication Research, 26,* 570–607.

Doob, A. N., & Macdonald, G. E. (1979). Television viewing and fear of victimization: Is the relationship causal? *Journal of Personality and Social Psychology, 37,* 170–179.

Dovidio, J. F., Kawakami, K., Johnson, C., Johnson, B., & Howard, A. (1997). On the nature of prejudice: Automatic and controlled processes. *Journal of Experimental Social Psychology, 33,* 510–540.

Entman, R. M. (1992). Blacks in the news: Television, modern racism and cultural change. *Journalism Quarterly, 69,* 341–361.

Entman, R. M., & Rojecki, A. (2000). *The Black image in the White mind: Media and race in America.* Chicago: University of Chicago Press.

Fazio, R. H. (1990). Multiple processes by which attitudes guide behavior: The MODE model as an integrative framework. In M. P. Zanna (Ed.), *Advances in experimental social psychology* (Vol. 23, pp. 75–109). San Diego, CA: Academic.

Fazio, R. H., & Towles-Schwen, T. (1999). The MODE model of attitude-behavior processes. In S. Chaiken & Y. Trope (Eds.), *Dual-process theories in social psychology* (pp. 97–116). New York: Guilford.

Ford, T. E. (1997). Effects of stereotypical television portrayals of African-Americans on person perception. *Social Psychology Quarterly, 60,* 266–275.

Freedman, J. L., & Sears, D. O. (1965). Selective exposure. In L. Berkowitz (Ed.), *Advances in experimental social psychology* (Vol. 2, pp. 57–97). San Diego, CA: Academic.

Frey, D. (1986). Recent research on selective exposure to information. In L. Berkowitz (Ed.), *Advances in experimental social psychology* (Vol. 19, pp. 41–80). San Diego, CA: Academic.

Fujioka, Y. (1999). Television portrayals and African American stereotypes: Examination of television effects when direct contact is lacking. *Journalism & Mass Communication Quarterly, 76,* 52–75.

Gerbner, G. (1998). Cultivation analysis: An overview. *Mass Communication & Society, 1,* 175–194.

Gerbner, G., Gross, L., Morgan, M., Signorielli, N., & Shanahan, J. (2002). Growing up with television: Cultivation processes. In J. Bryant & D. Zillmann (Eds.), *Media effects: Advances in theory and research* (2nd ed., pp. 43–67). Mahwah, NJ: Lawrence Erlbaum Associates.

Gibson, R., & Zillmann, D. (1994). Exaggerated versus representative exemplification in news reports: Perception of issues and personal consequences. *Communication Research, 21,* 603–624.

Gibson, R., & Zillmann, D. (2000). Reading between the photographs: The influence of incidental pictorial information on issue perception. *Journalism & Mass Communication Quarterly, 77,* 355–366.

Gilens, M. (1996). Race and poverty in America: Public misperceptions and the American news media. *Public Opinion Quarterly, 60,* 515–541.

Gilens, M. (1999). *Why Americans hate welfare: Race, media, and the politics of antipoverty policy.* Chicago: University of Chicago Press.

Gunther, A. C., & Chia, S. C. Y. (2001). Predicting pluralistic ignorance: The hostile media perception and its consequences. *Journalism & Mass Communication Quarterly, 78,* 688–701.

Gunther, A. C., & Schmitt, K. (2004). Mapping boundaries of the hostile media effect. *Journal of Communication, 54,* 55–70.

Hawkins, R. P., & Pingree, S. (1981). Uniform messages and habitual viewing: Unnecessary assumptions in social reality effects. *Human Communication Research, 7,* 291–301.

Hirsch, P. (1980). The "scary world" of the non viewer and other anomalies: A reanalysis of Gerbner et al.'s findings on cultivation analysis. Part I. *Communication Research, 7,* 403–456.

Hirsch, P. (1981). On not learning from one's own mistakes: A reanalysis of Gerbner et al.'s findings on cultivation analysis. *Communication Research, 8,* 3–37.

Jo, E., & Berkowitz, L. (1994). A priming effect analysis of media influences: An update. In J. Bryant & D. Zillmann (Eds.), *Media effects: Advances in theory and research* (pp. 43–60). Hillsdale, NJ: Lawrence Erlbaum Associates.

Johnson, J. D., Trawalter, S., & Dovidio, J. F. (2000). Converging interracial consequences of exposure to violent rap music on stereotypical attributions of Blacks. *Journal of Experimental Social Psychology, 36,* 233–251.

Josephson, W. L. (1986). Television violence and children's aggression: Testing the priming, social script, and disinhibition predictions. *Journal of Personality and Social Psychology, 53,* 882–890.

Oliver, M. B. (1994). Portrayals of crime, race, and aggression in reality-based police shows: A content-analysis. *Journal of Broadcasting & Electronic Media, 38,* 179–192.

Oliver, M. B. (1999). Caucasian viewers' memory of Black and White criminal suspects in the news. *Journal of Communication, 49,* 46–60.

Oliver, M. B., & Armstrong, G. B. (1995). Predictors of viewing and enjoyment of reality-based and fictional crime shows. *Journalism & Mass Communication Quarterly, 72,* 559–570.

Oliver, M. B., & Armstrong, G. B. (1998). The color of crime: Perceptions of Caucasians' and African Americans' involvement in crime. In M. Fishman & G. Cavender (Eds.), *Entertaining crime: Television reality programs* (pp. 19–35). New York: Aldine de Gruyter.

Oliver, M. B., & Fonash, D. (2002). Race and crime in the news: Whites' identification and misidentification of violent and nonviolent criminal suspects. *Media Psychology, 4,* 137–156.

Oliver, M. B., Jackson, R. L., Jr., Moses, N. M., & Dangerfield, C. L. (2004). The face of crime: Viewers' memory of race-related facial features of individuals pictured in the news. *Journal of Communication, 54,* 88–104.

Olson, M. A., & Fazio, R. H. (2001). Implicit attitude formation through classical conditioning. *Psychological Science, 12,* 413–417.

Olson, M. A., & Fazio, R. H. (2002). Implicit acquisition and manifestation of classically conditioned attitudes. *Social Cognition, 20,* 89–104.

Peffley, M., Hurwitz, J., & Sniderman, P. M. (1997). Racial stereotypes and Whites' political views of Blacks in the context of welfare and crime. *American Journal of Political Science, 41,* 30–60.

Peffley, M., Shields, T., & Williams, B. (1996). The intersection of race and crime in television news stories: An experimental study. *Political Communication, 13,* 309–327.

Perloff, R. M. (2002). The third-person effect. In J. Bryant & D. Zillmann (Eds.), *Media effects: Advances in theory and research* (2nd ed., pp. 489–506). Mahwah, NJ: Lawrence Erlbaum Associates.

Peterson, R. C., Thurstone, L. L., Shuttlesworth, F. K., & May, M. A. (1933). *Motion pictures and the social attitudes of children.* New York: Macmillan.

Potter, W. J. (1993). Cultivation theory and research: A conceptual critique. *Human Communication Research, 4,* 564–601.

Power, J. G., Murphy, S. T., & Coover, G. (1996). Priming prejudice: How stereotypes and counter-stereotypes influence attribution of responsibility and credibility among ingroups and outgroups. *Human Communication Research, 23,* 36–58.

Ramasubramanian, S. (2004). *Effects of media literacy training on explicit and implicit racial stereotypes.* Unpublished doctoral dissertation, Pennsylvania State University, University Park, PA.

Raney, A. A. (2003). Dispositon-based theories of enjoyment. In J. Bryant, D. Roskos-Ewoldsen, & J. Cantor (Eds.), *Communication and emotion: Essays in honor of Dolf Zillmann* (pp. 61–84). Mahwah, NJ: Lawrence Erlbaum Associates.

Roskos-Ewoldsen, D. R., Roskos-Ewoldsen, B., & Carpentier, F. R. D. (2002). Media priming: A synthesis. In J. Bryant & D. Zillmann (Eds.), *Media effects: Advances in theory and research* (2nd ed., pp. 97–120). Mahwah, NJ: Lawrence Erlbaum Associates.

Shrum, L. J. (1995). Assessing the social influence of television: A social cognition perspective on cultivation effects. *Communication Research, 22,* 402–429.

Shrum, L. J. (1996). Psychological processes underlying cultivation effects: Further tests of construct accessibility. *Human Communication Research, 22,* 482–509.

Shrum, L. J. (2002). Media consumption and perceptions of social reality: Effects and underlying processes. In J. Bryant & D. Zillmann (Eds.), *Media effects: Advances in theory and research* (2nd ed., pp. 69–95). Mahwah, NJ: Lawrence Erlbaum Associates.

Shrum, L. J., & Bischak, V. D. (2001). Mainstreaming, resonance, and impersonal impact: Testing moderators of the cultivation effect for estimates of crime risk. *Human Communication Research, 27,* 187–215.

Shrum, L. J., & O'Guinn, T. C. (1993). Processes and effects in the construction of social-reality: Construct accessibility as an explanatory variable. *Communication Research, 20,* 436–471.

Shrum, L. J., Wyer, R. S., Jr., & O'Guinn, T. C. (1998). The effects of television consumption on social perceptions: The use of priming procedures to investigate psychological processes. *Journal of Consumer Research, 24,* 447–458.

Tan, A., Fujioka, Y., & Lucht, N. (1997). Native American stereotypes, TV portrayals, and personal contact. *Journalism & Mass Communication Quarterly, 74,* 265–284.

Tversky, A., & Kahneman, D. (1973). Availability: A heuristic for judging. *Cognitive Psychology, 5,* 207–232.

Valentino, N. A. (1999). Crime news and the priming of racial attitudes during evaluations of the president. *Public Opinion Quarterly, 63,* 293–320.

Valentino, N. A., Traugott, M. W., & Hutchings, V. L. (2002). Group cues and ideological constraint: A replication of political advertising effects studies in the lab and in the field. *Political Communication, 19,* 29–48.

Vallone, R. P., Ross, L., & Lepper, M. R. (1985). The hostile media phenomenon: Biased perception and perceptions of media bias in coverage of the Beirut massacre. *Journal of Personality and Social Psychology, 49,* 577–585.

Vidmar, N., & Rokeach, M. (1974). Archie Bunker's bigotry: A study in selective perception and exposure. *Journal of Communication, 24,* 36–47.

Zillmann, D. (1985). The experimental exploration of gratifications from media entertainment. In K. E. Rosengren, L. A. Wenner & P. Palmgreen (Eds.), *Media gratifications research: Current perspectives* (pp. 225–239). Beverly Hills, CA: Sage.

Zillmann, D. (2002). Exemplification theory of media influence. In J. Bryant & D. Zillmann (Eds.), *Media effects: Advances in theory and research* (2nd ed., pp. 19–41). Mahwah, NJ: Lawrence Erlbaum Associates.

Zillmann, D., & Brosius, H. B. (2000). *Exemplification in communication: The influence of case reports on the perception of issues.* Mahwah, NJ: Lawrence Erlbaum Associates.

Zillmann, D., & Bryant, J. (1986). Exploring the entertainment experience. In J. Bryant & D. Zillmann (Eds.), *Perspectives on media effects* (pp. 303–324). Hillsdale, NJ: Lawrence Erlbaum Associates.

Zillmann, D., Gibson, R., Sundar, S. S., & Perkins, J. W. (1996). Effects of exemplification in news reports on the perception of social issues. *Journalism & Mass Communication Quarterly, 73,* 427–444.

13

News and Politics

William P. Eveland, Jr.
Mihye Seo
The Ohio State University

Roloff and Berger's (1982) *Social Cognition and Communication* was composed of nine chapters. Of these chapters, one was introductory, one pertained broadly to mass communication research, and the remainder covered topics such as impression formation, interpersonal communication, relational communication, and organizational communication. The mass communication chapter in that volume (Reeves, Chaffee, & Tims, 1982) is of central interest for this chapter given our focus on news (conveyed via mass media) and politics (which has, until the past decade or so, been primarily concerned with mass rather than interpersonal communication).

Reeves et al. (1982) were in a somewhat awkward position writing a chapter on mass communication for the Roloff and Berger book. The definition of social cognition set forth by that volume's authors was "the organized thoughts people have about human interaction" (p. 21). This definition makes the connection between social cognition and various forms of interpersonal interaction (mediated or otherwise) at the dyadic, small group, or organizational level obvious, but the relevance of traditional mass communication such as news and fictional entertainment is less clear. Realizing their position, Reeves et al. offered an alternative definition by dividing social cognition into "social *cognition*" (essentially a broadly cognitive approach to mass communication scholarship) and "*social* cognition" (the Roloff and Berger definition with a focus on cognitions about people). Much of the chapter focused on work that would fit the former definition but not the latter given the nature of mass communication research at the time. Thus, Reeves et al.

(1982) argued that "Since the interests of mass communication researchers obviously do not parallel the interests of personality psychologists, we should not be anxious to limit the application of cognitive models to social information" (p. 294).

Regarding social *cognition,* it was evident that scholars in political communication had been active for quite some time. In 1975, for instance, Becker, McCombs, and McLeod (1975) had written about "The Development of Political Cognitions," noting that research in political communication had already begun a transition by focusing on cognitive outcomes of mass media such as learning, socialization, and agenda setting. But, as Reeves et al. (1982) cautioned, "The research in social cognition is not directed at single *cognitive consequences* of exposure to stimuli, but at the *cognitive processes* that cause these results. This level of theorizing is not common in mass communication research" (p. 291).

Nonetheless, Reeves et al. (1982) were able to identify a number of lines of research in mass communication that fit their expanded definition of social cognition. However, in the realm of news and politics the pickings were rather slim. There were almost no references to work having been done in this area (at least not by communication scholars) fitting the label of social cognition. However, the Reeves et al. chapter did address a number of research areas that are at least relevant to news and politics, including differences in processing of various media, the effects of motivations on processing and learning, and socialization effects of media.

THEORETICAL AND METHODOLOGICAL DEVELOPMENTS SINCE 1982

In examining the trends in social cognition research in the domain of news and politics, we follow Reeves et al. (1982) by stressing social *cognition* and in particular cognitive processes. That is, we do not constrain ourselves by focusing solely on political communication and cognitions about people, nor do we focus broadly on cognitive outcomes. Although work in this more *social* cognition area has flourished since 1982, much of the relevant research is addressed more fully in other chapters (e.g., Oliver, Ramasubramanian, & Kim, chap. 12, this volume; Shrum, chap. 11, this volume).

Therefore, we focus our review on the developments in the political communication literature that have been most heavily influenced by cognitive psychological concepts that serve as the foundation of social cognition scholarship. This work addresses how information is stored in the mind, and includes theories of associative networks and schemas. From these broad models of human cognition comes an understanding of how information processing takes place (including concepts such as accessibility and the use of heuristics), more broadly notions of limited cognitive capacity, and the influence of emotion. We focus on the impact these concepts and the theories that employ them have had in political communication. By necessity, our review is selective, and we focus on work in a given area (e.g., agenda setting) that has been particularly influenced by the social cognition approach, ignoring other work in the same area if it has not approached the topic from a social cognition perspective. The areas of political communication that we address include processing of and learning from media, the influence of news on perceptions of opinion climates, agenda setting, media priming, framing effects, and the role of expertise or sophistication as a moderator of many of these effects.

IMPACT OF NEWS MEDIA ON KNOWLEDGE, PERCEPTIONS, AND BELIEFS

In this section, we focus on research on how individuals acquire various sorts of information from news media. Research on learning from the news addresses the recognition or recall of factual information derived from news texts. Work on perceptions of opinion climates addresses the role of the media in communicating public attitudes toward various issues or politicians. Finally, scholarship on agenda setting examines the impact of media coverage on public perceptions of which issues are the most important ones facing society.

Learning From the News

In the mid-1980s, several papers were published arguing for an information processing approach to the study of news and learning (Kellermann, 1985; Woodall, 1986; Woodall, Davis, & Sahin, 1983). These calls appear to have gotten a positive reception, as work on the effects of various content and structural factors of television news has tended to adopt the social cognition approach. Unfortunately, most of the experimental research has focused on television news to the exclusion of newspapers. The reason for this is not entirely clear, but likely has to do with issues of individual-level control over newspaper reading that make it more difficult to study.

Researchers from the experimental paradigm have examined the impact of numerous structural and content features to understand their impact on information processing and learning. The common theme in this work is the notion of limited cognitive capacity and how it is allocated based on structural or content features in the news (see Lang, 2000). The research generally assumes that some processing is automatic and thus does not require limited resources, whereas other processing is controlled or effortful and does consume resources. It also assumes that content and structural features of news media may encourage or require more or less attentional resources for processing, and that this has implications for recall. Scholars have examined the impact of variables such as story organization (Eveland, Marton, & Seo, 2004; Lang, 1989) and the use of cuts (Lang, Geiger, Strickwerda, & Sumner, 1993), tabloid production features (Grabe, Lang, & Zhao, 2003), live reports (Snoeijer, de Vreese, & Semetko, 2002), and news teasers (Cameron, Schleuder, & Thorson, 1991; Chang, 1998) on television news processing and learning.

Although research on structural features of television news and news characteristics such as teasers and live reports have been the object of study, two areas of research related to attentional capacity seem to be most prominent in the experimental paradigm of news learning research. The first is the effect of audiovisual correspondence and the second is the impact of negative images in the news. Regarding audiovisual correspondence, researchers have generally found that when the audio and visual messages in a television newscast conflict with one another or are simply not redundant, learning of the audio portion of the message can suffer (Brosius, Donsbach, & Birk, 1996; Drew & Grimes, 1987; Grimes, 1990, 1991; Lang, 1995; Reese, 1984; Son, Reese, & Davie, 1987). One possible reason for this effect is that nonredundant video and audio can produce an overload in the information processing system compared to audio-only or audio with redundant video, and this overload reduces the ability to recognize or recall the information presented in the audio channel (Lang, 1995). Another explanation is that consistent audiovisual messages enhance learning. This explanation is based on Paivio's (1971) dual coding hypothesis, which implies that when redundancy is high, recall of television news should be greater because the information is stored in both visual and verbal form in memory and thus becomes more accessible through a larger number of cues. By contrast, when the visual and verbal codes in television news do not correspond, no such positive effect for television over print would be observed.

This research has important implications because television news producers often "wallpaper" stories with at best semirelevant video even when it is not necessary to convey the information in the story. Some scholars (Walma van der Molen & van der Voort, 2000) have argued that the use of nonredundant video in experiments comparing the relative effectiveness of television news versus newspapers might explain the common finding of more learning from print. Others (Eveland, Seo, & Marton, 2002) have pointed out that because verbal–visual correspondence is in reality often low in television news (see

Graber, 1990), the effects of television news in the real world are unlikely to be superior to those of print media. This all suggests that low recall of television news stories may not be inherent to the medium, but instead could be altered by encouraging news producers to design newscasts to work with and not against human information processing realities (Graber, 2001; Lang, Potter, & Grabe, 2003).

The second dominant area of research related to attentional capacity and learning addresses the interaction between negative images and cognition. The impact of negative video compared to neutral video appears to depend in part on what aspect of news learning one is addressing—audio or visual memory, and memory of information before, during, or after the negative video. Negative video decreases memory for verbal information immediately preceding it (Lang, Newhagen, & Reeves, 1996; Newhagen & Reeves, 1992), but memory results during or after negative video are mixed (Lang et al., 1996; Mundorf, Drew, Zillmann, & Weaver, 1990; Newhagen & Reeves, 1992), potentially in part due to the time lag examined in each study and the nature of the memory measures employed. Delayed recall of factual information appears to favor stories without compelling negative images (Newhagen & Reeves, 1992).

Beyond helping to specify the aspects of television news that can encourage and discourage processing and memory (Lang et al., 2003) and helping to develop a theory of media processing (Lang, 2000), research from the experimental paradigm has served as a conduit through which new methodological procedures have flowed into media research. Among these are (a) secondary-task reaction time measures, which tap residual attentional resources not being used in the primary media processing task (e.g., Cameron et al., 1991); (b) heart rate measures that serve as operationalizations of orienting responses and thus direction of attentional resources (Lang et al., 1993); and (c) measures of skin conductance that tap arousal (Grabe, Lang, Zhou, & Bolls, 2000).

In addition to work from an experimental paradigm, survey researchers studying news media and learning have made attempts to ground their work in social cognition. In the mid-1980s, survey researchers began to realize that simple exposure might not be sufficient for learning from the news, and that a better (or at least complementary) measure would be the level of attention one paid to the news (e.g., Chaffee & Schleuder, 1986; McLeod & McDonald, 1985). Moving beyond attention, scholars then began to experiment with other measures derived from research on human information processing. Uses and gratifications researchers developed measures of audience activity (Levy, 1983), including cognitive activities like elaboration (Eveland, 2001; Perse, 1990), that were generally found to predict learning of news information. Others looked more broadly to self-reported information processing strategies (Kosicki & McLeod, 1990; Eveland, 2005), including selective scanning and reflective integration. Today it is uncommon to find survey research on news learning that does not at least include measures of news attention, but additional measures of information processing appear only occasionally.

Perceptions of Opinion Climates

Central to the more "social" notion of social cognition and news is the role of the news in how individuals perceive others. One important effect of news is in the development of stereotypes as addressed by Oliver et al. (chap. 12, this volume), and another is the impact of media generally and news specifically on perceptions of social reality (Shrum, chap. 11, this volume). A subset of these social reality assessments is particularly important in the area of news and politics: assessments of opinion distributions on public issues.

A number of scholars have discussed the potential role of news media in communicating information about what have been called *opinion climates,* most prominently among them Noelle-Neumann (1993). Noelle-Neuman argued that perceptions of the climate of opinion may come from either direct experience (i.e., interpersonal discussion) or through generally implicit cues in news media. Subsequently researchers have demonstrated that manipulations of representations of the climate of opinion in surveys (Moreno-Riaño, 2002) or via news reports (Gunther, 1998) can influence perceptions of public opinion.

Scholars also have examined how particular features or cues in the news may influence estimates of the climate of opinion. One distinction that has been made is between the effectiveness of base-rate information versus exemplars in news coverage in influencing perceptions of the climate of opinion. Base-rate information is statistical or factual information about opinion distributions, such as results of public opinion polls. This sort of information is often the subject of news coverage, especially the use of public opinion polls and "horse race" coverage in news coverage of election campaigns (Larson, 1999). Exemplars include examples, stories, and other anecdotal information that is used to illustrate base-rate information (Gibson & Zillmann, 1994) and is also a very common aspect of news coverage. The concern arises when conclusions drawn from base-rate information would be different from conclusions drawn from the distribution of exemplars in a given story—something that is not uncommon (Larson, 1999). Instances in which the distribution of exemplars does not reflect base-rate information may be the result of news bias or mere happenstance. Nonetheless, the more valid information is normally base-rate information, and so base-rate information would be the ideal basis for individuals to use in developing perceptions of opinion climates.

Using the terminology of the elaboration likelihood model (ELM; Petty & Priester, 1994), base-rate information may serve as central cues whereas exemplars may serve as peripheral cues (Perry & Gonzenbach, 1997). Put another way, individuals may use exemplars as heuristics to infer the climate of opinion instead of using the actual base-rate information. Research does in fact suggest that individuals are more likely to employ the peripheral cue of exemplar distribution when drawing conclusions (Daschmann, 2000; Perry & Gonzenbach, 1997). This can lead to a state of shared misperceptions (i.e., pluralistic ignorance) induced by the media because perceptions of the dominant opinion derived from exemplars are inconsistent with the actual dominant opinion as indicated by base-rate information.

Agenda Setting

Theories of the agenda-setting function of the news media (McCombs & Shaw, 1972) assume that news media must select some issues to present to the public to the exclusion of other issues, and this selective presentation of issues leads individuals to perceive the presented issues as more salient or important than those not presented. Agenda-setting research has contributed to a shifting focus of political communication from attitudinal and behavioral effects to cognitive effects of the media. That is, from the beginning, agenda-setting studies have focused on more subtle cognitive aspects of media effects compared to direct persuasion or behavioral outcomes.

Most early agenda-setting studies compared media agendas derived from content analysis with public agendas (e.g., What is the "most important problem" facing the country?) derived from sample surveys. In the mid-1980s, Iyengar and his colleagues (Behr & Iyengar, 1985; Iyengar & Kinder, 1987; Iyengar, Peters, & Kinder, 1982) worked to integrate agenda-setting findings with psychological theory. They not only provided some empirical support for agenda-setting effects at the individual as opposed to aggregate level, but also suggested a cognitive mechanism through which agenda-setting effects may occur.

According to Iyengar (1990), the accessibility bias is the fundamental cognitive process through which media influence public agendas. Based on work regarding the use of judgmental heuristics, he proposed that the agenda setting effect is a demonstration of general human "inclination to overvalue 'salient' evidence" (Iyengar et al., 1982, p. 855). Based on what Nisbett and Ross (1980) called the availability (not accessibility) heuristic, individuals make judgments about the frequency of events based on the availability of instances of those events for retrieval from memory. Extending this logic, Iyengar argued that prominent issues on the media agenda would be considered comparatively important by the public because these issues could be more easily retrieved from the memory. Thus, sheer frequency and repetition as well as prominent placement of issues in the news coverage (e.g., lead stories) could be a critical determinant of individual accessibility. This, in turn, influences the individual's perception of the importance of those issues.

In addition to Iyengar's approach to agenda setting, other scholars proposed alternative models derived either implicitly or explicitly from social cognition (Brosius & Kepplinger, 1990; Watt, Mazza, & Snyder, 1993; Zhu, Watt, Snyder, Yan, & Jiang, 1993). For instance, Watt et al. (1993) offered an "accumulated declining coverage effects" model of agenda setting, focusing on the memory decay process of individuals. Research on memory has generally indicated that memory decays exponentially, with most information forgotten soon after exposure and then remaining information slowly forgotten over time. However as the term *exponential* implies, the remaining memory for a given bit of information nears but never reaches zero. This exponential memory decay process generates an interesting but complicated model of agenda setting effects that requires a consideration of time lags between coverage and public perception. Having not taken memory decay into account, traditional agenda-setting studies assumed that agenda-setting effects should be linearly accumulated with increases in media coverage. When memory decay is accounted for, an expected model of accumulated agenda-setting effects would be nonlinear.

As mentioned before, most agenda-setting researchers have favored a cross-sectional survey approach. Yet recent studies have employed a longitudinal approach and time-series analysis to study agenda setting using macrolevel public opinion data (Smith, 1987; Soroka, 2002; Wanta & Foote, 1994; Zhu et al., 1993). What is most interesting is that these aggregate data were in some cases used to test microlevel processes like memory decay (Watt et al., 1993).

ATTITUDINAL EFFECTS OF NEWS MEDIA

Early research in political communication had concluded that the effects of the news media on attitudes and opinions were minimal. This led to a transition toward the study of cognitive effects, including agenda setting and learning. However, new theories of how news media could influence attitudes through cognitive processes emerged in the 1980s and 1990s. Most prominent among these were theories of media priming and framing effects.

Media Priming

The psychological concept of priming has been applied to various domains of media effects research. Research on priming has been particularly prominent in the domains of media sex and violence (Anderson, 1997; Anderson, Anderson, & Deuser, 1996; Bushman, 1988; Hansen, 1989; Hansen & Hansen, 1990; Josephson, 1987), but we do not address that research in this chapter. Instead, we focus on research on media priming in political communication scholarship for which the outcome variable is general evaluations of politicians.

Although it was not the first discussion of the topic, Iyengar and Kinder's (1987) *News That Matters* popularized the notion of media priming effects in the domain of politics. In a series of experiments, they found that when news media emphasized a specific issue (as in agenda setting), individuals were more likely to evaluate the president's general performance based on the specific evaluation of the president on that particular issue. Put differently, the relative weight given to an issue-specific evaluation of the president as a predictor of the overall evaluation of the president was found to vary based on how prominent that issue had been in the news. Thus, they defined media priming effects as "changes in the standards that people use to make political evaluations" (Iyengar & Kinder, 1987, p. 63). Similarly, Roskos-Ewoldsen and his colleagues labeled media priming as "the effects of the content of the media on people's later behavior or judgments related to the content" (Roskos-Ewoldsen, Roskos-Ewoldsen, & Carpentier, 2002, p. 97).

Since Iyengar and Kinder's (1987) original studies—which despite claims of powerful and consistent findings were actually quite mixed using standard judgments of statistical significance—other political communication researchers have accumulated empirical support for media priming effects (Domke, Shah, & Wackman, 1998; Krosnick & Kinder, 1990; McGraw & Ling, 2003; Pan & Kosicki, 1997; Valentino, 1999; Valentino, Traugott, & Hutchings, 2002). They have also worked to specify the underlying mechanisms involved in the media priming process and different conditions affecting the magnitude of media priming effects.

Controversies regarding the cognitive mechanism involved in the media priming process have been centered on competing approaches to the accessibility model (Iyengar, 1990) that has been employed in both agenda setting and priming research. Based on an associative network model of human memory (Collins & Loftus, 1975; Taylor & Fiske, 1978), the accessibility model in general assumes that political attitudes are stored in the form of nodes in the node-link structure of human memory. When a node is activated by some stimuli—such as a news report—it may remain active for some relatively short period of time, and thus increase the probability that related thoughts could be activated. This short-term increase in the activation of a node due to stimulation is called temporary accessibility, and it is the foundation of Iyengar and Kinder's (1987) explanation of media priming effects. The logic is that specific attitudes that are accessible in memory at the time a political judgment is made (e.g., Do I or don't I approve of the job George W. Bush is doing as president?) will be more heavily relied on in making that judgment than other equally relevant specific attitudes that have not been recently activated and thus are not as accessible.

Iyengar and Kinder's (1987) temporary accessibility model of media priming effects has been confronted with a number of critiques. Roskos-Ewoldsen et al. (2002) claimed that changes in temporary accessibility as assumed by Iyengar and Kinder for both priming and agenda setting are too transient to generate meaningful changes in opinions. Pointing out that previous studies of political priming have shown more enduring effects, they are skeptical of Iyengar and Kinder's assertion that the media priming effect is identical to the sort of priming effects studied by psychologists (Roskos-Ewoldsen et al., 2002). They suggest that only changes in chronic accessibility—when concepts are always accessible due to repeated activation over time (Bargh, Bond, Lombardi, & Tota, 1986)—could generate such relatively long-term effects (see also Pan & Kosicki, 1997; Price & Tewksbury, 1997). Miller and Krosnick (2000) demonstrated that temporary accessibility does not mediate media priming effects.

Although media priming researchers have favored laboratory experiments over surveys, some scholars have extended priming research to survey designs (e.g., Krosnick & Brannon, 1993; Krosnick & Kinder, 1990; Pan & Kosicki, 1997). In the surveys, instead of a priming condition moderating the effects of issue-specific evaluations on general evaluations, typically either time of interview (a measure of natural variation on issue attention in the media) or news media exposure (a measure of amount of contact with a given issue in the media) are employed as measured moderator variables. Then, either formal or informal content analyses are conducted to determine which issues were heavily covered in the news at a particular point in time. By employing data from both surveys and content analyses of news content, researchers can indirectly demonstrate the impact of media attention on certain issues and the impact of attitudes regarding those issues on general evaluations of politicians.

Framing Effects

The concept of framing in political communication research has multiple theoretical origins ranging from social interactionism (Goffman, 1974) and news discourse research (Gitlin, 1980), to cognitive psychology (Tversky & Kahneman, 1973). Reflecting these diverse research traditions, framing has been defined variously, such as news media templates for covering issues (Iyengar, 1991; Price & Tewksbury, 1997), symbolic constructions of issues that partisans use to influence public opinion

(Gamson, 1992; Snow & Benford, 1992), depictions of decision alternatives as a certain reference point such as a "gain" and a "loss" (Kahneman & Tversky, 1984), and personal cognitive maps of issues that individuals use to make sense of politics (Berinsky & Kinder, 2000). Despite the multiple sources of influence on framing research in political communication, it is hard to deny that research on the effects of framing in the media has been significantly influenced by the social cognition approach.

Framing effects roughly refer to the effects of different methods of issue presentation—using different rhetorical devices (Nelson, 2004) or taking different perspectives on the same factual information—on individuals' responses. Since the early 1990s, framing effects have emerged as a central area of research in political communication. Framing research has evolved around three related themes: (a) identifying framing effects on individuals' political judgments, issue interpretations, and other cognitive consequences; (b) understanding the cognitive process through which framing effects occur; and recently, (c) identification of contingent conditions for framing effects.

One hallmark of framing effects research is the identification of different or competing frames in the news, and then the use of manipulated news coverage using one or the other frame to test for effects of different frames on opinions or cognitions. For instance, Iyengar (1991) manipulated television news stories to employ either an episodic (focused on individual instances to represent a broad theme, much like exemplars) or thematic (using over time or aggregate data, much like base-rate information) frame. His evidence, although mixed, showed some impact of varying the frame on experimental participants' attribution of responsibility for the social problem addressed in the newscast. Episodic frames led individuals to blame individuals and see individuals as the locus of solving the problem, whereas thematic frames led to assessment of blame on society or the government and subsequent expectations of governmental responsibility for solving the problem.

Another series of noteworthy framing studies were conducted by Cappella and Jamieson (1997). These researchers made the distinction between issue frames and strategy frames. Issue frames address a topic by privileging information on policy proposals and issue information, whereas strategy frames focus on the horse race, the self-interest of politicians (getting elected), and political tactics employed to gain advantage. Overall, their findings comparing the effects of issue versus strategy frames in political news coverage suggested that the strategy frame enhanced political cynicism (see also Rhee, 1997). Other research suggests that different framing of the issue could influence the individual's issue position or issue-related policy judgment (Domke, 2001; Domke, McCoy, & Torres, 1999; Nelson, Clawson, & Oxley, 1997; Shah, Domke, & Wackman, 1996).

Beyond the usual attitudinal or opinion dependent variables in framing effects research, more recent studies have examined the impact of framing on other cognitive concepts such as cognitive complexity and mental representation. For instance, Shah, Kwak, Schmierbach, and Zubric (2004) demonstrated that some frames could produce more complicated mental structures than alternative frames (see also Berinsky & Kinder, 2000). Valkenburg, Semetko, and de Vreese (1999) found that exposure to differently framed news stories influenced readers' ability to recall the information presented in these stories. They found that those exposed to the human interest news frame had lower recall than those exposed to conflict, responsibility, or economic consequences frames.

As for agenda-setting and priming effects, the associative network model is highly relevant to framing effects studies. Most researchers explicitly or implicitly follow the accessibility model proposed by Iyengar (1991) or the applicability model of Price and Tewksbury (1997). Iyengar (1991) first argued that framing is mediated by concept accessibility, the same essential mechanism he believes underlies agenda-setting, priming, bandwagon, and cultivation effects. According to Iyengar, frames bring certain concepts, ideas, and feelings to the forefront of consciousness, where they are likely to affect subsequent opinions and judgments. The virtue of Iyengar's model is its parsimony, but that also could be its shortcoming. Although surely a great deal of communication phenomena can be understood as accessibility effects, many scholars believe that there are important differences among framing, agenda setting, and other kinds of communication effects and so they should not all be reduced to a single psychological explanation (e.g., Scheufele, 2000). Moreover, Iyengar's accessibility model of framing effects is susceptible to the same criticism aimed at its use in explaining priming and agenda setting (Roskos-Ewoldsen et al., 2002).

Price and Tewksbury (1997) also reported that "knowledge activation" mediated a number of communication effects (including agenda setting, priming, and framing), again relying on an underlying associative network model. However, according to their model, frames alter the applicability of knowledge about an issue stored in long-term memory. In other words, frames affect the perceived overlap or match between the attended features of a stimulus and stored knowledge (Hardin & Rothman, 1997; Higgins, 1996). Consequently, activated knowledge has a strong likelihood of influencing opinions, if it is both accessible in memory and applicable to the issue at hand (Higgins, 1996). Price and Tewksbury (1997) distinguished such processes from the psychological process of priming, in which stored knowledge temporarily becomes more accessible in memory. Despite their differences, both the accessibility model of Iyengar (1991) and the applicability model of Price and Tewksbury (1997) are based on the same basic associative network model of human memory.

On the other hand, Nelson and his colleagues (Nelson, Clawson, & Oxley, 1997; Nelson & Oxley, 1999; Nelson, Oxley, & Clawson, 1997) argued that framing effects are not mediated by accessibility (at least not temporary accessibility) but instead by an importance comparison among applicable considerations. They conducted a critical test between two competing models of framing effects and showed that accessibility measured in terms of reaction time did not mediate the framing effects. Instead framing tilted the balance among applicable considerations, which in turn influenced later decision making.

Framing effects are not without limits. Recipients actively filter incoming information based on their values, knowledge, interest, and experience. Several recent studies have shown that framing effects could be limited to certain conditions or groups. Druckman (2001), for example, indicated that framing effects were limited when the news source was not believed to be credible, and framing effects are not long term and are significantly weakened by interpersonal communication occurring after exposure to the frame (Druckman & Nelson, 2003). On the other hand, aspects of the individual's preexisting outlook that match the media frame could enhance the strength of framing effects (Gross, 2000; Haider-Markel & Joslyn, 2001).

Given the heavy influence of cognitive psychology in framing effects research, it is no surprise that scholars tend to work within a laboratory experimental paradigm. However, researchers also have extended framing research to survey designs with experimental manipulations (Haider-Markel & Joslyn, 2001; Nelson & Kinder, 1996; Shah et al., 2004) to help resolve issues of generalizability in laboratory experiments with students. In this approach, survey respondents are randomly assigned to different framing conditions by changing introductions to questions or question wordings before completing the dependent measures. In this way, researchers can gain the generalizability benefits of representative surveys while ensuring exposure to different frames and having the ability to draw clear causal conclusions. However, these studies are no longer truly studies of news media effects because telephone surveys cannot expose responses to television or print news media content. New approaches that combine the best of each approach are discussed later in the section on future directions.

EXPERTISE AS AN IMPORTANT MODERATOR OF NEWS MEDIA EFFECTS

Theory and research on knowledge organization and information processing has had an important impact on political communication scholarship. Political scientists had for years been concerned with how people thought about politics (e.g., Converse, 1964). However, it was not until the early 1980s that scholars really began to make use of psychological theory regarding knowledge organization and expertise to refine their theories of political thinking (see Lau & Sears, 1986). These theories are now being used to help understand how individuals process news media content and what effects news content has on learning and opinion. It turns out that one key moderator of many types of media effects, from learning to persuasion, may be political sophistication or expertise.

A volume could be filled discussing the consistencies and inconsistencies in conceptualizing and operationalizing concepts such as sophistication and expertise in this literature (Luskin, 1987; Wyckoff, 1987). Nonetheless, most operationalizations include at least some measure of factual knowledge and many include nothing more than a measure of factual knowledge. Given this, it should be no surprise that one of the most common findings is that prior expertise facilitates learning of new information (e.g., Fiske, Lau, & Smith, 1990; Rhee & Cappella, 1997). This finding is closely related to research on the knowledge gap, which predicts that those of higher socioeconomic status (SES) will learn information from media campaigns more quickly than those of low SES (Tichenor, Donohue, & Olien, 1970). Although the knowledge gap began as a primarily macrolevel theory, since its inception scholars have attacked this topic with psychological explanations. For instance, most surveys find that those high in SES—particularly education—are most likely to be political experts and have relatively high levels of political knowledge (Delli Carpini & Keeter, 1996). This simple transfer—from differential gain in knowledge based on SES or education to differential gain in knowledge based on prior knowledge or expertise, makes the knowledge gap amenable to an information processing explanation.

One explanation for the relation between expertise and learning is that expert knowledge structures are better organized and thus facilitate recall of new information (Fiske et al., 1990). Another explanation relates to how experts process incoming information. For instance, several studies have shown that experts generate more thoughts in response to news media than do novices (e.g., Fiske et al., 1990; Hsu & Price, 1993). These thoughts, sometimes known as elaborations, are important predictors of learning news content. Using panel data, Eveland, Shah, and Kwak (2003) demonstrated that political knowledge at one time point predicts cognitive elaboration on news content at a later time point controlling prior measures of news elaboration. Likewise, elaboration on news at one time point predicts political knowledge at a later time point, controlling prior knowledge. This suggests a spiral process of reciprocal influence between prior knowledge (expertise) and new learning through elaboration, and provides one psychological explanation for changes in knowledge gaps over time.

Although early experiments on media priming suggested that differences in political sophistication were largely irrelevant to priming effects (Iyengar & Kinder, 1987), subsequent studies have suggested that sophistication does matter. However, the evidence regarding whether sophistication increases or decreases media priming effects has been inconsistent. Whereas some researchers argue (and find) that novices are more vulnerable to priming effects (Iyengar, Peters, Kinder, & Krosnick, 1984; Krosnick & Kinder, 1990), others argue that priming effects are greatest among the most knowledgeable, as long as they have trust in the source of the appeal (Miller & Krosnick, 2000).

These conflicting theoretical explanations seem to stem from unresolved debates during the 1980s and 1990s over potentially different information processing strategies employed by political experts and novices. Findings of stronger priming effects on experts relied on the argument that they were more likely to engage in systematic and data-driven processing of political messages and also better able to interpret and use information when making decisions (Kuklinski, Metlay, & Kay, 1982). For instance, Fiske, Kinder, and Larter (1983) reported that political experts were better at processing and recalling information that was inconsistent with activated schema. Likewise, Sniderman, Brody, and Tetlock (1991) showed that the uninformed were more likely to use likeability heuristics than the informed.

Others believe that politically knowledgeable individuals are more likely to follow theory-based and heuristic information processing (Fiske et al., 1990). Because political experts have well-developed cognitive structures, they could be more sensitive to political cues. At the same time, experts are more likely to develop their own habitual or chronic shortcuts to make political decisions. McGraw, Lodge, and Stroh (1990) reported that political experts are more likely to engage in online processing and judgment formation. Findings that political experts are more sensitive to priming effects could rely on this line of argument (McGraw & Ling, 2003). As pointed out earlier, the role that political sophistication plays in the priming effects process is still unclear (McGraw, 2000). The confusing results may be at least partly due to the diverse conceptualizations and operationalizations of political sophistication to which we have already alluded.

PROJECTED TRENDS IN THE STUDY OF NEWS AND POLITICS

Although it is difficult to project how the social cognition perspective will alter the study of news and politics in the coming years, there are a number of theoretical and methodological trends that are likely to have a significant impact. On the theoretical side, most of the work in news and politics has been influenced by theories of associative networks (e.g., Collins & Loftus, 1975). However, more recent models of human memory, variously called connectionist or parallel distributed processing models (McClelland, 1988; McClelland & Rumelhart, 1985), are becoming more prominent in cognitive psychology and beginning to have an impact on work in social psychology (Smith, 1996; Smith & Queller, 2004). The implications of these models for research in communication are not yet clear, but it is possible that connectionist models may provide some new insights into how individuals process and store information that could change existing theories of news and politics that are based on the more traditional semantic associative network models.

Methodologically, one trend is the increasing use of experimental designs in the study of political communication. These designs—either in the form of traditional laboratory experiments or experiments embedded in traditional probability surveys (e.g., Mutz, 1998; Sniderman & Grob, 1996)—are important given the previous dominance of cross-sectional survey designs to test hypotheses in past political communication research. The increasing use of Web-based survey techniques introduces a number of possibilities to further integrate surveys and experiments by automating the delivery of audiovisual experimental stimuli into Web-based surveys (Birnbaum, 2004).

Despite the increasing role of experiments, however, even survey researchers have been working to employ more social cognition concepts like attention and elaboration in their studies (e.g., Eveland, 2001; Fredin, Kosicki, & Becker, 1996; McLeod & McDonald, 1985). Moreover, researchers are working to develop more complex and satisfying measures of cognitive structure using survey approaches. For instance, Eveland et al. (2004) used closed-ended measurements of concept similarity in conjunction with analytical methods from network analysis to tap a concept called knowledge structure density. Using open-ended responses, Shah et al. (2004) employed a cognitive mapping approach to measure cognitive complexity.

As already discussed, within experimental designs measures of physiological responses to news, including skin conductance and heart rate, are becoming more and more common (see Ravaja, 2004, for a review). Their use is only likely to increase in the future as new scholars are trained in their use and the research evidence regarding their validity and practicality continues to accumulate. Given that these measures are not under the conscious control of individuals and thus are not susceptible to social desirability effects—and given that they are susceptible to very short-term variation in response to stimuli—researchers should continue to expand the use of these measures into other areas of research on news and politics.

One final area of research that could transform the study of news and politics is the recent work on cognitive neuroscience. In just the past few years, a number of scholars have attempted to connect research on brain functioning to social and political cognition (Blakemore, Winston, & Frith, 2004; Graber, 2001; Lieberman, Schreiber, & Ochsner, 2003; Raichle, 2003). Realistically, it is unlikely that the use of neuroscience methods, including functional magnetic resonance imaging studies, will become common in the study of news and politics, if for no other reason than the expense of the equipment and the training required to use it appropriately. On the other hand, it is also unlikely that researchers studying in the area of news and politics will be able to ignore the implications of brain research. The greatest potential of cognitive neuroscience for the study of news and politics is linking our theories of information processing and cognition with actual physiological traces in the brain.

HOW DOES THE STUDY OF NEWS AND POLITICS COMPLEMENT OTHER AREAS OF DISCIPLINE?

We began this chapter noting that, using a traditional definition of social cognition, only a small subset of the research in news and politics that has been influenced by cognitive psychology would be fair game. Instead, we adopted the perspective of Reeves et al. (1982) that the impact of media (and in particular news media) on cognitions about other people or human interaction should not be considered theoretically separate from the impact of media on many other types of cognitions. This, we think, is one of the major contributions of work in the domain of news and politics; that a cognitive approach to both social and nonsocial (although socially constructed) objects can be fruitful.

Given this perspective, the research on news and politics from a social cognition perspective begins by putting social cognition into a truly macrosocial context. Politics has been defined as "a process whereby a group of people, whose opinions or interests are initially divergent, reach collective decisions which are generally regarded as binding on the group, and enforced as common policy" (Miller, 1987, p. 390). Thus, the study of news media effects on thinking about politics inherently links individual cognitive processes to the collective. More important, these individual cognitive processes are likely to have important implications for the well-being of the collective, including how informed it is and the basis of public opinion (which often drives public policy; see Monroe, 1998; Page & Shapiro, 1983) and voting decisions. Therefore, the research and theory discussed in this chapter helps us understand how cognitive processes might influence public policy and ultimately human history. To ignore this aspect of social cognition research by excluding it from the definition, then, would be a grave mistake.

POTENTIAL METHODOLOGICAL PITFALLS

Every area of research, and every specific research technique, has not only strengths but weaknesses. Often, the weaknesses are the flip side of the strength coin, and this is particularly true in the study of news and politics from a social cognition perspective. The attempt to transfer more micro and cognitive theory and research to a social level in an important context such as politics often leads researchers out of the laboratory to test theory in more generalizable contexts, including the study of public opinion in large, nationally representative samples. Thus, survey research has become one important approach for testing social cognition theories of political communication. This movement from micro, and often short-term, cognitive processes to a survey context can present researchers with a number of difficulties, among them problems of temporal consistency, measurement validity, and reactivity. We address each of these in turn.

When survey researchers ask about political communication behaviors, they typically ask individuals to report either typical behaviors or specific behaviors in some relatively wide time frame, whether that be over the course of a political campaign, during the past month, or shorter periods such as a week or a day. However, many of the theories we have addressed specify processes of communication and cognition that are based on substantially shorter time frames. For example, the notion of priming is a very short-term process, but researchers have examined it using panel survey data gathered over 6 months (Krosnick & Brannon, 1993), making the true theoretical connection to priming ambiguous. Others have attempted to model what in the psychological literature are considered short-term motivational and cognitive processes involved in learning using panel data with a 6-month time lag (Eveland et al., 2003). Thus, whereas theoretically our independent and dependent variables may vary in very short time increments, survey methods are unable to capture this sort of variation well. Thus, when employing survey methods researchers often must settle for what amounts to between-subject variation (individual differences) as opposed to over time within-subjects variation that is really more consistent with our theories. This is not to say that survey research is not valuable, but merely that researchers must be explicit about the temporal fit between theoretical concepts and the variables that are being measured.

Another issue is the ability of survey research to validly tap cognitive and motivational variables. For some time now scholars have debated the ability of respondents to self-report cognitive processes or to distinguish when they can and cannot reasonably do so (e.g., Nisbett & Wilson, 1977; Smith & Miller, 1978). There have also been questions raised about the ability of individuals to accurately report relatively nonsalient behaviors to survey researchers (Tourangeau, Rips, & Rasinski, 2000), among which may be various forms of interpersonal and mass-mediated communication. There are also potentially serious problems in measuring concepts such as political sophistication, expertise, and knowledge using traditional survey techniques (see Eveland et al., 2004, for a recent discussion). These concerns point to the need for more thorough validation—and a better understanding of the psychometric properties—of our survey measures than is the norm in the study of political communication.

A related concern about survey measurement is that of reactivity. Public opinion researchers have known for decades that the wording of questions, the number of and order of response options, the labels of endpoints on scales, and the order of questions can all influence responses to questions (e.g., Price, 1993; Schuman & Presser, 1981). Given this, survey researchers studying communication must always question what influence the context and wording of questions and response alternatives might have on responses to specific questions (Price, 1993; Schwarz & Bienias, 1990; Wright, Gaskell, & O'Muircheartaigh, 1994), and on the relation among responses to specific questions throughout the survey (Lasorsa, 2003). Especially among those who study political priming using survey research, the ability of various aspects of surveys to prime some considerations over others is an important issue to consider, as we cannot study media as a source of priming without considering surveys as a source of priming.

CONCLUSION

Without a doubt there has been considerable growth in research on both *social* cognition and social *cognition* in the domain of news and politics during the past two decades. Despite this impressive growth and the advances made, we foresee even more impressive growth in the coming decades as scholars develop new methodological approaches and adopt continuing advances in cognitive psychology. There remain many avenues yet to be explored, and many debates yet to be settled. Here's to the next 20 years!

REFERENCES

Anderson, C. A. (1997). Effects of violent movies and trait hostility on hostile feelings and aggressive thoughts. *Aggressive Behavior, 23,* 161–178.

Anderson, C. A., Anderson, K. B., & Deuser, W. E. (1996). Examining an affective aggression framework: Weapon and temperature effects on aggressive thoughts, affect, and attitudes. *Personality and Social Psychology Bulletin, 22,* 366–376.

Bargh, J. A., Bond, R. N., Lombardi, W. J., & Tota, M. E. (1986). The additive nature of chronic and temporal sources of construct accessibility. *Journal of Personality and Social Psychology, 50,* 869–878.

Becker, L. B., McCombs, M. E., & McLeod, J. M. (1975). The development of political cognitions. In S. H. Chaffee (Ed.), *Political communication: Issues and strategies for research* (pp. 21–63). Beverly Hills, CA: Sage.

Behr, R. L., & Iyengar, S. (1985). Television news, real-world cues, and changes in the public agenda. *Public Opinion Quarterly, 49,* 38–57.

Berinsky, A. J., & Kinder, D. (2000, August/September). *Making sense of issues through frames: Understanding the Kosovo crisis.* Paper presented at the annual meeting of the American Political Science Association, Washington, DC.

Birnbaum, M. H. (2004). Human research and data collection via the Internet. *Annual Review of Psychology, 55,* 803–832.

Blakemore, S.-J., Winston, J., & Frith, U. (2004). Social cognitive neuroscience: Where are we heading? *TRENDS in Cognitive Sciences, 8,* 216–222.

Brosius, H.-B., Donsbach, W., & Birk, M. (1996). How do text–picture relations affect the informational effectiveness of television newscasts? *Journal of Broadcasting & Electronic Media, 40,* 180–195.

Brosius, H.-B., & Kepplinger, H. M. (1990). The agenda-setting function of television news: Static and dynamic views. *Communication Research, 17,* 183–211.

Bushman, B. J. (1988). Priming effects of media violence on the accessibility of aggressive constructs in memory. *Personality and Social Psychological Bulletin, 24,* 537–545.

Cameron, G. T., Schleuder, J., & Thorson, E. (1991). The role of news teasers in processing TV news and commercials. *Communication Research, 18,* 667–684.

Cappella, J. N., & Jamieson, K. H. (1997). *Spiral of cynicism: The press and the public good.* New York: Oxford University Press.

Chaffee, S. H., & Schleuder, J. (1986). Measurement and effects of attention to media news. *Human Communication Research, 13,* 76–107.

Chang, H.-C. (1998). The effect of news teasers in processing TV news. *Journal of Broadcasting & Electronic Media, 42,* 327–339.

Collins, A. M., & Loftus, E. F. (1975). A spreading-activation theory of semantic processing. *Psychological Review, 82,* 407–428.

Converse, P. E. (1964). The nature of belief systems in mass publics. In D. E. Apter (Ed.), *Ideology and discontent* (pp. 206–261). London: Collier-Macmillan.

Daschmann, G. (2000). Vox pop & polls: The impact of poll results and voter statements in the media on the perception of a climate of opinion. *International Journal of Public Opinion Research, 12,* 160–179.

Delli Carpini, M. X., & Keeter, S. (1996). *What Americans know about politics and why it matters.* New Haven, CT: Yale University Press.

Domke, D. (2001). Racial cues and political ideology: An examination of associative priming. *Communication Research, 28,* 772–801.

Domke, D., McCoy, K., & Torres, M. (1999). News media, racial perceptions and political cognition. *Communication Research, 26,* 570–607.

Domke, D., Shah, D. V., & Wackman, D. (1998). Media priming effects: Accessibility, association and activation. *International Journal of Public Opinion Research, 1,* 51–74.

Drew, D. G., & Grimes, T. (1987). Audio-visual redundancy and TV news recall. *Communication Research, 14,* 452–461.

Druckman, J. N. (2001). On the limits of framing effects: Who can frame? *Journal of Politics, 63,* 1041–1066.

Druckman, J. N., & Nelson, K. R. (2003). Framing and deliberation: How citizens' conversations limit elite influence. *American Journal of Political Science, 47,* 729–745.

Eveland, W. P., Jr. (2001). The cognitive mediation model of learning from the news: Evidence from non-election, off-year election, and presidential election contexts. *Communication Research, 28,* 571–601.

Eveland, W. P., Jr. (2005). Information-processing strategies in mass communication research. In S. Dunwoody, L. B. Becker, D. M. McLeod, & G. M. Kosicki (Eds.), *The evolution of key mass communication concepts: Honoring Jack McLeod* (pp. 217–248). Cresskill, NJ: Hampton.

Eveland, W. P., Jr., Marton, K., & Seo, M. (2004). Moving beyond "just the facts": The influence of online news on the content and structure of public affairs knowledge. *Communication Research, 31,* 82–108.

Eveland, W. P., Jr., Seo, M., & Marton, K. (2002). Learning from the news in campaign 2000: An experimental comparison of TV news, newspapers, and online news. *Media Psychology, 4,* 353–378.

Eveland, W. P., Jr., Shah, D. V., & Kwak, N. (2003). Assessing causality in the cognitive mediation model: A panel study of motivations, information processing, and learning during campaign 2000. *Communication Research, 30,* 359–386.

Fiske, S. T., Kinder, D. R., & Larter, W. M. (1983). The novice and the expert: Knowledge-based strategies in political cognition. *Journal of Experimental Social Psychology, 19,* 381–400.

Fiske, S. T., Lau, R. R., & Smith, R. A. (1990). On the varieties and utilities of political expertise. *Social Cognition, 8,* 31–48.

Fredin, E. S., Kosicki, G. M., & Becker, L. B. (1996). Cognitive strategies for media use during a presidential campaign. *Political Communication, 13,* 23–42.

Gamson, W. (1992). *Talking politics.* New York: Cambridge University Press.

Gibson, R., & Zillmann, D. (1994). Exaggerated versus representative exemplification in news reports: Perception of issues and personal consequences. *Communication Research, 21,* 603–624.

Gitlin, T. (1980). *The whole world is watching: Mass media in the making and unmaking of the new left.* Los Angeles: University of California Press.

Goffman, E. (1974). *Frame analysis: An essay on the organization of experience.* New York: Harper & Row.

Grabe, M. E., Lang, A., & Zhao, X. (2003). News content and form: Implications for memory and audience evaluations. *Communication Research, 30,* 387–413.

Grabe, M. E., Lang, A., Zhou, S., & Bolls, P. D. (2000). Cognitive access to negatively arousing news: An experimental investigation of the knowledge gap. *Communication Research, 27,* 3–26.

Graber, D. A. (1990). Seeing is remembering: How visuals contribute to learning from television news. *Journal of Communication, 40*(3), 134–155.

Graber, D. A. (2001). *Processing politics: Learning from television in the Internet age.* Chicago: University of Chicago Press.

Grimes, T. (1990). Audio-visual correspondence and its role in attention and memory. *Educational Technology Research and Development, 38*(3), 15–25.

Grimes, T. (1991). Mild auditory-visual dissonance in television news may exceed viewer attentional capacity. *Human Communication Research, 18,* 268–298.

Gross, K. A. (2000, April). *The limits of framing: How framing effects may be limited or enhanced by individual level predispositions.* Paper presented at the annual meeting of the Midwest Political Science Association, Chicago.

Gunther, A. C. (1998). The persuasive press inference: Effects of mass media on perceived public opinion. *Communication Research, 25,* 486–504.

Haider-Markel, D. P., & Joslyn, M. R. (2001). Gun policy, opinion, tragedy, and blame attribution: The conditional influence of issue frames. *Journal of Politics, 63,* 520–543.

Hansen, C. H. (1989). Priming sex role stereotypic event schemas with rock music videos: Effects on impression favorability, trait inferences, and recall of a subsequent male–female interaction. *Basic and Applied Social Psychology, 10,* 371–391.

Hansen, C. H., & Hansen, R. D. (1990). The influence of sex and violence on the appeal of rock music videos. *Communication Research, 17,* 212–234.

Hardin, C. D., & Rothman, A. J. (1997). Rendering accessible information relevant: The applicability of everyday life. In R. S. Wyer (Ed.), *Advances in social cognition: Vol. 10. The automaticity of everyday life* (pp. 143–156). Mahwah, NJ: Lawrence Erlbaum Associates.

Higgins, E. T. (1996). Knowledge accessibility and activation: Accessibility, applicability, and salience. In E. T. Higgins & A. W. Kruglanski (Eds.), *Social psychology: Handbook of basic principles* (pp. 133–168). New York: Guilford.

Hsu, M.-L., & Price, V. (1993). Political expertise and affect: Effects on news processing. *Communication Research, 20,* 671–695.

Iyengar, S. (1990). The accessibility bias in politics: Television news and public opinion. *International Journal of Public Opinion Research, 2,* 1–15.

Iyengar, S. (1991). *Is anyone responsible?* Chicago: University of Chicago Press.

Iyengar, S., & Kinder, D. R. (1987). *News that matters: Television and American opinion.* Chicago: University of Chicago Press.

Iyengar, S., Peters, M. D., & Kinder, D. R. (1982). Experimental demonstrations of the "not so minimal" consequences of television news programs. *American Political Science Review, 76,* 848–858.

Iyengar, S., Peters, M. D., Kinder, D. R., & Krosnick, J. A. (1984). The evening news and presidential evaluations. *Journal of Personality and Social Psychology, 46,* 778–787.

Josephson, W. L. (1987). Television violence and children's aggregation: Testing the priming, social script and disinhibition predictions. *Journal of Personality and Social Psychology, 53,* 882–890.

Kahneman, D., & Tversky, A. (1984). Choices, values, and frames. *American Psychologist, 39,* 341–350.

Kellermann, K. (1985). Memory processes in media effects. *Communication Research, 12,* 83–131.

Kosicki, G. M., & McLeod, J. M. (1990). Learning from political news: Effects of media images and information-processing strategies. In S. Kraus (Ed.), *Mass communication and political information processing* (pp. 69–83). Hillsdale, NJ: Lawrence Erlbaum Associates.

Krosnick, J. A., & Brannon, L. A. (1993). The impact of the Gulf war on the ingredients of presidential evaluations: Multidimensional effects of political involvement. *American Political Science Review, 87,* 963–975.

Krosnick, J. A., & Kinder, D. R. (1990). Altering the foundations of popular support for the president through priming. *American Political Science Review, 84,* 497–512.

Kuklinski, J. H., Metlay, D. S., & Kay, W. D. (1982). Citizen knowledge and choices on the complex issues of nuclear energy. *American Journal of Political Science, 26,* 615–642.

Lang, A. (1989). Effects of chronological presentation of information on processing and memory for broadcast news. *Journal of Broadcasting and Electronic Media, 33,* 441–452.

Lang, A. (1995). Defining audio/video redundancy from a limited-capacity information processing perspective. *Communication Research, 22,* 86–115.
Lang, A. (2000). The limited capacity model of mediated message processing. *Journal of Communication, 50*(1), 46–70.
Lang, A., Geiger, S., Strickwerda, M., & Sumner, J. (1993). The effects of related and unrelated cuts on television viewers' attention, processing capacity, and memory. *Communication Research, 20,* 4–29.
Lang, A., Newhagen, J., & Reeves, B. (1996). Negative video as structure: Emotion, attention, capacity, and memory. *Journal of Broadcasting and Electronic Media, 40,* 460–477.
Lang, A., Potter, D., & Grabe, M. E. (2003). Making news memorable: Applying theory to the production of local television news. *Journal of Broadcasting and Electronic Media, 47,* 113–123.
Larson, S. G. (1999). Public opinion in television election news: Beyond polls. *Political Communication, 16,* 133–145.
Lasorsa, D. L. (2003). Question-order effects in surveys: The case of political interest, news attention, and knowledge. *Journalism and Mass Communication Quarterly, 80,* 499–512.
Lau, R. R., & Sears, D. O. (1986). *Political cognition.* Hillsdale, NJ: Lawrence Erlbaum Associates.
Levy, M. R. (1983). Conceptualizing and measuring aspects of audience "activity." *Journalism Quarterly, 60,* 109–115.
Lieberman, M. D., Schreiber, D., & Ochsner, K. N. (2003). Is political cognition like riding a bicycle? How cognitive neuroscience can inform research on political thinking. *Political Psychology, 24,* 681–704.
Luskin, R. C. (1987). Measuring political sophistication. *American Journal of Political Science, 31,* 856–899.
McClelland, J. L. (1988). Connectionist models and psychological evidence. *Journal of Memory and Language, 27,* 107–123.
McClelland, J. L., & Rumelhart, D. E. (1985). Distributed memory and the representation of general and specific information. *Journal of Experimental Psychology: General, 114,* 159–188.
McCombs, M. E., & Shaw, D. L. (1972). The agenda-setting function of mass media. *Public Opinion Quarterly, 36,* 176–187.
McGraw, K. M. (2000). Contributions of the cognitive approach to political psychology. *Political Psychology, 21,* 805–832.
McGraw, K. M., & Ling, C. (2003). Media priming of presidential and group evaluations. *Political Communication, 20,* 23–40.
McGraw, K. M., Lodge, M. G., & Stroh, P. (1990). On-line processing in candidate evaluation: The effects of issue order, issue importance and sophistication. *Political Behavior, 12,* 41–58.
McLeod, J. M., & McDonald, D. (1985). Beyond simple exposure: Media orientations and their impact on political processes. *Communication Research, 12,* 3–33.
Miller, D. (1987). *The Blackwell encyclopaedia of political thought.* New York: Basil Blackwell.
Miller, J. M., & Krosnick, J. A. (2000). News media impact on the ingredients of presidential evaluations: Political knowledgeable citizens are guided by a trusted source. *American Journal of Political Science, 44,* 301–315.
Monroe, A. D. (1998). Public opinion and public policy, 1980–1993. *Public Opinion Quarterly, 62,* 6–28.
Moreno-Riaño, G. (2002). Experimental implications for the spiral of silence. *Social Science Journal, 39,* 65–81.

Mundorf, N., Drew, D., Zillmann, D., & Weaver, J. (1990). Effects of disturbing news on recall of subsequently presented news. *Communication Research, 17*, 601–615.

Mutz, D. C. (1998). *Impersonal influence: How perceptions of mass collectives affect political attitudes*. New York: Cambridge University Press.

Nelson, T. E. (2004). Policy goals, public rhetoric, and political attitudes. *Journal of Politics, 66*, 581–605.

Nelson, T. E., Clawson, R. A., & Oxley, Z. M. (1997). Media framing of a civil liberties conflict and its effect on tolerance. *American Political Science Review, 91*, 567–583.

Nelson, T. E., & Kinder, D. R. (1996). Issue frames and group-centerism in American public opinion. *Journal of Politics, 58*, 1055–1078.

Nelson, T. E., & Oxley, Z. M. (1999). Issue framing effects on belief importance and opinion. *Journal of Politics, 61*, 1040–1067.

Nelson, T. E., & Oxley, Z. M., & Clawson, R. A. (1997). Toward a psychology of framing effects. *Political Behavior, 19*, 221–246.

Newhagen, J. E., & Reeves, B. (1992). The evening's bad news: Effects of compelling negative television news images on memory. *Journal of Communication, 42*(2), 25–41.

Nisbett, R., & Ross, L. (1980). *Human inference: Strategies and shortcomings of social judgment*. Englewood Cliffs, NJ: Prentice-Hall.

Nisbett, R., & Wilson, T. D. (1977). Telling more than we can know: Verbal reports on mental processes. *Psychological Review, 84*, 231–259.

Noelle-Neumann, E. (1993). *The spiral of silence: Public opinion—Our social skin* (2nd ed.). Chicago: University of Chicago Press.

Page, B. I., & Shapiro, R. Y. (1983). Effects of public opinion on policy. *American Political Science Review, 77*, 175–190.

Paivio, A. (1971). *Imagery and verbal processes*. New York: Holt, Rinehart, & Winston.

Pan, Z., & Kosicki, G. M. (1997). Priming and media impact on the evaluations of president's performance. *Communication Research, 24*, 3–30.

Perry, S. D., & Gonzenbach, W. J. (1997). Effects of news exemplification extended: Considerations of controversiality and perceived future opinion. *Journal of Broadcasting and Electronic Media, 41*, 229–244.

Perse, E. M. (1990). Media involvement and local news effects. *Journal of Broadcasting and Electronic Media, 34*, 17–36.

Petty, R. E., & Priester, J. R. (1994). Mass media attitude change: Implications of the elaboration likelihood model of persuasion. In J. Bryant & D. Zillmann (Eds.), *Media effects: Advances in theory and research* (pp. 91–122). Hillsdale, NJ: Lawrence Erlbaum Associates.

Price, V. (1993). The impact of varying reference periods in survey questions about media use. *Journalism Quarterly, 70*, 615–627.

Price, V., & Tewksbury, D. (1997). News values and public opinion: A theoretical account of media priming and framing. In G. A. Barnett & F. J. Boster (Eds.), *Progress in communication science: Advances in persuasion* (Vol. 13, pp. 173–212). Greenwich, CT: Ablex.

Raichle, M. E. (2003). Social neuroscience: A role for brain imaging. *Political Psychology, 24*, 759–764.

Ravaja, N. (2004). Contributions of psychophysiology to media research: Review and recommendations. *Media Psychology, 6*, 193–235.

Reese, S. D. (1984). Visual-verbal redundancy effects on television news learning. *Journal of Broadcasting, 28*, 79–87.

Reeves, B., Chaffee, S. H., & Tims, A. (1982). Social cognition and mass communication research. In M. E. Roloff & C. R. Berger (Eds.), *Social cognition and communication* (pp. 287–327). Beverly Hills, CA: Sage.

Rhee, J. W. (1997). Strategy and issue frames in election campaign coverage: A social cognitive account of framing effects. *Journal of Communication, 47*(3), 26–48.

Rhee, J. W., & Cappella, J. N. (1997). The role of political sophistication in learning from news: Measuring schema development. *Communication Research, 24,* 197–233.

Roloff, M. E., & Berger, C. R. (1982). *Social cognition and communication.* Beverly Hills, CA: Sage.

Roskos-Ewoldsen, D. R., Roskos-Ewoldsen, B., & Carpentier, F. R. D. (2002). Media priming: A synthesis. In J. Bryant & D. Zillmann (Eds.), *Media effects: Advances in theory and research* (2nd ed., pp. 97–120). Mahwah, NJ: Lawrence Erlbaum Associates.

Scheufele, D. A. (2000). Agenda-setting, priming and framing revisited: Another look at cognitive effects of political communication. *Mass Communication & Society, 3,* 297–316.

Schuman, H., & Presser, S. (1981). *Questions and answers in attitude surveys: Experiments on question form, wording, and context.* New York: Academic.

Schwarz, N., & Bienias, J. (1990). What mediates the impact of response alternatives on frequency reports of mundane behaviors? *Applied Cognitive Psychology, 4,* 61–72.

Shah, D. V., Domke, D., & Wackman, D. B. (1996). To thine own self be true: Value, framing and voter decision-making strategies. *Communication Research, 23,* 509–560.

Shah, D. V., Kwak, N., Schmierbach, M., & Zubric, J. (2004). The interplay of news frames on cognitive complexity. *Human Communication Research, 30,* 102–120.

Smith, E. R. (1996). What do connectionism and social psychology offer each other? *Journal of Personality and Social Psychology, 70,* 893–912.

Smith, E. R., & Miller, F. D. (1978). Limits on perception of cognitive processes: A reply to Nisbett and Wilson. *Psychological Review, 85,* 355–362.

Smith, E. R., & Queller, S. (2004). Mental representations. In M. B. Brewer & M. Hewstone (Eds.), *Social cognition* (pp. 5–27). Malden, MA: Blackwell.

Smith, K. A. (1987). Newspaper coverage and public concern about community issues. *Journalism Monographs, 101.*

Sniderman, P. M., Brody, R. A., & Tetlock, P. E. (1991). *Reasoning and choice: Explorations in political psychology.* New York: Cambridge University Press.

Sniderman, P. M., & Grob, D. B. (1996). Innovations in experimental design in attitude surveys. *Annual Review of Sociology, 22,* 377–399.

Snoeijer, R., de Vreese, C. H., & Semetko, H. A. (2002). Research note: The effects of live television reporting on recall and appreciation of political news. *European Journal of Communication, 17,* 85–101.

Snow, D. A., & Benford, R. D. (1992). Master frames and cycles of protest. In A. D. Morris & C. M. Mueller (Eds.), *Frontiers in social movement theory* (pp. 133–155). New Haven, CT: Yale University Press.

Son, J., Reese, S. D., & Davie, W. R. (1987). Effects of visual–verbal redundancy and recaps on television news learning. *Journal of Broadcasting and Electronic Media, 31,* 207–216.

Soroka, S. N. (2002). Issue attributes and agenda-setting by media, the public, and policy makers in Canada. *International Journal of Public Opinion Research, 14,* 264–285.

Taylor, S. E., & Fiske, S. T. (1978). Salience, attention and attribution: Top of the head phenomena. In L. Berkowitz (Ed.), *Advances in experimental social psychology* (Vol. 11, pp. 249–288). New York: Academic.

Tichenor, P. J., Donohue, G. A., & Olien, C. N. (1970). Mass media flow and differential growth in knowledge. *Public Opinion Quarterly, 34,* 159–170.

Tourangeau, R., Rips, L. J., & Rasinski, K. (2000). *The psychology of survey response.* Cambridge, UK: Cambridge University Press.

Tversky, A., & Kahneman, D. (1973). Availability: A heuristic for judging frequency and probability. *Cognitive Psychology, 5,* 207–232.

Valentino, N. A. (1999). Crime news and the priming of racial attitudes during evaluation of the president. *Public Opinion Quarterly, 63,* 293–320.

Valentino, N. A., Traugott, M., & Hutchings, V. L. (2002). Group cues and ideological constraints: A replication of political advertising effects studies in the lab and in the field. *Political Communication, 19,* 29–48.

Valkenburg, P. M., Semetko, H. A., & De Vreese, C. H. (1999). The effects of news frames on readers' thought and recall. *Communication Research, 26,* 550–569.

Walma van der Molen, J. H., & van der Voort, T. H. A. (2000). Children's and adults' recall of television and print news in children's and adult news formats. *Communication Research, 27,* 132–160.

Wanta, W., & Foote, J. (1994). The president–news media relationship: A time series analysis of agenda-setting. *Journal of Broadcasting and Electronic Media, 38,* 437–448.

Watt, J. A., Mazza, M., & Snyder, L. (1993). Agenda setting effects of television news coverage and the effects decay curve. *Communication Research, 20,* 408–435.

Woodall, W. G. (1986). Information-processing theory and television news. In J. P. Robinson & M. R. Levy (Eds.), *The main source: Learning from television news* (pp. 133–158). Beverly Hills, CA: Sage.

Woodall, W. G., Davis, D. K., & Sahin, H. (1983). From the boob tube to the black box: Television news comprehension from an information processing perspective. *Journal of Broadcasting, 27,* 1–23.

Wright, D. B., Gaskell, G. D., & O'Muircheartaigh, C. A. (1994). How much is "quite a bit"? Mapping between numerical values and vague quantifiers. *Applied Cognitive Psychology, 8,* 479–496.

Wyckoff, M. L. (1987). Issues of measuring ideological sophistication: Level of conceptualization, attitudinal consistency, and attitudinal stability. *Political Behavior, 9,* 193–224.

Zhu, J. H., Watt, J. H., Snyder, L. B., Yan, J., & Jiang, Y. (1993). Public issue priority formation: Media agenda setting and social interaction. *Journal of Communication, 43*(1), 8–29.

14

Comprehension of the Media

Beverly Roskos-Ewoldsen
David R. Roskos-Ewoldsen
Moonhee Yang
Mina Lee
University of Alabama

When people watch a movie, one of the viewers' basic goals is to have a coherent understanding of what they are watching. To accomplish this, viewers construct mental representations of the movie as the movie unfolds. This representation includes information about the characters and situations within the movie, and prior expectations based on knowledge about the genre of movies, the director, and the actors and actresses starring in the movie. This combination of information provides the basis for understanding the movie as it unfolds and for predicting future events in the movie. Unfortunately, little research has focused on how people create a coherent understanding of what they are watching (but see Livingstone, 1987, 1989, 1990a, 1990b; Morley, 1992, 19890/1999). That is, communication scholars have tended to ignore comprehension, including in the first edition of *Communication and Social Cognition* (Roloff & Berger, 1982). However, a major breakthrough in the study of comprehension occurred in cognitive psychology the year after the first edition was published.

The major breakthrough occurred when van Dijk and Kintsch (1983) published their volume detailing an early version of the construction-integration model of comprehension (see also Kintsch, 1998, 2005). The construction-integration model was important for several reasons. It was the first model to propose that comprehension involved both top-down theory-driven processes and bottom-up data-driven processing. Prior to this model, many models such as schema theory focused exclusively on top-down processing. No strictly bottom-up models had been proposed because comprehension clearly involved the use of prior knowledge.

A second innovation of the construction-integration model was the argument that comprehension involved three levels of representation: the surface level, the propositional level, and the situation model. The surface level representation simply involved the text as it was presented. The propositional level focused on local coherence because it represented each of the units of meaning of a text—typically, a sentence. The situation model was the most radical innovation of the theory. A situation model is a global representation of a story that involves both the propositions from a story, world knowledge, and inferences that are necessary for comprehension.

Unfortunately, the innovations proposed by van Dijk and Kintsch (1983) have been relatively ignored until recently by scholars interested in the study of the media. Fortunately, the innovations have not been ignored completely. In this chapter we present three research traditions that have sought to understand how we comprehend the media. One tradition can be traced back to Hall's (1980/2001) essay on the encoding/decoding model, which arose within British cultural studies. This research tradition focuses on the global comprehension and representation of media stories. A second tradition focuses on relationships between characters within a story and their role in forming a unified mental representation of the story (e.g., Livingstone, 1987). A third tradition focuses on the role of situation models in the comprehension of visual and text stories (e.g., Lee, Roskos-Ewoldsen, & Roskos-Ewoldsen, 2004; Yang, Roskos-Ewoldsen, & Roskos-Ewoldsen, 2004). These three traditions approach comprehension differently, each with their own methodologies. This chapter presents each tradition, focusing on their theoretical and methodological contributions to understanding how we understand the media. Before we present each of the traditions, we take a moment to define what we mean when we say that a person understands what he or she is watching.

There are several distinctions related to understanding that are used in the fields of psychology, communication studies, and semiotics. In psychology, there is the distinction of sensation and perception. Receptors in the body sense the patterns of energy impinging on them and, information from the receptors is combined with information from our memories and our emotions by nature of the pathways connecting the receptors to the brain. Further processing in the brain gives rise to the conscious perception of what it is that our body is sensing. This perception is part of how we understand what we watch; that is, how we know what it is that we are looking at. At a higher level, communication scholars make the distinction between comprehending a text or film and interpreting it. Comprehension involves understanding the story as it is written or seen, whereas interpretation involves explaining the potential deeper meanings of the story. Semiotics offers yet a third level to understanding. According to Eco (1990; see also Eco, 1979), understanding a text is a complex interplay between the creator of the text and the reader of the text, and this interplay includes shared cultural knowledge. The critical point from this perspective is that the reader's understanding of the text is based in part on his or her own experiences. As a result, two people with different experiences may understand the text differently. On the flip side, the more shared experiences and cultural knowledge, the more similar the understanding. For our purposes, we use two key points from this discussion. First, understanding involves the comprehension of, rather than interpretation of, a story. Second, comprehension is idiosyncratic to the reader, based on his or her past experiences; however, to the extent that people share experiences, comprehension will be similar.

THE ENCODING/DECODING MODEL

Hall's (1980/2001) essay, "Encoding/Decoding," brought into focus what was to become a major line of research within cultural studies: How do audiences comprehend or read a media text and what techniques do the media use to constrain how the text is read? The paper, first published in 1973 as a mimeograph, was originally a lecture that Hall presented at the Centre for Mass Communications Research at the University of Leicester. Hall later characterized the talk as a polemic against the standard media effects research at the time (Hall, 1994). Hall correctly characterized traditional effects research as assuming perfect communication. In other words, media effects researchers of the time assumed that all members of the audience understood a media message in perfect accord with each other. This assumption permitted the experimental testing of the effect of some message characteristic, such as violence, on some outcome variable, such as aggression, but it lacked a way to identify underlying individual differences in media effects. Hall also called into question the idea of a dominant media system presenting an ideology that the masses unwittingly are compelled to accept (Condit, 1989; Hall 1994). Hall's point was that an audience can decode—or read—a message at odds with the formulation intended by the individuals who formed (i.e., encoded) the message. The variability in how a message is read is driven by divergences in the codes that are used at encoding and decoding. The basic point that Hall made in this essay is that the audience is not just a passive recipient of a message; rather, it is the audience's reading of the message that influences the impact of that message on the audience (Hall, 1994; Morley, 1992).

Both points are illustrated by the idea that any message is polysemic in that it can be read in different ways. Hall (1980/2001) is careful to note that not all readings of a message are equal (see also Turner, 1990, however). The people involved in the production of the message will use different techniques to attempt to secure a preferred or dominant reading of the text (Hall, 1980/2001; Morley, 1992). How this is done involves the question of how the encoding of a message can constrain the reading of a text so that the reading favors the preferred or dominant reading. Drawing on Parkin's (1971) work on the influence of class on meaning systems, Hall's original formulation of the encoding/decoding model held that there were three categories of readings of a message. First, there is the *dominant reading* of the message, which is consistent with the reading intended by the message producers. Parkin argued that the ruling class, by definition, had the most access to the mechanisms for legitimizing their worldview. Consequently, the primary meaning system that arises within a culture reflects that dominant worldview and most people operate and interpret messages within that worldview. To borrow Hall's (1980/2001) example, a preferred reading of a text involving the government busting a strike would be to accept the obligation of the government to weaken unions because it is necessary for the economy. Second, there is a *negotiated reading,* which is in large part consistent with the preferred reading, but is situated in that it acknowledges the interests of the individual decoding (i.e., hearing, reading) the message. Parkin argued that the working class's meaning system is accommodationist—people are not particularly happy with their lot in life, but they accept it and make it work the best for them that they can. Parkin provides the example of trade unions. Trade unions do not call into question the dominant economic system, but rather seek to get the best it can for its members within the framework of the dominant system. To continue the example, a person hearing the same message on strike breaking may generally agree with the necessity of breaking strikes and decreasing the power of unions, but still maintain the necessity of workers at the plant where she works having a strong union because of their special status. Third, there is an *oppositional reading* of a message, which acknowledges the preferred reading of a message, but rejects that reading. Parkin characterized this as a radical meaning system. This recipient of the strike-busting message would understand that the purpose of the message is anti-union, but would reject that reading and instead decode the message as an example of a conservative government promoting the interests of the business class.

Clearly, understanding factors that influence how a message is read by an audience is central to understanding how people comprehend and interpret media stories. Within Hall's (1980/2001) original encoding/decoding model, how a message is read is closely tied to issues of class, drawing on Parkin's (1971) writings. However, it is important to note that Hall did not intend to argue that class deterministically shapes how a message will be read (Morley, 1992). Rather, social class will influence how a message is read through the various codes that different social classes acquire due to their economic standing. In other words, while Hall clearly acknowledged the role of cognition in the decoding process, his primary interest is in how sociological factors influence how the message is comprehended.

The classic study that grew out of the encoding/decoding model involved *Nationwide,* a British news program. *Nationwide* was a soft news program that was aired daily by the BBC. The program sought to have a populist appeal by emphasizing entertainment over hard news (Brunsdon & Morley, 1978/1999). The first *Nationwide* study by Brunsdon and Morley (1978/1999) involved a close textual analysis of a single episode of *Nationwide* (aired May 19, 1976) in an attempt to identify the preferred reading of the text of the episode, and the techniques that were used to constrain how the audience read the text. Some of the stories in the episode included a plant closure, a woman who went to an animal park to visit a lion that had attacked her, an interview with Ralph Nader, several stories focusing on students, and an interview with Patrick Meehan, who had just been released from prison for a murder he did not commit. Some of the techniques that the producers of *Nationwide* used to constrain the reading of the show, according to Brunsdon and Morley, included the use of inclusive pronouns such as *we* and *our* to create a sense of sharedness with the audience. To the extent that the audience shares responsibility for the program, they would not question what is presented. In addition, the program often appealed to common sense with its emphasis on the family and the home. Again, if something is common sense, then it will tend not to be questioned. The use of these and additional codes attempted to restrict the ability of the audience to read the program in a manner that was not intended by the creators of the program.

The second study by Morley (1980/1999) sought to understand how groups differing in social class, gender, and ethnicity would read this episode of *Nationwide.* This study involved a series of 29 focus groups. Nineteen of the focus groups watched the episode of *Nationwide* that Bronson and Morley had analyzed. The other 10 groups watched a second episode of *Nationwide* that focused on the British budget debate (aired March 29, 1977). Each of the groups watched one of the *Nationwide* episodes and then their reactions to different stories were queried. The findings of Morley's study are intriguing and suggest several modifications of the original encoding/decoding model. First, Morley found that the readings of the various groups did not fall neatly along class lines, as originally hypothesized. Rather, how audiences read a message was more complex than the encoding/decoding model's original formula (Turner, 1990). For example, bank managers would be expected to prefer the dominant meaning of *Nationwide* because of their middle-class cultural position, and they did accept the dominant reading. However, apprentices—who were clearly working class and should have had a negotiated reading—also appeared to accept the dominant reading (Fiske, 1987; Morley, 1980/1999; Storey, 2003). Second, the same audience had different, often contradictory, readings of the episode of *Nationwide* that they watched. This indicates that people can inhabit many different cultures (e.g., professor, parent, soccer fan, agnostic, etc.) and that cultural set of meanings that influences how a text is read can vary within the same individual (Radway, 1991; Storey, 2003). Third, the question arose as to what constituted the preferred reading of a text. As Morley (1992) put the question, is the preferred reading of a text inherent in the text or does the audience bring it to the text, with the consequence that the preferred reading could change across time? The answer is both. The early research on dominant or preferred readings was done in the context of news stories, where the ideological implications of one reading of a story over another are fairly clear. However, determining the preferred reading is usually more complicated than this. For example, what is the preferred reading of a soap opera, a tear-jerker or a situation comedy? The notion of a preferred reading seems better suited to documentary-style shows and does not work particularly well with entertainment shows (Brooker, 2000; Fiske, 1987; Morley, 1992).

If we may digress, the *Nationwide* studies reflect the primary methodologies that are used to this day to study the encoding/decoding model. Most of the research testing the encoding/decoding model involves a mix of both qualitative research methods (i.e., focus groups; e.g., Morley, 1980/1999) and textual or semiotic analysis of the message (i.e., content analysis, close textual reading; e.g., Brunsdon & Morley, 1978/1999; see also Ang, 1982/1985). However, other techniques have included ethnographic studies of children's TV viewing (Hodge & Tripp, 1986) or women's readings of romance novels (Radway, 1991). Sometimes these methods are used in combination with each other, such as Brunsdon and Morley's study of *Nationwide.* However, many studies rely on only one methodological tool, such as Ang's (1985) study of *Dallas* or Brooker's (2000) study of *Batman.* We think this is unfortunate because the complexity of comprehension demands a reliance on a multiplicity of research methods to gain a complete understanding of the text or the processes involved in reading that text.

The encoding/decoding model and Morley's (1980/1999) *Nationwide* studies resulted in several lines of related research (Turner, 1990). The first involves just how free an audience is to read a media message. Clearly, Hall (1980/2001) emphasized the polysemic nature of media messages, but the issue is just how polysemic media messages are. Both Hall and Morley (1992) pointed to the interplay between the producers of a media message and the audience in terms of how a message is read.

Indeed, when reading Hall's discussion of the dominant, oppositional, and resistance readings of a text, it is clear that each of these audiences "understands" the text to be about the same thing. That is, they share an understanding of the denotative meaning of the text. As Condit (1989) argued, what differs across these audiences is not the comprehension of the text, but rather the interpretation of the text, particularly whether it is good or bad. To continue our earlier example, different audiences may understand that a story is about strike busting, but the judgment of whether strike busting is a good practice may differ across the audiences. Condit referred to this as a *polyvalence* reading of a text, rather than a polysemic reading, because the text is understood to be about the same thing, but the valuation of story differs across audiences, which is consistent with Hall's argument in the encoding/decoding essay.

Others, such as Fiske (1987; Fiske & Hartley, 1978), emphasize the overwhelming power of the audience to find distinct meanings within a text (see also Storey, 2003). For example, Ang (1985), in her study of *Dallas,* argued that people read *Dallas* in relation to their lives and, given the multifaceted nature of people's lives, different readings of *Dallas* should emerge. This is what she found. As another example, consider the movie *Falling Down,* a Joel Schumacher film starring Michael Douglas. Douglas plays an unemployed engineer nicknamed D-Fens. D-Fens gets stuck in traffic one day, gets out of his car, and walks away, saying in reply to someone's query that he is going home. On his way home he encounters a rude convenience store owner overcharging for a can of soda, a ghetto gang that threatens him, and a White supremacist who mistakenly thinks that D-Fens shares his values. He deals with each situation with increasing violence, ultimately killing the supremacist. Meanwhile, his going home has more meaning than it first seemed, because his ex-wife is obviously terrified when he calls to say that he is coming home. Many viewers of the movie see D-Fens as an example of an individual who has gone over the edge of sanity. Other viewers see D-Fens as a hero who is taking on a society that has progressively gone insane. Yet other viewers see the movie as a comedy about the frustrations of everyday life. Like *Dallas,* this movie evokes different readings that may be related to individuals' lives.

Fiske (1987) further argued that, given the nature of the media system, the producers of media messages necessarily need to be ambiguous in how they produce a message so that it will appeal to the widest audience possible (see also Brooker, 2000). Consequently, Fiske argued that the reading of a TV show is the result of a negotiation between an ambiguous media text and a culturally situated audience. For example, Fiske notes a study by Hodge and Tripp (1986) involving the attraction of *The Prisoner* to young school children. *The Prisoner* was a soap opera set in a women's prison; it aired in Australia. The show was immensely popular with school-aged children. Based on a series of interviews with the children, the prison life portrayed in the show was decoded by the children as representing their life in school.

Still other researchers have emphasized intertextuality, which focuses on how other texts influence how a text is read (Bennett & Woolacott, 1987; Fiske, 1987). One recent study in this area is Brooker's (2000) study of Batman. Since the original Batman comic in 1939, there has been a common underlying Batman—the millionaire Bruce Wayne who fights criminals in Gotham. However, there have been a range of Batmans as well, ranging from the initial Batman who packed a gun and killed criminals to the more recent dark knight reincarnation (Brooker, 2000). Of particular interest to Booker was the Batman TV series. The *Batman* TV series of the mid-1960s had several readings. There was the serious reading focusing on Batman as a superhero, and the camp reading emphasizing the TV show as a comedy. The camp reading was favored by adults and was nominated for the Best Comedy Emmy Award in 1966. A third, queer reading involved a homosexual relationship between Batman and Robin. Brooker (2000) argued that these different readings of the show were driven, at least in part, by the intertextual connections that were drawn between the TV series and other media. For example, the hero interpretation of the *Batman* series may have been driven by viewers who watched TV action shows such as *Dragnet, I Spy,* and *The Avengers,* which shared many similarities with the *Batman* series, and those who also read the Batman comic books that emphasized Batman's superhero nature. The campy comedy reading of the series may have been driven by the series' similarity to other comedies that aired at the same time, such as *Bewitched, The Addams Family,* and *I Dream of Jeannie* (Brooker, 2000). The point of these examples is that these other texts were likely to have influenced the interpretation of the *Batman* series.

There are many issues that have arisen in response to Hall's (1980/1999) encoding/decoding model that are beyond the limits of this chapter to cover (see Morley, 1992). Indeed, there are many criticisms of the model that we have not presented (e.g., Evans, 1990; Jancovich, 1992; Wren-Lewis, 1983). However, we believe it is important to remember that when he presented the encoding/decoding paper at the University of Leicester, Hall did not think of the paper as presenting a full-blown model of how messages are comprehended or read (Hall, 1994). Rather, as indicated earlier, Hall saw the paper as a polemic against an untenable assumption of the effects tradition—that the text alone determines the reading. He hoped that a more detailed model would develop out of his preliminary framework, but he has not pursued the development of the model himself. We believe that it is time to assess how well the theoretical developments called for by the encoding/decoding model have been instantiated.

The next step, in our opinion, is to address three questions. First, under what circumstances is a reading of a text determined by the text and by the audience? Unfortunately, much of the writing on the polysemic nature of texts tends to focus on this as a characteristic of the text independent of the audience. Clearly, how a text is comprehended is a complex dynamic between the text and the audience. Determining the relative contributions of text and audience under different circumstances would go a long way toward understanding comprehension of the media. Second, whether a reading is polysemic or polyvalenced needs more clarification. As it is, the distinction between a reading and an evaluation of the reading is a difficult one to make and maintain. It is likely that this distinction involves the difference between the comprehension and interpretation of a text, although this remains to be seen. Third, many of the clear examples of a polysemic text strike us as dealing with how the story relates to a person's prior experiences, both in terms of their personal lives and in terms of their prior experiences with different media. In our view, more studies are needed that assess relevant aspects of a person's life, including media history, and then relating these different aspects of people's lives to different readings of a text.

THE UNDERLYING REPRESENTATION OF A MEDIA STORY: STUDYING THE RELATIONSHIPS AMONG CHARACTERS

The second wave of research to focus on comprehension of the media began in the late 1980s. These researchers built on the encoding/decoding model by providing psychological support for the arguments that Hall and others had advanced (Livingstone, 1989, 1990b). Specifically, they sought to answer whether people formed a unified mental representation of a movie or TV series. As Livingstone (1987) cogently argued, research has focused on the consequences of viewing the media without understanding how people comprehended the messages and, perhaps more important, represented the messages in memory. The focus on the mental representation of the show or series is important because that mental representation should directly reflect how people understand the show, including any influence of prior experiences, as suggested by the intertextuality literature. In other words, if watching situation comedies colored how audiences interpreted the *Batman* TV series, as Brooker (2000) argued, the nature of that influence will be tied to the representation of those situation comedies in memory.

Research using the mental representation approach has focused on people's perceptions of the characters within a story to identify the underlying representation of the story (Livingstone, 1987, 1989, 1990a, 1990b; Roskos-Ewoldsen, Roskos-Ewoldsen, Yang, & Crawford, 2003; Rowell & Moss, 1986). The research focused on perceptions of characters for several reasons. First, stories are often portrayed as conflicts between characters or sets of characters so that the story is understood as a dynamic between the various characters involved in the story. Second, perceptions of characters mediate the influence of media stories. How people identify with characters and how real those characters are perceived to be influences the impact of the media story on the viewer (Livingstone, 1990b; Roskos-Ewoldsen, Roskos-Ewoldsen, Yang, & Crawford, 2003). Finally, people's interpretation of a story is tied to how they perceive and identify with the main characters within a story (Livingstone, 1990a).

This research relies on multidimensional scaling (MDS) as a statistical technique for identifying the underlying mental representation of the story (Kruskal & Wish, 1986). As a statistical technique, MDS makes the assumption that information is stored in memory along dimensions and uses a spatial metaphor to understand the dimensional representations, such that characters that are closer in the dimensional representation are perceived as more similar than are those that are further away in the representation. As an aside, there is some discussion regarding whether this type of information is best represented as having discrete features (i.e., featurally) or as being located along a continuous dimension (i.e., dimensionally; Rosenberg, Nelson, & Vivekananthan, 1968; Rosenberg & Sedlak, 1972; Roskos-Ewoldsen, 1997; Tversky, 1977; Tversky & Hutchinson, 1986). Given the support for the dimensional representation of implicit personality theory (Rosenberg et al., 1968; Rosenberg & Sedlak, 1972), however, assuming that movie characters are represented dimensionally seems to be valid.

To use MDS, you need similarity ratings of a set of objects, or characters in our case. For example, Roskos-Ewoldsen et al. (2003) had participants watch the movie *Falling Down* and then rate the similarity of 10 major characters in the movie along a 11-point scale ranging from 0 (*not at all similar*) to 10 (*extremely similar*; see also Livingstone, 1987, Experiment 1). These similarity ratings are reverse-coded to transform them into dissimilarity scores so that higher numbers indicate greater differences. A second technique involves having people sort the objects into piles and then converting the sortings into dissimilarity scores (see Livingstone, 1987, Experiment 2; Livingstone, 1989; Rosenberg et al., 1968; Roskos-Ewoldsen, 1997). In either case, MDS produces an *n*-dimensional space where similar characters are closer in space and dissimilar characters are farther apart. Typically, one specifies a 1-D, 2-D, 3-D, and sometimes higher number of dimensions. Then, one jointly uses percentage of variance accounted for by the specific dimensional solutions, and stress, which is a measure of fit, to determine the number of dimensions that best capture the data. An excellent primer on MDS is Kruskal and Wish's (1986) short volume.

The earliest study within this tradition sought to determine whether MDS was a useful methodology for studying the representation of longer stories; specifically, whether representations that resulted from reading a book versus watching a fairly faithful film adaptation of the book differed (Rowell & Moss, 1986). In this study, participants either read Orwell's (1945) *Animal Farm* or watched Halas and Bachelor's (2004) animated adaptation of the book. Importantly, as Rowell and Moss (1986) noted, although the adaptation of the book is very close, one of the characters—the donkey—is treated more simplistically in the movie than in the book, which provides a potentially important point of comparison for the two representations. There were several interesting results of this study. First, the MDS representations for the book and the movie were meaningfully related to the major themes of the story. Second, the mental representation that resulted from watching the movie was simpler (only two dimensions) than the representation that resulted from reading the book (three dimensions). Finally, the differences in the two representations appeared to be tied to the complexity of the donkey character in the two different formats.

The most extensive line of research in this area was conducted by Livingstone (1987, 1989, 1990a, 1990b) and focused on the mental representations that resulted from watching soap operas such as *Dallas* and the BBC's *Coronation Street*. Besides testing whether people developed coherent representations of a TV series, Livingstone's (1987, 1989, 1990b) research focused on whether people used gender stereotypes, implicit personality theory, or narrative structures as identified by literary analysis to understand the stories. Across a series of studies, she found that, not only did people create coherent representations of TV series, but also that there was a high degree of consensus regarding these representations, as demonstrated by the fit of the MDS solutions to her similarity data, even when different methods were used to generate the similarity scores between the characters (Livingstone, 1987). Furthermore, the representations that emerged in these studies closely matched the decodings of the stories found in an analysis of the studies that relied on more traditional techniques used to test the encoding/decoding model (e.g., Brunsdon & Morley, 1978/1999; Hodge & Tripp, 1986). For example, gender was a clear dimension for both *Dallas* and *Coronation Street*, but the representation of gender for *Dallas* followed traditional gender themes (i.e., masculine was associated with potency or power) whereas the representation of gender for *Coronation Street* involved nontraditional gender roles (i.e., feminine was associated with potency or power). Likewise, morality and power emerged as important dimensions for both of the soaps, but morality and power were independent dimensions in the representation of *Dallas*, whereas they were negatively correlated in the representation of *Coronation Street* (Livingstone, 1987, 1989). These results demonstrate that the representation of the story reflected how the characters were depicted in the story, rather than more generic information such as gender stereotypes.

A final series of studies within this tradition explored whether people's representations of movies reflected the polysemic nature of the story. Earlier, we discussed the movie *Falling Down,* which is a story of an unemployed defense worker (D-Fens) who reacted with progressively higher levels of violence to the frustrations that he faced as he tried to walk home, where there was clearly something amiss in his relationship with his ex-wife. The movie is interpreted by some as a story of a man who is mentally ill, whereas others interpret it as a story of a hero who fought back against an insane world. Two studies confirmed these interpretations. Around 95% of the viewers perceived D-Fens as being mentally ill; approximately half of these viewers also perceived the main character as a hero in addition to being mentally ill, whereas the other half did not (Crawford, Roskos-Ewoldsen, & Roskos-Ewoldsen, 2004; Roskos-Ewoldsen et al., 2003). In the first study (Roskos-Ewoldsen et al., 2003), participants watched the entire movie and then rated the similarity of 10 main characters in the movie. MDS demonstrated clear differences in the underlying representation of the movie between participants who saw D-Fens as a hero and those who did not, indicating that people with different interpretations of the movie developed different underlying representations of the movie.

A follow-up study focused on how the mental representations of the movie evolved across time (Crawford et al., 2004). In this study, participants' underlying representation of the movie *Falling Down* was measured at three critical points in the movie or at the end of the movie. Not only did the representations of the movie change across time, reflecting the dynamics between the characters in the movie, but the changes were distinct for the different interpretations of the movie. In the hero interpretation, viewers' representations tended to focus on D-Fens versus everybody else. In the nonhero interpretation of the movie, the representation of the movie focused more on the relationships between the various characters who were trying to protect D-Fens's family while bringing him to justice.

Using MDS to capture the underlying representation of a media story clearly has its benefits. The number of dimensions in a best-fitting spatial solution corresponds to the complexity of the story in a meaningful way. In addition, the clustering of characters within a space reflects changes as the story unfolds, as well as differences between interpretations, in a meaningful way. However, despite the quantitative nature of data collection and analysis, interpretation of the dimensional solution is qualitative in nature. This is not a criticism, but an acknowledgment of the fact. There currently are no quantitative measures of changes in the locations of characters within a dimensional space across time because the space itself may change in dimensionality across time. Clearly, standardized ways of analyzing the clusters within a dimensional space are needed.

SITUATION MODELS AND COMPREHENSION

A third approach to studying comprehension is the mental models approach. A mental model is a dynamic mental representation of a situation, event, or object (van Dijk & Kintsch, 1983). We may use these mental models as a way to process, organize, and comprehend incoming information (Radvansky, Zwaan, Federico, & Franklin, 1998; Zwaan & Radvansky, 1998), make social judgments (Wyer & Radvansky, 1999), formulate predictions and inferences (Magliano, Dijkstra, & Zwaan, 1996), or generate descriptions and explanations of how a system operates (Rickheit & Sichelschmidt, 1999). A key notion of the mental model approach is that there is some correspondence between an external entity and our constructed mental representations of that entity (Johnson-Laird, 1983; van Dijk & Kintsch, 1983). However, psychologists disagree on the degree of association, and which aspects of an entity are incorporated into a model. Differences in opinion such as these make it difficult to provide an exact definition of mental models. The lack of a clear definition of mental models may be due to the fact that mental models capture a broad and diverse range of topics (Rickheit & Sichelschmidt, 1999).

One topic is how people understand complex, natural, or technical systems, such as gravity, calculators, VCRs, and computers (e.g., McCloskey, 1983). These are called mental models of the world. A second topic focuses on mental models of reasoning and decision making, including both inductive and deductive reasoning. With deductive reasoning, people are hypothesized to construct hypothetical mental models of possible outcomes and judge the validity of the outcomes based on the mental models (Johnson-Laird, 1983). With inductive reasoning, people's mental models are used to make inductive inferences about future events (e.g., Holland, Holyoak, Nisbett, & Thagard, 1986; Johnson-Laird, 1983, 1989). A third topic focuses primarily on spatial relations in the environment; a person uses these mental models to navigate in familiar and unfamiliar territory. These mental models are often referred to as cognitive maps (e.g., Taylor & Tversky, 1992). A final and most important topic for our purposes focuses on the mental representations of real or imagined situations, called *situation models* (Kintsch, 1998; van Dijk & Kintsch, 1983). According to van Dijk (1995), these situation models are constructs in memory that represent what a situation or event described in a text is about, rather than a literal representation of the text itself, and are used in the comprehension of text discourse and movies.

One question that is often raised about mental models is how they differ from schemas, or more generally, how mental models differ from one another. This is an important question because mental models and schemas are highly related. We and others have argued that mental models exist at many different levels (Roskos-Ewoldsen, Davies, & Roskos-Ewoldsen, 2004; Roskos-Ewoldsen, Roskos-Ewoldsen, & Carpentier, 2002; Wyer & Radvansky, 1999; Zwaan & Radvansky, 1998). However, we would argue that there is a continuum of abstractness along which mental representations exist, from a situation model to a mental model to a schema.

A situation model is a representation of a specific story or episode that has specific temporal and spatial constraints (Wyer, 2004). For example, a situation model of a *CSI: Crime Scene Investigation* episode would take place in the early 2000s in Las Vegas (e.g., the episode "Sounds of Silence" takes place primarily at a school for the deaf and at a coffee shop, both in Las Vegas) and features the characters of Gil Grissom, Catherine Willows, Warrick Brown, Nick Stokes, Sarah Sidle, Dr. Gilbert (the head of the school), among others. A mental model is a more abstract representation of a series of related stories. Like a situation model, a mental model has temporal and spatial constraints, but these constraints will typically be looser. A mental model of a series of reality-based crime shows such as *CSI: Miami, CSI: NY,* and *Cold Case* would take place throughout the early part of the 2000s and would be set in different locations such as New York City, Miami, and Las Vegas. Importantly, situation and mental models represent knowledge about some event or events. These representations are spatially and temporally contextualized. A schema is a more abstract representation that is knowledge of something (D'Andrade, 1995; Markman, 1999; Shore, 1996). For example, a schema for reality-based investigative shows would include little or no temporal or spatial information and that information would be related to items within the schema (e.g., time passes between finding physical clues and processing them; the crime scene and the lab are typically two different locations), but it does not contextualize the representation. Rather, the schema would include information about what the important elements of a typical reality-based investigative show are (e.g., a murder or other crime, an unknown perpetrator, a crime scene with physical clues, a crime lab, crime scene investigators, the possibility the crime will not be solved, etc.). There may be temporal elements to the schema (e.g., physical clues must be collected, analyzed with technical equipment, and put together before the crime is solved), but the schema itself is not contextualized within a specific time or place.

Despite the differences in their level of specificity, situation models and mental models, at least, have some similarities. The first similarity is that they are malleable. Norman (1983) observed that mental models are incomplete, lack clearly defined boundaries, and even contain errors. For example, people's mental models of how a calculator works often contain many errors. Similarly, Wyer and Radvansky (1999) argued that the components of a situation or mental model are interchangeable, much like building blocks that can be used to construct various shapes. My situation model of a specific episode of *CSI: Miami* may draw on situation models from other *CSI* episodes (e.g., the crime lab) to aid my comprehension of this episode. This characteristic of models distinguishes them from other approaches to cognition, such as semantic network models, or even schemas. Once a mental model or situation model is brought to mind these models interface with other knowledge structures such as networks or schemas in a much more dynamic way, which is highlighted by the second similarity: Both situation models and mental models are dynamic. That is, they are subject to user control and may be manipulated to generate inferences, test different scenarios, or draw conclusions about information that may or may not be contained in a text or situation. For example, when watching a crime mystery, people may construct a model of the crime and make online inferences about who did it or what the important clues are going to be (Dickinson & Givon, 1997). As another example, movie viewers may use cinematic features (e.g., editing techniques, costumes, music, dialogue, etc.) as cues to make predictions about future events or to make inferences about previous events. When anomalous information is foregrounded by filmmakers, viewers attempt to find out why such information is presented. Possible reasons why the information is foregrounded are generated through the manipulation of situation models about the film while viewers are watching the film (Magliano et al., 1996).

In addition, situation models and mental models both draw on real-world knowledge. Indeed, real-world experiences are essential in constructing them (Kintsch, 1998; Lakoff & Johnson, 1980; van Dijk & Kintsch, 1983). Long-term knowledge structures such as schemas that are based on our experience may be used to fill in the details of situation models. In the absence of firsthand experience with a particular situation, we may draw on our observations, others' explanations, analogous models, or components from analogous models, all of which we have experienced (Johnson-Laird, 1989).

These similarities between situation models and mental models make it difficult to distinguish between them. Nevertheless, we believe it is useful to do so. Therefore, we use the definitions outlined earlier. When we refer to a specific episode of a series or a particular movie, we use the term *situation model.* When we refer to an entire series or a genre of film, we use the term *mental model.* At this point, however, there is very little research on mental models as we have defined them, and all of the research we present here is based on situation models, rather than mental models. There is one caveat: When we use the phrase *mental models approach to studying comprehension,* we are referring to a general approach that incorporates all levels of models, including situation models, mental models, and schemas.

The Landscape Model: A Computation Approach to Situation Models

Within the broader mental models approach, the landscape model (van den Broek, Rapp, & Kendeou, 2005; van den Broek, Risden, Fletcher, & Thurlow, 1996; van den Broek, Young, Tzeng, & Linderholm, 1999) is concerned with how people generate a coherent understanding of a story. It is a computational model of text comprehension that focuses on coherence by looking at the relation between the online processing of a story and the memorial representation of that story. It incorporates both the level of activation of individual concepts in memory and their coactivation. It is the latter that provides the basis for coherence of a story and affords predictions about which concepts are more likely to be recalled, including those involving inferences drawn while reading the story. Most of the research using the landscape model focuses on recall, however, because arguably it provides a broader assessment of story comprehension than do measures of inference making.

The landscape model gets its name from the observation that, as one reads a story, information is being activated at various levels across time. If one were to construct a three-dimensional matrix of the concepts relevant to the movie along the x axis, the different scenes in the movie along the z axis, and the level of activations for each concept during each scene along the y axis, one would have a landscape of activations with hills and troughs corresponding to activation levels of the concepts across time. As an example, assume that there are 15 scenes within a movie and that there are a total of 75 concepts within these 15 scenes. Figure 14.1 is a hypothetical landscape of the activation of concepts within this movie. Higher elevations in the landscape indicate higher levels of activation of that concept. Troughs in the landscape would represent the absence of activation of that concept. This landscape forms the basis for the representation of the story's mental model in memory, but it is only one part of the representation—the other part being the coactivation of concepts within a scene.

The landscape model assumes that there are four general sources of activation of concepts while attending to a story (van den Broek et al., 1996; van den Broek et al., 1999). First, the immediate environment will activate concepts in memory. Specifically, concepts within the current sentence (for a book) or scene (for a movie) will be activated. Second, because activation dissipates across time (Higgins, Bargh, & Lombardi, 1985), concepts from

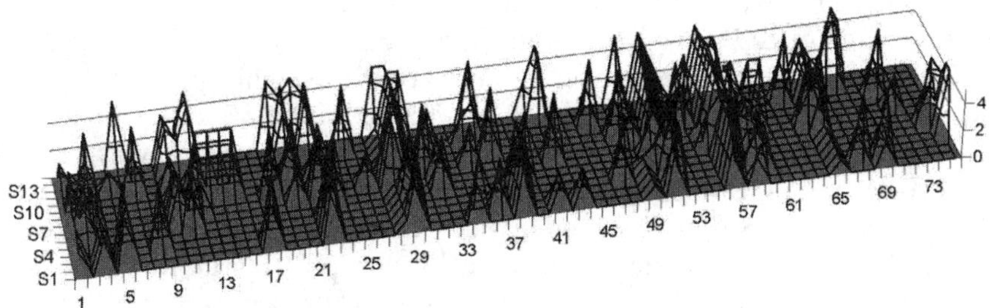

FIGURE 14.1. A landscape of activations for 75 concepts in a 15-sentence story.

the immediately proceeding sentence of scene should still be activated, albeit at a lower level of activation. Furthermore, concepts from previous scenes are hypothesized to have higher levels of activation if they were the focal point of the previous scene, they were related to active goals of the protagonists or antagonists in the previous scene, or they involved events that were antecedents to some subsequent event. Third, concepts from earlier in the story may be reactivated because they are necessary for maintaining the coherence of the story. Fourth, world knowledge that is necessary for understanding the story will be activated.

The landscape model has been tested with text-based stories (van den Broek et al., 1996; van den Broek et al., 1999). It has done an excellent job of accounting for participants' memory for a text-based story. Indeed, the landscape model appears to do a better job of predicting participants' memory for text than any existing model of text comprehension, although no direct tests have been made (van den Broek & Gustafson, 1990). However, the stories used to test the model were simple short stories. For example, one story about a knight and a dragon is 13 sentences long and includes 26 concepts. Therefore, it is unclear how well the landscape model would do with more complex stories, such as those found in many movies. This is because concepts may represent both visual and verbal information. In addition, both the text (i.e., dialogue) and the visual elements of the story can activate the concepts and therefore influence one's mental model of the story.

We tested the ability of the landscape model to explain comprehension of a video story by using a short clip (2 minutes, 17 seconds) from the one of the episodes of an animated series called *Cowboy Bebop* (Yang et al., 2004). The series recounts the story of three bounty hunters in a futuristic period. To test the landscape model, a video clip of the first 2 minutes of a single episode was divided into 23 segments based on the meaningful changes in the story, as judged by four media comprehension experts. The same four judges identified a total of 89 concepts in the video clip, including concepts based on both visual and verbal information.

A theoretically derived activation level for each of the 89 concepts across each of the 23 segments was determined by two trained judges who were blind to the experimental hypothesis. They used a 5-point scale to indicate the magnitude of activation. The intercoder reliability for the two judges was 86% overall. The result of this coding was a theoretically driven 89 (concepts) × 23 (segments) matrix of activation values, which constituted the landscape of activations for the video clip.

To develop an empirically derived landscape, 15 students watched the same 23 segments and rated how much the segment made them think of each concept. The empirically derived activation levels of the concepts within each segment were consistent ($\alpha = .77$), which made it possible to test the validity of the model's predictions concerning the levels of activation. The correlation between the theoretically derived activation from the trained judges and the perceived degree of activation from the participants' ratings (van den Broek et al., 1996) was .70, which means that there was good correspondence between the model's predicted activation and participants' ratings of how each segment made them think of each concept. However, when evaluating the model's prediction, it is important to remember that the reliability of the participants' ratings (.77) serves as an upper limit on the correlation between the model's predictions and the participants' ratings. At best, the model could account for 59% (77^2) of the variance in the participants' ratings. Therefore, the landscape model actually does a very good job of predicting the empirically derived activation levels even with a complex story with visual elements.

The next and final step in testing the model involved whether its landscape of activation could predict recall for the story. The landscape model assumes that the activation of a concept while watching the animated clip contributes to the formation of a memorial representation of the story (van den Broek et al., 1996), with concepts of higher activation contributing more to the representation than concepts of lower activation. The model also assumes that those concepts that are more central to the story, and therefore the representation, will be recalled at higher levels than concepts less central to the story. To test this aspect of the model, 14 participants from the same participant pool watched the clip from *Cowboy Bebop* in its entirety. After watching the clip, the participants completed several unrelated tasks for 10 minutes to avoid recency effects, and then completed a free recall test. Two trained coders decided whether the participant had recalled each of the 89 concepts. From this, the number of participants who recalled each concept was calculated; this vector served as the dependent variable. From the theoretically derived activations, the number of segments (out of 23) in which a concept had been activated was calculated, in addition to the activation vector described previously. Also, the extent to which two concepts were activated simultaneously within a segment was calculated. These three variables served as independent variables in a regression analysis (van den Broek et al., 1996). The regression analysis showed that together these variables accounted for 19% of the variance in participants' recall of the story (R = .44). In other words, the activations from the landscape model predicted recall moderately well, but there is clearly more to story comprehension than is predicted by the current instantiation of the model.

One aspect of the memorial representation of a story that may be important is its genre. Different genres can influence story comprehension simply by motivating the different goals of comprehension. For example, Zwaan (1994) found that people processed the same story differently, depending on whether it was a fiction or news story. When participants were told that it was a fictional story, they were likely to engage in developing a coherent narrative structure. On the other hand, when participants were told that it was a news story, they tended to focus on the text information itself.

Another aspect that may be important is the way information is presented. In news stories, meaningful correspondences between visual and verbal information is crucial; that is, verbal and visual information needs to be presented in such a way that its referent can be synchronized. The idea that visual and verbal information will differ to some extent, even though both types of information refer to the same topic, was investigated by Lee et al. (2004). In this study, a news story from CNN was used. To capture the differences between verbal and visual information, along with their synchronization, we introduced a modification to the landscape model based on the dual code theory of memory (Paivio, 1986, 1991). Dual code theory posits that verbal and visual information is represented separately in memory. Further, there are networks of connections within each type of representation. If a concept is represented in both systems, on presentation of the concept, activation in the two systems would be additive. In other words, concepts are remembered better when they are represented in two codes than when they are represented in only one code. Using this theory, we assumed that there would be two types of relations between verbal and visual information in the news story. One was a *representational correspondence.* The representational correspondence specified the instances that visual and verbal information referred to the same referent. The expected result from representational correspondence was that, on seeing simultaneous visual and verbal information about a referent, its representation would be activated in both types of codes, and the activations from each type would be additive. Thus, the likelihood of recalling that referent would be increased compared to referents that were not synchronized. In the study (Lee et al., 2004), we modified the total activation to reflect representational correspondence. First, the concept activations were recoded such that concept activation was coded separately for visual and verbal information. The verbal concepts were coded for activation while listening to the story only; the visual information was blocked from view. The visual concepts were coded while watching the story only; the sound was muted. The two matrices (i.e., landscapes of activation) were added, and then the resulting matrix of 79 concepts × 19 segments was collapsed across segments. This 79-concept vector reflected the additivity of representational correspondence.

The other relation was a *complementary representation.* In the complementary representation, we emphasized the elaborative power of verbal and visual information correspondence. Even though verbal and visual information may not represent the same referent, by coexisting in the story, visual and verbal concepts would complement each other, providing more associative power than concepts that do not coexist. Complementary representation was calculated for each segment by multiplying the activations of all possible pairs of concepts within each type of activation matrix (i.e., visual or verbal). Then, these two 79 × 19 matrices were summed. This matrix reflected the complementary representation by including associative relations from both verbal and visual concepts. For statistical purposes, this matrix was collapsed across segments to form a 79-concept association vector.

As in the *Cowboy Bebop* study, we gathered the recall data by having participants watch the entire 2.5-minute story, engage in unrelated tasks for 10 minutes, and then recall the story. The responses were coded for the number of times each concept occurred within the response. However, rather than counting the number of people who recalled each concept, as we did in the earlier study, we counted the number of times a concept was recalled in each participant's response and then averaged this number across participants. We hoped that this would be a more sensitive measure of concept recall, and it was. First, the regression model using the average number of times each concept was recalled as the dependent variable, and the modified activation vector as the independent variable, produced $R^2 = .66$. Second, replacing the modified activation vector with the modified association vector as the independent variable produced $R^2 = .42$. Finally, with both independent variables simultaneously entered as independent variables, $R^2 = .75$. Thus, the landscape model, modified to include visual and verbal information, captured recall of the news story quite well.

Brand Placement: A Conceptual Approach to Situation Models

The landscape model formed the theoretical basis for another investigation: how audiences process brand placements within a movie (Yang &

Roskos-Ewoldsen, 2005). According to the landscape model, the greater the activation of the brand while viewing the movie, the greater the likelihood that the brand will be recalled in the future. If a brand is tied to the comprehension of the show by serving as an enabler, it will receive a higher level of activation than brands that are in the background. A brand operates as an enabler when the brand plays a role in allowing some form of action or movement to occur within the story. For example, the Reese's Pieces that Elliot placed on the ground to lure an alien into his house in the movie *E.T.* were enablers because they played an important role in the story (luring the alien inside). Simply presenting the brand as a background in the scene in the movie will lead to a low level of activation because the brand placement is not related to story comprehension, and, consequently, later recall of the brand will be unlikely.

In the study (Yang & Roskos-Ewoldsen, 2005), we used three different levels of brand placement to test whether level of brand placement predicted recognition of the brand. The levels were (a) in the background, (b) used by the character, and (c) used as an enabler in the story. In the background condition, the product was shown with one of the main characters but the character did not use the product. In the used by character condition, the product was used by one of the main characters but was not central to the story. In the story enabler condition, the product played a role in the storyline, such as saving the main character or helping to solve a problem in the movie.

A total of 14 movie clips (5 for background, 5 for used by character, and 4 for story enabler) were edited to 20 minutes each. Participants watched one of these clips, completed an unrelated task for 10 minutes, and then took a recognition test. In the recognition test, participants were asked to indicate whether they remembered seeing a brand from the movie clips they watched (yes–no). The list included items that were not shown in the movies. The results for the recognition measure were consistent with the theoretical predictions from the landscape model. People were more likely to correctly recognize the brands placed in a movie when the brand was an enabler within the movie than when it was used by a character or was simply part of the background.

The Event Indexing Model: An Event-Related Approach to Situation Models

The landscape model is not the only model that focuses on story comprehension. Another is the event indexing model (Zwaan, Langston, & Graesser, 1995). The event indexing model focuses on events and their interconnectedness within the story. This emphasis is in contrast to the landscape model, which focuses on the activation pattern of the concepts in a story, rather than events. The event indexing model assumes that people process story information in an organized way. They monitor and cluster information while creating a situation model of the story. The clusters represent events in the story and, according to the event indexing model, people use specific indexes to create these clusters. Five indexes have been identified as important for clustering information into events (Magliano, Miller, & Zwaan, 2001; Zwaan, 1999; Zwaan et al., 1995; Zwaan, Radvansky, Hillard, & Curiel, 1998): changes in time, changes in space, establishment of a causal relation between antecedents and consequences, focus on the protagonists' goal, and focus on different agents or objects. These five indexes capture who is involved with what particular intention, when and where, and whether the current event is the cause of other events.

The event indexing model further assumes that the indexing process constitutes the process of updating situational models as new information in the story is encountered (Magliano et al., 2001; Zwaan et al., 1995; Zwaan et al., 1998). In particular, when a change is detected along any of the five dimensions, people are more likely to update their situation model of the story, compared to the situation where there is continuity. As part of the updating process, forward and backward inferences, as well as elaborations of the event, are made.

In a recent study, we investigated the extent to which people make inferences during the normal course of watching a movie (Lee & Roskos-Ewoldsen, 2004). We compared these inferences to a situation in which the usual comprehension process is disrupted: watching a movie in another language with English subtitles. In the study, we used two versions of *Rear Window* (Hitchcock, 1946); one was the English version and the other was the French-dubbed version with English subtitles. Participants watched the last half of the movie. As they watched the movie, they wrote down any thoughts that came to mind. Any inferences reported by the participants were coded as backward, current, and forward inferences (Trabasso & Magliano, 1996; van den Broek, Fletcher, & Risden, 1993). A backward inference was one that used information presented earlier in the movie and linked that information with what is currently occurring in the movie. Backward inferences play an important role in creating global coherence for the story. A forward inference was one that predicted future events, and a current inference was one that concerned only the immediate event. By linking events within the current scene together, current inferences aid in maintaining local coherence. We expected that more inferences would be made in the English version than in the French version, assuming that the normal updating process would be disrupted by viewers having to split their attention between the visual content of the French film and its subtitles.

To our surprise, there was no overall difference in the number of inferences made in the English and French conditions. However, there were significant differences in the types of inferences made. Participants generated more backward inferences in the English condition than in the French condition, whereas participants generated more current inferences in the French condition than in the English condition. There was no difference in the number of forward inferences made but, consistent with previous research on comprehension, there were very few forward inferences in either condition (van den Broek et al., 1993). The results of this experiment suggest that the presence of subtitles interferes with viewers' ability to make backward inferences. Given the role that backward inferences play in linking together information within situation models that are constructed while viewing a movie, interfering with backward inferences should impede the global coherence of the movie. Instead of making backward inferences, participants in the subtitle condition made more current inferences, which suggests that more of their attention was focused on tying events within the current situation model together so that there was local coherence in their understanding of the event in the film. These results suggest that when viewing films with subtitles, local coherence should not suffer because viewers devote working memory to linking together the information within the particular event (van den Broek et al., 1993). However, because reading the subtitles appears to interfere with participants' ability to make backward inferences, they are not as able to draw the events of the movie together into a coherent whole.

In a follow-up study, participants again watched the last half of the movie *Rear Window* in either English or French (Lee, Roskos-Ewoldsen, & Roskos-Ewoldsen, 2005). After watching the film, we gave participants descriptions of 78 events that occurred in the segment they watched, and asked them to sort the events into piles based on how similar the segments were to each other. The sorting data were then converted into similarity data (Roskos-Ewoldsen, 1997), which were submitted to a pathfinder analysis (Schvaneveldt, 1990). Pathfinder analysis creates an associative network representation of the connectedness of the events. It conveys both the linearity of events, as perceived by the participants, and the elaborateness of the connections among events. We view this representation as a situation model of the movie. We expected that in the English version one's situation model would be elaborated as in the normal course of watching a movie. That is, we expected more elaborations than when comprehension was disrupted, and we expected the elaborations to focus on the dimensions outlined by the event indexing model: time, space, causality, goals, and agents or objects. In contrast, we expected that the disruption of the normal comprehension process produced by the French version would result in a less elaborate situation model that incorporated fewer connections based on the event indexes.

The network representation for participants who watched the movie in English was much more complex than for participants who watched the movie in French. In addition, the network for students who watched the movie in English was structured around the characters in the movie and the enabling conditions that allowed the mystery to be solved. On the other hand, the network for students who watched the movie in French was structured around the characters within the movie and time. Thus, participants in both conditions were focusing on two dimensions from the event indexing model—causality and the agents in the English version and agents and time in the French version—but the focus on the characters and causality in the English version probably enabled them to draw more backward inferences and arguably, understand the movie more easily than when the focus was on the characters and time.

FUTURE DIRECTIONS

Clearly, research on the comprehension of the media is in its infancy. Although there is an expansive literature on text comprehension going back to and preceding van Dijk and Kintsch's (1983) seminal work in this area, there has been much less work on media comprehension. Although the research on text comprehension greatly informs our understanding of media comprehension, there are clear differences between text comprehension and media comprehension. Obviously, the media involves both verbal and visual information, and the integration of information across these different modalities. Similarly, music seems to play an important role in people's reactions to movies. However, it is not clear how music influences how people interpret scenes or what information it activates from memory to influence the construction of situation models. Likewise, there are numerous production techniques such as cuts, fade-aways, and zooms that are used to convey meaning within movies. How these are used to influence the comprehension of a media story is not well understood (Magliano et al., 1996).

A second area that deserves more attention involves how media comprehension influences the effects of the media. We have already reviewed research on how the landscape model informed our understanding of when product placements are likely to be explicitly remembered. Likewise, we have also argued that our understanding of cultivation theory would be enhanced if the event indexing model were used to explore cultivation effects (Roskos-Ewoldsen et al., 2004). For example, would heavy viewers of programs about World War II such as *Band of Brothers* really perceive New York City as a more dangerous place because of what they watch? Of course, cultivation theorists maintain that the genres of shows that people watch do not matter, but more recent research strongly implicates the role of genre in cultivation research (Segrin & Nabi, 2002). Using the event index model as a framework for studying cultivation theory would suggest that heavy viewers of these shows should not perceive New York City as more dangerous than light viewers of these shows do. Rather, these viewers would judge Europe during World War II as a more dangerous place than light viewers of these shows would because their comprehension of the programming is situated both temporally and spatially.

Finally, we believe that the role of comprehension should be explored across a number of domains. Kintsch (1998) argued that comprehension underlies many cognitive phenomena and that theories of comprehension may provide the unifying theoretical framework for cognitive science that has been missing. For example, Kintsch demonstrated how the construction integration model can account for many of the phenomena involved in person perception (Kunda & Thagard, 1996; Read, Vanman, & Miller, 1997; Thagard & Kunda, 1998). Of course, if you think about it, at its core, person perception fundamentally involves the comprehension of people's behaviors or what you are told about people. Likewise, theories of comprehension can explain many of the phenomena predicted by dual-process models of persuasion. For example, the elaboration likelihood model predicts that people with topic-relevant knowledge are better able to process messages than people with low levels of topic-relevant knowledge. From a comprehension standpoint, this finding makes perfect sense because people with more topic-relevant knowledge will construct more elaborate situation models of the persuasive messages. The bottom line is that much of our interaction within the social world involves our comprehension of what is occurring, and we believe that theories of communication and social cognition need to integrate comprehension processes much more than they have in the past.

CONCLUSIONS

Clearly, we believe that comprehension is a critical component of communication that has been largely ignored by communication and social cognition scholars. In many ways, not including comprehension was understandable. As we hope this chapter has demonstrated, this is an area of study that bridges a number of disciplinary boundaries. Scholars in cultural studies, English, communication studies, education, cognitive science, social cognition, linguistics, and critical studies all have conducted research focusing on some level of comprehension. Yet, despite this plurality of research, research on comprehension—particularly as it applies to the media—is in its infancy.

A second theme that we hope has emerged is this chapter is the multiplicity of research methods that are necessary to study comprehension.

The studies we have reviewed have included such diverse methodologies as close textual analysis, rhetorical criticism, focus groups, ethnography field work, reaction time measures, talk-aloud procedures, recognition and recall measures, multidimensional scaling and cluster analysis, and basic rating scales. Additional methodologies that we could add to this list include eye tracking techniques and basic physiological measurements as well as more sophisticated methods such as functional magnetic resonance imaging. The study of basic comprehension processes demands a commitment to triangulation in the use of various research methods to gain a more nuanced understanding of the phenomenon in question.

Despite the difficulties that the study of basic comprehension processes poses, we believe that it is a critical—and exciting—area of study.

REFERENCES

Ang, I. (1985). *Watching Dallas: Soap opera and the melodramatic imagination.* (D. Couling, Trans.) London: Methuen. (Original work published 1982)

Bennett, T., & Woolacott, J. (1987). *Bond and beyond: The political career of a popular hero.* Houndmills, UK: Macmillan Education.

Brooker, W. (2000). *Batman unmasked: Analyzing a cultural icon.* New York: Continuum.

Brunsdon, C., & Morley, D. (1999). Eveyday television: *Nationwide.* In D. Morley & C. Brunsdon (Eds.), *The Nationwide television studies* (pp. 19–110). London: Routledge. (Original work published 1978)

Condit, C. M. (1989). The rhetorical limits of polysemy. *Critical Studies in Mass Communication, 6,* 103–122.

Crawford, Z. A., Roskos-Ewoldsen, B., & Roskos-Ewoldsen, D. R. (2004, April). *Dynamic mental models of a movie.* Paper presented at the annual meeting of the Midwestern Psychological Association, Chicago.

D'Andrade, R. (1995). *The development of cognitive anthropology.* Cambridge, UK: Cambridge University Press.

Dickinson, C., & Givon, T. (1997). Memory and conversation: Toward an experimental paradigm. In T. Givon (Ed.), *Conversation: Cognitive, communicative, and social perspectives. Typological studies of language* (Vol. 34, pp. 91–132). Amsterdam: John Benjamins.

Eco, U. (1979). *The role of the reader.* Bloomington: Indiana University Press.

Eco, U. (1990). *The limits of interpretation.* Bloomington: Indiana University Press.

Evans, W. A. (1990). The interpretative turn in media research: Innovation, iteration, or illusion? *Critical Studies in Mass Communication, 7,* 147–168.

Fiske, J. (1987). *Television culture.* London: Methuen.

Fiske, J., & Hartley, J. (1978). *Reading television.* London: Routledge.

Halas, J., & Bachelor, J. (2004). *Animal farm* [DVD]. Chicago: Home Vision Entertainment.

Hall, S. (1994). Reflections upon the encoding/decoding model: An interview with Stuart Hall. In J. Cruz & J. Lewis (Eds.), *Viewing, reading, listening: Audiences and cultural reception* (pp. 253–274). Boulder, CO: Westview.

Hall, S. (2001). Encoding/decoding. In M. G. Durham & D. M. Kellner (Eds.), *Media and cultural studies: Keyworks* (pp. 166–176). Malden, MA: Blackwell. (Original work published 1980)

Higgins, E. T., Bargh, J. A., & Lombardi, W. (1985). Nature of priming effects on categorization. *Journal of Experimental Psychology: Learning, Memory, & Cognition, 11,* 59–69.

Hitchcock, A. (1954). *Rear Window.* Hollywood, CA: Paramount Pictures.

Hodge, R., & Tripp, D. (1986). *Children and television: A semiotic approach.* Cambridge, UK: Polity.

Holland, J. H., Holyoak, K. J., Nisbett, R. E., & Thagard, P. R. (1986). *Induction: Processes of inference, learning, and discovery.* Cambridge, MA: MIT Press.

Jancovich, M. (1992). David Morley, the *Nationwide* studies. In M. Barker & A. Beezer (Eds.), *Reading into cultural studies* (pp. 134–147). London: Routledge.

Johnson-Laird, P. N. (1983). *Mental models.* Cambridge, UK: Cambridge University Press.

Johnson-Laird, P. N. (1989). Mental models. In M. I. Posner (Ed.), *Foundations of cognitive science* (pp. 469–499). Cambridge, MA: Bradford.

Kintsch, W. (1998). *Comprehension: A paradigm for cognition.* Cambridge, UK: Cambridge University Press.

Kintsch, W. (2005). An overview of top-down and bottom-up effects in comprehension: The CI perspective. *Discourse Processes, 39,* 125–128.

Kruskal, J. B., & Wish, M. (1986). *Multidimensional scaling.* Beverly Hills, CA: Sage.

Kunda, Z., & Thagard, P. (1996). Forming impressions from stereotypes, traits, and behaviors: A parallel-constraint-satisfaction theory. *Psychological* Review, 103, 284–308.

Lakoff, G., & Johnson, M. (1980). *Metaphors we live by.* Chicago: University of Chicago Press.

Lee, M., Roskos-Ewoldsen, B., & Roskos-Ewoldsen, D. R. (2005, November). *Combining the landscape and event-indexing models in a conceptual PDP model of story comprehension.* Paper presented at the annual meeting of the National Communication Association, Boston.

Lee, M., & Roskos-Ewoldsen, D. R. (2004, May). *Subtitles, inferences, and movie comprehension: Predictions from the event indexing model.* Paper presented at the annual meeting of the International Communication Association, New Orleans, LA.

Lee, M., Roskos-Ewoldsen, D. R., & Roskos-Ewoldsen, B. (2004, May). *Mental representations of news stories.* Paper presented at the annual meeting of the International Communication Association, New Orleans, LA.

Livingstone, S. M. (1987). The implicit representation of characters in *Dallas*: A multidimensional scaling approach. *Human Communication Research, 13,* 399–420.

Livingstone, S. M. (1989). Interpretive viewers and structured programs: The implicit representations of soap opera characters. *Communication Research, 16,* 25–57.

Livingstone, S. M. (1990a). Interpreting a television narrative: How different viewers see a story. *Journal of Communication, 40*(1), 72–85.

Livingstone, S. M. (1990b). *Making sense of television: The psychology of audience interpretation.* Oxford, UK: Pergamon.

Magliano, J. P., Dijkstra, K., & Zwann, R. A. (1996). Generating predictive inferences while viewing a movie. *Discourse Processes, 22,* 199–224.

Magliano, J. P., Miller, J., & Zwann, R. A. (2001). Indexing space and time in film understanding. *Applied Cognitive Psychology, 15,* 533–545.

Markman, A. B. (1999). *Knowledge representation.* Mahwah, NJ: Lawrence Erlbaum Associates.

McCloskey, M. (1983). Naïve theories of motion. In D. Gentner & A. L. Stevens (Eds.), *Mental models* (pp. 299–324). Mahwah, NJ: Lawrence Erlbaum Associates.

Morley, D. (1992). *Television, audiences & cultural studies.* London: Routledge.

Morley, D. (1999). The *Nationwide* audience: Structure and decoding. In D. Morley & C. Brunsdon (Eds.), *The Nationwide television studies* (pp. 111–228). London: Routledge. (Original work published 1980)

Norman, D. A. (1983). Some observations on mental models. In D. Gentner & A. L. Stevens (Eds.), *Mental models* (pp. 299–324). Mahwah, NJ: Lawrence Erlbaum Associates.

Orwell, G. (1945). *Animal farm.* London: Penguin.

Paivio, A. (1986). *Mental representations.* New York: Oxford University Press.

Paivio, A. (1991). Dual coding theory: Retrospect and current status. *Canadian Journal of Psychology, 45,* 255–287.

Parkin, F. (1971). *Class inequality and political order.* New York: Praeger.

Radvansky, G. A., Zwann, R. A., Federico, T., & Franklin, N. (1998). Retrieval from temporally organized situation models. *Journal of Experimental Psychology: Learning, Memory and Cognition, 24,* 1224–1237.

Radway, J. A. (1991). *Reading the romance.* Chapel Hill: University of North Carolina Press.

Read, S. J., Vanman, E. J., & Miller, L. C. (1997). Connectionism, parallel constraint satisfaction processes, and Gestalt principles: (Re)introducing cognitive dynamics to social psychology. *Personality and Social Psychology Review, 1,* 26–53.

Rickheit, G., & Sichelschmidt, L. (1999). Mental models: Some answers, some questions, some suggestions. In G. Rickheit & C. Habel (Eds.), *Mental models in discourse processing and reasoning* (pp. 9–40). New York: Elsevier.

Roloff, M. E., & Berger, C. R. (Eds.). (1982). *Social cognition and communication.* Beverly Hills, CA: Sage.

Rosenberg, S., Nelson, C., & Vivekananthan, P. S. (1968). A multidimensional approach to the structure of personality impressions. *Journal of Personality and Social Psychology, 9,* 283–294.

Rosenberg, S., & Sedlak, A. (1972). Structural representations of implicit personality theory. In L. Berkowitz (Ed.), *Advances in experimental social psychology* (Vol. 6, pp. 235–297). New York: Academic.

Roskos-Ewoldsen, B., Davies, J., & Roskos-Ewoldsen, D. R. (2004). Implications of the mental models approach for cultivation theory. *Communications, 29,* 345–363.

Roskos-Ewoldsen, B., Roskos-Ewoldsen, D. R., Yang, M., & Crawford, Z. (2003, May–June). *Mental models of a movie.* Poster session presented at the annual meeting of the American Psychological Society, Atlanta, GA.

Roskos-Ewoldsen, D. R. (1997). Implicit theories of persuasion. *Human Communication Research, 24,* 31–63.

Roskos-Ewoldsen, D. R., Roskos-Ewoldsen, B., & Dillman Carpentier, F. (2002). Media priming: A synthesis. In J. B. Bryant & D. Zillmann (Eds.), *Media effects in theory and research* (2nd ed., pp. 97–120). Mahwah, NJ: Lawrence Erlbaum Associates.

Rowell, J. A., & Moss, P. D. (1986). Mental models of text and film: A multidimensional scaling analysis. *Educational Psychology, 6,* 321–333.

Schvaneveldt, D. W. (1990). *Pathfinder associative networks: Studies in knowledge organization.* Norwood, NJ: Ablex.

Segrin, C., & Nabi, R. L. (2002). Does television viewing cultivate unrealistic expectations about marriage? *Journal of Communication, 52,* 247–263.

Shore, B. (1996). *Culture in mind.* New York: Oxford University Press.

Storey, J. (2003). *Cultural studies and the study of popular culture* (2nd ed.). Athens: University of Georgia Press.

Taylor, H. A., & Tversky, B. (1992). Spatial mental models derived from survey and route descriptions. *Journal of Memory and Language, 31,* 261–292.

Thagard, P., & Kunda, Z. (1998). Making sense of people: Coherence mechanisms. In S. J. Read & L. C. Miller (Eds.), *Connectionist models of social reasoning and social behavior* (pp. 3–26). Mahwah, NJ: Lawrence Erlbaum Associates.

Trabasso, T., & Magliano, J. P. (1996). Conscious understanding during comprehension. *Discourse Processes, 21,* 255–287.

Turner, G. (1990). *British cultural studies: An introduction.* Boston: Unwin Hyman.

Tversky, A. (1977). Features of similarity. *Psychological Review, 84,* 327–352.

Tversky, A., & Hutchinson, J. W. (1986). Nearest neighbor analysis of psychological spaces. *Psychological Review, 93,* 3–22.

van den Broek, P., Fletcher, C. R., & Risden, K. (1993). Investigations of inferential processes in reading: A theoretical and methodological integration. *Discourse Processes, 16,* 169–180.

van den Broek, P., & Gustafson, M. (1990). Comprehension and memory for texts: Three generations of reading research. In S. R. Goldman, A. C. Graesser, & P. van den Broek (Eds.), *Narrative comprehension, causality, and coherence* (pp. 15–34). Mahwah, NJ: Lawrence Erlbaum Associates.

van den Broek, P., Rapp, D. N., & Kendeou, P. (2005). Integrating memory-based and constructionist processes in accounts of reading comprehension. *Discourse Processes, 39,* 299–316.

van den Broek, P., Risden, K., Fletcher, C., & Thurlow, R. (1996). A "landscape" view of reading: Fluctuating patterns of activation and the construction of a stable memory representation. In B. Britton & A. Graesser (Eds.), *Models of understanding text* (pp. 165–188). Mahwah, NJ: Lawrence Erlbaum Associates.

van den Broek, P., Young, M., Tzeng, Y., & Linderholm, T. (1999). The landscape model of reading: Inferences and the online construction of a memory representation. In H. van Oostendorp & S. R. Goldman (Eds.), *The construction of mental representations during reading* (pp. 71–98). Mahwah, NJ: Lawrence Erlbaum Associates.

van Dijk, T. A. (1995). On macrostructures, mental models, and other inventions: A brief personal history of the van Dijk-Kintsch theory. In C. A. Weaver, S. Mannes, & C. R. Fletcher (Eds.), *Discourse comprehension: Essays in honor of Walter Kintsch* (pp. 383–410). Hillsdale, NJ: Lawrence Erlbaum Associates.

van Dijk, T. A., & Kintsch, W. (1983). *Strategies of discourse comprehension.* New York: Academic.

Wren-Lewis, J. (1983). The encoding/decoding model: Criticisms and redevelopments for research on decoding. *Media, Culture & Society, 5,* 179–197.

Wyer, R. S. (2004). *Social comprehension and judgment: The role of situation models, narratives, and implicit theories.* Mahwah, NJ: Lawrence Erlbaum Associates.

Wyer, R. S., & Radvansky, G. A. (1999). The comprehension and validation of social information. *Psychological Review, 106,* 89–118.

Yang, M., Roskos-Ewoldsen, B., & Roskos-Ewoldsen, D. R. (2004). Implications of the landscape model of text memory for brand placement. In L. J. Shrum (Ed.), *Blurring the lines between entertainment and persuasion: The psychology of entertainment media* (pp. 79–98). Mahwah, NJ: Lawrence Erlbaum Associates.

Yang, M., & Roskos-Ewoldsen, D. R. (2005, May). *The effectiveness of brand placements in the movies: Levels of placements, explicit and implicit memory, and brand choice behavior.* Paper presented at the annual meeting of the International Communication Association, New York.

Zwaan, R. A. (1994). Effect of genre expectations on text comprehension. *Journal of Experimental Psychology: Learning, Memory, and Cognition, 20,* 920–933.

Zwaan, R. A. (1999). Five dimensions of narrative comprehension: The event-indexing model. In S. R. Goldman, A. C. Graesser, & P. van den Broek (Eds.), *Narrative comprehension, causality, and coherence: Essays in honor of Tom Trabasso* (pp. 93–111). Mahwah, NJ: Lawrence Erlbuam Associates.

Zwaan, R. A., Langston, M. C., & Graesser, A. C. (1995). The construction of situation models in narrative comprehension: An event-indexing model. *Psychological Science, 6,* 292–297.

Zwaan, R. A., & Radvansky, G. A. (1998). Situation models in language comprehension and memory. *Psychological Bulletin, 123,* 162–185.

Zwaan, R. A., Radvansky, G. A., Hilliard, A. E., & Curiel, J. M. (1998). Constructing multidimensional models during reading. *Scientific Studies of Reading, 2,* 199–220.

IV

Social Influence

15

Attitude Accessibility: Theory, Methods, and Future Directions

Laura Arpan
Florida State University

Nancy Rhodes
David R. Roskos-Ewoldsen
University of Alabama

A group of colleagues is discussing current events over dinner at a conference. A new topic comes up. Some of the people at the table immediately express their evaluation of the topic. Others at the table are a bit slower to express their views. In talking to this second group, it is clear that some of them have not thought about the issue much at all. Others have clearly thought about the issue but are unsure how they feel—they know the arguments on both sides, but have not decided which set of arguments is the most persuasive. Still others have a clearly defined attitude: They know how they feel, but they seem to just not have thought about the issue for a while and seem a bit rusty.

This vignette demonstrates some of the nuances of attitude accessibility. By *attitude accessibility* we refer to the ease with which an attitude is activated from memory. That is, some people, for some issues, know how they feel and can report on those feelings very quickly. These people have accessible attitudes toward the issue at hand. Other people respond more slowly to an attitude issue. They have a less accessible attitude. As we will see in this chapter, there could be a number of reasons why an attitude could be more or less accessible. Furthermore, the accessibility of an attitude has strong implications for how an attitude functions for an individual. This chapter addresses these issues. First, we quickly describe some of the early work that forms our understanding of what attitudes are and how they function.

When Roloff and Berger's (1982) volume appeared, the study of persuasion was beginning an explosion of research on dual-process models of persuasion (see Hamilton, chap. 18, this volume). At the same time, the pace of research into the nature of attitudes was somewhat sluggish. The little research that was being conducted on the nature of attitudes had been spurred by disappointments in the study of the attitude–behavior relation (Zanna & Fazio, 1982). However, an important outgrowth of this research on the connection between attitudes and behavior was work on attitude accessibility. Only a few articles had been published on attitude accessibility when Roloff and Berger's (1982) volume appeared (Fazio, Powell, & Herr, 1983; Fazio & Zanna, 1981), however, since that time, our understanding of attitude accessibility has advanced tremendously.

THE NATURE OF ATTITUDES

Attitudes have long been a focus of study by social scientists. From early on, definitions of attitudes have usually comprised three components—cognitive, affective, and behavioral (e.g., Allport, 1935)—that make up the tripartite model of attitudes. The tripartite model of attitudes has been extremely influential in shaping research on attitudes and research suggests that these three components of attitudes can function as both antecedents and consequences of attitudes (Eagly & Chaiken, 1983). For the most part, however, the concept of attitude generally refers to the evaluation of an object or concept. This evaluation is generally thought to encompass cognitive, behavioral, and affective components. This is, the beliefs one has about an attitude object, how one acts toward the object, and how one feels about the object are most often thought of as the main components of an attitude.

The cognitive component is generally thought to encompass the thoughts and beliefs related to the attitude object. For example, people generally believe that Diet Coke is low in calories (which is presumably positive). Of course, the beliefs about the attitude object are not necessarily evaluative in nature (e.g., the belief that Diet Coke is made of matter), although the preponderance of positive or negative thoughts is a good indication as to whether the attitude is favorable or unfavorable toward the issue (Cacioppo, Harkins, & Petty, 1981; Fishbein & Ajzen, 1975).

The affective component of an attitude is the emotional reaction to the attitude object; that is, one's feeling that the object is good or bad. The "yuck" reaction to a cockroach (or political leader) involves the affective component of the attitude. One way in which the affective component of an attitude is formed is by repeated associations of positive or negative feelings with the attitude object (Olson & Fazio, 2001, 2002). Likewise, the mere exposure effect—when people develop positive attitudes toward objects they are repeatedly exposed to—involves the affective component of attitudes (Fink, Monahan, & Kaplowitz, 1989; Monahan, Murphy, & Zajonc, 2000).

The behavioral component of an attitude refers to the actions of the individual with regard to the attitude object. In a sense, this is the component that has been considered the most important historically (Zanna & Fazio, 1982). Early in the history of social psychology there was an implicit assumption that the value of studying an attitude was to be able to predict behavior related to the attitude (Allport, 1935). However, as noted by Wicker (1969), a review of the research in attitudes demonstrated that the prediction of behavior from attitudes was far from certain. Although Wicker's findings were startling at the time, work since then has established that attitudes are related to behavior, albeit in a somewhat more complex fashion than originally assumed (Fazio & Roskos-Ewoldsen, 2005).

DEFINING ATTITUDE ACCESSIBILITY

During the 1980s and 1990s, research focused on the structure of attitudes in memory (Ajzen, 1989; Baron & Misovich, 1999; McGuire, 1986, 1989; Pratkanis, 1989; Smith & DeCoster, 1999; Wood, Rhodes, & Biek, 1995). Based on the idea of memory as a semantic network, the understanding of attitudes was that they are constructed of associated nodes in memory (Fazio, 1986; Fazio, Sanbonmatsu, Powell, & Kardes, 1986). In this model of memory, concepts that are frequently activated together form a strong association. Through the process of spreading activation, when one concept is activated, related concepts are also activated.

Within the attitude accessibility framework, we define attitudes as associations between objects and evaluations of those objects stored in memory (Fazio, 1986, 1989). Relating the network model to attitudes, then, the mental representation of the attitude object is stored as a node in this network. Similarly, the evaluation of this object is also represented as a node in the network.

There is variability in how easily constructs can be retrieved from memory. For example, the name of your best friend or your birthday are constructs that are easily and quickly accessed when you need them. In contrast, the name of your third-grade teacher (assuming you have been out of third grade for at least a few years) takes much longer to recall. You most likely have not forgotten the name of the teacher; that is, with some time and a few good memory cues, you are likely to eventually come up with the correct name. However, because it is not information that you use frequently, it is far less accessible to you than your birth date.

To the extent that an evaluation is strongly associated with the object, the evaluation will be highly accessible; that is, when the node for the attitude object is activated, the strength of the association will ensure that, due to spreading activation, the node containing the evaluation of the object is also activated. Indeed, this is the definition of an accessible attitude according to Fazio (1986): Attitudes for which there is a strong association between the object and the evaluation are highly accessible. When the strength of the connection reaches a certain level, the attitude becomes automatically accessible from memory. In this instance, when the attitude object (specifically, the mental representation thereof) is activated, the evaluation of that object is quickly and effortlessly accessed as well. In this way, judgments can be made rapidly and without extensive reflection.

In contrast, for attitudes that are not accessible, the associations between the object and the evaluation of that object are not as strong. In this case, the activation of the object does not spontaneously activate the evaluation of the object. Consequently, it may take more time to activate the judgment, or it could be that this object has no evaluation associated with it.

Of course, because we cannot possess an attitude toward everything (e.g., new objects in our environment or those toward which we have not been motivated to form an attitude), our responses to all possible attitude objects will fall somewhere on a nonattitude to attitude continuum. As described in the opening vignette, there is variability in the extent to which individuals have formed judgments about potential attitude objects. Some people will have extensively thought about an issue. They will be familiar with the arguments on both sides of the issue, and will have a clear understanding of relative merits of both sides. They will have thought about the ways in which the various sides of the argument are consistent with their own values. They will know whether they would expect to gain or lose personally if they engaged in behavior related to the issue. Furthermore, they will have examined their feelings about the issues and will have made an evaluation as to whether they have positive or negative feelings about the issue.

In contrast, a nonattitude refers to a construct that has not been associated with an evaluation. This might be something new, such as the first time someone heard about a new proposal for reforming health care funding. Or, it might be something that has not been important enough to the person to evaluate. For example, young adults may not form an evaluation of a particular brand of washing machine until they purchase their first home and are suddenly faced with needing to purchase such an appliance. Until the evaluation becomes relevant, they most likely have a nonattitude about specific washing machine brands.

Many attitudes lie somewhere between these two extremes. Most people, when asked, can report their evaluation of a wide range of attitude objects. For any given person, some of these attitudes will be strong and very quickly retrieved and others may be relatively weak and slowly accessed, but for most attitude objects, people are able to report where on a continuum their attitude lies.

FUNCTIONS OF ACCESSIBLE ATTITUDES

As we have already suggested, accessible attitudes are important predictors of various phenomenon of interest to communication scholars and psychologists (Roskos-Ewoldsen, 1997). We continue Fazio's (1989) practice of discussing the functions that accessible attitudes serve for the individual because we feel it is important to focus on what the attitude does for the individual. In other words, how does the accessible attitude influence how a person operates in her or his environment? We discuss several functions of accessible attitudes, but going back to the original functionalist theories of Smith, Bruner, and White (1956) and Katz (1960), accessible attitudes generally serve a knowledge function because, as we argue, accessible attitudes influence how a person understands and acts within a social environment. However, the basic argument for why accessible attitudes are more functional than less accessible ones is the observation that for an attitude toward some object in the environment to influence what a person perceives, or how a person understands a situation, or that person's behavior, the attitude must be activated in memory. Of course, accessible attitudes have a greater likelihood of being activated, which results in their being more functional for the individual. In this section, we briefly discuss the influence of attitude accessibility on attention, information processing, and behavior.

ATTENTION

Accessible attitudes attract our attention, literally determining what we notice in our environment. Roskos-Ewoldsen and Fazio (1992) found that research participants were more likely to orient their attention to objects in a complex visual field when they had more accessible attitudes toward those objects. Similarly, research participants who had more accessible attitudes toward particular consumer products were more likely to find those products on a shelf and choose them from a group of many other products toward which their attitudes were less accessible (Fazio, Powell, & Williams, 1989). Interestingly, when people did not have accessible attitudes toward the objects in a visual display, their attention was attracted to those items in the display that were more salient (Fazio et al., 1989). The implications are clear in a world full of information and visual clutter. We cannot act positively (or negatively) toward objects we do not "see." The orienting function of accessible attitudes will be the gateway to attitude-consistent behaviors in most cases.

The finding that accessible attitudes serve an orienting function suggests that, at some level, attitudes are activated extremely early in the processing of incoming stimuli (Roskos-Ewoldsen & Fazio, 1992). More recent research has focused on how early accessible attitudes play a role in the processing of incoming stimuli. Do attitudes influence other cognitive processes that occur at the early stages of the processing of incoming stimuli? One characteristic of social situations is that most stimuli are open to multiple classifications or interpretations. When interacting with a person, do we pay attention to that person's ethnicity, gender, age, physical characteristics, and so forth? Smith, Fazio, and Cejka (1996) established that the accessibility of our attitudes toward the various possible categorizations of an object ultimately influence how the object is categorized and perceived. Likewise, Fazio and Dunton (1997) found that as the accessibility of participants' attitudes toward a person's race increased, the more likely they were to categorize novel people in terms of race (see also Fazio, 2000; Fazio & Towles-Schwen, 1999). Apparently, accessible attitudes influence how ambiguous stimuli are categorized and what they come to mean.

INFORMATION PROCESSING

Accessible attitudes offer us an efficient, although not always desirable, means of processing myriad pieces of information we encounter each day by motivating us to attend to and carefully consider some messages and by facilitating avoidance or biased processing of other messages (Fazio & Towles-Schwen, 1999; Roskos-Ewoldsen, 1997).

Motivated Processing

Accessible attitudes often signal for us which topics or message sources are important, thereby encouraging us to attend to and elaborate on persuasive messages related to the important topic or delivered by a favored message source (Fabrigar, Priester, Petty, & Wegener, 1998; Roskos-Ewoldsen, Bichsel, & Hoffman, 2002). For example, Fabrigar et al. (1998) found that people with more accessible attitudes toward vegetarianism were more likely to centrally process a message about vegetarianism. Roskos-Ewoldsen et al. (2002) extended this finding by demonstrating that the activation of an attitude toward other components of the message could also increase central processing. In this experiment, participants with a more accessible positive attitude toward the source of the message were more likely to centrally process a message attributed to that source. Importantly, the attitude toward the source did not result in biased processing of the message. Rather, the accessible attitude toward the source of the message acted as a piece of information indicating the importance of the message, which motivated participants to more carefully process the message (see also Fabrigar et al., 1998; Roese & Olson, 1994). This attitude-as-information explanation is similar to research and theorizing on the effects of mood on judgment that has found that mood can both act as information that influences people's judgments and bias how information is interpreted (Clore, 1992).

Although studies of the elaboration likelihood model (ELM) and heuristic-systematic model (HSM) have shown that we tend to pay careful attention to messages about topics that are personally relevant or that relate to core values or desired outcomes (Johnson & Eagly, 1989), the evaluation of these topics as important must be accessible to start the elaborative process in a natural situation. For example, if we do not remember that we like or need to get more information about a particular political candidate, we might not read or listen to a news story about that candidate's most recent speech. The assumption here is that accessible attitudes toward the topic or the message source are one way to inform us that a message is important. The ELM and HSM suggest that we elaborate on messages we consider to be important to arrive at a correct decision with respect to the behavior or attitude advocated within the message (Chaiken, Liberman, & Eagly, 1989; Petty & Cacioppo, 1986). We would suggest that one way to think about the research on the ELM and HSM testing the role of motivation on how a message is processed is that the research involved experimental "primes" of the topic's importance. For example, studies involving messages advocating the research participants' having to take comprehensive exams before they would graduate certainly primed negative attitudes about exams. In short, accessible attitudes will often cause us to attend to and carefully scrutinize persuasive messages. However, this careful processing might not be intended to help us revisit and revise existing attitudes. Rather, such scrutiny might take the form of biased processing.

Biased Processing

Although accessible attitudes can influence us to studiously gather information to make correct decisions, they can also encourage us to cognitively reinforce our existing attitudes and past or ongoing behaviors. Early scholars recognized that attitudes can function as lenses through which we view and interpret our world (Allport, 1935; Katz, 1960; Smith et al., 1956). More recent research has shown that accessible attitudes often color our judgments of messages and attitude objects in a manner that is consistent with our attitudes (Fazio, 1990a; Fazio, Roskos-Ewoldsen, & Powell, 1994). For example, research participants with more accessible, positive attitudes toward a presidential candidate were more likely to say their favored candidate won a debate than were participants with equally positive, but less accessible attitudes (Fazio & Williams, 1986). Additionally, when it was more difficult to determine the winner in a televised vice-presidential debate, the same pattern of effects associated with accessible attitudes was found, but was even more pronounced (see also Houston & Fazio, 1989).

An important caveat to these studies is that accessible attitudes are more likely to bias processing when the information or situation is relatively ambiguous (Fazio & Williams, 1986; Roskos-Ewoldsen, 1997). In addition, the relation between attitude accessibility and biased processing is also typically attenuated among individuals who are motivated to make a correct decision and given the opportunity to arrive at a correct decision (Fazio, 1990b; Sanbonmatsu & Fazio, 1990; Schuette & Fazio, 1995). For example, Schuette and Fazio (1995) had research participants read a study that found that capital punishment either deterred crime or did not deter crime. When research participants expected their evaluations of a scientific study to be read by a panel of expert scientists, they showed less biased processing of the study. However, participants who did not expect their responses to be read by the experts showed biased processing of the study. When the results of the study were proattitudinal (consistent with participants' prior attitudes), participants with more accessible attitudes judged it to be much stronger and more convincing than participants with less accessible attitudes; when the study was counterattitudinal, they judged it to be weaker and less well conducted than participants with similar, but less accessible, attitudes (see also Houston & Fazio, 1989).

BEHAVIOR

Perhaps the most important contribution of the conceptualization and study of attitude accessibility in social psychological research is the identification of consistently strong correlations between accessible attitudes and behavior. Prior to work in this area, some scholars had rejected the existence of a relation between attitudes and behaviors, nearly sounding a death knell for research in attitudes and attitude structure in the early 1970s (Wicker, 1969). However, research has established that accessible attitudes are strongly correlated with eventual behaviors and behavioral intent (for general reviews, see Fazio, 1986, 1990a; Fazio & Roskos-Ewoldsen, 2005) in the areas of voting behavior, consumer product choice, loyalty to retail stores, intended charitable contributions, exercise behaviors, choice of a game to play, and racist behaviors (Bassili, 1995; Kokkinaki & Lunt, 1997; Posavac, Sanbonmatsu, & Fazio, 1997; Woodside & Trappey, 1996). Going back to our earlier observation, attitudes are most likely to affect behavior when they are activated from memory at the moment the attitude is initially observed. Of course, attitudes that are more accessible from memory are more likely to be activated and to influence behaviors.

Accessible attitudes most often affect behavior in situations that allow or require spontaneous decisions (e.g., deciding which gas station to turn into when your tank is empty), or in ambiguous social situations (Fazio, 1986, 1990a). With situations that facilitate or require spontaneous behaviors, highly accessible attitudes will likely determine which evaluations or objects come to mind when a behavioral decision must be made. For example, when research participants were asked to which charity they would donate monetary compensation for research participation, they chose the charities for which their attitudes were most accessible, even though they had evaluated other charities just as or more favorably in a pretest (Posavac et al., 1997).

With ambiguous objects or social situations, accessible attitudes can influence how we define or categorize the situation or object: This categorization, in turn, influences behavior (Fazio, 1986, 1990a). For example, imagine you are sitting in your car at an intersection and when someone walks toward your door. If you had recently been reading and worrying about local carjacking incidents (so that the concept of carjacking, as well as your attitude toward it, would be relatively accessible), you might automatically interpret the person as a carjacker and immediately lock your door. Someone who did not have accessible attitudes toward carjacking might not know how to interpret the intentions of this person. However, upon recognizing the name of a local charity on the person's shirt, one could interpret the person as a representative of a local charity who was asking for donations from people stuck at traffic lights. In the latter case, one might quickly start to look for change or try to avoid eye contact with the person. In the first case, spontaneous perceptions of the attitude object (the person walking up to the car) were driven by an accessible attitude, and attitude-consistent behavior followed spontaneously. In the second case, in which no relevant concepts were particularly accessible, a salient feature in the situation (the name of the charity on the person's shirt) drove the perception of the attitude object and the subsequent behavior. In essence, accessible attitudes can influence (sometimes incorrectly) perceptions of objects, people, and situations, causing the event or person to be defined or categorized according to accessible concepts and criteria, and situational behavior to follow from these perceptions and definitions.

So, in situations that call for spontaneous behavior, attitude accessibility should be most predictive of behavior (Fazio, 1990a; Sanbonmatsu & Fazio, 1990). However, in situations that require accurate decisions or a consideration of norms, we might reflect on the underpinnings or cognitive components of our attitude toward the behavior, social norms regarding the behavior, and the unique characteristics of the situation and then act accordingly (Ajzen, 1991; Ajzen & Fishbein, 1980; Fazio, 1990a). Hence, our behavior might not be strongly correlated with our attitudes in more deliberative situations that give us the opportunity to reflect on those attitudes. However, even in situations that involve careful, deliberative decision making, accessible attitudes can influence decisions (Roskos-Ewoldsen, 1997; Roskos-Ewoldsen, Yu, & Rhodes, 2004). As discussed earlier, the attitude-as-information hypothesis suggests that accessible attitudes can motivate deliberative decision making (Roskos-Ewoldsen et al., 2004). Consistent with this, Roskos-Ewoldsen et al. (2004) found that women with more accessible attitudes toward breast self-exams were more likely to intend to perform breast self-exams in the future. Likewise, accessible attitudes might bias how information is interpreted when making a more deliberative decision.

INCREASING ATTITUDE ACCESSIBILITY

Although few studies have systematically attempted to isolate effective methods of enhancing attitude accessibility, the transactive model of attitude accessibility (Roskos-Ewoldsen, 1997) suggests processes by which attitudes become accessible. Four basic means of making attitudes more accessible have been identified: recent activation, frequent activation, expectation of need, and cognitive elaboration.

Recency of activation is one mechanism for increasing attitude accessibility. However, recent activation of an attitude only temporarily increases accessibility. In network models of memory, recently activated nodes will temporarily be more accessible (Roskos-Ewoldsen, Klinger, & Roskos-Ewoldsen, 2006). Therefore, an attitude that has recently been reflected on, acted on, or activated via a pathway from a related concept or evaluation should be relatively accessible. This activation typically dissipates quickly, with accessibility returning to preactivation levels within about 550 to 600 milliseconds (Neeley, 1977). Even during this brief period of time when attitudes are made temporarily more accessible, they have been shown in experimental settings to influence attention to and processing of subsequently presented information (Bargh, Chaiken, Govender, & Pratto, 1992; Fazio, 1993; Fazio et al., 1986) and to influence judgments of ambiguous information for slightly longer periods of time (Fazio, Powell, & Herr, 1983; Roskos-Ewoldsen et al., 2006). In most research, attitudes are made temporarily more accessible via a priming procedure (see methodological considerations later).

In contrast to attitudes that are made accessible for a short time through priming techniques, some attitudes are chronically accessible. Attitudes that are activated frequently are likely to become chronically accessible (Powell & Fazio, 1984). Frequent activation and enhanced accessibility can occur via repeated judgments of an attitude object, expressions of one's attitude (e.g., giving a short speech), or through activation of related concepts or attitudes (Downing, Judd, & Brauer, 1992; Fazio et al., 1986; Houston & Fazio, 1989; Roskos-Ewoldsen & Fazio, 1992). Repeated expression of attitudes has been shown to enhance accessibility for up to 4 months (Zanna, Fazio, & Ross, 1994).

Third, merely expecting to need an attitude toward a particular object has been shown to increase chronic accessibility. For example, research participants who were told they would need to evaluate a novel object in the future were more likely to spontaneously form an attitude and had more accessible attitudes toward the object than participants who were not told they would need to evaluate the object (Fazio, Lenn, & Effrein, 1984). Similarly, participants in two studies of comparative advertising spontaneously developed attitudes toward the novel brand in the comparative ad, ostensibly because the message suggested a need to have an attitude toward the novel brand to evaluate its worth compared to the existing, well-liked brand (Mothersbaugh, Viosca, Phelps, & Roskos-Ewoldsen, 1998; Yi, Phelps, & Roskos-Ewoldsen, 1998). In short, when we perceive a need to have an attitude in the near future we will likely develop an accessible attitude toward the object in question.

Finally, cognitive elaboration is another manner by which attitudes are made accessible. Recall that an attitude is defined as an association of an evaluation with an object. In the network model, evaluations and attitude objects (or concepts) are considered to be nodes in memory that are connected to other relevant nodes. Activation of one node spreads to associated nodes. Each time these pathways are traveled as a result of activation of a related node, the pathways are strengthened. Therefore, considering or reconsidering one's evaluation of an object strengthens not only the association between the evaluation and the attitude object, but also the association with related nodes (related objects and evaluations). The result is a greater likelihood that the original attitude will be activated more frequently because of its stronger connection to more nodes in memory. Each subsequent activation of the attitude further strengthens its accessibility. The ELM and HSM suggest many ways in which individuals intrinsically or externally are motivated to engage in cognitive elaboration, and both models suggest that careful attention to the content of, or arguments within, a persuasive message results in more accessible attitudes (Chaiken et al., 1989; Kardes, 1988; Petty & Cacioppo, 1986, Sherman, 1987). Other processes that result in cognitive elaboration have also been shown to increase accessibility, such as direct experience with the attitude object (Fazio, 1986; Fazio & Zanna, 1981), exposure to fear appeals that results in a desire to control the danger (as opposed to the fear) associated with an unwanted outcome (Roskos-Ewoldsen et al., 2004), and the belief that possessing an attitude toward a particular object is personally important (Krosnick, 1989).

Concepts that are automatically accessible from memory will be come less accessible over time if the accessibility is not reinforced (Grant & Logan, 1993). Although this has not been demonstrated with accessible attitudes, certainly, the accessibility of attitudes must decrease over time if they are not reinforced. Consider your favorite TV character from your childhood. If you have not seen or thought of that character in a long time, the accessibility of your attitude toward that character has probably faded. Notice that we are not saying that the extremity of the attitudes will necessarily change, but the accessibility will weaken. However, according to the transactive model, accessible attitudes tend to operate in a manner that maintains their accessibility through frequent activation and through elaboration. For example, because accessible attitudes orient our attention to objects in our environment, they are reactivated or rehearsed via the automatic judgment that occurs when one attends to a liked or disliked object (Roskos-Ewoldsen, 1997). Additionally, because accessible attitudes motivate elaborative processing, more associations in memory to related nodes are created that will maintain or enhance the accessibility of the attitude. Finally, direct experience with an attitude object makes attitudes more accessible from memory, which can easily and consistently initiate the process from accessibility to attention to behavior that constitutes the remaining section of the transactive model described later (DeBono & Snyder, 1995; Fazio & Zanna, 1981). For example, in a recent study, cigarette smokers showed more biased processing of antismoking messages than nonsmokers (Rhodes & Roskos-Ewoldsen, 2005). In addition, as the smokers judged the antismoking ad to be more biased, they also indicated they were less likely to quit smoking. In other words, the antismoking ad created reactance in the smokers, which reinforced their desire to smoke. Importantly, the accessibility of the smokers' attitudes mediated this process. It was smokers with more accessible attitudes that judged the antismoking ads as more biased and were less likely to want to quit smoking. The accessible prosmoking attitude operated as a defense mechanism for these smokers to protect their smoking behavior from threats such as antismoking ads, and their accessible attitudes also strengthened the behavioral response to continue smoking.

METHODOLOGICAL AND STATISTICAL CONSIDERATIONS IN ATTITUDE ACCESSIBILITY RESEARCH

Research methodologies used to study attitude accessibility draw heavily from cognitive psychology, including the use of reaction time procedures to measure the accessibility of attitudes from memory (Bargh et al., 1992; Bassili, 1993; Berger & Mitchell, 1989; Fazio et al, 1986; Houston & Fazio, 1989; Powell & Fazio, 1984; Roskos-Ewoldsen & Fazio, 1992; Yi, Phelps, & Roskos-Ewoldsen, 1998). In a research setting, attitude accessibility can be measured or manipulated. Although measuring and manipulating accessibility can be fairly straightforward, researchers should keep in mind some individual and situational variables that may affect reaction times. For example, participants' motor operations or reading speeds naturally vary, such that some participants in an experimental setting will respond, on the average, more quickly than others. Furthermore, participants' attention levels vary during experiments, and this can be exacerbated by any extraneous noise or activity near where the experiment is being conducted. Additionally, differences in participants' desired decision-making confidence can affect their response times. Finally, researchers should expect reaction time data to be skewed. Techniques for managing these effects are described next.

Measuring Accessibility

Studies in which accessibility is measured rely on participant reaction times to attitude probes. Typically, research participants are first presented with the name or picture of an object (i.e., the attitude probe) on a computer screen and are then asked to press one of two keys or buttons to indicate whether they like or dislike the object. For example, a participant seated in front of a computer would be shown a photo of an ice cream cone and would be instructed to press either a + key (for a positive evaluation) or a – key (for a negative evaluation) as soon as he or she was able to form or recall an evaluation of ice cream cones. To equalize the distance from the resting area for the participants' hands, the Z key can be labeled + (positive), and the / key can be labeled – (negative). The elapsed time (captured by a computer) between presentation of the probe and the participant's pressing of the positive or negative key provides a measure of response latency. The assumption is that more accessible attitudes are associated with faster reaction times (Powell & Fazio, 1984; Roskos-Ewoldsen & Fazio, 1992). Software programs such as Superlab (http://www.superlab.com/), E-Prime (http://www.pstnet.com/products/e-prime/), and DirectRT (http://www.empirisoft.com/) are commonly used in this procedure. Although most accessibility experiments use words and pictures as stimuli, audio stimuli have also been employed in a study that required participants to listen to tape-recorded statements and respond to those statements by pressing a button on a response box (Fazio & Williams, 1986).

One limitation to the widespread use of the concept of attitude accessibility has been the necessity to engage research participants in a computerized reaction time task. In most cases, this has required bringing participants into the research lab to respond to programmed stimuli on individual computers. As a result, much of this type of work has been conducted using college student samples. However, reaction time procedures for phone surveys have recently seen an increase in use (Bassili & Krosnick, 2000). In particular, such surveys have employed reaction time techniques to assess the accessibility of political attitudes. Research employing these techniques has been used, for example, to demonstrate that the speed with which one retrieves a behavioral intention to vote predicts actual voting behavior up to a year later (Fletcher, 2000), and that individuals who are ambivalent toward abortion have less accessible attitudes than individuals who are not ambivalent (Huckfeldt & Sprague, 2000). The ready availability of such reaction time techniques should enable attitude researchers to more easily move beyond lab-based work with college student research participants.

Gathering and analyzing reaction time data presents a number of unique challenges. Reaction time data are inherently messy (Fazio, 1990b). The messiness of reaction time data results from a number of sources including a lack of practice sessions for participants, undesired variance in participants' speed of responding to probes and attention to the experiment, unintended effects of independent variables, and the order of attitude probes.

A major issue that accessibility researchers should consider is the general notion of speed–accuracy trade-off, which refers to the likelihood that participants will vary in terms of desired decision-making confidence and in their desire to pay attention during the experiment and subsequently respond to probes quickly. For example, some participants may want to be absolutely correct before responding to an attitudinal probe, whereas other participants will respond based on their initial reaction. Both tendencies can create variance in response latency that is unrelated to attitude accessibility. Therefore, participants should be instructed to respond to probes quickly, but accurately, and researchers should take care to keep participants on task and attentive during the study (Fazio, 1990b).

Additionally, research participants should perform several practice trials with probes unrelated to those in the eventual experiment before critical response latency measures are taken. Reaction times are a product of the time it takes participants to make a decision and the motor skills that are necessary to respond by pressing the key. These practice trials allow participants to become familiar with study procedures and to learn the motor skills necessary for responding to the attitude probes, thereby reducing natural variability in the speed of responding across participants. For example, Roskos-Ewoldsen et al. (2004) had participants complete two blocks of 20 trials using randomly ordered probes

"Press the like key" and "Press the dislike key" before having them complete a block of 20 practice trials with actual objects or concepts as probes. The fourth block contained the critical items ("breast cancer" and "breast self-exams" in this study), the probes "Press the like key" and "Press the dislike key," and 16 distracter items to generate a total of 20 trials. The probes in the third and fourth blocks were presented in a different random order to each participant. Although a total of three blocks of 20 practice trials each before the block of 20 items with the critical items may seem excessive, it ensures that participants are familiar with the task so that part of the reaction time does not reflect their hunting for the correct key to press after they made their decision.

Researchers should also plan to control for participants' individual response speeds. With between-subject designs, participants' mean response latencies in the filler trials (either the mean reaction time for responses to the "Press the like key" and "Press the dislike key" prompts presented in the fourth block or the harmonic mean of the reaction times for the 16 distracter items in the fourth block of trials) can be used to create an index of each participant's general response speed. This index can then be used as a control variable for responses to the critical attitude probes (e.g., as a covariate in an analysis of covariance). Latencies for filler trials can also be used to create difference scores that subtract mean filler latencies from latencies for key attitude probes (Fazio, 1990b; Fazio et al., 1984). The issue of individual response speeds is not as critical in within-subjects designs because the same participant is responding to all of the critical items.

With all designs, the number of response categories should be kept to a minimum. Most experiments employ a two-response option (yes–no, good–bad, like–dislike). Some experiments have successfully used 5-point, Likert-type response categories, but direct comparisons between the 2-point and 5-point options have not been made (Fazio, 1990b). If a greater number of response categories is essential to the design, a traditional questionnaire that includes more categories can be distributed after latency is measured with a dichotomous response system (Fazio, Powell, & Williams, 1989). In this case, participants will have two scores for each attitude object or two indexes for related objects: response latency from the dichotomous variables and an attitude score from the expanded set of response categories on the questionnaire.

Finally, there are several issues involved with the analysis of reaction time data. Reaction time data tend to be heavily skewed (Fazio, 1990b). When reporting reaction times, the skewness of the sample should always be reported. In addition, if the data are skewed, they need to be normalized prior to analysis using any parametric statistical test. Although the most common technique for transforming reaction time data involves a log-linear transformation, other methods of transforming the data are preferred. A better technique if several reaction times are going to be combined is to use the harmonic mean (Ratcliff, 1993). The harmonic mean involves reciprocally transforming each of the reaction times, averaging the reaction times, and then reciprocally transforming the mean back into the original metric of the reaction times (e.g., milliseconds). If only a single reaction time is being analyzed—as is often the case in attitude accessibility studies—a reciprocal transformation is still the preferred technique because it distorts the underlying distribution of reaction times less than other methods (Fazio, 1990b; Ratcliff, 1993). Another technique for dealing with the skewness of reaction time data is to discard scores that appear below a threshold (often 350 milliseconds) or longer than a threshold (often 2,000 or 2,500 milliseconds). However, this is a dangerous practice because simply discarding the error data can result in misinterpretations of the reaction time data. Ulrich and Miller (1994) did a series of simulations demonstrating that discarding as few as 0.5% of the reaction times from an analysis can make a main effect appear as a two-way interaction (see also Roskos-Ewoldsen & Franks, 1998).

Manipulating Accessibility

Because attitude accessibility is a measure of attitude strength, it is often correlated with attitude extremity. This correlation can cause difficulties for interpretation and data analysis (see, e.g., Fazio & Williams, 1986). Because of this, it is sometimes desirable to manipulate attitude accessibility. Experiments in which accessibility is manipulated typically employ a priming process or a repeated expression or judgment process. Such processes increase the accessibility of the attitudes without affecting the extremity of the attitudes (Roskos-Ewoldsen, 1997).

Asking a participant to make an attitude judgment about a given object several times is one way to manipulate accessibility, as repeated attitude judgments of an object have been shown to increase the chronic accessibility of the attitude toward that object from memory (Fazio, 1995; Fazio et al., 1986; Powell & Fazio, 1984; Roskos-Ewoldsen & Fazio, 1992). For example, if one wanted to manipulate the accessibility of an attitude toward candy bars, participants could be asked to indicate how much they liked candy bars during a pretest, using semantic differential or Likert-type response categories. The effect of repeated attitude judgments is found whether individuals make the same attitude judgment several times (e.g., good–bad; Fazio et al., 1986) or make multiple judgments using different evaluative scales (e.g., like–dislike, good–bad, pleasant–unpleasant; see Downing et al., 1992; Houston & Fazio, 1989; Powell & Fazio, 1984; Roskos-Ewoldsen & Fazio, 1992).

A priming procedure can also be used to temporarily increase the accessibility of an attitude. In this procedure the attitude object of interest is immediately preceded by an object for which participants have been shown to have highly accessible attitudes (Bargh et al., 1992; Fazio, 1993; Fazio et al., 1986). For example, if an earlier reaction time task had established that an individual had a highly accessible, negative attitude toward the word "bad," presenting the word "bad" (prime) immediately prior to the presentation of the word "snake" (target) would temporarily increase the accessibility of that individual's attitude toward snakes. However, for this type of priming to increase attitude accessibility for the target, the participant's attitude toward the target and his or her attitude toward the prime must have the same valence (e.g., a negative evaluation of the word "bad" and a negative evaluation of snakes).

Other methods can be used to manipulate attitude accessibility, such as asking participants to assign attitude objects of interest to the proper category or to rank-order objects in terms of favorability (Posavac et al., 1997); instructing participants that they will need to provide an evaluation of the object at a later time (Fazio, Blascovich, & Driscoll, 1992); or encouraging participants to elaborate on the attitude toward the object (Kardes, 1988; Stayman & Kardes, 1992).

RECENT DEVELOPMENTS AND FUTURE DIRECTIONS IN ATTITUDE ACCESSIBILITY RESEARCH

The study of attitude accessibility has been extensive since the early 1980s and our knowledge of the causes and consequences of attitude accessibility has grown due to this research. Research continues to expand our understanding of attitude accessibility. First, we discuss research on implicit racism and implicit attitudes. Second, we discuss recent research exploring attitude and norm accessibility.

Implicit Racism

Although the study of racist attitudes has a long history in the social sciences, there is also a long history of difficulty associated with measuring racist attitudes. Whereas the explicit disclosure of racist attitudes was socially acceptable many years ago, the change in consciousness of racial issues resulting from the civil rights movement has made it generally undesirable to endorse racist attitudes in most social contexts today. Because of this, the measurement and study of racism has changed over the past few decades. Researchers have recognized that in direct assessments of attitudes toward minority groups respondents are likely to deny racist attitudes and beliefs to present themselves in a favorable light. A variety of techniques have been developed to try to circumvent this socially desirable responding. Perhaps the most clever technique was the development of the bogus pipeline. This technique deceived participants into believing that their true feelings could be seen by researchers through a variety of physiological measurements that the participant believed were being taken. Participants in the bogus pipeline condition reported more racist attitudes than those in the control condition (Jones & Sigall, 1971; Sigall & Page, 1971).

More recently, building on the work in attitude accessibility, techniques have been developed to assess racist attitudes in ways that circumvent the self-presentation concerns of research participants. In particular, Fazio, Jackson, Dunton, and Williams (1995) described a technique for measuring attitudes toward minority groups that build directly on work in attitude accessibility. In this research paradigm, research participants are led to believe that their primary task is to remember a series of faces they are shown on the computer monitor. Later during the experimental session, participants are told that the task will be made more difficult by presenting words between each of the faces, and their task is to indicate whether they like or dislike the word as quickly as possible. The critical issue is whether the faces of African Americans influence how quickly participants respond to positive or negative words. Participants for whom faces of African Americans accelerated how quickly they responded to the negative words (e.g., the face of the African American primed a negative attitude) were much more likely to respond in a racist manner later in the experiment. In other words, the task involved a priming paradigm to implicitly measure people's racist responses.

This work and related work by other researchers has furthered our understanding of the functions of attitudes and stereotypes in thinking about members of minority groups (Devine, Monteith, & Zuwerink, 1991; Dovidio, Kawakami, & Johnson, 1997; Fazio & Dunton, 1997; see Oliver, Ramasubramanian, & Kim, chap. 12, this volume). In particular, these findings have been largely consistent with dual-process accounts of stereotype activation. That is, under most circumstances, the initial response to a minority group member is the automatic and rapid retrieval of the concepts stored in the stereotype. Because of spreading activation processes, the evaluations associated with those concepts are also activated, enabling a quick, stereotype-based judgment of the person. In dual-process accounts, the second process is a deliberative override of the initial judgment. This override occurs when the person making the judgment is both motivated and able to reflect on the judgment, bring additional information to bear, and correct the initial judgment.

The research on implicit racism points to the importance of measuring implicit social reactions (Greenwald & Banaji, 1995). Most of the research on attitudes has measured people's explicit attitudes because people are asked to indicate their attitudes. However, attitudes can influence behavior without conscious recollection of the attitude. Consider Roskos-Ewoldsen and Fazio's (1992) study where participants' attention was more likely to be drawn to distracter items in a visual search task if their attitudes toward the distracter items were more accessible from memory. In that task, participants probably did not consciously think about their attitude while completing the search task (the reaction times were fast enough to rule out this possibility). However, their attitudes did influence how they performed on this task. More research needs to consider the influence of implicit attitudes on persuasion and to measure effects of persuasion via implicit attitude measures.

Norm Accessibility

Research demonstrating the importance of norms in explaining social behavior includes work by Cialdini and his colleagues (Cialdini, Reno, & Kallgren, 1990; Kallgren, Reno, & Cialdini, 2000; Reno, Cialdini, & Kallgren, 1993) showing strong social influences on behaviors such as littering. Likewise, beliefs about the typical behavior of members of a personally important peer group, even if erroneous, have been shown to influence behavior (Miller, Monin, & Prentice, 2000; Prentice & Miller, 1993; Terry & Hogg, 1996). In particular, studies of misperceived norms of drinking behavior affect the drinking behavior of college undergraduates. Further examples of social influence on judgments include polarization of attitudes on the basis of information regarding in-group norms (Mackie, 1986) and judgments made under the scrutiny of others (e.g., Asch, 1956). Clearly, there is substantial evidence for normative influence on behavior.

Often, however, in tests of models of the attitude–behavior relations such as the theory of planned behavior, attitude emerges as a more important predictor of behavior than subjective norm. To better understand the dynamic interplay of attitudes and subjective norms, recent work has begun to examine the accessibility of the subjective norm (Rhodes & Roskos-Ewoldsen, 2005). Just as accessible attitudes are more strongly related to behavior, it is believed that accessible norms will also more strongly predict actions.

Rhodes and Roskos-Ewoldsen (2005) developed a methodology to assess norm accessibility that is similar to that used to assess attitude accessibility. The stimuli used are patterned after the paper-and-pencil measures of subjective norms described by Ajzen and Fishbein (1980). Specifically, participants are asked to respond quickly but accurately to a series of questions inquiring whether each of a number of important people in their lives (e.g., parents, siblings, best friend, boyfriend or girlfriend) wants them to engage in a number of behaviors (e.g., smoking cigarettes, drinking alcohol, and filler items). Each prompt is shown on the screen until the participant presses either the "yes" key or the "no" key.

Although the findings are somewhat preliminary as yet, there is evidence that norm accessibility can be a useful construct in predicting behavior. Attitude and norm accessibility together have been found to account for variance in smoking and drinking behavior (R^2 = .78) beyond that accounted for by traditional measures of attitude and subjective norm (R^2 = .35). Furthermore, norm accessibility is strongly related to other measures of social pressure to smoke and drink, such as the percentage of one's peers who engage in these behaviors and self–reported peer influence to smoke.

Future research also needs to explore how norms become chronically accessible. Self-reported peer influence to smoke was related to norm accessibility (Rhodes & Roskos-Ewoldsen, 2005). Research suggests that at least part of the influence of peers on smoking behavior occurs because of repeated offers of cigarettes and discussions of smoking (Jacobson et al., 2001). The finding that peer influence is related to norm accessibility suggests that repeated expression of the social norms probably increases norm accessibility in the same way that it influences attitude accessibility (Fazio, 1986). Clearly, more research is necessary to explore the mechanisms by which norms become more accessible from memory.

A further direction for future research in this area is to understand how the accessibility of norms might bias perceptions of information in situations. Just as accessible attitudes color perceptions, when one has a clear idea of the normative expectations for behavior, persuasive appeals might be interpreted accordingly. We believe that there is great potential to capitalize on norm accessibility in constructing health-related persuasive appeals.

CONCLUSIONS

As a result of a research tradition spanning more than 70 years of study, the understanding of the interrelation between attitudes and persuasion has flourished and is still growing. The growth of this knowledge is, in part, due to increases in our understanding of the characteristics of attitudes. This chapter has focused primarily on attitude accessibility, although other characteristics of attitudes, such as ambivalence, are also relevant. Attitude accessibility has been a concern for attitude scholars for close to 20 years, and more recently, research has begun to look at the interrelations between attitude accessibility and persuasion (Roskos-Ewoldsen, 1997; Roskos-Ewoldsen et al., 2002; Roskos-Ewoldsen et al., 2004). Accessible attitudes are more resistant to attempts at persuasion, longer lasting, better at predicting behavior, and more likely to bias how future information is interpreted.

Although there has been extensive research on attitude accessibility, this research has tended to focus on the consequences of accessible attitudes—the consequences of accessible attitudes on the orienting of attention, the processing of messages, and future behavior. However, research to further our understanding of the development of accessible attitudes is still in its infancy. Importantly, the research on attitude accessibility suggests that attitude accessibility should be one of the dependent and independent variables of choice for persuasion scholars. Future research needs to focus both on how messages influence attitudes (i.e., attitude accessibility as dependent variable), and on how attitudes influence attention to, and processing of, persuasive messages (i.e., attitude accessibility as independent variable). In addition, research and theorizing needs to include a consideration of implicit attitudes and norms. Research is beginning to suggest the importance of norm accessibility in predicting behavior. Future research in this area will demonstrate, once again, the importance of understanding the cognitive underpinnings of social behavior.

ACKNOWLEDGMENTS

The preparation of this chapter was supported in part by R49/CE000191 from the U.S. Department of Health and Human Services Center for Disease Control and Prevention, National Center for Injury Prevention and Control to the University of Alabama at Birmingham Injury Control Research Center.

REFERENCES

Ajzen, I. (1989). Attitude structure and behavior. In *Attitude structure and function* (pp. 241–274). Hillsdale, NJ: Lawrence Erlbaum Associates.

Ajzen, I. (1991). The theory of planned behavior. *Organizational Behavior and Human Decision Processes, 50,* 179–211.

Ajzen, I., & Fishbein, M. (1980). *Understanding attitudes and predicting social behavior.* Upper Saddle River, NJ: Prentice-Hall.

Allport, G. W. (1935). Attitudes. In C. A. Murchison (Ed.), *Handbook of social psychology* (Vol. 2, pp. 798–844). Worcester, MA: Clark University Press.

Asch, S. E. (1956). Studies of independence and conformity: I. A minority of one against a unanimous majority. *Psychological Monographs, 70*(9, Whole No. 416).

Bargh, J. A., Chaiken, S., Govender, R., & Pratto, F. (1992). The generality of the automatic attitude activation effect. *Journal of Personality and Social Psychology, 62,* 893–912.

Baron, R. M., & Misovich, S. J. (1999). On the relationship between social and cognitive modes of organization. In S. Chaiken & Y. Trope (Eds.), *Dual-process theories in social psychology* (pp. 586–605). New York: Guilford.

Bassili, J. N. (1995). Response latency and the accessibility of voting intentions: What contributes to accessibility and how it affects vote choice. *Personality and Social Psychology Bulletin, 21,* 686–695.

Bassili, J. N., & Krosnick, J. A. (2000). Do strength-related attitude properties determine susceptibility to response effects? New evidence from response latency, attitude extremity, and aggregate indices. *Political Psychology, 21,* 107–132.

Berger, I. E., & Mitchell, A. A. (1989). The effect of advertising on attitude accessibility, attitude confidence, and the attitude–behavior relationship. *Journal of Consumer Research, 16,* 269–279.

Cacioppo, J. T., Harkins, S. G., & Petty, R. E. (1981). The nature of attitudes and cognitive responses and their relationships to behavior. In R. E. Petty, T. M. Ostom, & T. C. Brock (Eds.), *Cognitive responses in persuasion* (pp. 31–54). Hillsdale, NJ: Lawrence Erlbaum Associates.

Chaiken, S., Liberman, A., & Eagly, A. H. (1989). Heuristic and systematic information processing within and beyond the persuasion context. In J. S. Uleman & J. A. Bargh (Eds.), *Unintended thought* (pp. 212–252). New York: Guilford.

Cialdini, R. B., Reno, R. R., & Kallgren, C. A. (1990). A focus theory of normative conduct: Recycling the concept of norms to reduce littering in public places. *Journal of Personality and Social Psychology, 58,* 1015–1026.

Clore, G. L. (1992). Cognitive phenomenology: Feelings and the construction of judgment. In L .Martin & A. Tesser (Eds.), *Construction of social judgments* (pp. 133–163). Hillsdale, NJ: Lawrence Erlbaum Associates.

DeBono, K. G., & Snyder, M. (1995). Acting on one's attitudes: The role of a history of choosing situations. *Personality and Social Psychology Bulletin, 21,* 620–628.

Devine, P. G., Monteith, M. J., & Zuwerink, J. R. (1991). Prejudice with and without compunction. *Journal of Personality and Social Psychology, 60,* 817–830.

Dovidio, J. F., Kawakami, K., & Johnson, C. (1997). On the nature of prejudice: Automatic and controlled processes. *Journal of Experimental Social Psychology, 33,* 510–540.

Downing, J. W., Judd, C. M., & Brauer, M. (1992). Effects of repeated expressions on attitude extremity. *Journal of Personality and Social Psychology, 63,* 17–29.

Eagly, A. H., & Chaiken, S. (1983). Communication modality as a determinant of persuasion: The role of communicator salience. *Journal of Personality and Social Psychology, 45,* 241–256.

Fabrigar, L. R., Priester, J. R., Petty, R. E., & Wegener, D. T. (1998). The impact of attitude accessibility on elaboration of persuasive messages. *Personality and Social Psychology Bulletin, 24,* 339–352.

Fazio, R. H. (1986). How do attitudes guide behavior? In R. H. Sorrentino & E. T. Higgins (Eds.), *The handbook of motivation and cognition: Foundations of social behavior* (pp. 204–243). New York: Guilford.

Fazio, R. H. (1989). On the power and functionality of attitudes: The role of attitude accessibility. In A. R. Pratkanis & S. J. Breckler (Eds.), *Attitude structure and function* (pp. 153–179). Hillsdale, NJ: Lawrence Erlbaum Associates.

Fazio, R. H. (1990a). Multiple processes by which attitudes guide behavior: The MODE model as an integrative framework. In M. Zanna (Ed.), *Advances in experimental social psychology* (Vol. 23, pp. 75–109). Orlando, FL: Academic.

Fazio, R. H. (1990b). A practical guide to the use of response latency in social psychological research. In C. Hendrick & M. S. Clark (Eds.), *Research methods in personality and social psychology* (Vol. 11, pp. 74–97). Newbury Park, CA: Sage.

Fazio, R. H. (1993). Variability in the likelihood of automatic attitude activation: Data reanalysis and commentary on Bargh, Chaiken, Govender, and Pratto (1992). *Journal of Personality and Social Psychology, 64,* 753–758.

Fazio, R. H. (1995). Attitudes as object evaluation associations: Determinants, consequences, and correlates of attitude accessibility. In R. E. Petty & J. A. Krosnick (Eds.), *Attitude strength: Antecedents and consequences* (pp. 247–282). Hillsdale, NJ: Lawrence Erlbaum Associates.

Fazio, R. H. (2000). Accessible attitudes as tools for object appraisal: Their costs and benefits. In G. Maio & J. M. Olson (Eds.), *Why we evaluate: Functions of attitudes* (pp. 1–36). Mahwah, NJ: Lawrence Erlbaum Associates.

Fazio, R. H., Blascovich, J., & Driscoll, D. M. (1992). On the functional value of attitudes: The influence of accessible attitudes upon the ease and quality of decision making. *Personality and Social Psychology Bulletin, 18,* 388–401.

Fazio, R. H., & Dunton, B. C. (1997). Categorization by race: The impact of automatic and controlled components of racial prejudice. *Journal of Experimental Social Psychology, 33,* 451–470.

Fazio, R. H., Jackson, J. R., Dunton, B. C., & Williams, C. J. (1995).Variability in automatic activation as an unobtrusive measure of racial attitudes: A bona fide pipeline? *Journal of Personality and Social Psychology, 69,* 1013–1027.

Fazio, R. H., Lenn, T. M., & Effrein, E. A. (1984). Spontaneous attitude formation. *Social Cognition, 2,* 217–234.

Fazio, R. H., Powell, M. C., & Herr, P. M. (1983). Toward a process model of the attitude–behavior relation: Accessing one's attitude upon mere observation of the attitude object. *Journal of Personality and Social Psychology, 44,* 723–735.

Fazio, R. H., Powell, M. C., & Williams, C. J. (1989). The role of attitude accessibility in the attitude to behavior process. *Journal of Consumer Research, 16,* 280–288.

Fazio, R. H., & Roskos-Ewoldsen, D. R. (2005). Acting as we feel: When and how attitudes guide behavior. In T. C. Brock & M. C. Green (Eds.), *Persuasion: Psychological insights and perspectives* (2nd ed., pp. 41–62). Thousand Oaks, CA: Sage.

Fazio, R. H., Roskos-Ewoldsen, D. R., & Powell, M. C. (1994). Attitudes, perception, and attention. In P. M. Niedenthal & S. Kitayama (Eds.), *The heart's eye: Emotional influences in perception and attention* (pp. 197–216). Orlando, FL: Academic.

Fazio, R. H., Sanbonmatsu, D. M., Powell, M. C., & Kardes, F. F. (1986). On the automatic activation of attitudes. *Journal of Personality and Social Psychology, 50,* 229–238.

Fazio, R. H., & Towles-Schwen, T. (1999). The MODE model of attitude–behavior processes. In S. Chaiken & Y. Trope (Eds.), *Dual process theories in social psychology* (pp. 97–116). New York: Guilford.

Fazio, R. H., & Williams, C. J. (1986). Attitude accessibility as a moderator of the attitude–perception and attitude–behavior relations: An investigation of the 1984 presidential election. *Journal of Personality and Social Psychology, 51,* 505–514.

Fazio, R. H., & Zanna, M. P. (1981). *Direct experience and attitude–behavior consistency: Advances in experimental social psychology* (Vol. 14, pp. 161–202). Orlando, FL: Academic.

Fink, E. L., Monahan, J. L., & Kaplowitz, S. A. (1989). A spatial model of the mere exposure effect. *Communication Research, 16,* 746–769.

Fishbein, M., & Ajzen, I. (1975). *Belief, attitude, intention, and behavior.* Reading, MA: Addison-Wesley.

Fletcher, J. F. (2000). Two-timing: Politics and response latencies in a bilingual survey. *Political Psychology, 21,* 27–55.

Grant, S. C., & Logan, G. D. (1993). The loss of repetition priming and automaticity over time as a function of degree of initial learning. *Memory and Cognition, 21,* 611–618.

Greenwald, A. G., & Banaji, M. R. (1995). Implicit social cognition: Attitudes, self-esteem, and stereotypes. *Psychological Review, 102,* 4–27.

Houston, D. A., & Fazio, R. H. (1989). Biased processing as a function of attitude accessibility: Making objective judgments subjectively. *Social Cognition, 7,* 51–66.

Huckfeldt, R., & Sprague, J. (2000). Political consequences of inconsistency: The accessibility and stability of abortion attitudes. *Political Psychology, 21,* 57–79.

Jacobson, P. D., Lantz, P. M., Warner, K. E., Wasserman, J., Pollack, H. A., & Ahlstrom, A. K. (2001). *Combatting teen smoking: Research and policy strategies.* Ann Arbor: University of Michigan Press.

Johnson, B. T., & Eagly, A. H. (1989). The effects of involvement on persuasion: Meta-analytic perspectives. *Personality and Social Psychology Bulletin, 17,* 289–299.

Jones, E. E., & Sigall, H. (1971). The bogus pipeline: A new paradigm for measuring affect and attitude. *Psychological Bulletin, 76,* 349–364.

Kallgren, C. A., Reno, R. R., & Cialdini, R. B. (2000). A focus theory of normative conduct: When norms do and do not affect behavior. *Personality and Social Psychology Bulletin, 26,* 1002–1012.

Kardes, F. R. (1988). Spontaneous inference processes in advertising: The effects of conclusion omission and involvement on persuasion. *Journal of Consumer Research, 15,* 225–233.

Katz, D. (1960). The functional approach to the study of attitudes. *Public Opinion Quarterly, 24,* 163–204.

Kokkinaki, F., & Lunt, P. (1997). The relationship between involvement, attitude accessibility, and attitude–behaviour consistency. *British Journal of Social Psychology, 36,* 497–509.

Krosnick, J. A. (1989). Attitude importance and attitude accessibility. *Personality and Social Psychology Bulletin, 15,* 297–308.

Mackie, D. (1986). Social identification effects in group polarization. *Journal of Personality and Social Psychology, 50,* 720–728.

McGuire, W. J. (1986). The vicissitudes of attitudes and similar representational constructs in twentieth century psychology. *European Journal of Social Psychology, 16,* 89–130.

McGuire, W. J. (1989). The structure of individual attitudes and attitude systems. In A. R. Pratkanis & S. J. Breckler (Eds.), *Attitude structure and function* (pp. 37–69). Hillsdale, NJ: Lawrence Erlbaum Associates.

Miller, D. T., Monin, B., & Prentice, D. A. (2000). Pluralistic ignorance and inconsistency between private attitudes and public behaviors. In D. J. Terry & M. A. Hogg (Eds.), *Attitudes, behavior, and social context: The role of norms and group membership* (pp. 95–113). Mahwah, NJ: Lawrence Erlbaum Associates.

Monahan, J. L., Murphy, S. T., & Zajonc, R. B. (2000). Subliminal mere exposure: Specific, general, and diffuse effects. *Psychological Science, 11,* 462–466.

Mothersbaugh, D., Viosca, M., Phelps, J., & Roskos-Ewoldsen. D. R. (1998). *The relationship between comparative advertising and attitude accessibility: What are the mechanisms?*

Neeley, J. H. (1977). Semantic priming and retrieval from lexical memory: Roles of inhibitionless spreading activation and limited-capacity attention. *Journal of Experimental Psychology: General, 106,* 225–254.

Olson, M. A., & Fazio, R. H. (2001). Implicit attitude formation through classical conditioning. *Psychological Science, 12,* 413–417.

Olson, M. A., & Fazio, R. H. (2002). Implicit acquisition and manifestation of classically conditioned attitudes. *Social Cognition, 20,* 89–104.

Petty, R. E., & Cacioppo, J. T. (1986). *Communication and persuasion: Central and peripheral routes to attitude change.* New York: Springer-Verlag.

Posavac, S. S., Sanbonmatsu, D. M., & Fazio, R. H. (1997). Considering the best choice: Effects of the salience and accessibility of alternatives on attitude–decision consistency. *Journal of Personality and Social Psychology, 72,* 253–261.

Powell, M. C., & Fazio, R. H. (1984). Attitude accessibility as a function of repeated attitudinal expression. *Personality and Social Psychology Bulletin, 10,* 139–148.

Pratkanis, A. R. (1989). *The cognitive representation of attitudes.* In A. R. Pratkanis & S. J. Breckler (Eds.), *Attitude structure and function* (pp. 71–98). Hillsdale, NJ: Lawrence Erlbaum Associates.

Prentice, D. A., & Miller, D. T. (1993). Pluralistic ignorance and alcohol use on campus: Some consequences of misperceiving the social norm. *Journal of Personality and Social Psychology, 64,* 243–256.

Ratcliff, R. (1993). Methods for dealing with reaction time outliers. *Psychological Bulletin, 114,* 510–532.

Reno, R. R., Cialdini, R. B., & Kallgren, C. A. (1993). The transsituational influence of social norms. *Journal of Personality and Social Psychology, 64,* 104–112.

Rhodes, N., & Roskos-Ewoldsen, D. R. (2005). *Norm and attitude accessibility.* Manuscript submitted for publication.

Roese, N. J., & Olson, J. M. (1994). Attitude importance as a function of repeated attitude expression. *Journal of Experimental Social Psychology, 30,* 39–51.

Roloff, M. E., & Berger, C. R. (1982). *Social cognition and communication.* Beverly Hills, CA: Sage.

Roskos-Ewoldsen, D. R. (1997). Attitude accessibility and persuasion: Review and a transactive model. In B. Burleson (Ed.), *Communication yearbook 20* (pp. 185–225). Beverly Hills, CA: Sage.

Roskos-Ewoldsen, D. R., Bichsel, J., & Hoffman, K. (2002). The influence of accessibility of source likability on persuasion. *Journal of Experimental Social Psychology, 38,* 137–143.

Roskos-Ewoldsen, D. R., & Fazio, R. H. (1992). On the orienting value of attitudes: Attitude accessibility as a determinant of an object's attraction of visual attention. *Journal of Personality and Social Psychology, 63,* 198–211.

Roskos-Ewoldsen, D. R. & Franks, J. J. (1998, April). *Associative attitude priming: An artifact?* Invited paper presented at the annual meeting of the Midwest Communication Association, Chicago.

Roskos-Ewoldsen, D. R., Klinger, M., & Roskos-Ewoldsen, B. (2006). Media priming. In G. Preiss, A. Burrell, & J. Bryant (Eds.), *Mass media theories and processes: Advances through meta-analysis* (pp. 58–80). Mahwah, NJ: Lawrence Erlbaum Associates.

Roskos-Ewoldsen, D. R., Yu, H. J., & Rhodes, N. (2004). Fear appeal messages affect accessibility of attitudes toward the threat and adaptive behaviors. *Communication Monographs, 71,* 49–69.

Sanbonmatsu, D. M., & Fazio, R. H. (1990). The role of attitudes in memory-based decision making. *Journal of Personality and Social Psychology, 59,* 614–622.

Schuette, R. A., & Fazio, R. H. (1995). Attitude accessibility and motivation as determinants of biased processing: A test of the MODE model. *Personality and Social Psychology Bulletin, 21,* 704–710.

Sherman, S. J. (1987). Cognitive processes in the formation, change, and expression of attitudes. In M. P. Zanna, J. M. Olson, & C. P. Herman (Eds.), *Social influence:*

The Ontario symposium (Vol. 5, pp. 75–106). Hillsdale, NJ: Lawrence Erlbaum Associates.

Sigall, H., & Page, R. (1971). Current stereotypes: A little fading, a little faking. *Journal of Personality and Social Psychology, 18,* 247–255.

Smith, E. R., & DeCoster, J. (1999). Associative and rule-based processing: A connectionist interpretation of dual-process models. In S. Chaiken & Y. Trope (Eds.), *Dual-process theories in social psychology* (pp. 323–336). New York: Guilford.

Smith, E. R., Fazio, R. H., & Cejka, M. A. (1996). Accessible attitudes influence categorization of multiply categorizable objects. *Journal of Personality and Social Psychology, 71,* 888–898.

Smith, M., Bruner, J. S., & White, R. W. (1956). *Opinions and personality.* Oxford, UK: Wiley.

Stayman, D. M., & Kardes, F. R. (1992). Spontaneous inference processes in advertising: Effects of need for cognition and self-monitoring on inference generation and utilization. *Journal of Consumer Psychology, 1,* 125–142.

Terry, D. J., & Hogg, M. A. (1996). Group norms and the attitude–behavior relationship: A role for group identification. *Personality and Social Psychology Bulletin, 22,* 776–793.

Ulrich, R., & Miller, J. (1994). Effects of truncation on reaction time analysis. *Journal of Experimental Psychology: General, 123,* 34–80.

Wicker, A. W. (1969). Attitudes versus actions: The relationship of verbal and overt behavioral responses to attitude objects. *Journal of Social Issues, 25,* 41–78.

Wood, W., Rhodes, N., & Biek, M. (1995). Working knowledge and attitude strength: An information-processing analysis. In R. E. Petty & J. A. Krosnick (Eds.), *Attitude strength: Antecedents and consequences* (pp. 283–313). Mahwah, NJ: Lawrence Erlbaum Associates.

Woodside, A. G., & Trappey, R. J. (1996). Customer portfolio analysis among competing retail stores. *Journal of Business Research, 32,* 189–200.

Yi, H., Phelps, J. E., & Roskos-Ewoldsen, D. R. (1998). Examining the effectiveness of comparative advertising: The role of attitude accessibility. *Journal of Current Issues and Research in Advertising, 20,* 61–74.

Zanna, M. P., & Fazio, R. H. (1982). The attitude–behavior relation: Moving toward a third generation of research. In M. P. Zanna, E. T. Higgins, & C. P. Herman (Eds.), *Consistency in social behavior: The Ontario Symposium* (Vol. 2, pp. 283–301). Hillsdale, NJ: Lawrence Erlbaum Associates.

Zanna, M. P., Fazio, R. H., & Ross, M. (1994). The persistence of persuasion. In R. C. Schank & E. Langer (Eds.), *Beliefs, reasoning, and decision making: Psychologic in honor of Bob Abelson* (pp. 347–362). Hillsdale, NJ: Lawrence Erlbaum Associates.

16

Emotion and Persuasion: A Social Cognitive Perspective

Robin L. Nabi
University of California, Santa Barbara

In our current intellectual climate, it should come as no surprise to find a chapter focused on emotion in a volume highlighting social cognition. Indeed, the connection between thought and feeling is currently well-accepted, with evidence originating from multiple domains of psychology, including neurobiology, memory, information processing, personality, and others (see Forgas, 2001, for a range of related perspectives). However, at the time Roloff and Berger's (1982) volume was published, the study of emotion and persuasion was primarily confined to the study of fear appeals, which had taken a decidedly cognitively based turn, replacing the motivational perspective that had dominated from midcentury into the 1970s (e.g., Leventhal, 1970; Rogers, 1975, 1983). Since then, growing interest in emotion throughout psychology has led to increased theorizing, not only about the persuasive effects of fear (e.g., Witte, 1992) but also an array of other emotions (e.g., Nabi, 1999). Further, dominant paradigms of persuasion have recently begun to incorporate affect-based constructs to better understand the role emotions may play in the processes of attitude and behavior change.

This chapter, then, aims to address three questions, central to which is the interplay between emotion and cognition. First, how have models of fear appeals (and other emotions) developed since the mid-1980s? Second, how have popular persuasion theories, each oriented around cognitively based devices (elaboration likelihood model, theory of reasoned action, and framing), conceptualized the role of emotion and affect? Third, how has affect more generally been considered in the persuasion literature? The chapter then turns to methodological issues involved in the study of emotions' persuasive influence, including emotional arousal techniques, measurement, and research design.

Before we begin, though, it may be helpful to be clear on the terms used throughout the chapter. Affect, broadly speaking, encompasses both emotion and mood. Emotions are generally short-lived, intense states directed at some external stimuli, whereas moods are untargeted and more enduring experiences (see Fiske & Taylor, 1991, for a review). Further, affect can be either relevant or irrelevant to a persuasion context. Relevant affect is in response to the message or target object (e.g., fear about cancer in response to an antismoking public service announcement) whereas irrelevant affect stems from some other source (e.g., negative feedback on a test prior to exposure to a persuasive appeal). This review focuses primarily, although not exclusively, on message-relevant emotion.

RECENT MODELS OF EMOTION AND PERSUASION

Since the first systematic investigation of fear appeals in the 1950s (Hovland, Janis, & Kelley, 1953; Janis & Feshbach, 1953), social cognition has played an increasingly important role in the research on emotion and persuasion. Indeed, a meta-analysis published in the mid-1980s (Boster & Mongeau, 1984) indicated not only that higher levels of fear are reliably associated with attitude change ($r = .21$), but also that four cognitions—perceived severity, susceptibility, response, and self-efficacy—are central to that process. Despite this finding, the data did not endorse any particular model of fear appeals as accurately capturing the persuasive process (see Eagly & Chaiken, 1993, for a more thorough discussion). It was not until nearly a decade later that the next innovation in fear appeal theorizing, and perhaps the first model to give careful attention to how emotion and cognition might interact, was introduced.

Extended Parallel Process Model

Combining the response elements of Leventhal's parallel response model and the appraisal elements of Rogers's (1975, 1983) protection motivation theory (PMT), Witte's (1992) extended parallel process model (EPPM) suggests that a fear appeal should contain information related to threat susceptibility and severity as well as response and self-efficacy. From a processing perspective, perceived susceptibility and severity combine to create perceived threat. The higher the perceived threat, the stronger the emotional reaction. Assuming fear is aroused, appraisal of perceived efficacy (i.e., thoughts related to self and response efficacy) is made. If perceived efficacy exceeds perceived threat (one believes they can effectively cope with the danger), the EPPM suggests desire to control danger will result in adaptive change. If, however, perceived threat outweighs perceived efficacy, fear control and maladaptive change (like reactance, defensive avoidance, or denial) will occur.

In the EPPM's initial test, Witte (1994) found some support for her model in that fear did not directly associate with message acceptance, whereas perceived efficacy did associate with message acceptance. However, the critical notion of perceived threat mediating the relation between fear and attitudes when efficacy was high was not supported. Indeed, in a meta-analysis, Witte and Allen (2000) found evidence for positive associations between each of the four perceptions (severity, susceptibility, response, and self-efficacy) and message acceptance variables. However, a nonsignificant interaction between threat and efficacy suggests the effects of threat may not be dependent on the degree of perceived efficacy. Additional analysis revealed high-threat/high-efficacy designs yielded greater persuasion than high-threat/low-efficacy and low-threat/high-efficacy designs, which did not differ from one another, and all three pairings were more persuasive than the low-threat/low-efficacy design (see also Roskos-Ewoldsen, Yu, & Rhodes, 2004).

So what does this mean for emotion, cognition, and persuasion? Without doubt, the evidence shows that cognitive appraisals and emotional arousal are inextricably intertwined, and we must consider both as we continue sorting out the process through which fear and other emotions impact persuasive outcomes. Indeed, this is the foundation for the next, more general model of persuasion and emotion.

Cognitive Functional Model

The cognitive functional model (CFM; Nabi, 1999) was strongly influenced by appraisal theories of emotion (e.g., Frijda, 1986; Izard, 1977; Lazarus, 1991; Plutchik, 1980; Tomkins, 1963) and was developed at a time when dual-processing cognitive response theories were guiding a considerable amount of persuasion research (e.g., Chaiken, 1987; Petty & Cacioppo, 1986). The CFM draws together key elements from these perspectives to explain how message-relevant negative emotions (fear, anger, sadness, etc.) affect the direction and stability of persuasive outcome (see Nabi, 1999). The CFM assumes that emotions are discrete, meaning they each reflect a unique person–environment relationship and thus are associated with different goals and action tendencies designed to achieve those goals (see Lazarus, 1991). For instance, fear arises when one perceives the environment to contain a threat to physical safety, thus motivating protective behavior, whereas anger arises from perception of a demeaning offense or goal blockage, thus motivating retributive action.

The CFM posits that a message evokes an emotion if its content reflects the emotion's core relational theme and if the receiver recognizes both the theme and its personal relevance. The emotional response then triggers two simultaneous motivations: motivation to attend to or avoid the message content, topic, or both (i.e., motivated attention) and motivation to satisfy the emotion-induced goal (i.e., motivated processing). Based on the type of emotion experienced, motivated attention sets a baseline attention level that will either impede (for avoidance emotions, like fear) or facilitate (for approach emotions, like anger) subsequent information processing.

Apart from the initial avoidance or approach response to an emotionally evocative stimulus, receivers are motivated to resolve the perceived problematic situation by taking emotion-consistent action. Toward this end, people should willingly process and act on valid and relevant efficacy, or reassuring, information. Receivers' expectation of whether a message will offer such reassurance (i.e., expectation of reassurance) will ultimately determine information processing depth. Relative uncertainty should stimulate closer information processing, regardless of emotion type. Relative certainty that reassuring information will not be forthcoming should encourage message avoidance in favor of other potential information sources. Finally, the effects of certainty that reassuring information is forthcoming are expected to depend on the type of emotion aroused—careful processing if experiencing an approach emotion and less careful processing if experiencing an avoidance emotion.

In the initial test of the CFM (Nabi, 2002), the effects of anger and fear on information processing and persuasion were compared. Anger led to closer information processing than fear, and uncertainty of receiving reassurance from the message led to closer information processing than certainty. The posited interaction between the two variables, though, was not found. While awaiting future tests, the CFM is open to possible revision. However, it stands as the most recent theoretical development geared toward understanding how discrete emotions and cognition interact to affect persuasive outcome.

As the reader can see, there is growing, although still limited, understanding of the role cognition plays in emotions' effects on persuasive outcomes. Relatedly, the rather extensive theorizing on persuasion pays only limited attention to the role of specific emotions in such processes. The next section reviews three popular orientations to persuasion—cognitive response, expectancy value, and framing—with an eye toward how, if at all, these perspectives have included the role of emotion and potential fruitful directions for future research.

PERSUASION THEORIES AND EMOTION

Cognitive Response Theories

Hitting its stride in the early 1980s, the cognitive response perspective assumes that the thoughts people have during message exposure predict persuasive outcome (e.g., Cacioppo, Harkins, & Petty, 1981; Petty, Ostrom, & Brock, 1981). The two most prominent theories from this tradition, the elaboration likelihood model (ELM; Petty & Cacioppo, 1986) and the heuristic systematic model (HSM; Chaiken, 1987), suggest that different levels of motivation and ability to process information can result in different styles of decision making based on more or less cognitive effort (see Hamilton, chap. 18, this volume, for a more complete discussion of these models).

With their concentration on cognition, it is unsurprising that the role of emotion was initially overlooked in these models. By the late 1980s, however, Petty, Cacioppo, and their colleagues made several efforts to explain the influence of predominantly message-irrelevant affect within the context of the ELM (e.g., Petty, Cacioppo, & Kasmer, 1988; Petty, Fabrigar, & Wegener, 2003; Petty, Gleicher, & Baker, 1991). In essence, they suggested that affect can influence attitudes: (a) as a peripheral cue when elaboration is low, (b) as issue-relevant information when elaboration is high, (c) by influencing the extent of information processing activity when elaboration is moderate, or (d) by influencing the direction or type of thoughts brought to mind when information is ambiguous.

Despite their thoughtful analysis of the role of affect generally, the authors paid little attention to the impact of discrete emotion on information processing. It was this state of affairs that led to the development of the CFM (Nabi, 1999), which focuses on how message-relevant discrete emotions impact motivation and ability to process information and thus direct elaboration rather than be constrained by it. Future research on the CFM focusing on how different emotions impact processing motivation and ability as well as potential moderating variables to the process will make useful contributions to our understanding of emotion and persuasion.

Before moving on, I would like to focus for a moment on the HSM as it suggests distinctive directions for future research. The ELM and HSM share many similarities. However, unique to the HSM is the concept of the sufficiency criterion; that is, the psychological mechanism that theoretically predicts that systematic processing will augment use of heuristics when heuristics alone do not leave one sufficiently confident in the correctness of his or her decision (Chaiken, Liberman, & Eagly, 1989). A second unique element of the HSM is the concept of multiple motives. That is, the HSM suggests a "right decision" could be based not only on accuracy but also on impression management or ego-defensive goals.

Minimal research unites the HSM and discrete emotions (Hale, LeMieux, & Mongeau, 1995; Meijnders, Midden, & Wilke, 2001). Yet by considering the impact of emotion on decisional confidence level, we see exciting opportunities to better understand how emotions might impact information processing depth. For example, fear might increase the desired threshold for confidence that one is making the right decision about, say, a medical procedure, and thus increase the likelihood of systematic processing. Anger might cause one to (a) lower the sufficiency threshold (e.g., rush to judgment), (b) reach the threshold more quickly (e.g., expedite processing), or (c) encourage information processing even after the threshold has been reached due to residual arousal. Further, the motives of impression management and ego defensiveness are themselves likely to arouse emotions, like anxiety or anger, and thus are critical to understanding the persuasion process when such motives are engaged.

In sum, the cognitive response perspective has generated much persuasion research, with only minimal attention to affect generally and emotion in particular. However, by considering how discrete emotions impact processing motivation and ability, judgmental confidence, and thoughts generated about message topics, both areas of research stand to be enhanced.

Expectancy Value Theories

Rising to prominence in the 1970s, expectancy value theories of persuasion conceptualize people as rational decision makers, weighing outcome likelihood and outcome value. The theory of reasoned action (TRA; Fishbein, 1979; Fishbein & Ajzen, 1975) is a prototypical example of this perspective, and in essence, it suggests that volitional behaviors are best predicted by behavioral intentions. Behavioral intentions, in turn, are based on two types of cognitive antecedents: attitudes toward performing a particular behavior and perceptions of the social norm surrounding that behavior. From this perspective, other variables affect behavior insofar as they affect the individual's attitudes about the behavior, subjective norms concerning that behavior, or both. Further, the strength of the attitude–behavior relation is impacted by the stability of one's intentions over time and the extent to which the translation of an intention into behavior is under volitional control.

Given the general (mis)perception that reason and emotion represent contradictory processes (e.g., Damasio, 1994; Tomkins, 1963) it is not surprising that theories with an expectancy value orientation would pay limited attention to issues related to affect. Indeed, there is no published study in which emotion is projected to play a meaningful role in the expectancy value calculus, even though the PMT (Rogers, 1975, 1983), itself a theory with expectancy value roots, is evidence that these are not incompatible perspectives.

Recently, Cappella and his colleagues (e.g., Cappella, Romantan, & Lerman, 2004) found evidence that emotion may play an important role in a TRA-related context. In their research, they considered if discrete emotions (proud, disgusted, angry, apprehensive, and hopeful) toward intentions to quit smoking and toward current levels of smoking might explain variance in intentions to quit among a representative sample of 18- to 25-year-old smokers. Their results suggested that the set of emotions (proud, hopeful, and disgust in particular) explained an additional 21% of the variance in intentions to quit smoking beyond what was attributable to the other variables in the model (demographics, attitude toward quitting smoking, self-efficacy, perceived social norms, sensation seeking, and past smoking behavior). Indeed, Cappella and his colleagues have some preliminary evidence that quitting intentions predicted by these emotions are associated with subsequent quitting behavior a year later (personal communication, September 2004).

Although preliminary, this research offers compelling evidence that emotions may play a significant role in both attitude and behavior change. It further opens the door to considering additional ways in which emotions might be integrated into expectancy value models of persuasion. The preceding research suggests that feelings can associate with intentions to act. In addition, one could consider how feelings toward a behavior, in conjunction with behavioral beliefs, might impact attitudes toward the behavior. For example, not only might the belief that smoking is unattractive impact one's attitude toward smoking, but feeling that smoking is disgusting could as well. Further, one's feelings about important others (family members, friends) may impact motivation to comply with their views.

Finally, beyond the expectancy value paradigm, emotions likely play an integral role in strengthening the attitude–behavior relation. Indeed, a quick examination of past variables believed to enhance this relation, like vested interest (Sivacek & Crano, 1982) or direct experience (Regan & Fazio, 1977), suggests emotions may be involved. For example, research on vested interest considers situations with "hedonic relevance" or personal stake. Indeed, personal relevance is a key precursor to emotional arousal, according to appraisal theorists (e.g., Lazarus, 1991). Thus, situations in which one has a vested interest are likely to be emotionally arousing. Similarly, when one has direct experience, there is a stronger likelihood that emotions will be involved. Taking Regan and Fazio's (1977) seminal work on the campus housing crisis at Cornell, one could easily imagine that those sleeping on cots in their dorm lounges would not only have direct experience but, as a result, be far angrier than those sleeping in a (relatively) comfortable bed in a private room. It is likely that those with direct experience were more inclined to act in response to the housing crisis compared to others with equally negative attitudes, not because of their negative experience per se, but because of their feelings about their experience, which, in turn, motivated action.

In sum, despite a history of expectancy value theories and the attitude–behavior literature more generally overlooking the role of emotion, current research supports the importance of exploring ways in which emotions fit into our decision-making processes and actions.

Framing Theory

Framing theory posits that the way in which information is presented, or the perspective taken in a message, influences the responses individuals will have to the issue at hand. As Entman (1993) stated, "[t]o frame is to select some aspects of a perceived reality and make them more salient in a communicating text in such a way as to promote a particular problem definition, causal interpretation, moral evaluation, and/or treatment recommendation" (p. 52). These claims are supported by numerous prominent programs of research in many fields, including political communication and health decision making (e.g., Cappella & Jamieson, 1997; Iyengar, 1991; Kahneman & Tversky, 1984; Rothman & Salovey, 1997). Framing research offers an alternative to expectancy value perspectives on decision making in that if people were truly rational decision makers, style of information presentation should not dramatically influence choice. Yet as Kahneman and Tversky (1984) demonstrated, this is far from the case. In their classic study on choice between two action alternatives to address an expected disease outbreak, they showed that when two options (one more risky than the other) were framed in terms of the number of lives saved, 72% of respondents selected the risk-averse option that assured saving 200 lives. Yet when the same options were presented in terms of lives lost, 78% selected the risk-seeking option that offered a one-third probability of saving everyone and a two-thirds probability of saving no one. More recently, Salovey and his colleagues have found that in health contexts, gain frames, which emphasize the benefits of adopting a behavior, are generally more effective when used to encourage prevention health behaviors, like sunscreen use or regular exercise. Conversely, loss frames, which emphasize the costs of not adopting the advocated behavior, are more effective when used in the context of detection health behaviors, like breast self-examination and mammography use (Rothman &

Salovey, 1997; Salovey, Schneider, & Apanovitch, 2002). Although framing research makes it clear that people's decisions are influenced not just by information but how that information is presented, the role of emotion has yet to be systematically studied in this context. This is somewhat surprising given the remarkable similarity between loss-framed messages and fear appeals, both of which focus on costs that might be life-threatening, as well as response efficacy information via recommended behaviors. Salovey and his colleagues have begun to explore anticipated affect, or the emotions people expect to feel if they engage in a behavior (or not), as a potential mediator of framing effects.[1] However, this work is still in its infancy, and at this point it is only evident that differently framed messages may be associated with different feeling states (e.g., loss frames evoke more negative affect than gain frames). Close examination of the role of not just anticipated emotions but actual emotional experience (and the relation between the two) on framing outcomes would greatly benefit both domains of research.

As the research on prospect theory edges toward determining how emotion might fit into its paradigm, a complementary approach integrates cognitive appraisal theories and framing theory to argue that emotions are themselves frames that, once evoked, differentially impact information processing and decision making (Nabi, 2003). If emotions do systematically and predictably influence perceptions as frames do, we would expect the same selective cognitive processes as found in framing research to be engaged. That is, the information made accessible from memory, the information we seek out or avoid, and the decisions that we make will be guided by the particular emotion (i.e., frame) experienced, especially for more relevant or familiar topics (see Figure 16.1).

In an initial test of this notion, Nabi (2003) evoked fear and anger about either drunk driving (high relevant topic) or gun violence (low relevant topic) in a sample of undergraduates and then asked for perceptions of causes and potential solutions for those social problems and preferences for various policy initiatives. Results were largely supportive of the emotion-as-frame hypothesis. For the more familiar topic of drunk driving, those primed with anger or fear evidenced differences in information accessibility, desired information, and policy preference generally consistent with those emotional states. Yet, no significant differences were found for the low-relevant context of gun violence. By considering the message features that lead to discrete emotion evoca-

[1]This is remarkably similar to how Hovland and his colleagues viewed fear in their drive models. That is, one would "try on" the recommendation to see if it would alleviate fear. If so, the recommendation would be adopted. If not, maladaptive action would occur.

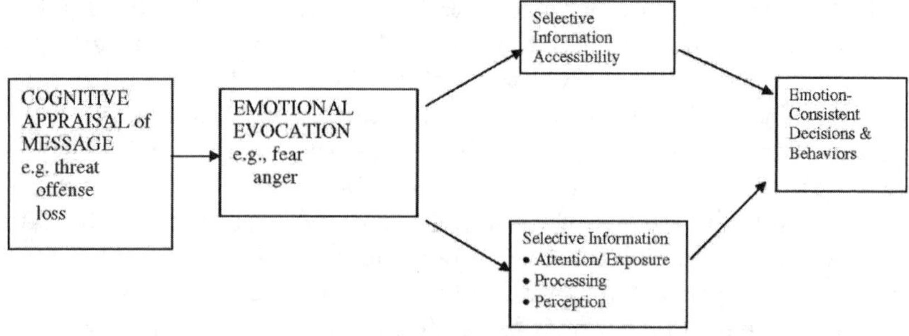

FIGURE 16.1. Model of framing view of emotion.

tion, we may ultimately have a better understanding of the potentially central role emotions may play in understanding how message frames impact attitudes and behaviors.

Summary

The dominant paradigms of persuasion research have been slow to consider how emotions might help to explain information processing and attitudinal or behavioral outcomes. Yet, the ways in which discrete emotions might impact cognitive responses, message processing style, attitude–behavior associations, information accessibility, perceptions of decisional options, and the like are exciting directions for future research in the coming years.

MOOD AND PERSUASION

Although this chapter focuses on discrete emotions, I would be remiss to ignore the significant body of research on mood and persuasion that has been building since the 1980s and explained largely via cognitively based mechanisms (e.g., Dillard & Meijnders, 2002; Eagly & Chaiken, 1993; Fiedler, 2001; Petty et al., 2003). In general, positive moods are associated with more simplified, heuristic, and creative processing, characterized by little attention to detail (see Isen, 1987; Schwarz, Bless, & Bohner, 1991, for reviews; see also Mackie & Worth, 1991). A recent meta-analysis by Hullett (2005) indeed suggested that positive moods may reduce message processing depth. However, the results also suggested that this effect may be contingent on the hedonic implications of the message itself. That is, only if a receiver is in a good mood and expects a message to interfere with that positive state might message processing be compromised. Further, it appears that such reductions in message processing depth are a function of reduced motivation, not ability, to process information.

In contrast, negative moods are believed to induce more systematic processing and thus closer attention to message argument (see Bohner, Crow, Erb, & Schwarz, 1992; Schwarz, 1990). Isen (1993) argued that these effects stem from respondents' desires to distract themselves from unpleasant thoughts, leading to more careful processing of other, affect-irrelevant messages. However, others contend that bad moods signal potential threats and thus trigger careful evaluation of the environment to promote effective problem solving (e.g., Bless, Bohner, Schwarz, & Strack, 1990; 1988; Schwarz, 1990; Schwarz et al., 1991).

This notion of mood-as-information (Schwarz, 1990; Schwarz & Clore, 1988) has gained substantial attention recently, suggesting good moods signal safe and stable environments not requiring close attention, whereas bad moods signal problems to be addressed. In the past decade, two cognitive assessments—expectations and interpretations—have been shown to moderate the use of moods as information sources. The hedonic contingency model (Wegener & Petty, 1994) suggests that people are motivated to perpetuate good moods and avoid negative states. Thus, expectations about the potential outcomes of message processing can moderate the impact of good or bad moods. For example, if one expects message processing to ruin a good mood, peripheral processing is likely. If one thinks message processing might enhance a good mood, closer processing is likely (Wegener, Petty, & Smith, 1995).[2] Further, the mood-as-input model (Bohner & Weinerth, 2001) suggests that the same affective state can have different processing effects, depending on people's interpretation of their moods. If one identifies the source of the mood and it is not relevant to a decision, its effects will be mitigated. Thus, it is clear that cognitive assessments of one's social environment are critical to understanding the effect moods may have on information processing and social influence.

The role of cognitive appraisals is brought closer to the fore with the growing interest in the role of specific mood states on attitudes. Little is known about the role of discrete mood states—anger, sadness, and the like—on information processing and persuasion (Fiedler, 2001). However, a small but growing body of research supports the notion that incidental emotional states can promote different perceptions of event likelihood (DeSteno, Petty, Wegener, & Rucker, 2000; Keltner, Ellsworth, & Edwards, 1993; Lerner & Keltner, 2000, 2001). For example,

[2]Schwarz and Clore (1996) argued that the mood-as-information and hedonic contingency models are complementary in that the mood management is engaged only after the initial evaluation of the environment proves reasonably secure.

DeSteno et al. (2000) found that mild sadness and anger arousal enhanced likelihood estimates of sadness and anger-arousing events.

In addition, specific mood states have been associated with different degrees of message processing depth (e.g., Bodenhausen, Sheppard, & Kramer, 1994; Tiedens & Linton, 2001). Sad moods specifically have been found to prompt analytic or systematic information processing (Bless et al., 1990; Bless, Mackie, & Schwarz. 1992; Bohner, Chaiken, & Hunyadi, 1994; Bohner et al., 1992; Schwarz, 1990). Conversely, angry moods seem to promote a more heuristic processing strategy (Bodenhausen, Sheppard, & Kramer, 1994; Tiedens & Linton, 2001).

Recently, DeSteno, Petty, Rucker, Wegener, and Braverman (2004) integrated the study of relevant and incidental emotion to test the emotion-specificity hypothesis. They predicted that those already in a specific mood state, such as anger or sadness, would be more influenced by a message framed to match their mood state, assuming the messages were scrutinized and contained sound arguments. In their research, mood was induced by reading news magazine articles on either a natural disaster in Africa (sadness) or an anti-American war protest in the Middle East (anger). Respondents then read news stories proposing city tax increases to be allocated to sources evoking either sadness (special needs children) or anger (traffic delays). Results suggested that as long as messages were scrutinized, the groups whose mood matched the message-relevant emotion were more persuaded than other groups (see also Rucker & Petty, 2004, for related findings). Despite several caveats limiting the conditions under which such effects can be expected (e.g., situational or individual factors associated with close scrutiny in the absence of strongly held attitudes), this research marks an innovative integration of the interplay between not only emotion and cognition, but message-relevant and irrelevant emotion as well.

ISSUES OF METHODOLOGY

As with any research pursuit, our confidence in the results can be only as solid as the methods used to obtain them. Given the study of discrete emotions in persuasion is gaining momentum, both theoretically and empirically, it is important to reflect on how such research has been conducted in the past and how best to proceed. In this section, I address issues relating to emotional arousal techniques, emotion measurement, and research designs and analyses. As these issues could constitute a book chapter in themselves, I restrict the discussion to message-relevant emotions (although see Fiedler, 2001, and especially Parrott & Hertel, 1999, for broader discussions on these matters).

Emotional Inductions

As noted earlier, most research on discrete emotions and persuasion has focused on fear appeals, and there is little variation in the methods used for emotional induction. The vast majority of this research occurs in experimental settings in which messages are designed to evoke more or less fear through manipulation of message features varying in their degree of threat. For example, in their dental hygiene experiment, Janis and Feshbach (1953) evoked high threat by presenting the negative consequences of tooth decay (e.g., pain from toothaches) along with graphic images of diseased teeth and gums, whereas low threat was induced through more benign statements (e.g., references to cavities) and visuals (e.g., X-rays).

More recent studies on specific emotions, including fear, anger, and guilt, take similar approaches, using stimuli ranging from health brochures (e.g., Witte, 1994) to advertisements (Coulter & Pinto, 1995) to news stories (e.g., Nabi, 2002). In general these efforts are successful in arousing different levels of the target emotion in different conditions. However, several limitations and pitfalls suggest we be realistic about this method's value. First, given both ethical concerns and situational constraints, experimental contexts do not lend themselves to assessing the effects of truly high levels of fear (or other negative emotions) as might occur in more real-world settings (Eagly & Chaiken, 1993; Witte, 1998). However, provided the messages used are representative of those likely to be encountered in the real world, it may be that scaring people senseless in experiments, even if it were allowed by institutional review boards, would not help us to better understand the effects of messages as they are processed in everyday life.

Second, emotional appeals are generally classified based on the emotions they arouse. As noted by others (e.g., Dillard & Wilson, 1993; O'Keefe, 2003), defining messages based on their effects rather than their intrinsic properties virtually precludes our ability to understand what message features associate not only with emotional arousal but with persuasive outcome. Understanding the message characteristics, both concrete and abstract, textual and visual, that reliably evoke particular emotions in particular audiences for various topics and behaviors is essential to eliminating the conflation between the stimulus and the response, and hence an important topic for future research. Functional emotion theory (e.g., Lazarus, 1991), with its focus on perception and cognitive appraisals, can serve as a useful guide in this endeavor.

Third, exposure to persuasive messages has been shown to promote both intentional and unintentional emotional arousal. Dillard, Plotnick, Godbold, Freimuth, and Edgar (1996) provided evidence that nearly all of the 31 AIDS public service announcements shown to a sample of undergraduates evoked significant amounts of at least one other emotion besides fear. As different emotions likely have different effects on persuasive outcomes (e.g., Coulter & Pinto, 1995; Dillard & Peck, 2000), this is a critical potential threat to research purporting to speak to specific emotions and thus should be factored into construct measurement as described later.

Fourth, attempts to evoke different levels of emotion or, indeed, different emotions, often differ in the information presented to the audience. For example, one group may view diseased teeth and gums (high fear), whereas another group sees an X-ray or a healthy smile (low fear). Similarly, one group may be told they are likely to become victims of crime (fear), whereas another group may be told that criminals are not being suitably punished (anger). The different sets of information, although perhaps effective in their emotional arousal goals, are also likely to filter into decision-making processes, according to theories like the TRA and the ELM. Thus, it may be difficult to conclude from such research that the different emotional experiences, and not the different information provided, lead to differences in persuasive outcomes.

As we think about future directions for inducing message-relevant discrete emotions, there is little doubt that exposure to audio, textual, or visual stimuli will continue to be the primary focus. A key goal, then, is to gain insight into the message features that might reliably evoke particular emotions in particular audiences—a priority for communication scholars. However, we should also keep an eye toward holding constant the information to which audiences are exposed, perhaps by borrowing from various mood induction techniques. For example, asking respondents to write about the aspects of an issue that make them sad or angry or fearful will likely arouse the intended emotion (see Nabi, 2003), and although it may lead to differential thought accessibility and may not help with message design, it avoids the introduction of confounding information. It would further allow us to explore persuasive efforts designed to take advantage of latent emotions associated with social issues, health concerns, or commercial products, and how accessing such emotions might shape information processing and decision making. Thus, simply asking participants to think about how they feel about, say, gun control or mammograms, prior to other tasks may prove insightful, especially for research conducted in less controlled environments.

Measuring Emotional Arousal

The vast majority of emotion and persuasion studies rely on self-reports of emotional experience. Although this confines the realm of study to conscious emotional experience and is constrained by respondents' abilities to understand and report their particular emotional states, self-report is accepted as a valid measure of emotion (see Parrott & Hertel, 1999). The published literature includes several validated measures of emotion and affect, like the Positive and Negative Affect Scale (Watson, Clark, & Tellegen, 1988), the UWIST Mood Adjective Checklist (Matthews, Jones, & Chamberlain, 1990), the Multiple Affective Adjective Checklist–Revised (Zuckerman & Lubin, 1985), the Discrete Emotions Scale (Izard, 1972), the Emotional Assessment Scale (Carlson et al., 1989), as well as the scales of State–Trait Anxiety (Spielberger, Gorsuch, & Lushene, 1970), State–Trait Anger (Spielberger, Jacobs, Russell, & Crane, 1983), and State–Trait Guilt (Otterbacher & Mutz, 1973). However, these measures are rarely used in full in emotion and persuasion research. Instead, most researchers tend to develop their own sets of items to assess targeted emotions. Although not a fatal flaw, it does make comparability across studies more difficult. Thus, as the research moves forward, it would be wise to pay attention to consistency in measure use.

Also, by using consistent measures, we can then avoid the troublesome habit of combining a range of emotion items that, although all negative, reflect different discrete emotions. For example, in the past, items like anger (Leventhal, Singer, & Jones, 1965), sad (Leventhal & Singer, 1966), nauseous (Witte, 1994), and nauseated (Gleicher & Petty, 1992) have been included in scaled measures of fear. By combining words that represent different affective states associated with different underlying cognitive appraisal patterns and action tendencies, we lose the ability to draw reliable conclusions about any one emotion. More recent studies have become sensitive to these issues and have set examples for not only measuring a range of emotions, but using them as separate variables in analyses (e.g., Dillard & Peck, 2000; Nabi, 2002).

In addition to self-reported emotion, other measures, like facial expression, physiological measures (e.g., heart rate, eye movement, skin conductance), and neurophysiological tests (e.g., EEGs), could be considered to validate levels of arousal, although they are of little use in distinguishing among particular emotions. However, as unique facial expressions have been associated with discrete emotions (Ekman & Friesen, 1971), emotional reactions could be assessed by facial coding schemes, like the Facial Action Coding System (Ekman & Friesen, 1978) and the Specific Affect Coding System (see Gottman, 1993). Although a nice complement to subjective reports of emotional experience, such techniques can be consuming in terms of both time (training coders, coding time) and resources (e.g., videotaping each participant). Facial electromyography (EMG), although more invasive and requiring specialized equipment, can measure action potential or movement of facial muscles during stimulus exposure. Arguably a more reliable indicator than self-report measures or coding systems, this technique may be limited in its application as it can be a time-consuming procedure perhaps best used in response to visual stimuli. Still, by linking video segments to EMG output, this procedure could be very helpful in identifying images that can arouse discrete emotions to be used in later research. Given the increasing availability and accessibility of equipment to measure physiological response, it is likely that the next decade will see increasing use of these and other procedures to gain insight into issues related to emotional arousal.

Research Design and Analysis

Most research on discrete emotions and persuasion is confined to experimental designs in which participants (generally students) are randomly assigned to groups in which they receive a message designed to elicit high or low levels of an emotion (sometimes moderate levels or control groups are also included). Measures of attitudes then follow, and analysis of variance or related tests to compare means between or among the groups are performed. Although this controlled environment is essential to have confidence in claims derived regarding the effect of emotional arousal on attitudes, several cautionary notes are warranted.

First, given the artificial circumstances under which the data are gathered, and particularly when carefully designed stimuli are not drawn from the population of actual messages, it is only reasonable to question how well such research can generalize to natural environments. Of course, collecting data in more real-world settings may interfere with the ability to make causal claims about the relation between emotions and persuasive outcomes, but such research would surely compliment ongoing laboratory-based investigations.

Second, the stimuli generally used tend to be presented in more rational, rather than narrative, form. Yet, the increasing interest in entertainment education (see Singhal & Rogers, 1999), in which persuasive messages are embedded in dramatic content, suggests we should broaden our research to narrative messages in which drama—and thus emotion—are deemed critical to attention and processing. This poses a particularly interesting context as audiences' identification with characters lays the groundwork for strong emotional arousal. Understanding the relations among narrative, emotions, and attitude and behavior change should be a priority in the coming decade.

Third, assuming we stick with experimental designs, we should consider the effects of emotions on a broader range of outcomes. In recent years, the notions of expectancies and event likelihood have been introduced, but surely other outcomes remain ready to be explored. As McGuire (1968) noted in his information processing theory, there are, depending on how you slice it, 6 to 12 steps in the process of attitude change. Focusing on the 6-step model, most research targets the fourth step, yielding or acceptance. Yet, we know little about how emotional appeals might impact exposure, attention, comprehension, retention, or behavior. Each of these represents a viable path in the course toward understanding emotion's role in persuasion.

Fourth, to the extent we wish to compare the relative effects of different emotions, or even the effects of high and low arousal of a particular emotion, it is important to consider the level of emotional intensity in each condition. For example, in comparing fear and anger, the fear-inducing message must not only evoke more fear than anger and vice versa, but the levels of fear and anger should themselves be comparable (i.e., both moderate or both high). Similarly, if high and low fear groups significantly differ in reported fear arousal, one might claim a successful manipulation. However, if the means differ by less than a full scale point, one should be cautious about drawing inferences about high and low fear. Interpreting results based on more objective standards of arousal, rather than relative ones, would help to clarify what a collection of studies has to contribute to our knowledge in this area.

Finally, as anyone who has tested emotional appeals may tell you, there are inevitably people who, for example, report strong fear reactions to a mild fear appeal or no fear reaction to a strong fear appeal. Although random assignment to condition should, theoretically, neutralize such effects across groups, it does raise an interesting question about how to best analyze data. Should we continue to stick with the groups we predetermined by design? Or might we consider using the representation of their psychological state (e.g., self-reported emotional arousal) in the analysis? O'Keefe (2003) argued that this type of research might best proceed by manipulating message features, determining how those features impact the psychological state of interest (in our case emotions), and finally looking at how the state impacts persuasive outcome. In so doing, measures of fear, or any other emotion, serve not as manipulation checks but as critical mediators or moderators in the persuasion process. This approach, then, suggests that natural variation in emotional reactions is acceptable data for learning about the effects of emotions on persuasive outcomes.[3]

The relation between emotion and cognition may not be easy to capture, and integrating one into the domain of the other, especially within persuasion research, may seem quite a challenge. Rather than seeing the two as competing constructs, we are far better served recognizing and appreciating their functional interdependence. To make an automotive

[3]Of note, this approach requires that measures of emotion be placed carefully within the surveying instrument. If measured too late, they may not reflect the emotional state during message processing.

analogy, we might think of cognition as a car and emotion as its fuel. Cognition may form the bulk of the entity, but emotion plays a critical, if less obvious, role in motivating any action that occurs. Both are essential for progress to be made, and whereas the right combination can motivate effective behavior, the wrong combination will most assuredly backfire. Finding the most effective blending of cognitive and emotional persuasive elements, then, should be both our challenge and our goal.

REFERENCES

Bless, H., Bohner, G., Schwarz, N., & Strack, F. (1990). Mood and persuasion: A cognitive response analysis. *Personality and Social Psychology Bulletin, 16,* 331–345.

Bless, H., Mackie, D. M., & Schwarz, N. (1992). Mood effects on attitude judgments: Independent effects of mood before and after message elaboration. *Journal of Personality and Social Psychology, 63,* 585–595.

Bodenhausen, G. V., Sheppard, L., & Kramer, G. (1994). Negative affect and social judgment: The differential impact of anger and sadness. *European Journal of Social Psychology, 24,* 45–62.

Bohner, G., Chaiken, S., & Hunyadi, P. (1994). The role of mood and message ambiguity in the interplay of heuristic and systematic processing. *European Journal of Social Psychology, 24,* 207–221.

Bohner, G., Crow, K., Erb, H., & Schwarz, N. (1992). Affect and persuasion: Mood effects on the processing of message content and context cues and on subsequent behaviour. *European Journal of Social Psychology, 22,* 511–530.

Bohner, G., & Weinerth, T. (2001). Negative affect can increase or decrease message scrutiny: The affect interpretation hypothesis. *Personality and Social Psychology Bulletin, 27,* 1417–1428.

Boster, F. J., & Mongeau, P. (1984). Fear-arousing persuasive messages. In R. N. Bostrom (Ed.), *Communication yearbook 8* (pp. 330–375). Beverly Hills, CA: Sage.

Cacioppo, J. T., Harkins, S. G., & Petty, R. E. (1981). The nature of attitudes and cognitive responses and their relationship to behavior. In R. E. Petty, T. M. Ostrom, & T. C. Brock (Eds.), *Cognitive responses in persuasion* (pp. 32–54). Hillsdale, NJ: Lawrence Erlbaum Associates.

Cappella, J. N., & Jamieson, K. H. (1997). *Spiral of cynicism: The press and the public good.* New York: Oxford University Press.

Cappella, J. N., Romantan, A., & Lerman, C. (2004). *Emotional bases for quitting smoking: Extending the integrated theory of behavior change.* Unpublished manuscript.

Carlson, C. R., Collins, F. L., Stewart, J. F., Porzelius, J., Nitz, J. A., & Lind, C. O. (1989). The assessment of emotional reactivity: A scale development and validation study. *Journal of Psychopathology and Behavioral Assessment, 11,* 313–325.

Chaiken, S. (1987). The heuristic model of persuasion. In M. P. Zanna, J. M. Olson, & C. P. Herman (Eds.), *Social influence: The Ontario Symposium* (Vol. 5, pp. 3–39). Hillsdale, NJ: Lawrence Erlbaum Associates.

Chaiken, S., Liberman, A., & Eagly, A. H. (1989). Heuristic and systematic information processing within and beyond the persuasion context. In J. S. Uleman & J. A. Bargh (Eds.), *Unintended thought* (pp. 212–252). New York: Guilford.

Coulter, R. H., & Pinto, M. B. (1995). Guilt appeals in advertising: What are their effects? *Journal of Applied Psychology, 80,* 697–705.

Damasio, A. R. (1994). *Descartes' error: Emotion, reason, and the human brain.* New York: Grosset/Putnam.

DeSteno, D., Petty, R. E., Rucker, D. D., Wegener, D. T., & Braverman, J. (2004). Discrete emotions and persuasion: The role of emotion-induced expectancies. *Journal of Personality and Social Psychology, 86,* 43–56.

DeSteno, D., Petty, R. E., Wegener, D. T., & Rucker, D. D. (2000). Beyond valence in the perception of likelihood: The role of emotion specificity. *Journal of Personality and Social Psychology, 78,* 397–416.

Dillard, J. P., & Meijnders, A. (2002). Persuasion and the structure of affect. In J. P. Dillard & M. Pfau (Eds.), *The persuasion handbook: Developments in theory and practice* (pp. 309–327). Thousand Oaks, CA: Sage.

Dillard, J. P., & Peck, E. (2000). Affect and persuasion: Emotional responses to public service announcements. *Communication Research, 27,* 461–495.

Dillard, J. P., Plotnick, C. A., Godbold, L. C., Freimuth, V. S., & Edgar, T. (1996). The multiple affective outcomes of AIDS PSAs: Fear appeals do more than scare people. *Communication Research, 23,* 44–72.

Dillard, J. P., & Wilson, B. (1993). Communication and affect: Thoughts, feelings, and issues for the future. *Communication Research, 20,* 637–646.

Eagly, A. H., & Chaiken, S. (1993). *The psychology of attitudes.* Fort Worth, TX: Harcourt Brace Jovanovich.

Ekman, P., & Friesen, W. V. (1971). Constants across cultures in the face and emotion. *Journal of Personality and Social Psychology, 17,* 124–129.

Ekman, P., & Friesen, W. V. (1978). *Facial action coding system: A technique for the measurement of facial movement.* Palo Alto, CA: Consulting Psychologists Press.

Entman, R. M. (1993). Framing: Toward clarification of a fractured paradigm. *Journal of Communication, 43*(4), 51–58.

Fiedler, K. (2001). Affective influences on social information processing. In J. Forgas (Ed.), *Handbook of affect and cognition* (pp. 165–185). Mahwah, NJ: Lawrence Erlbaum Associates.

Fishbein, M. (1979). A theory of reasoned action: Some applications and implications. *Nebraska Symposium on Motivation, 27,* 65–116.

Fishbein, M., & Ajzen, I. (1975). *Belief, attitude, intention, and behavior: An introduction to theory and research.* Reading, MA: Addison-Wesley.

Fiske, S. T., & Taylor, S. E. (1991). *Social cognition.* New York: McGraw-Hill.

Forgas, J. P. (2001). *Handbook of affect and cognition.* Mahwah, NJ: Lawrence Erlbaum Associates.

Frijda, N. H. (1986). *The emotions.* New York: Cambridge University Press.

Gleicher, F., & Petty, R. E. (1992). Expectations of reassurance influence the nature of fear-stimulated attitude change. *Journal of Experimental Social Psychology, 28,* 86–100.

Gottman, J. M. (1993). Studying emotion in social interaction. In M. Lewis & J. M. Haviland (Eds.), *Handbook of emotions* (pp. 475–487). New York: Guilford.

Hale, J. L., LeMieux, R., & Mongeau, P. A. (1995). Cognitive processing of fear-arousing message content. *Communication Research, 22,* 459–474.

Hovland, C. I., Janis, I. L., & Kelley, H. H. (1953). *Communication and persuasion.* New Haven, CT: Yale University Press.

Hullett, C. R. (2005). The impact of mood on persuasion: A meta-analysis. *Communication Research, 32,* 423–442.

Isen, A. M. (1987). Positive affect, cognitive processes, and social behavior. *Advances in Experimental Social Psychology, 20,* 203–253.

Isen, A. M. (1993). Positive affect and decision making. In M. Lewis & J. M. Haviland (Eds.), *Handbook of emotions* (pp. 261–277). New York: Guilford Press.

Iyengar, S. (1991). *Is anyone responsible? How television frames political issues.* Chicago: University of Chicago Press.

Izard, C. E. (1972). *Patterns of emotions: A new analysis of anxiety and depression.* New York: Academic.

Izard, C. E. (1977). *Human emotions.* New York: Plenum.

Janis, I. L., & Feshbach, S. (1953). Effects of fear-arousing communications. *Journal of Abnormal and Social Psychology, 48,* 78–92.

Kahneman, D., & Tversky, A. (1984). Choices, values, and frames. *American Psychologist, 39,* 341–350.

Keltner, D., Ellsworth, P. C., & Edwards, K. (1993). Beyond simple pessimism: Effects of sadness and anger on social perceptions. *Journal of Personality and Social Psychology, 64,* 740–752.

Lazarus, R. S. (1991). *Emotion and adaptation.* New York: Oxford University Press.

Lerner, J. S., & Keltner, D. (2000). Beyond valence: Toward a model of emotion-specific influences on judgment and choice. *Cognition and Emotion, 14,* 473–493.

Lerner, J. S., & Keltner, D. (2001). Fear, anger, and risk. *Journal of Personality and Social Psychology, 81,* 146–159.

Leventhal, H. (1970). Findings and theory in the study of fear communications. In L. Berkowitz (Ed.), *Advances in experimental social psychology* (Vol. 5, pp. 119–186). New York: Academic.

Leventhal, H., & Singer, R. P. (1966). Affect arousal and positioning of recommendations in persuasive communications. *Journal of Personality and Social Psychology, 4,* 137–146.

Leventhal, H., Singer, R. P., & Jones, S. (1965). Effects of fear and specificity of recommendation upon attitudes and behavior. *Journal of Personality and Social Psychology, 2,* 20–29.

Mackie, D. M., & Worth, L. T. (1991). Feeling good, but not thinking straight: The impact of positive mood on persuasion. In J. P. Forgas (Ed.), *Emotion and social judgments* (pp. 201–219). New York: Pergamon.

Matthews, G., Jones, D. M., & Chamberlain, A. G. (1990). Refining the measurement of mood: The UWIST mood adjective checklist. *British Journal of Psychology, 81,* 17–42.

McGuire, W. J. (1968). Personality and attitude change: An information processing theory. In A. G. Greenwald, T. C. Brock, & T. M. Ostrom (Eds.), *Psychological foundations of attitudes* (pp. 171–196). New York: Academic.

Meijnders, A. L., Midden, C. J. H., & Wilke, H. A. M. (2001). Role of negative emotion in communication about CO risks. *Risk Analysis, 21,* 955–966.

Nabi, R. L. (1999). A cognitive-functional model for the effects of discrete negative emotions on information processing, attitude change, and recall. *Communication Theory, 9,* 292–320.

Nabi, R. L. (2002). Anger, fear, uncertainty, and attitudes: A test of the cognitive-functional model. *Communication Monographs, 69,* 204–216.

Nabi, R. L. (2003). The framing effects of emotion: Can discrete emotions influence information recall and policy preference? *Communication Research, 30,* 224–247.

O'Keefe, D. J. (2003). Message properties, mediating states, and manipulation checks: Claims, evidence, and data analysis in experimental persuasive message effects research. *Communication Theory, 13,* 251–274.

Otterbacher, J. R., & Munz, D. C. (1973). State–trait measure of experiential guilt. *Journal of Consulting and Clinical Psychology, 40,* 115–121.

Parrott, W. G., & Hertel, P. (1999). Research methods in cognition and emotion. In T. Dalgleish & M. J. Power (Eds.), *Handbook of cognition and emotion* (pp. 61–81). New York: Wiley.

Petty, R. E., & Cacioppo, J. T. (1986). The elaboration likelihood model of persuasion. In L. Berkowitz (Ed.), *Advances in experimental social psychology* (Vol. 19, pp. 123–205). New York: Academic.

Petty, R. E., Cacioppo, J. T., & Kasmer, J. A. (1988). The role of affect in the elaboration likelihood model of persuasion. In L. Donohew, H. E. Sypher, & E. T. Higgins (Eds.), *Communication, social cognition, and affect* (pp. 117–146). Hillsdale, NJ: Lawrence Erlbaum Associates.

Petty, R. E., Fabrigar, L. R., & Wegener, D. T. (2003). Emotional factors in attitudes and persuasion. In R. J. Davidson, K. R. Scherer, & H. H. Goldsmith (Eds.), *Handbook of affective sciences* (pp. 752–772). New York: Oxford University Press.

Petty, R. E., Gleicher, F., & Baker, S. M. (1991). Multiple roles for affect in persuasion. In J. Forgas (Ed.), *Emotion and social judgments* (pp. 181–200). New York: Pergamon.

Petty, R. E., Ostrom, T. M., & Brock, T. C. (1981). *Cognitive responses in persuasion.* Hillsdale, NJ: Lawrence Erlbaum Associates.

Plutchik, R. (1980). *Emotion: A psychoevolutionary synthesis.* New York: Harper & Row.

Regan, D. T., & Fazio, R. H. (1977). On the consistency between attitudes and behavior: Look to the method of attitude formation. *Journal of Experimental Social Psychology, 13,* 28–45.

Rogers, R. W. (1975). A protection motivation theory of fear appeals and attitude change. *Journal of Psychology, 91,* 93–114.

Rogers, R. W. (1983). Cognitive and physiological processes in fear appeals and attitude change: A revised theory of protection motivation. In J. T. Cacioppo & R. E. Petty (Eds.), *Social psychophysiology* (pp. 153–176). New York: Guilford.

Roloff, M. E., & Berger, C. R. (1982). *Social cognition and communication.* Beverly Hills, CA: Sage.

Roskos-Ewoldsen, D., Yu, H. J., & Rhodes, N. (2004). Fear appeal messages affect accessibility of attitudes toward the threat and adaptive behaviors. *Communication Monographs, 71,* 49–69.

Rothman, A. J., & Salovey, P. (1997). Shaping perceptions to motivate healthy behavior: The role of message framing. *Psychological Bulletin, 121,* 3–19.

Rucker, D. D., & Petty, R. E. (2004). Emotion specificity and consumer behavior: Anger, sadness, and preference for activity. *Motivation and Emotion, 28,* 3–21.

Salovey, P., Schneider, T. R., & Apanovitch, A. M. (2002). Message framing in the prevention and early detection of illness. In J. P. Dillard & M. Pfau (Eds.), *The persuasion handbook: Developments in theory and practice* (pp. 391–406). Thousand Oaks, CA: Sage.

Schwarz, N. (1990). Feelings as information: Informational and motivational functions of affective states. In E. T. Higgins & R. M. Sorrentino (Eds.), *Handbook of motivation and cognition: Foundations of social behavior* (Vol. 2, pp. 527–561). New York: Guilford.

Schwarz, N., Bless, H., & Bohner, G. (1991). Mood and persuasion: Affective states influence the processing of persuasive communications. In M. P. Zanna (Ed.), *Advances in experimental social psychology* (Vol. 24, pp. 161–199). San Diego, CA: Academic.

Schwarz, N., & Clore, G. L. (1988). How do I feel about it? The informative function of affective states. In K. Fielder & J. Forgas (Eds.), *Affect, cognition, and social behavior* (pp. 44–62) Toronto: Hogrefe International.

Schwarz, N., & Clore, G. L. (1996). Feelings and phenomenal experiences. In E. T. Higgins & A. W. Kruglanski (Eds.), *Social psychology: Handbook of basic principles* (pp. 433–465) New York: Guilford.

Singhal, A., & Rogers, E. M. (1999). *Entertainment-education: A communication strategy for social change.* Mahwah, NJ: Lawrence Erlbaum Associates.

Sivacek, J., & Crano, W. D. (1982). Vested interest as a moderator of attitude–behavior consistency. *Journal of Personality and Social Psychology, 43,* 210–221.

Spielberger, C. D., Gorsuch, R. L., & Lushene, R. E. (1970). *STAI manual for the State–Trait Anxiety Inventory.* Palo Alto, CA: Consulting Psychologists Press.

Spielberger, C. D., Jacobs, G., Russell, S., & Crane, R. S. (1983). Assessment of anger: The state–trait anger scale. In J. Butcher & C. Spielberger (Eds.), *Advances in personality assessment* (Vol. 2, pp. 161–189). Hillsdale, NJ: Lawrence Erlbaum Associates.

Tiedens, L. Z., & Linton, S. (2001). Judgment under emotional certainty and uncertainty: The effects of specific emotions on information processing. *Journal of Personality and Social Psychology, 81,* 973–988.

Tomkins, S. S. (1963). *Affect, imagery, consciousness: Vol. II. The negative affects.* New York: Springer.

Watson, D., Clark, L. A., & Tellegen, A. (1988). Development and validation of brief measures of positive and negative affect: The PANAS scales. *Journal of Personality and Social Psychology, 54,* 1063–1070.

Wegener, D. T., & Petty, R. E. (1994). Mood-management across affective states: The hedonic contingency hypothesis. *Journal of Personality and Social Psychology, 66,* 1034–1048.

Wegener, D. T., Petty, R. E., & Smith, S. M. (1995). Positive mood can increase or decrease message scrutiny: The hedonic contingency view of mood and message processing. *Journal of Personality and Social Psychology, 69,* 5–15.

Witte, K. (1992). Putting the fear back into fear appeals: The extended parallel process model. *Communication Monographs, 59,* 329–349.

Witte, K. (1994). Fear control and danger control: A test of the extended parallel process model (EPPM). *Communication Monographs, 61,* 113–134.

Witte, K. (1998). Fear as motivator, fear as inhibitor: Using the extended parallel process model to explain fear appeal successes and failures. In P. A. Anderson & L. K. Guerrero (Eds.), *Handbook of communication and emotion: Research, theory, applications, and contexts* (pp. 423–450). San Diego, CA: Academic.

Witte, K., & Allen, M. (2000). A meta-analysis of fear appeals: Implications for effective public health campaigns. *Health Education and Behavior, 27,* 591–615.

Zuckerman, M., & Lubin, B. (1985). *Manual for the multiple affect adjective check list-revise.* San Diego, CA: EdITS/Educational and Industrial Testing Service.

17

Compliance Gaining

Janet R. Meyer
Kent State University

One of the more frequent goals of everyday communication is to persuade another to comply with a request. The ability to seek compliance in a manner that is effective and contextually appropriate is an important aspect of communication competence. Such skills are often a necessary condition to the realization of broader goals in organizational, group, health, legal, and political contexts. Thus, it is not surprising that one of the larger bodies of research on interpersonal communication has focused on how persons seek compliance.

Despite a substantial literature on interpersonal influence, many questions about the design of compliance-seeking messages have yet to be answered. For example, the manner in which a speaker's representation of an influence goal leads to the retrieval of knowledge about how to make requests in a specific type of situation is not well understood. Whereas it is generally agreed that persons differ in the ability to adapt the language of a request to a situation or person (Burleson & Caplan, 1998), the processing underlying this learning has seldom been investigated directly. Nor is it clear what plans or strategies for seeking compliance persons store in long-term memory. Arguably, questions like these are best answered by research based on cognitive models of message production. A main purpose of this chapter is to consider the application of cognitive theory to explaining how persons seek compliance.

For present purposes, a compliance-seeking message is defined as a message produced with the intent of persuading a single hearer to engage in an action. In the language of speech act theory (Labov & Fanshel, 1977), a compliance-seeking message typically includes an explicit or implicit request for action and may include additional speech acts, such as an apology, explanation, promise, or assertion. When coupled with content, the sequence of acts in a message may correspond to a particular strategy (e.g., moral appeal, debt, promise).

This chapter begins with an overview of early work on compliance gaining and criticisms of several aspects of that research. New directions in research on interpersonal influence that emerged in the mid-1980s are then noted. The subsequent section considers cognitive approaches to the study of compliance seeking, with emphasis on the assumptions of the implicit rules model (IRM; Meyer, 1990, 1997). Questions about the production of requests made salient by the IRM and findings of research bearing on these questions are discussed. Issues pertinent to the quality of cognitive research on compliance seeking are then considered, as are future trends in compliance-gaining research.

EARLY COMPLIANCE-GAINING RESEARCH

Research on compliance gaining in the communication field was stimulated by the publication of a study by Miller, Boster, Roloff, and Seibold (1977). The MBRS study, which employed 16 compliance-gaining strategies developed by sociologists Marwell and Schmitt (1967), generated a large body of research on compliance gaining that continues today, albeit with dependent variables encompassing a broader range of message features than strategy use alone.

Early research on compliance gaining often focused on one or more of four issues. One objective was to identify the perceptual dimensions of compliance-gaining situations. An oft-cited study by Cody and McLaughlin (1980) revealed six such dimensions (intimacy, hearer dominance, personal benefits, rights, resistance, and long-term consequences; also see Boster & Stiff, 1984). A second goal was to determine how values on the situation dimensions influence strategy use. These efforts yielded a large body of research (for reviews, see Seibold, Cantrill, & Meyers, 1985; Wilson, 2002.) By the mid-1980s, however, many researchers had concluded that the effects of single situation dimensions on strategy use were inconsistent and small in size (Cody et al., 1986; Dillard & Burgoon, 1985).

A third purpose of compliance-gaining research was to investigate individual differences in strategy use. Whereas a number of traits were found to predict strategy use, effect sizes were typically small to moderate (Seibold et al., 1985; Wilson, 2002). A fourth pursuit was to identify typologies of compliance-gaining strategies. One of the better known typologies, an inductively derived set of strategies developed by Schenck-Hamlin, Wiseman, and Georgacarakos (1982) contained oft-used strategies not included in the widely used Marwell and Schmitt (1967) typology (see Kellermann & Cole, 1994).

In a typical compliance-gaining study, participants read hypothetical situations written to instantiate particular features, such as low intimacy and high hearer status. They then read messages representing each strategy in a typology and indicated the likelihood they would use each message in a given situation. In the mid-1980s, this research came under attack for a number of reasons. These issues have been summarized elsewhere and will be mentioned only briefly (Miller, Boster, Roloff, & Seibold, 1987; Seibold et al., 1985; Wilson, 2002). A frequent criticism was that compliance-gaining research was atheoretical. Critics also noted that (a) the use of a single message to represent a strategy confounded the strategy with the message, (b) the use of a single situation to represent a configuration of features confounded the effect of the features with the effect of the situation, and (c) studies often failed to control for variability across conditions in features other than those manipulated.

Also criticized was the strategy selection procedure used in much research. Burleson et al. (1988) argued that a message construction procedure (where participants write messages) provided more valid data than the strategy selection procedure (where participants rate the likelihood of using messages). Based on seven studies, Burleson et al. concluded that the strategy selection procedure is subject to an item desirability bias and that nonsignificant effects of situation features and individual differences found in research using strategy selection are due, at least partly, to the item desirability bias.

In a comprehensive analysis of 74 compliance-gaining taxonomies in the literature, Kellermann and Cole (1994) identified a number of problems with existing taxonomies. They found, for example, that (a) the strategies vary considerably across typologies, suggesting that classification schemes are seldom exhaustive; (b) definitions of strategies are often insufficient or ambiguous, resulting in overlap between strategies; (c) taxonomies are typically atheoretical in that a rationale for the strategies in them is not provided; and (d) messages written to instantiate strategies are frequently invalid representations of the strategy. Kellermann and Cole recommended that strategies be distinguished on theoretically meaningful dimensions. They noted, "When theoretically meaningful distinctions between compliance gaining message behaviors are available, theoretically meaningful classification systems can be developed" (p. 48).

NEW DIRECTIONS IN RESEARCH ON INTERPERSONAL INFLUENCE

By the early 1990s, many scholars had begun to explore alternative approaches to the study of how persons seek to persuade. These new directions were influenced by a growing recognition that speakers pursue multiple goals in request messages (O'Keefe & Delia, 1982), the adoption of Brown and Levinson's (1987) politeness theory by communication scholars (Baxter, 1984; Leichty & Applegate, 1991), and increased attention to the type of influence goal pursued (Cody, Canary, & Smith, 1994; Dillard, 1990b).

Research on Multiple Goals

When designing messages, persons are concerned not only with instrumental goals, but with goals related to identity management and relationship maintenance (Clark & Delia, 1979). That persons differ in the extent to which they pursue multiple goals in messages was an implicit assumption of much constructivist research (Burleson & Caplan, 1998; O'Keefe & Delia, 1982). The manner in which multiple goals influence compliance seeking has been explored in a number of research programs.

Early compliance-gaining research verified that persons choose not to endorse some strategies. The criteria used to make such decisions were investigated by Hample and Dallinger in a line of research on cognitive editing. Hample and Dallinger (1987) noted that a speaker may decide a compliance-gaining message is unacceptable for a variety of reasons. For example, the message might be seen as ineffective; as conflicting with the speaker's principles; or as harmful to the speaker's self-image, the other, or the relationship. Cognitive editing research has investigated variables predicting the use of particular editing criteria (see Hample, chap. 5, this volume).

In developing the goals-planning-action model of social influence, Dillard (1990a) argued that pursuit of an influence goal is constrained by a range of secondary goals (also see Dillard, Anderson, & Knobloch, 2002). In a multiphase study, Dillard, Segrin, and Harden (1989) identified six goals of concern to speakers designing influence messages. In addition to a (primary) influence goal, the typology includes five secondary goals: an interaction goal (concerned with impression management and facework), a goal to protect personal resources, a relational maintenance goal, an arousal management goal, and an identity goal (to act consistently with one's ethical standards).

Research investigating cross-cultural differences in compliance seeking has also been guided by a set of conversational constraints thought to influence the design of requests. Kim and Wilson (1994) proposed that these constraints include (a) concern to avoid hurting the hearer's feelings, (b) concern for minimizing imposition, (c) concern for avoiding negative evaluation by the hearer, (d) concern for clarity, and (e) concern for effectiveness. The perceived importance of the constraints has been found to vary across individualistic and collectivist cultures (Kim & Wilson, 1994).

To separate short-lived secondary goals from more enduring goals, Meyer (2001) distinguished situated secondary goals from habitual (chronic) secondary goals. Whereas a situated goal is one important to a speaker in a current situation, a chronic goal is one the person considers important and pursues across many communication contexts (Meyer, 1997; also see Srull & Wyer, 1986). Extant findings suggest that the importance of chronic goals to be supportive, maintain a positive relationship, and make a good impression are positively related to self-monitoring and negatively related to verbal aggressiveness (Meyer, 2001).

Research Stimulated by Politeness Theory

In the mid-1980s, some communication scholars began employing Brown and Levinson's (1987) politeness theory as a theoretical framework for research on interpersonal influence (Baxter, 1984; Leichty & Applegate, 1991; Lim & Bowers, 1991; Meyer, 1994a). Among the factors encouraging a shift in focus from strategy selection to politeness were studies suggesting that typologies of compliance-gaining strategies failed to capture important variations in the content of requests (Craig, Tracy, & Spisak, 1986; Tracy, Craig, Smith, & Spisak, 1984). Politeness theory recognized that speakers often word their requests to incorporate negative politeness (implying they do not wish to impose) or positive politeness (conveying approval or acceptance). As politeness theory is discussed by Wilson and Feng (chap. 4, this volume), its assumptions are not reiterated here.

Although politeness theory generated numerous studies, it was not uncommon for communication scholars to question or criticize it (Craig et al., 1986; Leichty & Applegate, 1991; Lim, 1990; Wilson, Aleman, & Leatham, 1998). The theory implies, for example, that the importance of facework in a request should be greater when the hearer has relatively more power, social distance is greater, or the imposition is greater. Evidence supporting these predictions has been mixed and inconsistent (Baxter, 1984; Leichty & Applegate, 1991; Meyer, 1994a, 2001). Extant findings suggest that facework in compliance requests can be influenced by features not recognized in politeness theory, such as rights, resistance, and liking (Lim, 1990; Meyer, 1994a) and that the effect on facework of a single feature often depends on other features, traits, or the kind of influence goal (Meyer, 2001, 2002; Roloff & Janiszewski, 1989).

Types of Request Goals

Early research on compliance-gaining seemed to imply that strategy use could be predicted by situational features or individual differences. This perspective treated the speaker's goal as a "goal to gain compliance." By the early 1990s, several communication scholars had identified typologies of influence goals. Cody et al. (1994) proposed a typology of 11 types of influence goals that include, for instance, a gain assistance goal, share activity goal, give advice goal, and protect right goal (see Canary, Cody, & Marston, 1986). In a multiphase study of influence goals in close relationships, Dillard (1990b) identified six categories of influence goals: give advice-lifestyle, gain assistance, share activity, change political stance, give advice-health, and change relationship.

The typologies of influence goals stimulated research on how the type of request goal affects compliance seeking. Current findings suggest that the type of request affects the influence strategies preferred (Canary et al., 1986), perceptions of face threat and the importance of facework (Wilson et al., 1998), and which secondary goals are important (Schrader & Dillard, 1998). The effects of situation features on secondary goal importance also depend on the kind of request pursued. Greater intimacy appears to be associated with more facework when asking a favor but with less facework in borrow requests (Roloff & Janiszewski, 1989). The effects of six situation features on the importance of five secondary goals have been found to vary across four types of request goals (borrow, share activity, stop annoyance, request for permission; Meyer, 2002).

COGNITIVE APPROACHES TO THE STUDY OF COMPLIANCE GAINING

In the late 1970s, cognitive approaches to the study of behavior, influenced by work in artificial intelligence (Anderson, 1983) and experimental psychology, began to influence the study of social behavior in social psychology (Bargh, 1989; Higgins, 1989; Srull & Wyer, 1986) and communication (Greene, 1984; Roloff & Berger, 1982). Cognitive explanations take as axiomatic that all social perception and behavior is influenced by knowledge in the individual's long-term memory. Cognitive research is often based on specific assumptions about the cognitive structures that organize this knowledge and underlie the behavior to be explained. Whereas some researchers focus on structures, such as schemas, that organize beliefs about concepts, persons, and situations (Fiske & Taylor, 1984; Meyer, 1996b), others focus on structures connecting goals and contextual features to behaviors (Greene, 1984, 1997; Meyer, 1990, 1997).

Cognitive Models of Interpersonal Influence

Communication scholars have developed a number of cognitive models to explain the production of persuasive messages (Dillard et al., 2002; Wilson, 2002). The first detailed cognitive model to account for message production in the communication field was action assembly theory (Greene, 1984, 1997). Although intended to account for all messages, not just requests, the cognitive structures and processes assumed in action assembly theory apply to interpersonal influence messages (Greene, 1990; Greene, Smith, & Lindsey, 1990). (The reader is referred to Greene & Graves, chap. 2, this volume, for discussion of this theory.)

One of the first models to explain the production of influence messages, per se, was the goals-planning-action (GPA) model (Dillard, 1990a, 1990b). The GPA model assumes that secondary goals act as constraints on the pursuit of an influence goal. The model holds that message planning can take one of two paths. On the one hand, awareness of an influence goal can lead to a decision to engage the target. Plans are then generated, a plan is chosen, and action follows. Alternatively, an influence goal can lead initially to the generation of plans. After considering the plans, the source then decides whether to engage the target. If the decision is to pursue the request, a plan is selected and implemented.

Another model from the 1990s, the cognitive rules model (CRM), was designed to account for the formation of interaction goals (Wilson, 1990, 1995). The CRM views long-term memory as an associative network of nodes. A cognitive rule involves a pattern of association between nodes. Wilson (1990) noted, "In verbal form, a cognitive rule might read 'if conditions X, Y, and Z are encountered, then set A as a goal.'" (p. 82). For a goal to be formed, the level of activation of a rule must exceed a threshold such that the rule is triggered. The likelihood that a rule will be triggered increases with the accessibility of the rule and the degree of fit to the current situation. The relative importance of these factors in causing a rule to be triggered depends on the degree of fit between the rule and situation.

A third theoretical model, the IRM, was designed initially to explain how perceptions of a request situation influence the retrieval of compliance-gaining behaviors (Meyer, 1990). Meyer (1997) extended the model to account for the cognitive processes involved in designing a request, anticipating outcomes of a message plan, and editing the plan. An overview of the IRM is given next.

The IRM holds that the design of a request involves two types of cognitive structures: situation–action associations and action–consequence associations. Both are viewed as implicit rules in a distributed model of memory (McClelland & Rumelhart, 1985). A situation–action association connects a situation schema containing a goal and situation features to actions appropriate to pursuing that goal in that kind of situation. If translated to words, such a rule might specify, "If the goal is to ask for a ride to the airport and the hearer won't mind, then use a direct request." A single situation schema can be connected to actions at multiple levels of linguistic output (e.g., words, phrases, speech acts, tactics, plans, and nonverbal cues).

An action–consequence association connects a cognitive representation of an action and contextual features to knowledge about consequences of that action in that context. If stated in words, such a rule might specify, "Asking for a large favor can have the consequence of making the hearer feel imposed upon." A single action can be connected to multiple consequences.

According to the IRM, a speaker about to design a request retrieves a situation schema partially matched to his or her influence goal (e.g., to ask for a ride) and current situational features. The retrieved schema makes accessible actions appropriate to seeking compliance in that situation. One such action might be an indirect request. A decision to implement the action would activate a situation–action rule specifying a goal to make an indirect request and situational features. Linguistic cues made accessible by the latter rule (e.g., "I was wondering ... ") might then interact in a bottom-up manner with a preliminary message plan ("John, I need a ride") to transform the plan into an output plan adapted to current features ("John, I was wondering if you could possibly give me a ride").

Once a message plan is formulated, any component of the plan may become matched to the action component of an action–consequence rule. Once such a rule is activated, activation spreading from the action component makes accessible consequences of that action in a similar context. Consequences of a message are activated initially at a preconscious level. The likelihood of becoming aware that a not-yet-spoken message would conflict with (or realize) a secondary goal increases with the accessibility of the same knowledge and decreases with competing demands on processing capacity. The accessibility of knowledge about the relevance of a message consequence to a secondary goal is thought to be higher if the goal is more highly activated or the consequence is more highly activated. Having realized a message would conflict with a goal (e.g, it would damage the relationship), the speaker may then edit the message (see Meyer, 1997).

The IRM provides a general framework for conceptualizing the cognitive processes underlying the design and editing of a request. The model's assumptions make salient a number of more specific questions about the exact nature of these cognitive processes. Some questions raised by the model and the findings of studies conducted to investigate these issues are considered next.

Questions About Cognitive Processes

How Does a Cognitive Representation of a Request Goal and Situational Features Lead to the Retrieval of Knowledge About Similar Situations? According to the IRM, a speaker's representation of an influence goal and situation features leads to the retrieval of a situation schema containing a similar goal and features. In this respect, the model implies that the wording of a request is influenced by a type of request goal and situational features acting in concert. This assumption receives support from studies showing that the effect of situation features on facework or the importance of other secondary goals depends on the kind of request goal pursued (Meyer, 2002; Roloff & Janiszewski, 1989).

The factors determining which of several situation schemas might be considered the best matched to a situation are not well understood. Not clear, for example, is whether speakers would be more likely to retrieve (a) a schema containing a more specific representation of their current goal but poorer match to current situational features, or (b) a schema containing a more general goal but close match to current features. In one study investigating this issue, participants rated the similarity of abstract goal–feature configurations to a target situation involving a request to borrow a book (Meyer, 2003). The goal–feature configurations varied in the extent to which they contained a goal closely matched to the situation and in the number of situation features matched to the situation. The findings suggested that a speaker making a request to borrow a book would consider a rule with a borrow item goal and values of familiarity, status, and resistance matched to the situation a better match than a rule containing a more specific borrow book goal but one or two features mismatched to the situation. On the other hand, a rule containing a borrow item goal and one mismatched feature and a rule with a more general gain assistance goal and three matched features would be considered equally well matched. The study suggested that the most general level at which persons represent abstract goal knowledge when asking to borrow a book is at the level of a gain assistance goal (as opposed to a very general change behavior goal; Meyer, 2003, Study 1). A second study produced similar results. Future work on this issue will need to investigate how variations in the strength of situation schemas influence which schema is retrieved. If two schemas are equally well matched to a situation, the one that is permanently more accessible (stronger) due to frequency of activation should be retrieved over the one with less strength, all else equal (also see Greene, 1984, 1997; Wilson, 1990).

Are Strategies or Scripts for Seeking Compliance Stored in Memory? Early compliance-gaining research seemed to imply that persons possess a repertoire of compliance-gaining strategies and select from this repertoire a strategy appropriate to a situation. Thus far, empirical evidence that persons store strategies of the sort found in typologies is somewhat limited. Reservations about whether persons select a strategy from a repertoire have been noted by a number of scholars (Miller et al., 1987; O'Keefe, 1997; Seibold et al., 1985). Nonetheless, it is possible that persons do store compliance-seeking strategies in memory.

Research on sentence production and comprehension makes it clear that persons rely on abstract knowledge about familiar sequences of actions (scripts) at multiple levels of message planning. Both speaking and comprehension rely on scripts for the sequence of sounds in a word and sequence of letters in a word. Persons also store scripts indicating the typical sequence of actions in familiar activities such as going to a restaurant (Schank & Abelson, 1977). Thus, persons are capable of acquiring abstract knowledge specifying an ordered sequence.

A cognitive structure specifying a sequence of actions relevant to planning a request might take different forms. Schank and Abelson (1977) suggested persons possess an ordered sequence of alternative plans for making a request. If the first plan fails, a plan later in the sequence may be tried. Building on this work, Rule and Bisanz (1987) proposed that persons possess a persuasion schema that orders 15 tactics from the most preferred (direct request) to least preferred. Actors can "skip" tactics in the list. One implication of the IRM is that the tactic(s) most likely to be employed in a request will be those activated to the highest level by a situation schema containing a request goal and features similar to those in the current situation. A situation schema could send activation to several tactics. The level of activation of a given tactic should be positively related to (a) its strength in long-term memory (which would increase with frequency of use), and (b) the amount of activation it receives from the situation schema (which would increase with the frequency of use of the tactic in that type of situation). Consistent with this idea, Cody et al. (1994) provided evidence that the order of preference of tactics varies with the kind of influence goal pursued.

A somewhat different possibility is that persons possess scripts specifying an abstract sequence of speech acts to be employed in a single request message. Such scripts might specify a sequence such as explanation-request for action, compliment-request for action, or request for action-promise. Such a script could serve as the action part of either a situation–action rule or action–consequence rule. The possibility that persons store strategies consisting of sequences of speech acts was investigated by Meyer (1994b). Requests generated in response to 15 hypothetical situations were coded for speech acts such as request for action, promise, apology, and explanation. The frequency of each possible sequence of speech acts was then tabulated. The study found that consistency in the sequences of speech acts used by a given respondent was greater across situations containing the same request goal (borrow or stop action) than across situations containing different request goals. The results tentatively suggest that the type of request goal is a better predictor of consistency in the use of speech act sequences than are configurations of situation features. Conceivably, the request goal constrains the sequence of speech acts used, whereas situation features influence other aspects of the language of a request. Further research is needed to determine whether scripts specifying sequences of speech acts for making requests are stored in memory. One series of studies found that memory for strategies defined by unfamiliar sequences of tactics was relatively poor (Greene et al., 1990).

Whereas the preceding considerations suggest that strategies might be stored in memory as a sequence of actions, abstract knowledge about a strategy might also be stored in memory as a configuration of values on dimensions found to distinguish compliance-gaining strategies (Kellermann & Cole, 1994). Roskos-Ewoldsen (1997) argued, for example, that persons possess implicit persuasion schemas that order strategies for changing another's beliefs or attitudes along two dimensions: a social acceptability dimension and a tactic dimension. The tactic dimension ranges from message-oriented strategies (e.g., providing detailed arguments) to association strategies (e.g., associating the attitude object with valued objects or persons). Strategies for seeking compliance might be stored as values along dimensions pertinent to explicitness, inclusion of reasons for asking, mention of incentives, amount of negative politeness, and so on (see Dillard, Wilson, Tusing, & Kinney, 1997; Lim & Bowers; 1991; Wiseman & Schenck-Hamlin, 1981).

What Factors Influence Whether Consequences of a Message Are Anticipated Prior to Speaking? Prior to making a request, a speaker may or may not realize that a planned message would conflict with a secondary goal. According to the IRM, the likelihood of becoming aware of the knowledge that a message would conflict with goal will increase with the level of activation of the same knowledge in working memory and decrease with competing demands on capacity (Meyer, 1997). The level of activation of knowledge about the relevance of a message consequence to a goal should increase with the level of activation of the relevant goal and level of activation of the consequence. A secondary goal could be activated to a higher level temporarily if the situation were of a type where the goal is typically pursued. A goal would have a higher permanent level of activation (strength) if it is a frequently activated chronic goal for the person (Meyer, 2001).

These assumptions predict that the likelihood of realizing a planned message would conflict with a goal should be greater if (a) the chronic importance of the goal is greater, or (b) the situated importance of the goal is greater. Support for these predictions has been stronger for situated than for chronic goals. Current findings suggest that speakers judge supplied messages as more likely to conflict with a not offend goal and a relationship maintenance goal to the extent that the respective goal is more important to them in the immediate situation. The effect of chronic goal importance on the perceived likelihood that a message would conflict with the same goal appears to vary with the secondary goal and kind of request situation (Meyer, 2005). Whether persons anticipate that a message would conflict with a secondary goal also depends on personality differences. At least two studies indicate that persons higher in verbal aggressiveness are less inclined to judge request messages unacceptable on the grounds that the message would offend or hurt the hearer (Hample & Dallinger, 1987; Meyer, 2004).

According to the IRM, the likelihood of realizing that a not-yet-spoken message would conflict with a secondary goal also depends on the level of activation of the consequence. If the permanent level of activation of a message consequence is higher (i.e., stronger) due to frequency of activation in the same or numerous contexts, then the same amount of activation from the action part of an action–consequence rule should cause the consequence to become activated to a relatively higher level. Under such conditions, the IRM holds that knowledge about the relevance of the message consequence to a secondary goal would also be activated to a higher level (all else equal). Thus, the likelihood of realizing that a not-yet-spoken message would conflict with a goal should generally be greater if the consequence relevant to the goal is one experienced on a frequent basis. To my knowledge, this prediction has not been tested.

What Cognitive Differences Underlie Individual Differences in the Ability to Adapt a Request to a Specific Situation? The IRM implies that the ability to adapt a request to a specific goal and situation will increase with two factors: the specificity of the goal in the retrieved situation schema and the number of situational features in the schema. The features in a schema will be those the speaker has perceived to be relevant to how requests of that type should be made. For example, a schema specifying high hearer status should make accessible more actions conveying deference than would a schema specifying equal status.

A situation–action rule containing a more specific goal and more features may be said to be more highly differentiated. For example, the language of a request should be better adapted to the situation if the design of the request were guided by a situation schema specifying a goal to ask for a ride to the airport and the features high intimacy, equal status, low rights, and high resistance than if it were guided by a less differentiated schema specifying a goal to ask for a favor and the features high intimacy and equal status. Individual differences in the ability to produce a request adapted to a situation should also be influenced by the degree of differentiation in the action–consequence rule used to anticipate consequences of a message. To the extent that the contextual features in the action component of such a rule match all critical features of the situation, the consequences made accessible by the rule should be a more accurate prediction of message outcomes.

What Learning Processes Underlie the Acquisition of More Highly Differentiated Situation–Action Rules and Action–Consequence Rules? How persons develop more highly differentiated implicit rules is not well understood. The acquisition of more specific rules likely relies on both explicit and implicit learning. Whereas explicit learning involves a conscious effort to articulate a new rule, implicit learning relies on relatively unconscious, automatic processes of schema abstraction (Reber, Kassin, Lewis, & Cantor, 1980).

A person might acquire a situation–action rule with a more specific request goal (e.g., a borrow goal vs. a gain assistance goal) after observing that the optimal actions for seeking assistance depend on the assistance goal pursued. A rule specifying a goal to gain assistance might be supplemented with a more specific situation–action rule linking a goal to borrow and contextual features to actions appropriate in borrow requests (e.g., promising to take care of the borrowed item).

Acquisition of a rule containing a relatively greater number of situation features could result from being reminded to a situation where an existing situation–action rule failed (Berger & Jordan, 1992). Remembering the earlier situation, the speaker might recall that the message failed because it did not address a critical situation feature, high resistance. Identification of the critical feature not addressed in the earlier request could lead to the eventual acquisition of a more highly differentiated situation–action rule connecting features in the rule used previously plus the feature, high resistance, to actions suitable in high-resistance situations.

Few studies have investigated the processes whereby persons acquire situation–action rules. Two studies exploring this issue asked whether persons acquire implicit situation–action rules from repeated experiences of similar request situations (Meyer, 1996a). In each study, participants learned, based on feedback, which request behavior was "correct" for multiple instances of several situation schemas. Each schema was defined by values on five dimensions. As predicted, the results suggested that participants abstracted situation schemas from repeated experiences of similar request situations during a learning phase and acquired rules associating abstract configurations of elements to a communication behavior.

Issues of Concern in Social Cognitive Research

The value of studies investigating the cognitive processes underlying compliance seeking can be enhanced by attention to several issues. First, for the findings to be meaningful and comparable to results of other studies, it is essential that researchers provide clear definitions of constructs referring to cognitive structures, such as schema (Fiske &

Taylor, 1984), script (Schank & Abelson, 1977), chronic goal (Meyer, 2001; Srull & Wyer, 1986), and rule (Meyer, 1997; Wilson, 1990). Equally important are definitions of constructs referring to variability in the level of action of cognitive structures, such as strength (Anderson, 1983; Greene, 1984; Meyer, 1997), accessibility (Higgins, 1989), working memory (Anderson, Reder, & Lebiere, 1996; Baddeley, 1986), and priming (Bargh & Barndollar, 1996). Definitions of cognitive concepts should be consistent with the origins and definitions of the construct in cognitive psychology.

Second, the theoretical implications of cognitive research are often clearer when researchers' assumptions about the cognitive structures and processes thought to underlie the phenomenon being studied are made explicit. For example, research on how a request is adapted to a specific hearer might be based on a specific model of person memory (Fiske & Taylor, 1984; Meyer, 1996b; Park, 1989). Third, variations in the accessibility of constructs should be investigated using reaction time measures, onset latency measures, or priming manipulations whenever possible (see Arpan, Rhodes, & Roskos-Ewoldsen, chap. 15, this volume; Bargh & Barndollar, 1996; Higgins, 1989; Meyer, 1996b; Wilson, 1990). Fourth, as a number of scholars have noted, cognitive accounts of compliance seeking should be consistent with what is known about the planning and production of sentences (Harley, 1995; O'Keefe, 1997; O'Keefe & Lambert, 1995).

FUTURE TRENDS

Research investigating the preceding questions and related ones could yield a more detailed understanding than has heretofore been possible of how persons design requests, anticipate message outcomes, edit messages, reflect on communication failures, and acquire more highly differentiated situation–action rules and action–consequence rules. The centrality of these issues to explanations of interpersonal influence suggests that cognitive research on compliance seeking should increase over the next decade. In the same time span, increased attention to five additional areas of inquiry can be expected. First, a greater number of studies will investigate factors influencing the effectiveness of compliance-seeking messages (e.g., Boster, Fediuk, & Kotowski, 2001). Second, findings of research on message effectiveness will be applied with increasing frequency to the study of interpersonal influence in applied contexts such as doctor–patient communication, risk-prevention communication, and communicating with the elderly. Third, current trends predict a greater number of meta-analyses of various subsets of the literature on interpersonal influence. Fourth, it will become increasingly evident that the situation features important to adapting the language of a request differ across types of requests and social contexts. Finally, the future should see a greater number of studies investigating interpersonal influence in the various forms of computer-mediated communication.

REFERENCES

Anderson, J. R. (1983). *The architecture of cognition.* Cambridge, MA: Harvard University Press.

Anderson, J. R., Reder, L. M., & Lebiere, C. (1996). Working memory: Activation limitations on retrieval. *Cognitive Psychology, 30,* 221–256.

Baddeley, A. D. (1986). *Working memory.* Oxford, UK: Oxford University Press.

Bargh, J. A. (1989). Conditional automaticity: Varieties of automatic influence in social perception and cognition. In J. S. Uleman & J. A. Bargh (Eds.), *Unintended thought* (pp. 3–51). New York: Guilford.

Bargh, J. A., & Barndollar, K. (1996). Automaticity in action: The unconscious as repository of chronic goals and motives. In P. M. Gollwitzer & J. A. Bargh (Eds.), *The psychology of action: Linking cognition and motivation to behavior* (pp. 457–481). New York: Guilford.

Baxter, L. A. (1984). An investigation of compliance-gaining as politeness. *Human Communication Research, 10,* 427–456.

Berger, C. R., & Jordan, J. M. (1992). Planning sources, planning difficulty and verbal fluency. *Communication Monographs, 59,* 130–149.

Boster, F. J., Fediuk, T. A., & Kotowski, M. R. (2001). The effectiveness of an altruistic appeal in the presence and absence of favors. *Communication Monographs, 68,* 347–359.

Boster, F. J., & Stiff, J. B. (1984). Compliance gaining message selection behavior. *Human Communication Research, 10,* 539–556.

Brown, P., & Levinson, S. C. (1987). *Politeness: Some universals in language usage.* Cambridge, UK: Cambridge University Press.

Burleson, B. R., & Caplan, S. E. (1998). Cognitive complexity. In J. C. McCroskey, J. A. Daly, M. M. Martin, & M. J. Beatty (Eds.), *Communication and personality: Trait perspectives* (pp. 233–286). Creskill, NJ: Hampton.

Burleson, B. R., Wilson, S. R., Waltman, M. S., Goering, E. M., Ely, T. K., & Whaley, B. B. (1988). Item desirability effects in compliance-gaining research: Seven studies documenting artifacts in the strategy selection procedure. *Human Communication Research, 14,* 429–486.

Canary, D. J., Cody, M. J., & Marston, P. J. (1986). Goal types, compliance gaining and locus of control. *Journal of Language and Social Psychology, 5,* 249–269.

Clark, R. A., & Delia, J. G. (1979). *Topoi* and rhetorical competence. *Quarterly Journal of Speech, 65,* 187–206.

Cody, M. J., Canary, D. J., & Smith, S. W. (1994). Compliance-gaining goals: An inductive analysis of actors' goal types, strategies, and successes. In J. A. Daly & J. M. Wiemann (Eds.), *Strategic interpersonal communication* (pp. 33–90). Hillsdale, NJ: Lawrence Erlbaum Associates.

Cody, M. J., Greene, J. O., Marston, P., O'Hair, H. D., Baaske, K. T., & Schneider, M. J. (1986). Situation perception and message strategy selection. In M. L. McLaughlin (Ed.), *Communication yearbook 9* (pp. 390–420). Beverly Hills, CA: Sage.

Cody, M. J., & McLaughlin, M. L. (1980). Perceptions of compliance-gaining situations: A dimensional analysis. *Communication Monographs, 47,* 132–148.

Craig, R. T., Tracy, K., & Spisak, F. (1986). The discourse of requests: Assessment of a politeness approach. *Human Communication Research, 12,* 437–468.

Dillard, J. P. (1990a). A goal-driven model of interpersonal influence. In J. P. Dillard (Ed.), *Seeking compliance: The production of interpersonal influence messages* (pp. 41–56). Scottsdale, AZ: Gorsuch Scarisbrick.

Dillard, J. P. (1990b). The nature and substance of goals in tactical communication. In M. J. Cody & M. L. McLaughlin (Eds.), *The psychology of tactical communication* (pp. 70–90). Clevedon, UK: Multilingual Matters.

Dillard, J. P., Anderson, J. W., & Knobloch, L. K. (2002). Interpersonal influence. In M. L. Knapp & J. A. Daly (Eds.), *Handbook of interpersonal communication* (3rd ed., pp. 425–474). Thousand Oaks, CA: Sage.

Dillard, J. P., & Burgoon, M. (1985). Situational influences on the selection of compliance-gaining messages: Two tests of the predictive utility of the Cody–McLaughlin typology. *Communication Monographs, 52,* 289–304.

Dillard, J. P., Segrin, C., & Harden, J. M. (1989). Primary and relational goals in the production of interpersonal influence messages. *Communication Monographs, 56,* 19–38.

Dillard, J. P., Wilson, S. R., Tusing, K. J., & Kinney, T. A. (1997). Politeness judgments in personal relationships. *Journal of Language and Social Psychology, 16,* 297–325.

Fiske, S. T., & Taylor, S. E. (1984). *Social cognition.* New York: Random House.

Greene, J. O. (1984). A cognitive approach to human communication: An action- assembly theory. *Communication Monographs, 51,* 289–306.

Greene, J. O. (1990). Tactical social action: Towards some strategies for theory. In M. J. Cody & M. L. McLaughlin (Eds.), *The psychology of tactical communication* (pp. 31–47). Clevedon, UK: Multilingual Matters.

Greene, J. O. (1997). A second generation action assembly theory. In J. O. Greene (Ed.), *Message production: Advances in communication theory* (pp. 151–170). Mahwah, NJ: Lawrence Erlbaum Associates.

Greene, J. O., Smith, S. W., & Lindsey, A. E. (1990). Memory representations of compliance-gaining strategies and tactics. *Human Communication Research, 17,* 195–231.

Hample, D., & Dallinger, J. M. (1987). Individual differences in cognitive editing standards. *Human Communication Research, 14,* 123–144.

Harley, T. A. (1995). *The psychology of language: From data to theory.* East Sussex, UK: Taylor & Francis.

Higgins, E. T. (1989). Knowledge accessibility and activation: Subjectivity and suffering from unconscious sources. In J. S. Uleman & J. A. Bargh (Eds.), *Unintended thought* (pp. 75–123). New York: Guilford.

Kellermann, K., & Cole, T. (1994). Classifying compliance gaining messages: Taxonomic disorder and strategic confusion. *Communication Theory, 4,* 3–60.

Kim, M.-S., & Wilson, S. R. (1994). A cross-cultural comparison of implicit theories of requesting. *Communication Monographs, 61,* 210–235.

Labov, W., & Fanshel, D. (1977). *Therapeutic discourse: Psychotherapy as conversation.* New York: Academic.

Leichty, G., & Applegate, J. O. (1991). Social-cognitive and situation influences on the use of face-saving persuasive strategies. *Human Communication Research, 17,* 451–484.

Lim, T.-S. (1990). Politeness behavior in social influence situations. In J. P. Dillard (Ed.), *Seeking compliance: The production of interpersonal influence messages* (pp. 75–86). Scottsdale, AZ: Gorsuch Scarisbrick.

Lim, T.-S., & Bowers, J. W. (1991). Face-work: Solidarity, approbation, and tact. *Human Communication Research, 17,* 415–450.

Marwell, G., & Schmitt, D. R. (1967). Dimensions of compliance-gaining behavior: An empirical analysis. *Sociometry, 30,* 350–364.

McClelland, J. L., & Rumelhart, D. E. (1985). Distributed memory and the representation of general and specific information. *Journal of Experimental Psychology: General, 114,* 159–188.

Meyer, J. R. (1990). Cognitive processes underlying the retrieval of compliance-gaining strategies: An implicit rules model. In J. P. Dillard (Ed.), *Seeking compliance: The production of interpersonal influence messages* (pp. 57–73). Scottsdale, AZ: Gorsuch Scarisbrick.

Meyer, J. R. (1994a). Effect of situational features on the likelihood of addressing face needs in requests. *Southern Communication Journal, 59,* 240–254.

Meyer, J. R. (1994b). Formulating plans for requests: An investigation of retrieval processes. *Communication Studies, 45,* 131–144.

Meyer, J. R. (1996a). Retrieving knowledge in social situations: A test of the implicit rules model. *Communication Research, 23,* 581–611.

Meyer, J. R. (1996b). What cognitive differences are measured by the Role Category Questionnaire? *Western Journal of Communication, 60,* 233–253.

Meyer, J. R. (1997). Cognitive influences on the ability to address interaction goals. In J. O. Greene (Ed.), *Message production: Advances in communication theory* (pp. 71–90). Mahwah, NJ: Lawrence Erlbaum Associates.

Meyer, J. R. (2001). Pursuing relational goals in requests: The effects of dispositional factors and type of relationship. *Southern Communication Journal, 67,* 51–65.

Meyer, J. R. (2002). Contextual influences on the pursuit of secondary goals in request messages. *Communication Monographs, 69,* 189–203.

Meyer, J. R. (2003). Cognitive representations of request situations: The relative importance of goal specificity and situation features. *Western Journal of Communication, 67,* 292–314.

Meyer, J. R. (2004). Effect of verbal aggressiveness on the perceived importance of secondary goals in messages. *Communication Studies, 55,* 168–184.

Meyer, J. R. (2005). Effect of secondary goal importance on the anticipation of message outcomes. *Southern Communication Journal, 70,* 109–122.

Miller, G. R., Boster, F. J., Roloff, M. E., & Seibold, D. (1977). Compliance-gaining message strategies: A typology and some findings concerning effects of situational differences. *Communication Monographs, 44,* 37–51.

Miller, G. R., Boster, F. J., Roloff, M. E., & Seibold, D. (1987). MBRS rekindled: Some thoughts on compliance gaining in interpersonal settings. In M. E. Roloff & G. R. Miller (Eds.), *Interpersonal processes: New directions in communication research* (pp. 89–117). Newbury Park, CA: Sage.

O'Keefe, B. J. (1997). Variation, adaptation, and functional explanation in the study of message design. In G. Philipsen & T. L. Albrecht (Eds.), *Developing communication theories* (pp. 85–118). Albany: State University of New York Press.

O'Keefe, B. J., & Delia, J. G. (1982). Impression formation and message production. In M. E. Roloff & C. R. Berger (Eds.), *Social cognition and communication* (pp. 33–72). Beverly Hills, CA: Sage.

O'Keefe, B. J., & Lambert, B. L. (1995). Managing the flow of ideas: A local management approach to message design. In B. Burleson (Ed.), *Communication yearbook 18* (pp. 54–82). Thousand Oaks, CA: Sage.

Park, B. (1989). Trait attributes as on-line organizers in person impressions. In J. N. Bassili (Ed.), *On-line cognition in person perception* (pp. 39–59). Hillsdale, NJ: Lawrence Erlbaum Associates.

Reber, A. S., Kassin, S. M., Lewis, S., & Cantor, G. (1980). On the relationship between implicit and explicit modes in the learning of a complex rule structure. *Journal of Experimental Psychology: Human Learning & Memory, 6,* 492–502.

Roloff, M. E., & Berger, C. R. (1982). *Social cognition and communication.* Beverly Hills, CA: Sage.

Roloff, M. E., & Janiszewski, C. A. (1989). Overcoming obstacles to interpersonal compliance: A principle of message construction. *Human Communication Research, 16,* 33–61.

Roskos-Ewoldsen, D. R. (1997). Implicit theories of persuasion. *Human Communication Research, 24,* 31–63.

Rule, B. G., & Bisanz, G. L. (1987). Goals and strategies of persuasion: A cognitive schema for understanding social events. In M. P. Zanna & J. M. Olson (Eds.), *Social influence: The Ontario Symposium* (Vol. 5, pp. 185–206). Hillsdale, NJ: Lawrence Erlbaum Associates..

Schank, R., & Abelson, R. (1977). *Scripts, plans, goals and understanding: An inquiry into human knowledge structures.* Hillsdale, NJ: Lawrence Erlbaum Associates.

Schenck-Hamlin, W. J., Wiseman, R. L., & Georgacarakos, G. N. (1982). A model of properties of compliance-gaining strategies. *Communication Quarterly, 30,* 92–100.

Schrader, D. C., & Dillard, J. P. (1998). Goal structures and interpersonal influence. *Communication Studies, 49,* 276–293.

Seibold, D. R., Cantrill, J. G., & Meyers, R. A. (1985). Communication and interpersonal influence. In M. L. Knapp & G. R. Miller (Eds.), *Handbook of interpersonal communication* (pp. 551–611). Beverly Hills, CA: Sage.

Srull, T. K., & Wyer, R. S. (1986). The role of chronic and temporary goals in social information processing. In R. M. Sorentino & E. T. Higgins (Eds.), *Handbook of motivation and cognition: Foundations of social behavior* (pp. 503–549). New York: Guilford.

Tracy, K., Craig, R. T., Smith, M., & Spisak, F. (1984). The discourse of requests: Assessment of a compliance-gaining approach. *Human Communication Research, 10,* 513–538.

Wilson, S. R. (1990). Development and test of a cognitive rules model of interaction goals. *Communication Monographs, 57,* 81–103.

Wilson, S. R. (1995). Elaborating the cognitive rules model of interaction goals: The problem of accounting for individual differences in goal formation. In B. Burleson (Ed.), *Communication yearbook 18* (pp. 3–25). Thousand Oaks, CA: Sage.

Wilson, S. R. (2002). *Seeking and resisting compliance: Why people say what they do when trying to influence others.* Thousand Oaks, CA: Sage.

Wilson, S. R., Aleman, C. G., & Leatham, G. B. (1998). Identity implications of influence goals: A revised analysis of face-threatening acts and application to seeking compliance with same-sex friends. *Human Communication Research, 25,* 64–96.

Wiseman, R. L., & Schenck-Hamlin, W. (1981). A multidimensional scaling validation of an inductively-derived set of compliance-gaining strategies. *Communication Monographs, 48,* 251–270.

18

Motivation, Social Context, and Cognitive Processing as Evolving Concepts in Persuasion Theory

Mark A. Hamilton
University of Connecticut

Current evolutionary theory (Eldredge & Gould, 1972; Gould, 1982, 1983; Mayr, 1992) holds that species develop in punctuated equilibria that are characterized by long periods of stasis interrupted by abrupt morphological change. I became interested in the parallels between memes and genes while writing an article on types of concepts used by communication researchers covering a span of 20 years (Hamilton & Nowak, 2005). Although the periodicity of conceptual change in the social sciences is on a minute scale compared to species change across epochs, our data suggested that concepts, like species, do not develop gradually or at a uniform rate. Rather, social scientific concepts evolve in punctuated equilibria marked by periods of intense change brought about by the introduction of new ideas, theories, or approaches. These new ideas can account for anomalous findings within the scientific community that have disturbed the flow of normal science. These new ideas transform the conceptual landscape by altering the paradigm within a discipline. Following such dynamic periods are static periods of conventional studies that seek to establish the boundaries of the new paradigm.

Concept life cycles in the social sciences generate larger patterns of theory development that appear to follow the 20-year cycle of the typical academic publishing career. After the appearance of a theory that transforms a discipline, its advocates tend to the unresolved details of the theory (Kuhn, 1962), and adherents to rival theories retire—or die (Planck, 1949/1962). In the social science ecosystem, compelling theories often hold sway for a generation of researchers (approximately two decades) before finally losing their struggle to survive, displaced by a theory with better fit. Extending the metaphor, the surviving theory is better able to adapt to selection pressure exerted by crucial experiments in a harsh empirical environment. The niche occupied by a fallen theory is sometimes replaced generations later by a new theory that outwardly resembles the failed theory but is quite different in its inner workings. The rhinoceros is in some respects the successor to the triceratops in the niche it occupies, the giraffe succeeds the diplodocus. In the evolution of scientific concepts, particularly in the field of persuasion, form also follows function.

ERAS OF THEORY DEVELOPMENT IN SOCIAL INFLUENCE

The study of persuasion following World War II has undergone three eras of theory development that fit the template of a 20-year cycle to conceptual upheaval. One era brackets the year 1960, another the year 1980, and a third the year 2000. The three eras reflect the stages of learning, suggesting that disciplines build knowledge structures in a manner that parallels that of individuals. The subsumption theory of learning (Ausubel, 1963) argues that for people to engage in meaningful learning, they proceed from accreting information to progressive differentiation to integrative reconciliation. Each stage is founded on the stage that precedes it, such that differentiation depends on accreted information, and integration depends on differentiation.

The 1960 era can be viewed as extensive theorizing about the possible processes that occur in persuasion. It produced a long list of processes that may influence beliefs and attitudes. This era of accreting information was essentially an informal group brainstorming session on processes, a session that had thousands of participants over two decades, and much "piggy-backing" of ideas. Research interest in the concept of process has, in fact, continued to this day and is even surging (Hamilton & Nowak, 2005).

The 1980 era can be viewed as theorizing about how the various persuasion processes identified during the earlier era of process accretion differ from one another. The result was a bevy of theories about modes of processing. Typically, these theories contrasted two modes of processing, arguing that they are qualitatively different. Dual process theories have differentiated deep from shallow processing (Craik, 1979; Craik & Tulving, 1975), mindful from mindless processing (Langer, 1975, 1978; Langer, Blank, & Chanowitz, 1978), automatic from controlled processing (Bargh, 1984; Schneider & Shiffrin, 1977; Shiffrin & Schneider, 1977), central from peripheral processing (Petty & Cacioppo, 1981), systematic from heuristic processing (Chaiken, 1980), and spontaneous from deliberative processing (Fazio, Chen, McDonel, &

Sherman, 1982; Fazio, Powell, & Herr, 1983). Some of these theorists followed up their distinctions with a description of the sequence of events associated with each process, whereas other theorists did not.

In the years that immediately preceded and followed 2000, theorizing addressed how various forms of processing persuasive messages relate to one another. The result has been theories that see similarities and matters of degree in what were previously thought to be qualitatively different modes of processing. That is, these more integrative theories take a quantitative approach to the qualitative distinctions made by dual process models. The unimodel of persuasion (Kruglanski, Thompson, & Spiegel, 1999) removes the "partition" between the processing of message content and source variables first proposed by Laswell (1948). Similarly, the omnistructure model (Hamilton, 1997) proposes that message evaluation and source evaluation sequences influence one another at each stage of information processing.

An Era of Accreting Processes

The publication of the SMCR model (Berlo, 1960) had a profound impact on the field of communication. The model described the role of source, message, channel, and receiver variables (thus, the acronym) in the communication process. The dominant social influence theories of the 1960s were also enamored with process, but the norm was to propose a process model that describes a single sequence of events most individuals would follow after exposure to a persuasive message (Petty, 1994). A major focus of persuasion research in the 1960s era was the effect of message variables on attitudes. Message effects studies manipulated variables such as language intensity (consisting of opinionated language, obscene language, specific language, and emotional language), message discrepancy (the difference between the position advocated by the source and the premessage attitude of receivers), fear appeals, message-sidedness, primacy–recency, rhetorical questions, type of conclusion, and comprehensibility. Source variables—credibility (Berlo, Lemert, & Mertz, 1963; McCroskey, 1966) in particular—were often included in research designs of this era as potential moderators of message effects. Channel variables, most notably the distinction between mass media and interpersonal communication (Katz & Lazersfeld, 1955; Lazersfeld & Menzel, 1963; Lazersfeld & Merton, 1964; Rogers & Beal, 1958), were treated as nominal, indicating qualitatively different domains of communication.

When receiver variables were included in research designs, it was typically as potential moderators of message effects. This meant that researchers would necessarily focus more on state variables, which could be manipulated into binary independent variables, rather than trait variables, which would be measured on continuous metrics. Continuous predictor variables pose a problem for those who rely on analysis of variance (ANOVA) for their statistical analysis. Most of the single-motive distinct-sequence theories of the 1960s assumed that attitude change was the result of receivers resolving incongruities between the material presented in a source's message and audience members' beliefs or attitudes. Thus, the implicit receiver goal was to have a veridical belief system.[1] To address receiver differences in processing, persuasion theories were frequently supplemented with auxiliary social cognitive models to explain the nature of subjective knowledge. Conversely, some theories of social cognition were developed to model subjective knowledge and were later extended to apply to persuasion.

Social Cognitive Models. Message learning theory (Hovland, Janis, & Kelly, 1953) is a prominent example of a persuasion theory that was supplemented with an auxiliary treatment of receiver variables—both the work on personality and persuasibility (Hovland & Janis, 1959) and subjective knowledge (Hovland & Rosenberg, 1960). The opposite pattern was for a persuasion theory to develop as a supplement to a main social cognitive theory. Consider the case of social judgment theory (Hovland, Harvey, & Sherif, 1957; Hovland & Pritzker, 1957; Hovland & Sherif, 1952). It began as a theory of perception (Sherif, 1935) and social norms (Sherif, 1936) and was later applied to the study of attitude change (Sherif & Hovland, 1953, 1961). In the same vein, field theory (Lewin, 1935) gave rise to affective consistency models of attitude organization such as balance theory (Heider, 1946). This social cognitive model of subjective knowledge was then extended to persuasion and interpersonal influence (Heider, 1958). Similarly, the syllogistic consistency model (McGuire, 1960a, 1960b) influenced the development of information processing theory (McGuire, 1968, 1969); cognitive dissonance theory (Festinger, 1957; Festinger & Carlsmith, 1959) was extended to cover persuasion (Aronson, Turner, & Carlsmith, 1963); and belief systems theory (Rokeach, 1956, 1960) was a

[1]A belief is the subjective probability that a proposition about an attitude object is true (Fishbein & Ajzen, 1975). Beliefs are organized into systems in which a given belief can range from general to specific, depending on its place in a hierarchy (Katz, 1960). Attitudes are the evaluative, affect-laden consequences of beliefs, so an attitude hierarchy should follow from the presence of a belief hierarchy. Given that values are global attitudes within attitude hierarchies (Hunter et al., 1976), values follow from general beliefs (Smith, 1991) and lower level attitudes follow from specific beliefs. Attitudes within a system vary as to their salience—how central or marginal they are to the person's self-concept (Smith et al., 1956). Salience is the recognition of a particular need, with that need activating a particular process. This conceptualization of salience predates the ELM concept of personal relevance which differentiates central from peripheral processing.

precursor to congruity theory (Osgood, Suci, & Tannenbaum, 1957; Rokeach & Rothman, 1965).

Single-motive distinct-sequence persuasion theories, even when supplemented by social cognitive theories of subjective knowledge, propose that receivers pursue a limited set of goals. That is, the single motive drives a particular goal, and that goal initiates a particular sequence. Individuals might differ in the degree to which they pursue the goal or they might differ on values for variables in the sequence, but the sequence was assumed to apply to everyone.

Multiple Motives. Theories in the 1960s that proposed multiple discrete sequences of variables as part of the persuasion process were overshadowed by single-process distinct-sequence theories. Multimotive theories were treated as somewhat obscure so they generated less research than the single-motive theories of the day (Insko, 1965; Keisler et al., 1967). In multimotive theories, individuals were assumed to differ on personality factors linked to motivation. Research on personality differences in need (Atkinson & Litwin, 1960; McClelland, 1962) buttressed this assumption. A second key assumption of multimotive theories is that either the message itself (Kelman, 1961) or the social context (Smith, Bruner, & White, 1956) can increase perceived need, leading to the simultaneous activation of several sequences, each of which can influence beliefs and opinions. This principle of parallel processing implies that for most receivers under most circumstances, situational cues activate more than one sequence (Kelman, 1961; Smith et al., 1956).

The multimotive theories were specific about which text variables (message features) or social context variables (mainly source features) act as antecedents to a given sequence, although the antecedents varied from theory to theory. The theories were vague about two aspects of these causal connections: (a) which antecedents are associated with which needs, and (b) which needs are associated with which sequences. Both sets of associations can be expressed as correlations. The multimotive theories also lacked detail about the sequences themselves—for a given sequence, which variables mediate the effect of message variables on beliefs, attitudes, and behavior. Nonetheless, the theories were relatively consistent in the process model they implied. Receivers were supposed to follow the series of stages shown in Figure 18.1 (see Smith, 1969; Smith et al., 1956). The six stages consist of exposure, perception, orientation, goal-directed evaluation, judgment, and finally belief and attitude change (or more generally information integration).

An Era of Differentiating Processes

Drawing from social psychology, the social cognitive approach to communication was transformational in that it focused researcher attention

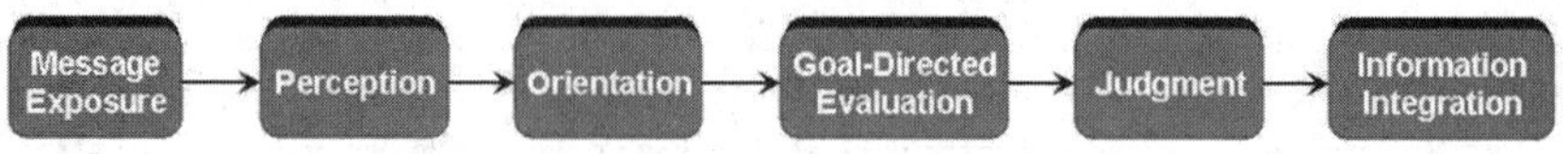

FIGURE 18.1. Universal stages of the persuasion process.

on individual differences in message processing. The publication of *Social Cognition and Communication* (Roloff & Berger, 1982) was part of that social cognitive revolution. Circa 1980, the multimotive, distinct-sequence models were in ascension and the single-motive, distinct-sequence models were in decline. The key works in persuasion leading up to and immediately following 1980 were those that formulated two dual-process models—the elaboration likelihood model (ELM; Petty, 1977; Petty & Cacioppo, 1981) and the heuristic-systematic model (HSM; Chaiken, 1980).

The processes described in dual-process models were substantially influenced by personality function models, message learning theory (Hovland et al., 1953), and early information processing theory (McGuire, 1968, 1969). The concept of multiple processes was merged with cognitive response theory (Greenwald, 1968) to create the first dual-process model (see Petty & Cacioppo, 1981). This first dual-process model (Petty, 1977) provides a link between cognitive response theory and the basic principles of the most popular dual-process models, the ELM and the HSM.

An Era of Integrating Processes

The period surrounding 2000 saw the emergence of multimotive, interconnected-sequence models. In these models, processes assigned to separate and distinct sequences in dual-process models are modified to be interconnected and fused at each stage of the persuasion process. Like modern information processing theory (Hamilton, 1997, 1998), the unified model of persuasion (Kruglanski et al., 2000; Shah & Kruglanski, 1999, 2000) proposes that the evaluation of evidence to support message claims is influenced by a variety of motives but that the general form of this evaluation and the objective of understanding message claims is paramount.

Both the unimodel and the omnistructure emphasize message clarity and possess a facility to accommodate diverse forms of message evaluation such as systematic and heuristic processing of evidence (Hamilton & Nowak, 2005). The unimodel directly addresses the dichotomies identified by dual-process models, seeking to uncover the continua beneath the binary variables (Kruglanski et al., 1999; Uleman, 1999). In light of this, it is worth noting that moving from binary variables to variables with higher precision is a sign of a maturing discipline (Hunter & Hamilton, in press). The social cognitive theory that served as the basis for the unimodel was lay epistemic theory (LET; Kruglanski, 1980, 1989). LET explains how subjective knowledge is formed, such that lay epistemologies are processes by which a person evaluates message content. Similarly, the social cognitive basis for the omnistructure model is belief systems theory (BST; Hamilton & Mineo, 1996, 1999; Rokeach, 1956, 1960, 1968). Like LET, BST proposes a set of ethnologics that people use to justify their beliefs about their world.

THE STRUCTURE UNDERLYING THE PHASES OF THE PERSUASION PROCESS

Nearly all persuasion theories, from those constructed in the late 1950s up to the present, assume that receivers proceed through a sequence of stages that can culminate in attitude change. Single-motive, distinct-sequence theories propose that this set of stages applies to all receivers. Message learning theory (Hovland et al., 1953) was perhaps the most influential single-motive, distinct-sequence theory. The six-stage sequence it proposes consists of exposure, attention, comprehension, acceptance, opinion change, and attitude change. Note the similarity between this sequence and the one depicted in Figure 18.1. Suppose that a person has been exposed to message content, attends to the content, and comprehends the content. The person can then evaluate the message by comparing the information it contains to that stored in memory. This information comparison process is responsible for judgments of message discrepancy (Hovland et al., 1957; Hovland & Pritzker, 1957; Hovland & Sherif, 1952). The information comparison process results in a degree of acceptance (due to bolstering arguments) or rejection (due to counterarguments) of the message conclusion. Message conclusions that meet with a degree of acceptance can be internalized into memory structures.

As a direct descendent of message learning theory, classic information processing theory (McGuire, 1968, 1969) offered a comparable set of six stages: exposure, attention, comprehension, message evaluation (bolstering thoughts or counterarguments), belief change, and attitude change. These stages are shown in Figure 18.2. The information comparison process developed by message learning theory became the key variable *message evaluation* under information processing theory (McGuire, 1969). Note how premessage source evaluations (reputation) and message comprehension (the extent to which message content is clear to receivers) influence message evaluation.

The ELM claims that receivers pass through the stages of exposure, motivation, ability, message evaluation and cognitive elaboration, be-

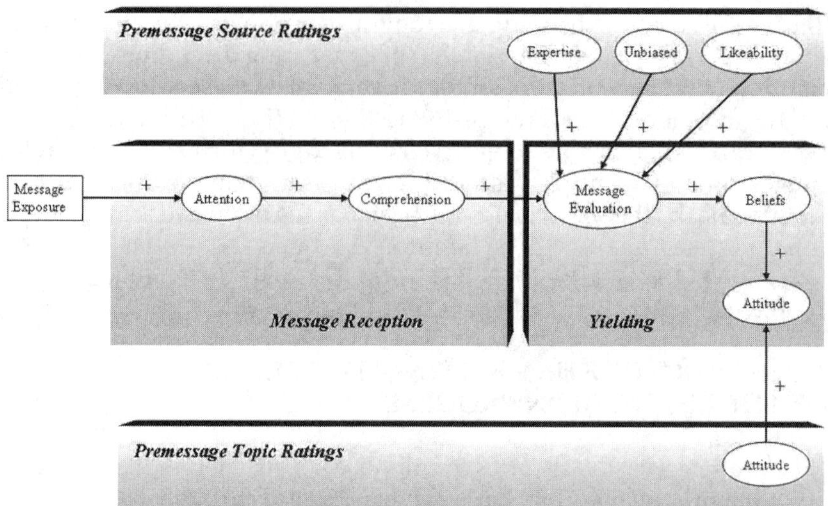

FIGURE 18.2. Process model for classic information processing theory.

lief change, and attitude change (Petty & Cacioppo, 1981, 1986). The prevailing theories of the 1960s, with their single-motive distinct-sequence structure shared two assumptions with the multimotive distinct-sequence theories of the 1980s: (a) Receivers follow a sequence of stages, and (b) the processing of persuasive messages occurs as a discrete mental operation.

The next three sections of this chapter describe the development of multiple-motive theories. The three sections correspond to the three 20-year eras of research in persuasion, marked by the appearance of personality function models around 1960, dual-process models around 1980, and unified models around 2000.

THE FUNCTIONALIST MANIFESTO IN AN ERA OF SINGLE-MOTIVE THEORIES

Attitude researchers have speculated as to why people form, maintain, and change their attitudes. This section examines the three early multimotive discrete-sequence models. These models were quite sophisticated for their day in that they specified both the message content and the social contexts that make a given motive salient, with that motive triggering one or more specific processes. Each of the theories identifies three basic processes that can influence the persuasiveness of a message. These shared, basic processes are described in Figure 18.3.

During orientation (Smith et al., 1956), a perceived need activates a related persuasion process as the receiver seeks to comprehend the position advocated by the source. The more specific the position advocated, the greater the clarity of the message, as shown in Figure 18.3. Motivation moderates the effect of the process that ensues, such that the need amplifies the effect of the process on belief structures (the effect multipliers in Figure 18.3). Any effect of a sequence requires the receiver to understand the position advocated. Function theories assume that clarification of the source's position facilitates persuasion. Hence, message clarity (comprehension or cognitive clarity) is assumed for each of the three processes, although the role of clarity is more prominent in some processes than others.

A Combined Personality Function Model

The triadic functional model (Smith et al., 1956) emerged from the collaboration of Smith with his broad interest in personality, including identity and values (Smith, 1969, 1991), Bruner with his interest in knowledge acquisition (Bruner, 1957, 1973), and White with his interest in ego psychology (White, 1963). The triadic functional model posits that beliefs and attitudes serve three functions: object appraisal, social adjustment, and ego defense. Attitudes based on any of the three functions can be expressed as an opinion in the triadic functional model. The

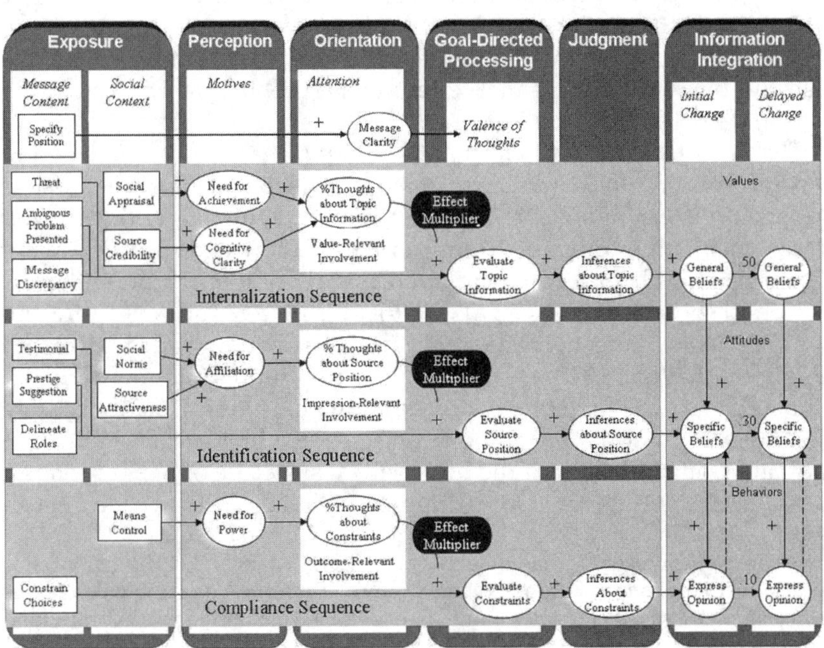

FIGURE 18.3. Generic three-motive process model.

eclecticism of this model seems more a result of an accidental collection of diverse interest among the three authors rather than an intentional effort to merge competing theories.

The multiple-process model of Katz (1960; Katz & Stotland, 1959; Sarnoff & Katz, 1954) had much in common with the triadic functional model.[2] Both theories contain knowledge acquisition, ego defense, and social adjustment functions, although they employ different labels for these processes. In fact, the two personality function theories are sufficiently similar as to be quite compatible.

Knowledge Acquisition. When the receiver encounters an ambiguous problem that invites closer scrutiny, this increases the perceived need for cognitive clarity (Katz, 1960; Smith et al., 1956). The need for cognitive clarity, in turn, causes an increase in the relevance of accumulating information (thoughts devoted to problem solving) and more processing devoted to knowledge acquisition. The knowledge function described by Katz (1960) is quite similar to the object appraisal function proposed by Smith et al. (1956) in that both processes can have an impact on general beliefs and subsequent values. New information or rational arguments in a source's message are supposed to lead to an evaluation of the information contained in the message. This evaluation involves a comparison of the new information contained in the message with the old information the receiver holds in memory. This comparison process is similar to that elicited by exposure to a discrepant message (see the message discrepancy effect in Figure 18.3) as described by Hovland et al. (1953).

The need for cognitive clarity should amplify the positive effect of new information and rational arguments on deep and effortful message appraisal. Alternatively, preexisting belief structures provide an inner framework for organizing the environment, allowing simplification of incoming stimuli, and enhancing perceptual accuracy through the use of mental shortcuts (Smith et al., 1956). This distinction was a forerunner to the systematic–heuristic processing distinction made in the HSM (Eagly & Chaiken, 1993). A veridical internal representation of reality obtained via the knowledge sequence allows receivers to make accurate predictions about the behavior of objects, enabling greater control of their environment. Within the hierarchical structure of belief systems, messages that influence central, high-level beliefs will have indirect ef-

[2]In later versions of the theory (Katz, 1960; Katz & Stotland, 1959), values that contribute to the consolidation of identity play an important role in ego defense by increasing self-esteem. Yet when values tied to the self-definition process culminate in the expression of opinion, this is supposed to be a fourth function of attitudes. However, Smith et al. (1956) correctly noted that any attitude could be expressed as an opinion or not. Hence, the fourth function is not unique.

fects on regional, low-level beliefs. That is, the more general beliefs change global attitudes (values), exerting downward pressure on specific attitudes (Hunter, Levine, & Sayers, 1976).

Ego Defense. In their function theory, Smith et al. (1956) were concerned with adjustment strategies that include ego defense mechanisms. The ego defense process was described more generally in the psychoanalytic theory of attitudes (Katz, Sarnoff, & McClintock, 1956; Sarnoff, I., 1960, 1962, Sarnoff, D., 1965; Sarnoff & Katz, 1954; Sarnoff & Zimbardo, 1961). Although Katz did not specify which motive triggers his ego defense function, he did suggest a motive such as need for achievement. Psychoanalytic theory conceptualizes the ego as a configuration of perceptual and motor skills that constitutes the self-concept, a mental construct that develops over time. The ego invokes coping mechanisms to reduce the tension caused by external or internal threats,[3] where this threat is conveyed when the source makes a specific point on an issue that is perceived as a threat (see the effect of threat in Figure 18.3).

A threatening message evokes negative affect (fear, anger, sadness). Experiencing negative affect is supposed to be perceived as socially unacceptable, and acknowledging these culturally unacceptable responses would damage the concept of self. That is, stress destabilizes the ego by causing fluctuations in attitude toward self. This is in keeping with the notion of neuroticism as variation in self-esteem (Rosenberg, 1965). During reality testing, there is an inverse relation between realistic responses that produce a pragmatic orientation toward self (pushing the receiver toward the knowledge acquisition sequence) and autistic responses that produce an idealistic orientation toward the self (pushing the receiver toward the ego defense sequence). That is, realistic responses are grounded in the tendency to be socially adjustive, whereas autistic responses are grounded in the tendency to be ego defensive (Smith, 1969). The distinction between a pragmatic–objective orientation and an idealistic–subjective orientation was later realized in the ELM as the difference between objective processing and biased processing (see Petty & Cacioppo, 1986).

Social Adjustment Processes. The social adjustment function as described by Smith (1969) is similar to Katz's instrumental-adjustment function. Smith et al. (1956) had proposed an adjustment process based

[3]Motives that evoke intolerable fear threaten the ego and are kept from consciousness by ego defense mechanisms. The defenses against tension caused by internal threat include projection (externalization), repression, and reaction formation. The defenses against tension caused by external threats include denial and identification with aggressor.

on identification that facilitates relationships with important others in a person's environment. Social norms such as group cohesiveness make the need for affiliation (nAFF; McClelland, 1962) salient to receivers. In turn, nAFF should increase the personal significance of identification.

Motivational Processes Model

The motivational processes model of Kelman (1958) provides a template for interpreting the personality function theories of Smith et al. (1956) and Katz (1960). The motivational processes model emphasizes the importance of message content and social cues as antecedents to multiple parallel processes that influence beliefs, attitudes, and expressed opinions. The motivational processes model differs from the personality function model in that Smith et al. and Katz portrayed needs triggered by social context, whereas Kelman suggested the source's message triggers receiver needs. These two views are reconcilable given that a message is part of the social context.

The chief contribution of the motivational processes model is its observation that different processes (a) produce attitudes that vary in their quality and durability, and (b) result in different kinds of behavior. One such behavioral difference is the expression of opinion—some processes yield opinions that are more consistent with privately held beliefs, whereas other processes may yield opinions that show less consistency. The model (Kelman, 1961) was revolutionary in that it tied type of process to the consequences of attitudes—their quality (resilience resulting from belief integration), persistence over time, and their ability to predict behavior. Figure 18.3 shows the internalization, identification, and compliance processes in the motivational processes model.

Internalization Processes. Both the personality function models and the Kelman model feature a knowledge acquisition process. This process influences values through general beliefs that are central to the person's self-concept. The models allow for the rational evaluation of message content motivated by the need for cognitive clarity (as shown in Figure 18.3). Both models also allow for the irrational evaluation of message content, although Katz's model provides much more detail about this subjective–autistic processing alternative. The advantage of the Kelman model is that it groups rational and irrational evaluation processes together, assembling the two based on the similar effects they have on general beliefs and global attitudes.

Identification and Other Social Adjustment Processes. Both the personality function models and the motivational processes model propose that social adjustment processes influence lower level attitudes through specific beliefs. Katz (1960) described this social adjustment process as reinforcement driven by classical conditioning. By contrast, the Kelman (1961) model, like Smith et al. (1956) describes this adjustment process as based on identification. The advantage of the Kelman model is that it characterizes these identification effects on attitudes as being short-term and less durable. Belief change due to identification will continue only so long as receivers care about their relationship with the source (or the group the source represents).

The Compliance Process. Compliance is part of the motivational processes model (Kelman, 1961) but not the functional theories.[4] The compliance process in Figure 18.3 is activated when receivers orient to the incentives under the control of the source. A key mediating variable in this compliance process is the reinforcement of the source's position on the topic. This involves the association of the position advocated by the source with the incentives. Surveillance, the ability to monitor receiver behavior, should increase the pressure that receivers feel to express support for the position advocated by the source. The impact of the choice-limiting message on this reinforcement of the source's position will be amplified by the surveillance potential of the source (Kelman, 1961; McGuire, 1969).

Receivers' decision to publicly embrace a source's position that is discrepant from their own, and the opinion conformity that follows, may influence specific beliefs and low-level attitudes through cognitive dissonance or counterattitudinal advocacy (Smith, 1969). This concept of dissonance-driven attitude change was later featured in the ELM (Petty, 1977; Petty & Cacioppo, 1981).

THE DUAL-ROUTE MOVEMENT

Cognitive response theorists (Brock, 1968; Greenwald, 1968) criticized message learning theory for not sufficiently appreciating the reaction of the individual to message content. They believed that a person's cognitive response to message content is a much better predictor of attitude change than a person's retention of that content. This perspective on persuasion was a prevailing view in social psychology at Ohio State University (OSU), as was the notion that most theories in persuasion were not logically flawed; rather their authors had incorrectly specified the domain of the theory (Greenwald, 1968). The first model presented

[4]Neither Smith et al. (1956) nor Katz (1960) seemed interested in compliance, perhaps because its only effect on attitudes is indirect, mediated by dissonance-arousing inconsistencies stemming from the advocacy of an attitude-discrepant position by receivers.

in this section is the cognitive response model of attitude persistence that served as the prototype for the ELM (Petty, 1977; Petty & Cacioppo, 1981). As this model is analyzed, it is referred to by its descriptor—the cognitive response model of persistence (CRMP).

Cognitive Response and the Processing of Persuasion Cues

The CRMP proposed a series of all-or-nothing decision points that audience members may encounter while processing message content. Figure 18.4 shows these binary choices represented as decision points in the process model. Four of these decisions occur in the cognitive response route and one occurs in the persuasion cue route.[5] The process model proposes that receivers must make each of the decisions one at a time in the sequence specified so these binary outcomes cannot occur simultaneously. This means that the model shown in Figure 18.4 entails sequential rather than parallel processing.

In addition to conceptualizing the choice points in the model as binary yes–no alternatives, Petty dichotomized the duration of the attitude change variable into two categories—long-term and short-term—just like earlier functional models. Thus, enduring atti-

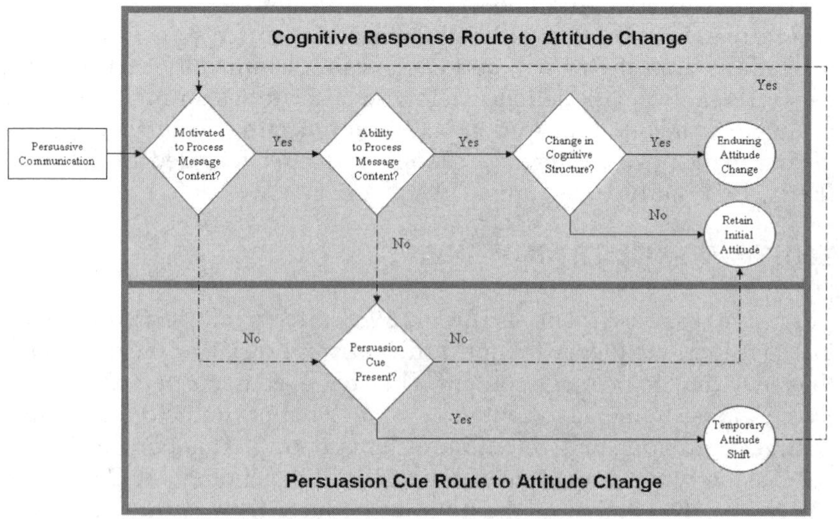

FIGURE 18.4. Cognitive response model of persistence.

[5]The verbal description of the model in Petty's dissertation and a chapter in their edited volume that was in press at the time of the dissertation indicate that the series of binary outcomes are sequential.

tude change occurs at the end of the cognitive response route. Temporary attitude shift occurs at the end of the persuasion cue route. This dichotomization is a consequence of fitting the model to a format that is amenable to ANOVA (Hamilton, Hunter, & Boster, 1993). That is, the predictor variables are all categorical and the dependent variables are considered one at a time.

The Cognitive Response Route. The CRMP represented in Figure 18.4 specifies four steps or necessary conditions along the cognitive response route to enduring attitude change. If receivers are motivated and able to process message content, their cognitive response to that content will be integrated into existing memory structures (Petty, 1977). This change in beliefs should result in enduring attitude change. If receivers are unmotivated or unable to process message content, then persuasion cues are irrelevant: "If motivation and ability are present, then persuasion cues become immaterial as the person will process the communication" (Petty, 1977, p. 152). That is, unless receivers are able to process message content, they will drop down to the peripheral cue route (indicated in Figure 18.4 with broken lines).

The Persuasion Cue Route. When receivers lack the motivation to process, the ability to process the message, a predominance of favorable or unfavorable thoughts, or have no change in cognitive structure, then they are supposed to look for prompts as to which position to take on an issue—cues present in the persuasion setting. Petty (1977) listed a set of persuasion cues that can temporarily influence attitudes. One set of cues is related to the message source. Drawing on the model of Kelman (1961), Petty included the compliance process (power is the salient cue), identification process (attraction is the salient cue), and inferred credibility (reputation is the salient cue).

Only one cue can be processed at a time within the persuasion cue route. If more than one cue were processed at a time, the model would not be able to predict which of two conflicting cue effects would prevail. The cue generates "one prominent cognitive response" (Petty, 1977, p. 151). Given that persuasion cue processing is rapid (a single thought), it should be possible for receivers to evaluate persuasion cues in sequence, giving the appearance of parallel cue processing. All the peripheral cues that are present in the persuasion context could conceivably influence attitudes because the model does not propose that receivers must stop their search after they have discovered just one cue. The search for persuasion cues would depend on receiver motivation. After each of the cues had been processed with the resulting short-term adjustment to attitudes, the receiver would remain open to considering more persuasion cues, returning to the beginning of the persuasion cue route (the broken line in

Figure 18.4). If audience members do not find any persuasion cues, temporary attitude shift cannot occur.

AN EXPLICIT ROLE FOR ATTENTION AND COMPREHENSION IN DUAL-PROCESS MODELS

The concept of motivation as a variable that moderates the effect of message and source variables on attitude change evolved from the primordial triadic function model and motivational processes model to the more robust dual-process models such as the ELM and HSM. In the verbal descriptions of the triadic function model, motivation was treated as a continuous variable (Smith et al., 1956). Decision points in the CRMP were dichotomous and that was still the case with the early ELM (Petty & Cacioppo, 1981) and early HSM (Chaiken, 1980). There is an advantage to converting continuous variables into binary (yes–no) variables: The binary variable is isomorphic with the manipulated high versus low independent variable in an experimental design. The disadvantage of converting continua to dichotomies is that it distorts the process model and results in a loss of statistical power (due to range restriction) when significance tests are conducted.

Subsequent conceptualizations of the HSM conceptualized motivation as a set of continuous variables (Chaiken, Lieberman, & Eagly, 1989; Chen & Chaiken, 1999; Eagly & Chaiken, 1993). Later versions of the ELM acknowledged that motivational moderators are continua (Petty & Cacioppo, 1986; Petty, Wegener, Fabrigar, Priester, & Cacioppo, 1993). Yet its advocates have an unfortunate verbal habit of describing those continua in terms of their endpoints, as binary variables (Petty & Cacioppo, 1986; Petty & Wegener, 1999). In part, this is because continuous variables such as need for cognition and personal relevance were dichotomized so that they could be fit into ANOVAs, where their amplifying effect could be analyzed as an interaction term. To gain greater power, these continuous moderator variables should be left as continuous variables and analyzed as interaction terms using multiple regression.

Motivation to Process Message Content or Preexisting Beliefs

The ELM (Petty & Cacioppo, 1981) distinguishes the motivation to process message content from the motivation to ponder preexisting beliefs, a distinction that can be traced back to the motivational processes model of Kelman (1961). Exposure to a persuasive communication should increase receivers' motivation to process the message, which should increase their orientation toward the message (see Figure 18.5). Greater interest in the message enables an objective–realistic processing of the persuasive communication, a rational evaluation of message content that should register on measures of argument quality. Thus, as the motivation to process the message increases, receivers will be more likely to elaborate on the evidence presented by the source in support of the conclusion advocated in the message.

Some research suggests that message content is unnecessary for attitude change to occur (Tesser, 1976, 1978; Tesser & Conlee, 1975; Tesser & Cowan, 1975; Tesser & Danheiser, 1978; Tesser & Johnsin, 1974; Tesser & Leone, 1977). Exposure to a simple message that induces the activation of schema should increase receivers' motivation to elaborate on preexisting beliefs, which should increase their orientation toward their initial attitude (see Figure 18.5). Greater interest in existing attitudes enables a subjective–autistic examination of memory structures, a less rational evaluation of attitudes that should influence judgments of the position taken by the source, as compared to preexisting beliefs. Thus, as the motivation to ponder preexisting beliefs increases, receivers will be more likely to compare the position advocated by the source (conclusion) to information contained in existing belief structures. If receivers do not engage in this information comparison process, then they will resort to a search for peripheral cues (indicated by the broken line in Figure 18.5).

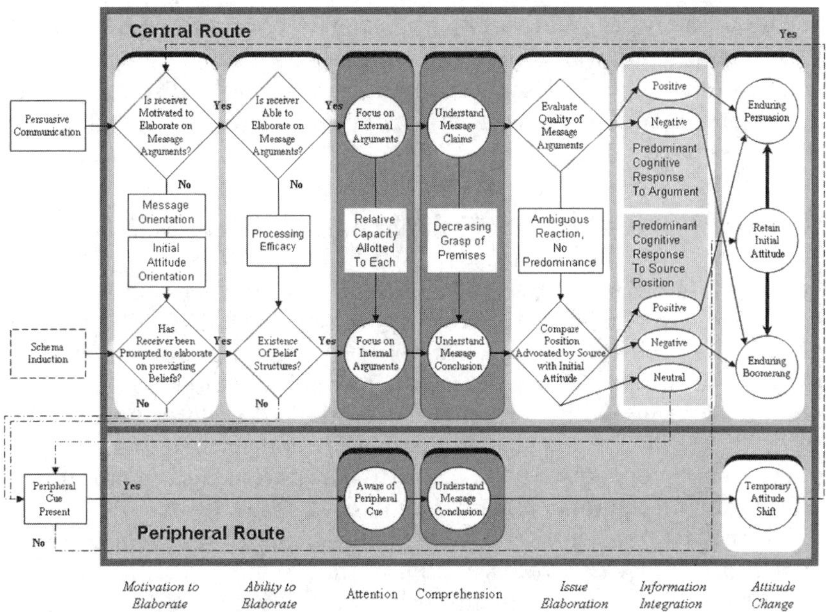

FIGURE 18.5. The elaboration likelihood model with attention and comprehension made explicit.

In the HSM, the three main motives are accuracy, defense, and impression management (Chaiken et al., 1989). Receivers are assumed to have multiple motives most of the time, although the motive that takes precedence depends on receiver mood (Chen & Chaiken, 1999). Receivers in a neutral mood tend toward impression management, whereas those in a positive mood tend toward accuracy motives. Each motive is associated with a sequence consisting of both systematic and heuristic processing (Chaiken et al., 1989). The ratio of systematic to heuristic processing depends on the *sufficiency principle.* Receivers are assumed to expend only as much mental energy as necessary to address their needs (Chaiken, 1980).

The sufficiency principle holds that receivers weigh the cost of cognitive effort against their need to satisfy their accuracy, defense, or impression management motives. It is based on the assumption that receivers equate greater mental effort with increased judgmental confidence. The principle places two variables along a continuum of judgmental confidence, ranging from no confidence at the low end to complete confidence at the high end. The first variable is actual confidence, the point on the confidence continuum that represents receivers' self-assessment of their current amount of information. The second variable is *desired* confidence, the point on the confidence continuum that represents a sufficient amount of information to satisfy their needs. The discrepancy between the two points on the continuum (desired confidence minus actual confidence) is supposed to predict the ratio of systematic to heuristic processing, such that the larger the discrepancy, the higher the ratio of systematic to heuristic processing (Chaiken, Giner-Sorolla, & Chen, 1996).

Ability to Process Message Content or Preexisting Beliefs

The ELM distinction between the motivation to process the message and the motivation to elaborate on preexisting beliefs reverberates through the rest of the model. There is a corresponding distinction between the ability to process the message and the extent to which the receiver has developed belief structures on the issue (Petty & Cacioppo, 1986). The HSM makes a similar distinction, conceptualizing ability to process as a consequence of cognitive capacity and accumulated information on the topic (Chen & Chaiken, 1999).

The process model of the ELM in Figure 18.5 suggests three sequences for motivated receivers. First, those who have the ability to elaborate on message arguments will proceed to elaborate on message arguments. Second, those who lack the ability to elaborate on message arguments will resort to pondering preexisting belief structures. If receivers determine that their existing belief structures are sufficient to allow cognitive elaboration, then they will proceed to compare the position advocated by the source with their initial attitude. If they determine that their existing belief structures are insufficient as a basis for judgment, then they will begin a search for peripheral cues (indicated by the broken line in Figure 18.5).

Issue Elaboration

The ELM distinction between the ability to process message arguments and the ability to process preexisting beliefs carries over to issue elaboration. Receivers who have the ability to elaborate on message content will evaluate argument quality. The model describes three categories of outcome from cognitive response: (a) a predominance of favorable thoughts, (b) a predominance of neutral thoughts (neither favorable nor unfavorable thoughts predominate), and (c) a predominance of unfavorable thoughts. Information integration in the ELM has historically been defined both conceptually and operationally as additive in that belief change is predicted to be the number of positive thoughts minus the number of negative thoughts (Hamilton et al., 1993).

If receivers' predominant cognitive response to message arguments is favorable, then there will be a corresponding favorable change to belief systems and subsequent attitude change will be positive (persuasion). If their predominant cognitive response to message arguments is unfavorable, then there will be a corresponding unfavorable change to belief systems and subsequent attitude change will be negative (boomerang). The ELM prediction of boomerang effects whenever profuse counterarguing occurs is not supported by the frequency of boomerang effects in the literature (Hamilton et al., 1993). Later tests of the ELM have employed an averaging integration equation that predicts no attitude change when profuse counterarguing occurs, where the averaging equation is now consistent with verbal descriptions of belief change in the ELM and process model (Petty & Wegener, 1999).

Underlying the ELM's three categories of cognitive response in an averaging integration equation is the variable polarity of cognitive response, which can be defined as the absolute value of the difference between number of positive thoughts about the message and number of negative thoughts about the message divided by the total number of thoughts (including neutral thoughts). Ability to elaborate on message content leads to a polarization of cognitive response in response to perceived argument quality, inhibiting elaboration on preexisting beliefs. Information garnered during cognitive elaboration on message content or preexisting beliefs can be integrated into memory structures. Thus, cognitive elaboration should not only lead to more differentiated memory structures, it should make those memory structures more accessible.

Peripheral Processes. The ELM describes the possible conditions for peripheral processing as (a) low motivation to process, (b) low ability to process, or (c) a lack of polarity in cognitive response to discrepancy, due to either a predominance of neutral thoughts or a lack of predominance in positive or negative thoughts. The peripheral processes described in the CRMP (credibility effects, attractiveness effects, and compliance effects) were incorporated directly from the motivational processes model of Kelman (1961). The peripheral processes described in the ELM (Petty & Cacioppo, 1981, 1986), however, were drawn from reinforcement theory (Staats & Staats, 1958), affective consistency theory (Heider, 1958), and social judgment theory (Sherif, Sherif, & Nebergall, 1965). Hence, peripheral cues are supposed to generate conditioning effects, balance effects, or judgmental distortion effects. Figure 18.5 indicates that for any of these three effects to occur, receivers must be aware of the presence of the cue and possess a minimal understanding of the conclusion of the message (the position advocated by the source).

UNIFYING PROCESSES IN MULTIPLE-MOTIVE SINGLE-SEQUENCE MODELS

There are general processes with which people respond to messages, regardless of message content or context. The processes are ubiquitous because they are rooted in physiology—there is a tendency for mammals to respond to a wide variety of objects with the same stimulus evaluation sequence (Scherer, 1984). This biologically based sequence or *omnistructure* provides receivers with a general-purpose mechanism for evaluating messages and their sources on a given topic (Hamilton, 1997, 1998; Hamilton & Nowak, 2005). Although these sequences can operate independently and in parallel, they most often interact with one another. The degree of interaction and direction of the influence varies with the phase of message processing. The phases closely resemble the stages of the persuasion process illustrated in Figure 18.1 and the stages of information processing theory (McGuire, 1968, 1969, 1989).

The immediacy of the stimulus and the depth of cognitive processing interact to determine source evaluation, as shown in Figure 18.6. When a source is proximate in space and time, cognitive processing tends to be shallow and impulsive, even instinctive. The dynamism (or power) of a source will be most relevant to receivers when the source is temporally and spatially proximate, where cognitive processing is shallow and impulsive. As the emotional immediacy of the source diminishes, the relative impact of the cognitive processing grows. The competence (or expertise) of a source will be salient to receivers during goal-directed evaluation, when depth of cognitive processing is at a moderate level.

The trustworthiness (or character) of a source will be most pertinent to receivers when they reflect on causal attributions, placing the greatest demand on cognitive capacity. Finally, liking of a source (attitude toward the source) will be most relevant during the process of information integration, when emotional immediacy declines to its most distal point and cognitive processing tapers off.

The model in Figure 18.6 implies a source evaluation sequence consisting of dynamism (power), competence, trustworthiness, and liking (attitude toward the source). The four variables have been found to be linked by strong positive effects during message processing, a pattern referred to as a *charisma sequence* (Hamilton, 1997). Past exposure to messages causes this source evaluation sequence to be represented in memory (Hamilton & Stewart, 1993). These source-related engrams or personae can be activated by simple messages that prompt receivers to think about a source. Curiously, the causal links between these variables tend to be stronger in memory than during message processing (Hamilton, 1997). Similar engrams exist for topic evaluation, with emotional involvement with and accumulated information on topic leading to premessage attitude toward topic (Hamilton & Stewart, 1993). Premessage topic and source evaluation sequences interact during message processing to produce postmessage topic and source evaluations (Hamilton & Thompson,

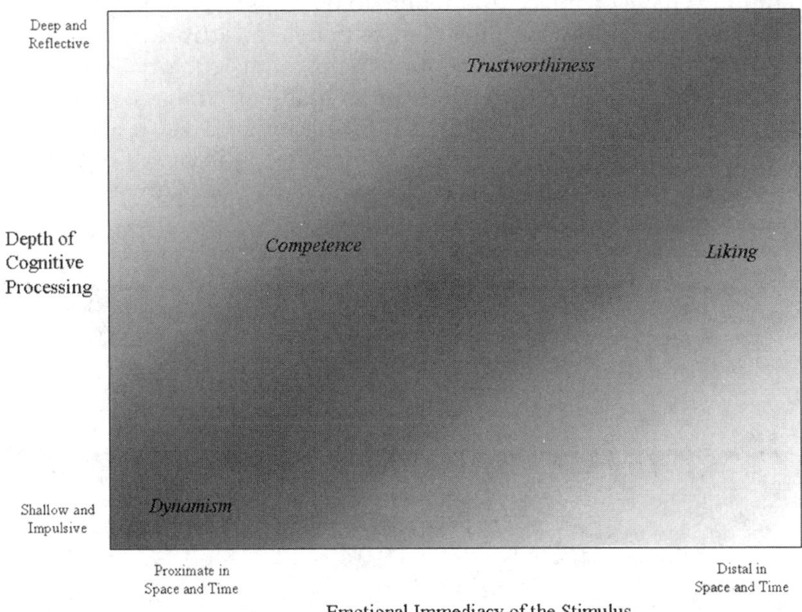

FIGURE 18.6. Impact of emotional immediacy and depth of processing on source evaluation.

1994). Figure 18.7 illustrates the charisma sequence. Note the mutual influence of emotion and cognition during this sequence.

The Effect of Message Processing on Source and Topic Evaluation

The message processing sequence parallels the charisma sequence as shown in the omnistructure model presented in Figure 18.8. Message processing begins with the perception of content and delivery, and continues through orientation, which includes the allocation of mental effort and the filling of cognitive capacity. During goal-directed processing, arguments (claims and evidence) are evaluated, followed by causal attributions related to evaluations of mental effort and emotional equilibrium. Finally, information is integrated into belief structures and weighted by emotional response to influence attitudes. Figure 18.8 also shows the impact of premessage evaluations (in memory) of accumulated information, value-relevant involvement, and attitude on the online reception of and yielding to messages.

The nature and degree of interaction between the modules of the omnistructure depends on which phase of the structure is operating, as described in greater detail in Hamilton (1997, 1998). Causal modeling techniques have enabled researchers to track the effects of exposure to message variables through to changes in beliefs, attitudes, and behavior. First, consider message reception in the omnistructure. Attention to message content is influenced by both dynamism (from the source evaluation module) and accumulated information and value-relevant involvement (from the topic evaluation module). Allotments of attention depend on the relative influence exerted by the source and topic evaluation modules.

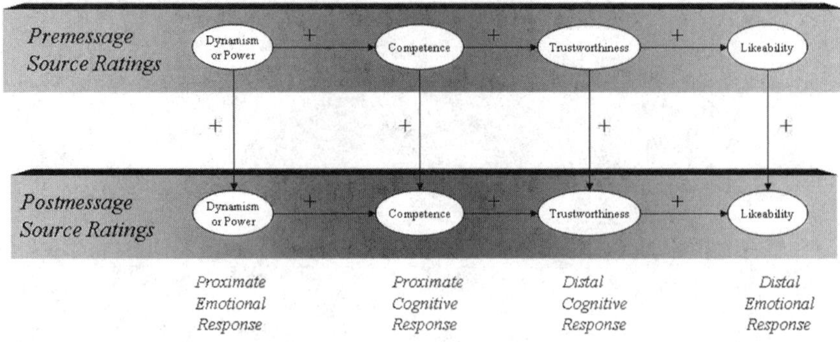

FIGURE 18.7. The role of emotion and cognition in the charisma sequence.

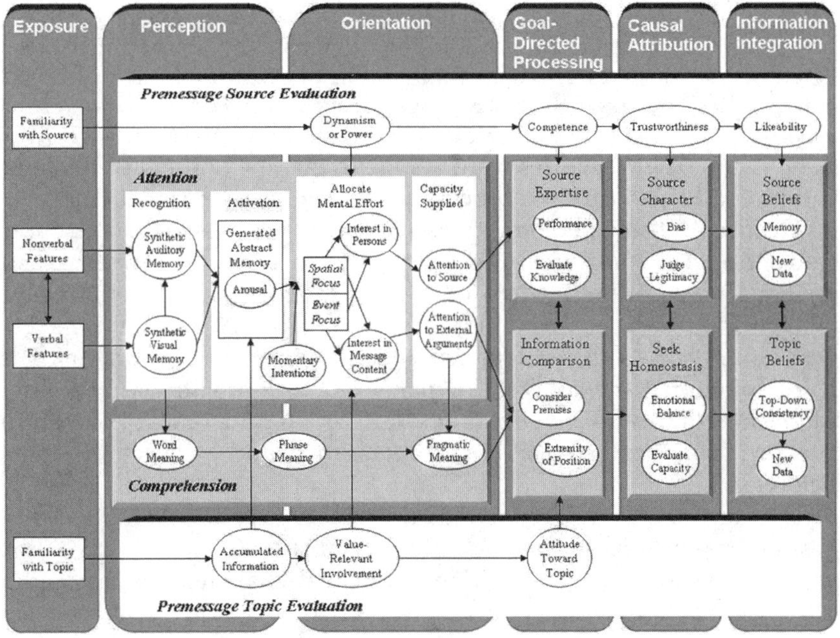

FIGURE 18.8. Omnistructure model of attitude change.

Next, compare yielding to the message in the omnistructure to that described in classic information processing theory. The omnistructure model treats message evaluation as a component of goal-directed processing, adds causal attribution processes, and equates opinion change with belief change as explained by information integration theory (Anderson, 1971). The omnistructure model shows source competence evaluations in memory plus premessage attitude toward topic influencing online, goal-directed processing. Similarly, source trustworthiness evaluations in memory influence online causal attributions and source likeability evaluations in memory influence the online information integration process.

CONCLUSIONS

The late 1950s and early 1960s witnessed an explosion of persuasion theories. Fundamentally different assumptions regarding the cognitive mediation process differentiate these theories. One set of theories assumed a process in which receivers compared their existing attitudes based on the information they possess in memory to the position advocated by the source based on any new information contained in the message.[6] Another set of theories assumed a process in which receivers considered the cognitive and affective consistency among attitudes.[7] The third set of theories, those that were the focus of a large portion of this chapter, assumed that a cognitive orientation was one of several a receiver might take, where orientation was a function of the receiver's personality. These theories were unique in that they proposed that attitudes result from multiple processes that operate in parallel.[8]

The first of these personality function theories was the triadic functional model of Smith et al. (1956). The schematic or "map" of personality effects was offered as a proto-causal model (Smith, 1969). In this chapter the triadic function model was merged with the multiple-process model of Katz (1960) to generate a combined function model. The third functional theory was Kelman's (1961) motivational processes model (see Figure 18.2), with its emphasis on the outcomes of the multiple processes of persuasion—persistence and predictability of behavior.

The shift from single-motive distinct-sequence models to dual-process models in the persuasion discipline, circa 1980, coincided with the social cognition movement. Methodological challenges had posed a barrier to testing the older personality function theories. Dual-process models such as the ELM simplified the individual difference aspect by reducing the number of motive conditions in their designs to two: knowledge acquisition and other processes (Eagly & Chaiken, 1993). Multiple-motive distinct process models, from Kelman's motivated processes model to the ELM and HSM, have sought to directly incorporate social cognitive theory to generalize their applicability (Petty, 1992). By contrast, single-sequence models (whether they have included one or several motives) have proposed auxiliary social cognitive theories to extend their applicability. Although this difference may seem subtle, it does have implications for the methods employed to test

---

[6]These message discrepancy theories included message learning theory (Hovland, Janis & Kelly, 1953), social judgment theory (Sherif & Hovland, 1961; Sherif & Sherif, 1967; Sherif et al., 1965; Sherif, Taub & Hovland, 1958), and adaptation-level theory (Helson, 1959).

[7]These consistency theories included the syllogistic consistency model (McGuire, 1960a, 1960b, 1960c), dissonance theory (Aronson, Turner, & Carlsmith, 1963; Festinger, 1962; Festinger & Carlsmith, 1959), and sequels to congruity theory (Osgood et al., 1957) such as belief congruity theory (Rokeach & Rothman, 1965).

[8]Message discrepancy theories and consistency theories modeled a single process of attitude formation and change. Individual differences were acknowledged within that process, for example a person's degree of ego-involvement within social judgment theory (Sherif & Cantril, 1947; Sherif et al., 1965). By contrast, function theories take into account individual differences in motivation, claiming that understanding such motivational differences is essential for the prediction of attitude change (Insko, 1967; Keisler, Collins, & Miller, 1969).

a given model. Social cognitive theories such as BST and LET assume people use natural logic as they process messages. These theories have been applied to such diverse phenomena as motivation, therapy, and ethnocentrism. Both BST and LET are complex theories in their own right and can be tested as such. This allows researchers to test the underlying logic of the theory outside a persuasive setting.

The 20-year upheavals in persuasion at 1960, 1980, and 2000 have been accompanied by an evolution in methodological tools such as causal and mathematical modeling. Ostrom (1981) argued that advances in the analysis of designs, including techniques for handling more predictor and criterion variables, have enabled researchers to test more sophisticated conceptualizations of persuasion processes. Yet reflection on the impact that advances in methods has had on the two largest paradigm shifts in persuasion reveals that conceptual advances precede the availability of more powerful modeling techniques. Modeling techniques disseminate at a relatively slow pace.

It remains to be seen which of the developments surrounding the year 2000 will have a lasting impact on the persuasion area, so discussing the contributions of various developments in the field would be premature. Nonetheless, there are two areas of progress suggested by issues discussed in this chapter that might leave a legacy in persuasion. One avenue for research would be to examine the relations among motives and how they affect the structure of belief and attitude hierarchies. This suggestion was first offered by McGuire (1985). A second possibility would be to examine the degree to which the parallel processes in multisequence models interact with one another at the various stages of the persuasion sequence, from exposure to information integration. Suppose that the central and peripheral sequences are relatively discrete; this would mean they operate more or less as routes like the ELM suggests (Petty & Cacioppo, 1981, 1986). Variables in the central route sequence would have little influence on those in the peripheral route sequence, and vice versa. If, on the other hand, the variables at a given stage of processing interact with one another to a large degree, this indicates stronger support for the unified models discussed in this chapter.

ACKNOWLEDGMENTS

I would like to thank Paul J. Mineo and Linda A. Patrylak for their comments on an earlier draft of this chapter.

REFERENCES

Anderson, N. H. (1971). Integration theory and attitude change. *Psychological Review, 78,* 171–206.

Aronson, E., Turner, J., & Carlsmith, J. M. (1963). Communication credibility and communication discrepancy as determinants of opinion change. *Journal of Abnormal and Social Psychology, 67*, 31–36.

Atkinson, J. W., & Litwin, G. H. (1960). Achievement motive and text anxiety conceived as motive to approach success and motive to avoid failure. *Journal of Abnormal and Social Psychology, 60*, S2–63.

Ausubel, D. (1963). *The psychology of meaningful verbal learning.* New York: Grune & Stratton.

Bargh, J. A. ((1984). Automatic and conscious processing of social information. In R. S. Wyer Jr., & T. K. Srull (Eds.), *Handbook of social cognition, Vol. 3.* Hillsdale, NJ: Lawrence Erlbaum Associates.

Berlo, D. (1960). *The process of Communication.* New York: Holt, Rinehart, and Winston.

Berlo, D., Lemmert, J., & Mertz, R. (1969). Dimensions for evaluating the acceptability of message sources. *Public Quarterly, 33*, 563–576.

Brock, T. C. (1968). Commodity and value change. In A. G. Greenwald, T. C. Brock, & T. M. Ostrom (Eds.), *Psychological foundations of attitudes* (pp. 243–275). New York: Academic Press.

Bruner, J. (1973). *Beyond the information given.* New York: Norton.

Bruner, J. S. (1957). Neural mechanisms in perception. *Psychological Review, 64*, 340–358.

Chaiken, S. (1980). Heuristic versus systematic information processing and the use of source versus message cues in persuasion. *Journal of Personality and Social Psychology, 39*, 752–766.

Chaiken, S., Giner-Sorolla, R., & Chen, S. (1996). Beyond accuracy: Defense. In P. M. Golllwitzer & J. A. Bargh (Eds.), *The psychology of action: Linking cognition and motivation to behavior* (pp. 553–578). New York: Guilford.

Chaiken, S., Liberman, A., & Eagly, A. H. (1989). Heuristic and systematic information processing within and beyond the persuasion context. In J. S. Uleman & J. A. Bargh (Eds.), *Unintended thought* (pp. 212–252). New York: Guilford.

Chen, S., & Chaiken, S. (1999). The heuristic–systematic model in its broader context. In S. Chaiken & Y. Trope (Eds.), *Dual-process theories in social psychology* (pp. 73–96). New York: Guilford.

Craik, F. I. M. (1979). Human memory. *Annual Review of Psychology, 30*, 63–102.

Craik, F. I. M., & Tulving, E. (1975). Depth of processing and the retention of words in episodic memory. *Journal of Experimental Psychology, 104*, 268–294.

Eagly, A. H., & Chaiken, S. (1993). *The psychology of attitudes.* Fort Worth, TX: Harcourt Brace Jovanovich.

Eldredge, N., & Gould, S. J. (1972). Punctuated equilibria: An alternative to phyletic gradualism. In T. J. M. Schopf (Ed.), *Models in paleobiology* (pp. 82–115). San Francisco: Freeman, Cooper.

Fazio, R. H., Chen, J., McDonel, E. C., & Sherman, S. J. (1982). Attitude accessibility, attitude-behavior consistency and the strength of the object-evaluation association. *Journal of Experimental Social Psychology, 18*, 339–357.

Fazio, R. H., Powell, M. C., & Herr, P. M. (1983). Toward a process model of the attitude–behavior relation: Accessing one's attitude upon mere observation of the attitude object. *Journal of Personality and Social Psychology, 44*, 723–735.

Festinger, L. (1957). *A theory of cognitive dissonance.* Stanford, CA: Stanford University Press.

Festinger, L. (1962). Cognitive dissonance. *Scientific American, 207*, 93–106.

Festinger, L., & Carlsmith, J. M. (1959). Cognitive consequences of forced compliance. *Journal of Abnormal and Social Psychology, 58,* 203–211.

Fishbein, M., & Ajzen, I. (1975). *Belief, attitude, intention, and behavior: An introduction to theory and research.* Reading, MA: Addison-Wesley.

Gould, S. J. (1982). The meaning of punctuated equilibrium and its role in validating a hierarchical approach to macroevolution. In R. Milkman (Ed.), *Perspectives on evolution* (pp. 83–104). Sunderland, MA: Sinauer Associates.

Gould, S. J. (1983). Irrelevance, submission, and partnership: The changing role of paleontology in Darwin's three centennials, and a modest proposal for macroevolution. In D. S. Bendall (Ed.), *Evolution from molecules to men* (pp. 347–366). Cambridge, UK: Cambridge University Press.

Greenwald, A. G. (1968). Cognitive learning, cognitive response to persuasion, and attitude change. In A. G. Greenwald, T. C. Brock, & T. M. Ostrom (Eds.), *Psychological foundations of attitudes* (pp. 147–170). New York: Academic.

Hamilton, M. (1997). The phase interfaced omnistructure underlying the processing of persuasive messages. In F. J. Boster & G. Barnett (Eds.), *Progress in communication science* (pp. 1–38). Norwood, NJ: Ablex.

Hamilton, M. A. (1998). Message variables that mediate and moderate the effect of equivocal language on source credibility. *Journal of Language and Social Psychology, 17,* 109–143.

Hamilton, M. A., Hunter, J. E., & Boster, F. J. (1993). The elaboration likelihood model as a theory of attitude formation: A mathematical analysis. *Communication Theory, 3,* 50–65.

Hamilton, M. A., & Mineo, P. J. (1996). Personality and persuasibility: Developing a multidimensional model of belief systems. *World Communication, 24,* 1–16.

Hamilton, M. A., & Mineo, P. J. (1999). Self-worth and negative affect as antecedents to the authoritarian justification of conservatism and rigidity. *Politics, Groups, and the Individual, 8,* 85–110.

Hamilton, M. A., & Nowak, K. J. (2005). Information systems concepts across two decades: An empirical analysis of trends in theory, methods, process, and research domains. *Journal of Communication, 8,* 85–110.

Hamilton, M. A., & Stewart, B. (1993). Extending an information processing model of language intensity effects. *Communication Quarterly, 41,* 231–246.

Hamilton, M. A., & Thompson, W. (1994). Testing an information processing account of message intensity effects. *World Communication, 23,* 1–14.

Heider, F. (1946). Attitudes and cognitive organization. *Journal of Psychology, 21,* 107–112.

Heider, F. (1958). *The psychology of interpersonal relations.* New York: John Wiley & Sons.

Helson, H. (1959). Adaptation level theory. In S. Koch (Ed.), *Psychology: A study of a science* (Vol. 1, pp. 565–621). New York: McGraw-Hill.

Hovland, C. I., & Janis, I. L. (1959). *Personality and persuasibility.* New Haven, CT: Yale University Press.

Hovland, C. I., Janis, I. L., & Kelley, H. H. (1953). *Communications and persuasion: Psychological studies in opinion change.* New Haven, CT: Yale University Press.

Hovland, C. I., Harvey, O. J., & Sherif, M. (1957). Assimilation and contrast effects in reaction to communication and attitude change. *Journal of Abnormal and Social Psychology, 55,* 242–252.

Hovland, C. I., & Pritzker, H. A. (1957). Extent of opinion change as a function of amount of change advocated. *Journal of Abnormal and Social Psychology, 54,* 257–261.

Hovland, C. I., & Rosenberg, M. J. (1960). *Attitude organization and change.* New Haven, CT: Yale University Press.

Hovland, C. I., & Sherif, M. (1952). Judgmental phenomena and scales of attitude measurement: Item displacement in Thurstone scales. *Journal of Abnormal Social Psychology, 47,* 822–832.

Hunter, J. E., & Hamilton, M. A. (in press). *Analyzing individual differences in experimental design.* Sage.

Hunter, J. E., Levine, R. L, & Sayers, S. E. (1976). Attitude change in hierarchical belief systems and its relationship to persuasibility, dogmatism, and rigidity. *Human Communication Research, 3,* 1–28.

Insko, C. A. (1967). *Theories of attitude change.* New York: Appleton-Century-Crofts.

Katz, D. (1960). The functional approach to the study of attitudes. *Public Opinion Quarterly, 24,* 163–177.

Katz, D., Sarnoff, I., & McClintock, C. (1956). Ego-defense and attitude change. *Human Relations, 9,* 27–45.

Katz, D., & Stotland, E. (1959). A preliminary statement in theory of attitude structure and change. In S. Koch (Ed.), *Psychology: A study of a science* (Vol. 3, pp. 423–475). New York: McGraw-Hill.

Katz, E., & Lazarsfeld, P. F. (1955). *Personal influence.* New York: The Free Press.

Keisler, C. A., Collins, B. E., & Miller, N. (1969). *Altitude chance: A critical analysis of theoretical approaches.* New York: Wiley.

Kelman, H. C. (1958). Compliance, identification, and internalization: Three processes of attitude change. *Journal of Conflict Resolution, 2,* 51–60.

Kelman, H. C. (1961). Processes of opinion change. *Public Opinion Quarterly, 25,* 57–78.

Kruglanski, A. (1980). Lay epistemological process and contents: Another look at attribution theory. *Psychological Review, 87,* 70–87.

Kruglanski, A. W. (1989). The psychology of being "right": On the problem of accuracy in social perception and cognition. *Psychological Bulletin, 106,* 395–409.

Kruglanski, A. W., Thompson, E. P., & Spiegel, S. (1999). Separate or equal? Bimodel notions of persuasion and a single-process "unimodel". In S. Chaiken & Y. Trope (Eds.), *Dual process models in social cognition: A source book.* New York: Guilford.

Kruglanski, A. W., Thompson,, E. P., Higgins, E. T., Atash, M. N., Pierro, A., Shah, J. Y., & Spiegel, S. (2000). To do the right thing! or to just do it! Locomotion and assessment as distinct self-regulatory imperatives. *Journal of Personality and Social Psychology, 79,* 793–815.

Kuhn, T. (1962). *The structure of scientific revolutions.* Chicago: University of Chicago Press.

Langer, E. J. (1975). The illusion of control. *Journal of Personality and Social Psychology, 32,* 311–328.

Langer, E. J. (1978). Rethinking the role of thought in social interaction. In J. Harvey, W. Ickes, R. Kiss, (Eds.), *New Directions in Attribution Research, 2,* 35–58.

Langer, E. J., Bashner, R., & Chanowitz, B. (1985). Decreasing prejudice by increasing discrimination. *Journal of Personality and Social Psychology, 49,* 113–120.

Langer, E. J., Blank, A., & Chanowitz, B. (1978). The mindlessness of ostensibly thoughtful action: The role of "placebic" information in interpersonal interaction. *Journal of Personality and Social Psychology, 36,* 635–642.

Laswell, H. (1948). *The structure and function of communication and society: The communication of ideas.* New York: Institute for Religious and Social Studies, 203–243.

Lazersfeld, P., & Menzel, H. (1963). Mass media and personal influence. In Schramm (Ed.), The science of human communication (pp. 94–115).

Lazresfeld, P., & Merton, R. (1964). Mass communication, popular taste, and organized social action. In L. Bryson (ed.), *The communication of ideas*. New York: Institute for Religious and Social Studies.

Lewin, K. (1935). *A dynamic theory of personality*. New York: McGraw-Hill.

Mayr, E. (1992). Speciational evolution or punctuated equilibria. In A. Somit & S. Peterson (Eds.), *The dynamics of evolution* (pp. 21–48). New York: Cornell University Press.

McClelland, D. (1962). Business drive and national achievement. *Harvard Business Review, 40*, 99–112.

McCroskey, J. (1966). Scales for the measurement of ethos. *Speech Monographs, 33*, 65–72.

McGuire, W. J. (1960a). A syllogistic analysis of cognitive relationships. In M. J. Rosenberg, C. I. Hovland, W. J. McGuire, R. P. Abelson, & J. W. Brehm (Eds.), *Attitude organization and change: An analysis of consistency among attitude components* (pp. 65–111).

McGuire, W. J. (1960b). Cognitive consistency and attitude change. *Journal of Abnormal and Social Psychology, 60*, 345–353.

McGuire, W. J. (1960c). Direct and indirect effects of dissonance-producing messages. *Journal of Abnormal and Social Psychology, 60*, 354–358.

McGuire, W. J. (1968). Personality and attitude change: An information processing theory. In A. G. Greenwald, T. C. Brock, & T. M. Ostrom (Eds.), *Psychological foundations of attitudes* (pp. 171–196). San Diego, CA: Academic.

McGuire, W. J. (1969). The nature of attitudes and attitude change. In G. Lindzey & E. Aronson (Eds.), *The handbook of social psychology* (pp. 156–180). Reading, MA: Addison-Wesley.

McGuire, W. J. (1985). Attitudes and attitude change. In G. Lindzey & A. Elliot (Eds.), *The handbook of social psychology* (Vol. 2, pp. 233–346). New York: Random House.

McGuire, W. J. (1989). Theoretical foundations of campaigns. In R. Rice & C. Atkins (Eds.), *Public communication campaigns*. Newbury Park: Sage.

Osgood, C., Suci, G., & Tannenbaum, P. (1957). *The measurement of meaning*. Urbana: University of Illinois Press.

Ostrom, T. M. (1981). Theoretical perspectives in the analysis of cognitive responses. In R. E. Petty, T. M. Ostrom, & T. C. Brock (Eds.), *Cognitive responses in persuasion* (pp. 283–290). Hillsdale, NJ: Lawrence Erlbaum Associates.

Petty, R. E. (1977). *A cognitive response analysis of the temporal persistence of attitude changes induced by persuasive communications*. Unpublished doctoral dissertation, Ohio State University. Columbus, OH.

Petty, R. E. (1994). Two routes to persuasion: State of the art. In G. d'Ydewale, P. Eelen, & P. Bertelsen (Eds.), *International perspectives on psychological science* (Vol. 2, pp. 229–247). Hillsdale, NJ: Lawrence Erlbaum Associates.

Petty, R. E., & Cacioppo, J. T. (1981). *Attitudes and persuasion: Classic and contemporary approaches*. Dubuque, IA: Wm C. Brown.

Petty, R. E., & Cacioppo, J. T. (1986). The elaboration likelihood model of persuasion. In L. Berkowitz (Ed.), *Advances in experimental social psychology* (pp. 123–205). San Diego, CA: Academic.

Petty, R. E., & Wegener, D. T. (1999). The elaboration likelihood model: Current status and controversies. In S. Chaiken & Y. Trope (Eds.), *Dual process theories in social psychology* (pp. 41–72). New York: Guilford.

Petty, R. E., Wegener, D. T., Fabrigar, L. R., Priester, J. R., & Cacioppo, J. T. (1993). Conceptual and methodological issues in the elaboration likelihood model of persuasion: A reply to the Michigan State critics. *Communication Theory, 3,* 336–362.

Planck, M. (1962). *Scientific autobiography and other papers* (F. Gaynor, Trans.) New York: Greenwood Press. (Original work published 1949)

Rogers, E. M., & Beal, G. M. (1958). *Reference group influence in adoption of agricultural technology.* Iowa State University Press.

Rokeach, M. (1956). Political and religious dogmatism: An alternative to the authoritarian personality. *Psychology Monographs, 70,* No. 425.

Rokeach, M. (1960). *The open and closed mind.* New York: Basic Books.

Rokeach, M. (1968). *Beliefs, attitudes and values.* San Francisco, CA: Jossey-Bass.

Rokeach, M., & Rothman, G. (1965). The principle of belief congruence and the congruity principle as models of cognitive interaction. *Psychological Review, 72,* 128–142.

Roloff, M. E., & Berger, C. R. (Eds.). (1982). *Social cognition and communication.* Newbury Park, C: Sage.

Rosenberg, M. (1965). *Society and the adolescent self-image.* Princeton, NJ: Princeton University Press.

Sarnoff, D., (1965). The experimental evaluation of psychoanalytic hypothesis. *Transactions of the New York Academy of Sciences, 28,* 272–290.

Sarnoff, D., & Katz, D. (1954). The motivational bases of attitude change. *Journal of Abnormal and Social Psychology, 49,* 115–124.

Sarnoff, I. (1960). Psychoanalytic theory and social attitudes. *Public Opinion Quarterly, 24,* 251–279.

Sarnoff, I. (1962). *Personality dynamics and development.* New York: Wiley.

Sarnoff, I., & Zimbardo, P. (1961). Anxiety, fear, and social affiliation. *Journal of Abnormal and Social Psychology, 62,* 356–363.

Scherer, K. R. (1984). On the nature and function of emotion: A component process approach. In P. Ekman & K. Scherer (Eds.), *Approaches to emotion* (pp. 293–316). Hillsdale, NJ: Lawrence Erlbaum Associates.

Shah, J. Y., & Kruglanski, A. W. (1999). Aspects of goal-networks: Implications for self-regulation. In M. Boekaerts, P. R. Pintrich, & M. Zeidner (Eds.), *Handbook of self-regulation.* San Diego, Academic Press.

Shah, J. Y., & Kruglanski, A. W. (2000). The structure and substance of intrinsic motivation. In C. Sansone & J. M. Harackiewicz (Eds.), *Intrinsic motivation: Controversies and new directions.* San Diego: Academic Press.

Sherif, C. W., Sherif, M., & Nebergall, R. E. (1965). *Attitude and attitude change: The social judgment-involvement approach.* Philadelphia: Saunders.

Sherif, M. (1935). A study of some social factors in perception. *Arch. Psychology.,* No 187.

Sherif, M., & Cantril, H. (1947). *The psychology of ego-involvements.* New York: Wiley.

Sherif, M. & Hovland, C. I. (1953). Judgmental phenomena and scales of attitude measurement: Placement of items with individual choice of number of categories. *Journal of Abnormal and Social Psychology, 48,* 135–141.

Sherif, M., & Hovland, C. I. (1961). *Social judgment: Assimilation and contrast effects in communication and attitude change.* New Haven, CT: Yale University Press.

Sherif, M., & Sherif, C. W. (1967). Attitudes as the individual's own categories: The social-judgment approach to attitude and attitude change. In C. W. Sherif & M. Sherif (Eds.), *Attitude, ego-involvement and change* (pp. 105–139). New York: Wiley.

Sherif, M., Taub, D., & Hovland, C. I. (1958). Assimilation and contrast effects of anchoring stimuli on judgments. *Journal of Experimental Psychology, 55,* 150–155.

Shiffrin, R. M, & Schneider, W. (1977). Controlled and automatic human information porcessing: 1. detection, search, and attention. *Psychological Review, 84*, 1–66.

Smith, M. B. (1969). *Social psychology and human values.* Chicago: Aldine.

Smith, M. B. (1974). *Humanizing social psychology.* San Francisco: Jossey-Bass.

Smith, M. B. (1991). *Values, self, and society: Toward a humanist social psychology.* New Brunswick, NJ: Transaction.

Smith, M. B., Bruner, J. S., & White, R. W. (1956). *Opinions and personality.* New York: Wiley.

Staats, A. W., & Staats, C. K. (1958). Attitudes established by classical conditioning. *Journal of Abnormal and Social Psychology, 57*, 37–40.

Tesser, A. (1976). Thought and reality constraints as determinants of attitude polarization. *Journal of Research in Personality, 10*, 183–194.

Tesser, A. (1978). Self-generated attitude change. In L. Berkowitz (Ed.), *Advances in experimental social psychology* (Vol. 11, pp. 289–338). Orlando, FL: Academic.

Tesser, A., & Conlee, M. C. (1975). Some effects of time and thought on attitude polarization. *Journal of Personality and Social Psychology, 31*, 262–270.

Tesser, A., & Cowan, C. L. (1975). Some effects of thought and number of cognitions on attitude change. *Social Behavior and Personality, 3*, 216–226.

Tesser, A., & Cowan, C. L. (1977). Some attitudinal and cognitive consequences of thought. *Journal of Research in Personality, 11*, 216–226.

Tesser, A., & Danheiser, P. (1978). Anticipated relationship, salience of partner and attitude change. *Personality and Social Psychology Bulletin, 4*, 35–38.

Tesser, A., & Johnsin, R. D. (1974). Thought and dependence as determinants of interpersonal hostility. *Bulletin of the Psychonomic Society, 2*, 425–430.

Tesser, A., & Leone, C. (1977). Cognitive schemas and thought as determinants of attitude change. *Journal of Experimental Social Psychology, 13*, 340–356.

Uleman, J. S. (1999). Spontaneous versus intentional inferences in impression formation. In S. Chaiken & Y. Trope (Eds.), *Dual-process theories in social psychology* (pp. 141–160). New York: Guilford.

White, R. W. (1963). Ego and reality in psychoanalytic theory: A proposal regarding independent ego energies. In *Psychological issues* (Vol. 3, pp. 1–210). New York: International Universities Press.

Author Index

A

B

C

F

G

H

I

J

K

L

M

N

Q

R

S

T

U

V

W

Y

Z

Subject Index

A

J

K

L

M

U

V

W